Legal Restrictions on Third-Country Nationals in EU Emergencies

Ius, Lex et Res Publica
Studies in Law, Philosophy and Political Cultures

Edited by Barbara Janusz-Pohl

Vol. 45

Jacek Chlebny (ed.)

Legal Restrictions on Third-Country Nationals in EU Emergencies

PETER LANG
Berlin · Bruxelles · Chennai · Lausanne · New York · Oxford

Bibliographic Information published by the Deutsche Nationalbibliothek
The Deutsche Nationalbibliothek lists this publication in the Deutsche Nationalbibliografie; detailed bibliographic data is available online at http://dnb.d-nb.de.

Library of Congress Cataloging-in-Publication Data
Names: Chlebny, Jacek editor
Title: Legal Restrictions on Third-Country Nationals in EU Emergencies / edited by Professor Jacek Chlebny.
Description: Berlin ; New York : Peter Lang, 2026. | Series: Ius, Lex et Res Publica : Studies in Law, Philosophy and Political Cultures, 2191-3250 ; vol. 45 | Includes bibliographical references and index.
Identifiers: LCCN 2025042948 (print) | LCCN 2025042949 (ebook) | ISBN 9783631925201 hardback | ISBN 9783631925218 pdf | ISBN 9783631945919 epub
Subjects: LCSH: Emigration and immigration law—European Union countries | Stateless persons—European Union countries | Noncitizens—European Union countries | Asylum, Right of—European Union countries | Emergency management—Law and legislation—European Union countries
Classification: LCC KJE6044 .L44 2026 (print) | LCC KJE6044 (ebook)
LC record available at https://lccn.loc.gov/2025042948
LC ebook record available at https://lccn.loc.gov/2025042949

The monograph is a part of the research project: “Legal Restrictions on Third-Country Nationals in EU Emergencies” (No. 2020/37/B/HS5/00975), financed by the National Science Centre, Poland.

Editorial Reviewer: Doc. JUDr. Lukáš Potěšil, Ph.D. (Masaryk University)

ISSN 2191-3250
ISBN 978-3-631-92520-1 (Print)
ISBN 978-3-631-92521-8 (ePDF)
ISBN 978-3-631-94591-9 (ePUB)
DOI 10.3726/b23374

Published by Peter Lang GmbH, Berlin, Germany

info@peterlang.com

www.peterlang.com

Contact for General Product Safety Regulation (GPSR): gpsr@peterlang.com

Contents

Introduction (Jacek Chlebny) 17

1 European law perspective: are there any special provisions on entry and residence of third-country nationals necessary in times of emergency? 23

1.1 Definitions of emergency and crisis in the context of migration (Wojciech Piątek) 23

1.2 Time of emergency—legal sources (Wojciech Piątek) 29

1.3 The emergency response mechanism (Rafał Rogala) 34

1.3.1 Introduction 34

1.3.2 The 2015–2016 migration crisis 38

1.3.2.1 Schengen border code reform 42

1.3.2.2 Actions prior to the apogee of the crisis 44

1.3.2.3 Hotspots 48

1.3.2.4 Relocation and resettlement 57

1.3.2.5 Activation of crisis management mechanisms 65

1.3.2.6 Externalization of migration 66

1.3.2.7 The EU-Turkey Agreement (Statement) 68

1.3.2.8 European Trust Fund 76

1.3.2.9 Establishment of the European Border and Coast Guard 78

1.3.2.10 The 2015–2016 migration crisis—a summary 79

1.3.3 The migration crisis triggered by the COVID-19 pandemic 82

1.3.3.1 First reactions to the pandemic crisis 83

1.3.3.2 The response to the COVID-19 pandemic from EU bodies 89
1.3.3.3 Labor migrants during the COVID-19 pandemic 95
1.3.3.4 The situation of applicants for international protection during the COVID-19 pandemic 98
1.3.3.5 Application of soft law in the practice of managing the crisis caused by the COVID-19 pandemic 99
1.3.3.6 Poland's response to the pandemic and the crisis it caused 102
1.3.3.7 Conclusions 106
1.3.4 Instrumentalization of migration 108
1.3.4.1 Examples of the instrumentalization of migration in Europe in the twenty-first century 109
1.3.4.2 From securitization to the instrumentalization of migration 113
1.3.4.3 European Union legislative offensive: The Migration and Asylum Pact and Acts 117
1.3.4.4 Poland's response to the migrant crisis on the Polish-Belarusian border 127
1.3.5 Ukraine crisis 133
1.3.5.1 Poland's response to the influx of refugees from Ukraine 140
1.3.6 Conclusions 143
1.4 Human rights in times of emergency: EU law perspective (Barbara Opalska) 146
1.4.1 Introduction 146
1.4.2 EU Law, the European Pact on Migration and Asylum, and the pivotal Principle of Non-Refoulement 148
1.4.3 Conclusions 164
1.5 Human rights in times of emergency: international law perspective (Anna Chmielarz-Grochal) 164
1.5.1 Introduction 164
1.5.2 Fundamental rights of migrants in international law 167
1.5.3 The principle of *non-refoulement* in international human rights law 172

1.5.4 Guarantees of migrants' rights in the European Convention on Human Rights ... 176
1.5.5 The permissibility of restrictions on human rights in the light of acts of international law ... 183
1.5.6 Standards of protection of migrants' rights in the case law of the European Court of Human Rights ... 186
1.5.7 Conclusions ... 197
1.6 Derogations in time of emergency (Jacek Chlebny) ... 201
1.6.1 Derogating from the application of obligations in a state of public emergency in the ECHR ... 201
1.6.1.1 Application of the derogation clause ... 201
1.6.1.2 A state of public danger threatening the life of the nation ... 204
1.6.1.3 Measures taken on the basis of a derogation clause ... 207
1.6.1.4 Effects of the derogation on the rights of refugees and immigrants ... 208
1.6.2 Suspension of obligations under the ICCPR due to exceptional public danger threatening the existence of the nation ... 210
1.6.2.1 Principles governing the suspension of rights and freedoms guaranteed in the ICCPR ... 210
1.6.2.2 Conditions for the suspension of obligations under the Covenant pursuant to Article 4 of the ICCPR ... 212
1.6.3 Restriction of the rights and freedoms guaranteed in the Charter of Fundamental Rights of the European Union ... 215
1.6.4 Conclusions ... 216

2 Substantive and procedural law perspective: human rights of migrants in times of emergency in selected countries ... 219
2.1 Belgium (Geert Debersaques, Anke Meskens) ... 219
2.1.1 Substantive law perspective: human rights of migrants in times of emergency in Belgium ... 219
2.1.1.1 The state of emergency in Belgium ... 220
2.1.1.1.1 Article 187 of the Constitution ... 220
2.1.1.2 Human rights related to migration ... 222

2.1.1.2.1 Introduction: the legal framework in Belgium 222
2.1.1.2.2 The right to private and family life under Article 8 ECHR 223
2.1.1.2.2.1 Introduction 223
2.1.1.2.2.2 The right to residence in the context of Article 8 ECHR 224
2.1.1.2.2.3 Expulsion of migrants under Belgian legislation in the context of Article 8 ECHR 228
2.1.1.2.3 The prohibition of torture, inhumane or degrading treatment or punishment under Article 3 ECHR 232
2.1.1.2.3.1 Introduction 232
2.1.1.2.3.2 The right to residence in the context of Article 3 ECHR 232
2.1.1.2.3.3 Expulsion of migrants under Belgian legislation in the context of Article 3 ECHR 243
2.1.1.3 Personal rights for third-country nationals 244
2.1.1.3.1 Article 10, 11 and 191 Constitution 244
2.1.1.4 Political rights for third-country nationals 246
2.1.1.4.1 The right to civil service 246
2.1.1.5 Economic, social, and cultural rights for third-country nationals 249
2.1.1.5.1 Introduction 249
2.1.1.5.2 The right to education 250
2.1.1.5.3 The right to social allowances 254
2.1.1.6 Solidarity rights for third-country nationals 257
2.1.1.6.1 The right to live in peace 257
2.1.1.6.1.1 The inviolability of the home 264
2.1.2 Procedural law perspective: human rights of migrants in times of emergency in Belgium 264
2.1.2.1 Special procedures on entry and residence of the third-country nationals 264

2.1.2.1.1 Legal framework in Belgium 264
2.1.2.1.2 The (general) procedure on entry and residence 266
2.1.2.1.3 Deprivation of liberty, restriction of liberty and use of coercion 267
2.1.2.1.3.1 Deprivation of liberty and restriction of liberty 267
2.1.2.1.3.2 Use of coercion 271
2.1.2.2 Identification of standards for proper organization of administrative authorities and courts 274
2.1.2.2.1 Basic standards for proper functioning administrative authorities and courts 274
2.1.2.2.2 The effect of times of emergency on the standards for proper organization of administrative authorities and courts 282
2.1.2.2.3 How do public authorities and courts cope with the amount of applications for international protection? 283
2.1.2.3 Application of new technologies into administrative and court proceedings 286
2.2 Czech Republic (Ivo Pospíšil) 286
2.2.1 Constitutional definition of states of emergency in the Czech Republic 286
2.2.1.1 General background 286
2.2.1.2 The constitutional and sub-constitutional regulation of states of emergency 288
2.2.2 Substantive law perspective: the human rights of migrants in the Czech Republic 291
2.2.2.1 Institutional framework of protection 291
2.2.2.2 Selected issues of human rights of migrants 296
2.2.3 Restrictions on human rights in states of emergency and the status of aliens 300
2.2.3.1 Limitation of rights in general 300
2.2.3.2 Restrictions on the rights of foreigners in states of emergency 304
2.2.3.3 Procedural guarantees for the protection of rights in states of emergency 306

2.3 France (Fanny Jacquelot) ... 309
2.3.1 Substantive law perspective: emergency standards in France ... 309
2.3.1.1 Introduction ... 309
2.3.1.2 The state of emergency provided for the Constitution ... 309
2.3.1.3 The state of emergency provided by law ... 310
2.3.2 Human rights related to migration: the right to asylum ... 310
2.3.2.1 Introduction ... 310
2.3.2.2 The right to migrate ... 311
2.3.2.3 Temporary protection ... 311
2.3.2.4 Sources of the right to asylum in France ... 313
2.3.2.4.1 Domestic sources of asylum law ... 313
2.3.2.4.2 External sources of asylum law ... 314
2.3.2.5 The different types of protection granted for asylum applications ... 314
2.3.2.5.1 Introduction ... 314
2.3.2.5.2 Constitutional asylum ... 316
2.3.2.5.3 Conventional asylum ... 317
2.3.2.5.4 Subsidiary protection ... 318
2.3.2.6 The malfunctioning of the asylum system during the state of health emergency ... 319
2.3.2.7 Restrictions on fundamental rights during a state of health emergency ... 321
2.3.2.7.1 Restrictions on freedom of movement ... 321
2.3.2.7.2 Restrictions on family reunification ... 322
2.3.3 Personal rights for third-country nationals ... 323
2.3.3.1 Introduction ... 323
2.3.3.2 Health ... 323
2.3.3.3 Individual freedom ... 324
2.3.3.3.1 Administrative detention ... 324
2.3.3.3.2 House arrest ... 325
2.3.3.3.3 Personal freedom of foreign nationals during a state of emergency ... 326

2.3.3.3.3.1 Problems during states of emergency under the 1955 law 326
2.3.3.3.3.2 Problems during the state of health emergency 327
2.3.3.4 Privacy 327
2.3.3.5 Data protection 329
2.3.4 Political rights for third-country nationals 329
2.3.5 Economic, social, and cultural rights for third-country nationals 329
2.3.5.1 Introduction 329
2.3.5.2 Right to work 330
2.3.5.2.1 General law 330
2.3.5.2.2 Adaptations during emergency periods 331
2.3.6 Human rights of the specific vulnerable groups: unaccompanied minors 331
2.3.7 Procedural law perspective 332
2.3.7.1 Special procedures on the entry and residence of third-country nationals 332
2.3.7.1.1 Introduction 332
2.3.7.1.2 The standard entry and residence procedure for third-country nationals in France 333
2.3.7.1.2.1 Entering France 333
2.3.7.1.2.2 Removal from French territory 333
2.3.7.1.3 Special entry and residence procedures in times of emergency 334
2.3.7.2 Identification of standards for proper organization of administrative authorities and courts 335
2.3.7.2.1 Introduction 335
2.3.7.2.2 Relations between third-country nationals and the authorities 335
2.3.7.2.3 The right to a judge for third-country nationals 336

2.3.7.2.4 Adaptations during a state of health emergency 338
2.3.7.2.4.1 Administrative authorities 338
2.3.7.2.4.2 Administrative justice 338
2.3.7.3 Application of new technologies in administrative and courts proceedings 339
2.3.7.3.1 Introduction 339
2.3.7.3.2 New technologies in administrative and legal proceedings 339
2.3.7.3.3 New technologies specifically for third-country nationals 340
2.4 Italy (Paola Pannia) 341
2.4.1 Introduction 341
2.4.2 A diachronic overview on the legislative framework regulating the rights of migrants in Italy: emergency as an overarching keyword 343
2.4.2.1 A (quite) recent history of immigration 343
2.4.2.2 The Italian constitutional framework on third-country nationals and their rights 346
2.4.2.3 The most relevant legislative provisions: an overview on the legal status of third-country nationals 348
2.4.2.4 The evolution of the Italian Immigration law 351
2.4.3 The Italian legislation on foreigners' rights in time of emergency: a substantial and procedural perspective 356
2.4.3.1 The Balkan "emergencies" 357
2.4.3.2 The "Arab Spring" 360
2.4.3.3 The EU "refugee crisis" of 2015 363
2.4.3.3.1 The management of arrivals and the hotspots approach 363
2.4.3.3.2 Reforms meant to restructure the national reception system 365
2.4.3.3.3 Reforms aimed at speeding up the international protection procedure 368
2.4.3.4 The covid emergency and the regularization 369

2.4.3.5 The current “state of emergency”: the Ukraine war and beyond 371
2.4.3.5.1 The state of emergency declared after the Ukraine war 371
2.4.3.5.2 The rapid succession of reforms and the declaration of a new “state of emergency” 374
2.4.3.5.3 The Agreement Italy-Albania and the issue of the “safe third countries of origin” 377
2.4.4 Conclusive remarks: tools, reasons and implications surrounding the construction of a regime of permanent emergency 379
2.5 Poland 383
2.5.1 Substantive law (Michał Kowalski) 383
2.5.1.1 Introductory remarks 383
2.5.1.2 Constitutional standard 386
2.5.1.3 Statutory guarantees 400
2.5.1.4 Conclusions 410
2.5.2 Procedural law perspective 412
2.5.2.1 Special procedures on the entry and residence of third-country nationals (Paweł Dańczak) 412
2.5.2.1.1 General overview 412
2.5.2.1.2 The COVID-19 pandemic 413
2.5.2.1.3 Inflow of Ukrainian nationals in connection with the invasion of Ukraine by the Russian Federation 416
2.5.2.1.4 General procedure 420
2.5.2.1.5 Special procedures 427
2.5.2.1.5.1 Crisis at the EU external border—the Polish-Belarusian border 427
2.5.2.2 Deprivation of liberty, restriction of liberty and coercion (Paweł Dańczak) 439
2.5.2.2.1 Deprivation and restriction of liberty 439
2.5.2.2.2 Direct coercion 443

2.5.2.3 Cooperation with the European Border and Coast Guard Agency (Paweł Dańczak) 443
2.5.2.4 Identification of basic standards for public administration bodies and administrative courts adjudicating cases concerning entry and residence of third-country nationals in the territory of the Republic of Poland (Grzegorz Rząsa) 448
2.5.2.4.1 Introductory remarks 448
2.5.2.4.2 The principle of equal treatment of foreigners residing in the territory of Poland and Polish citizens 451
2.5.2.4.3 The standards applicable to proceedings before public administration authorities in cases concerning the entry and stay of a foreigner in the territory of Poland (in context of the right to good administration) 453
2.5.2.4.4 Standards applicable to proceedings before an administrative court in cases concerning the entry and stay of a foreigner in the territory (in the context of the right to an effective remedy before a court) 466
2.5.2.4.5 Selected cases of restrictions on foreigners' rights due to crisis situations 473
2.5.2.4.6 Conclusions 482
2.6 Slovakia (Lilla Garayova) 483
2.6.1 Introduction 483
2.6.2 Substantive law perspective: the human rights of migrants in times of emergency in Slovakia 484
2.6.2.1 Human rights related to migration 495
2.6.2.2 Personal rights for third-country nationals 508
2.6.2.3 Political rights for third-country nationals 513

2.6.2.4 Economic, social and cultural rights for third-country nationals 517
2.6.2.5 Solidarity rights for third-country nationals 521
2.6.2.6 Human rights of specific vulnerable groups 525
2.6.3 Procedural law perspective 531
2.6.3.1 Special procedures on the entry and residence of the third-country nationals 532
2.6.3.2 Identification of standards for the proper organization of administrative authorities and courts 533
2.6.3.3 Application of new technologies in administrative and courts proceedings 537
2.6.4 Conclusions 540

Summary (Jacek Chlebny) 543

Bibliography 553

Notes on contributors 569

Index 571

Introduction

Jacek Chlebny

This monograph is a study in the field of foreigners' protection law, focusing on the conditions of entry and residence in the European Union for third-country nationals and stateless persons during states of emergency, such as threats of terrorism, risks to health and life, and mass migration. These threats are becoming increasingly frequent. The starting point for these considerations is the view that the existing legal regulations, both at the national and EU level, are inadequate to deal with such situations. Therefore, there is a pressing need to assess the current legal framework and propose new solutions, both *de lege lata* and *de lege ferenda*.

The need to amend the existing asylum law regulations was recognized by the EU legislator, who decided in 2024 to adopt the so-called New Pact on Migration and Asylum. This Pact includes nine regulations and one directive. Its drafters intended for it to establish a new, coherent system for managing irregular migration in Europe.[1] However, it does not explicitly address specific regulations governing the entry and residence of third-country nationals in the EU during states of emergency.[2] Although the adopted regulations have not yet entered into force, they will be considered within the analytical

[1] For further information in this field, see the website of the European Commission: Pact on Migration and Asylum. A common EU system to manage migration <https://home-affairs.ec.europa.eu/policies/migration-and-asylum/pact-migration-and-asylum_en> accessed December 7, 2024.

[2] Particularly noteworthy in this regard are the provisions of Regulation (EU) 2024/1359 of the European Parliament and of the Council on responding to crisis and force majeure situations in the areas of migration and asylum and amending Regulation

framework to assess their potential to achieve the intended objectives. The primary task in the present deliberations is to determine the degree to which the new regulations are adapted to threats related to the aforementioned states of emergency and to evaluate their impact on the functioning of individual states and the European Union as a whole.

Extraordinary situations require extraordinary legal measures. They should exist both at the level of proceedings before public administrations and during their judicial review. On the one hand, they should be characterized by a high level of flexibility in their application, depending on the circumstances. On the other hand, it is essential to maintain specific protection standards for third-country nationals. The existence of a state of emergency does not exempt public administrative authorities and courts from adhering to the principle of procedural fairness. This means that prompt action by state authorities in a state of emergency is at least as critical as in ordinary times, if not more so.

The importance of the efficient operation of public administration bodies and courts became apparent during the COVID-19 pandemic. The questions that became pressing at that time—concerning how the work of bodies and courts is organized in a state of emergency,[3] the validity of the principles of openness of proceedings,[4] equal treatment of parties,[5] and the prompt resolution of cases[6]—continue to demand new answers, if only due to ongoing technological progress.

There is no doubt that third-country nationals decide to migrate to Europe, among other reasons, because of the emergencies occurring in their countries

(EU) 2021/1147. This regulation regulates temporary measures in the event of a crisis situation in the areas of migration and asylum.

3 Horvat M., Piątek W., Potesil L., Rozsnyai K. F., "Public Administration's Adaptation to Covid-19 Pandemic—Czech, Hungarian, Polish and Slovak Experience" (2021) 1(19) *Central European Public Administration Review* <https://doi.org/10.17573/cepar.2021.1.06>.

4 Piątek W., "A Right to a Public Hearing in Times of Emergency—Online or Physical?" (2023) 14(2) *International Journal for Court Administration* <https://doi.org/10.36745/ijca.444>.

5 See the report of the European Union Agency for Fundamental Rights «The coronavirus pandemic and fundamental rights: a year in review» (2021) 21.

6 See the report titled Impact of COVID-19 on the courts and litigation time limits accessible at the webpage <https://beauchamps.ie/publications/857> accessed December 7, 2024.

of previous residence. The mere fact of their mass influx to the borders of the European Union—irrespective of security considerations—creates an emergency situation, at least at the state border where they gather. A conflict may then arise between the interests of the persons staying at the border and the interests of the state into whose territory they wish to enter.[7] Is it then acceptable to assert that the public interest of the host state should take precedence over the individual interest of the third-country national? Or would it be more justifiable to invoke the principle of proportionality and seek an answer to this question *ad casum*?

The considerations in this study will be divided into two parts. The first focuses on EU law, examining the very concept of times of emergency, including its presence in EU legal acts. It then analyses the legal framework governing the impact of such emergencies on state functioning and the rights of third-country nationals. Within this framework, the analysis will determine the extent to which the EU legislator permits derogations from certain rights to protect the public interest, particularly in matters of state security, and how such derogations align with the principles of international human rights protection.

The second part of the discussion focuses on the national regulations of selected legal orders. The legal situation of a migration emergency will be presented in the context of national regulations on personal, political and economic rights. In addition, a procedural perspective will be taken into account, covering the right to an administrative process, the right to a court, and the right to an effective remedy. The impact of new technologies on the conduct of administrative and judicial proceedings will also be considered. While the research concerns a general problematic framework intended to provide a common denominator for the reflections carried out in the monograph, it is not rigid in nature. This approach ensured that the authors retained their freedom and academic autonomy in selecting what, from the perspective of the country and the subject matter under discussion, they deemed truly relevant and what could be ascribed less cognitive significance. In addition,

---

7 According to Cardinal Gerhard Müller, no one has a natural right to live where he or she wishes. For more information, see Cardinal Müller, The State Has the Right to Defend Its Borders. Catholic News Agency Service November 13, 2024 <https://www.ekai.pl/kard-muller-nie-jestem-rozczarowany-ze-ameryka-wybrala-trumpa/> accessed on December 7, 2024.

for various reasons, not all the authors were able to collect and elaborate their research results to a degree comparable to the others. However, even the narrower scope of these reflections provided enough valuable insights that it would be a mistake not to present them.

The selection of countries covered by the analysis—Belgium, the Czech Republic, France, Poland, Slovakia and Italy—is not random. It is based on several interrelated criteria. Firstly, the list includes both Central and Eastern European and Western European countries, which allows for capturing the diversity of experiences and legal traditions in the field of regulations concerning foreigners and responding to emergency situations. Poland, the Czech Republic and Slovakia represent the perspective of new Member States, which, after joining the European Union, have gradually built their migration law systems, often based on model solutions developed within the *acquis communautaire*. Belgium, France and Italy, on the other hand, are countries with a long legal and administrative tradition in the field of migration and the protection of foreigners, and also play a significant role in shaping EU migration and asylum policy.

Secondly, the selected countries differ in terms of their geographical location, which determines their role in the European migration management system. Poland, the Czech Republic and Slovakia constitute the external or transit border of the European Union, which means that they are particularly affected by migration in crisis situations. Belgium, France and Italy, on the other hand, are destination countries that face problems related to the residence, integration and protection of foreigners on their territory. This combination allows us to show how the geopolitical context influences the application of provisions on the entry and residence of third-country nationals in emergency situations.

Thirdly, the selection of these countries is justified by their diverse normative and jurisprudential achievements in the field of migration law and administrative law applied in emergency situations. France and Italy have extensive experience in regulating states of emergency, which allows for an analysis of the limits of permissible restrictions on individual rights in situations of public security threats. Belgium's participation in the process of creating European Union law in the area of migration and asylum means that an analysis of its legal system allows us not only to understand the specifics of national solutions but also to assess their significance and impact on the development of common EU standards.

The diversity of the countries studied in terms of their geographical location, their place and importance in the European migration system (border and destination countries), and their experience in the use of emergency instruments allows for a comparative analysis. Such a broad perspective also makes it possible to determine the extent to which EU and international law influence national solutions in the area of migration and whether the mechanisms adopted ensure a response to crisis situations that is consistent with European and constitutional standards of human rights protection.

The research was conducted using the dogmatic-legal method, encompassing both acts of EU law, primary and derived, as well as selected legal orders of the Member States. The evolutionary method plays an auxiliary role, highlighting the changes that migration law has undergone over time. Finally, given the inclusion of multiple legal systems in this study, the comparative law method also plays an important role.

The study is based on the state of the law, literature and case law as of March 1, 2026.

European law perspective: are there any special provisions on entry and residence of third-country nationals necessary in times of emergency?

1.1 Definitions of emergency and crisis in the context of migration (Wojciech Piątek)

Our contemporary world is characterized by a succession of emergencies, ranging from the outbreak of the COVID-19 pandemic to armed conflicts, including Russia's aggression against Ukraine and hostilities in the Middle East. Another growing emergency is climate change, which is has led to climatic anomalies in some parts of the world, including droughts and floods. Such emergencies force people to migrate in search of more favorable living conditions. In 2015, more than two million African refugees arrived in Europe.[8] Further groups of African refugees continue to arrive, with fluctuating intensity, off the coasts of Italy and Greece.[9] In 2022, millions of Ukrainians fled their country as a result of Russian aggression.[10] From 2021 onwards, groups of migrants, mainly from the Middle East and Africa, have

8 See Asylum and Migration into the EU in 2015. European Union Agency for Fundamental Rights (2016) 5.

9 The regular influx of migrants from Africa to Italy began in the 1970s. See Marek Bodziany, Anna Kotasińska, "Europejski kryzys migracyjny—włoskie studium przypadku, Pogranicze" (2017) 5(2) *Polish Borderlands Studies*, 111.

10 The living and economic situation of Ukrainian refugees in Poland. Report of the questionnaire survey conducted by NBP Regional Branches, Department of Statistics 2022, p. 7. See also Witold Klaus, Monika Szulecka, "Departing or Being Deported? Poland's Approach Toward Humanitarian Migrants" (2022) *Journal of Refugee Studies*, 6–8.

attempted to cross the eastern border of the European Union, with varying intensity.[11]

According to one dictionary definition, an emergency is "an unexpected and usually dangerous situation that calls for immediate action."[12] The concept of a state of emergency, as described in the legal literature, refers to a crisis identified and designated by a state as reaching a severity threshold that necessitates urgent, exceptional and temporary measures that would not be permissible under normal conditions.[13] These definitions encapsulate three constitutive features of an emergency: the unpredictability of the phenomenon, the seriousness of the danger posed, and the need for a rapid response. The question of the extent to which an emergency can be equated with a crisis, and whether the two concepts can be used interchangeably, also requires consideration.

The emergencies referred to above are unpredictable and, in the case of climate change, sometimes even denied. As a result, they are difficult to anticipate and effectively prevent. Their magnitude even makes thorough preparation impossible. They usually occur suddenly and take those affected by surprise. This was the case with both the outbreak of the COVID-19 pandemic and Russia's aggression against Ukraine. Even if the emergency builds up gradually, as with climate change, the severity of the threat to fundamental values such as human health and life limits the available responses. Often, the only solution is to flee a place threatened by warfare or made uninhabitable due to drought or flooding. The decision has to be taken immediately, without time for in-depth calculation based on empirical data. The effectiveness of protective measures often depends on the appropriateness and speed of the decision.

A feature of modern emergencies is that they are no longer short-lived, measured in hours or days. They can last for months or even years. However,

---

11 The Polish government described these attacks as hybrid aggression. See A hybrid attack on Poland, special service on the website of the Republic of Poland from August 9, 2022 <https://www.gov.pl/web/special-services/a-hybrid-attack-on-poland> accessed November 29, 2024.

12 <https://www.britannica.com/dictionary/emergency> and <https://www.britannica.com/dictionary/emergency> accessed November 26, 2024.

13 Greene A., *Permanent States of Emergency and the Rule of Law: Constitutions in an Age of Crisis* (Hart Publishing 2018) 30.

this does not mean that emergencies should be treated as something permanent, escaping any temporal constraints. Each recognized state of emergency is a temporary response to an exceptional and temporary situation.[14] The prolongation of an emergency and the lack of a clearly defined temporal framework pose an additional threat to people, as they result in extraordinary legal and factual conditions being maintained for an extended period of time.

It is important to consider the extent to which an emergency can be equated with the concept of a crisis. Undoubtedly, they can create crises—whether humanitarian, health, or economic. However, this is not a necessary condition. At the core of an emergency is the threat of a particular good being lost. A real threat capable of causing a humanitarian, health or economic crisis is sufficient. The greater the importance of the threatened good (such as human life or health), the greater the concern. Nevertheless, an emergency does not have to automatically escalate into a crisis requiring radical solutions that might further destabilize states and societies.

Emergencies should be understood objectively, as existing realities. Nevertheless, due to the threat of certain goods, such as human health or life, being lost, their occurrence may evoke subjective emotions.[15] This state of affairs may give rise to another danger: the potential for public authorities to exploit the situation to justify granting themselves broader powers than necessary. The level of public acceptance for such decisions may be disproportionately high relative to the actual threat being addressed. Although this phenomenon is sociological rather than legal in nature, it should not be underestimated when considering legal responses to emergencies, particularly those involving restrictions on the entry and residence of third-country nationals in the EU. It can easily influence their wording and their social acceptance.

These examples of emergency situations have a direct impact on life across the entire planet, including the functioning of states and international organizations. These entities, on the one hand, can cause emergencies and, on the other hand, should have clearly defined legal regulations indicating how to act in response to such situations. An example of such regulation is

---

14 Greene A., *Emergency Powers in a Time of Pandemic* (Bristol University Press 2020) 12.
15 Greene A., *Emergency Powers in a Time of Pandemic* (Bristol University Press 2020) 14.

provided by the provisions of Chapter XI of the Polish Constitution, entitled "states of emergency." Article 228(1) of the Polish Constitution lists three types of states of emergency: martial law, a state of emergency and a state of natural disaster. Each of these may be introduced only in exceptional circumstances, when the ordinary constitutional measures prove insufficient.[16] In Germany, Article 115a(1) of the Basic Law[17] provides for the imposition of martial law (*Verteidigungsfall*) in the event of an attack or imminent threat of an armed attack on German territory. Earlier provisions refer to the need to maintain or restore public order, the possibility of the police requesting military assistance,[18] and the protection of the democratic order,[19] including cooperation between the police and other services of the various Länder in this connection. In France, a state of emergency is provided for by Article 16 of the Constitution, which deals with a serious and imminent threat to the institutions of the Republic, the independence of the State, the integrity of its territory, or the performance of international obligations. An additional condition for the application of emergency measures is the interruption of the regular functioning of the public authorities defined in the Constitution.[20] Article 43(4) of the Constitution of the Czech Republic allows for the presence of foreign troops in the Czech Republic and Czech troops abroad in the event of the need to fulfill international obligations to defend against aggression and to participate in operations related to the occurrence of natural, industrial and environmental disasters.

---

16 For a more detailed discussion, see Brzeziński M., "Wybrane zasady stanów nadzwyczajnych w konstytucji z dnia 2 kwietnia 1997 r.—uwagi de lege lata i de lege ferenda" (2017) 45 *Studia Politologiczne*, 278–280; Dzimińska-Mosio M., "Instytucja stanów nadzwyczajnych a stan wojenny" (2019) 3 *Biblioteka Nauki*, 169–170.

17 Grundgesetz für die Bundesrepublik Deutschland (BGBl. vom December 19, 2022, I S. 2478).

18 Article 35(2) GG stipulates, among other things, natural disasters and particularly dangerous accidents.

19 Article 91(2) GG.

20 At the same time, the Constitution of the Fifth Republic upheld the institution of the state of siege in Article 36, without specifying the circumstances in which it could be introduced, thus prolonging the formal validity of the laws on the state of siege of 1849 and 1878. See Complak K., "Stany nadzwyczajne á la française oraz á la polonaise" (2014) 22 *Studia Iuridica Lublinensia*, 51–54.

However, there are also some legal orders that lack constitutional or statutory provisions for managing emergencies.[21] These states are dependent on ad hoc responses to a specific emergency that has occurred at a particular time. Any legal and factual action they take is, on the one hand, determined by the nature of the threat that has arisen and, on the other, made at short notice, sometimes under the heavy influence of the threat, without any broader understanding of its implications.

A question worth asking concerns the scope of existing regulations in the context of the observed crises and their effectiveness in preventing them. Are the regulations in force in individual countries sufficient to counteract the effects of ever-new crises? A negative answer to this question may stem, for example, from the limited scope of national regulations. Crisis situations often transcend the boundaries of a single state and require a joint response from many countries. Coordination of their action is therefore essential. The increasing regulation of migration crises at the EU level is, therefore, not surprising. Successive crises may necessitate new and more extensive measures to prevent them. The consequence of successive emergencies, including their worsening, may be the need to strengthen cooperation between different states and to adopt new forms of collaboration. At the same time, states may, for various reasons, refrain from declaring a state of emergency even when there are objective grounds for doing so and when legal frameworks are already in place.[22] Finally, the rationale for the imposition of a state of emergency does not necessarily align with the actual need to prevent crisis situations. In other words, contemporary emergencies resist simple categorization under national state of emergency regulations. In particular, not every migration crisis can be categorized as a state of emergency. The final decision depends on a number of factors, both objective, concerning the degree of threat to a specific good, and subjective, related to the assessment of the seriousness of the threat.

---

21 The Swiss Constitution is an example of such a solution. See Czeszejko-Sochacki Z., *System konstytucyjny Szwajcarii* (Warszawa 2002), 87.

22 Such a situation was encountered in Poland during the COVID-19 pandemic. The government shied away from declaring a state of disaster because of the need to compensate those whose rights and freedoms (for example, concerning the way they do business) had been restricted.

What the various legal regulations on emergencies have in common is their wording, which aims to prevent the dangers associated with the nature of the threat in question. To achieve this goal, the participation of law enforcement and uniformed services of the respective states is envisaged. Depending on the situation, their powers to perform factual and legal acts are extended. This is usually combined with a limitation of the rights of individual subjects. The question remains: to what extent can the executive be endowed with powers that interfere with the rights and freedoms of individuals? How can these rights be restricted? Where is the limit beyond which this restriction is not permissible, in view of the need to protect human dignity and the rule of law? Is this limit fixed, or is it fluid, depending on the nature of the right at stake?

An example of a regulation that explicitly allows for the possibility of restrictions (derogations) is Article 15(1) of the Convention for the Protection of Human Rights and Fundamental Freedoms, which permits each High Contracting Party to take measures derogating from the application of its obligations under the Convention to the extent strictly required by the situation. The rationale for taking these measures is the outbreak of war or other public danger threatening the life of the nation.[23] A similar provision is found in Article 4 of the International Covenant on Civil and Political Rights, which allows for derogations in cases of a public emergency threatening the existence of a nation. States Parties to the Covenant may then take steps to suspend their obligations under the Covenant with the exception of actions entailing discrimination solely based on race, color, sex, language, religion or social origin.

On the one hand, it is clear that both national and EU law allow for restrictions on the rights and freedoms of individuals in the event of an emergency. On the other hand, such restrictions cannot be absolute. They must always be proportionate to the emergency. This statement, general in its content, will need to be further elaborated based on the specific legal and factual circumstances of the states of emergency triggered by the influx of successive waves of migrants into the EU.

---

23 Further paragraphs of this provision mention the impossibility of derogating from Article 2 of the Convention (right to life), as well as Article 3 (prohibition of torture) and Article 4 (prohibition of slavery and forced labour).

It is clear from the regulations presented above that a state of emergency is linked to a threat arising from an unexpected phenomenon that disrupts the normal functioning of states and societies. During such times, certain values and rights may not be fully protected by the state. The justification for reducing the level of legal protection lies in the need to safeguard higher-order goods. However, the curtailment of existing rights must have temporal limits. The measures adopted should be proportionate to their intended effects. Otherwise, an emergency could easily develop into a permanent crisis, with lasting effects on the rights and freedoms of individuals.

1.2 Time of emergency—legal sources (Wojciech Piątek)

Given the subject of these considerations, it is appropriate to consider the impact of the above-defined state of emergency on the right of entry and residence of third-country nationals in the territory of the European Union. When searching for the sources of legal regulations in force in this area, it is worth starting the analysis by outlining the threats that give rise to a state of emergency before turning to regulations which directly address emergencies.

The EU legislator, in Directive 2003/109/EC, identifies three types of threats: threats to public policy, public security, and public health. All three appear in the preamble. The first two serve as negative grounds for third-country nationals to apply for residence status in an EU country.[24] All threats, including those related to public health, fall within the competence of the Member State. Examining whether any of these risks apply to long-term residents remains essential.[25] The provisions outlined in the preamble are reflected in the specific provisions of Directive 2003/109/EC, such as those relating to the withdrawal of resident status,[26] exceptions to protection against

---

24 According to recital 8, third-country nationals who wish to acquire and maintain long-term resident status should not constitute a threat to public policy or public security. The notion of public policy may cover a conviction for committing a serious crime.

25 According to Recital 21, the Member State in which a long-term resident intends to exercise his/her right of residence should be able to check that the person concerned meets the conditions for residing in its territory. It should also be able to check that the person concerned does not constitute a threat to public policy, public security or public health.

26 Article 9(3) and (7) of Directive 2003/109/EC.

expulsion,[27] and outright refusal to consider a residence permit on the grounds of a threat to public policy and public security,[28] or public health.[29] A threat to public policy and security provides grounds for refusing family reunification.[30] The types of threats indicated provide grounds for Member States to deny third-country nationals the right to enter and stay on their territory.

In Directive 2008/115/EC, threats to public policy, public security, or national security, are referred to in Article 7(4) in the context of a justification for a Member State to either refrain from setting a period for the voluntary departure of a third-country national or to set a departure period shorter than 7 days.[31] On the other hand, the notion of a serious threat to public policy, public security, or national security appears in Article 11(2), in the context of the duration of an entry ban imposed on a third-country national entering the territory of an EU Member State. The occurrence of such threats allows the entry ban to be extended beyond the 5-year period provided for in Article 11(1) of Directive 2008/115/EC.

A threat to Member States in the form of internal security, public policy, public health and international relations is presented in the preamble of the Schengen Borders Code as a justification for the existence of border controls.[32] A public health threat is defined in Article 2(21) of the Schengen Borders Code as any disease with epidemic potential, as defined by the International Health Regulations of the World Health Organization, as well as other infectious diseases or contagious parasitic diseases if they are the subject of protection

---

27 Article 12(1) of Directive 2003/109/EC.

28 Article 17 of Directive 2003/109/EC.

29 Article 18 of Directive 2003/109/EC. Noteworthy is the wording of Article 18(2), according to which only diseases that may justify a refusal to allow entry or the right of residence in the territory of the second Member State shall be the diseases as defined by the relevant applicable instruments of the World Health Organization, and such other infectious or contagious parasite-based diseases that are the subject of protective provisions in relation to nationals in the host country. Member States shall not introduce new more restrictive provisions or practices.

30 Recital 14 of Directive 2003/86/EC. According to the wording of the second sentence of recital 14, the person who wishes to be granted family reunification should not constitute a threat to public policy or public security.

31 The end result is that exit from the territory of the Member State occurs more quickly than the standard deadline of between 7 and 30 days provided for in Article 7(1) of Directive 2008/115/EC.

32 Recitals 6 and 8 of Regulation 2016/399.

provisions applicable to nationals of the Member States.[33] In the provisions of this regulation, the EU legislator repeatedly refers to the concept of threat in one or all of these areas. The notion of threat is particularly significant in the provisions of Chapter II, which addresses the temporary introduction of controls at internal EU borders.[34]

The Regulation establishing the Community Customs Code also mentions threats to public policy, internal security, or public health. When verifying whether an applicant fulfills the conditions of entry, one of the considerations is whether the individual is considered to be a threat to public policy, internal security, or public health.[35] Such a threat constitutes grounds for refusing to grant a visa.[36]

The EU legislator introduced the new terminology in the preamble to Regulation 2024/1347. Here, the justification for exclusion from international protection is based on the applicant's threat to commit a terrorist attack.[37] In contrast, Regulation 2024/1348 approaches the threat from the opposite perspective, focusing on the persecution of the applicant due to race, religion, nationality, or membership in a social or political group. The terminology refers to the concept of the country of first asylum and the concept of a safe third country.[38]

To sum up this strand of the considerations, the types of threat addressed by the Regulations and Directives on the entry and residence of third-country nationals in the territory of the EU are public policy, internal security and public health. The occurrence of any of these risks necessitates the adoption of measures to prevent or address them.

Turning to the regulations that address emergency situations, the wording of Article 18 of Directive 2008/115/EC deserves attention. It pertains to emergency situations in which an exceptionally large number of third-country nationals subject to return obligations place an unforeseen and significant burden on a Member State's detention facilities or on its administrative or judicial staff. In such circumstances, the Member State

33 Article 2(21) of Regulation 2016/399.
34 Articles 25–30 of Regulation 2016/399.
35 Article 21(3)(d) of Regulation 810/2009.
36 Article 32(1)(a)(6) of Regulation 810/2009.
37 Recital 45 of Regulation 2024/1347.
38 Article 59 of Regulation 2024/1348.

may, for the duration of this exceptional situation, set longer time limits for judicial review[39] and take urgent action regarding detention conditions that deviate from those stipulated in the Directive.[40] The Member State is obliged to inform the Commission when exceptional measures have been implemented and when the reasons for their continued application cease to exist. At the same time, the EU legislator emphasized the exceptional nature of these regulations, clarifying that they cannot be interpreted as allowing a derogation from the general obligation to take all appropriate measures, whether general or specific, to ensure compliance with the Directive.

A similar premise—mass arrivals of third-country nationals in a Member State resulting in the collapse of the asylum system, and the situation of instrumentalization, whereby a third country or a hostile non-state actor encourages or facilitates the movement of third-country nationals or stateless persons to the external borders or to a Member State, with the aim of destabilizing the Union or a Member State—is referred to in Article 1(4) of Regulation 2024/1359 as a crisis situation. The provisions of this regulation establish solidarity mechanisms, consisting of assistance from other Member States to the affected country. The primary means of assistance is the relocation of refugees.[41] Another form is financial contributions for activities relevant to the emergency response.[42] The Regulation also provides for derogations in registering applications for international protection[43] and an accelerated procedure.[44]

Emergency situations are dealt with by the EU legislator in Directive 2008/115/EC, particularly in the context of emergency health care and the needs of vulnerable persons.[45] In such emergencies, the treatment of third-country nationals may not be less favorable than the coercive measures and grounds for withholding of removal provided for in the

---

39 Article 15(2) of Directive 2008/115/EC provides for an accelerated judicial review of the detention measure as soon as possible after its application.

40 These conditions are provided for in Articles 16(1) and 17(2) of Directive 2008/115/EC.

41 Article 4(2)(b)(1) of Regulation 2024/1359.

42 Article 8(1)(b) of Regulation 2024/1359.

43 Articles 10–13 of Regulation 2024/1359.

44 Article 14 of Regulation 2024/1359.

45 Article 4(4)(a) of Directive 2008/115/EC.

Directive. Emergencies involving the need for essential health care and medical treatment must be considered for third-country nationals pending return before the expiry of the voluntary departure period or the period for which removal was withheld.[46] The same considerations regarding the need for emergency health care and essential treatment should apply to persons in detention.[47]

An emergency situation also justifies waiving the requirement to present a travel document valid for at least three months after the intended date of departure from the territory of the Member States when applying for a visa.[48] Similarly, the Schengen Borders Code waives this requirement for the entry of third-country nationals into the EU.[49]

It is clear from the regulations presented that, in practice, three types of emergencies can occur. The first type involves a threat from third-country nationals related to a breach of security rules, public health, or public policy. The second type refers to specific situations involving a large number of third-country nationals and the need to provide them with a specific type of assistance, such as health care. The third type is linked to conditions in the refugee's country of origin. Each type of emergency is associated with specific legal regulations. As demonstrated by the examples presented above, such regulations may concern time limits for certain actions[50] or a relaxation of formal requirements for entry or residence in the EU by third-country nationals.[51]

The first type of emergency—a specific threat from third-country nationals involving the risk of breaching security, public health or public policy rules, whether they are residing in the territory of an EU Member State or applying for the right of residence—will be considered further.

---

46 Article 14(1)(b) of Directive 2008/115/EC.

47 Article 16(3) of Directive 2008/115/EC.

48 Article 12 of Regulation 810/2009.

49 Article 6(1)(a)(i) of Regulation 2016/399.

50 For example, Article 18 of Directive 2008/115/EC provides for longer periods of judicial review.

51 Article 12 of Regulation 810/2009, Article 6(1)(a)(i) of Regulation 2016/399.

1.3 The emergency response mechanism (Rafał Rogala)

1.3.1 Introduction

A crisis should be understood as a situation in which a specific social system—a community, organization, political sector, state or region—faces an imminent threat to its basic structures or fundamental values, characterized by suddenness and a high degree of uncertainty, necessitating rapid and far-reaching actions. Thus, a crisis is defined by three essential elements: threat, suddenness and uncertainty.[52] Crises have also been an inherent feature of public and political debates for years, especially in the context of social stability and security. Many crises lead to massive population displacement. Armed conflicts, natural disasters, economic crises and climate change often force people to migrate in search of security and better living conditions.[53] It is not uncommon for modern migration crises to extend far beyond the classic categories of random incidents. Increasingly, they are the consequence of deliberate and premeditated actions aimed at the political and social structures of individual countries and the European Union itself. Perceived as a disruption to the "normal" order of life, a migration crisis can, therefore, be a tool of hybrid threat to the EU Member States.[54]

In this way, crisis and migration become interconnected, creating one of the most important and emotionally charged axes of the contemporary European debate. As A. Lindley points out, we live in an "era of crisis" and an "era of migration." Migration, in turn, is often seen as a threat to

---

52 Lipscy P.Y., "COVID-19 and the Politics of Crisis" (2020) 74(S1) *International Organization* E98, 99; Boin A., Hart P., Stern E., and Sundelius B., *The Politics of Crisis Management: Public Leadership under Pressure* (2nd edn, Cambridge University Press 2016) 5; Kriesi H., "Crisis Policymaking in the EU: The COVID-19 Crisis and the Refugee Crisis 2015–16 Compared" (First published online: December 2024) *Elements in European Politics*.

53 Lindley A., "Exploring Crisis and Migration Concepts and Issues" in *Crisis and Migration. Critical Perspectives* (Routledge 2014) 1.

54 Greenhill K. M., "Weapons of Mass Migration: Forced Displacement as an Instrument of Coercion" (2010) 9(1) *Strategic Insights* (Spring-Summer 2010) Monterey, California: Naval Postgraduate School; Sascha-Dominik Oliver Vladimir Bachmann, Anthony Paphiti, "Mass Migration as a Hybrid Threat?—A Legal Perspective" (June 30, 2021) 50(1) *Polish Political Science Yearbook* 119–145 <https://ssrn.com/abstract=3897464>.

the sovereignty and integrity of states and is provoking increasingly strong reactions—both social and political.[55]

Faced with massive population movements triggered by factors such as armed conflicts or deepening economic inequality, the European Union and individual Member States, including Poland, must respond swiftly to migration crises.

A. Lindley presents classical models for responding to crises, which reflect the complexity of the phenomena and the multifaceted nature of the actions taken by communities, institutions and governments in the face of threats. Prevention, one of the key elements of crisis management, focuses on identifying and minimizing risks before a crisis occurs. Mechanisms such as early warning systems, income diversification programs or measures to increase community resilience provide the foundation for building stability and preventing potential crises. These efforts are usually reinforced by legal instruments designed to support their implementation. On the other hand, responses of a reactive nature include actions taken in the face of a crisis to mitigate its effects. The third form of response consists of long-term strategies, which focus on socio-economic and political reconstruction after the crisis is over.[56] Political and institutional actions include legislative changes, the creation of specialized management units and the introduction of exceptional administrative measures, such as tighter border controls or states of emergency. While effective in the short term, such measures can lead to social tensions and restrictions on individual rights. Crises are also sometimes used strategically by political actors to achieve their own goals. Crisis narratives are used to mobilize the public, legitimize controversial reforms or consolidate power, which often distracts attention from the real causes and hinders effective governance.[57]

Thus, in the above-described context, migration becomes an area not only of crisis intervention but also of deep-rooted legal change and institutional change. Against this backdrop, temporary processes conducted in a state of

---

55 Lindley A., "Exploring Crisis and Migration Concepts and Issues" in *Crisis and Migration. Critical Perspectives* (Routledge 2014) 1.

56 Lindley A., "Exploring Crisis and Migration Concepts and Issues" in *Crisis and Migration. Critical Perspectives* (Routledge 2014) 1, 6.

57 Lindley A., "Exploring Crisis and Migration Concepts and Issues" in *Crisis and Migration. Critical Perspectives* (Routledge 2014) 1, 7.

emergency gradually become permanent elements of the European Union's migration policy. As a result, states of emergency cease to be mere responses to crises and instead begin to shape regular practices and legal solutions, so that "crisis tools" become an everyday reality.

The emergence of a new reality that normalizes a permanent state of emergency has drawn the attention of researchers.[58] These phenomena require analysis, and the question of whether they are a permanent part of the new reality must be answered. In the context of migration, the phenomenon of permanent emergency confronts us with the question of what direction and shape the response of the European Union and the Member States will take toward such a problem.[59] Migration, perceived as a security problem, shapes and will shape the political discourse, the public perception of this phenomenon, and the legislative environment, and will significantly affect the rights and obligations of both the Union as a whole and its citizens, especially citizens of third countries, i.e., migrants.

The author of this chapter examines the interplay between crisis and migration, looking at how the European Union, individual Member States, and Poland, in particular, are responding to migration challenges in crisis situations. He pays special attention to migrants, both those seeking protection and those migrating for economic reasons, as they are often at the center of disputes over security, human rights and national sovereignty. Invoking the concept of migration as a security issue, the author addresses the growing concerns and tensions surrounding migration issues, as well as

---

58 Gerbaudo M., "The European Commission's Instrumentalization Strategy: Normalising Border Procedures and De Facto Detention" (2022) 7 *European Papers* 615, 626 <https://www.europeanpapers.eu/en/europeanforum/european-commission-instrumentalization-strategy-border-procedures-detention#_ftnref56>.

59 This phenomenon has also been recognized at the level of European institutions, which clearly indicate that they have been operating for many years in a state of permanent crisis. Cf. European Parliamentary Research, Rebecca Torpeywith, Christoffer Nielsen, PE 757.822—June 2024: "Since 2009, the European Council has been operating in a permanent state of crisis—addressing economic, migration, foreign affairs and health crises—some simultaneously. These crises have varied in their cause as well as their impact on the EU. Some, even though external (e.g., Libya and Syria), had knock-on effects that impacted the European continent or were linked to other crises the EU faced (e.g., migration)" <https://www.europarl.europa.eu/RegData/etudes/BRIE/2024/757822/EPRS_BRI(2024)757822_EN.pdf>.

the perpetuation of the legal state of emergency, which may eventually lead to a redefinition of the concept of protection and humanitarianism on the European continent.

It is worth noting that the actions in question do not result solely from the mere fact of the crisis but are also shaped by various factors, such as political motivations, media narratives and public perceptions of the situation. This relationship is not a direct result of increased migration but rather the interaction of objective migration processes with subjective narratives created by the media, politicians and other actors involved in migration issues. The phenomenon should be viewed constructively, which means that the analysis should consider how migration is interpreted and presented in different social and political contexts.[60]

Historical analysis reveals that refugee migrations in the so-called migration age of the twentieth century—from the aftermath of World War II to decolonization processes to the current conflicts in the Middle East and Ukraine—have consistently been portrayed as crises that required extraordinary political action. States have always struggled with the challenges of controlling migration, but in the era of globalization and economic deregulation, these problems have taken on particular intensity. While most governments have abandoned the old mechanisms of exit control, the regulation of immigration has reached an unprecedented level of sophistication, requiring intensive bilateral, regional and international action.

Until the 1980s, international migration was not a central political issue in many Western countries. The rise of interest in international migration management began in the late 1980s, when migration became a topic of discussion in international political forums.[61] One of the key elements of global migration management was the introduction of freedom of movement arrangements within regional unions such as the European Union (EU), the Economic Community of West African States (ECOWAS), the Association of Southeast Asian Nations (ASEAN) and the Common Market of the South (Mercosur). In the case of the EU, the signing of the Schengen Agreement

---

60 Cantat C., Pécoud A., and Thiollet H., "Migration as Crisis" (OnlineFirst, SAGE Journals) 3 <https://doi.org/10.1177/000276422311828892023>.

61 de Haas C., Castles H., and Miller M. J., *The Age of Migration: International Population Movements in the Modern World* (6th edn, Guilford Press 2020).

in 1985,[62] and its full implementation in 1999,[63] made it possible to eliminate internal borders between Member States, but at the same time posed challenges in terms of joint control of external borders and harmonization of visa and immigration policies.[64] This undoubted achievement became an asset that, in the perception of politicians, also required protection. A prosperous and peaceful Europe, in turn, became the target of increased migration driven by the aforementioned factors. A crisis emerged at the boundary between these two spaces.

1.3.2 The 2015–2016 migration crisis

Undoubtedly, the apogee of the migration crisis occurred in 2015. However, its signs were already visible much earlier. Despite this, defining exact time frames within which this phenomenon can be situated is problematic.[65] Taking into account the criterion of purposeful presentation, the response of states and the European Union to the crisis was framed as broadly as possible,

---

62 The Agreement of June 14, 1985 between the Governments of the States of the Benelux Economic Union, the Federal Republic of Germany and the French Republic on the gradual abolition of controls at their common borders, OJ L 239, September 22, 2000, 13–18.

63 Under the Treaty of Amsterdam of October 2, 1997, amending the Treaty on European Union, the Treaties establishing the European Communities and certain related acts OJ C 340, November 10, 1997, 115, which entered into force on May 1, 1999, the Schengen acquis was incorporated into European Union law.

64 de Haas C., Castles H., and Miller M. J., *The Age of Migration: International Population Movements in the Modern World* (6th edn, Guilford Press 2020).

65 U.N. agencies have questioned the validity of the term, pointing out that countries with fewer resources have coped with larger migrant flows (Miles T. “U.N. View on the European Migrant Crisis? There Isn’t One” (2018) *Reuters* <https://www.reuters.com/article/world/un-view-on-the-european-migrant-crisis-there-isnt-one-idUSKBN1JW22N/>). It has been suggested that the EU was deliberately creating a crisis for political gain, justifying the characterization of the situation as a political crisis (de Bellis M., “European Leaders Are Manufacturing a ‘Migration Crisis’ for Political Gain” (January 18, 2019) *Amnesty International Blog* <https://www.amnesty.org/en/latest/news/2019/01/european-leaders-are-manufacturing-a-migration-crisis-for-political-gain/>). The European Commission, which adopted the rhetoric of the crisis in 2015–2016, later itself criticized the perpetuation of this narrative as disinformation (Rankin J, “EU Declares Migration Crisis Over as It Hits Out at ‘Fake News’” (2019) *Guardian* <https://www.theguardian.com/world/2019/mar/06/eu-declares-migration-crisis-over-hits-out-fake-news-european-commission>).

considering as its beginning the potentially most significant trigger—the Arab Spring and its repercussions. In turn, in view of the continuous influx of migrants, varying in terms of intensity, it is not possible to establish a specific end date for this phenomenon.

Since the beginning of the twenty-first century, the regulation of migration flows has been at the heart of EU policy toward neighboring countries, particularly in southern Europe. The range of instruments at the time was limited to the blunt reinforcement of external borders, the introduction of stricter regulations on illegal migration, or the conclusion of bilateral border cooperation treaties—especially between the EU's Southern Member States and the EU's southern neighbors.[66] These measures initially seemed sufficient to keep illegal migration to the EU under control.[67] However, in light of the events that followed the outbreak of the so-called Arab Spring, the above solutions proved unreliable. The reconfiguration of *the status quo* since 2011 has destabilized the European Union's southern neighborhood. In particular, the complex political situation and the escalation of armed conflicts in Syria and Libya led to a loosening of border controls and mass migration. As a result, the EU faced mixed migration flows of unprecedented scale.[68]

The overthrow of Mu'ammar al-Gaddafi's regime in Libya, which had paradoxically stemmed the tide of migration from the African continent to Europe, had a significant impact on the increase in the number of refugees heading to Europe.[69] The number of illegal crossings at the external

---

66 An example is the treaty of friendship, partnership and cooperation signed between Italy and Libya on August 30, 2008, under which Italy was to finance Libyan infrastructure projects totaling $5 billion over 20 years in exchange for guarantees of cooperation in the fight against illegal migration (Ronzitti N., "The Treaty on Friendship, Partnership and Cooperation between Italy and Libya: New Prospects for Cooperation in the Mediterranean?" (2009) 1(1) *Bulletin of Italian Politics* 129–130 <https://www.gla.ac.uk/bip>). A similar agreement was concluded in 1992 between Spain and Morocco. Although it did not enter into force until 20 years after it was signed, the two countries have cooperated in combating illegal migration. (Carrera S., Cassarino J. P., Den Hertog L., et al., "EU-Morocco Cooperation on Readmission, Borders and Protection: A Model to Follow?" (2016) *CEPS* www.ceps.eu.

67 Strazzari F., *Dissecting the EU Response to the "Migration Crisis"* (Manchester University Press eBooks 2021) Academia.edu, 1.

68 Strazzari F., *Dissecting...*, 1–2.

69 Dahl M., and Dziudzik A., "States of the European Union towards the 2015 Immigration Crisis" (2017) 3(244) *European Union.co.uk*.

borders of EU Member States increased by 35 % in 2011 compared to 2009–2010, reaching almost 141,000 cases. The migrants mainly came from Tunisia (20 %), Afghanistan (16 %) and Pakistan (11 %). A significant increase in detections was recorded in the Mediterranean, where the number of illegal crossings surged from 5,000 in 2010 to more than 64,000 in 2011.[70]

Italy, Malta, and Greece proved to be the hardest-hit countries, and their responses to the crisis had a domino effect throughout the European Union.

Faced with migratory pressures, Italy implemented measures that reflect the specificity of its approach to migration crises in the Mediterranean region. A particularly significant event was the so-called "Lampedusa Crisis" of 2011.[71] Italy's actions were multidirectional. On February 12, 2011, a state of humanitarian emergency was declared throughout the country under Article 5 of Law No. 225/1992 on the Protection of Civilians, which allowed the delegation of emergency powers to special commissioners. The commissioners were given the authority to establish centers and temporary spaces where migrants could be detained.[72] Such facilities often operated outside the standard legal framework, leading to a state of "legal indeterminacy" and arbitrary deprivation of migrants' liberty.[73]

Following previous practices, a diplomatic initiative was launched with the migrants' countries of origin. A key moment was the signing of an agreement with Tunisia on April 5, 2011 concerning police cooperation and the readmission of migrants residing illegally. All those who arrived in Italy from Tunisia after that time were considered illegal border crossers and returned to Tunisia under the agreement. With regard to the migrants residing in Lampedusa, the Italian authorities used the national temporary protection procedure outlined in Article 20 of the Italian Immigration Law. Temporary residence permits on humanitarian grounds were granted to migrants who arrived by April 5, 2011, in order to reduce pressure on the national asylum

---

70 General Report 2011, Frontex, frontex.europa.eu/General_Report_2011.

71 Campesi G., "The Arab Spring and the Crisis of the European Border Regime: Manufacturing Emergency in the Lampedusa Crisis" (2018) <https://www.eui.eu/documents/rscas/research/mwg/201011/5-25-campesi.pdf>.

72 Campesi G. (2018) 5–7.

73 Campesi G. (2018) 12.

system and facilitate their onward movement to other EU countries such as France and Germany. However, this solution provoked controversy within the Schengen framework, with other Member States, such as France and Germany, accusing Italy of violating the spirit of cooperation on migration control.[74] In response, the French government decided to close the southern border with Italy and resume border controls.[75] This development had two key consequences. On the one hand, it set a precedent for Schengen Member States to reintroduce controls at the EU's internal borders. On the other, it initiated efforts to reform EU legislation in this area and strengthen the position of EU institutions overseeing the proper understanding of the "Schengen spirit."[76] Italy was criticized for prioritizing security over human rights, particularly for its prolonged detention of migrants in conditions that violated international law, including Directive 2008/115/EC on the return of illegal migrants.[77] The situation in Lampedusa became a catalyst for broader reflection on the European border regime and the division of responsibilities in managing migration crises. It is noteworthy that the Member State most affected by the crisis inadvertently caused a secondary crisis in its response. As we will see later, this model would be successfully adopted by other countries and would contribute to in-depth discussions on the instrumentalization of migration.

The refugee crisis triggered by the civil war in Libya in 2011 presented the European Union with the challenge of balancing humanitarian action with migration control policies. On the one hand, the Union encouraged Member States to provide humanitarian assistance and asylum to refugees. On the other hand, measures were implemented to prevent

---

74 Campesi G. (2018) 12.

75 Collett E., "Faltering Movement: Explaining Europe's Schengen Struggle" (November 2, 2011) *Migration Policy Institute* <https://www.migrationpolicy.org/article/faltering-movement-explaining-europes-schengen-struggle>.

76 Guild E., Carrera S., Vosyliūtė L., Groenendijk K., Brouwer E., Bigo D., Jeandesboz J., and Martin-Mazé M., *Internal Border Controls in the Schengen Area: Is Schengen Crisis Proof?* (2016) Policy Department C: Citizens' Rights and Constitutional Affairs, European Parliament <https://www.europarl.europa.eu/RegData/etudes/STUD/2016/571356/IPOL_STU%282016%29571356_EN.pdf>.

77 Directive 2008/115/EC of the European Parliament and of the Council of December 16, 2008 on common standards and procedures in Member States for returning illegally staying third-country nationals (OJ EU. L. 2008, No. 348, 98, as amended).

a massive influx of irregular migrants, often exploited by organized crime networks.[78] A May 2011 European Commission communiqué acknowledged that 650,000 people had fled Libya due to the conflict. In response, the Union repatriated 50,000 third-country nationals to their countries of origin and allocated 80.5 million euros in humanitarian aid for refugees in North Africa.[79]

In December 2011, the European Commission launched the Regional Protection Program in North Africa. A key element of the program was the resettlement of refugees in EU Member States to strengthen international cooperation within the its framework.[80] The European Commission sought to persuade Member States of the need to resettle some of refugees from the Arab Spring countries. Despite these appeals, Europe resettled only 700 refugees in 2011. The Union's response to the crisis was criticized by Cecilia Malmström, then Commissioner for Home Affairs, who stated in a speech at Harvard University in 2012 that no Member State had taken a serious initiative to provide shelter for those in need of international protection.[81] She also stressed that instead of showing solidarity, Member States—such as France and Italy—focused on securing their internal borders, even reinforcing controls at the French-Italian border.[82]

1.3.2.1 Schengen border code reform

In response to unilateral actions taken by Member States, such as the reintroduction of internal border controls, the European Commission proposed

---

78 Fargues, P., and Fandrich C., *Migration after the Arab Spring*. MPC Research Report 2012/09 (Migration Policy Center, European University Institute 2012).

79 European Commission, "Communication on Migration" (Communication) COM (2011) 248 final, May 4, 2011.

80 Fargues P., and Fandrich C., *Migration after the Arab Spring* (MPC Research Report 2012/09, Migration Policy Centre 2012) <https://cadmus.eui.eu/bitstream/handle/1814/23504/MPC-RR-2012-09.pdf?sequence=1>.

81 Malmström C., *Responding to the Arab Spring and Rising Populism: The Challenges of Building a European Migration and Asylum Policy*. Lecture at Harvard University's Minda de Gunzburg Center for European Studies (Boston, Massachusetts 2012). Retrieved from <http://europa.eu/rapid/pressReleasesAction.do?reference=SPEECH/12/312&format=HTML&aged=0&language=EN&guiLanguage=en>.

82 European Commission, *Communication on Migration* [COM (2011) 248 final].

reforms to Schengen governance.[83] Recognizing the security of external borders as crucial to the functioning of the Schengen area, the Commission proposed a mechanism for automatically suspending the free movement of people in situations where Member States fail to meet their obligations to protect external borders.[84] However, the proposals met with criticism from the European Parliament, which stressed that existing rules already sufficiently regulate the temporary reintroduction of controls and that new exceptions are unnecessary. It also pointed out that migration should not be seen as a threat to public order and internal security. As a result of the 2013 amendments to the Schengen Borders Code and the Schengen Evaluation and Monitoring Mechanism, significant modifications were made to the governance of the Schengen area. The most important change was the introduction of the possibility of temporarily reintroducing internal controls for up to two years in the event of deficits at external borders, which required a recommendation from the Council on a proposal from the European Commission. The reformed Schengen evaluation and monitoring mechanism, integrated into EU law, gave the Commission a key role in overseeing and evaluating Member States' actions, increasing transparency and accountability through detailed reports and annual reports. New rules on procedures and criteria for reintroducing controls were intended to improve Schengen governance, by striking a balance between freedom of movement and internal security.[85] However, the EU's overall response to the refugee crisis remained primarily security-oriented, which often conflicted with the principles of solidarity and humanitarianism.[86]

---

83 European Commission, Proposal for a Regulation of the European Parliament and of the Council Amending Regulation (EC), No. 562/2006 in order to provide for common rules on the temporary reintroduction of border control at internal borders in exceptional circumstances [COM (2011) 560 final], Brussels, September 16, 2011.

84 Carrera S., "An Assessment of the Commission's 2011 Schengen Governance Package: Preventing Abuse by EU Member States of Freedom of Movement?" (2012) 47 *CEPS Paper in Liberty and Security in Europe*.

85 Guild E., Carrera S., Vosyliūtė L., Groenendijk K., Brouwer E., Bigo D., Jeandesboz J., and Martin-Mazé M., *Internal Border Controls in the Schengen Area: Is Schengen Crisis Proof?* (Policy Department C: Citizens' Rights and Constitutional Affairs, European Parliament 2016).

86 Fargues P., and Fandrich C., *Migration after the Arab Spring* (MPC Research Report 2012/09, Migration Policy Centre, European University Institute 2012).

1.3.2.2 Actions prior to the apogee of the crisis

In the period leading up to the height of the migration crisis, there were key turning points that significantly influenced the EU and Member States' response to the crisis, contributing, as it were, to a consolidated approach. These are mainly the tragic incidents at sea that resulted in the loss of hundreds of migrants' lives as they attempted to reach Europe. The first of these occurred on October 3, 2013, off the coast of the Italian island of Lampedusa, when a boat sank, resulting in the deaths of 366 people traveling from Libya to Italy.[87] Another tragic incident was the sinking of a ship carrying migrants and asylum seekers from Libya to Italy on April 19, 2015, claiming more than 800 lives. The UNHCR later described the incident as "the most serious humanitarian disaster of recent times."[88]

In response to the tragic events of 2013, the European Union addressed only isolated aspects of the problem, sidestepping, as it were, the broader issues of the emerging crisis. *Task Force Mediterranean (TFM)* was established, led by the Italian government and the European Commission as part of Operation *Mare Nostrum*.[89] It should be noted that more than 100,000 people were rescued during the following year as part of this operation.[90] In 2013, the European Border Surveillance System (EUROSUR) was also established as a framework for information exchange and cooperation between Member States and Frontex.[91] Its main objectives were to improve situational awareness and increase response capabilities at the European Union's external borders.

---

87 Reachel Dickson sees the very beginning of the migration crisis in this date. Dickson R., *Migration Law, Policy and Human Rights: The Impact of Crisis in Europe* (Routledge, 2022).

88 Bonomolo A., and Kirchgaessner S., "UN Says 800 Migrants Dead in Boat Disaster as Italy Launches Rescue of Two More Vessels" (April 20, 2015) *The Guardian* <https://www.theguardian.com/world/2015/apr/20/italy-pm-matteo-renzi-migrant-shipwreck-crisis-srebrenica-massacre>.

89 3336th Council Meeting Justice and Home Affairs October 9–10, 2014, 14044/14.

90 Adam Taylor, "Italy Ran an Operation That Saved Thousands of Migrants from Drowning in the Mediterranean. Why Did It Stop?" (April 20, 2015) *The Washington Post* <www.washingtonpost.com/news/worldviews/wp/2015/04/20/italy-ran-an-operation-that-save-thousands-of-migrants-from-drowning-in-the-mediterranean-why-did-it-stop/>.

91 European Commission, "EUROSUR" (Home Affairs: Schengen, Borders and Visa) <https://home-affairs.ec.europa.eu/policies/schengen-borders-and-visa/border-crossing/eurosur_en>.

EUROSUR was created to prevent cross-border crime, counter irregular migration, and contribute to the protection of migrants' lives.[92] Despite a growing sense of urgency—partly triggered by Operation *Mare Nostrum*—initial policy efforts failed to bring about significant systemic change. The December 2013 *Task Force Mediterranean* report mainly reiterated existing approaches, such as the Global Approach to Migration and Mobility, Frontex operations, and EUROSUR. It was not until June 2014 that EU leaders agreed on new strategic guidelines to shape policy for the next few years, yet these failed to deliver substantial breakthroughs.[93]

The European Commission identified the main areas of action for *Task Force Mediterranean*: cooperation with third countries; regional protection, resettlement and strengthening of legal migration routes to Europe; combating human trafficking, smuggling and organized crime; strengthening border surveillance; improving the situational maritime picture and protecting and saving migrant lives in the Mediterranean; and support and solidarity with Member States facing migration pressures. In practice, these activities were limited to only a few meetings and the development of guidelines. While *the TFM* was not recognized as an effective crisis response mechanism, the general thrust of the migration strategy remains a key element of contemporary policy initiatives.[94]

The migration crisis peaked in 2015 when the number of asylum applications filed in European countries reached an unprecedented level of nearly 1.3 million.[95] This was almost double the previous record of 700,000 applications, recorded in 1992 following the fall of the Berlin Wall. The

---

92 Dickson R., *Migration Law, Policy and Human Rights: The Impact of Crisis in Europe* (Routledge, 2022).

93 Collett E., and Le Coz C., *After the Storm: Learning from the EU Response to the Migration Crisis* (Migration Policy Institute, June 2018) <https://www.migrationpolicy.org/research/after-storm-eu-response-migration-crisis>.

94 Collett E., and Le Coz C., "After the Storm: Learning from the EU Response to the Migration Crisis" (June 2018) *Migration Policy Institute* <https://www.migrationpolicy.org/research/after-storm-eu-response-migration-crisis>; European Commission, "Communication from the Commission to the European Parliament and the Council on the Work of the Task Force Mediterranean" (COM [2013] 869 final, December 4, 2013).

95 Eurostat: Statistics | Eurostat <https://ec.europa.eu/eurostat/databrowser/view/migr_asyappctza__custom_15611029/default/table?lang=en>.

predominant countries of origin of the applicants were Syria, Afghanistan and Iraq, which were then engulfed in bloody armed conflicts. Half of the asylum seekers in 2015 came from these three countries. In contrast, the main countries receiving applications were Germany (442,000), Hungary (174,000) and Sweden (156,000). However, the geographic distribution of the number of asylum applications in Europe was highly uneven. The average number of applications was 250 per 100,000 inhabitants. Hungary had the highest rate, with 1,770 applications per 100,000 residents, followed by Sweden with 1,600. Germany accepted 540 applications per 100,000 residents, which was significantly above the European average. In comparison, France and the UK recorded 110 and 60 applications per 100,000 residents, respectively. It is worth noting that between 1985 and 2015, a total of approximately 11.6 million asylum applications were filed in Europe, with about 10 % of this number submitted in 2015 alone.[96] The most intensive migration flows took place in the Aegean Sea, between Turkey and Greece, where more than 850,000 people, mainly from Syria, Iraq and Afghanistan, crossed in 2015. However, the dynamics of migration along this route were altered by the controversial agreement between the European Union and Turkey, concluded in March 2016, which significantly restricted migration toward southeastern Europe.

The tragedy that occurred on April 19, 2015 off the coast of Lampedusa, where more than 800 people died, shocked public opinion around the world and revealed the scale of the migration crisis facing the European Union. The disaster became a symbol of the dramatic challenges of migration and the urgent need for an effective and solidarity-based response to the influx of refugees and migrants. In response to these events, the European Commission adopted the European Agenda on Migration in May 2015, which was intended as a comprehensive approach to migration management, border protection and humanitarian support.[97] The Agenda set out both short-term and medium-term actions to deal with the unprecedented influx of migrants. The EU recognized that migration required a coherent and comprehensive approach,

---

96 Eurostat: <https://tiny.pl/rmr_6hry>.

97 European Commission, *Communication from the Commission to the European Parliament, the Council, the European Economic and Social Committee and the Committee of the Regions: A European Agenda on Migration* (COM(2015) 240 final) (Brussels 2015, May 13). Retrieved from <https://eur-lex.europa.eu/legal-content/PL/TXT/?uri=CELEX%3A52015DC0240>.

including both European and national action. A key objective of the program was to reduce the impact of the migration crisis in the Mediterranean, while addressing long-term solutions related to migration management. For this reason, the solutions adopted were divided into immediate actions and long-term solutions.

The Agenda stressed the need for immediate action, which was crucial in responding to the humanitarian crisis. One of the key elements was the intensification of search and rescue operations in the Mediterranean. Operations *Triton* and *Poseidon*, led by Frontex, were significantly strengthened with a threefold increase in budget and resources. These operations were aimed not only at protecting the EU's external borders, but above all at saving human lives at sea, which had become a priority of the EU's migration policy in the face of a growing number of accidents.[98]

At the same time, the Agenda included the fight against organized crime, including human trafficking networks that exploited migrants, putting them at risk. The European Commission introduced an action plan against human trafficking, which included operations under Operation *EUNAVFOR MED* (also known as Operation Sophia), aimed at identifying and destroying vessels used by traffickers. These activities were aimed not only at disrupting trafficking activities but also at discouraging the use of illegal migration routes.[99] The Agenda also included mechanisms for the relocation and resettlement of migrants and refugees. The solutions were intended only to precede the adoption of permanent systemic solutions, the preparation of which the European Commission announced in the document. Temporary relocation schemes were designed to support frontline countries, such as Greece and Italy, which were most burdened by the influx of migrants. The mechanism provided for the relocation of 40,000 people in need of international protection, which was expected to provide important assistance in managing the crisis. In addition, the resettlement of 20,000 non-EU refugees by 2020 in cooperation with the Office of the High Commissioner for Refugees (UNHCR) was proposed, with a budget of €50 million for 2015–2016. While these mechanisms were innovative, their implementation faced significant difficulties, including a lack of solidarity from some Member States, which

---

98 European Commission, *Communication from the Commission* (2015, May 13) 4.
99 European Commission, *Communication from the Commission* (2015, May 13) 5.

limited their effectiveness.[100] These solutions will be presented in more detail later, as they have permanently entered the canon of measures adopted in emergency situations in the European Union. As such, they have also become the subject of intense political and social discussions and disputes.

Faced with the migration crisis, the European Union also took steps to support the countries most affected by the influx of refugees and to strengthen migration management at the regional and global levels. A key element was the expansion of protection and development programs in North Africa, the Horn of Africa and the Middle East, which received €30 million in 2015–2016, to reduce migration pressures by improving the living conditions of refugees in their regions of origin.

In Niger, for example, a multifunctional pilot center was established and implemented with international partners, which provided protection, information and support for the voluntary return of migrants. At the same time, migration was integrated into Common Security and Defense Policy (CSDP) missions, such as operations in Niger and Mali, enabling more effective border management and combating smuggling. Cooperation with African and Middle Eastern countries also led to a summit in Malta to develop a common approach to managing migration and combating smuggling and human trafficking. In response to the Syrian crisis, the EU allocated €3.6 billion in humanitarian and stabilization aid for refugees in Syria and neighboring countries.[101]

1.3.2.3 Hotspots

The next step was the innovative use of the hotspot approach, which aimed to streamline the identification, registration and fingerprinting of migrants in particularly affected areas. This initiative was supported by EU agencies such as Frontex, Europol and the European Asylum Support Office (EASO). Their task was to assist local authorities in Greece and Italy. The agencies' activities were coordinated as follows: EASO supported asylum procedures, Frontex handled the organization of the return of persons not entitled to protection, and Europol and Eurojust conducted investigations to dismantle smuggling and trafficking networks. This ensured that asylum seekers could

100 European Commission, *Communication from the Commission* (2015, May 13) 5–6.

101 European Commission, *Communication from the Commission* (2015, May 13) 6–7.

be swiftly referred to the appropriate procedures and that those illegally present in the EU could be returned more efficiently to their countries of origin. The hotspot approach became one of the pillars of the EU's response to the migration crisis. However, it required further improvements to meet the growing challenges and ensure that the solutions implemented were fully effective.

A key problem was the lack of a clear legal framework governing the operation of "hotspots." Although the hotspot approach was formally introduced as part of the European Agenda on Migration, its implementation was mainly based on executive decisions and national regulations in Greece and Italy.

The lack of clear guidelines and standards led to uneven treatment of migrants and potential violations of their fundamental rights.[102] Hotspot management was based on a patchwork of legal and policy documents from different European, international and national levels, leading to fragmentation and difficulty in applying them consistently.[103] At the European level, the key document introducing this approach was the 2015 *European Agenda on Migration*. Regulations of individual EU agencies provide additional information on their role in hotspots[104] but lack a precise definition of the

---

102 Halilovic A., "Executive Migration Governance and Law-making in the European Union: Towards a State of Exception," (2024) 9(2) *European Papers* 518.

103 Tas S., "Fundamental Rights Violations in the Hotspots: Who Is Watching over Them?" (2022) 7(1) *European Papers*, 217–219.

104 European Asylum Support Office (EASO): Regulation (EU) No. 439/2010 of the European Parliament and of the Council of May 19, 2010 establishing the European Asylum Support Office, in particular Article 2 and Article 10 stipulate the possibility of sending asylum support teams in situations of special needs in Member States under migratory pressure; Frontex Agency (European Border and Coast Guard Agency): Regulation (EU) 2016/1624 of the European Parliament and of the Council of September 14, 2016 on the European Border and Coast Guard Agency, Article 16 and Article 17 describe Frontex's involvement in the identification, registration, fingerprinting and support in organizing the return of migrants; Europol: Regulation (EU) 2016/794 of the European Parliament and of the Council of May 11, 2016. on the European Union Agency for the Cooperation of Law Enforcement Agencies (Europol), Article 4 and Article 5 indicate that Europol supports the fight against human smuggling and trafficking, and carries out intelligence activities and coordinates hotspot operations; Eurojust: Regulation (EU) 2018/1727 of the European Parliament and of the Council of November 14, 2018. on the European Union Agency for Criminal Justice Cooperation (Eurojust), Articles 2–3 highlight Eurojust's role in combating organized crime, including supporting human smuggling activities

mechanism.[105] While there is no formal definition of the approach, in practice, hotspots have become a key component of migrant relocation in Greece and Italy, according to Council Decisions 2015/1523[106] and 2015/1601[107] of September 2015.

In Greece, "Hotspots" were introduced by Law No. 4375/2016,[108] which transformed the existing migrant reception system established by Law No. 3907/2011.[109] Newly arrived migrants were directed to Reception and Identification Centres (RICs) located on the islands of Lesbos, Chios, Samos, Kos and Leros. Registration and verification procedures included a restriction on freedom of movement within the center for three days, extendable to a maximum of 25 days. Initially, the hotspots operated as open registration and support centers, but over time they evolved into more restrictive processing centers in accordance with national and EU regulations.

In Italy, the "Hotspot" approach was implemented in key border points such as Puglia (Taranto) and Sicily (Lampedusa, Pozzallo, Messina). By the end of 2018, four such centers were in operation, using the existing infrastructure.

---

in hotspot operations; Eurodac: Regulation (EU) No. 603/2013 of the European Parliament and of the Council of June 26, 2013 on the establishment of Eurodac, Articles 8 and 9 indicate the procedures involved in fingerprinting migrants and entering them into the database.

105 Tas S., "Fundamental Rights Violations in the Hotspots: Who Is Watching over Them?" (2022) 7(1) *European Papers* 218.

106 Council of the European Union, *Decision (EU) 2015/1523 of September 14, 2015 Establishing Provisional Measures in the Area of International Protection in Favor of Italy and Greece* [2015] OJ L239/146.

107 Council of the European Union, Decision (EU) 2015/1601 *of September 22 2015 Establishing Provisional Measures in the Area of International Protection in Favor of Italy and Greece* [2015] OJ L248/80.

108 Law No. 4375/2016: This law regulates the organization and functioning of the Asylum Service, the Appeals Office, the Reception and Identification Service, and establishes the General Secretariat for Reception. It also brings Greek law into line with Directive 2013/32/EU of the European Parliament and the Council on common procedures for granting and withdrawing international protection status <https://migrant-integration.ec.europa.eu/library-document/greek-asylum-law-43752016_en>.

109 Law No. 3907/2011: This law establishes the Asylum Service and the First Reception Service, bringing Greek law in line with Directive 2008/115/EC concerning common standards and procedures in the Member States for the return of illegally staying third-country nationals <https://migrant-integration.ec.europa.eu/library-document/law-no-39072011-gg-726012011-establishment-asylum-service-and-service-first_en>.

Italian "hotspots" focused on quickly identifying migrants and registering them, avoiding the need to create new facilities.

The "hotspot" approach was intended to support frontline states in effectively managing migration, but it encountered many challenges in practice. While, on the one hand, it allowed for better cooperation between EU agencies and national authorities, supporting the identification of migrants and the separation of those in need of international protection from those to be returned, on the other hand, it revealed serious shortcomings. The system struggled with infrastructure deficiencies, administrative overload, and limited support and solidarity from other EU Member States. Conditions at the hotspots were subject to harsh criticism from civil society organizations, which alleged overcrowding at the centers, lack of access to essential services, and inhumane and even illegal detention conditions. Amnesty International and Human Rights Watch have repeatedly pointed out serious shortcomings in the operation of hotspots, such as inadequate medical care, poor-quality food and accommodation, and overcrowded facilities.[110] Although the hotspot approach was initially seen as a practical emergency tool to respond quickly to an exceptional influx of migrants at the EU's borders, serious operational, legal and humanitarian problems emerged during its implementation. These difficulties limited its effectiveness and made it the target of widespread criticism from NGOs and international institutions. A 2016 report by Amnesty International examined in detail the problems associated with the operation of hotspots in Greece and Italy, highlighting their numerous shortcomings and human rights violations. The document described cases of arbitrary deprivation of liberty, which often took place in conditions that violated Article 3 of the European Convention on Human Rights, which prohibits inhuman and degrading treatment.[111]

---

110 Amnesty International, "Hotspot Approach: How EU's Flagship Approach Leads to Inhumane and Ineffective Treatment of Refugees and Migrants," EUR 30/5004/2016 (2016) <https://www.amnesty.org/en/documents/eur30/5004/2016/en/>. "EU Hotspots and Breaches of Human Security" (2016); Human Rights Watch, *Greece: Refugee "Hotspots" Unsafe, Unsanitary—Women, Children Fearful, Unprotected; Lack Basic Shelter* (May 19, 2016) Greece: Refugee "Hotspots" Unsafe, Unsanitary | Human Rights Watch.

111 Amnesty International, *Hotspot Approach: How the EU's Flagship Approach Leads to Inhumane and Ineffective Treatment of Refugees and Migrants* (2016) 14–16, 18.

Amnesty International criticized the excessive focus of the hotspot approach on crisis management and security at the expense of protecting human rights. Migrants in hotspots were often seen as "objects of risk," and the lack of transparency in procedures and limited access to legal assistance led to the marginalization of their fundamental rights. Many were denied access to asylum procedures or prevented from fully understanding their rights, resulting in violations of basic principles of refugee law, including the principle of non-refoulement, which prohibits returning people to countries where they could face persecution.[112] The report also stressed that hotspots have failed to live up to expectations as a migration management tool. Numerous delays in administrative processes, a lack of effective coordination between EU agencies and limited resources led to significant difficulties in achieving the intended goals. The relocation of migrants from Greece and Italy to other Member States was poorly implemented, revealing a lack of real solidarity within the European Union.[113]

The most criticized issue in the report was the documented use of illegal *pushback* practices. Greece and Italy have been repeatedly accused of returning migrants to third countries, such as Turkey, without providing them with the opportunity to apply for asylum. Amnesty International considered these actions a serious violation of international law and EU human rights standards. The organization stressed that such practices not only pose a threat to the lives and safety of migrants but also undermine the legal foundations underlying EU migration policy.[114] The situation in Greece in 2020 raised particular concern when the Greek government and Frontex were accused of using *pushbacks*, that is, pushing migrants and asylum seekers back to Turkey without allowing them to apply for protection. These actions were found to violate both the Geneva Convention and other international human rights obligations.[115] The consequences of these practices were serious, not only for asylum seekers but also for the reputation of the EU's migration management

---

112 Amnesty International, *Hotspot approach…*, 20, 22–23, 26–28.

113 Amnesty International, *Hotspot approach…*, 30–32.

114 Amnesty International, *Hotspot approach…*, 34–36.

115 Calarco G., "Conditions in Hotspots: Overcrowding and Inhumane Practices" in Cantat C., Pécoud A., Thiollet H. (eds), *Migration as Crisis* (2023) 9.

mechanisms. Ultimately, the controversy led to the resignation of the Frontex director in 2022.[116]

One of the key aspects of the criticism was the transformation of the perception of migrants from "subjects of protection" to "subjects of risk." This process was reflected not only in the political discourse of the EU but also in the public debate on the operation of hotspots. The introduction of advanced intelligence mechanisms on the front lines of the migration crisis, such as biometric and risk analysis systems, has created tensions between the logic of security management and human rights protection in the EU. As Jeandesboz noted, these "heavy intelligence mechanisms" have reinforced tensions between a security-focused approach and one based on humanitarian protection.[117] The European Parliament has repeatedly noted the need to ensure that the categorization of migrants in hotspots is carried out with full respect for human rights.[118] One resolution stressed that it is crucial to focus on protection and humanitarian assistance rather than solely on security. One came from outside the EU institutions, particularly from NGOs, which accused the EU of using "anti-migrant security measures" and repressive treatment of asylum seekers. Practices such as prolonged detention, lack of access to asylum procedures, and rapid deportations were widely criticized for their incompatibility with international refugee law.[119]

At the international level, the 2016 EU-Turkey agreement[120] had a particular impact on the operation of hotspots. In Greece, the agreement transformed hotspots from open reception centers to return and detention centers, thereby

---

116 Politico, "EU Border Agency Chief Resigns after Critical Watchdog Probe" (April 29, 2022) <https://www.politico.eu/article/eu-border-agency-fabrice-leggeri-resigns-watchdog-probe-findings-released-misconduct/>.

117 Jeandesboz J., "European Border Policing: EUROSUR, Knowledge, Calculation" (2017) 18(3) *Global Crime* 256–285 <https://doi.org/10.1080/17440572.2017.1347043>.

118 European Parliament, "The Situation in the Mediterranean and the Need for a Holistic EU Approach to Migration (2015/2095(INI))" (April 12, 2016) P8_TA(2016)0102, rec. 81–85 <http://www.europarl.europa.eu/sides/getDoc.do?pubRef=-%2f%2fEP%2f%2fTEXT%2bTA%2bP8-TA-2016-0102%2b0%2bDOC%2bXML%2bV0%2f%2fEN&language=EN>; European Parliament (2016d).

119 Amnesty International, *Hotspot Approach: How EU's Flagship Approach Leads to Inhumane and Ineffective Treatment of Refugees and Migrants* (2016).

120 EU-Turkey Statement of March 18, 2016, in European Council Press Release 144/16 of March 18, 2016.

sparking considerable human rights controversies. At the national level, hotspots have been regulated differently: Italy adopted *Standard Operating Procedures* in 2015, while Greece introduced the aforementioned *Law No. 4375*, which implemented the agreement with Turkey but lacked detailed regulations on the operation of hotspots.

The lack of independent mechanisms to monitor activities at hotspots is a significant shortcoming. The Fundamental Rights Agency (FRA), though mentioned as a potential entity with influence over the activities of EU agencies, has not been formally tasked with overseeing the operation of these centers.[121]

The hotspot approach illustrates the fragmented nature of migration governance in the EU. Regulatory fragmentation and the lack of a comprehensive legal framework lead to difficulties in implementing the principles of transparency, accountability and protection of migrants' fundamental rights—issues that must be urgently addressed in future EU migration reforms. Hotspots were intended as an effective tool to support frontline states in dealing with the influx of migrants. In practice, however, they have largely functioned as a technocratic solution, focused more on managing migration as a security threat than on providing humanitarian protection. The introduction of biometric technologies, such as the Eurodac system, and the systematic collection of data on migrants have been widely perceived as shifting the focus from protection to control and security.

The hotspot approach, initially conceived as a temporary solution in response to the 2015 migration crisis, has over time become a permanent feature of EU migration policy. Although hotspots were originally intended as a temporary measure, they have never been abolished, even after a reduction in the number of migrants arriving in the EU in 2015–2016.[122] In Italy, hotspots continue to operate as centers for identification and redistribution. In Greece, the function of hotspots has been further transformed as a result of the March 2016 EU-Turkey agreement, which converted Greece's identification centers into places of detention, where migrants waited for asylum applications to

---

121 European Parliament, *Explanatory Note on the "Hotspot" Approach* (no date) <https://www.europarl.europa.eu/cmsdata/226729/Session_1_-_Explanatory_note_on_the_Hotspot_approach.pdf>.

122 Gerbaudo M., *The European Commission's Instrumentalization Strategy: Normalising Border Procedures and De Facto Detention* (European Papers 2022).

be processed or deportation decisions to be made. The transformation was a symbolic shift from the original reception function to a model focused on control and detention.[123] The COVID-19 pandemic further exposed the limitations of this system. Extended periods of detention, overcrowding, and inadequate hygiene measures intensified criticism of the hotspot approach, culminating in the humanitarian catastrophe of the September 2020 fire at Greece's largest hotspot on Lesbos, Moria.[124]

The European Commission announced the New Pact on Migration and Asylum on September 23, 2020, which was supposed to be a fresh start for EU migration policy. Although presented as a reform, the New Pact actually institutionalized the hotspot approach.[125] The proposed regulations on screening and asylum procedures formalize hotspot measures, such as identity, security and health checks near external borders. Detaining migrants at the border has thus become a standard element of EU migration policy, rather than an emergency tool. While hotspots were initially intended to mitigate the effects of the migration crisis, their entrenchment and transformation into a permanent mechanism for migration management is highly controversial. Critics point to the lack of a unified legal framework governing their activities and an excessive focus on aspects of control at the expense of humanitarian protection, exacerbating tensions in the European discourse on migration.[126]

As Halilović points out, the transformation of the hotspot approach from a temporary emergency response measure to a permanent migration management mechanism is an example of the transformation of a state of emergency to a state of exception in European Union migration policy.[127] The legal and

---

123 Gerbaudo M., *The European Commission's Instrumentalization Strategy …*

124 BBC News, "*Moria Migrants: Fire Destroys Greek Camp Leaving 13,000 Without Shelter*" (September 9, 2020) <https://www.bbc.com/news/world-europe-54082201>.

125 European Commission, *Communication from the Commission on the New Pact on Migration and Asylum*, COM(2020) 609 final (Brussels, September 23, 2020) accessed online at <https://eur-lex.europa.eu/legal-content/PL/TXT/?qid=1601287338054&uri=COM%3A2020%3A609%3AFIN>.

126 Gkliati M., "Let's Call It What It Is: Hybrid Threats and Instrumentalisation as the Evolution of Securitisation in Migration Management" (European Papers, 2023) <https://www.europeanpapers.eu/en/europeanforum/lets-call-it-what-it-is-hybrid-threats-and-instrumentalisation>.

127 Halilovic A., "Executive Migration Governance and Law-making in the European Union: Towards a State of Exception," *European Papers*, accessed online at

policy literature distinguishes between a state of emergency and a state of exception. A state of emergency involves a temporary deviation from the ordinary rules of law to address a crisis situation but remains anchored in the norms of the legal order. An example of this in the EU is the refugee relocation mechanism, introduced under Article 78(3) of the TFEU, which allows temporary measures to be taken in response to migration crises. This mechanism, while departing from the Dublin system, is within the framework of EU law.[128] A state of exception, on the other hand, according to Schmitt's theory, means the suspension of legal norms by the executive in a way that goes beyond the established legal order. It is a mechanism that violates the foundations of the democratic legal order.[129] Hotspots, introduced as a political initiative of the European Commission, exhibit the characteristics of a state of exception, as they lack a basis in formal EU law and a clearly defined legal framework, and thus risk violating human rights and the rule of law.[130] The transformation of Greek hotspots in connection with the signing of the 2016 EU-Turkey agreement from reception centers to detention centers has led to legitimate controversy over restrictions on the freedom of movement of migrants and refugees and violations of their fundamental rights.[131] In addition, the introduction of legislative proposals such as the Screening Regulation indicates the further institutionalization of this mechanism.[132] The new legislation makes it mandatory for migrants to be detained at the

---

<https://www.europeanpapers.eu/en/system/files/pdf_version/EP_eJ_2024_2_Aida_Halilovic_00769.pdf>.

128 Fatovic C., *Outside the Law: Emergency and Executive Power* (Johns Hopkins University Press 2009) 67; Curtin D., "Challenging Executive Dominance in European Democracy" (2014) *Modern Law Review*, 3.

129 Schmitt C., *Political Theology: Four Chapters on the Concept of Sovereignty* (University of Chicago Press 2005) 6 and 12.

130 Neville D., Sy S., and Rigon A., "On the Frontline: The Hotspot Approach to Managing Migration" (2016) *Study for the European Parliament*; Stępka M., "Identifying Security Logics in the EU Policy Discourse: the "Migration Crisis" and the EU" (Springer 2022) 89.

131 Halilovic A., *Executive Migration Governance*, 522.

132 Regulation (EU) 2024/1356 of the European Parliament and of the Council of May 14, 2024 on the introduction of screening of third-country nationals at the external borders and amending Regulations (EC) No. 767/2008, (EU) 2017/2226, (EU) 2018/1240 and (EU) 2019/818, OJ L 1356 (May 14, 2024) 1–29 <https://eur-lex.europa.eu/eli/reg/2024/1356/oj>.

border for security, health and identity checks, bringing hotspot practices closer to a permanent feature of EU border management policy.[133]

From there, it is only a short step to the full instrumentalization of crisis mechanisms.[134] A solution that was supposed to be the exception is increasingly becoming the norm. From a political perspective, hotspots have come to symbolize the securitization of migration, where the protection of human rights is subordinated to security imperatives.

1.3.2.4 Relocation and resettlement

The 2015 migration crisis exposed the European Union's unpreparedness for the massive influx of migrants. Initially, underestimated data and the disregard of rising arrivals through the Eastern Mediterranean led to a delayed response. The short and safer route from Turkey to the Greek islands did not raise concerns, and the summer vacation of EU institutions further hampered action. It was not until September, when daily migrant numbers reached into the thousands, that the problem was fully recognized, with abandoned life jackets on Greek beaches becoming a symbol of the crisis.[135] No longer able to withstand the onslaught, Greece and the countries of the Balkan Peninsula allowed migrants to continue moving to the countries they indicated as destinations.[136] The 2015 migration crisis also highlighted the European Union's legal and organizational limitations in managing mass migrant flows. Although the Temporary Protection Directive 2001/55/EC could have been activated in response to the above situation, the lack of consensus among Member States prevented its application. Meanwhile,

---

[133] Articles 6, 9, 12 and 15 of the Regulation (EU) 2024/1356. *Cf. also* Gerbaudo M., "The European Commission's Instrumentalization Strategy: Normalising Border Procedures and De Facto Detention" *European Papers—European Forum* (2024) <https://www.europeanpapers.eu/en/europeanforum/european-commission-instrumentalization-strategy-border-procedures-detention>.

[134] Gerbaudo M., "The European Commission's Instrumentalization Strategy: Normalising Border Procedures and De Facto Detention" (2024) *European Papers—European Forum* <https://www.europeanpapers.eu/en/europeanforum/european-commission-instrumentalization-strategy-border-procedures-detention>.

[135] Collett E., and Le Coz C., *After the Storm: Learning from the EU Response to the Migration Crisis* (Migration Policy Institute, June 2018), 13 <https://www.migrationpolicy.org/research/after-storm-eu-response-migration-crisis>.

[136] The most common were Germany, Sweden, Austria, the Netherlands and Denmark.

countries such as Austria and Slovenia began informal cooperation, while others sought legal clarification from the European Commission on the legal basis for "letting through" migrants—without receiving a response.[137] At this point, the European Union was faced with a crisis not only at its external borders but also deep within its territory, confronting the EU administration with an unprecedented challenge. It was not the proactive efforts of EU institutions that shaped the course of emerging solutions; rather, the dynamics of events compelled certain actions.

On July 20, 2015, the Justice and Home Affairs Council adopted an important position, which the Council of the European Union subsequently incorporated into its conclusions on the resettlement of persons in need of international protection. These conclusions formed part of the EU's response to the migration crisis.[138] The document, referring to the earlier findings of the European Council's statement of April 23, 2015 and its conclusions of June 26, 2015, aimed to establish a mechanism for the resettlement of refugees within the European Union and associated countries. The core objective was to create legal and safe routes for refugees and distribute responsibilities among Member States. The conclusions provided for the resettlement of 20,000 people from third countries, where they had already received temporary protection, to EU Member States and four countries outside the Union (Norway, Iceland, Liechtenstein and Switzerland). The final number of people covered by the program was 22,504, of whom 18,415 were to go to 27 EU Member States (excluding Hungary) and 4,089 to associated countries. Poland pledged to accept 900 people, which was an expression of international solidarity and its obligations under the Union's migration policy. The conclusions also identified priority resettlement regions, including North Africa, the Middle East and the Horn of Africa, with a focus on countries participating in Regional Development and Protection Programs. The mechanism had an external burden-sharing character, emphasizing the

---

137 Collett E., and Le Coz C., *After the Storm: Learning from the EU Response to the Migration Crisis* (Migration Policy Institute, June 2018), 13 <https://www.migrationpolicy.org/research/after-storm-eu-response-migration-crisis>.

138 Council of the European Union, "Conclusions on the Resettlement of Persons in Need of International Protection (Brussels, July 22, 2015), document 11130/15 ASIM 62 RELEX 633, accessed by Council of the EU, 11130/15 <https://data.consilium.europa.eu/doc/document/ST-11130-2015-INIT/pl/pdf>.

Union's commitment to realizing international solidarity and assisting third countries in managing migration flows.[139]

In May 2015, the European Commission proposed relocating 20,000 refugees, and in June, the European Council increased the number by an additional 40,000.[140] However, the evolving situation tested the proposed solutions, still making them insufficient. During the summer, the number of migrants on the Eastern Mediterranean route increased, reaching a peak of more than 210,000 new arrivals in October.[141] On August 24, Germany announced that it would process the asylum applications of Syrians for whom other countries were responsible under the Dublin regulations, a move that won the support of Angela Merkel, who declared "wir schaffen das" ("we can handle it").[142] The crisis worsened after two major tragedies: the discovery of 71 migrant bodies in a truck in Austria (August 28) and the death of Aylan Kurdi (September 2). In response, on September 22, the Council decided to relocate another 120,000 refugees, despite opposition from the Czech Republic, Slovakia, Hungary, and Romania, which criticized Germany for the consequences of opening its borders.[143] The fragmented approach of individual EU countries in attempting to resolve their specific issues related to the crisis required an immediate and systemic response from the European Union. In September, Hungary closed its borders and built a wall on its border with Serbia, and other Balkan countries followed suit, leading to the closure of the Balkan route. In 2016, Austria limited the number of asylum applications it accepted to 37,500.[144] All of these measures only reinforced the erosion of solidarity within the EU. One of the

---

139 Kosman M. M., "Kryzys imigracyjny w UE w latach 2015–2017: Aspekty prawne i polityczne," (2017) 11 *Rocznik Integracji Europejskiej*, 283–284.

140 Šabić S. S., *The Relocation of Refugees in the European Union* (Zagreb: Friedrich Ebert Stiftung 2017).

141 IOM, "Migration Flows—Mediterranean Route." *International Organization for Migration* (2015) <https://iom.int/>.

142 Merkel A., Government Press Conference (Bundespressekonferenz), Berlin, August 31, 2015, documented in: "We Can Do It!": Angela Merkel on Welcoming Refugees (August 31, 2015), German History in Documents and Images, German Historical Institute Washington <https://germanhistorydocs.org/en/a-new-germany-1990-2023/ghdi:video-5097> [accessed: 7 April 2026].

143 Šabić S. S., *The Relocation of Refugees in the European Union* (Zagreb: Friedrich Ebert Stiftung 2017).

144 Triandafyllidou A., "A "Refugee Crisis" Unfolding: "Real" Events and Their Interpretation in Media and Political Debates," (2018) 16 *Journal of Immigrant & Refugees Studies* 198–216.

most controversial ideas was the establishment of the Temporary Relocation System in the EU, aimed at redistributing asylum seekers among EU Member States. Its main significance lay in the temporary suspension of the guiding principle under the so-called "EU Dublin system," under which the first country of entry into the EU is responsible for processing an asylum application.[145]

In spring 2015, the European Commission proposed a mechanism to relocate asylum seekers from countries such as Italy and Greece to other EU countries to show solidarity with those on the front lines. Before the summer, the European Council unveiled a plan to voluntarily relocate 40,000 refugees. As migrant arrivals in Greece surged over the summer, a mandatory relocation scheme was proposed, but it met with resistance. In September, the Council, voting with a qualified majority, agreed to relocate 120,000 refugees, triggering political tensions within the EU.

The mechanism posed practical challenges, including determining how many people each country would receive and organizing transfers. The Commission developed a distribution formula based on population size, GDP, the number of asylum applications and the unemployment rate. Implementation required cooperation between Member States, EASO, and other agencies. In July 2015, EU Member States also pledged to resettle more than 22,000 people from outside Europe. This initiative became a key policy during this period and dominated the political debate for many years. The transition from a voluntary system of relocating asylum seekers to a mandatory mechanism became a flashpoint in relations between Member States.

The legal analysis of this mechanism demonstrates both its importance and the challenges that emerged during implementation.[146] The mandatory relocation mechanism was introduced by Council Decision (EU) 2015/1523 and Council Decision (EU) 2015/1601, which established temporary measures in the area of international protection in favor of Italy and Greece.[147] These

---

145 Carrera S., Blockmans S., Gros D., and Guild E., "The EU's Response to the Refugee Crisis: Taking Stock and Setting Policy Priorities" (December 16, 2015) 20 *CEPS* 5 <https://cdn.ceps.eu/wp-content/uploads/2015/12/EU%20Response%20to%20the%202015%20Refugee%20Crisis_0.pdf>.

146 Collett E., and Le Coz C., *After the Storm: Learning from the EU Response to the Migration Crisis* (Migration Policy Institute, June 2018), 13 <https://www.migrationpolicy.org/research/after-storm-eu-response-migration-crisis>.

147 "Council Decision (EU) 2015/1523 of September 14, 2015 Establishing Provisional Measures in the Area of International Protection for the Benefit of Italy and of

decisions were based on Article 78(3) of the TFEU, which allows the Council to adopt emergency measures in crisis situations involving a massive influx of refugees into the European Union. However, the fact that their adoption required a qualified majority vote revealed the lack of unanimity and deepened political divisions.[148] The mechanism also required the establishment of national contact points and coordination with EASO to organize transfers. However, the process encountered numerous difficulties, such as initial delays in implementation and a lack of consensus on specific commitments.[149] The transition to a mandatory relocation system was a turning point that exacerbated existing tensions between Member States. Countries such as Hungary, the Czech Republic and Poland explicitly opposed the mechanism, questioning its legality and arguing that it violated the principle of subsidiarity.[150] Italy and Greece, on the other hand, felt that the support provided by the EU was insufficient, which only exacerbated the sense of injustice.

The CJEU's September 6, 2017, judgment in Joined Cases C-643/15 and C-647/15 was a significant moment in the legal assessment of the Council's decision-making and implementation process.[151] The Slovak Republic and Hungary, in their actions for the annulment of Council Decision 2015/1601, raised a number of objections, which the Court dismissed in full. The CJEU found that the Council's decision met the legal requirements under Article 78(3) TFEU and complied with the principles of proportionality and legal certainty. The judgment stressed that the relocation mechanism was

---

Greece" (2015 L239/146, September 15, 2015) *Official Journal of the European Union*.

148 "Council Decision (EU) 2015/1601 of September 22 2015 Establishing Provisional Measures in the Area of International Protection for the Benefit of Italy and Greece" (2015 L248/80, September 24, 2015) *Official Journal of the European Union*.

149 European Commission, *Relocation & Resettlement: Sharing Responsibility and Opening Legal Pathways to Europe* (Brussels, September 2017).

150 European Commission, *Fact Sheet: Refugee Crisis—Q&A on Emergency Relocation*, press release, September 22, 2015.

151 Judgment of the Court of Justice of September 6, 2017 in the Slovak Republic and Hungary v. Council of the European Union in the Action for annulment of Decision (EU) 2015/1601. Pietras-Eichberger M., *Prawne i polityczne konsekwencje wyroku Trybunału Sprawiedliwości z dnia 6 września 2017 roku w sprawie Republiki Słowackiej i Węgier przeciwko Radzie Unii Europejskiej w przedmiocie skargi o stwierdzenie nieważności decyzji (UE) 2015/1601*, (2024) 1(88/2) *Politeja*, 79–90 <https://doi.org/10.12797/Politeja.20.2024.88.2.05> Joined Cases C-643/15 and C-647/15, ECLI:EU:2017:631, CELEX: 62015CJ0643.

a temporary measure to counter the effects of the sudden influx of migrants to Italy and Greece, and its compatibility with the Treaties was beyond question.[152]

Regarding the use of Article 78(3) TFEU as the legal basis for EU Council Decision 2015/1601, the Court of Justice of the European Union (CJEU) analyzed the legal nature of the act in detail. In its ruling, the CJEU explained that Article 78(3) TFEU allows for the adoption of "temporary measures" in the event of a sudden influx of migrants, aligning with the purpose of establishing the relocation mechanism. The Court clarified that the acts adopted based on this provision are not legislative in nature, as they are issued under a non-legislative procedure, meaning that they are not subject to the requirement that national parliaments participate in the legislative process.[153] Measures adopted based on Article 78(3) TFEU are of an emergency nature and do not require a legislative procedure, allowing for a rapid response to migration crises.

The CJEU also ruled that the validity of an act of Union law cannot depend on subsequent assessments of its effectiveness. The assessment of an act's compatibility with the treaties must be based on the data available at the time of its adoption. In the case of EU Council Decision 2015/1601, concerning the relocation mechanism, the CJEU found that Slovakia's and Hungary's allegations that the act was inadequate to achieve its objectives were unfounded.[154] The CJEU found that the decision was proportionate and in line with the treaties and that the problems with its implementation were due to Member States' resistance, not legislative errors.[155] The ruling confirmed that the effectiveness of an act cannot be a basis for invalidating it unless a manifest error in the adoption process is proven. It reinforced the principle that regulations should be assessed in the context of the information available at the time of their creation.[156]

As M. Pietras-Eichberger pointed out, the Republic of Poland, acting as an intervener on the side of Hungary and Slovakia, raised the argument about the difficulty of implementing the relocation mechanism in countries with

---

152 §§ 86–103 of the Court's judgment C-643/15 and C-647/15.

153 §§ 57–66 of the Court's judgment C-643/15 and C-647/15.

154 § 224 of the Court's judgment C-643/15 and C-647/15.

155 §§ 299 and 301 of the Court's judgment C-643/15 and C-647/15.

156 §§ 218–221 of the Court's judgment C-643/15 and C-647/15.

an almost uniform ethnic composition, such as Poland.[157] It was claimed that cultural and linguistic differences between Polish citizens and migrants subject to relocation could pose significant challenges to social integration. However, the CJEU rejected this argument as inadmissible for two reasons. First, the CJEU found that the argument went beyond the objections raised by Hungary and Slovakia, meaning that it fell outside the scope of the dispute at hand.[158] Second, the CJEU stressed that granting international protection conditional on the ethnicity of asylum seekers is contrary to Article 21 of the EU Charter of Fundamental Rights, which prohibits discrimination, including on ethnic and cultural grounds.[159]

In turn, the judgment of the Court of Justice of the European Union (CJEU) of April 2, 2020, in Joined Cases C-715/17, C-718/17 and C-719/17 addressed a key issue in managing the migration crisis in the European Union—the violation by Poland, Hungary and the Czech Republic of the principles of solidarity and obligations under EU law.[160] The ruling serves as an important reference point for analyzing the relationship between the principles of solidarity and internal security within the EU legal framework.

The 2015 EU Council decisions (2015/1601 and 2015/1523) established a temporary relocation mechanism for applicants for international protection to alleviate migratory pressures on Greece and Italy. The mechanism provided for the relocation of 120,000 people, and its implementation was the responsibility of all EU Member States. However, Poland, Hungary and the Czech Republic refused to implement their obligations. Hungary completely ignored the mechanism, while Poland and the Czech Republic, despite initial declarations, failed to implement any measures.[161] As a result, the European

---

157 Pietras-Eichberger M., "Prawne i polityczne konsekwencje wyroku Trybunału Sprawiedliwości z dnia 6 września 2017 roku w sprawie Republiki Słowackiej i Węgier przeciwko Radzie Unii Europejskiej w przedmiocie skargi o stwierdzenie nieważności decyzji (UE)," 2015/1601 (2024) 1(88/2) *Politeja*, 86.

158 § 303 of the Court's judgment C-643/15 and C-647/15.

159 § 3 05 of the Court's judgment C-643/15 and C-647/15.

160 CJEU Judgment of 2.04.2020, C-715/17, European Commission v. Republic of Poland and Hungary, LEX No. 2891851 <https://sip.lex.pl/#/jurisprudence/522985547/1/c-715-17-niezastosowanie-sie-przez-polske-czechy-i-wegry-do-decyzji-ue-dotyczacych-relokacji … ?cm=URELATIONS>.

161 The Czech Republic eventually relocated 12 people, Poland none.

Commission filed a complaint under Article 258 of the TFEU against these countries for non-compliance.

The countries invoked Article 72 of the Treaty on the Functioning of the European Union (TFEU), which allows Member States to derogate from EU law in situations requiring the protection of public order and internal security. They argued that the relocation mechanism threatened their security. The CJEU unequivocally rejected this line of defense in its April 2, 2020 ruling, pointing out that Article 72 TFEU cannot be applied unilaterally and arbitrarily.[162] The Court stressed that Member States must provide evidence of a real and concrete threat, which Poland, Hungary and the Czech Republic had failed to do.[163]

The CJEU ruled that the Council's decisions were binding and could not be subject to unilateral evaluation by Member States.[164] The relocation mechanism was an important element of the EU's typical response to the migration crisis, and its effective implementation depended on the cooperation of all Member States. The Court stressed that solidarity is a fundamental principle of the EU legal order, and its violation undermines trust between Member States and the effectiveness of the common policy.[165]

The 2020 CJEU ruling has far-reaching legal and political implications. First, it confirms that Member States cannot evade their obligations based on unilateral interpretations of security threats. Second, the judgment reinforces the principle of solidarity as the foundation of EU cooperation. It underscores the need for joint action in the face of crises and responsibility for the implementation of accepted commitments while also pointing to the need for further reforms in EU migration and asylum policy.

The Court's 2017 and 2020 judgments also stressed that the relocation mechanism should be implemented in a spirit of solidarity and cooperation among Member States. The CJEU's jurisprudence has strengthened

---

162 Judgment of the CJEU of April 2, 2020, C-715/17, European Commission v. Republic of Poland and Hungary, § 160.

163 Judgment of the CJ of 2.04.2020, C-715/17, European Commission v. Republic of Poland and Hungary, § 159.

164 Judgment of the CJ of 2.04.2020, C-715/17, European Commission v. Republic of Poland and Hungary, §§ 143, 145–147.

165 Judgment of the CJ of 2.04.2020, C-715/17, European Commission v. Republic of Poland and Hungary, §§ 1180–1181.

the European Commission's position as the guardian of the EU treaties and emphasized the need to uphold the principles enshrined in the TFEU.

1.3.2.5 Activation of crisis management mechanisms

In late October 2015, three main coordination mechanisms emerged in response to the escalating migration crisis: The Western Balkans Contact Group, the ARGUS system[166] and the Integrated Political Crisis Response (IPCR).[167] Although their implementation was somewhat delayed, they had a significant impact on the European Union's coordination capacity. These mechanisms allowed political and operational representatives to meet regularly to identify challenges and develop responses. Each of these instruments had distinct functions, and their evaluation provides valuable lessons on crisis management at the EU level.[168] ARGUS, activated on October 29, 2015, enabled the rapid exchange of information between European Commission departments, supporting the monitoring of migratory movements and protecting Member States' borders. Seen as a tool for managing hybrid threats, the mechanism allowed the EU to treat the crisis as a security challenge rather than a humanitarian disaster.[169]

In turn, the IPCR mechanism operates in three modes: monitoring, information sharing and full activation, enabling rapid political coordination and response to wide-ranging crises. Supported by advanced communications technologies, the IPCR ensured the efficient data flow between EU institutions and Member States, strengthening the ability to respond strategically to a crisis.[170] Both mechanisms highlighted once again the EU's changing

166 European Commission, "Communication from the Commission to the European Parliament, the Council, the European Economic and Social Committee and the Committee of the Regions: Commission Provisions on 'ARGUS' General Rapid Alert System" (COM [2005] 662 final, December 23, 2015).

167 Council of the EU, *Council Implementing Decision (EU) 2018/1993 of December 11, 2018 on EU Integrated Arrangements for Responding at the Political Level in Crisis Situations* [2018] OJ L 320/28.

168 Collett E., and Le Coz C., *After the Storm: Learning from the EU Response to the Migration Crisis…*, 17.

169 Wasilewski K., "The Role of Information and Communication Technology in the EU Response to the 2015 Refugee Crisis" (2020) 2(176) *Studia Migracyjne—Przegląd Polonijny* 83 <https://doi.org/10.4467/25444972SMPP.20.012.12328>.

170 Wasilewski K., *The Role of Information …* (2020) 84.

approach to the refugee crisis—from humanitarian support to the perception of the situation as a threat to security and stability. Their implementation demonstrated the importance of integrated crisis management, although challenges remained due to the varied approaches of Member States and limited operational resources.[171]

1.3.2.6 Externalization of migration

The significant drop in arrivals to Greece, while migrants to Italy reached record levels, resulted from the EU-Turkey agreement and the tightening of border controls in the Western Balkans. To deal with what has been termed the "migration crisis," the EU adopted a strategy based on externalizing migration controls. Along with securitization and privatization of migration, externalization of migration is one of the of the tools that states in the so-called Global North, including the EU, are using to manage largely unwanted migration flows.[172] They enter into agreements with countries such as Turkey, Libya and Morocco that commit to stopping migrants from reaching European borders. These measures, while effective in the short term, remain controversial due to concerns over compliance with international human rights standards.[173]

C. Rodier states that externalization means a partial shift of border management to the territory of a third country.[174] In order to speak of externalization, two elements are necessary: the transfer of a state's physical border to the outside and the creation of a metaphorical border in a third country, but with such an effect that the Member State gains real and direct control over the border in that country.[175] In practice, the externalization of border

---

171 Wasilewski K., *The Role of Information …* (2020) 84.

172 Spijkerboer T., "The Global Mobility Infrastructure: Reconceptualising the Externalisation of Migration Control" (2018) 20(4) *European Journal of Migration and Law*, 452–469 <https://doi.org/10.1163/15718166-12340038>.

173 Calarco G., "Conditions in Hotspots: Overcrowding and Inhumane Practices" in C. Cantat, A. Pécoud, and H. Thiollet (eds) *Migration as Crisis* (2023) 9–10.

174 Rodier C., *Analysis of the External Dimension of the EU's Asylum and Immigration Policies—Summary and Recommendations for the European Parliament* (Brussels 2006) 8 <http://www.europarl.europa.eu/meetdocs/2004 2009/documents/dt/619/619330/619330en.pdf>.

175 More extensively Rogala R., in J. Chlebny (ed), *Prawo o cudzoziemcach. Komentarz* (Warszawa 2020), commentary to Article 459 after McNamara F., "Member State

management transforms the border into a remote space where legal obligations and international responsibilities are blurred.[176] Wessel points out that tensions between externalization, border management and legal validity arise in bilateral migration "agreements" adopted in the form of soft law.[177] Reviglio stresses that in pursuing a policy of externalization, states introduce soft-law instruments to build a securitized border through securitization practices[178] or border-induced displacement,[179] thereby prioritizing the politics of legal effectiveness over the politics of validity.[180] The implementation of agreements operating under soft law poses certain challenges for lawmaking as well as for political and judicial oversight. It seems that the legal effectiveness of these agreements is a more important criterion than their formal legal validity. Managing such complex phenomena through complicated law is too static and slow. Consequently, management instruments in the form of soft law are more flexible and better suited to the political goal of reducing the number of people arriving in Europe.[181] These solutions became

---

Responsibility for Migration Control within Third States—Externalization Revisited" (2013) 15 *European Journal of Migration and Law* 327.

176 Reviglio M., "The Shift to Soft Law at Europe Borders: Between Legal Efficiency and Legal Validity," (2023) 23(1) *Global Jurist*, 23–41 <https://doi.org/10.1515/gj-2022-0040>.

177 Wessel, R. A., "Normative Transformations in EU External Relations: The Phenomenon of 'Soft' International Agreements." (2021) 44 (1) *West European Politics* 72–92 <https://doi.org/10.1080/01402382.2020.1738094.Search in Google Scholar>.

178 Campesi G., "Crisis, Migration and the Consolidation of the EU Border Control Regime." (2018) 4(3) *International Journal of Migration and Border Studies*, 196–221 <https://doi.org/10.1504/ijmbs.2018.10015056.Search in Google Scholar>.

179 Moreno-Lax V., and Lemberg-Petersen M., "Border-induced Displacement: The Ethical and Legal Implications of Distance-Creation through Externalization" (2019) 56 (1) *Questions of International Law*, 5–33. Search in Google Scholar <https://scholar.google.com/scholar?q=Moreno%20Lax%2C%20V.%2C%20and%20M.%20Lemberg-Petersen.%202019.%20%E2%80%9CBorder-induced%20Displacement%3A%20The%20Ethical%20and%20Legal%20Implications%20of%20Distance-Creation%20through%20Externalization.%E2%80%9D%20Questions%20of%20International%20Law%2056%20%281%29%3A%205%E2%80%9333>.

180 Reviglio M., "The Shift to Soft Law at Europe Borders: Between Legal Efficiency and Legal Validity," (2023) 23(1) *Global Jurist*.

181 Reviglio M., "The Shift to Soft Law at Europe Borders: Between Legal Efficiency and Legal Validity," (2023) 23(1) *Global Jurist*, 23–41 <https://doi.org/10.1515/gj-2022-0040>.

particularly evident during the migration crisis of 2015 leading to a preference for soft-law instruments in crisis management.[182] They allowed a rapid response to evolving circumstances without being subject to often formalized state procedures. This shift was even more pronounced in subsequent crises, such as the COVID-19 pandemic, which is discussed in detail in the chapter on pandemics.[183]

As Reviglio points out, the EU and Member States have made financial and political support, as well as development cooperation, conditional on the effective implementation of exit controls by third countries.[184] The EU's new Migration Partnership Framework Mechanism is based on "effective incentives and appropriate conditionality," the European Council stated, stressing that "cooperation on readmission and return will be a key test of the partnership between the EU and its partners."[185]

1.3.2.7 The EU-Turkey Agreement (Statement)

The bilateral agreement between the EU and Turkey was adopted on March 18, 2016, in a European Council statement in the form of a press release.[186] The EU and Turkey reached an agreement that provided for the "rapid return of all migrants who do not need international protection crossing the border from Turkey to Greece, and the taking back of all irregular migrants detained

182 For a closer look at the concept of soft law in EU law, see, among others, Stefan, Oana Andreea and Stefan, Oana Andreea and Avbelj, Matej and Eliantonio, M. and Hartlapp, Miriam and Korkea-aho, Emilia and Rubio, Nathalie, *EU Soft Law in the EU Legal Order: A Literature Review*. King's College London Law School Research Paper Forthcoming (March 4, 2019) <https://ssrn.com/abstract=3346629> or <http://dx.doi.org/10.2139/ssrn.3346629>, 8 ff.

183 Oana Stefan, "COVID-19 Soft Law: Voluminous, Effective, Legitimate? A Research Agenda," *Insight, European Papers* <https://www.europeanpapers.eu/en/authors/oana-stefan>.

184 EU-Turkey Statement (2016) and Memorandum of Understanding between Libya and Italy (2017) described by Reviglio M., "The Shift to Soft Law at Europe Borders: Between Legal Efficiency and Legal Validity," (2023) 23(1) *Global Jurist*.

185 European Council, "European Council meeting (June 28, 2016)—Conclusions" (Brussels, EUCO 26/16, June 28, 2016) <chrome-extension://efaidnbmnnnibpcajpcglclefindmkaj/https://www.consilium.europa.eu/media/21645/28-euco-conclusions.pdf>.

186 European Council (2016) *EU-Turkey Statement*, March 18, Press Release <https://www.consilium.europa.eu/en/press/press-releases/2016/03/18/eu-turkey-statement/>.

in Turkish waters" (point 1). The joint statement provides a mechanism for the systematic and "speedy return" of these individuals. The agreement states that migrants arriving in Greece will be properly registered, and their asylum applications will be processed in accordance with Directive 2013/32/EU. In addition, for every Syrian taken back to Turkey, another Syrian was to be resettled from Turkey to the EU, with priority given to those who had not previously attempted to enter the EU illegally. Turkey also pledged to take measures to prevent new illegal arrivals to the Greek islands (point 2).[187] In addition, plans were made to intensify talks on visa liberalization for Turkish citizens, assuming the possibility of visa abolition by the end of June 2016 (point 5). In addition, the agreement adopted a two-phase financing plan for measures to curb migration, allocating a total of €6 billion by the end of 2018 (point 6), as well as a commitment to speed up Turkey's accession process (point 8). Significant changes were made by Council Decision 2016/1754 of September 29, 2016, which supplemented earlier provisions of Council Decision 2015/1601 of September 22, 2015, regarding the relocation of 120,000 migrants. The decision was made in favor of the resettlement of Syrian refugees from Turkey instead of the originally planned relocations from Greece and Italy. Thus, the intra-EU relocation mechanism was partially replaced by a procedure for resetting people from outside the Union, particularly from Turkey, to Member States.[188] The 2016 EU-Turkey statement thus aimed to curb irregular migration from Turkey to the European Union by implementing mutual commitments. The EU and its Member States pledged to disburse €6 billion under the Refugee Facility for Turkey (FRiT) and to implement a refugee resettlement program on a 1:1 ratio. These two commitments have been fulfilled, but the EU has failed to deliver on key policy promises, such as visa liberalization for Turkish citizens, progress in accession negotiations and modernization of the customs union. Turkey, on the other hand, initially took steps to curb migration, introducing visa requirements for Syrians and building walls on its borders with Syria and Iran. However, in 2020, in response to the Idlib crisis, Turkey opened its borders

---

187 Kosman M. M., "Kryzys imigracyjny w UE w latach 2015–2017: Aspekty prawne i polityczne" (2017) 11, *Rocznik Integracji Europejskiej*, 285.

188 Kosman M. M., *Immigration Crisis in the EU 2015–2017: Legal and Political Aspects*, *Yearbook of European Integration*, No. 11 (2017) 286.

to migrants, undermining the effectiveness of the Statement.[189] In addition, Turkey suspended the implementation of the readmission agreement as it applies to third-country nationals other than Syria, making it conditional on the EU lifting visas.

Although the EU-Turkey agreement explicitly refers to the *non-refoulement* obligation and the ban on collective expulsions, it lacks reference to the unique sensitivities of those landing on the Greek islands.

The EU-Turkey Statement of March 18, 2016 is one of the key actions taken by the European Union in response to the migration crisis to manage migration flows and reduce irregular migration on the Eastern Mediterranean migration route.[190] The Statement is based on the concept of containing and deterring illegal flows and strengthening cooperation with third countries, which is part of the strategy of externalizing EU migration policy. While the statement has effectively reduced the number of irregular migrants entering the EU, it has raised numerous controversies over human rights and compliance with international asylum law.[191]

In April 2016, two Pakistani and one Afghan national residing in Greece challenged the legality of the EU-Turkey Statement before the Court of Justice of the EU. The applicants argued that the EU-Turkey Statement was unlawful because it violated the principle of *non-refoulement* and the prohibition of collective expulsion. In addition, they questioned its legality, arguing that it unlawfully assumed that Turkey could be considered a "safe third country."[192] They also argued that the EU-Turkey Statement *de jure* constituted an

---

189 Ineli-Ciger M., and Yigit Ö., "Country Fiche TURKEY" (2020) *ASILE* <https://www.asileproject.eu/wp-content/uploads/2021/03/Country-Fiche_Turkey_Final_Pub.pdf>; Beste İşleyen, and Sibel Karadağ, "Engineered Migration at the Greek-Turkish Border: A Spectacle of Violence and Humanitarian Space" (2023) 54(5) *Security Dialogue*, 475–492.

190 Carrera S., den Hertog L., and Stefan M., *It Wasn't Me! The Luxembourg Court Orders on the EU-Turkey Refugee Deal* (CEPS Policy Insights No. 2017-15, April 2017) 1.

191 Carrera S., den Hertog L., and Stefan M., *It Wasn't Me!* …, 1; Costello C., "It Need Not To Be Like This" (2016) 51 *Forced Migration Review*, 12–4; Peers S., "The Final EU/Turkey Refugee Deal: A Legal Assessment" (2016) *EU Law Analysis*.

192 According to Article 38 of Directive 2013/32/EU of the European Parliament and of the Council of June 26, 2013 on common procedures for granting and withdrawing international protection (recast)," L 180/60, June 29, 2013, *Official Journal of the European Union*, A safe third country is a third country that treats an applicant for

international agreement attributable to the European Council. This would mean that it should be subject to the decision-making procedures of Article 218 TFEU (which sets out the procedure for concluding international agreements) and/or Article 78 TFEU (which sets out the legal basis for EU asylum policy). The applicants argued that failure to comply with these articles invalidates the EU-Turkey Statement.

The General Court issued its conclusions in the form of three court orders (NF, NG and NM v. European Council, T-192/16, T-193/16 and T-257/16) published on February 28, 2017.[193] The orders of the General Court were appealed before the Court of Justice, but CJEU rejected the appeal. In light of the court's ruling, the EU-Turkey Statement does not constitute a formal international agreement but is a political declaration by representatives of what were then the 28 EU Member States and Turkey, which means that it is not legally binding on either the EU or Turkey.[194] It is not subject to formal scrutiny by the European Parliament and excludes the involvement of the Court of Justice in Luxembourg from monitoring the agreement's compliance with the EU's refugee rights obligations and the EU Charter of Fundamental Rights, raising questions about its transparency and legal accountability.[195]

---

international protection in accordance with accepted international standards, in particular:
(a) life and liberty are not threatened on the basis of race, religion, nationality, membership in a particular social group or political opinion;
(b) there is no risk of serious harm within the meaning of Directive 2011/95/EU (the recast Qualification Directive);
(c) the principle of non-refoulement in accordance with the Geneva Convention and Protocol relating to the status of refugees is observed;
(d) the prohibition of expulsion in violation of the right to freedom from torture and cruel, inhuman or degrading treatment, as established by international law, is respected; and
(e) it is possible to apply for refugee status and, if recognized as a refugee, to receive protection in accordance with the Convention and the Geneva Protocol relating to the Status of Refugees.

193 Cases C-208/17 P, C-209/17 P and 210/17 P, NF, NG and NM v European Council <https://curia.europa.eu/jcms/upload/docs/application/pdf/2017-02/cp170019en.pdf>.

194 den Heijer M., and Spijkerboer T., "Is the EU-Turkey Refugee and Migration Deal a Treaty?" (2017) *EU Law Analysis Blog* <https://eulawanalysis.blogspot.com/search?q=Is+the+EU-Turkey+refugee+and+migration+deal+a+treaty>.

195 Carrera S., den Hertog L., and Stefan M. M., *It Wasn't Me!* ..., 8.

All the European institutions involved have distanced themselves from authorship and legal responsibility for the EU-Turkey Statement, arguing before the Court that it does not, in fact, constitute an agreement to which they are parties. The European Council argued that "to the best of its knowledge, no agreement or treaty [...] has been concluded." It added that the EU-Turkey Statement was merely "the fruit of an international dialogue between the Member States and the [Republic of] Turkey and—in light of its content and the intentions of its authors—[was] not intended to have legally binding effects or constitute an agreement or treaty." The Commission argued that "no agreement" had been concluded between the EU and the Republic of Turkey. The Commission argued that "from the context of the vocabulary" it appears that the EU-Turkey Statement constituted a "political agreement" reached by the heads of state or government of the Member States.[196]

The agreement reached, as an action that does not fall within the legal framework of the treaty, is *a novelty* in the field of anti-crisis measures and sets a precedent that European Union bodies may be tempted to follow in the future. As S. Carrera, L. den Hertog and M. Stefan point out, this is a serious challenge to the transparency, accountability and quality of decision-making in the EU.[197] The main objective of the Lisbon Treaty in the area of Freedom, Security and Justice was to expand the use of the "Community method" of cooperation in border, asylum and migration policy. This was intended to address the democratic and judicial deficits that had characterized European cooperation under the former "Third Pillar" in some of these areas.[198] Critics of the adopted solution stressed that the EU should not have two conflicting approaches. It is illogical that the EU is heavily involved in the implementation of the agreement through its legal, budgetary and operational powers, while at the same time, it does not legally consider itself a party to any agreement that underpins these activities. This approach undermines the transparency and accountability of EU governance under the Lisbon Treaty.

The proliferation of decision-making outside the Treaties in migration and asylum policy leads to negative consequences, including violations of the fundamental rights of asylum applicants. Shifting legal responsibility

---

196 Carrera S., den Hertog L., and Stefan M., *It Wasn't Me!* ..., 4–5.
197 Carrera S., den Hertog L., and Stefan M., *It Wasn't Me!* ..., 7–8.
198 Carrera S., den Hertog L.,. and Stefan M., *It Wasn't Me!* ..., 8.

for measures such as the EU-Turkey Statement has serious repercussions. Growing political instability and widespread violations of the rule of law and human rights demonstrate that Turkey cannot be considered a "safe" country for asylum seekers.[199] Such agreements leave the EU in a vulnerable and dependent position vis-à-vis the Turkish government, which weakens the EU's ability to deal with the situation in Turkey and undermines the EU's legitimacy both vis-à-vis Turkey and internationally. There is a need to reform the Dublin system and return to policymaking in accordance with the rule of law set forth in the Treaties.[200]

The EU-Turkey Statement, while effective in reducing the number of irregular migrants, has highlighted the tensions between migration policy goals, especially in times of crisis, and human rights standards. The lack of formal institutionalization and legal control over its implementation remains one of the key challenges for the future of EU migration policy. The EU-Turkey agreement aimed to reduce the number of irregular migrants entering Greece from Turkey but did not comprehensively solve the refugee crisis.

Implementation of the agreement may violate the principle of *non-refoulement* and the concept of the first country of asylum and safe third country described in the Procedures Directive. Refugees in Turkey face the risk of being returned to their country of origin or being subjected to degrading treatment. In addition, the resettlement system in place has shortcomings, including discrimination based on the nationality of refugees and failure to meet resettlement goals.[201]

The main findings indicate that externalization policies, which aim to outsource migration control and limit inflows through technical and financial support to third countries, ultimately threaten the fundamental rights

---

199 Amnesty International, "Turkey: Illegal Mass Returns of Syrian Refugees Expose Fatal Flaws in EU-Turkey Deal" (April 1, 2016) <www.amnesty.org>; Fernández Arribas G., "The EU-Turkey Agreement: A Controversial Attempt at Patching up a Major Problem" (2016) 1(3) *European Papers* 1097–1104; European Forum (October 17, 2016); Parliamentary Assembly of the Council of Europe (PACE), Resolution 2109 (2016) "The Situation of Refugees and Migrants within the EU-Turkey Agreement of March 18, 2016" <http://bit.ly/2fISxlY>; UN Human Rights Council, "Report of the Special Rapporteur on the Human Rights of Migrants on Mission in Greece" (A/HRC/35/25/Add.2, April 24, 2017) <http://bit.ly/2rHF7kl>, § 31.

200 Carrera S., den Hertog L., and Stefan M., *It Wasn't Me! …*, 12–13.

201 Arribas G. F., *The EU-Turkey Agreement*, 1103–1104.

of refugees. Rather than protecting states from liability, externalization practices may violate European states' international obligations, including the principle of *non-refoulement* and the right to leave.

From a crisis management perspective, the EU-Turkey agreement was another attempt to develop an operational approach to solving a complex, multidimensional political problem. At the time the agreement was signed, preparations for its implementation were inadequate, even though its entry into force was scheduled within 48 hours. The Greek authorities found themselves in a situation where they had to act quickly with only general guidelines derived from the agreement's content. This was particularly problematic in terms of compliance with EU and Greek asylum law, as noted both during the implementation of the agreement and in retrospect. This shows that the EU is still gaining experience in simultaneously managing crises and resolving urgent problems on the ground, especially under intense political pressure.[202]

In retrospect, an assessment of the validity of this agreement should take into account the specific reality in which this agreement was concluded. The immediate goal of the agreement was to stop the uncontrolled flow of refugees from Turkish territory to Greece. The intended effect of drastically reducing the number of people crossing the external border of the European Union was achieved later that year. Nevertheless, to assume that this was due solely to the EU-Turkey Statement is incorrect.[203] The agreement undoubtedly represents a glaring example of the European Union externalizing policy and is judged as such by contemporary experts on the subject.[204] The EU-Turkey Statement has faced criticism for its negative impact on the human rights of migrants and refugees[205] and its detrimental effects on international

202 Collett E., and Le Coz C., *After the Storm: Learning from the EU Response to the Migration Crisis*, 20.

203 Ovacık G., Ineli-Ciger M., and Ulusoy O., "Taking Stock of the EU-Turkey Statement in 2024" (2024) 26(2) *European Journal of Migration and Law*, Published online June 18, 2024.

204 Ovacık G., Ineli-Ciger M., and Ulusoy O., "Taking Stock of the EU-Turkey Statement in 2024" (2024) 26(2) *European Journal of Migration and Law*. Published online June 18, 2024 <https://brill.com/view/journals/emil/26/2/article-p154_2.xml>.

205 ECHR, *Akkad v. Turkey*, Application No. 1557/19, Judgment of June 21, 2022; cf. also Ulusoy O., and Battjes H., "Situation of Readmitted Migrants and Refugees from Greece to Turkey under the EU-Turkey Statement" (2017) 15 *VU Migration Law Series*.

migration law, as well as its use of migrants as a tool in international politics and policymaking.[206]

Turkey has been repeatedly criticized for its deportation and detention practices in the context of the implementation of the EU-Turkey Statement. The European Court of Human Rights (ECHR) has found numerous violations of human rights, including the prohibition of torture, inhuman and degrading treatment, and the right to an effective remedy. One example is the case of *Akkad v. Turkey*, in which the Court found that the deportation of a Syrian refugee was incompatible with the European Convention on Human Rights.[207] Similar violations were found in the cases of Iraqi nationals[208] and Iranian nationals,[209] where the Turkish authorities failed to provide access to effective remedies and violated the right to protection from deportation. The aforementioned rulings indicate that Turkey does not fully meet the standards necessary to be considered a safe third country. Restrictions on access to legal protection, forced returns, and inadequate conditions of detention show that these practices are contrary to international human rights law.[210] As a result, the continued recognition of Turkey as a safe third country requires a thorough analysis and verification of compliance with international refugee protection standards.

The agreement has been partially successful—financial commitments have been met and resettlement has been partially implemented, but the failure to fulfill key promises and the changing political situation in Turkey limited its long-term effectiveness. The contemporary situation requires a new approach to analyzing the EU-Turkey Statement. Both the mechanisms for stopping illegal migration and the EU's border externalization policy should

---

206 Helme K., "The Implications of the EU-Turkey Refugee Agreement on the EU's Role as an International Human Rights Actor" (2021) 10(2) *Australian and New Zealand Journal of European Studies*, 68–73.

207 ECHR, *Akkad v. Turkey*, Application No. 1557/19, judgment of June 21, 2022, §§ 70–76.

208 ECHR, *J.A. and A.A. v. Turkey*, Application No. 80206/17, judgment of February 6, 2024, §§ 73–75.

209 ECHR, *B.S. v. Turkey*, Application No. 14820/19, judgment of March 21, 2024, §§ 1–8.

210 Ovacık G., Ineli-Ciger M., and Ulusoy O., "Taking Stock of the EU-Turkey Statement in 2024" (2024) 26(2) *European Journal of Migration and Law*, Published online June 18, 2024.

be evaluated from the perspective of their effectiveness and compliance with international human rights standards. In the face of ongoing migration challenges, the need to revise existing cooperation and adapt it to the changing political and humanitarian realities has become evident.[211]

1.3.2.8 European Trust Fund

The European Union has taken significant financial actions as one part of a complementary response to the crisis. In terms of funding, the EU has increased resources for migration management by creating trust funds such as the European Trust Fund and increasing financial support to frontline countries. The European *Trust Fund for Stability* and Countering the Root Causes of Irregular Migration and Forced Displacement in Africa (*Emergency Trust Fund for Africa*) was established in November 2015 during the Valletta Summit.[212] Its main objective was to counter destabilization, forced displacement and irregular migration in Africa by promoting stability and improving migration flow management in three key regions: Sahel and Lake Chad, the Horn of Africa and North Africa. The Fund was also intended to support economic development, build societies' resilience, and promote legal migration pathways. As of August 2024, €5 billion had been disbursed from the Fund.[213]

However, back in 2018, the European Court of Auditors conducted its first audit of the Fund's activities, pointing out the need for better targeting.[214] The Court noted that while the Fund is a flexible tool, the initiatives undertaken were too broad and covered too many areas, limiting their effectiveness. In the course of subsequent audits, the Court found that earlier recommendations had been only partially implemented. The Fund did not fully address human rights risks and did not provide

---

211 Ovacık G., Ineli-Ciger M., and Ulusoy O., "Taking Stock of the EU-Turkey Statement in 2024" (2024) 26(2) *European Journal of Migration and Law*, Published online June 18, 2024.

212 European Commission, *EU Emergency Trust Fund for Africa* (2024). Downloaded from: <https://trust-fund-for-africa.europa.eu/index_en>.

213 European Commission, *EUTF MLS HoA S1 2024 Report* (Pobrano 2024) <https://trust-fund-for-africa.europa.eu/document/download/c67c3504-ab93-42ed-b085-1f159ef2e254_en?filename=EUTF%20MLS%20HoA%20S1%202024%20Report.pdf>.

214 European Court of Auditors, Special report No. 32/2018: European Union Emergency Trust Fund for Africa: Flexible But Lacking Focus (2018) <https://www.eca.europa.eu/en/Pages/DocItem.aspx?did=48342>.

adequate targeting of support, which meant that projects did not always address the most urgent needs of beneficiaries.[215] In addition, the Court noted that the Fund's activities were often subordinated to the European Union's migration policy, raising concerns about the instrumentalization of development assistance. Expenditures were sometimes contingent on the cooperation of African countries in the readmission of migrants and border management. An example was Libya, where funds were allocated to support the coast guard, despite allegations of human rights violations and complicity in human trafficking. A similar controversy arose in the case of Niger, where the implementation of migration restrictions negatively affected local communities and economies.[216]

In its 2024 report, the Court reiterated the need for better support targeting, recommending that the European Commission increase evidence-based targeting of specific geographic areas and beneficiaries, improve identification of human rights risks, and implement more effective mechanisms for monitoring results.[217]

Contrary to the intentions and declarations of the European Union, the Fund has become a tool for the implementation of short-term objectives of the European Union's migration policy, which has provoked widespread criticism. The most significant objections relate to the subordination of the Fund's activities to the political interests of the EU, mainly its focus on reducing migration to Europe at the expense of long-term development goals. The Fund has often been used to pressure African countries to conclude migrant readmission agreements and strengthen border controls. Critics point out that this approach undermines the coherence of EU development policy and undermines the effectiveness of efforts to combat poverty, inequality and instability.[218] As a result, in addition to being seen as an instrument of

215 Oxfam International, *The EU Trust Fund for Africa: Trapped between Aid Policy and Migration Politics* (2020). Retrieved from: <https://oxfamilibrary.openrepository.com/bitstream/10546/620936/1/bp-eu-trust-fund-africa-migration-politics-300120-en.pdf>.

216 Oxfam International, *The EU Trust Fund for Africa: Trapped between Aid Policy and Migration Politics* (2020) 11.

217 European Court of Auditors, *Special Report 17/2024: The EU Trust Fund for Africa—Despite New Approaches, Support Remained Unfocused* (2024). Retrieved from: <https://www.eca.europa.eu/en/publications?ref=SR-2024-17>, 5.

218 Oxfam International, *The EU Trust Fund for Africa: Trapped between Aid Policy and Migration Politics* (2020) 11 after: Molenaar F., Ursu A., Tinni B., Hoffmann A., and

development support, the Fund is also an instrument of migration policy and an example of the instrumentalization of development aid and ignoring human rights issues.

1.3.2.9 Establishment of the European Border and Coast Guard

The European Union has also taken steps to strengthen its own institutional structures to better manage crisis situations and increase its resilience in the future should similar crises occur. On September 4, 2016, The Council of the European Union approved the establishment of the European Border and Coast Guard, which became operational on October 6, 2016. Its main goal became integrated management of the EU's external borders, improving control of migration flows and ensuring a high level of security. The Guard was formed from Frontex (with expanded competencies) and national border authorities. As part of its tasks, the Guard conducted an assessment of countries' border control capabilities, organized joint operations and rapid interventions, supported countries under migratory pressure, assisted in search and rescue operations, established a rapid reserve of 1,500 officers, coordinated the return of irregular migrants, and established cooperation with third countries. In addition, it has improved cooperation with the European Fisheries Control Agency and the European Maritime Safety Agency.[219]

Meester J., *A Line in the Sand: Roadmap for Sustainable Migration Management in Agadez* (Clingendael: Netherlands Institute of International Relations 2017) <https://www.clingendael.org/publication/roadmapsustainable-migration-management-agadez>.

219 European Parliament and Council of the European Union (2016), *Regulation (EU) 2016/1624 of September 14, 2016, on the European Border and Coast Guard and amending Regulation (EU) 2016/399 and repealing Regulations (EC) No. 863/2007, (EC) No. 2007/2004 and Decision 2005/267/EC*. OJ L 251, September 16, 2016, 1–76. Retrieved from: <http://data.europa.eu/eli/reg/2016/1624/oj>, repealed by the European Parliament and the Council of the European Union (2019), *Regulation (EU) 2019/1896 of November 13 2019 on the European Border and Coast Guard and repealing Regulations (EU) No. 1052/2013 and (EU) 2016/1624*. OJ L 295, November 14, 2019, 1–131. Downloaded from: <http://data.europa.eu/eli/reg/2019/1896/oj>; Council of the European Union, *European Border and Coast Guard: Council Approved New Rules* (2016). Retrieved from: <https://www.consilium.europa.eu/pl/press/press-releases/2016/09/14/european-border-coast-guard/>.

1.3.2.10 The 2015–2016 migration crisis—a summary

Despite the passage of time since the culmination of the migrant crisis, many of the mechanisms implemented in 2015–2016, such as the EU-Turkey agreement or the coordination structures at the Council level, remain active, even if they function only to a limited extent. The conservative approach to the *deactivation* of these structures stems from the fear of overlooking signs of a new crisis, but also from the assessment of the situation that de facto the migration crisis cannot unequivocally be said to be over. Its intensity has fluctuated, yet the influx of irregular migrants or those seeking protection continues. Despite the decline in migration to Europe in 2024, largely due to the reduced movement of Ukrainian refugees, it is expected to increase again in 2025.[220] A fact highlighted by commentators is the inadequate timing of the EU institutions' response. At a time when they should have acted, they hesitated or made decisions insufficient to address the challenges at hand.[221] This attitude resulted from a lack of certainty about the right course of action, as well as a lack of coherent goals and narratives that could unite stakeholders. It also highlighted the unpreparedness of EU structures to deal effectively with dynamic changes in migration flows, necessitating improvised responses.[222] The events of 2013–2019 exposed the shortcomings and limitations of existing EU migration policies. Prior to 2013, migration management was based on scattered initiatives, such as the European Neighborhood Policy and the Common Foreign and Security Policy. Despite measures such as strengthening borders, cooperation with third countries and increased humanitarian assistance, the EU faced the need to transform its migration policies.[223] After 2015, an attempt was made to consolidate them and create a more comprehensive approach to migration issues.

---

220 International Centre for Migration Policy Development, *Migration Outlook 2025: Inflows to Europe Stabilize, but Trump 2.0, Ukraine and Syria Pose Looming Challenges for the EU* <https://www.icmpd.org/news/migration-outlook-2025-inflows-to-europe-stabilise-but-trump-2.0-ukraine-and-syria-pose-looming-challenges-for-the-eu>.

221 Collett E., and Le Coz C., *After the Storm: Learning from the EU Response to the Migration Crisis*, 22.

222 Collett E., and Le Coz C., *After the Storm: Learning from the EU Response to the Migration Crisis*, 22.

223 Strazzari F., *Dissecting the EU Response to the "Migration Crisis"* (Manchester University Press eBooks, 2021), Academia.edu, 1.

The migration crisis has highlighted the inability of existing European Union policies to effectively manage dynamic and complex migration flows. The events outlined by the author have provided the impetus for a more profound reform of the approach to migration and the development of more integrated policy and operational tools that could meet similar challenges in the future. Restrictive practices previously used at the EU's external borders, especially by Greece, have been transferred to the internal policies of other Member States. Attempts to liberalize migration policy have proved ineffective in the face of the EU's systemic reliance on measures restricting migrants' rights. In view of this, violations of the principles of international protection have become part of standard migration management within the EU. Consequently, the integration of internal and external control mechanisms in the European Union prevents the complete abandonment of repressive practices at the expense of the fundamental rights of applicants for international protection.[224] Contemporary approaches to migration management continue this tradition, with a significant challenge remaining the ineffectiveness of current management mechanisms, which often exacerbate crises. An example is the restriction of legal migration channels, leading to an increase in irregular migration and an increased risk of human rights violations such as violence against migrants or exploitation in destination countries.[225]

The scale of migration and the resulting fears have led to a change in the perception of the phenomenon. Media and political discourses increasingly described the situation as a "migration crisis" or "asylum crisis."[226] Although this approach has been questioned,[227] it has significantly influenced the formation of public opinion and put pressure on European leaders to take swift action. However, the complexity of the migration crisis—involving

224 Skleparis D., *European Governments' Responses to the "Refugee Crisis": The Interdependence of EU Internal and External Controls* (University of Glasgow 2017) <https://eprints.gla.ac.uk/147595/7/147595.pdf>.

225 Cantat, Pécoud, and Thiollet, *Migration as Crisis* (2023), 6.

226 Berry M., Garcia-Blanco I., and Moore K., "Press Coverage of the Refugee and Migrant Crisis in the EU: A Content Analysis of Five European Countries," *UNHCR* (2015).

227 Jeandesboz S., and Pallister-Wilkins M., "Crisis, Enforcement and Control at the EU Borders," in A. Lindley, *Crisis and Migration* (Academia.edu 2016).

humanitarian, security, economic and identity aspects—has made the development of an appropriate response strategy a highly divisive issue across Europe.

As Kriesi writes, the political decision-making process in crisis situations is strongly determined by the characteristics of the crisis itself. Functional pressures arising from specific problems with material, temporal and spatial backgrounds play an important role, as do the institutional conditions of the European Union and the political tensions that emerge at different stages of the crisis. Crises are complex in nature, involving many policy areas, with the result that their course and responses can vary considerably depending on the specifics of each sector. Although the main assumptions are based on a structuralist approach, the impact of the actions of individual actors, who may shape decisions within the constraints imposed by the crisis situation, is also considered.[228]

Member States' response to the migration crisis and migration flows is noteworthy. It is based on a variety of political and administrative mechanisms, which often focus on controlling and managing the flow of people.[229] One of the main approaches is the tightening of border controls and the securitization of migration, as seen, for instance, during the COVID-19 pandemic or the crisis on the EU's eastern border. Countries are introducing surveillance technologies, building physical barriers such as walls or obstacles, and expanding the powers of institutions such as border guards. The European Union has significantly increased its budget for border control, which has risen from €13 billion in 2007–2013 to €35 billion in 2021–2027.[230] These measures, while effective in reducing irregular migration, often lead to severe humanitarian consequences.[231]

Countries are also using migration as a political tool, a particularly controversial aspect of their crisis management strategies. Examples of such actions

---

228 Kriesi H., *Crisis Policymaking in the EU: The COVID-19 Crisis and the Refugee Crisis 2015–16 Compared*. (Cambridge University Press 2025).

229 Cantat C., Pécoud A., and Thiollet H., *Migration as Crisis* (2023) 16.

230 European Commission, *Granice UE z finansowym wsparciem—zwiększenie budżetu na migrację i zarządzanie granicami do 34,9 mld euro w latach 2021–2027*, June 12, 2018, accessed online at <https://poland.representation.ec.europa.eu/news/granice-ue-z-finansowym-wsparciem-2018-06-12_pl>.

231 Cantat C., Pécoud A., and Thiollet H., *Migration as Crisis* (2023) 8, 16.

include Turkey, which in 2020 orchestrated an increased flow of migrants to Greece in violation of previous agreements with the EU, or Belarus, which in 2021 directed migrants to the borders of Poland, Latvia and Lithuania as part of political pressure.[232] Such instrumentalization of migration leads to an escalation of international tensions and undermines regional stability.[233]

In isolated cases, states have taken more humanitarian approaches, as was the case in the European Union's response to the 2022 migration of Ukrainian citizens. At the time, the EU activated a 2001 directive, providing immediate protection for those fleeing the war. This action differed from previous crisis responses, which were often more restrictive and focused on border control, demonstrating that alternative models for responding to migration in a crisis context are possible.[234]

These various strategies indicate that states' responses to migration crises focus primarily on security and controlling flows, often at the expense of protecting human rights and long-term systemic solutions.

1.3.3 The migration crisis triggered by the COVID-19 pandemic

The COVID-19 pandemic had far-reaching consequences for the entire world, including Europe. The crisis, which resulted in the deaths of more than 7 million people worldwide, affected every area of the functioning of both countries and their citizens.[235] In addition to the undeniably tragic consequences in the area of health and human life, the pandemic also took its toll on other spheres, including the movement of people. Europe quickly found itself at the epicenter of events. The pandemic significantly disrupted the free movement of people, arguably the most tangible and cherished achievement of European integration, and hampered the European Union's collective ability to manage migration. European coordination on borders and mobility in the Schengen area was again partially undermined as the sovereignty of states to control their borders became dominant in the face of the emerging health crisis.

---

232 ibid., 9.

233 ibid., 15, 17.

234 ibid., 10.

235 Data as of December 29, 2024 World Health Organization (n.d.). *COVID-19 Dashboard: Deaths* <https://data.who.int/dashboards/covid19/deaths?n=c>.

1.3.3.1 First reactions to the pandemic crisis

In March 2020, following the announcement of the COVID-19 pandemic by the World Health Organization (WHO),[236] EU Member States were the first to react. They began to impose a series of restrictions on the movement of people, both within their territories and restricting border crossings, by reintroducing border controls. Thus, the principle of free movement of people, one of the four fundamental freedoms of the EU, the essence of which is based on the absence of border controls at internal borders, was severely disrupted. Italy, being one of the first countries affected by the pandemic, was the first to decide to impose strict lockdown measures and restrictions on mobility.[237] Spain, Belgium and France soon followed with similar decisions. As a result, the closure of borders and the resumption of border controls in the Schengen area for reasons dictated by the COVID-19 pandemic occurred 188 times.[238] However, it is worth noting that some of the countries that activated the special border control mechanism cited arguments relating to aspects of the threat of irregular migration flows and terrorism.[239] Particularly striking in this regard was the fact that in arguing this, the states pointed to new factual grounds every now and then, justifying the extension of temporary border controls in name only.[240]

These measures were unprecedented, mainly due to the number of instances in which border controls were simultaneously reintroduced and operated at the internal borders of the Schengen zone. However, countries

---

236 World Health Organization (2020, March 11). *WHO Director-General's opening remarks at the media briefing on COVID-19—March 11, 2020.* Retrieved from <https://www.who.int/director-general/speeches/detail/who-director-general-s-opening-remarks-at-the-media-briefing-on-covid-19-11-march-2020>.

237 Horowitz J., "Italy Announces Restrictions Over Entire Country in Attempt to Halt Coronavirus," *The New York Times.*

238 European Commission. (n.d.). *Full List of MS Notification.* European Commission <https://home-affairs.ec.europa.eu/document/download/11934a69-6a45-4842-af94-18400fd274b7_en?filename=Full%20list%20of%20MS%20notification_en.pdf>.

239 De Somer M., "Schengen: Quo Vadis?" (2020) *European Journal of Migration and Law,* 180; Schengen: Quo Vadis? (2020) 22(2) *European Journal of Migration and Law.*

240 ibid., 181., The impermissibility of such action by the Schengen Borders Code is pointed out by Carrera S., in S. Carrera and N. Chun Luk (eds), "In the Name of Covid-19: An Assessment of the EU Border Controls and Travel Restrictions in the EU" (European Parliament 2020), Study requested by the LIBE Committee, 48.

differed in their approach to implementing these measures. Some countries decided to completely close their borders to all EU and EFTA members. This group included Belgium, Cyprus, Denmark, Estonia, Finland, France, Iceland, Lithuania, Norway, Romania, Slovakia and Spain. Full border controls were reintroduced in these countries, resulting in a significant reduction in cross-border traffic. Another group of countries applied selective border controls that covered selected borders or depended on the epidemiological situation in particular countries. Austria, the Czech Republic, Germany, Hungary, Malta, Poland, Portugal, Slovenia and Switzerland opted for this solution, focusing mainly on controls with countries with higher infection rates.

In contrast, Bulgaria, Croatia, Greece, Ireland, Italy, Latvia, Liechtenstein, Luxembourg, the Netherlands and Sweden did not implement formal border controls or apply minimal restrictions. However, these countries may have imposed regional movement restrictions that de facto affected border crossings, despite the lack of official notifications to the European Commission.[241] The restrictions that were put in place had a significant impact on the functioning of the common market and border regions, which rely heavily on cross-border economic and social cooperation.

During the COVID-19 pandemic, many countries combined border controls with strict travel restrictions, which in practice meant closing borders.[242] Border controls are a nuisance, but they do not prevent border crossings, whereas travel restrictions block them altogether. Some countries distinguished between "essential" and "non-essential" travel, while others imposed only internal restrictions without implementing border controls.[243] Member

241 Frey L., *Coordination Breakdown: The Impacts of COVID-19 on Migration in Europe* (Migration Policy Institute, March 2024) <https://www.migrationpolicy.org/sites/default/files/publications/mpi_covid-mobility-europe_final.pdf>; Peyrony J., Rubiom J., Viaggi R., *The Effects of COVID-19-Induced Border Closures on Cross-Border Regions: An Empirical Report Covering the Period March to June 2020* (Luxembourg: Publications Office of the European Union 2021); European Commission, "*Temporary Reintroduction of Border Control*," accessed December 23, 2022.

242 Thym D., and Bornemann J., "Schengen and Free Movement Law During the First Phase of the Covid-19 Pandemic: Of Symbolism, Law and Politics," (2020) 5(3) *European Papers*, 1143–1170 <https://doi.org/10.15166/2499-8249/420>.

243 Delhomme V. N., "The Legality of Covid-19 Travel Restrictions in an "Area without Internal Frontiers": Court of Justice (Grand Chamber) December 5, 2023, Case

States exercised powers under Articles 25 and 28 of the Schengen Borders Code, allowing for the temporary resumption of border controls.[244] As Thym points out, states saw such action as a partially independent decision, as evidenced, for example, by the failure to complete the procedure for justifying all relevant circumstances when notifying the Commission of such a decision.[245]

The Schengen Borders Code (SBC) provides three mechanisms for the temporary reintroduction of internal border controls.[246] Article 29 of the SBC, which refers to "exceptional circumstances," applies to situations arising from serious negligence in the control of external borders, making its application less relevant in the context of the COVID-19 pandemic. Instead, recourse to Articles 25 and 28 of the SBC remains legitimate. Article 25 regulates the procedure for reintroducing control in the event of foreseeable threats to public order or internal security, requiring prior notification to other Member States and the European Commission. Article 28, by contrast, allows for the immediate introduction of control in emergency situations, with notification occurring simultaneously with the implementation of measures. Under Article 25, the maximum duration of controls was six months, whereas under Article 28, it could be up to two months. Each measure had to comply with the principles of proportionality and necessity. At this point, it should be noted that these solutions have been subject to revision and have undergone significant changes, which will be discussed later in the chapter.

On this subject, too, the COVID-19 pandemic revealed significant differences in the way Member States applied the Schengen Borders Code. Some countries, such as Germany, Austria and Norway, made use of Article 28 of the SBC, which allows for the immediate reintroduction of border controls in emergency situations. Others, such as Finland, Denmark and France,

---

C-128/22, Nordic Info," (2024) 20(2) *European Constitutional Law Review*, 307–328 <https://doi.org/10.1017/S1574019624000245>.

244 Regulation (EU) 2016/399 of the European Parliament and of the Council of March 9, 2016, on the EU Code on the rules governing the movement of persons across borders (Schengen Borders Code).

245 Thym D., and Bornemann J., Schengen and Free Movement Law During the First Phase of the Covid-19 Pandemic: Of Symbolism, 1148.

246 Regulation (EU) 2016/399 of the European Parliament and of the Council of March 9, 2016 on the EU Code on the rules governing the movement of persons across borders (Schengen Borders Code) (consolidated text) [2016] OJ L 77/1 <http://data.europa.eu/eli/reg/2016/399/oj>.

invoked Article 25 of the SBC, which addresses foreseeable threats. France and Denmark linked the pandemic to already existing reasons such as terrorist threats and secondary migration flows. The Czech Republic, by contrast, left its borders with Poland and Slovakia open, diverging from other countries' decisions to close their borders completely.[247]

As S. Montaldo points out, from a legal perspective, the temporary reintroduction of border controls by EU Member States in response to the COVID-19 pandemic did not raise significant concerns. Although Articles 25 and 28 of the Schengen Borders Code do not directly address the issue of public health, the jurisprudence of the Court of Justice of the European Union recognizes that serious and imminent threats—such as the rapid spread of an epidemic—can be considered threats to public order and internal security.[248] This is because the concept of public order includes the protection of key social interests, while internal security concerns threats to the stability of the operation of essential public services. The COVID-19 pandemic could, therefore, be considered a real, present and serious threat to both public order and public security. The scale and intensity of the health crisis justified extraordinary measures, such as the reintroduction of border controls or restrictions on movement, in accordance with the provisions of the Schengen Borders Code and CJEU case law.

In Case C-128/22[249] the CJEU confirmed that infectious diseases with pandemic potential, such as COVID-19, can justify restrictions on freedom of movement under Articles 27(1) and 29(1) of Directive 2004/38.[250] Member States may restrict the right to enter and leave the territory and impose protective measures such as quarantine or testing, provided they are proportionate and consistent.[251] Such restrictions may be of a general nature,

247 Montaldo S., "The COVID-19 Emergency and the Reintroduction of Internal Border Controls in the Schengen Area" (2020) 5(1) *European Papers* 527 <www.europeanpapers.eu>.

248 Court of Justice of the European Union, Judgment of September 13, 2016, Secretary of State for the Home Department v. CS, C-304/14, §§ 38–39 and extensive case law cited in this ruling.

249 Court of Justice of the European Union (Grand Chamber), Judgment of December 5, 2023, C-128/22, Nordic Info, ECLI:EU:C:2023:XYZ <https://eur-lex.europa.eu/legal-content/PL/TXT/PDF/?uri=CELEX:62022CJ0128>.

250 *Nordic Info*, par. 52–54.

251 *Nordic Info*, par. 58–59.

without individual behavioral analysis.[252] The Court pointed out that restrictive measures must be published in a manner that makes them easy to understand and subject to judicial or administrative challenge.[253] It also expressed a rather controversial position in which it questioned whether, in light of the precautionary principle, alternative measures—such as maintaining social distance, wearing masks or regular testing—could have been equally effective in reducing the spread of the virus.[254] Although quarantine is considered a highly restrictive measure, the Court deemed it proportionate, along with testing, as both help minimize the risk of spreading the virus.[255] Regarding controls, the Court stressed the difference between police and border controls, holding that measures aimed at protecting public health do not violate the Schengen Borders Code.[256] The temporary reintroduction of border controls must be linked to a threat to public order and comply with the conditions of Articles 25–28 of the Code.[257] While states have limited discretion in implementing such measures, they must act in accordance with the precautionary principle and EU law.[258]

The *Nordic Info* ruling is a key reference point for the application of EU law in emergency situations such as the COVID-19 pandemic, particularly in its interpretation of the provisions of Directive 2004/38/EC and the Schengen Borders Code.[259] The Court of Justice of the EU has indicated that under Articles 27(1) and 29 of the Directive, measures restricting freedom of movement may be justified on public health grounds, provided they are proportionate, necessary and non-discriminatory.[260] A flexible interpretation of

252 *Nordic Info*, par. 64, 67–70.
253 *Nordic Info*, par.71–72.
254 *Nordic Info*, par. 90–91.
255 *Nordic Info*, par. 97.
256 *Nordic Info*, par. 117.
257 *Nordic Info*, par. 124–127.
258 *Nordic Info*, par. 129.
259 Delhomme V. N., "Legality of COVID-19 Travel Restrictions in an Area Without Internal Frontiers" (2024) *European Constitutional Law Review* <https://www.cambridge.org/core/journals/european-constitutional-law-review/article/legality-of-covid19-travel-restrictions-in-an-area-without-internal-frontiers/ABF12B6908D428E2BBAAF8F6ACDAAA53>, 316.
260 Delhomme V. N., *Legality of COVID-19 Travel Restrictions in an Area Without Internal Frontiers* (Cambridge University Press 2024) 316.

"freedom of movement" has made it possible to include both the right to enter and to leave the territory of a Member State.[261] Despite inaccuracies in the Directive's drafting, the Court recognized the possibility of general restrictions in exceptional situations, such as a pandemic, stressing their compatibility with Article 72 TFEU if they meet the conditions of proportionality. The Schengen Borders Code lacked direct references to public health, but the Court, taking into account the particular seriousness of a pandemic, accepted measures to protect the public from an epidemic threat. As *Delhomme* argues, in its assessment of proportionality, the Court referred to Articles 7 and 16 of the EU Charter of Fundamental Rights,[262] but did not fully exploit the potential of Article 35 on the right to health, which could have provided a stronger legal basis for the measures taken.[263] The judgment reiterates the need to balance public health protection with individuals' rights and stresses the need to adapt EU legislation to modern challenges. Thus, *Nordic Info* sets a precedent for the future development of jurisprudence on EU law, considering the balance between the public interest and fundamental rights.[264]

Similarly, D. Thym presents a position that cautiously allows for the possibility of justifying the reinstatement of border controls during the COVID-19 pandemic by referring to the concept of "public order" while stressing that this concept cannot be wholly equated with "protection of public health." According to Thym, serious threats to public health, such as a pandemic, may justify such measures due to their significant social and economic impact. At the same time, he points out that less serious health threats, such as the presence of people with infectious diseases, could only justify individual movement restrictions but did not warrant the reintroduction of border controls. Thym also points out that even if there were doubts about the compatibility of such measures with the Schengen Borders Code (SBC), Article 35 of the Charter of Fundamental Rights of the European Union and

261 ibid., 317.

262 Charter of Fundamental Rights of the European Union (OJ EU. C. 2007 No. 303, 1, as amended).

263 ibid., 327.

264 ibid., 328.

Article 72 of the Treaty on the Functioning of the European Union (TFEU) could have provided an adequate legal basis to justify them.[265]

S. Carrera takes a more critical view of the actions of EU Member States during the COVID-19 pandemic, stressing that decisions to impose travel bans and entry restrictions were, in many cases, inconsistent with the provisions of the Schengen Borders Code. His analysis indicates that Member States had no formal SBC-based legal basis for imposing travel bans that temporarily prevented entry of citizens and residents of other Schengen countries. Carrera argues that such actions undermined the foundations of the Schengen area and contradicted the principles of EU law, which require that restrictions on movement be lawful, proportionate and temporary.[266]

1.3.3.2 The response to the COVID-19 pandemic from EU bodies

The European Union and its bodies played a key role in coordinating the response to the COVID-19 pandemic, even though these actions gained momentum and intensity over time. While accepting the use of border controls as part of Member States' efforts to combat the pandemic, the European Commission stressed the need to strike a balance between protecting health and ensuring the smooth movement of people and the supply of goods.[267] Member States often took unilateral decisions to reintroduce border controls, which limited the effectiveness of standard policies and cooperation within the Schengen area. This situation has highlighted the need to strengthen emergency coordination mechanisms and solidarity among EU countries.[268]

---

265 Thym D., and Bornemann J., *Schengen and Free Movement Law During the First Phase of the Covid-19 Pandemic* …, 1148.

266 Carrera S. in Carrera S., and Chun Luk N., "In the Name of Covid-19: An Assessment of the EU Border Controls and Travel Restrictions in the EU" (European Parliament 2020), Study requested by the LIBE committee, 49.

267 Council Recommendation (EU) 2020/912 of June 30, 2020 concerning the temporary restriction of non-essential travel to the EU and the possibility of lifting this restriction, EUR-Lex - 32020H0912 - EN - EUR-Lex <https://eur-lex.europa.eu/legal-content/PL/TXT/?uri=uriserv%3AOJ.LI.2020.208.01.0001.01.ENG&toc=OJ%3AL%3A2020%3A208I%3ATOC>.

268 Communication from the Commission Coordinated step-by-step approach toward restoring freedom of movement and removing internal border controls—COVID-19 (2020/C 169/03) C_2020169EN.01003001.xml <https://eur-lex.europa.eu/legal-content/PL/TXT/HTML/?uri=CELEX:52020XC0515(05)>.

Excessive discretion for states to reinstate border controls can lead to their abuse. The examples of Austria and France, which used the regulations not only to combat pandemics, but also to control migration and counter terrorism, show that there is a risk of the Schengen Borders Code regulations being instrumentalized.[269] These actions have harmed fundamental principles of the European Union, such as the free movement of people and goods. In addition, the pandemic exposed deficiencies in the transparency of Member States' actions. Although the introduction of regulations requires notification to the European Commission and other Member States, not all countries fully and clearly communicated the measures they were implementing.[270] It proved necessary to strengthen monitoring and reporting mechanisms to ensure compliance with the principles of EU law.[271] Balancing security and freedom of movement also proved to be a key challenge. The pandemic showed how difficult it is to maintain a balance between protecting public health and citizens' rights.

The first major document issued in response to the COVID-19 pandemic was the European Commission's Communication on the temporary restriction of non-essential travel to the EU.[272] The document emphasized the need to restrict international mobility to slow the spread of the SARS-CoV-2 virus. The communiqué was temporary and originally covered a period of 30 days but was extended several times. The European Commission recommended temporary travel restrictions on entry to the EU to curb the spread of COVID-19. These were to include drastically limiting the flow of people to the Union's external borders, except for essential travel, such as returning EU citizens, health workers and diplomats. Those authorized to enter were to be subject to coordinated health checks. The restrictions were to be in effect for 30 days, with the possibility of extension depending on developments. The

---

269 Thym D., and Bornemann J., *Schengen and Free Movement Law During the First Phase of the Covid-19 Pandemic* …, 1147.

270 Carrera S. in Carrera S., and Chun Luk N. (eds) *In the Name of Covid-19: An Assessment of the EU Border Controls and Travel Restrictions in the EU* (European Parliament 2020), Study requested by the LIBE committee, 49.

271 ibid., 50.

272 European Commission, *COVID-19: Temporary Restriction of Non-essential Travel to the EU* (COM/2020/115 final) (2020). Downloaded January 19, 2025 from <https://eur-lex.europa.eu/legal-content/PL/TXT/?uri=CELEX%3A52020DC0115>.

Commission asked the European Council to swiftly adopt these measures at all external borders of the Schengen zone. On June 30, 2020. The Council of the European Union adopted Recommendation (EU) 2020/912 on the temporary restriction of non-essential travel to the EU and the possibility of lifting the restriction.[273] The document included criteria and methodology that should be used in deciding whether to lift travel restrictions, considering factors such as the epidemiological situation, preventive measures and economic and social considerations. The recommendation also stressed the need for a coordinated approach by Member States to lift external border restrictions and introduce a list of third countries whose residents should not be subject to temporary travel restrictions. At the summit in October 2020, the European Council adopted a recommendation on coordinating the response to the pandemic.[274] The document stressed the importance of a coordinated approach to restricting the free movement of people, managing testing strategies and quarantine. The document set out standard criteria and thresholds that Member States should consider when deciding whether to impose such restrictions, as well as principles for mapping risk areas and coordinating action among Member States.

In March 2021, the European Commission published a communication entitled *A common path to a safe and sustainable reopening*.[275] The document presented a strategy for the gradual lifting of pandemic restrictions and the introduction of "digital green certificates" (EU Digital COVID Certificate). The authors pointed to the need for investment in digital tools and harmonization of procedures between Member States. June 14, 2021. The European Parliament and the EU Council adopted Regulation (EU) 2021/953, which

273 Council Recommendation (EU) 2020/912 of June 30, 2020 concerning the temporary restriction of non-essential travel to the EU and the possibility of lifting this restriction, EUR-Lex - 32020H0912 - EN - EUR-Lex <https://eur-lex.europa.eu/legal-content/PL/TXT/?uri=uriserv%3AOJ.LI.2020.208.01.0001.01.ENG&toc=OJ%3AL%3A2020%3A208I%3ATOC>.

274 Council Recommendation (EU) 2020/1475 of October 13 2020 on a coordinated approach to restricting free movement in response to the COVID-19 pandemic, EUR-Lex - 32020H1475 - EN <https://eur-lex.europa.eu/legal-content/PL/TXT/?uri=celex%3A32020H1475>.

275 European Commission, *Wspólna droga do bezpiecznego i trwałego ponownego otwarcia, komunikat z dnia 17 marca 2021 r* <https://commission.europa.eu/document/07e9facf-2410-4bfe-97df-840eb6bca56e_pl>.

introduced the EU Digital COVID Certificate.[276] The act aimed to simplify international travel within the EU by standardizing the confirmation of vaccination, negative test results, or recovery from COVID-19. The regulation was key to restoring the free movement of people after the problematic pandemic period. Provisions to ensure the protection of personal data and mechanisms for mutual recognition of certificates by Member States were also included. The document helped improve coordination between EU countries in the field of public health. The key document in the last phase of the pandemic was Council Recommendation (EU) 2022/2548, which adapted measures to the current epidemiological situation.[277] The document pointed out the need to ensure a coordinated approach to travel to the EU while respecting the principle of proportionality. The Council stressed the need to monitor variants of the virus and maintain rapid response mechanisms in case the situation worsens. The recommendation replaced earlier acts and focused on long-term pandemic management. It was the latest in a series of measures that strengthened the EU's preparedness for future health crises. Actions in the financial area were not insignificant. In response to the crisis caused by the COVID-19 pandemic, a Recovery Plan for Europe, known as Next Generation EU, was developed.[278] Its goal is to make the European economy more dynamic and support the ecological and digital transformation to prepare and make the European Union more resilient to future challenges. The plan includes a €750 billion emergency reconstruction mechanism that

---

276 Regulation (EU) 2021/953 of the European Parliament and of the Council of June 14, 2021 on a framework for the issuance, verification and recognition of interoperable certificates of vaccination, test result and recovery in connection with COVID-19 (EU digital COVID certificate) to facilitate free movement during the COVID-19 pandemic (OJ L 211, June 15, 2021, 1–22) <http://data.europa.eu/eli/reg/2021/953/oj> (not applicable).

277 Council Recommendation (EU) 2022/2548 of December 13, 2022 on a coordinated approach to travel to the Union during the COVID-19 pandemic and replacing Council Recommendation (EU) 2020/912 (OJ L 328, December 22, 2022, 146–152). Accessed January 19, 2025 <http://data.europa.eu/eli/reco/2022/2548/oj>.

278 Communication from the Commission to the European Parliament, the European Council, the Council, the European Economic and Social Committee and the Committee of the Regions Europe's moment: Repair and Prepare for the Next Generation, COM/2020/456 final (Brussels, May 27, 2020) <https://eur-lex.europa.eu/legal-content/EN/TXT/?uri=celex:52020DC0456>.

is part of an overall package worth €1,824.3 billion, which also consists of a multi-year financial framework for 2021–2027. Next Generation EU funds are distributed as loans and grants under seven programs, including the Instrument for Reconstruction and Enhanced Resilience and the REACT-EU program.

During the initial phase of the pandemic, the European Commission was unable to develop uniform criteria for evaluating measures introduced by Member States based on the standards of the European Centre for Disease Prevention and Control (ECDC). In particular, solutions were sought that could provide alternatives to closing borders and resuming controls at the European Union's internal borders.[279] Among the instruments that were used, it is worth mentioning a few that were applied in the fight against the pandemic.

The first mechanism used was a list of safe third countries, established by the European Council in June 2020. The list included countries considered epidemiologically safe, and Member States were recommended to lift entry restrictions for their citizens.[280] The list was subject to systematic updates: it initially included 15 countries but was reduced to seven countries in early 2021 and expanded again to 14 countries in 2022.[281] Implementation of the recommendations by Member States was not uniform. Some followed the guidelines, introducing additional precautions in the form of mandatory testing or quarantine, while others banned the entry of third-country nationals altogether or applied less restrictive regulations, allowing entry under certain conditions.[282]

The second tool was the introduction of a traffic light system by the European Commission in September 2020 to coordinate Member States'

---

279 Thym D., and Bornemann J., *Schengen and Free Movement Law During the First Phase of the Covid-19 Pandemic…*, 1149.

280 Council of the European Union, *Council Recommendation on the Temporary Restriction on Non-essential Travel Into the EU and the Possible Lifting of Such Restriction* (Brussels, June 30, 2020) 9208/20 <https://data.consilium.europa.eu/doc/document/ST-9208-2020-INIT/en/pdf>.

281 Schengen News, *EU's List of Epidemiologically Safe Countries Amid COVID-19* <https://schengen.news/eu-list-of-epidemiologically-safe-countries-amid-covid-19/>.

282 Frey, Lindsay, *Coordination Breakdown: The Impacts of COVID-19 on Migration in Europe* (Migration Policy Institute, March 2024) <https://www.migrationpolicy.org/sites/default/files/publications/mpi_covid-mobility-europe_final.pdf>.

internal travel activities. The system classified Member States of the European Union, the European Economic Area, and the United Kingdom (during the transition period after Brexit) according to the degree of epidemiological risk by assigning them green, orange, or red colors. Although this system was an example of effective coordination, not all Member States followed its guidelines. France, for example, developed its own health risk assessment system,[283] while Hungary decided to close its borders to most of the European Union, except for the Visegrad Group countries.[284]

The third mechanism involved testing and quarantine measures, introduced as reliable diagnostic tests became available. European Union Member States took varied approaches to testing and isolation obligations, implementing different regulations depending on the status of travelers (EU or third-country nationals) and the type of tests accepted.[285]

The final mechanism was exceptions to travel restrictions, designed to allow key sectors of the economy to operate. Despite the rapid closure of borders, Member States introduced exceptions for workers employed in sensitive sectors such as health care, transportation, agriculture and the food industry. Some countries, including Belgium, Croatia, the Czech Republic, Denmark, Greece, Latvia and Slovenia, implemented the European Commission's guidelines for industries exempted from restrictions,[286] while others tailored regulations to local economic needs.[287] Only on October 13, 2020, did the Council of the European Union adopt the aforementioned recommendation for a coordinated approach to the restrictions on freedom of movement in

---

283 Benton M., Batalova J., Davidoff-Gore S., and Schmidt T., *COVID-19 and the State of Global Mobility in 2020* (Migration Policy Institute) <https://www.migrationpolicy.org/research/covid-19-state-global-mobility-2020>.

284 Januzi S., "Hungary Amends Travel Restrictions for V4 Countries" (October 7, 2020) *Schengen News* <https://schengen.news/hungary-amends-travel-restrictions-for-v4-countries/>.

285 European Migration Network (EMN) and Organization for Economic Cooperation and Development (OECD), "The Impact of COVID-19 in the Migration Area in EU and OECD Countries" (EMN OECD Umbrella Inform, April 2021).

286 European Commission, "Guidelines Concerning the Exercise of the Free Movement of Workers during COVID-19 Outbreak" (C 102 I/03, March 30, 2020) *Official Journal of the European Union*.

287 EMN and OECD, "Maintaining Labour Migration in Essential Sectors in Times of Pandemic" (EMN OECD Inform 3, October 21, 2020).

response to the emergency situation caused by the COVID-19 pandemic. The Council deemed it necessary to take measures to reduce the negative effects of fragmented border policies and provide greater transparency and predictability for citizens and businesses.[288]

The COVID-19 pandemic highlighted challenges in border management, interstate solidarity and compliance with EU law, revealing limitations in coordination. The EU's external borders have gained symbolic importance as a protection tool, but border closures have been implemented unilaterally, violating the principles of the internal market and the Schengen system. The European Commission, supported by Frontex, EASO and Europol, sought to coordinate actions, emphasizing the dependence between countries in medical supplies and key services. However, the lack of effective oversight of the implementation of measures by Member States has led to discrepancies in the application of EU rules. The crisis demonstrated the need for more effective mechanisms to enforce common legal standards.

1.3.3.3 Labor migrants during the COVID-19 pandemic

The COVID-19 pandemic significantly affected migration flows in Europe, leading to drastic declines in labor, student, family and refugee migration. In 2020, most EU Member States issued significantly fewer work permits for third-country nationals, and in nine countries the number of permits issued fell by more than 40 % compared to 2019. Germany recorded the most significant decline, with a nearly 80 % reduction in permits issued, followed by the Czech Republic, Slovenia and Greece. The exceptions were Spain and Lithuania, which increased the number of permits issued, with Spain responding to agricultural labor shortages, increasing the number by more than 25 %. Despite a 20 % drop, Poland remained the leader in issuing permits, mainly for Ukrainian workers, thanks to simplified visa procedures.[289]

---

288 Council of the European Union, COUNCIL RECOMMENDATION (EU) 2020/1475 of October 13, 2020 on a coordinated approach to restricting free movement in response to the COVID-19 pandemic (L 337/3, October 14, 2020) *Official Journal of the European Union* <https://eur-lex.europa.eu/legal-content/PL/TXT/HTML/?uri=OJ:L:2020:337:FULL>.

289 Frey L., *Coordination Breakdown: The Impacts of COVID-19 on Migration in Europe* (Migration Policy Institute, March 2024) 9–10.

In response to these challenges, EU Member States have implemented various solutions. Spain and Italy introduced labor legalization programs for irregular migrants to alleviate labor shortages. Poland simplified entry and legalization procedures for Ukrainian workers, allowing labor migration to recover quickly. Following Russia's aggression against Ukraine in 2022, the European Union adopted Directive 2001/55/EC, which allowed Ukrainian refugees to stay legally and access the labor market.

Despite the restrictions, the movement of workers was not completely halted. As mentioned earlier, certain occupational groups deemed crucial to the functioning of the economy, such as workers in the healthcare, transportation and agricultural sectors, were still able to move freely. This resulted from a selective approach to mobility, which allowed only the most necessary workers to move. Although introduced as a crisis measure, this selection suggested a potential regression in the free movement of workers in the future. At the same time, it became a tool to stimulate workers' movement within the European Union. Instead of restricting freedom of movement, it was used to support strategic economic sectors and strengthen the single labor market. The pandemic revealed the need to develop mechanisms to balance public health and safety with workers' rights, potentially contributing to a more flexible and resilient labor market in the future.[290]

During the COVID-19 pandemic, the free movement of workers in the European Union was subject to special rationing, which resulted in two categories of cross-border workers, depending on the nature of the work they performed and their affiliation with specific economic sectors. The first category included workers whose mobility was based on the nature of the work they performed, i.e., frontier, posted and seasonal workers. The second category included those employed in sectors considered crucial from the perspective of public security and public order, such as health care, social welfare, goods supply logistics, information and communications technology, engineering, critical infrastructure, civil security, the food sector and transportation.[291]

---

290 Robin-Olivier S., "Free Movement of Workers in the Light of the COVID-19 Sanitary Crisis: From Restrictive Selection to Selective Mobility." *European Papers* (2020). Retrieved from <https://www.europeanpapers.eu/en/europeanforum/free-movement-of-workers-covid-19-sanitary-crisis#_ftnref1>.

291 Robin-Olivier S., "Free Movement of Workers in the Light of the COVID-19 Sanitary Crisis: From Restrictive Selection to Selective Mobility," *European*

When the prerequisites for belonging to both categories were cumulative, priority was given to ensuring the unimpeded exercise of freedom of movement, in accordance with Article 45 of the Treaty on the Functioning of the European Union (TFEU) and the provisions of the Schengen Borders Code. It was important that border workers performing professional duties in the health care sector, the food industry or other essential services (such as childcare, elderly care, maintenance of critical infrastructure, among others) retain the right to cross the borders of Member States in order to carry out their professional duties. The European Commission stressed that similar rules should apply to posted and seasonal workers, especially in the area of health care, maintenance of medical infrastructure, production of medical equipment and supply logistics, as their work played a key role in ensuring the continuity of essential public services.[292]

Similarly, for workers performing tasks fundamental to the protection of public health, safety and public order, Member States were obliged to apply measures ensuring their free movement in accordance with the principle of proportionality and non-discrimination. Temporary restrictions on movement could only be applied to the extent necessary to protect the public interest, in accordance with Article 45(3) TFEU, and could not affect the essence of the right to free movement of workers. Maintaining freedom of movement only for specific categories of workers was considered inadequate and seen as a failure of single market principles.

In response to the COVID-19 pandemic, the European Commission presented guidelines to prevent uncoordinated and disparate actions by Member States that could violate single market principles and fundamental rights. Developed with the support of the European Asylum Support Office (EASO) and the European Border and Coast Guard Agency (Frontex), the document aimed to integrate COVID-19 containment measures into the European Union legal order. The Commission recalled that any restrictions on fundamental rights must comply with the rule of law and, in particular, meet

---

Papers—European Forum <https://www.europeanpapers.eu/en/europeanforum/free-movement-of-workers-covid-19-sanitary-crisis>.

292 Commission Communication C, 1753 final of March 16, 2020. *Guidelines on Border Management Measures to Protect Health and Ensure the Availability of Essential Goods and Services* (2020).

the criteria of legality, necessity, proportionality and non-discrimination. In addition, these measures must respect the principle of *non-refoulement* and other obligations under international law.

1.3.3.4 The situation of applicants for international protection during the COVID-19 pandemic

The COVID-19 pandemic caused significant restrictions on the right to apply for asylum, which was reflected in a drastic drop in the number of asylum applications submitted in 2020. The closure of the European Union's external borders and the reduction in the activities of the authorities responsible for conducting asylum procedures prevented migrants from formally registering as applicants for international protection. Some Member States introduced measures that directly restricted access to the asylum procedure.[293] For example, Italy and Malta declared their ports "unsafe" for disembarkation, resulting in a renewed politicization of the migration issue. Hungary and Spain declared a state of emergency, suspending asylum applications. Belgium and the Netherlands closed reception centers for asylum seekers, while Malta and Greece suspended asylum hearings and halted access to detention centers for visitors.[294]

However, there were also exceptions. For instance, Portugal implemented a policy of full access to public health services for all migrants and asylum seekers, recognizing that protecting public health requires providing universal access to medical care.

In sum, the emergency measures adopted by Member States in the wake of the COVID-19 pandemic restricted rights guaranteed by European Union law, including the right to asylum protected by Article 18 of the Charter of Fundamental Rights of the European Union. Member States' differing responses resulted from the fragmented nature of the Common European Asylum System, which relies heavily on national administrative mechanisms

293 Marin L., *COVID-19 Crisis and Closure of External Borders: Another Stress Test Challenging Solidarity in the EU?*, European Papers <https://www.europeanpapers.eu/en/europeanforum/covid-19-crisis-closure-external-borders-another-stress-test-challenging-solidarity#_ftnref34>.

294 ibid.

and procedures, leading to a lack of uniformity in applying EU standards of international protection.

1.3.3.5 Application of soft law in the practice of managing the crisis caused by the COVID-19 pandemic

The use of soft-law instruments by the European Union provided for in Article 288 (5) TFEU played a significant role in managing the COVID-19 crisis and was widely utilized as an important regulatory element in the fight against the pandemic.[295] Soft law, such as guidelines, recommendations or communications, allowed EU institutions, particularly the European Commission and the Council, to act swiftly in emergency situations.[296] A key advantage of these instruments was that they could be implemented immediately, without requiring lengthy legislative procedures. In the context of a dynamically changing epidemiological situation, this enabled the Union to respond effectively to public health threats and problems arising from the fragmentation of national systems.

Soft-law instruments were also characterized by flexibility, allowing Member States to adapt guidelines to local circumstances. For example, in border management, the Commission's guidelines provided a basis for Member States to implement policies that took into account their administrative and geographic specificities. In addition, soft law played a preliminary role, allowing solutions to be tested and a common position to be developed before their potential introduction as binding legislation.[297]

Despite its many advantages, soft law also revealed its significant drawbacks. The most serious of these was its lack of binding force, which led to

---

295 Stefan O., *COVID-19 Soft Law: Voluminous, Effective, Legitimate? A Research Agenda*, European Papers <https://www.europeanpapers.eu/en/authors/oana-stefan>; Marin L., "The COVID-19 Crisis and the Closure of External Borders: Another Stress-test for the Challenging Construction of Solidarity Within the EU?" (2020) 5(2) *European Papers, European Forum*, Insight of October 28, 2020, 1071–1086, ISSN 2499-8249 <https://doi.org/10.15166/2499-8249/398>; Daniel Thym, and Jonas Bornemann, *Schengen and Free Movement Law During the First Phase of the Covid-19 Pandemic …*, 1157–1158.

296 Stefan O., *COVID-19 Soft Law: Voluminous, Effective, Legitimate?*, 663.

297 ibid., p. 664.

inconsistencies in the implementation of the guidelines adopted.[298] Member States could selectively apply the Commission's recommendations, which undermined the uniformity of action taken. Thym and Bornemann point out that such fragmentation undermines the effectiveness of the Union's coordination mechanisms and hinders progress toward a common health and migration policy.[299]

Another drawback was that the democratic legitimacy of these instruments was limited. The lack of clear consultation procedures with Member States, the European Parliament and other stakeholders raised questions about the transparency of the legislative process.[300] For example, regarding the Commission's guidelines on mobile applications, it is unclear to what extent national authorities were consulted, which weakened public trust in the process.[301] The European Parliament, despite its calls for more coordinated action at the EU level, was largely excluded from the process of developing soft-law instruments, further limiting the democratic legitimacy of these measures.[302] Soft law also suffers from significant legitimacy flaws because its legal effects are diluted. In the Commission's view, there was a lack of clear delineation between soft and hard law, which hindered effective implementation and oversight of compliance with EU regulations. This gap revealed the need for mechanisms to enable the Commission to adopt binding legal acts in emergency situations, which would allow it to respond more quickly and effectively to crises.[303]

---

298 Daniel Thym, and Jonas Bornemann, *Schengen and Free Movement Law During the First Phase of the Covid-19 Pandemic …*, 1158.

299 ibid., 1158.

300 Eliantonio M., and Ştefan O., "The Elusive Legitimacy of EU Soft Law: An Analysis of Consultation and Participation in the Process of Adopting COVID-19 Soft Law in the EU," (2021) 12 *European Journal of Risk Regulation*, 169.

301 Stefan O., *COVID-19 Soft Law: Voluminous, Effective, Legitimate?*, 665; Daniel Thym, and Jonas Bornemann, *Schengen and Free Movement Law During the First Phase of the Covid-19 Pandemic …*, 1158.

302 Eliantonio M., and Ştefan O., *The Elusive Legitimacy of EU Soft Law …*, 169.

303 Luisa Marin, "COVID-19 Crisis and Closure of External Borders: Another Stress Test Challenging Solidarity in the EU?," *European Papers* <https://www.europeanpapers.eu/en/europeanforum/covid-19-crisis-closure-external-borders-another-stress-test-challenging-solidarity#_ftnref34>.

Another problem that undermined their effectiveness was the lack of transparency in the process of adopting soft laws. Ambiguities about how these instruments were consulted and adopted, as well as a lack of public access to detailed information about the decision-making process, limited their public acceptance.

Finally, a significant challenge is the limited ability to enforce soft law. The lack of binding legal effect prevents effective *ex post* judicial review in the event of violations of these guidelines by Member States. As commentators point out, the Court of Justice of the EU has repeatedly refused to recognize the Commission's recommendations as actionable acts, stressing that their non-binding nature precludes the possibility of pursuing claims related to them.[304]

Soft law has again become a distinctive tool for times of crisis, on this occasion triggered by a pandemic. Its use was widespread not only in Europe but also in other countries across different continents. For example, M. McLeod analyses how governments around the world, including Australia, used soft law during the COVID-19 pandemic.[305] The author points out that while it is effective and flexible it also raises serious questions about accountability and oversight, challenging Australia's concept of the separation of powers.[306] In the European Union, the dominance of soft-law instruments was reflected both in the number of documents issued as well as in the range of specific types of instruments, such as communications and recommendations, which, while flexible, did not provide an adequate level of legal certainty.[307]

Perceived as a crisis to be managed, the pandemic once again highlighted the need for uniform procedures for adopting and implementing soft law,

304 Stefan O., *COVID-19 Soft Law: Voluminous, Effective, Legitimate?*, 666.

305 McLeod M., "Distancing from Accountability? Governments' Use of Soft Law in the COVID-19 Pandemic" (2022) 50(1) *Federal Law Review*, 3–19.

306 Similarly, Stefan O., "COVID-19 Soft Law: Voluminous, Effective, Legitimate? A Research Agenda," *European Papers* <https://www.europeanpapers.eu/en/authors/oana-stefan>; Luisa Marin, "COVID-19 Crisis and Closure of External Borders: Another Stress Test Challenging Solidarity in the EU?," *European Papers* <https://www.europeanpapers.eu/en/europeanforum/covid-19-crisis-closure-external-borders-another-stress-test-challenging-solidarity#_ftnref34>.

307 Stefan O., "COVID-19 Soft Law: Voluminous, Effective, Legitimate? A Research Agenda," *European Papers* <https://www.europeanpapers.eu/en/authors/oana-stefan>.

which should include consultation with the European Parliament and other stakeholders. Soft-law instruments do not have binding legal effects, but their effectiveness depends on the trust of citizens and Member States. Experience shows that soft regulations can effectively shape public behavior, a crucial factor in managing a pandemic. Gaining public and political support is crucial, and it requires transparency in the actions of EU institutions. In response, the European Commission has committed to consultation and stakeholder dialogue to increase transparency and effectiveness. The COVID-19 pandemic highlighted the need to reform the mechanisms for adopting and implementing soft law, requiring greater public involvement and unification of legislative procedures.

1.3.3.6 Poland's response to the pandemic and the crisis it caused

Poland was one of the first European Union countries to introduce strict measures in response to the COVID-19 pandemic.[308] The Polish authorities implemented a number of legislative and administrative measures to limit the spread of the virus and minimize its socio-economic impact. By Decree of the Minister of Health on March 14, 2020, a state of epidemic emergency was introduced,[309] which was later transformed into an epidemic state effective from March 20, 2020, to May 15, 2022.[310] After that date, a state of epidemic emergency was again declared, lasting until July 1, 2023.[311] The state allowed

308 Gruszczynski L., Zatonski M., and McKee M., *Do Regulations Matter in Fighting the COVID-19 Pandemic? Lessons from Poland* (Cambridge University Press) <https://www.cambridge.org/core/services/aop-cambridge-core/content/view/2323EDEA35F83F1E4BF4FC6F97084546/S1867299X21000532a.pdf>, 747.

309 Ordinance of the Minister of Health of March 13, 2020, on the declaration of an epidemic emergency in the territory of the Republic of Poland, *Journal of Laws*, item 433, as amended.

310 Ordinance of the Minister of Health of March 20, 2020 on the declaration of an epidemic state in the territory of the Republic of Poland (i.e., Journal of Laws of 2022, item 340).

311 Ordinance of the Minister of Health of May 12, 2022 on the declaration of an epidemic emergency in the territory of the Republic of Poland (Journal of Laws, item 1028) and Ordinance of the Minister of Health of June 14, 2023 on the cancellation of an epidemic emergency in the territory of the Republic of Poland, *Journal of Laws*, item 1118.

for a number of restrictions, such as border closures,[312] a ban on public gatherings, and the mandatory wearing of protective masks.

In response to the pandemic outbreak, the Polish Parliament passed the Law of March 2, 2020, on Special Solutions Related to the Prevention, Prevention and Control of COVID-19, Other Infectious Diseases and Emergencies Caused by Them.[313] This law introduced a number of solutions that regulated health, social and economic spheres, enabling legal and practical adaptations to the radically changed situation. The Council of Ministers as well as its members issued a number of executive regulations that significantly restricted civil rights and freedoms, raising legitimate concerns about the legality of these acts.[314]

In response to the COVID-19 pandemic, the Polish authorities introduced a number of emergency measures, such as the organization of mass vaccinations, the establishment of temporary hospitals, the introduction of distance learning, and support for entrepreneurs.

Despite emerging calls for the introduction of a state of disaster in connection with the COVID-19 pandemic, none of the states of emergency provided for in the Constitution was ultimately declared. The pandemic met the criteria for a natural disaster set forth in Article 232 of the Constitution, as evidenced by Article 3(1)(2) of the April 18, 2002 Law on the state of natural disaster,[315] defining a natural disaster as an event related to natural forces, including infectious diseases in humans. Furthermore, Article 3(1)(1) of the

---

312 Decree of the Minister of Internal Affairs and Administration of March 13, 2020 on the reintroduction of temporary border control of persons crossing the state border constituting an internal border, *Journal of Laws*, item 434, as amended.

313 Law of March 2, 2020 on special solutions related to the prevention, prevention and control of COVID-19, other infectious diseases and emergencies caused by them (i.e., Journal of Laws of 2024, item 340, as amended).

314 Florczak-Wątor M., "Niekonstytucyjność ograniczeń praw i wolności jednostki wprowadzonych w związku z epidemią COVID-19 jako przesłanka odpowiedzialności odszkodowawczej państwa" (2020) 12 *Państwo i Prawo*, 5–20. Accessed online: sip.lex.pl <https://sip.lex.pl/get/publication/pdf/pip/pdf/2020/12/pip_2020_12_005.pdf>; Wąsikowski A., "Prawa i wolności obywatelskie w warunkach epidemii Covid-19" (2021) XVII(1) *Zeszyty Cywilistyczne* <https://dx.doi.org/10.21784/ZC.2021.002>.

315 OJ 2017, item 1897.

same law supports the classification of a pandemic could be considered a natural disaster, as its effects threaten the life and health of a large number of people, and an effective response requires extraordinary measures, the cooperation of authorities, and the operation of specialized services under unified leadership.[316]

Restrictions on internal mobility, including a ban on movement except in emergencies, were supplemented by measures at the borders. Poland closed its borders to foreigners, suspended international air and rail traffic, and imposed a mandatory 14-day quarantine for those entering the country. Exceptions were made for transport drivers and daily commuters to neighboring countries, among others.

The introduction of a state of epidemic emergency and then a state of epidemic on the territory of the Republic of Poland necessitated the adoption of special legal solutions that allowed foreigners to maintain legal residence and perform their work despite the restrictions resulting from the COVID-19 pandemic. These solutions, set forth in the so-called COVID-19 Special Law,[317] were aimed at protecting the rights of foreigners in a crisis situation, while counteracting the negative economic effects resulting from the labor shortage.

Among the key solutions were provisions allowing the automatic extension of foreigners' legal stay. The validity periods of national visas, temporary residence permits and work permits that expired during an epidemic emergency or epidemic state were extended by law until the 30th day following the cancellation of whichever state was last in effect.[318] Analogous provisions applied to extending the deadlines for applying for residence permits and extending residency under the visa-free regime.[319] In addition, the law recognized the stay of foreigners on Polish territory as legal by law, as long as they stayed in the country based on short-term residence titles, such as a Schengen

---

316 Florczak-Wątor M., *Konstytucyjna regulacja stanów nadzwyczajnych w świetle dotychczasowej praktyki jej (nie)stosowania* (Państwo i Prawo 2022),) No 10, 333–350 <https://sip.lex.pl/>.

317 Law of March 2, 2020 on special solutions related to the prevention, prevention and control of COVID-19, other infectious diseases and emergencies caused by them (i.e., Journal of Laws of 2024, item 340, as amended).

318 Article 15zd of the COVID Law-19.

319 Article 15z of the COVID Law-19.

visa or a residence permit issued by another Schengen state.[320] Thanks to these regulations, foreigners were able to continue living and working in Poland without having to take additional administrative actions. The law also introduced changes in terms of foreigners' access to the labor market. Work permits, seasonal work permits and declarations of entrustment of work to a foreigner, the validity of which expired during a state of epidemic emergency or a state of epidemic, were extended by law until the 30th day following the cancellation of the last of these states.[321] In addition, foreigners were allowed to continue working under changed conditions, resulting from employers' decisions, without having to change their permits.[322] In the case of seasonal work, it was possible to perform work without obtaining new work permits.[323] Additional solutions included extending the validity of foreigners' identity documents, such as residence cards, Polish identity cards or "consent for tolerated stay" documents.[324] The deadlines for voluntary departure from the Polish territory were also extended, as were the deadlines for return specified in decisions on the foreigner's obligation to return.[325] The special legal solutions introduced during the COVID-19 pandemic made it possible to preserve the stability of the legal situation of foreigners residing in Poland while at the same time ensuring that the Polish labor market could continue functioning under the conditions of the epidemic crisis.

However, the COVID-19 pandemic highlighted the divisive treatment of migrants in Poland, pointing to the government's instrumentalization of migration according to economic and political interests.[326] As W. Klaus argues, the Polish authorities took a differentiated approach toward labor migrants and refugees, basing their actions on economic calculations and xenophobic narratives.[327] Poland demonstrated a selective approach to

320 Article $15z^{1}$ of the COVID Law-19.
321 Article 15zzq(1) of the COVID-19 Law.
322 Article $15z^{5}$ of the COVID Law-19.
323 Article $15z^{7}$ of the COVID Law-19.
324 Article $15z^{2}$ of the COVID Law-19.
325 Article 15zzza of the COVID Law-19.
326 Klaus W., "The Porous Border Woven with Prejudices and Economic Interests. Polish Border Admission Practices in the Time of COVID-19."
327 Klaus W., "The Porous Border Woven with Prejudices and Economic Interests. Polish Border Admission Practices in the Time of COVID-19" <https://www.mdpi.com/2076-0760/10/11/435>.

migration during the pandemic. While borders were opened to Belarusians fleeing the Lukashenko regime, they were simultaneously closed to refugees from other countries. Those attempting to cross the Polish-Belarusian border were turned back or placed in in detention centers, violating the non-discrimination principle and international protection standards.[328]

The COVID-19 pandemic did not lead to a paradigm shift in Polish migration policy but rather reinforced existing trends of economization. Economic needs, including pressure from employers, were a key influence on decisions to liberalize regulations for labor migrants, even at the expense of devaluing the importance of refugee migration. Despite the crisis, the dominant patterns of migration management remained unchanged, and economic factors continued to play an overriding role.[329] During the COVID-19 pandemic, access to the refugee procedure in Poland was severely restricted, violating domestic and international legal obligations such as the Geneva Convention, Article 18 of the EU Charter of Fundamental Rights and Article 56 of the Polish Constitution. The MIAA's March 13, 2020 regulation did not include applicants for international protection in the exceptions to border movement restrictions, making it impossible in practice to submit applications at the borders. The closure of key crossings, such as Terespol, and the lack of clear guidelines from the Border Guard exacerbated the problems of foreigners, who often did not know how or where they could apply for protection. The only help came from social organizations and social workers.[330]

1.3.3.7 Conclusions

On May 5, 2023, the World Health Organization (WHO) announced the cancellation of the global public health emergency related to the COVID-19

---

328 Klaus W., "The Porous Border Woven with Prejudices and Economic Interests. Polish Border Admission Practices in the Time of COVID-19."

329 Jaroszewicz M., Krępa M., and Pachocka M., "The Discourse and Practices of Polish Migration Policy During the COVID-19 Pandemic: Economisation as a Form of Emergency Governance" (2024) *Comparative Migration Studies* <https://doi.org/10.1186/s40878-024-00388-x>.

330 Ombudsman, Expert Committee on Migrants, Position Paper of the Commission of Experts on Migrants on the Situation of Migrants and Migrant Women during the COVID-19 Pandemic (2020). Available at: <https://bip.brpo.gov.pl/sites/default/files/Stanowisko%20Komisji%20Ekspert%C3%B3w%20ds.%20Migrant%C3%B3w%2C%2013.05.2020.pdf>.

pandemic.[331] Following this decision, in Poland, the Minister of Health by Decree of June 14, 2023, cancelled the state of epidemic emergency as of July 1, 2023.[332] The cancellation of the state of epidemic emergency marked the end of the special legal solutions introduced for foreigners under the so-called COVID-19 law. In accordance with the regulations, all of these extended entitlements expired on July 31, 2023, and as of August 1, 2023, foreigners benefiting from these solutions lost their right to legal residence in the territory of the Republic of Poland unless their stay was recognized as legal under other legal provisions.

In conclusion, the COVID-19 pandemic caused a profound crisis in migration flows in Europe, but the flexible actions of Member States and the European Union, especially with the use of soft-law instruments, contributed to a relatively rapid recovery of labor and, to some extent, student migration. However, refugee migration is unlikely to return to pre-pandemic levels for the foreseeable future. In 2022, the biggest impact on European labor markets and the refugee system came from the influx of refugees from Ukraine, which continues to shape the migration situation in the region. The uncoordinated initial response of countries to the pandemic crisis was a reminder that the Schengen concept remains a sensitive and fragile creation—legally, politically and socially.[333]

Poland's response to the COVID-19 pandemic was characterized by the rapid introduction of stringent restrictions, both internally and externally, but their implementation disregarded standard legislative and constitutional procedures. The consequences were chaotic regulations and violations of fundamental rights. Despite the solutions adopted, the COVID-19 pandemic significantly worsened the situation of foreign workers in the Polish labor market. The pandemic also highlighted how migration narratives can contribute

---

331 WHO Director-General, *WHO Director-General's opening remarks at the media briefing—May 5, 2023* (World Health Organization 2023, May 5) <https://www.who.int/news-room/speeches/item/who-director-general-s-opening-remarks-at-the-media-briefing-5-may-2023>.

332 Ordinance of the Minister of Health of June 14, 2023 on the cancellation of an epidemic emergency in the territory of the Republic of Poland (2023) *Journal of Laws*, item 1118.

333 Beaucillon C. (ed), "European Solidarity in Times of Emergency: An Introduction to the Special Focus on COVID-19 and the EU" (2020) 5(1) *European Papers* 687 et seq <www.europeanpapers.eu>.

to the marginalization of specific professional groups. Migrants were at risk of being employed on unstable contracts or in the shadow economy, making them more vulnerable to dismissal in the face of the economic crisis. Notably, the solutions adopted in this regard were national in nature, which often led to their non-compensation or non-application by other EU Member States, which limited rights under the European Union's common market, including the free movement of people and services.

The pandemic also contributed to the reinforcement of orthodox approaches to migration, in which migrants were seen as a potential source of virus transmission. Combined with the authorities' actions, such a reaction was part of a broader securitization of migration. Combined with the events on the European Union's eastern border, which resulted from the instrumental treatment of migrants, these developments led to a further erosion of the humanitarian dimension of the phenomenon and reinforced externalization, securitization and, ultimately, instrumentalization in migration policy.

1.3.4 Instrumentalization of migration

Twentieth-century history and literature document numerous examples of ethnic and national groups being used to destabilize other democratic states.[334] This phenomenon has been referred to as the instrumentalization or weaponization of migration. This concept was introduced to the scientific literature by K. M. Greenhill, who argued that forced migration is used as a tool of pressure in international negotiations, with actors using migrants as a means of coercion.[335] The instrumentalization of migrants, which Greenhill also refers to as migration engineering, describes the deliberate generation or manipulation of cross-border population flows for political, military or economic gain by states or other actors.[336] The scale of measures used ranges

---

334 Szachoń-Pszenny A., and Zaręba A., Etapowość instrumentalizacji migrantów na przykładzie granicy z Białorusią—wyzwania współczesności (Przegląd Geopolityczny 2024) 49–68.

335 Greenhill K. M., "Weapons of Mass Migration: Forced Displacement as an Instrument of Coercion" (2010) 9(1) *Strategic Insights* (Spring-Summer 2010) 116–117 <http://hdl.handle.net/10945/11515> 116–117.

336 Greenhill K. M., "Weapons of Mass Migration: Forced Displacement as an Instrument of Coercion" (2010) 9(1) *Strategic Insights* (Spring-Summer 2010) 116–117 <http://hdl.handle.net/10945/11515> 116–117.

from soft tactics to the use of direct coercion. While the process may appear voluntary, it is the result of deliberate political action. Democratic systems are particularly susceptible to this type of action because they operate under legal norms that guarantee the preservation and protection of the fundamental rights of migrants. Additionally, democratic decision-making processes are also more conflict-ridden, making them vulnerable to the destabilization caused by migration crises.[337] In his work, Greenhill identifies dozens of situations that align with the rationale for instrumentalization.[338]

1.3.4.1 Examples of the instrumentalization of migration in Europe in the twenty-first century

Although not a new phenomenon, the instrumentalization of migration intensified during the COVID-19 pandemic, amplifying the pressure it generated and increasing its destabilizing potential.

Morocco has used migration as a tool to pressure Spain in the context of the Western Sahara dispute. In May 2021, after Spain admitted the Polisario Front leader Brahim Ghali for medical treatment, Morocco deliberately allowed a massive influx of migrants into the Spanish enclave of Ceuta.[339] Within two days, several thousand migrants crossed the border, triggering a humanitarian and political crisis. Morocco used the situation to exert pressure on Spain and the European Union, demanding recognition of its claim to Western Sahara. These actions were intended to force Spain to change its policy toward Western Sahara and to gain political and economic concessions.[340] In response, Spain used so-called "hot returns"—immediate deportations without individual consideration. Surprisingly, the jurisprudence of the Grand Chamber of the European Court of Human Rights (*ND and NT v. Spain*)

---

337 Greenhill K. M., "Weapons of Mass Migration: Forced Displacement as an Instrument of Coercion" (2010) *Strategic Insights*, 118.

338 Greenhill K. M., "Weapons of Mass Migration: Forced Displacement as an Instrument of Coercion" (2010) *Strategic Insights*, 120–121.

339 Torreblanca J. I., "This Time Is Different: Spain, Morocco, and Weaponized Migration" (ECFR, May 21, 2021) <https://ecfr.eu/article/this-time-is-different-spain-morocco-and-weaponised-migration>.

340 Cassarino J.-P., "An Unsettling Déjà-vu: The May 2021 Ceuta Events" (2022) 7(1) *European Papers, European Forum, Insight*, 79–85 <https:doi/org/10.15166/2499-8249/548>.

supported this Spanish political decision.[341] The Court indicated that such actions can be considered lawful under certain conditions.[342] At the political level, the EU, through Commission President *Ursula von der Leyen*, also expressed support for Spain, stressing the need for standard solutions in migration management.[343]

Turkey has repeatedly used migration as a tool to pressure the European Union, especially in the context of the Syrian crisis. In February 2020, thousands of migrants gathered at the Turkish-Greek border after Turkey announced it would no longer prevent refugees from attempting to cross into Greece. Turkey demanded more financial aid from the EU and support for its military operations in Syria. Using migration as a tool of leverage, Turkey sought more political and financial support from the European Union while demonstrating its ability to control the flow of migrants into Europe.[344] The crisis has once again revealed the EU's vulnerability to forced migration engineering and its lack of effective countermeasures.[345]

Belarus, under Alexander Lukashenko, has used migration as a tool to pressure the European Union in response to sanctions imposed on the regime after the rigged 2020 presidential election. In 2021, Belarusian authorities

---

341 Grand Chamber, Case of *N.D. and N.T. v. Spain* (Applications nos 8675/15 and 8697/15), Judgment of February 13, 2020, HUDOC, accessed at <https://hudoc.echr.coe.int/fre#{%22itemid%22:[%22001-201353%22]>.

342 More Rogala R., "Prawo cudzoziemca do ubiegania się na granicy o udzielenie ochrony międzynarodowej," (2021) 11 *Europejski Przegląd Sądowy* <https://www.wolterskluwer.com/pl-pl/news/europejski-przeglad-sadowy-11-2021>.

343 "Spain and Morocco Clash After Thousands of Migrants Enter Ceuta," *CNBC*, May 19, 2021, accessed at <https://www.cnbc.com/2021/05/19/spain-and-morocco-clash-after-thousands-of-migrants-enter-ceuta.html>.

344 Gkliati M., "Let's Call It What It Is: Hybrid Threats and Instrumentalisation as the Evolution of Securitisation in Migration Management" (2022) *European Papers* <https://www.europeanpapers.eu/en/europeanforum/lets-call-it-what-it-is-hybrid-threats-and-instrumentalisation#_ftnref1>; Dhian Ho S., Wijnkoop M., "The Instrumentalization of Migration: A Geopolitical Perspective" (December 6, 2022) *Clingendael Institute* <https://www.clingendael.org/publication/instrumentalization-migration>.

345 Howson K. T., "The Weaponization of Migration: How Has Forced Displacement been Utilized as an Instrument of Coercion?" (2022) *Foreign Policy Analysis, Refugee Studies, European Foreign Policy, Migration Studies* <https://www.academia.edu/117885144/The_Weaponization_of_Migration_How_has_forced_displacement_been_utilised_as_an_instrument_of_coercion>, 8–9.

actively attracted migrants from countries such as Afghanistan, Iraq and Syria, encouraging them to cross the borders with Poland, Lithuania and Latvia. Thousands of migrants found themselves in difficult conditions at the border, triggering a humanitarian and political crisis. Belarus exploited the situation to put pressure on the European Union, seeking to ease sanctions and secure political gains. These actions were aimed at destabilizing the EU's borders and creating a migration crisis to weaken the European Union's position on the international stage. However, according to available sources, the history of instrumentalizing migration on Poland's eastern border began long before 2021. After the collapse of the communist system, it was assumed that migration engineering would cease to play a role in interstate relations.[346] However, systemic changes and restrictions on the protection of democracy and human rights led to the reappearance of this phenomenon. An example is the actions of Russian and Belarusian special services, which in 2010 initiated Operation Sluice.[347] The purpose of this operation was to test the capacity of the European Union's eastern border, destabilize the region and obtain EU funds to seal it. Migrants, recruited from Caucasus countries as well as from students and residents in Belarus, were allowed to illegally cross the EU border for high fees. The operation was revived in 2021 with the aim of destabilizing the situation and deepening social divisions in Poland, including stirring up controversy over the admission of migrants, as well as diverting international attention from repression and human rights violations in Belarus. It is now widely accepted that this operation constituted the first, non-obvious, hybrid unveiling of the armed conflict in Ukraine.[348]

---

346 Szachoń-Pszenny A., and Zaręba A., "Instrumentalizacja migrantów jako forma destabilizacji bezpieczeństwa na wschodniej granicy zewnętrznej UE w kontekście wojny w Ukrainie" (2024) 1(88/3) *Politeja*, 89–104 <https://doi.org/10.12797/Politeja.21.2024.88.3.06>, 97–99.

347 Konieczny M., Operacja "Śluza"—Kryzys uchodźczy związany z przerzutem nielegalnych migrantów przez polsko-białoruską granicę (2022) XX, z. 2, *Roczniki Administracji i Prawa*, 89–102 <https://doi.org/10.5604/01.3001.0016.0948>.

348 Szachoń-Pszenny A., and Zaręba A., Instrumentalizacja migrantów jako forma destabilizacji bezpieczeństwa na wschodniej granicy zewnętrznej UE w kontekście wojny w Ukrainie (2024) 1(88/3) *Politeja*, 89–104 <https://doi.org/10.12797/Politeja.21.2024.88.3.06>, 97–99. Operation Sluice was part of a hybrid war waged by Belarus and Russia, which began as early as 2021 as a prelude to the aggression against Ukraine. The model of forced migration engineering ("weapon D—demographic")

In the literature, the phenomenon of instrumentalization itself is usually the subject of research. However, our primary area of interest remains how states respond when placed under pressure from agents of provocation, as Greenhill calls them.[349] Hence, in the following section, the author will focus on issues related to responses to the instrumentalization of migration flows.

According to Greenhill, states react to the instrumentalization of migration in various ways. The most natural and obvious response is to tighten border controls, restrict asylum rights and introduce emergency legislation.[350] States also frequently attempt to shift responsibility to third countries by entering into readmission agreements. Interestingly, these countries are usually those that engage in instrumentalization, as was the case with Turkey in the 2016 EU-Turkey agreement. This suggests that, to some extent, states recognize the effectiveness of instrumentalization actions, confirming its effectiveness in the eyes of provocateurs.

Some countries go further, employing economic sanctions or even military interventions to eliminate sources of migration and restore the status quo, as was the case with the US in Central America. It is also worth examining the internal actions of states under migration pressure due to the instrumentalization of migration. Democratic states take advantage of the situation to advance their own political goals through the use of strategic public narratives. As a result, they portray migrants as a threat in order to undermine public support for their admission, leading to further instrumentalization of migrants and aligns with the broader securitization of migration.[351] States

---

was used to put pressure on Poland, combining this with propaganda and disinformation. Belarus concealed its perpetration, portraying the crisis as a spontaneous event, while Polish services pointed to the organized nature of the activities supported by criminal structures. "Operation Sluice" was the first stage of Russia's planned invasion of Ukraine, All That Matters <https://wszystkoconajwazniejsze.pl/pepites/operacja-sluza-byla-pierwszym-etapem-planowanej-inwazji-rosji-na-ukraine/>.

349 Greenhill K. M., "Weapons of Mass Migration: Forced Displacement as an Instrument of Coercion" (2010) 9(1) *Strategic Insights* (Spring-Summer 2010) 116–117 <http://hdl.handle.net/10945/11515>.

350 Greenhill K. M., "Weapons of Mass Migration: Forced Displacement as an Instrument of Coercion" (2010) 9(1) *Strategic Insights* (Spring-Summer 2010) 116–117 <http://hdl.handle.net/10945/11515>.

351 Bigo D. "Security and Immigration: Toward a Critique of the Governmentality of Unease" (2002) 27(1_suppl) *Alternatives: Global, Local, Political*, 63–92 <https://journals.sagepub.com/doi/10.1177/03043754020270S105>, 68–69.

and security actors anticipate threats using what D. Bigo refers to as "ban-optics." This approach focuses on selective surveillance and managing social unrest, which in turn leads to increased inequality and social exclusion. These actions, while sometimes effective, can lead to human rights violations and escalating tensions, making compliance with international law and cooperation between states essential.

1.3.4.2 From securitization to the instrumentalization of migration

It is fitting to pause at this point and devote a few moments to the phenomenon of securitization itself. The relationship between migration and security has always been complex, often generating deeply politicized and polarized debates in political, social, journalistic and academic circles.[352] The instrumentalization of migration reflects the natural continuation and intensification of the securitization trend that has characterized EU migration policy for the past four decades.[353] In this sense, instrumentalization represents an evolution of securitization, according to which exceptional and extraordinary situations, described as crises, necessitate new security measures. Migration is one of the main issues perceived as a security threat in the EU, justifying introducing "emergency measures" that would not otherwise be acceptable.[354] Migration management in Europe has become synonymous with security crisis management, manifested through "border processes" and deterrence, with negative consequences for the fundamental rights of migrants.

According to the evolving narrative, the threat extends beyond security concerns and becomes a national security issue, raising the need for defense.

---

352 Stępka M., Identifying Security Logics in the EU Policy Discourse: the "Migration Crisis" and the EU, in Joanna Dyduch, Sylwia Wojciechowska-Lodyga (eds), *Crisis and Migration: Critical Perspectives* (Springer, Cham, 2022) 1–21.

353 Gkliati M., "Let's Call It What It Is: Hybrid Threats and Instrumentalisation as the Evolution of Securitisation in Migration Management" (2022) *European Papers*. Retrieved from <https://www.europeanpapers.eu/en/europeanforum/lets-call-it-what-it-is-hybrid-threats-and-instrumentalisation#_ftnref1>.

354 Waever O., Buzan B., and De Wilde J., *Security: A* New *Framework for Analysis* (1st ed, Boulder: Lynne Riener Publishers 1998); Léonard S., "EU Border Security and Migration into the European Union: FRONTEX and Securitisation through Practices" (2010) *European Security* 235.

While securitization has led to the related trend of "crimmigration,"[355] instrumentalization perceives not only a criminal or terrorist threat, but also a threat to the territorial integrity and political stability of Member States and the EU as a whole. The narrative of crimmigration uses the language of criminal law, while instrumentalization uses the language of the law of war (weaponization) to justify even more extreme responses to an increasingly acute and existential threat.[356]

Although securitization is increasingly employed, it is widely criticized. A comprehensive critique of the securitization of migration as a social and political construct is formulated by Bigo. He argues that this process does not result from objective threats but from the political and institutional management of anxiety, in which the threat narrative is used to legitimize government actions. Bigo indicates that the central mechanism of migration management is creating and escalating a sense of threat.[357] The author stresses that the securitization of migration blurs the boundaries between internal and external security, portraying migrants as both an external threat (mass and unregulated border crossings) and an internal threat (integration problems, crime).[358]

Institutions set up to protect security, such as Europol, are playing an increasingly important role in migration management, gaining access to large-scale IT systems that collect data on migrants.[359] Bigo notes that security institutions are not only responding to threats but also defining them and prioritizing them, using tools such as risk categories and profiling, and

---

355 van den Driesche F., "Crimmigration: What It Is, and Its Practical Implications" (2019, December 20) *Leiden University*. Retrieved from <https://www.universiteitleiden.nl/en/news/2019/12/crimmigration-what-it-is-and-its-practical-implications>; García Hernández C. C., *Crimmigration law* (2nd edn, Chicago, Illinois: American Bar Association 2021).

356 Gkliati M., *Let's Call It What It Is: Hybrid Threats and Instrumentalisation as the Evolution of Securitisation in Migration Management* (2022).

357 Bigo D., "Security and Immigration: Toward a Critique of the Governmentality of Unease," 67–69.

358 ibid., p. 77.

359 Jones Ch., *Eurodac: Member States Want Wider Police Access to Biometric Database Despite Most Having Never Made Use of It* (Statewatch, December 2016) <https://www.statewatch.org/media/documents/analyses/no-303-eurodac-lea-access.pdf>.

the discourse about threats often serves to legitimize the actions of these institutions, even when the threats are marginal or unclear.[360]

The securitization of migration is not an answer that directly addresses and defines the relevant migration problems. M. Gkliati stresses that the EU and its Member States, seeing the instrumentalization of migrants by countries such as Belarus and Turkey as a hybrid threat, introduce extraordinary measures that often violate human rights.[361] This is evidenced by the tightening of border regulations in Greece, Poland and Lithuania, as well as legislative proposals at the EU level that allow for the suspension of rules to protect migrants' rights in crisis situations. Gkliati criticizes this approach, saying the EU's responses are exaggerated and based more on security rhetoric than on real border protection needs, ultimately leading to the normalization of human rights violations.[362]

The crisis, especially when viewed as a hybrid threat, poses challenges to states and institutions, often requiring swift and decisive responses. In the context of the European Union, there is a clear shift in the approach to managing the migrant crisis, especially in the face of threats related to the so-called instrumentalization of migration, where migrants are used by third countries as a tool for political pressure. These responses take various forms, from tightening border controls to introducing exceptional legislation that de facto restricts human rights and asylum law principles.[363] The EU's response to the phenomenon of the instrumentalization of migrants should focus on addressing the related structural problems of migration diplomacy, considering the interdependence of the EU and third countries in the context of migration.[364]

---

360 Bigo D., "Security and Immigration: Toward a Critique of the Governmentality of Unease," 75–77; Cantat C., Pécoud A., and Thiollet H., *Migration as Crisis* (2023), 9.

361 Gkliati M., *Let's Call It What It Is: Hybrid Threats and Instrumentalisation as the Evolution of Securitisation in Migration Management* (2022).

362 Gkliati M., *Let's Call It What It Is: Hybrid Threats and Instrumentalisation as the Evolution of Securitisation in Migration Management* (2022).

363 Cantat C., Pécoud A., and Thiollet H., *Migration as Crisis* (2023), 17.

364 European Economic and Social Committee, *Instrumentalization of Migrants and the Ukrainian Refugee Crisis Require a Rethink of Migration Policy* (June 20, 2022) <https://www.eesc.europa.eu/pl/news-media/news/instrumentalizacja-migrantow-i-ukrainski-kryzys-uchodzczy-wymagaja-ponownego-namyslu-nad-polityka-migracyjna>.

One recent example of the EU institutions' activities that confirm the paradigm shift in the approach to migration is the European Commission's communication from December 11, 2024 (COM(2024) 570 final).[365] The communication has startled many experts in migration and humanitarian law by acknowledging that EU Member States have become the target of hybrid attacks from Russia and Belarus. The Commission explicitly recognizes the need for exceptional measures to counter these attacks, marking a significant paradigm shift in the approach to border management and human rights protection. The Commission acknowledges that, in the face of growing threats from hostile states, Member States must be able to take necessary actions to protect their national security and territorial integrity. The document underscores that the measures taken must adhere to the principles of proportionality, necessity, and temporariness, which is crucial in the context of human rights protection. In the legal context, the Commission emphasizes that, under the Schengen Borders Code, the Member States are obligated to protect the EU's external borders and prevent unauthorized crossings. At the same time, they must respect the principle of non-refoulement and other fundamental rights enshrined in international treaties, such as the Geneva Convention and the EU Charter of Fundamental Rights. The Commission highlights that Russia and Belarus are using migration as a weapon to destabilize the European Union, necessitating a decisive response. The document outlines the possibility of introducing temporary measures that restrict certain fundamental rights, provided they are absolutely necessary and aim to protect public order and national security.

This controversial shift in language and approach to border management in the context of hybrid threats requires careful justification, as any measures that could seriously interfere with human rights must be time-limited.

[365] European Commission, Communication from the Commission to the European Parliament and the Council on Countering Hybrid Threats Arising from the Use of Migration as a Weapon and on Enhancing Security at the EU's External Borders (2024) *COM*, 570 final, December 11, 2024.

1.3.4.3 European Union legislative offensive: The Migration and Asylum Pact and Acts

The issue under discussion is essentially related to events whose origins can be traced back to the migration crisis of 2015–2016. Nevertheless, its placement at this point in the chapter is not accidental. The author seeks to indicate the trends and the confluence of events that ultimately shaped the legislative framework of the legal instruments adopted in the European Union in connection with the ongoing crises. The migration crisis of 2015, the outbreak of the COVID-19 pandemic, the instrumental actions of third countries—but also of Member States—as well as the EU's response to the influx of refugees from Ukraine following Russia's aggression, have all given the legal instruments adopted by EU bodies a specific shape and content. There is no escaping the conclusion that the dominant trend in shaping these measures is the instrumentalization and securitization of migration. In view of the above, this seems to be the most opportune moment to discuss legal solutions, with the Pact on Migration and Asylum and its accompanying legislation at the forefront.

As of 2019, the European Union took a series of steps to manage the migration and asylum crisis, responding to the challenges of increasing migratory pressures and the instrumentalization of migrants by third countries. That year, EU interior ministers, drawing on a report prepared by the Finnish presidency, stressed the need for a comprehensive approach to migration, considering entire migration routes and cooperation at all levels of government.[366] Work began on a New Pact on Migration and Asylum, which aimed to reform the EU's asylum laws and propose temporary solutions for the reception of migrants from rescue ships.

On September 23, 2020, the European Commission formally presented a New Pact on Migration and Asylum, including five legislative proposals. Key elements of the Pact included a pre-entry phase, solidarity mechanisms,

---

366 Presidency Perspectives on EU migration and asylum policy—results of the discussion. NOTA Brussels, November 22, 2019 (OR. en) 14364/19 LIMITE JAI 1228 ASIM 144 RELEX 1095th Committee of Permanent Representatives / Council. Justice and Home Affairs Council, December 2–3, 2019 <https://www.consilium.europa.eu/pl/meetings/jha/2019/12/02-03/>.

streamlining returns, and internal migration and asylum management. In parallel, work was undertaken to improve the standard asylum system. A crucial development was the migration crisis at the EU-Belarus border in 2021, triggered by the deliberate actions of Alexander Lukashenko's regime, which attracted migrants and directed them to EU borders to cause destabilization. This crisis had a significant impact on the content of the legislative acts under discussion. In response, the European Commission presented a package of legislative proposals in December 2021 to address the instrumentalization of migration. This package included a revised Schengen Borders Code[367] and a new Instrumentalization Regulation,[368] both aimed at creating a legal framework for Member States to effectively respond to migration instrumentalization.

The proposal to amend Regulation (EU) 2016/399, known as the Schengen Borders Code, responded to challenges that have undermined the coherence and effectiveness of the Schengen area in recent years. The proposed regulations aimed to strengthen the management of the European Union's external and internal borders and enhance the ability to respond to crises related to migration, public health and security.

It is important to note that the European Commission's proposal was made during the ongoing coronavirus pandemic, a period when Member States had reintroduced border controls. However, as part of this proposal, the European Commission also introduced a definition of "instrumentalization of migration" allowing Member States to apply precise measures to counter the destabilizing actions of third countries.[369] Instrumentalization was defined as a situation in which a third country initiates illegal migration flows into the

367 European Commission. Proposal for a Regulation of the European Parliament and of the Council amending Regulation (EU) 2016/399 on a Union Code on the rules governing the movement of persons across borders (COM/2021/891 final) (2021) <https://eur-lex.europa.eu/legal-content/EN/TXT/?uri=COM%3A2021%3A891%3AFIN&qid=1639608649722>.

368 European Commission, Proposal for a Regulation of the European Parliament and of the Council addressing situations of instrumentalisation in the field of migration and asylum, *COM* (2021) 890 final 2021/0427 (COD) <https://eur-lex.europa.eu/legal-content/PL/TXT/HTML/?uri=CELEX:52021PC0890>.

369 Article 2(27) Proposal for a Regulation of the European Parliament and of the Council amending Regulation (EU) 2016/399 on a Union Code on the rules governing the movement of persons across borders (2021) *COM*, 891 final.

Union by actively encouraging or facilitating the movement of third-country nationals to the EU's external borders. In addition, the drafters stated that such actions must indicate the third country's intention to destabilize the Union or a Member State. These actions could threaten the core functions of the state, including territorial integrity, law and order, or national security.

The proposal allowed Member States to limit the number of border crossings and their opening hours in response to the instrumentalization of migration. The Council adopted a general approach, adding non-state actors to the definition as potential perpetrators of instrumentalization. Smuggling and humanitarian aid operations were not classified as instrumentalization unless they were intended to destabilize the Union. The Schengen Borders Code granted Member States the right to take necessary measures to maintain security, law and order. Migrants attempting to enter by force *en masse*, using violence, could be dealt with under the code.[370]

The Commission also proposed the creation of a European-level response mechanism for crises affecting most Schengen Member States. The mechanism would allow the EU Council to make binding decisions on temporary travel restrictions at external borders in crisis situations, such as the COVID-19 pandemic. The aim was to prevent fragmented responses by individual Member States and ensure consistency in crisis management. The proposal also included procedural changes to ensure that Member States' unilateral reintroduction of internal border controls would remain a measure of last resort. A detailed risk analysis and consideration of alternative measures were required before deciding to reintroduce border controls.[371] The regulations also emphasized the need to minimize the negative impact of such measures on cross-border regions, especially regarding the freedom of movement of citizens and economic activity. As part of the proposed changes, the Commission also focused on promoting alternative control measures, such as monitoring border areas, which were expected to allow threats to be countered more effectively without the need to fully reintroduce border controls.

---

370 Articles 5 and 13 Proposal for a Regulation of the European Parliament and of the Council Amending Regulation (EU) 2016/399 on a Union Code on the rules governing the movement of persons across borders (2021) *COM*, 891 final.

371 Articles 25–28 Proposal for a Regulation of the European Parliament and of the Council Amending Regulation (EU) 2016/399 on a Union Code on the rules governing the movement of persons across borders (2021) *COM*, 891 final.

Increased cooperation between Member States, including the exchange of information and technological support, were key to the effectiveness of these measures. The amendments to the Schengen Borders Code were adopted on June 13, 2024 and have already entered into force.[372] In the final version of the regulation, only the provision allowing the closure of border crossings was retained, leaving it up to Member States to decide on closures in emergency situations.[373]

In contrast, the proposed Regulation on the Instrumentalization of Migration was highly controversial.[374] First, it gave Member States a disproportionate tool to override existing asylum law, potentially restricting access to international protection at EU borders.[375] As a result, third countries could take advantage of this situation to accuse the EU of double standards in fundamental rights, leading to the so-called "hypocrisy trap."[376] Second, both the proposed regulation and the planned toolkit were shaped mainly by the Belarusian episode, which limited their application to other instrumentalization situations. They did not take into account structural factors or the role of the EU itself in contributing to the instrumentalization of migration by third countries. Ultimately, the regulation was not adopted, as the proposal failed to gain support in the Council.

---

372 Regulation (EU) 2024/1717 of the European Parliament and of the Council of June 13, 2024 amending Regulation (EU) 2016/399 on the EU Code on the rules governing the movement of persons across borders, (June 20 2024) *Official Journal of the European Union*, L 1717 <https://eur-lex.europa.eu/legal-content/PL/TXT/HTML/?uri=OJ:L_202401717>.

373 Article 5 (4) of Regulation (EU) 2016/399 of the European Parliament and of the Council of March 9, 2016 on the EU Code on the rules governing the movement of persons across borders (Schengen Borders Code) (OJ EU. L. 2016 No. 77, 1, as amended).

374 European Commission, "Proposal for a Regulation of the European Parliament and of the Council on Addressing Situations of Instrumentalisation in the Field of Migration and Asylum" (2021) *COM* 890 final, 2021/0427(COD).

375 Article 2 European Commission, "Proposal for a Regulation of the European Parliament and of the Council on Addressing Situations of Instrumentalisation in the Field of Migration and Asylum" (2021) *COM* 890 final.

376 Rasche L., *The Instrumentalization of Migration—How Should the EU Respond?* (Jacques Delors Centre) <https://www.delorscentre.eu/en/publications/the-instrumentalisation-of-migration>.

In contrast, the content relating to the instrumentalization of migration was transferred to the content of Regulation (EU) 2024/1359 of the European Parliament and of the Council of May 14, 2024, on responding to emergencies and force majeure situations in the field of migration and asylum and amending Regulation (EU) 2021/1147.[377] The Regulation defines an instrumentalization situation as a type of crisis situation in which a third country or hostile non-state actor encourages third-country nationals and stateless persons to move to the external borders of the Union or to a Member State, to destabilize the Union or a Member State.[378]

Article 3 of Regulation (EU) 2024/1359 sets out the procedure for responding to emergencies and force majeure situations in the field of migration and asylum, including the instrumentalization of migration. A Member State may request the application of derogations and solidarity measures, providing a description of the situation, justification and actions taken. The European Commission evaluates the request and submits a draft decision to the Council, which quickly decides to grant derogations for up to three months, with the possibility of extension.

Member States can deviate from normal asylum rules by extending the time for registering an asylum application to four weeks[379] and extending border procedures for an additional six weeks.[380] They can also adjust the threshold for decisions to grant international protection.[381] These derogations must be approved by the Council, with the approval of the Commission.[382] States must ensure that fundamental rights are respected, with derogations applied only in exceptional circumstances.[383] The regulation also allows for the temporary closure or restriction of border crossings.[384]

---

377 Regulation (EU) 2024/1359 of the European Parliament and of the Council of May 14, 2024 addressing situations of crisis and force majeure in the field of migration and asylum and amending Regulation (EU) 2021/1147, L 1359, May 22, 2024, *Official Journal of the European Union*, ELI <http://data.europa.eu/eli/reg/2024/1359/oj>.

378 Article 1(4)(b) of EU Parliament and Council Regulation 2024/1359.

379 Article 10(1) of Regulation (EU) 2024/1359.

380 Article 11(1) of Regulation (EU) 2024/1359.

381 Article 11 (3) and (4) of Regulation (EU) 2024/1359.

382 Article 2(2)(a)(ii), Article 3, Article 4(3) of Regulation (EU) 2024/1359.

383 Article 1(2) and (3) of Regulation (EU) 2024/1359.

384 Article 1(3) of Regulation (EU) 2024/1359.

I. Goldner Lang stresses that the EU's new rules on the instrumentalization of migrants represent a significant step forward, preventing unilateral and excessive action by Member States.[385] The rules are designed to ensure that measures taken by Member States are proportionate and in accordance with international and EU law. The author points out that even if migrants are instrumentalized, they have the right to seek asylum in accordance with international and EU law. Lang notes that practical implementation of these provisions will be key to ensuring the effectiveness of the right to seek asylum. As the example of Polish legislation described later indicates, national distinctions will not be too difficult to achieve.

Subsequent years saw the main development of the proposed solutions. In 2022, the European Union focused on managing the refugee crisis related to Russia's invasion of Ukraine (this issue will be discussed separately). The Temporary Protection Directive was implemented, offering Ukrainian refugees clear legal status throughout the EU. Support also included mobilizing resources from cohesion policy funds and the approval by Council of negotiating mandates for two pieces of legislation related to migration and asylum. Key legislative work on the reform of the common asylum and migration policy was completed in 2023. Agreement was reached on five legislative acts, including screening, biometric data collection and asylum procedures. Solidarity among Member States and responding to crises, such as the instrumentalization of migration, became a priority. In December 2023, the Spanish presidency presented a progress report on the legislative work on the Pact on Migration and Asylum, marking the end of an intensive phase of reforms in this area,[386] a December 20, 2023. EU Parliament and Council reached an agreement on the measure.[387]

On May 14, 2024, the Council of the European Union adopted the EU Pact on Migration and Asylum, a comprehensive migration and asylum

---

385 Goldner Lang I., "Instrumentalisation of Migrants: It is Necessary to Act, but How?" (2024) *EU Migration Law Blog* <https://eumigrationlawblog.eu/instrumentalisation-of-migrants-it-is-necessary-to-act-but-how/>.

386 Council of the European Union, *Rada ds. Wymiaru Sprawiedliwości i Spraw Wewnętrznych, 4–5 grudnia 2023* <https://www.consilium.europa.eu/pl/meetings/jha/2023/12/04-05/>.

387 Council of the European Union, *Przełomowe porozumienie Rady i Parlamentu co do reformy systemu azylowo-migracyjnego UE* (December 20, 2023) <https://www.consilium.europa.eu/pl/press/press-releases/2023/12/20/the-council-and-the-european-parliament-reach-breakthrough-in-reform-of-eu-asylum-and-migration-system/>.

management reform.[388] It introduces a set of rules aimed at the orderly management of the influx of migrants.

The Pact on Migration and Asylum is new legislation introduced by the European Union to create a standard system for managing migration and granting international protection, based on European values.[389] The reforms aim to integrate key policies on migration, asylum, border and integration, providing Member States with the necessary tools to address various migration challenges. The Pact entered into force on June 11, 2024, with full implementation expected within two years. The reform is based on four main pillars. The first focuses on external border protection, covering border procedures and improvements to the Eurodac system for identifying migrants. The second pillar introduces simplified and efficient asylum procedures and uniform standards of protection. The third pillar establishes a system of solidarity and responsibility among EU countries, allowing them to choose how to support each other, such as through relocation or financial assistance. The fourth pillar relies on cooperation with partner countries, supporting border management, combating human smuggling and promoting legal migration routes, such as the Talent Partnerships program or the EU Talent Pool platform. These reforms are an important step toward a fair and sustainable system for managing migration in the EU.

In 2024, with the adoption of the Asylum and Migration Pact, EU regulations on asylum and refugee protection were modernized with the introduction of the third phase of the Common European Asylum System (CEAS), replacing the 2013 regulations. The new set of instruments covers all stages of the asylum process, from arrival in the EU to the expulsion of those denied protection. E. Guild points out that the new EU legal instruments on asylum and refugee protection include three interrelated systems of legal responsibility.[390]

---

388 Council of the European Union, Rada przyjmuje unijny pakt o migracji i azylu (14 maja 2024) *Komunikat prasowy* <https://www.consilium.europa.eu/pl/press/press-releases/2024/05/14/the-council-ad>.

389 European Commission, *Pakt o migracji i azylu: Wspólny unijny system zarządzania migracją* <https://home-affairs.ec.europa.eu/policies/migration-and-asylum/pact-migration-and-asylum_pl>.

390 Guild E., "EU Pact Instruments on Asylum and Minimum Human Rights Standards" (October 21, 2024) *EU Migration Law Blog* <https://eumigrationlawblog.eu/eu-pact-instruments-on-asylum-and-minimum-human-rights-standards/>.

The first concerns Member States' sovereignty in controlling borders, which has been modified by the EU's binding rules in accordance with the Charter of Fundamental Rights. The second involves European human rights law, including the European Convention on Human Rights (ECHR), which emphasizes the principle of *non-refoulement* and other obligations related to international protection through ECtHR case law. The third system refers to international refugee and human rights law, including the 1951 Geneva Convention Relating to the Status of Refugees and the 1967 Protocol, which set standards for the treatment of persons seeking protection.[391]

The new EU asylum and migration legislation creates a comprehensive system of regulations aimed at improving migration management, enhancing solidarity among Member States and harmonizing protection standards and procedures. The Screening Regulation introduces the mandatory registration and verification of irregular migrants, including identity, security and health checks.[392] This is intended to strengthen border control and improve the management of migration flows. At the same time, the Asylum and Migration Management Regulation establishes a solidarity mechanism between Member States, distributing the responsibility for processing asylum applications in a more balanced way to counter the unequal burden on some countries, particularly border states.[393] The Asylum Procedure Regulation harmonizes asylum decision-making processes while introducing a mandatory border procedure to speed up proceedings and prevent secondary movements within the EU.[394] This is complemented by the Qualification Regulation, which harmonizes refugee protection standards across the EU, ensuring uniform rights

391 ibid.

392 Regulation (EU) 2024/1356 of the European Parliament and of the Council of May 14, 2024 on the introduction of screening of third-country nationals at external borders and amending Regulations (EC) No. 767/2008, (EU) 2017/2226, (EU) 2018/1240 and (EU) 2019/817 *Official Journal of the European Union*, series L 1356, May 22, 2024.

393 Regulation (EU) 2024/1351 of the European Parliament and of the Council of May 14, 2024 on asylum and migration management, amending Regulations (EU) 2021/1147 and (EU) 2021/1060 and repealing Regulation (EU) 604/2013 *Official Journal of the European Union*, series L 1351, May 22, 2024.

394 Regulation (EU) 2024/1348 of the European Parliament and of the Council of May 14, 2024 on the establishment of a common procedure for applying for international protection in the Union and repealing Directive 2013/32/EU *Official Journal of the European Union*, series L 1348, May 22, 2024.

and preventing "asylum tourism."[395] For optimized crisis management, the Crisis and Force Majeure Response Regulation, already discussed in greater detail, provides for rapid protocols for handling, particularly in the context of the instrumentalization of migration. These measures can be supplemented with operational and financial assistance, allowing for a flexible response in exceptional circumstances.[396] To enhance data management and improve system interoperability, the Eurodac Regulation introduces an asylum and migration database, supporting the implementation of resettlement and temporary protection legislation.[397]

At the same time, the Reception Conditions Directive harmonizes standards for the dignified reception of migrants across the EU, with the aim of preventing secondary movements and ensuring consistency among Member States.[398] The EU has also introduced the EU Resettlement Framework Regulation, which establishes a common mechanism for resetting refugees

---

395 Regulation (EU) 2024/1347 of the European Parliament and of the Council of May 14, 2024 on standards for the qualification of third-country nationals or stateless persons as beneficiaries of international protection, for a uniform status for refugees or for persons eligible for subsidiary protection, and for the content of the protection granted, amending Council Directive 2003/109/EC and repealing Directive 2011/95/EU of the European Parliament and of the Council, *Official Journal of the European Union*, series L 1347, May 22, 2024.

396 Regulation (EU) 2024/1359 of the European Parliament and of the Council of May 14, 2024 on responding to emergencies and force majeure situations in the field of migration and asylum and amending Regulation (EU) 2021/1147 *Official Journal of the European Union*, series L 1359, May 22, 2024.

397 Regulation (EU) 2024/1358 of the European Parliament and of the Council of May 14, 2024. on the establishment of Eurodac for the comparison of biometric data for the effective application of Regulations (EU) 2024/1351 and (EU) 2024/1350 of the European Parliament and of the Council and Council Directive 2001/55/EC, as well as for the identification of illegally staying third-country nationals and stateless persons, requesting comparisons with Eurodac data by law enforcement authorities of Member States and Europol for law enforcement purposes, amending Regulations (EU) 2018/1240 and (EU) 2019/818 of the European Parliament and of the Council and repealing Regulation (EU) 603/2013 of the European Parliament and of the Council, *Official Journal of the European Union*, series L 1358, May 22, 2024.

398 Directive (EU) 2024/1346 of the European Parliament and of the Council of May 14 2024 on the establishment of standards for the reception of applicants for international protection (recast), *Official Journal of the European Union*, series L 1346, May 22, 2024.

from outside the EU, strengthening international solidarity.[399] In this context, the European Union Asylum Agency (EUAA) plays an important role, providing technical and operational support to Member States both in normal situations and under migration pressure.[400] The regulations that have been put in place are aimed at increasing the effectiveness of migration management, ensuring solidarity and balance among Member States, as well as harmonizing protection standards across the EU. On the one hand, they respond to the challenges of uncontrolled migration and crises, while on the other, they strengthen the EU's ability to protect human rights and promote legal forms of migration. However, one of the key challenges remains their full implementation at the level of Member States and ensuring that the new mechanisms are not abused in a way that limits access to international protection.

Despite the European Union's political pronouncements, in her article, E. Guild is critical of the opportunities that the new regulations of the EU Pact on Migration and Asylum provide Member States with to limit their obligations or adopt restrictive interpretations of asylum rights.[401] She stresses that the proposed instruments could be used to evade responsibility for accepting refugees and migrants through a selective approach to the principles of solidarity among Member States. In her view, of particular concern is the mechanism for cooperation with third countries, which could lead to externalization of migration control. Guild also highlights the risk of crisis situations, where new regulations may allow deviations from basic principles of human rights protection. The lack of unambiguous guarantees for the protection of rights in such conditions could lead to abuse and

---

399 Regulation (EU) 2024/1350 of the European Parliament and of the Council of May 14, 2024 establishing an EU framework for resettlement and reception for humanitarian reasons and amending Regulation (EU) 2021/1147 *Official Journal of the European Union*, series L 1350, May 22, 2024.

400 Regulation (EU) 2021/2303 of the European Parliament and of the Council of December 15 2021 establishing a European Union Agency for Asylum and repealing Regulation (EU) No. 439/2010 *Official Journal of the European Union*, series L 468/1, December 15, 2021.

401 Guild E., "EU Pact Instruments on Asylum and Minimum Human Rights Standards," *EU Migration Law Blog.*

further erosion of the rights of asylum seekers, which, as we will see soon, is a legitimate concern.[402]

Analyzing these systems, it can be seen that the coexistence of state sovereignty with the principles of EU law and international human rights standards requires strict adherence to principles such as *non-refoulement*. The EU acts as a coordinator and guarantor of the coherence of these obligations while respecting the autonomy of Member States. However, practical challenges, such as differences in implementation and tensions between sovereignty and human rights, remain key issues that require further attention.

1.3.4.4 Poland's response to the migrant crisis on the Polish-Belarusian border

The events originating at the eastern external border of the European Union, including the Polish-Belarusian border in 2021, became the next installment of the migration crisis. They were quickly defined as an instance of the instrumentalization of migrants, a designation first made by EU Migration Commissioner Ylva Johansson,[403] and also considered a tool of hybrid warfare, as expressed by Lithuanian Foreign Minister Gabrielius Landsbergis.[404] Contrary to expectations, the Commission did not condemn the actions taken by the countries of the eastern flank, but, following the model of earlier declarations relating to Greece and Spain, these actions were deemed appropriate in response to the instrumentalization actions of the Belarusian regime.[405] Poland, Lithuania and Latvia were targeted by Belarus, which

---

402 Guild E., "EU Pact Instruments on Asylum and Minimum Human Rights Standards," *EU Migration Law Blog*.

403 Mc Mahon M., and Johansson Y., "It's not really a migration crisis. It's a geopolitical crisis" (2021, November 23) *Euronews*. Retrieved from <https://www.euronews.com/2021/11/23/ylva-johansson-it-s-not-really-a-migration-crisis-it-s-a-geopolitical-crisis>.

404 Shelton J., "Lithuania: Minsk using refugees as "weapon against EU"" (2021, July 12) *Deutsche Welle*. Retrieved from <https://www.dw.com/en/lithuanian-fm-belarus-using-refugees-as-hybrid-weapon-against-eu/a-58245160>.

405 "Instrumentalization of migrants" is defined in the Commission Communication COM(2021) 891 final of December 14, 2021 on the proposal to amend Regulation (EU) 2016/399 on the EU Code on the rules governing the movement of persons across borders as "a situation in which a third country initiates irregular migration flows into the Union by actively encouraging or facilitating the movement of third-country nationals to the external borders [...] where such actions indicate the third country's

organized migration routes for foreigners, mainly from the Middle East and Africa.[406] In response to the destabilization of the EU's eastern borders and the international community's refusal to recognize Alexander Lukashenko, the European Union imposed sanctions covering the Belarusian authorities and related entities.

Following the launch of Russia's full-scale aggression against Ukraine in February 2022 and the entry of Finland and Sweden into NATO, the Russian Federation has also used migration as an element of hybrid warfare, as was evident at the Finnish-Russian border, where migrants attempted to cross the border using bicycles, as they did in 2015. In response to these challenges, Finland closed its borders with Russia, limiting asylum options.[407] Lithuania, Latvia and Poland responded to the instrumentalization of migrants by the Belarusian government by changing their laws and introducing restrictive border control measures that affected the rights of people on the move.[408] As a first step, soldiers were deployed to protect the state border on the section with Belarus to support Border Guard officers.[409]

At the same time, on September 2, 2021, the President of the Republic of Poland imposed a state of emergency on part of the territory of Podlaskie and Lubelskie provinces, which was in force until November 30, 2021.[410] In addition, on October 29, 2021, the Law on the construction of border security state border was enacted, which came into force as a key act regulating the construction of physical barriers along the border with Belarus.[411] During the

---

intention to destabilize the Union or a Member State, where the nature of such actions may jeopardize the essential functions of the State, including its territorial integrity, the maintenance of public order or the protection of its national security."

406 Statement by the Prime Ministers of Poland, Lithuania, Latvia and Estonia.

407 Hofverberg E., "Finland: Government Closes Entire Land Border with Russia" (2023, November 28) *Law Library of Congress*.

408 Forti M., "Belarus-sponsored Migration Movements and the Response by Lithuania, Latvia, and Poland: A Critical Appraisal," *European Papers* <https://www.europeanpapers.eu/en/europeanforum/belarus-sponsored-migration-movements-and-response-by-lithuania-latvia-and-poland>.

409 Article 11b of the Act of October 12, 1990, on the Border Guard (2021) *Journal of Laws*, item 1486.

410 Presidential Decree of September 2, 2021, OJ (2021), item 1612.

411 Law of October 29 2021 on the construction of state border security (i.e., *Journal of Laws* 2023, item 1390).

same period, the Law on foreigners of December 12, 2013 and the Law on granting protection to foreigners on the territory of the Republic of Poland of June 13, 2003 were amended. Among other things, the amendments made it possible not to examine applications for international protection in the case of illegal crossing of the external border of the EU unless the foreigner proved that he came directly from the territory where he was threatened with persecution.[412]

These measures are set to continue, as on October 12, 2024, Prime Minister Donald Tusk announced Poland's new migration strategy, which included a key solution involving the possibility of "temporary, territorial suspension of the right to asylum" in cases of instrumentalization of migration flows.[413] The Council of Ministers adopted the document "Take Back Control. Ensure Security. Poland's Comprehensive and Responsible Migration Strategy for 2025–2030" on October 15, 2024.[414]

On December 18, 2024, the Council of Ministers adopted a draft law amending the law granting protection to foreigners on the territory of the Republic of Poland. The draft law's first reading was held in the Sejm on January 9, 2025.[415] At the time of writing, the bill is scheduled for a public hearing on February 4, 2025.

It is worth considering the proposed solutions, as they constitute a novelty and, being a turning point in the area of refugee law, introduce new derogatory institutions and a definition of instrumentalization into the Polish legal order. The 2024 draft law is a reaction to the escalation of the phenomenon of instrumentalization of migration, particularly visible since July 2021, as a tool for destabilizing the internal situation of Poland and other EU Member States on the eastern flank. The Belarusian

---

412 Law of October 14 2021 on amending the Law on foreigners and certain other laws, *Journal of Laws*, item 1918.

413 *Propozycja Tuska może prowadzić do niebezpiecznego efektu domina* <https://tvn24.pl/swiat/zawieszenie-prawa-do-azylu-propozycja-donalda-tuska-komentarze-europejskich-mediow-st8135907>.

414 Council of Ministers, *Uchwała w sprawie przyjęcia dokumentu "Odzyskać kontrolę. Zapewnić bezpieczeństwo. Kompleksowa i odpowiedzialna strategia migracyjna Polski na lata 2025–2030,"* <https://www.gov.pl/web/premier/uchwala-w-sprawie-przyjecia-dokumentu-odzyskac-kontrole-zapewnic-bezpieczenstwo-kompleksowa-i-odpowiedzialna-strategia-migracyjna-polski-na-lata-2025-2030>.

415 <https://www.sejm.gov.pl/Sejm10.nsf/PrzebiegProc.xsp?nr=924>.

authorities, in cooperation with Russia and international criminal groups, organized large-scale attempts to cross the Polish border illegally. This situation prompted the legislator to propose amendments to the Law on granting protection to foreigners, aimed at creating effective legal tools to counter similar threats in the future.[416]

A key element of the draft is the introduction of a legal definition of the term "instrumentalization of migration." In light of the proposed definition, migration instrumentalization includes systemic actions of the state bordering Poland or other entities aimed at enabling illegal crossing of the EU external border, often using violence against public officials and destruction of border infrastructure.[417] Such a definition, which is broader than the one contained in the Regulation of the European Parliament and of the Council (EU) 2024/1359,[418] also indicates the purpose of these actions—the destabilization of the internal situation of the target country.

The draft also provides for the introduction of a new Article 33a, which regulates the substantive legal grounds for restricting the right to file an application for international protection.[419] These restrictions may only be applied in situations where instrumentalization is occurring, when there is a serious and real threat to the security of the state or society. A further condition for their introduction is the need to temporarily restrict the right to apply in order to prevent the threat. The restrictions will be temporary—not exceeding 60 days at a time—and will be introduced by a decree of the Council of Ministers, with the possibility of extension upon approval by the Diet. A further step is to expand the grounds for deprivation of refugee status. The draft also introduces new grounds for deprivation of this status, such as posing a threat to state security or society, or the conviction of a foreigner

416 Explanatory memorandum to the draft law on amendments to the law on granting protection to foreigners on the territory of the Republic of Poland, Print No. 924, Sejm of the Republic of Poland.

417 Article 1 item 1 of the draft law on amending the law on granting protection to foreigners on the territory of the Republic of Poland.

418 Regulation (EU) 2024/1359 of the European Parliament and of the Council of May 14, 2024 on responding to emergencies and force majeure situations in the field of migration and asylum and amending Regulation (EU) 2021/1147 (OJ EU. L. 2024, item 1359).

419 Article 1 item 4 of the draft law on amending the law on granting protection to foreigners on the territory of the Republic of Poland.

for a particularly serious crime.[420] The previous legislation did not provide for such possibilities, which, in the opinion of the legislator, constituted a legal loophole.[421]

In conclusion, the draft law amending the Law on granting protection to foreigners on the territory of the Republic of Poland aims to introduce effective legislative tools to counteract the internal destabilization of Poland due to the instrumentalization of migration. However, the declared goals behind the introduced solutions are not recognized and are criticized.[422]

These actions align with the new paradigm at the EU level, mentioned earlier, in which third-country nationals subjected to instrumentalization are classified as hybrid threats. M. Forti argues that the crisis on the EU's eastern border with Belarus and the migration policies of countries such as Poland, Lithuania and Latvia clearly demonstrate the securitized nature of the EU's response.[423] In response to migration pressures, these countries have introduced restrictive laws and declared states of emergency, which restrict migrants' rights, including the right to asylum and the prohibition of inhumane treatment. Poland has taken a step further by refusing to implement the Pact on Migration and Asylum, claiming that

---

420 Article 1(2) of the draft law on amending the law on granting protection to foreigners on the territory of the Republic of Poland.

421 Justification of the draft law on amending the law on granting protection to foreigners on the territory of the Republic of Poland.

422 *Prawa do azylu nie da się zawiesić—analiza prawna*, Association for Legal Intervention, November 7, 2024, accessed January 27, 2025 <https://interwencjaprawna.pl/prawa-do-azylu-nie-da-sie-zawiesic-analiza-prawna/>; Horna-Cieślak M., *Stanowisko Rzecznika Praw Dziecka do projektu nowelizacji ustawy o udzielaniu cudzoziemcom ochrony—zawieszenie prawa do azylu*, Office of the Children's Rights Ombudsman, December 2024, accessed January 27, 2025 <https://brpd.gov.pl/wp-content/uploads/2024/12/WG-RPD-do-MSWiA-stanowisko-do-projektu-noweli-do-u.u.c.o.-zawieszenie-prawa-do-azylu.pdf>; *Opinia dotycząca rządowego projektu zmiany ustawy o udzielaniu cudzoziemcom ochrony na terytorium RP*, Amnesty International Poland <https://www.amnesty.org.pl/opinia-dotyczaca-rzadowego-projektu-zmiany-ustawy-o-udzielaniu-cudzoziemcom-ochrony-na-terytorium-rp/>.

423 Forti M., "Belarus-sponsored Migration Movements and the Response by Lithuania, Latvia, and Poland: A Critical Appraisal," *European Papers* <https://www.europeanpapers.eu/en/europeanforum/belarus-sponsored-migration-movements-and-response-by-lithuania-latvia-and-poland>.

the current government was not involved in negotiating the accompanying documents.[424] Moreover, Polish government's decision to temporarily suspend asylum procedures appears to validate the concerns expressed by commentators on the Pact.

As Gkliati writes, while the Pact on Migration and Asylum was meant to establish a predictable framework for migration management, in practice, it perpetuates these emergency mechanisms, turning them into standard tools.[425] An example is the hotspot approach, which was introduced in 2015 as an ad hoc solution, and which is now a standard tool for migration control (screening), as has already been widely reported by the author.[426] Temporary solutions implemented during a crisis have become a permanent feature of EU migration policy, leading to the creation of permanent derogation regimes, i.e., deviations from standard legal norms in favor of exceptional measures, raising legitimate concerns about the impact on the rule of law and the protection of human rights.[427] The Pact on Migration and Asylum has undergone permanent changes due to events at the eastern border, and, as Gerbaudo writes, the stated goal of "putting in place a 'new, sustainable European framework' that provides 'certainty, clarity and decent conditions for [people] coming to the EU' is no longer valid."[428] The European Commission's strategy of instrumentalizing migration by normalizing border procedures and de

424 PAP, *Unia decyduje w sprawie migracji. Co zrobi Polska?*, December 17, 2024 <https://www.pap.pl/aktualnosci/unia-decyduje-w-sprawie-migracji-co-zrobi-polska>.

425 Gkliati M., *Let's Call It What It Is: Hybrid Threats and Instrumentalisation as the Evolution of Securitisation in Migration Management* (2022).

426 Gerbaudo M., "The European Commission's Instrumentalization Strategy: Normalising Border Procedures and De Facto Detention" (2022) 7(2) *European Papers*, 615–626 <https://doi.org/10.15166/2499-8249/582> and <https://www.europeanpapers.eu/en/europeanforum/european-commission-instrumentalization-strategy-border-procedures-detention#_ftn18>.

427 Halilovic A., "Executive Migration Governance and Law-making in the European Union: Towards a State of Exception" (2024) *European Papers* <https://www.europeanpapers.eu/en/e-journal/executive-migration-governance-law-making-in-european-union-towards-state-exception>.

428 Halilovic A., "Executive Migration Governance and Law-making in the European Union: Towards a State of Exception" (2024) *European Papers* <https://www.europeanpapers.eu/en/e-journal/executive-migration-governance-law-making-in-european-union-towards-state-exception>.

facto detention reinforces a securitarian approach to migration management, dehumanizing migrants and treating them as a political tool.[429]

1.3.5 Ukraine crisis

On February 24, 2022, Russian troops entered Ukrainian territory, carrying out "unprovoked and unjustified military aggression."[430] Because of this sudden armed invasion, which included bombing and rocket attacks on various targets throughout Ukrainian territory, hundreds of thousands of war refugees headed west, triggering the largest humanitarian crisis in Europe since World War II. According to the Office of the UN High Commissioner for Refugees (UNHCR), 3,725,806 people, mostly women, children and the elderly, left Ukraine in the first month after the Russian aggression began.[431] At the time of writing, UNHCR estimates that there are 6,863,400 registered refugees from Ukraine worldwide, almost 92 % of whom are in Europe.[432] As of January 14, 2025, there are 993,795 registered refugees from Ukraine. Of these, 1,903,100 have applied for asylum and received temporary protection or similar national protection programs. As of February 24, 2022, there were 27,473,825 border crossings from Ukraine to Poland and 25,481,455 border crossings from Poland to Ukraine. The scale of the movements required an immediate response from both Member States and the European Union itself.[433]

---

429 ibid.

430 European Council, *European Council conclusions on the unprovoked and unjustified military aggression of Russia against Ukraine* (February 24, 2022) <https://www.consilium.europa.eu/pl/press/press-releases/2022/02/24/european-council-conclusions-24-february-2022/>.

431 Żołędowski C., "Nowi uchodźcy w Europie. Przemieszczenia zewnętrzne z Ukrainy między 24.02. i 24.03.2022 r," in G. Firlit-Fesnak, E. Jaroszewska, Ł. Łotocki, J. Łukaszewska-Bezulska, M. Ołdak, P. Zawadzki, C. Żołędowski, and T. Żukowski (red.), *Inwazja Rosji na Ukrainę. Społeczeństwo i polityka wobec kryzysu uchodźczego w pierwszym miesiącu wojny* (Warszawa 2022) 4–9, Based on UNHCR data <https://data2.unhcr.org/en/situations/ukraine> accessed March 25, 2022.

432 Data current as of January 18, 2025. UNHCR <https://data.unhcr.org/en/situations/ukraine>.

433 UNHCR Data current as of January 14, 2025. UNHCR <https://data.unhcr.org/en/situations/ukraine>.

In response to Russia's invasion of Ukraine, the Council of the European Union adopted an important measure in the area of asylum law by deciding to activate Council Directive 2001/55/EC of July 20, 2001, on minimum standards for granting temporary protection in the event of a mass influx of displaced persons and on measures to promote a balance of efforts between Member States in receiving such persons and managing the consequences.[434]

The directive was the first international protection instrument adopted by the European Union on the basis of its new powers under the Treaty of Amsterdam. It establishes an emergency procedure to provide immediate and temporary protection in situations of a mass influx or imminent threat of such an influx of displaced persons from third countries who cannot return to their country of origin. The procedure was developed on the basis of the experience of the influx of refugees from the former Yugoslavia in the 1990s.

The term "temporary protection" is defined in Article 2(a) of the Directive, and as Polish law does not define this legal institution, the definition set forth in the Directive should be used.[435] Temporary protection regimes are used as emergency measures in situations of mass influx, providing group protection to prevent the overloading of asylum systems and immediately protect those in need. Unlike the 1951 Geneva Convention, which is based on individual processing, temporary protection expanded the definition of "refugee," although it is treated as an exceptional measure in special situations such as the Yugoslav conflict mentioned above.[436] Thus, it means "a special type of procedure, with the aim of providing, in the event of a threat of the

---

434 Council Implementing Decision (EU) 2022/382 of March 4, 2022, Establishing the existence of a mass influx of displaced persons from Ukraine within the meaning of Article 5 of Directive 2001/55/EC and resulting in the introduction of temporary protection; OJ L 71, March 4, 2022, 1–6.

435 Council Directive 2001/55/EC of July 20, 2001 on minimum standards for giving temporary protection in the event of a mass influx of displaced persons and on measures promoting a balance of efforts between the Member States in receiving such persons and bearing the consequences thereof, OJ L 212, August 7, 2001, 12–23, *ELI* <http://data.europa.eu/eli/dir/2001/55/oj>.

436 Beirens H., Maas S., Petronella S., and van der Velden M., *Study on the Temporary Protection Directive: Final Report* (European Commission, January 2016), accessed at <https://home-affairs.ec.europa.eu/system/files/2020-09/final_report_evaluation_tpd_en.pdf>, 4.

occurrence or actual occurrence of a massive influx of displaced persons from third countries who cannot return to their country of origin, and whose purpose is to grant immediate temporary protection to such persons, particularly when it is reasonable to believe that the asylum system will not be able to bear the burden of such an influx without adverse effects on the operation of that system, to the detriment of those concerned and other persons seeking protection." As Sergio Carrera and M. Ineli-Ciger point out, Council Directive 2001/55/EC came into force in 2001 and was the first EU directive on international protection adopted after the entry into force of the Amsterdam Treaty in 1999.[437] Nevertheless, the question most often posed by researchers of the topic was why the crisis mechanism specified in the directive was activated only during the armed conflict in Ukraine and not earlier.

Indeed, one can point to several events that could have justified an appropriate response by the EU Council, resulting in the activation of the mechanisms of Directive 2001/55/EC. The first could be the situation that arose after the events of the Arab Spring. The Italian government asked the EU Council to activate the procedure specified in Directive 2001/55/EC to grant temporary protection to those who had already arrived or were likely to arrive from North Africa in the coming months.[438] At the April 11–12, 2011 meeting of the Justice and Home Affairs (JHA) Council, the request by Italy, supported by Malta, to activate the temporary protection mechanism was not accepted, despite declarations of solidarity toward these countries. It was argued that the conditions outlined in Directive 2001/55/EC were not met. Commissioner Malmström first proposed using the temporary protection

---

437 Ineli-Ciger M., *The Missing Piece in the European Agenda on Migration: the Temporary Protection Directive*, 2015 <https://eulawanalysis.blogspot.com/search?q=temporary+protection>; Carrera S., and Ineli-Ciger M., *EU Responses to the Large-Scale Refugee Displacement from Ukraine: An Analysis on the Temporary Protection Directive and Its Implications for the Future EU Asylum Policy. Preface* (Migration Policy Centre, Robert Schuman Centre, European University Institute 2023) <https://cadmus.eui.eu/bitstream/handle/1814/75377/ASILE%20E-Book.pdf?sequence=7&isAllowed=y>.

438 Nascimbene B., and Di Pascale A., "The 'Arab Spring' and the Extraordinary Influx of People Who Arrived in Italy from North Africa," (2011) 13 *European Journal of Migration and Law*, 347–348.

mechanism in the event of a mass influx of refugees, but the proposal did not receive the required support.[439]

Similarly, nearly one million refugees and migrants arrived irregularly in Europe by sea in 2015. In view of the Syrian conflict and the Mediterranean migration crisis, the question arose as to whether the legal conditions for activating the Temporary Protection Directive (2001/55/EC) had been met and whether a corresponding proposal should be submitted to the EU Council. Despite this, the Directive was once again not applied.[440]

M. Ineli Ciğer, who has been researching the Directive since 2010, pointed out several aspects in her earlier work that, in her opinion, could explain the failure to trigger the process provided for in Directive 2001/55/EC. One of the key challenges in the context of Directive 2001/55/EC was the unclear definition of mass influx. The directive defines the phenomenon as the arrival of large numbers of people displaced from a particular country or geographic region, regardless of whether their arrival was spontaneous or organized, such as through evacuation programs. The lack of precise criteria to unambiguously determine when a situation qualifies as a mass influx was considered to be a factor hindering the application of the Directive in the past. However, such a definition, based on general and vague terms, was intended to provide decision-making flexibility for host countries, allowing them to act more quickly without the need for detailed consideration of individual refugee claims as a result of international refugee law obligations.[441] As the report's authors point out, the definition of mass influx is deliberately broad and

---

439 Nascimbene B., and Di Pascale A., "The 'Arab Spring' and the Extraordinary Influx of People Who Arrived in Italy from North Africa," 13 (2011) *European Journal of Migration and Law*, 349.

440 Ciğer M. İ., "Reasons Why: Understanding the Reasons Behind the Activation of the Temporary Protection Directive in 2022" (2022) *5 EU Migration Law Blog*. Retrieved from <https://eumigrationlawblog.eu/5-reasons-why-understanding-the-reasons-behind-the-activation-of-the-temporary-protection-directive-in-2022/>.

441 Ineli-Ciger M., *The Missing Piece in the European Agenda on Migration: the Temporary Protection Directive*, 2015 <https://eulawanalysis.blogspot.com/search?q=temporary+protection>; Ineli-Ciger M., "Reasons for the Activation of the Temporary Protection Directive in 2022: A Tale of Double Standards," in Carrera S., Ineli-Ciger M. (eds), *EU Responses to the Large-Scale Refugee Displacement from Ukraine: An Analysis on the Temporary Protection Directive and Its Implications for the Future EU Asylum Policy*, 61.

flexible to allow for responses to a variety of scenarios—from sudden influxes to gradual increases in asylum claims to evacuation programs. This flexibility is both a strength of the Directive, but also a weakness, as the lack of clear criteria for the number of people in need of protection makes it difficult to get Member States to agree to its activation. In practice, despite various situations exerting pressure on national asylum systems, the Directive has not been applied because Member States have interpreted the concept of "mass influx" and the legitimacy of activating the temporary protection mechanism differently. In conclusion, the broad definition of "mass influx" was intended to provide flexibility to the Directive, but in practice it leads to ambiguity and lack of consensus among Member States, which significantly limits its effectiveness as an emergency measure.[442] A. Skordas points out that the lack of a prior concept of international law in this regard creates leeway for the authorized bodies of the European Union to decide on the scope and timing of the activation of the institution of temporary protection.[443]

Another obstacle to earlier activation of Directive 2001/55/EC was said to be, in Ciğer's reasoning, the long and complicated decision-making process. The procedure for activating the Temporary Protection Directive is characterized by both flexibility and limitations. It has the advantage of being adaptable to a variety of mass influx situations, such as sudden migration crises, a gradual increase in the number of refugees, or evacuation programs. The directive makes it possible to provide immediate protection to displaced persons and promotes solidarity among Member States by enabling burden sharing. However, the activation procedure is said to be complicated and time-consuming, as it requires a qualified majority in the EU Council, making it prone to delays and political tensions. The exclusive role of the European Commission in submitting applications limits the initiative of

442 Beirens H., Maas S., Petronella S., and van der Velden M., *Study on the Temporary Protection Directive: Final Report,* European Commission, January 2016), accessed at <https://home-affairs.ec.europa.eu/system/files/2020-09/final_report_evaluation_tpd_en.pdf>, 16–17. These doubts were also shared by R. Rogala in his commentary on Article 106 of the Law on granting protection to foreigners on the territory of the Republic of Poland; Rogala R., in J. Chlebny (ed), *Prawo o cudzoziemcach. Komentarz* (Warszawa 2020).

443 Skordas A., "Temporary Protection Directive 2001/55/EC," in: Daniel Thym, and Kay Hailbronner (eds), *EU Immigration and Asylum Law* (C.H. Beck/Hart/Nomos 2022) 1177–1228.

Member States, while the aforementioned lack of precise guidelines on the definition of "mass influx" and activation rules causes differences in interpretation. As a result, the procedure was perceived as inefficient and difficult to apply in emergency situations. However, as it turned out in the case of the Directive's activation after the outbreak of war in Ukraine, the process was carried out with remarkable speed. Member States expressed broad support for the application of Directive 2001/55/EC at the EU Council meeting on February 27, 2022, and the European Commission already proposed a draft decision activating the Directive on March 2. In accordance with Article 5 of Directive 2001/55/EC, on March 4, 2022, the Council of the EU adopted Executive Decision (EU) 2022/382 recognizing the existence of a mass influx of displaced persons from Ukraine within the meaning of Article 5 of Directive 2001/55/EC, resulting in the introduction of temporary protection, which in practice meant that it was already in force from that date. Other obstacles to the swift implementation of the Directive, as identified by Ciğer, were the difficulties with obtaining a qualified majority in the Council of the European Union in situations of mass influxes of refugees, which mainly affected a limited number of Member States. Indeed, most displaced people arrived in a few selected countries (Poland, Slovakia, Hungary, Romania), which limited the involvement of the remaining countries and contributed to political reluctance to activate the Directive. Another factor was the fear of creating a so-called "pull factor" effect, i.e., a situation in activating the temporary protection mechanism might encourage a larger number of migrants wishing to seek protection and enter the European Union.[444] In addition, an important barrier was the perception that the Directive offers beneficiaries of temporary protection too high a level of rights, such as access to health care, the labor market, education or shelter. According to a report evaluating the functioning of the Directive, some Member States felt that these guarantees were too costly and could discourage activation of the Directive. These factors, combined with political reluctance and fears about the consequences of activating the act in question, effectively blocked its implementation for

---

[444] Ciğer M. İ., *5 Reasons Why: Understanding the Reasons Behind the Activation of the Temporary Protection Directive in 2022* (EU Migration Law Blog 2022). Retrieved from <https://eumigrationlawblog.eu/5-reasons-why-understanding-the-reasons-behind-the-activation-of-the-temporary-protection-directive-in-2022/>.

many years, even though it could have been an effective tool for responding to migration crises. However, as has already been demonstrated, the speed with which the directive was activated contradicts the claim that objective obstacles prevented its activation, raising the question: What was the missing element in the previously indicated examples? Ciğer provides a concise yet factual answer. The missing element was political will—the willingness to use the mechanism provided by the Directive.[445]

It is necessary to discuss the legal act by which the Council activated the provisions of the Directive since only together do the two create a complementary legal environment for the application of the Directive's provisions. Council Implementing Decision (EU) 2022/382 of March 4, 2022—as it is referred to—concerns the recognition of a mass influx of displaced persons from Ukraine within the meaning of Article 5 of Directive 2001/55/EC and the introduction of temporary protection for these persons. The scope of the decision includes the recognition that the influx of displaced persons from Ukraine, caused by the military invasion of the Russian Federation, constitutes a mass influx within the meaning of Directive 2001/55/EC. The decision introduces temporary protection for those covered by the subjective scope of the Council Decision.[446] Regarding the subjective scope of the EU Council Implementing Decision, it should be read together with the provisions of Directive 2001/55/EC, which, in Article 5 (3) (a), specifies the groups eligible for temporary protection, although Member States may extend the regime to other groups of displaced persons from the same country or region of origin. The decision applies to Ukrainian citizens residing in Ukraine before February 24, 2022, as well as stateless persons and citizens of third countries other than Ukraine who enjoyed international protection or equivalent national protection in Ukraine before February 24, 2022. It also covers family members of such persons, including spouses, partners,

---

445 Ciğer M. İ., *5 Reasons Why: Understanding the Reasons Behind the Activation of the Temporary Protection Directive in 2022* (2022).

446 Council of the European Union, Council Implementing Decision (EU) 2022/382 of March 4, 2022, determining the existence of a mass influx of displaced persons from Ukraine within the meaning of Article 5 of Directive 2001/55/EC and resulting in the introduction of temporary protection (2022) L 71/1 *Official Journal of the European Union*, Article 1.

minor children and other close relatives who lived together as one family and were dependent on the person under temporary protection. Member States may also extend temporary protection to other persons who legally resided in Ukraine before February 24, 2022, but who cannot safely return to their country or region of origin.[447] Temporary protection for Ukrainian nationals was extended until March 4, 2026, by Council Executive Decision (EU) 2024/1836 of June 25, 2024.[448]

1.3.5.1 Poland's response to the influx of refugees from Ukraine

Implementation of the provisions of Directive 2001/55/EC and the EU Council Decision required the preparation of appropriate national regulations. Although work on regulations to address the mass influx of refugees from Ukraine had already begun, the adoption by the EU Council of Executive Decision (EU) 2022/382 created the need to include its provisions in the proposed law. In addition, amendments had to be made to the Law of June 13, 2003 on granting protection to foreigners on the territory of the Republic of Poland.[449] Despite the formal implementation of the Directive in the 2003 legislation, its scope and adaptation method did not fully meet current challenges, necessitating further legislative action. As a result, the Law on Assistance to Citizens of Ukraine in Connection with the Armed Conflict on the Territory of Ukraine was passed on March 12, 2022.[450] The new regulation, which has the character of a special law, adapted the existing

447 Council of the European Union, Council Implementing Decision (EU) 2022/382 of March 4, 2022, establishing the existence of a mass influx of displaced persons from Ukraine within the meaning of Article 5 of Directive 2001/55/EC and resulting in the introduction of temporary protection (2022) L 71/1 *Official Journal of the European Union* Article 2.

448 Council of the European Union, Council Implementing Decision (EU) 2024/1836 of June 25 2024 on the extension of the temporary protection introduced by Implementing Decision (EU) 2022/382 (2024) L 1836 *Official Journal of the European Union*. L_202401836EN.000101.fmx <https://eur-lex.europa.eu/legal-content/PL/TXT/HTML/?uri=OJ:L_202401836>.

449 Article 106 et seq. of the Law of June 13, 2003 on granting protection to foreigners on the territory of the Republic of Poland (i.e., Journal of Laws of 2023, item 1504, as amended).

450 Law of March 12, 2022, on Assistance to Citizens of Ukraine in Connection with the Armed Conflict on the Territory of Ukraine (i.e., Journal of Laws of 2024, item 167, as amended).

migration and asylum law to the dynamic situation, providing effective support for refugees while also addressing legislative shortcomings and filling legal gaps that had emerged during its implementation.[451]

According to Article 1(1) of the special law, it establishes special rules for legalizing the stay of Ukrainian citizens who came to Poland from Ukraine in connection with the hostilities, as well as for Ukrainian citizens holding the Card of the Pole who, together with their immediate family, came to Poland for the same reason. The legislator defined the Act's subjective scope in Article 1(2) by referring to the categories of persons defined by Decision 2022/382 but chose not to indicate the complete list of beneficiaries defined by the decision, regulating the status of some of them by the Act on granting protection to foreigners on the territory of the Republic of Poland. Successive amendments to the Act changed its subject and object scope, adapting it to the dynamically changing reality, while also correcting legislative errors and filling the legal gaps that arose and were revealed in the practice of applying the act. It should be noted that within the framework of the Law of March 12, 2022, on assistance to citizens of Ukraine,[452]special procedures and solutions are provided, which cannot be fully discussed in this study. Therefore, only the current scope of the law and key changes are presented. Citizens of Ukraine who arrived in Poland legally after February 24, 2022, are entitled to temporary protection, which includes the legalization of their stay until March 4, 2024 (Article 2, paragraph 1). Along with the assignment of a PESEL number with "UKR" status, which a Ukrainian citizen should obtain immediately upon arrival in the territory of Poland, these individuals are granted access to public services such as health care and education, as well as access to the trusted profile system (Article 4). Those with a trusted profile can, in turn, obtain Diia.pl, an electronic document available in the mCitizen application, which serves as a residence permit and allows movement within the Schengen area under the terms of Article 6(1). This document, along with a valid passport, also allows crossing the external borders of the EU. Citizens of Ukraine under temporary protection may take up employment in Poland without obtaining a work permit (Article 22). The employer is only obliged to report the fact of entrusting work to the district labor office

451 The law has been amended to a greater or lesser extent some 30 times.

452 Journal of Laws of 2023, item 103, as amended (hereinafter: "Special Law").

within 7 days of its commencement. Under an amendment to the Special Law, the legal stay of Ukrainian citizens who enjoy temporary protection has been extended until September 30, 2025 (Article 42a). The possibility of obtaining temporary residence permits for the purpose of business or family reunification has also been extended (Articles 158–159 of the Law on foreigners), thus introducing an alternative to temporary protection. Indeed, a person who obtains said temporary residence permit loses his status as a beneficiary of temporary protection and is treated as any other foreigner residing in Poland. The special law does not apply to persons who have other forms of legal stay in Poland, such as refugee status, a permanent residence permit, or a long-term EU resident status (Article 1, paragraph 4).

It is worth summarizing the European Union's actions in response to the refugee crisis triggered by the Russian invasion of Ukraine in order to understand both the positive aspects and the challenges the EU continues to face. Following D. Vitiello, it is optimistic to see the EU's response encompassing a sense of shared threat, which has prompted Member States to take a more humane approach to sheltering refugees and a collective responsibility in responding to the crisis.[453] The Visegrad Group countries, which had previously questioned the principles of solidarity and sharing of responsibility, stood at the forefront of those who provided the earliest and most intensive support. The European Commission, which had previously focused on strengthening border controls, quickly adopted operational guidelines to ease external border management, facilitating border crossings between the EU and Ukraine.[454]

However, the EU's response to this refugee crisis also warrants a critical examination. The paradigm of containing migration is outdated and deceptive, and refugee crises can be triggered or exacerbated by inappropriate policy responses as Vitiello writes.[455] The broad consensus in his view is that

---

453 Vitiello D., "The Nansen Passport and the EU Temporary Protection Directive: Reflections on Solidarity, Mobility Rights and the Future of Asylum in Europe," (2022) 7(1) *European Papers*, European Forum, Insight of March 30, 2022, 15–30. ISSN 2499-8249 <https://doi.org/10.15166/2499-8249/542>.

454 Communication COM(2022) 107 final from the Commission of March 8, 2022 on European solidarity with refugees and those fleeing war in Ukraine.

455 Vitiello D., "The Nansen Passport and the EU Temporary Protection Directive: Reflections on Solidarity, Mobility Rights and the Future of Asylum in Europe" (2022) *European Papers*,

the effectiveness of EU migration and asylum policy depends on the political will of Member States.

The EU's response to the Ukraine-related refugee crisis could become a key strategic asset in the current confrontation with Russia. However, double standards in EU migration policy are becoming increasingly evident.[456] During the 2021 Belarus-Poland border crisis, the EU considered 3,000 migrants—mostly Kurds from Iraq and Syria—as a security threat, yet not long afterward it successfully settled some 8 million refugees from Ukraine.[457] European politicians actively portray some mass migrations as a threat to state security, while others are accepted. The Belarusian border incident, although deliberately orchestrated by Lukashenko, did not absolve the EU of its international legal obligations to protect refugees on European soil.[458] The EU could have condemned Lukashenko's tactics while simultaneously providing humanitarian aid and protection to refugees on the Polish border. Comparing the EU's official responses to the Belarusian border crisis and the Ukraine-related refugee crisis, it becomes evident that the EU has systematically denied some groups of refugees their rights while protecting others.[459] One situation was portrayed as an existential crisis, while the other was managed in an organized and cooperative manner.[460]

1.3.6 Conclusions

Summarizing these reflections on the migration crises that have affected Europe in the last dozen years or so, several key conclusions emerge. These crises, although diverse in their causes, course and effects, have highlighted

---

456 Swan E., "The Double Standard in the EU's Treatment of Refugees from Ukraine and the Global South" (2023) *Columbia Political Review* <https://shorturl.at/5Y7c1>.

457 Swan E., "The Double Standard in the EU's Treatment of Refugees from Ukraine and the Global South" (2023) *Columbia Political Review* <https://shorturl.at/5Y7c1>.

458 Ineli-Ciger M., "Reasons for the Activation of the Temporary Protection Directive in 2022: A Tale of Double Standards" (2023) *EU Responses to the Large-Scale Refugee Displacement from Ukraine: An Analysis on the Temporary Protection Directive and Its Implications for the Future EU Asylum Policy* <https://shorturl.at/c5xJ9>, 68–71.

459 Peers S., "Temporary Protection for Ukrainians in the EU? Q and A" (2022) *EU Law Analysis* <https://shorturl.at/RRMW1>.

460 Swan E., "The Double Standard in the EU's Treatment of Refugees from Ukraine and the Global South" (2023) *Columbia Political Review* <https://shorturl.at/5Y7c1>.

structural and political problems in the European Union and the evolution of approaches to migration as a socio-political phenomenon.

The first of the crises discussed was the migration crisis of 2015–2016, triggered by the massive influx of refugees from the Middle East and North Africa. These events highlighted the lack of cohesion and solidarity within the European Union. Although the European Commission proposed mechanisms such as relocation and resettlement, their effectiveness was limited by the lack of consensus among Member States and the resistance of some of them to mandatory quotas. At the same time, securitization increased in importance—migration began to be seen not only as a humanitarian challenge but also as a potential threat to internal security.

The migration crisis triggered by the COVID-19 pandemic posed new challenges for the European Union, which revealed the weaknesses of the Schengen mechanism. Faced with a rapidly changing health situation, many Member States introduced unilateral border closures and movement restrictions, often without adequate coordination at the EU level. The lack of a common approach to border management and differences in the measures used hampered the internal market and undermined the principle of the free movement of people. At the time, the European Union exercised its authority mainly through soft-law acts, such as guidelines and recommendations, which were not binding. While such instruments were intended to provide flexibility and tailor actions to local needs, they undermined the principle of legal certainty and citizens' trust in EU institutions. This crisis highlighted the need to strengthen the Schengen coordination mechanisms and develop a stronger, binding legal framework to effectively respond to similar situations in the future.

Another crisis was the situation on the European Union's eastern border in 2021, where migrants became a tool in the hands of the Lukashenko regime, which instrumentally used them to destabilize the European Union. The response of Poland, Lithuania and Latvia, as well as the EU itself, was characterized by the further strengthening of border controls, the construction of physical barriers and the use of legal measures restricting access to asylum procedures. The crisis highlighted how easily migrants can become pawns in geopolitical games and exacerbated the tendency to treat them primarily through the lens of security policy.

Russia's aggression against Ukraine in 2022 and the refugee crisis it triggered, in turn, revealed another face of the European Union's migration policy. The response was swift and decisive—refugees from Ukraine received immediate protection, access to the labor market and extensive social support. This example shows that political will can significantly affect the effectiveness of action and solidarity within the EU. At the same time, however, this crisis highlighted double standards in the treatment of different groups of migrants. While refugees from Ukraine were met with widespread support, migrants from the Middle East and Africa were often treated as a threat, raising questions about the consistency of the values professed by the European Union.

Over the years, the externalization of EU migration policy has also become increasingly evident. Agreements with third countries, such as the 2016 agreement with Turkey, have sought to shift the burden of migration management beyond the EU's borders. While this approach has helped reduce the influx of migrants, it has raised controversy over respect for human rights and responsibility for the fate of those detained in third countries.

Instrumentalization, externalization and securitization of migration have become permanent features of European migration policy. The use of migrants as political tools, the shifting of responsibility to third countries, and the treatment of migration as a security threat show how the perception of the phenomenon has changed in recent years. Unfortunately, these approaches lead to the marginalization of the humanitarian dimension of migration and the erosion of human rights. The rationale for protecting refugee rights under customary international law is to ensure that refugee protection is not subject to political or geopolitical considerations. Increasingly, however, the EU strategically invokes and rejects humanitarian principles and concerns based on political expediency.

As E. Swan argues, EU migration policy today is so fragmented that it functions more as an illusion of cooperation than a genuinely integrated system for managing migration. While the EU continues to declare its commitment to humanitarian values, it increasingly operates solely within state safeguards, allowing states to avoid responsibility for protecting human rights. Europe's approach to migration focuses on keeping migrants out by strengthening the EU's external borders, drawing strength from the instrumentalization of fear and portraying the "migrant" as a burden on government resources.[461] Strikingly, the EU's migration policy does little to establish cooperation between Member States in resettling migrants and refugees within the Schengen zone. The EU frames migration as a matter of state security, where migrants and refugees pose a threat to Europe's imaginary solidarity. The lack of institutionalized procedures for managing migration internally and the absence of effective accountability for sharing the asylum burden explain why the EU encounters a crisis during every sudden migratory influx. The lessons are clear: Europe needs a more balanced and coherent approach to migration management. Instead of treating migration as a problem, it should be recognized as a potential opportunity for development. It is also crucial to ensure equal treatment for all migrants, regardless of their origin. Double standards not only undermine the values on which the European Union is based but also lead to deeper divisions in European societies. Today's migration crises, while difficult and complex, are also an opportunity to redefine migration policies in a spirit of solidarity, humanity and responsibility. If the European Union wants to meet the challenges of the future, it must move away from short-sighted solutions based on fear and securitization and instead focus on building a more inclusive and open community.

1.4 Human rights in times of emergency: EU law perspective (Barbara Opalska)

1.4.1 Introduction

Respect for human rights is one of the core values of the European Union, as outlined in Article 2 of the Treaty on European Union.[462] The Charter of Fundamental Rights of the European Union[463] plays a crucial role in upholding these rights. It is legally binding on EU institutions, agencies and bodies, as well as on Member States when applying EU law. This is particularly

---

[461] Swan E., *The Double Standard in the EU's Treatment of Refugees from Ukraine and the Global South* (2023).

[462] Treaty on European Union (TEU) <https://eur-lex.europa.eu/resource.html?uri=-cellar:2bf140bf-a3f8-4ab2-b506-fd71826e6da6.0023.02/DOC_1&format=PDF> Consolidated Version of the Treaty on European Union [2012] OJ C 326/13.

[463] Charter of Fundamental Rights of the European Union (CFR) [2000], OJ C 326, October 26, 2012 (as adopted in 2007, entered into force December 1, 2009).

significant in the context of Article 78 of the Treaty on the Functioning of the European Union,[464] which serves as the legal foundation for the Common European Asylum System[465] (CEAS).

The purpose of this chapter is to map the human rights of migrants and asylum applicants within the full scope of EU law, particularly legal acts adopted under the European Pact on Migration and Asylum (hereinafter also "the Pact"),[466] which presents a significant challenge. In its communication of September 23, 2020,[467] titled "A New Pact on Migration and Asylum,"[468] the European Commission acknowledges the broad and complex nature of the Pact, which makes it difficult to delineate its precise content and boundaries.

The analysis will examine the protection of the fundamental rights of migrants and asylum applicants within the European Union, drawing its legal basis from both EU primary law and secondary legislation, including the newly adopted European Pact on Migration and Asylum.[469] These legal frameworks uphold the *principle of non-refoulement*, the right to asylum and fair treatment, while emphasizing the importance of solidarity among Member States in the management of asylum responsibilities.

---

464 Treaty on the Functioning of the European Union (TFEU) <https://eur-lex.europa.eu/legal-content/EN/TXT/PDF/?uri=CELEX:12012E/TXT&from=EN> consolidated version as amended by the Lisbon Treaty (December 1, 2009) [2012] OJ C 326/47.

465 European Commission, *Common European Asylum System* (no date) <https://home-affairs.ec.europa.eu/policies/migration-and-asylum/common-european-asylum-system_en> accessed February 10, 2025.

466 European Commission (2023) "Delivering on the EU Pact on Migration and Asylum" <https://commission.europa.eu/strategy-and-policy/priorities-2019-2024/promoting-our-european-way-life/migration-and-asylum/pact-migration-and-asylum/delivering-eu-pact-migration-and-asylum_en> accessed February 10, 2025.

467 European Commission (2023) *Historic Agreement Reached Today by the European Parliament and Council on the Pact on Migration and Asylum* <https://home-affairs.ec.europa.eu/news/historic-agreement-reached-today-european-parliament-and-council-pact-migration-and-asylum-2023-12-20_en> accessed February 10, 2025.

468 European Commission, "A New Pact on Migration and Asylum" (Communication) *COM* (2020) 609 final, September 23 <https://eur-lex.europa.eu/resource.html?uri=cellar:85ff8b4f-ff13-11ea-b44f-01aa75ed71a1.0002.02/DOC_3&format=PDF> accessed February 10, 2025.

469 European Commission, "New Pact on Migration and Asylum" <https://eur-lex.europa.eu/legal-content/EN/TXT/?uri=CELEX%3A52020DC0609> (2025) (Communication) *COM* (2020) 609 final, September 23, accessed February 10, 2025.

1.4.2 EU Law, the European Pact on Migration and Asylum, and the pivotal Principle of Non-Refoulement

The protection of the human rights of migrants and asylum applicants within the EU is grounded in several key legal provisions. The first legal framework is EU primary law, which includes the Treaty on European Union[470] (TEU), the Treaty on the Functioning of the European Union[471] (TFEU), and the EU Charter of Fundamental Rights of the European Union[472] (CFR), as well as secondary law, in particular the New Pact on Migration and Asylum, all of which must be applied in accordance with the CFR. The second legal regime is European human rights law, which includes the European Convention on Human Rights[473] (ECHR). This convention applies to all EU Member States and is incorporated into the Treaty on European Union[474] (TEU). While the ECHR does not explicitly address migrants or asylum applicants, the jurisprudence of the European Court of Human Rights (ECtHR) has established that several provisions—which include the fundamental *principle of non-refoulement*—are relevant to their protection and serve as the basis for other related obligations. International refugee and human rights law, which includes conventions adopted by the United Nations and ratified by EU Member States, makes a third legal framework. Among these instruments, the Refugee Convention[475] and its Protocol are particularly significant, as they are explicitly referenced in both the Treaty on the Functioning of the European Union (TFEU) and the EU Charter of Fundamental Rights.[476] Further discussion of the ECtHR's case law can be found in the chapter on human rights of migrants in times of emergency from an international law perspective.

Human rights are guaranteed under European law regardless of nationality. This section aims to examine the extensive legal provisions related

470 TEU, art 6; CFR, art 52.
471 TFEU, art 78.
472 CFR, art 19(2).
473 European Court of Human Rights, *European Convention on Human Rights* (Council of Europe) <https://www.echr.coe.int/documents/d/echr/convention_ENG> accessed February 10, 2025.
474 TEU, art 6; CFR, art 52.
475 UNHCR, *1951 Refugee Convention* <https://www.unhcr.org/uk/about-unhcr/overview/1951-refugee-convention> accessed February 10, 2025.
476 CFR, art 19(2).

to human rights within the framework of primary EU law and the new instruments introduced under the Pact, specifically focusing on protections afforded to migrants and asylum applicants. While it is essential to reference the relevant articles within the legal framework, a comprehensive analysis of each exceeds the scope of this chapter. Consequently, I will enumerate them without providing a detailed examination of each.

1. Treaty-based human rights protections. These treaties obligate EU Member States to adhere to fundamental rights when acting within the scope of EU law. Together, these instruments ensure a comprehensive legal framework for the protection of human rights across the EU.
   1.1. Treaty on European Union[477] (TEU) articles:
      1. Founding values of the EU, Article 2: This Article forms the basis for the protection of human rights, including those of migrants and asylum applicants. It highlights the EU's foundational values, including respect for human dignity, freedom, democracy, equality, the rule of law, and respect for human rights, including those of persons belonging to minorities.
      2. Broader commitment to promoting the EU's values in external relations, Article 3: This Article indirectly supports the human rights of migrants and asylum applicants by framing human rights protection as a key component of the EU's external and internal policies, including migration and asylum law
      3. Union's Accession to the European Convention on Human Rights, Article 6: This Article ensures that the EU is committed to respecting fundamental rights as guaranteed by the European Convention on Human Rights (ECHR). It also underscores the binding nature of the Charter of Fundamental Rights of the European Union (CFR) for EU institutions and Member States when implementing EU law.
   1.2. Treaty on the Functioning of the European Union[478] (TFEU) relevant Articles:

477 TEU <https://eur-lex.europa.eu/resource.html?uri=cellar:2bf140bf-a3f8-4ab2-b506-fd71826e6da6.0023.02/DOC_1&format=PDF> [2012] OJ C 326/13.

478 TFEU <https://eur-lex.europa.eu/legal-content/EN/TXT/PDF/?uri=CELEX:12012E/TXT&from=EN> [2012] OJ C 326/47.

1. Area of Freedom, Security and Justice, Article 67: Affirms the EU's commitment to ensuring a common policy on asylum, immigration, and external border control, based on solidarity and fair treatment, which includes the protection of fundamental rights, including the rights of asylum seekers and migrants.

Chapter 2 Policies on border checks, asylum and immigration:

2. Common European Asylum System (CEAS), Article 78: This Article establishes the legal foundation for a common asylum policy within the European Union, ensuring adherence to the 1951 Refugee Convention and other relevant international treaties. It serves as the legal basis for the development of the Common European Asylum System (CEAS) and outlines uniform standards for the treatment of third-country nationals in need of international protection. Moreover, it explicitly reaffirms compliance with the principle of non-refoulement.
3. Legal framework for the EU's common immigration policy, Article 79: Focuses on the conditions of entry and residence, and the rights of third-country nationals. It provides the basis for legislative measures concerning legal migration, including the integration of migrants and measures to prevent and combat irregular migration and human trafficking.
4. Solidarity and Fair Sharing of Responsibility, Article 80: Establishes the fundamental principle of solidarity and fair distribution of responsibilities among EU Member States in the implementation of asylum and migration policies. It underscores the necessity of a collective and coordinated approach to effectively manage these areas within the European Union.

1.3. The Charter of Fundamental Rights of the European Union[479]

The Charter consolidates the fundamental rights applicable within the EU and has been legally binding since the Treaty of Lisbon in 2009. It is organized into six titles: Dignity, Freedoms, Equality, Solidarity, Citizens' Rights, and

[479] European Parliament, "Charter of Fundamental Rights of the European Union" (2012) OJ C 326/391 <https://www.europarl.europa.eu/charter/pdf/text_en.pdf> accessed February 10, 2025.

Justice. The broad system of rights enjoyed by Europeans, including migrants and asylum applicants, must be upheld both in the actions of EU institutions and in the implementation of EU law by Member States. These are the relevant provisions of the Charter of Fundamental Rights (CFR) in the context of the human rights of migrants and asylum applicants in times of emergency:

1. Right to Human Dignity, Article 1: This Article upholds the principle of human dignity, which serves as the foundational element of all rights enshrined within the Charter.
2. Prohibition of Torture, Inhuman, or Degrading Treatment or Punishment, Article 4: This fundamental right is absolute and applies universally, guaranteeing that no individual, including migrants and asylum seekers, may be subjected to such inhumane practices under any circumstances.
3. Right to Liberty and Security, Article 6: This provision affirms that no individual shall be deprived of their liberty except in narrowly defined situations, such as lawful detention following a criminal conviction or during immigration control procedures, and solely in accordance with established legal norms. The right to liberty and security protects individuals from arbitrary detention, ensuring that any deprivation of liberty is lawful, necessary, proportionate and subject to judicial scrutiny. This right is essential for safeguarding both citizens and non-citizens, including migrants and asylum seekers, within the EU.
4. Right to Respect for Private and Family Life, including Family Reunification under EU Law, Article 7: In the realm of migration, this right encompasses family reunification, permitting migrants and asylum seekers to be reunited with their family members under specified conditions. EU law underscores that any limitations on family life must be proportionate and legally substantiated. This right serves as a vital protection for the preservation of family unity within the EU, particularly for migrants and refugees seeking protection or legal residency.
5. Right to the Protection of Personal Data, Article 8: This provision guarantees individuals control over their personal information, ensuring that such data is processed in a fair, transparent, and secure manner. It further establishes that personal data can only be collected and utilized for specific, legitimate purposes, and that individuals must be duly

informed regarding the use of their data. In the context of migration, this right assumes particular importance, as the processing of personal data—such as biometric information, asylum applications, and other sensitive details—must adhere to stringent privacy protection standards.

6. Freedom of Expression and Information, Article 11: This provision encompasses the freedom to hold opinions, express ideas, and receive and disseminate information without interference from public authorities. It protects the diversity of the media and the right of individuals, including migrants and asylum seekers, to seek, receive and impart information freely.
7. Right to Education, Article 14: This provision guarantees access to educational opportunities for all individuals, without discrimination, and ensures that education contributes to the development of personal abilities and full societal participation. In the context of migration, this right is of particular significance for children of migrants and asylum seekers, as it ensures their access to the same educational opportunities as nationals. The Article further underscores that access to education must be available at all levels, from primary to higher education, and that individuals, including those with special educational needs, should receive adequate support to fully benefit from education.
8. Freedom to Choose an Occupation and Right to Engage in Work, Article 15: This provision affirms that individuals, including migrants and asylum seekers, have the right to seek employment, pursue their chosen profession, and engage in work under conditions of equality and non-discrimination. The right to choose an occupation is fundamental to personal freedom and economic empowerment, and in the context of migration, it plays a pivotal role in facilitating the integration of migrants and asylum seekers into the labor market.
9. Right to Asylum, Article 18: This provision explicitly recognizes the right to asylum in accordance with the 1951 Geneva Convention on Refugees and EU treaties. It affirms that individuals fleeing persecution are entitled to seek asylum within the EU, in line with both the Refugee Convention and EU asylum policies. It ensures protection for those at risk of persecution based on factors such as race, religion, nationality, membership in a particular social group, or political opinion. The right to asylum is essential in safeguarding human rights, ensuring

that individuals with a genuine need for international protection are not returned to countries where they face significant harm or danger. Although the application of this right is subject to legal procedures and conditions, the Charter highlights the EU's commitment to uphold the dignity of asylum seekers and provide them with a fair and transparent process.

10. Principle of Non-Refoulement, Article 19: This provision prohibits collective expulsions and ensures that no individual is returned to a country where they face serious risks, such as the death penalty, torture, or inhuman or degrading treatment or punishment. As a fundamental principle of international refugee law, it is vital for the protection of migrants, asylum seekers and refugees within the EU. It guarantees that no individual will be deported to a place where their life, freedom, or safety would be threatened. The prohibition of refoulement applies not only to those seeking asylum but also to individuals at risk of serious harm upon return. This principle reflects the EU's commitment to uphold human rights and dignity, and serves as a critical safeguard in protecting vulnerable individuals within its borders.
11. Prohibition of Discrimination, Article 21: This provision prohibits discrimination on various grounds, including race, ethnicity, nationality, sex, religion, language, disability, age, or sexual orientation. It ensures that all individuals, including asylum seekers and migrants, are treated with equality and dignity, regardless of their background or status. In the context of asylum seekers, this prohibition is particularly significant, as it guarantees that they will not be subjected to discriminatory treatment during the asylum process. It protects them from unequal or unjust treatment based on factors such as race, ethnicity, nationality, or any other characteristic irrelevant to their eligibility for protection.
12. Equality between Women and Men, Article 23: This provision guarantees gender equality in all spheres, including within the contexts of migration and asylum. It ensures that no discrimination occurs based on gender, thereby affirming the equal entitlement of both women and men to fair treatment and opportunities. In the context of asylum seekers and migrants, this right is particularly vital for safeguarding women against gender-based violence, exploitation and discrimination—issues that disproportionately affect female asylum seekers.

13. Rights of the Child, Article 24: This Article ensures that children, including those who are migrants or asylum seekers, receive special protection and care in all matters affecting their welfare. It affirms that children have the right to freely express their views on matters that affect them, with due consideration given to their age and maturity, and that their best interests must be a primary consideration in all actions and decisions. The provision also ensures children's access to education, healthcare, and social services. In the context of migration and asylum, this Article underscores the importance of protecting children's rights, ensuring their protection from exploitation, neglect, or harm, and prioritizing their welfare throughout the asylum process. It reflects the EU's commitment to safeguarding the rights and dignity of children, particularly vulnerable groups such as unaccompanied minors.
14. Social Security and Social Assistance, Article 34: This provision guarantees access to social security and social assistance, ensuring that individuals, including migrants and asylum seekers, can access essential social services and benefits when in need. It aims to protect individuals from poverty and social exclusion by ensuring access to necessary resources such as healthcare, unemployment benefits, and housing support, in accordance with national laws and practices. In the context of migration, this right is especially significant, as it ensures that individuals who are temporarily unable to work or support themselves due to their status as asylum seekers or migrants are not left without basic necessities. The provision reflects the EU's commitment to fostering social inclusion and ensuring that vulnerable individuals, including migrants, have access to the resources and support necessary for their well-being and integration into society.
15. Healthcare, Article 35: This Article guarantees the right to medical care for all individuals, including migrants and asylum seekers, in the event of illness or injury. It upholds the principle that healthcare services must be available, accessible and of adequate quality, with particular attention to the needs of vulnerable groups, including migrants. In the context of migration and asylum, this provision is especially important for ensuring that asylum seekers, refugees, and other migrants receive necessary healthcare, including both physical and mental health services, during their stay in the EU. While Member States retain responsibility

for organizing and financing their healthcare systems, the provision mandates that individuals cannot be denied essential health services, particularly in emergency situations or where specific needs arise due to their status.

16. Right to Good Administration, Article 41: This provision guarantees that every individual, including migrants and asylum seekers, has the right to have their affairs handled impartially, fairly and within a reasonable time by EU institutions and bodies. It includes the right to be heard before decisions affecting one's rights are made, the right to access one's file, and the obligation for the administration to provide reasons for its decisions. In the context of asylum procedures, this right is critical for ensuring that individuals are treated with fairness and transparency throughout the application process for international protection. It requires authorities to act efficiently, with respect for individual rights, ensuring that asylum seekers and migrants are not subjected to arbitrary or unjust treatment by administrative bodies. The right to good administration is fundamental to ensuring accountability and maintaining trust in the functioning of EU institutions, particularly in migration and asylum processes.
17. Right to an Effective Remedy and a Fair Trial, Article 47: This provision guarantees the right to an effective remedy and a fair trial, a fundamental right for asylum seekers challenging decisions on their claims.

1.4. The European Pact on Migration and Asylum[480]

1.4.1. Reform of the CEAS 2016 and the European Pact on Migration and Asylum 2020

In response to the dramatic influx of approximately one million migrants entering EU territory in 2015, the Commission acted swiftly by proposing new, robust and sustainable Common European Asylum System.[481]

---

480 European Commission, *Delivering on the New Pact on Migration and Asylum* (no date) <https://commission.europa.eu/strategy-and-policy/priorities-2019-2024/promoting-our-european-way-life/migration-and-asylum/pact-migration-and-asylum/delivering-eu-pact-migration-and-asylum_en> accessed February 10, 2025.

481 European Commission, "Communication from the Commission to the European Parliament, the European Council and the Council: The Reform of the Common European Asylum System and Enhancing Legal Migration" (2016) *COM* 197 final

It presented seven proposals in 2016[482] to create a fairer, more efficient and more sustainable system for allocating asylum applications among Member States,[483] which however proved unsuccessful. In 2021, only Regulation 2021/2303,[484] establishing the EU Asylum Agency, was formally adopted. This Regulation was separated from the broader reform package.[485]

The Pact was relaunched when the Commission presented the so-called New Pact on Migration and Asylum on September 23, 2020.[486] Alongside non-legislative initiatives, the Pact represents a new approach to managing migration. Over three years later, the European Parliament[487] and the Council reached a political agreement on five of the key files in a historic breakthrough.[488] Following a political agreement on December 20, 2023,

---

<https://eur-lex.europa.eu/legal-content/EN/TXT/PDF/?uri=CELEX:52016DC0197> accessed February 10, 2025.

482 European Parliament, "Reform of the Common European Asylum System (CEAS)" (no date) <https://www.europarl.europa.eu/legislative-train/carriage/reform-of-the-common-european-asylum-system-(ceas)/report?sid=7901> accessed February 10, 2025.

483 European Commission, "Press Release: The Reform of the Common European Asylum System and Enhancing Legal Migration" (2016) (December 16, 6) <https://ec.europa.eu/commission/presscorner/detail/en/ip_16_1620> accessed February 10, 2025.

484 Regulation (EU) 2021/2303 of the European Parliament and of the Council of December 15, 2021 establishing the European Union Agency for Asylum [2021] OJ L 468/1 <https://eur-lex.europa.eu/legal-content/EN/TXT/PDF/?uri=CELEX:32021R2303> accessed February 10, 2025.

485 European Council on Refugees and Exiles (ECRE), "Editorial: EU Asylum Agency Moving Forward and the End of the Package Approach" (ECRE [publication date]) <https://ecre.org/editorial-eu-asylum-agency-moving-forward-and-the-end-of-the-package-approach/> accessed February 10, 2025.

486 European Commission, "Proposal for a Regulation of the European Parliament and of the Council Establishing a Common European Asylum System and a Union Resettlement Framework" (2020) COM (2020) 610 final <https://eur-lex.europa.eu/resource.html?uri=cellar:85ff8b4f-ff13-11ea-b44f-01aa75ed71a1.0002.02/DOC_3&format=PDF> accessed February 10, 2025.

487 European Parliament, "Study on the Implementation of the Common European Asylum System: Challenges and Opportunities" (2021) IPOL/STU2021697130 EN <https://cdn.ceps.eu/wp-content/uploads/2021/09/IPOL_STU2021697130_EN.pdf> accessed February 10, 2025.

488 European Commission, *Historic Agreement Reached Today by the European Parliament and Council on the Pact on Migration and Asylum* (2023) <https://home-affairs.ec.europa.eu/news/historic-agreement-reached-today-european-

a total of ten new legislative texts were adopted by the European Parliament on April 10, 2024, and subsequently by the Council on May 14. On April 10, 2024, the European Parliament voted in favor of the new rules on migration, followed by their formal adoption by the Council of the EU, on May 14, 2024.[489] The legal instruments of the Pact entered into force on June 11, 2024 and will enter into force in June 2026. Together, these reforms will establish a new legal foundation for a fairer and more efficient system of migration management.

The term "Pact" was selected to reflect the Commission's attempt to reconcile the divisions among Member States in the Council, with the initial proposals incorporating compromises to address the varying positions of different groups. Eastern Member States, particularly the Visegrad Group,[490] resisted the relocation of asylum seekers, while Northern and Western Member States emphasized responsibility, and Southern Member States—the so-called EU Med Group[491]—championed the principle of solidarity. An agreement has been reached on legislative acts covering various aspects, from arrival in the EU territory to reception conditions, the rights of individuals in need of international protection, the processing of asylum claims, and the expulsion of those deemed not to require such protection. These instruments represent the third phase of the Common European Asylum System (CEAS), replacing the second-phase instruments adopted in 2013.

The European Pact on Migration and Asylum comprises ten key legislative instruments designed to harmonize asylum and migration policies across the European Union. Spanning approximately 1,500 pages, the Pact introduces the following ten instruments along with their key developments:

---

parliament-and-council-pact-migration-and-asylum-2023-12-20_en> accessed February 10, 2025.

489 European Commission, "Timeline Progress on the Pact—Adoption" (May 2024) <https://home-affairs.ec.europa.eu/sites/default/files/styles/oe_theme_medium_no_crop/public/2024-05/timeline%20progress%20on%20the%20pact-adoption-05-2024.jpg?itok=zsYppfh5> accessed February 10, 2025.

490 Zielonka J., *The Visegrad Group: A Study in Regional Cooperation* (Oxford: Oxford University Press 2017).

491 European Parliament, "The Role of the EU Med Group in Shaping Migration Policy" (2020) IPOL/STU20201234 EN <https://www.europarl.europa.eu/thinktank/en/document.html?reference=IPOL-STU20201234> accessed February 10, 2025.

1. The Asylum Procedures Regulation[492] establishes one truly common procedure for international protection, ensuring timely, fair and efficient assessments. It enhances procedural guarantees for asylum seekers, including access to legal assistance and safeguards against arbitrary detention. It establishes a common procedure for deciding on an asylum application, while trying to limit abuse and remove incentives for secondary movements across the EU. Chapter III provides special procedures (accelerated, border and subsequent application) as well as the concept of a safe country. Together with the Return Border Procedure Regulation it also establishes a mandatory border procedure for both the asylum and return process at the external border.
2. The Return Border Procedure Regulation[493] revises the rules governing the return of third-country nationals who do not have legal residence status within the EU. The regulation emphasizes the humane treatment of such individuals and the effective enforcement of the return decisions.
3. The revised Reception Conditions Directive[494] establishes minimum standards for the treatment of applicants, encompassing housing, healthcare and education, to ensure adequate living conditions for individuals arriving in the EU and seeking international protection. Additionally, it introduces new grounds for detention and grants earlier access to the labor market.

---

492 "Proposal for a Regulation of the European Parliament and of the Council Establishing a Common Procedure for International Protection in the Union and Repealing Directive 2013/32/EU" [2016] COM(2016) 467 final <https://eur-lex.europa.eu/legal-content/EN/TXT/?uri=celex:52016PC0467> accessed February 10, 2025.

493 Regulation (EU) 2024/1349 of the European Parliament and of the Council of May 14, 2024 establishing a return border procedure, and amending Regulation (EU) 2021/1148 [2024] OJ L119/1, Regulation - EU - 2024/1349 - EN - EUR-Lex <https://eur-lex.europa.eu/eli/reg/2024/1349/oj> accessed February 10, 2025.

494 Directive (EU) 2024/1346 of the European Parliament and of the Council of May 14, 2024 laying down standards for the reception of applicants for international protection (recast) <https://eur-lex.europa.eu/legal-content/EN/TXT/PDF/?uri=CELEX:32024L1346> accessed February 10, 2025.

4. The Qualification Regulation[495] replaces the Qualification Directive, incorporating the principles of the Geneva Convention into EU law. Its primary objective is to ensure that Member States apply common criteria for determining eligibility for international protection. Additionally, it defines the rights and obligations of beneficiaries of international protection, thereby harmonizing the recognition of refugee status and subsidiary protection across the European Union. The regulation also introduces measures to discourage secondary movements and provides for the potential mandatory participation in integration programs.
5. The EU Asylum Agency Regulation[496] (EUAA): establishes the European Union Agency for Asylum to support Member States in implementing EU asylum policies and provide operational assistance.
6. The Eurodac Regulation[497] will transform the existing Eurodac database from an asylum-focused system into a comprehensive asylum and migration database. The updated database is designed to support the asylum system, facilitate the management of irregular migration, and contribute to the implementation of the Resettlement Regulation and the Temporary Protection Directive. It will be integrated into the EU's interoperability framework, ensuring seamless connectivity with other EU databases. Key developments include enhancements in the collection and storage of biometric data, including fingerprints, to strengthen security and improve the identification process; an expanded scope covering a broader range of individuals and incorporating more comprehensive information, a transition from an application-centered to an applicant-centered approach.

---

495 Regulation (EU) 2024/1347 of the European Parliament and of the Council of May 14, 2024 on standards for the qualification of third-country nationals or stateless persons as beneficiaries of international protection <https://eur-lex.europa.eu/legal-content/EN/TXT/PDF/?uri=CELEX:32024R1347> accessed February 10, 2025.

496 Regulation (EU) 2021/2303 of the European Parliament and of the Council of December 15, 2021 on the European Union Agency for Asylum and repealing Regulation (EU) No. 439/2010 [2021] OJ L468/1 <https://eur-lex.europa.eu/legal-content/EN/TXT/?uri=CELEX:32021R2303> accessed February 10, 2025.

497 Regulation (EU) 2024/1347 of the European Parliament and of the Council of May 14, 2024 on the establishment of "Euroda" <https://eur-lex.europa.eu/eli/reg/2024/1358/oj/eng> accessed February 10, 2025.

7. The Asylum and Migration Management Regulation[498] (AMMR) introduces a replacement for the Dublin Regulation and establishes a solidarity mechanism aimed at enhancing EU migration and asylum policies. The regulation outlines the nature and structure of this solidarity mechanism, specifying the timelines and scope for the inclusion of beneficiaries. Additionally, it emphasizes the role of the European Union Agency for Asylum (EUAA) in supporting the solidarity mechanism, managing migration, providing information, and coordinating the Dublin network. Articles 3, 4, and 5 of the AMMR set out key provisions that contribute to the regulation's comprehensive approach to asylum and migration management. Recital 2 of the AMMR states that this comprehensive approach comprises both internal and external components. The internal component, defined in Article 4 of the AMMR, includes cooperation and mutual partnerships between EU institutions and Member States, ensuring prompt and efficient access to asylum procedures and reception conditions for applicants, effective border management, prevention of onward movement, and efficient management of returns. The external component, as outlined in Article 5, establishes a direct link between asylum policies and external relations. It includes initiatives such as the promotion of legal migration and pathways, addressing the root causes and drivers of irregular migration and forced displacement, and enhancing the effectiveness of return, readmission and reintegration processes, as well as visa policies.
8. The Union Resettlement and Humanitarian Admission Framework Regulation[499] aims to enhance safe and legal pathways to the EU for individuals in need of protection, while also strengthening international partnerships with non-EU countries hosting significant refugee populations. Participation is voluntary, and the regulation provides the

---

498 Regulation (EU) 2024/1351 of the European Parliament and of the Council of May 14, 2024 on asylum and migration management [2024] OJ L 186/1 <https://eur-lex.europa.eu/eli/reg/2024/1351/oj/eng> accessed February 10, 2025.

499 Regulation (EU) 2024/1350 of the European Parliament and of the Council of May 14, 2024 establishing a Union Resettlement and Humanitarian Admission Framework, and amending Regulation (EU) 2021/1147 [2024] OJ L119/1 <https://eur-lex.europa.eu/eli/reg/2024/1350/oj/eng> accessed February 10, 2025.

possibility to assist Member States in implementing their plans. The EUAA is tasked with coordinating technical cooperation in this context.

9. The Crisis and Force Majeure Regulation[500] establishes mechanisms to address crisis situations, including cases of instrumentalization or force majeure, by enabling temporary measures to manage exceptional migratory pressures. It also provides for derogations and solidarity measures for Member States.
10. The Screening Regulation[501] establishes uniform rules to ensure the thorough screening and proper registration of irregular migrants and asylum seekers entering the EU, creating a seamless link to subsequent return or asylum procedures. It sets out procedures for screening individuals at the EU's external borders to identify vulnerabilities and determine the appropriate course of action.

Key aspects of the Screening Regulation include the establishment of a screening procedure at the EU's external borders, provisions on the location of screening and the legal fiction of non-entry, and the role of EUAA in the screening process, including information provision, debriefing, and other related activities.

1.4.2 The Common Implementation Plan for the European Pact on Migration and Asylum[502]

Based on the common implementation plan, Member States were required to establish a National Implementation Plan by December 12, 2024. This plan was to have outlined the necessary actions and a timeline for their

500 Regulation (EU) 2024/1359 of the European Parliament and of the Council *of* May 14, 2024 addressing situations of crisis and force majeure in the field of migration and asylum and amending Regulation (EU) 2021/1147 [2024] OJ L119/98 <https://eur-lex.europa.eu/eli/reg/2024/1359/oj/eng> accessed February 10, 2025.

501 Regulation (EU) 2024/1356 of the European Parliament and of the Council of May 14, 2024 introducing the screening of third-country nationals at the external borders and amending Regulations (EC) No. 767/2008 (EU) 2017/2226, (EU) 2018/1240, and (EU) 2019/817 [2024] OJ L119/58 <https://eur-lex.europa.eu/eli/reg/2024/1356/oj/eng> accessed February 10, 2025.

502 European Commission, *Migration and Asylum: Commission Presents Common Implementation Plan to Ensure Readiness by July 2026*, Press Release, June 12, 2024) <https://ec.europa.eu/commission/presscorner/detail/en/ip_24_3161>.

implementation. Each Member State must complete the full implementation of its plan by July 1, 2026. As part of the measures to be undertaken by Member States to implement the new system, the European Commission encourages a comprehensive review of existing capacities, particularly in terms of human resources. This includes assessing current personnel levels, identifying recruitment needs, and ensuring adequate training. The National Implementation Plan should provide a clear framework reflecting the present workforce, specifying required increases, and detailing a structured approach for recruitment and training, including specific timelines for implementation. The successful execution of the Common Implementation Plan depends on the parallel development of several interdependent legal, technical and operational building blocks, which include:

1. A Common Migration and Asylum Information System (Eurodac): The reformed Eurodac system is a large-scale IT database designed to support Member States in determining responsibility for asylum claims and monitoring secondary movements. Its timely development and operationalization are critical preconditions for the implementation of the broader elements of the Pact.
2. A New System for Managing Migration at the EU External Borders: This system aims to regulate the irregular arrival of non-EU nationals through fast, efficient and harmonized asylum and return procedures while ensuring strong legal safeguards. The Screening Regulation, the Asylum Procedure Regulation, and the Regulation on a Return Border Procedure introduce a standardized process in which all irregular migrants undergo screening for identity, security risk, vulnerability and health. Additionally, a mandatory border procedure applies to those unlikely to qualify for international protection or those presenting security concerns.
3. Ensuring Adequate Reception Conditions: Reception standards are aligned with the specific needs of applicants, including earlier access to the labor market (six months instead of nine), enhanced physical and mental healthcare, and strengthened protections for families, children and vulnerable applicants. The revised Reception Conditions Directive introduces measures to enhance the efficiency of reception systems and prevent secondary movements. For instance, Member States may assign

applicants to specific accommodations or geographic locations, and may link the provision of material reception conditions to compliance with designated residence requirements.

4. Fair, Efficient and Convergent Asylum Procedures: The Asylum Procedure Regulation and the Qualification Regulation harmonize asylum decision-making processes across Member States. These regulations ensure procedural efficiency while reinforcing safeguards, rights, and guarantees for applicants and beneficiaries of international protection.
5. Effective and Fair Return Procedures: A sustainable EU migration policy necessitates the efficient return of individuals without a legal right to remain in the EU. The newly established Return Coordinator will oversee joint planning of return operations, optimize Frontex support, and facilitate cooperation on returnees, including those posing security risks.
6. A Fair and Efficient Responsibility-Sharing Mechanism: The new responsibility-sharing framework seeks to establish a more effective and stable allocation of responsibilities across the EU while reducing incentives for secondary movements. This includes the introduction of "take-back" notifications and measures to prevent system abuse, such as the obligation for applicants to submit their asylum claims in the first Member State of entry.
7. A Legally Binding but still Flexible Solidarity Mechanism: For the first time, the EU has introduced a permanent and legally binding solidarity framework to ensure that no Member State faces migratory pressure alone.
8. Preparedness, Contingency Planning and Crisis Response: Enhanced mechanisms will strengthen Member States' resilience to evolving migratory situations and mitigate potential crises.
9. Enhanced Safeguards for Asylum Applicants and Vulnerable Persons: Fundamental rights monitoring has been strengthened to ensure procedural fairness while safeguarding human dignity and ensuring an effective right to asylum, particularly for vulnerable groups such as children.
10. Resettlement, Inclusion, and Integration: Increased efforts will be dedicated to supporting Member States in integrating and including

migrants, which remains a cornerstone of a sustainable migration and asylum policy.

1.4.3 Conclusions

In conclusion, while the European Union has made significant strides in advancing the protection of migrants' and asylum applicants' human rights through a combination of primary and secondary legal frameworks, the ultimate success of these efforts will depend on the effective implementation of the European Pact on Migration and Asylum. The Pact introduces a series of legislative instruments that aim to create a more cohesive and equitable migration system across the EU. However, the true test lies in its practical application. Despite the absence of a transposition phase—since most of the adopted instruments are regulations—the implementation phase will likely present considerable challenges. Only time will tell if the EU can successfully navigate the complexities of these reforms, addressing the varying national interests and ensuring that the fundamental rights of migrants and asylum applicants are adequately protected in practice. The transition from adoption to execution may prove to be as demanding as the negotiation and approval phases—if not more so—and will ultimately determine the long-term effectiveness of the EU's human rights protections for migrants and asylum applicants.

1.5 Human rights in times of emergency: international law perspective (Anna Chmielarz-Grochal)

1.5.1 Introduction

Human rights protection has been—and continues to be—a persistent challenge for modern states at both national and international levels. It has acquired particular importance in the era of migration, especially in emergency situations, which may be caused by such specific circumstances as war, terrorism, pandemics, economic crisis, or climate change.[503] The mass migrations observed over recent years, driven by economic, social, and religious factors—and intensified by the COVID-19 pandemic and the war

---

503 See more <https://publications.iom.int/system/files/pdf/pub2023-047-l-world-migration-report-2024_0.pdf> accessed September 30, 2024.

in Ukraine—raise important questions about the scope and effectiveness of international legal protection. International human rights law is aimed at protecting fundamental rights even in crisis situations, while respecting the state sovereignty. Furthermore, among the rights guaranteed by international law are the fundamental rights to which every human being is entitled, regardless of nationality and circumstances.[504] Universal standards for the protection of human rights are set by the 1948 Universal Declaration of Human Rights (UDHR).[505] Although it is not legally binding (a *soft-law* source), its provisions have provided a model for many international human rights treaties. The Declaration is based on the premise that fundamental freedoms and rights belong to every human being, and that they are inalienable and equally applicable to everyone. It sets out the fundamental principles of human rights, such as universality, interdependence, indivisibility, equality and non-discrimination.

Mass migration is a social phenomenon that European countries must address, particularly with the support of international organizations such as the Council of Europe or the European Union (EU).[506] In situations of particular risk, such as armed conflicts or pandemics, like the recent COVID-19 pandemic, appropriate instruments and effective mechanisms for the protection of fundamental rights should be applied.[507] European law provides a sufficiently high standard of human rights protection, but does not eliminate the risk to state and citizen security, especially with increased influxes of irregular migrants, including third-country nationals. This entails the need for European countries to introduce and apply legal restrictions on the entry and stay of foreigners on their territories.

---

504 See "Note on International Protection: Note by the High Commissioner" (2022) 34(3–4) *International Journal of Refugee Law*, 489–504 <https://doi.org/10.1093/ijrl/eeac044>.

505 See <https://www.un.org/en/about-us/universal-declaration-of-human-rights> accessed September 30, 2024.

506 For a general characterization of European standards for the protection of human rights, their instruments and mechanisms, see Karska E., Morawska E. H., Czepek J., Dąbrowski Ł. D., Oręziak B., and Gałka K., *Human Rights in the European Paradigm of the Protection of Aliens* (Warszawa 2023) 21–70.

507 See *inter alia* de Pooter H., "Pandemie et migrations," in T. Fleury Graff, P. Jacob (eds), *Migrations et droit international* (Paris 2022) 273–302; Lagrance P., *La protection internationale face aux nouveaux conflits*, in *Migrations* …, 439–454.

The multiplicity of international human rights instruments makes it impossible to discuss them in detail, even with regard to the legal situation of migrants[508] in times of emergency. In this chapter I focus my attention on the human rights guarantees set out in the Convention for the Protection of Human Rights and Fundamental Freedoms (1950)[509] and its additional protocols. The Convention does not *verba legis* refer to migration or migrants' rights, but its provisions guarantee the rights and freedoms of all persons who are under the jurisdiction of a State Party, regardless of their citizenship of that state. Foreign nationals may therefore enjoy the protection guaranteed by the ECHR, but in situations of particular risk, the Convention rights may be subject to limitations. The provisions of the ECHR also play a crucial role in shaping the interpretation of European Union regulations concerning foreigners, including those seeking international protection. European standards for the protection of human rights, including those of migrants, are defined and developed by the European Court of Human Rights (ECtHR). The jurisprudence of the ECtHR confirms the dynamism of the Convention and makes it a "living instrument" for the protection of human rights, adapted to changing living conditions, views, and events—such as the migration of people in emergency situations.[510] The Court takes into account the universal standards of human rights protection under international law. Its jurisprudence often serves as a point of reference for national courts and tribunals in cases related to the entry and residence of foreigners on the territories of individual European countries. The analysis of the ECHR's provisions and the ECtHR's jurisprudence should make it possible to answer the question of whether the Convention system allows for effective protection of the rights

508 The term "migrants" is used in this text in a broad sense, encompassing all persons moving voluntarily to improve their quality of life, as well as those forced to leave due to circumstances beyond their control, such as armed conflict, persecution or natural disasters. See: Office of the UN High Commissioner for Refugees, *Migrant Definition* <https://emergency.unhcr.org/protection/legal-framework/migrant-definition#0> accessed September 30, 2024.

509 Hereinafter also as: "European Convention on Human Rights," "Convention" or "ECHR." See <https://www.echr.coe.int/european-convention-on-human-rights> accessed September 30, 2024.

510 See more: Çalı B., Bianku L., and Motoc I., *Migration and the European Convention on Human Rights*, in B. Çalı, L. Bianku, and I. Motoc (eds), *Migration and the European Convention on Human Rights* (Oxford University Press 2021) 3–18.

of migrants—third-country nationals who seek protection in EU Member States in situations of particular risk.

1.5.2 Fundamental rights of migrants in international law

Migrants from countries outside the European Union who find themselves in crisis situations benefit from guarantees under the principles and norms of international law, most of which are contained in international agreements regulating human rights. These are both universal, such as the International Covenant on Civil and Political Rights (1966) and the International Covenant on Economic, Social and Cultural Rights (1966),[511] and regional, such as the Convention for the Protection of Human Rights and Fundamental Freedoms.[512] International human rights law is based on the recognition of the inherent dignity and the equal and inalienable rights of all members of the human community, which is the foundation of freedom, justice and world peace.[513] There are also international agreements that deal strictly with migrants. One can mention, for example, the International Convention on the Protection of the Rights of All Migrant Workers and Members of Their Families (1990).[514] In the case of refugees, the key document governing the scope of their protection is the Convention relating to the Status of Refugees, drawn up in Geneva on July 28, 1951 and supplemented by the 1967 Protocol.[515] The Convention not only addresses refugee status, but also defines

---

511 Other universal sources of international human rights law include, e.g., the International Convention on the Elimination of All Forms of Racial Discrimination (1965), Convention on the Elimination of All Forms of Discrimination against Women (1979), Convention against Torture and Other Cruel, Inhuman or Degrading Treatment or Punishment (1984), Convention on the Rights of the Child (1989), Declaration on the Protection of All Persons from Enforced Disappearances (1992), Convention on the Rights of Persons with Disabilities (2006).

512 Other regional sources of international human rights law include e.g., the African Charter on Human and Peoples' Rights (1981), the American Convention on Human Rights (1969), the Inter-American Convention to Prevent and Punish Torture (1985, the Inter-American Convention on Forced Disappearance of Persons (1994), the European Social Charter (1961) and the European Social Charter (Revised) (1996).

513 See the preambles to the UDHR, ICCPR and ICESCR.

514 See <https://www.ohchr.org/en/instruments-mechanisms/instruments/international-convention-protection-rights-all-migrant-workers> accessed September 30, 2024.

515 See: <https://www.unhcr.org/media/convention-and-protocol-relating-status-refugees> accessed September 30, 2024.

the right to asylum as a fundamental right for those who meet the criteria set out in the Convention. International human rights standards applicable to migrants can thus be found in various legal instruments. Nevertheless, migrants face various challenges or obstacles in the migration process and also in the countries of destination, especially irregular (undocumented) migrants.[516] The issue of human rights protection is very relevant today, as in addition to armed conflicts, international human rights law is confronted with challenges such as terrorism,[517] poverty,[518] climate change,[519] and pandemics.[520]

Human rights have historically been shaped in response to the needs of society, in connection with the development of states and democratic society, as well as in the wake of global phenomena or technological change.[521] Human rights scholarship generally distinguishes three generations of these rights: civil and political rights, economic, social and cultural rights, and freedoms and solidarity rights.[522] There are calls for the existence of a fourth generation of human rights, which is linked to, *inter alia*, the development of new technologies, bioethics, etc.[523] The basic content of human rights under

---

516 Arowolo G. A., "Protecting the Rights of Migrants: the Challenges and the Prospects" (2021) 105 *Journal of Law, Policy and Globalization*, 92–105.

517 Scheinin M., "Terrorism," in D. Moeckli, S. Shah, S. Sivakumaran, and D. J. Harris (eds), *International Human Rights Law* (Oxford University Press 2022) 605–621.

518 Marks S. P., "Poverty," in *International …*, 622–642.

519 Rajamani L., "Climate Change," in *International …*, 644–660.

520 Abraham M., "Pandemics," in *International …*, 661–679.

521 See *inter alia* Bates E., "History," in *International …*, 3–21; Nowak M., *Introduction to the International Human Rights Regime* (Leiden, Boston 2003) 9–32; Donnelly J., and Whelan D. J., *International Human Rights*, (London, New York: Routledge 2020) 3–16.

522 See *inter alia*: Pocar F., "Some Thoughts on the Universal Declaration of Human Rights and the "Generations" of Human Rights" (2015) 10 *Intercultural Human Rights Review*, 43–53; cf. Domaradzki S., Khvostova M., and Pupovac D., "Karel Vasak's Generations of Rights and the Contemporary Human Rights Discourse" (2019) 20 *Human Rights Review*, 423–443 <https://doi.org/10.1007/s12142-019-00565-x>.

523 See *inter alia*: Perepolkin S. M., Perepolkin D. S., Averianova M. V., "Typology of the Fourth Generation of Human Rights" (2021) 1 *Journal of International Legal Communication*, 91–101 <https://doi.org/10.32612/uw.27201643.2021.1>; López Baroni M. J., "Fourth Generation Human Rights in View of the Fourth Industrial Revolution" (2024) 9 *Philosophies*, 39–54 <https://doi.org/10.3390/philosophies9020039> / <https://www.mdpi.com/journal/philosophies>.

international law is based on three levels of regulation. The first plane is basic human rights, which apply to everyone and in all circumstances, including in emergency situations. The second tier is the limitations on human rights permitted by law. The third tier comprises the derogation mechanism provided for in some human rights conventions.

Fundamental rights are guaranteed and protected in international law and are enjoyed by every human being, irrespective of nationality or social standing and regardless of circumstances. They are treated as inherent and inalienable rights of the individual, deriving from human dignity.[524] They are, in particular, the right to life, the right to protection of health, freedom from torture, inhuman or degrading treatment, the prohibition of forced labor and slavery. These are guaranteed by all universal sources of international human rights law, in particular the UDHR, the ICCPR and the ICESCR, and in the European region the ECHR.[525] In addition to the guarantees of life, liberty, personal rights and security, other rights or freedoms of a personal nature—as well as political rights and economic, social and cultural rights—are (respectively) normalized in these acts. The following can be mentioned: the right to privacy, freedom of thought, conscience and religion, freedom of expression, the right to freedom of movement, the right of assembly and association, the right to property, the right to work, the right to education, the right to social security, among others. Today, the Council of Europe's human rights system is the most developed in Europe and is based on values such as the rule of law, pluralism, democracy, human rights and civil liberties. The primary source of human rights in this system is the ECHR, whose provisions, subject to ongoing interpretation by the ECtHR, have a significant impact on the level of human rights protection in European countries. The condition of human rights is also influenced by other Council of Europe bodies and institutions.

Focusing specifically on migrants, the following principles of international law apply: 1) the principle of *non-refoulement*; 2) the prohibition of collective expulsion; 3) the principle of non-discrimination; and 4) the prohibition of

---

524 Wellman C., *An Approach to Rights: Studies in the Philosophy of Laws and Morals* (Dordrecht 1997), 81.

525 See Kälin W., and Künzli J., *The Law of International Human Rights Protection* (Oxford University Press 2019), 520–550.

racism and incitement to national, racial or religious hatred.[526] They set minimum standards for the protection of human rights. They can be described as principles of international migration law. They are legally binding on all states under customary international law and frequently under international agreements, which reinforces their normative significance. In addition, they are absolute and cannot be subject to any exceptions or derogations in any circumstances, including crisis situations. They apply to all migrants regardless of their legal status and factual circumstances.

For foreigners migrating in situations of acute emergency (war, political repression, a pandemic, etc.), access to international protection is fundamental. The Universal Declaration of Human Rights guarantees in Article 14(1) the right of everyone to seek and enjoy asylum in another country in the event of persecution. This means that, while states are not obliged to provide foreigners with access to territory, they should ensure that they have access to asylum procedures when they come under their jurisdiction. In turn, based on Article 13 of International Covenant on Civil and Political Rights, "An alien lawfully in the territory of a State Party to the present Covenant may be expelled therefrom only in pursuance of a decision reached in accordance with law and shall, except where compelling reasons of national security otherwise require, be allowed to submit the reasons against his expulsion and to have his case reviewed by, and be represented for the purpose before, the competent authority or a person or persons especially designated by the competent authority." Also, according to the Geneva Convention Relating to the Status of Refugees, asylum is a fundamental right and anyone fleeing persecution or other inhuman and degrading treatment in their country of origin has the right to seek such protection. Parties to this international agreement, including EU Member States, are obliged to grant this right to any person who fulfills the criteria set out therein. In contrast, while the European Convention on Human Rights does not regulate the issue of applying for or obtaining international protection, the ECtHR, in its jurisprudence, refers to the rules concerning the entry, exit and residence of foreigners on the territory of the States Parties to the Convention.[527]

---

526 More extensively Chetail V., *International Migration Law* (Oxford University Press 2019), 119–164.

527 This issue is covered more extensively in the following section.

The vast majority of human rights are not absolute and may be subject to limitations. Acts of international human rights law set a framework (criteria) for the permissibility of limitations to the rights guaranteed therein (so-called limitation clauses).[528] Most often, these clauses refer to specific human rights, which is justified by the possibility to adapt the basis of limitation to the specifics of individual rights.[529] However, they may be general in nature.[530] Irrespective of the construction of a limitation clause, limitations on fundamental rights are exceptionally permissible, and their application may arise from the need to protect both individual and public interests. Interference with fundamental rights must meet certain conditions, such as: (1) lawfulness, (2) necessity in a democratic society, and (3) pursuit of a legitimate aim. Subject to the principle of proportionality, restrictions may only be imposed if they are necessary and genuinely correspond to a legitimate aim, being compatible with other human rights, including the principle of non-discrimination. They must therefore be neither arbitrary nor discriminatory. The legitimate objectives of the restrictions are national security, public safety, public order, public health, public morals, or the rights and freedoms of others, etc. At the same time, the restrictions imposed must not affect the essence of the right in question.[531] Limitation clauses are relevant for the state as the entity empowered to impose restrictions on human rights, but also for the addressee of the right in question, who can challenge the permissibility of the interference. With regard to migrants, rights of a relative nature may include: the right to leave any country, the right to family life (as an obstacle to expulsion or as a basis for family reunification), the right to liberty and the prohibition of arbitrary detention, the right to freedom of movement within the territory of the state. In contrast, rights such as the prohibition of torture and the prohibition of inhuman or degrading treatment (absolute rights) are absolute.

---

528 See *inter alia* Bilgorajski A., "Boundaries an Limitations of Human Rights: A Contribution to the Discussion" (2023) 27 *Scientific Journal of Bielsko-Biala School of Finance and Law*, 70; Badar M. E., "Basic Principles Governing Limitations on Individual Rights and Freedoms in Human Rights Instruments" (2003) 7 *The International Journal of Human Rights*, 63–92.

529 See, notably, Article 8(2) and Article 10(2) ECHR, Article 12(3) and Article 19(3) ICCPR.

530 Article 29(2) of the Universal Declaration of Human Rights.

531 See, notably, Article 12(3) ICCPR and Article 4 ICESCR.

Some human rights conventions introduce a mechanism of so-called derogation.[532] It consists of the fact that, in particularly exceptional circumstances, states may derogate from their Convention obligations and thus suspend certain freedoms or rights, but provided that the conditions set out in international law are met together. The act of derogation results in state actions that violate freedoms and rights being treated as lawful. In contrast, there are some fundamental rights that cannot be subject to derogation, including, for example, the right to life; the prohibition of torture or cruel, inhuman or degrading treatment; the prohibition of slavery and servitude; and the rights to freedom of thought, conscience and religion. The catalog of such rights may vary slightly depending on the convention that provides for a derogation mechanism. In turn, the derogations applied by a state must be consistent with other legal obligations under customary international law and treaty law. Such a universal obligation requiring compliance in all circumstances is, in particular, the prohibition of discrimination. The protection of human life and health also falls into this category of international obligations that states must respect in all circumstances.[533]

1.5.3 The principle of *non-refoulement* in international human rights law

The principle of *non-refoulement* is a principle of international law that plays an important role in the protection of human rights. It provides a guarantee for the realization of the human right to seek international protection. This

---

532 See *inter alia*: Article 4(1) of International Covenant on Civil and Political Rights (ICCPR); Article 15(1) of European Convention on Human Rights; Article 27(1) American Convention on Human Rights; Article 4(1) Arab Charter on Human Rights; Article 35(1) Commonwealth of Independent States Convention on Human Rights and Fundamental Freedoms. However, the vast majority of human rights and migration conventions do not provide for a derogation mechanism, e.g., International Covenant on Economic, Social and Cultural Rights (ICESCR), Convention on the Elimination of All Forms of Racial Discrimination, Convention on the Rights of the Child, Convention on the Protection of the Rights of All Migrant Workers and Members of their Families, International Labour Organization (ILO) Migration for Employment Convention, ILO Migrant Workers (Supplementary Provisions) Convention, Protocol against the Smuggling of Migrants by Land, Sea and Air, and Protocol to Prevent, Suppress and Punish Trafficking in Persons.

533 See, more extensively, Chapter 1.6: Chlebny J., "Derogations in Time of Emergency," in *Legal Restrictions on Third-Country Nationals in EU Emergencies* (Peter Lang 2026).

principle has its basis in Article 33(1) of the Refugee Convention.[534] This provision prohibits the expulsion (*return*) or return (*rejection*) of an alien to the border of territories where his or her life or freedom would be threatened on account of his or her race, religion, nationality, membership of a particular social group or political opinion. In view of the need to respect the principle of *non-refoulement*, states are therefore obliged to allow a foreigner into their territory and to refrain from transferring him/her to the borders of another state where his/her rights would be threatened. On the other hand, granting protection to a person with a well-founded fear of persecution is a discretionary act of the state, undertaken in accordance with the provisions of national law, also taking into account European Union regulations. Thus, *non-refoulement* sets the limits of the responsibility of the state which expelled the foreigner or refused him/her entry.[535]

Non-refoulement is also referred to in other international law and human rights instruments, universal and regional, binding and *soft law*.[536] The personal and material scope of *non-refoulement* in international refugee law and international human rights law is not the same.[537] The scope of protection vis-à-vis foreigners is broader in the human rights legal system.[538]

In international human rights law, the prohibition of *refoulement* protects not only refugees but foreigners in general from being returned to a country where they would be at risk of torture or other inhuman and degrading treatment or punishment. It also covers those seeking international protection

534 Cf. Chlebny J., *Proceedings on the Granting of Refugee Status* (Warszawa 2011) 115–128; Moreno-Lax V., *Accessing Asylum in Europe, Extraterritorial Border Controls and Refugee Rights under EU Law* (Oxford University Press 2017) 286.

535 Chlebny J., *Proceedings …*, 120. See more extensively Chodorowska A., and Trylińska A., "The Concept of the Principle of Non-Refoulement in Refugee Law" (2021) 2 *Dyskurs Prawniczy i Administracyjny*, 7–23.

536 See more extensively Goodwin-Gil G. S., McAdam J., and Dunlop E., *The Refugee in International Law* (Oxford University Press 2021) 241–306.

537 Gilbert G., "Human Rights, Refugees and Other Displaced Persons in International Law," in E. de Wer, and J. Vidmar (eds), *Hierarchy in International Law: The Place of Human Rights* (Oxford University Press 2012) 189; Ragheboom H., *The International Legal Status and Protection of Environmentally Displaced Persons: A European Perspective* (Boston: Leiden 2017) 182.

538 See more extensively Moran C. F., "Strengthening the Principle of Non-refoulement" (2020) 25 *The International Journal of Human Rights*, 1032–1052 <https://doi.org/10.1080/13642987.2020.1811690> accessed September 30, 2024.

who have entered and are on the territory of the state concerned and those who have just reached the border, regardless of whether they have applied for international protection. Against being returned to a country where a foreigner would be at risk of torture, Article 3 of the Convention against Torture and Other Cruel, Inhuman or Degrading Treatment or Punishment (1984)[539] protects explicitly. This guarantee is complemented by the prohibition in Article 7 of the ICCPR of subjecting anyone to torture or cruel, inhuman or degrading treatment or punishment. In addition, from the requirement expressed in Article 2 of the ICCPR to respect and ensure the rights contained in the Covenant to all persons under the jurisdiction of a State Party follows the prohibition of extradition, deportation, expulsion or any other form of removal of a person from their territory if there is a real danger that irreparable harm, such as deprivation of life or torture or cruel, inhuman or degrading treatment, will be inflicted on that person, either in the country to which he or she is to be expelled or in any other country to which that person may consequently be expelled.[540]

While the principle of *non-refoulement* does not derive directly from the ECHR, it is affirmed and developed through ECtHR jurisprudence.[541] The Convention's prohibition of torture or cruel, inhuman or degrading treatment or punishment (Article 3) and the right to life (Article 2) complement *non-refoulement* and at the same time international protection standards.[542] In practice, these provisions of the Convention extend protection from

539 See <https://www.ohchr.org/en/instruments-mechanisms/instruments/convention-against-torture-and-other-cruel-inhuman-or-degrading> accessed September 30, 2024.

540 General comment No. 31 (80), The nature of the general legal obligation imposed on States Parties to the Covenant. Adopted by the Human Rights Committee at the Eightieth Session, CCPR/C/21/Rev.1/Add.13, March 29, 2004, §§ 10 and 12 <https://www.refworld.org/legal/general/hrc/2004/en/52451> accessed September 30, 2024.

541 See Furramani E., Bushati R., "The Principle of "Non-Refoulement" and its Evolution in the Jurisprudence of the European Court of Human Rights" (2022) 11 (3) *Academic Journal of Interdisciplinary Studies*, 107–120. <https://doi.org/10.36941/ajis-2022-007> accessed September 30, 2024.

542 See inter alia Wouters C. W., *International Legal Standards for the Protection from Refoulement: A Legal Analysis on the Prohibitions on Refoulement Contained in the Refugee Convention, the European Convention on Human Rights, the International Covenant on Civil and Political Rights, and the Convention Against Torture* (Leiden 2009).

refoulement to persons who wish to apply for international protection or whose applications have been rejected.[543] The application of the prohibition of *refoulement* is also linked to the right to liberty and security of person (Article 5) and guarantees of judicial protection (Article 6).[544]

Furthermore, in international human rights law the obligation to respect the principle of *non-refoulement* is absolute, which is justified by the absolute nature of the prohibition of torture and other cruel, inhuman or degrading treatment or punishment.[545] In contrast, exceptions to the prohibition of *refoulement* are permitted in the Geneva Convention, on the basis of Article 33(2), as well as Article 1(F), but at the same time the prohibition cannot be derogated from.[546] Finally, acts such as the ECHR provide for a mechanism for judicial review of compliance with the principle of *non-refoulement* in situations of violations of the rights of aliens.[547]

In conclusion, the principle of *non-refoulement* is one of the most important standards for dealing with migrants. It is central to international refugee law, although it covers all forms of international protection, not just refugee status as regulated by the Geneva Convention. The adoption of this principle in international human rights law has expanded the scope of the protection that it entails, as well as making *non-refoulement* an indispensable human rights protection requirement for states to respect. However, the contemporary migration crisis, especially in the European region, including the Polish-Belarusian border, does not favor the development of the principle

---

543 Chodorowska A., and Trylińska A., *The Concept …*, 9.

544 Cf. Ktistakis Y., *Protecting Migrants under the European Convention on Human Rights and the European Social Charter. A Handbook for Legal Practitioners* (Council of Europe, February 2013) 81–93.

545 Dean M., "Bridging the Gap: Humanitarian Protection and the Convergence of Laws in Europe" (2014) 20 *European Law Journal*, 45.

546 UNHCR, *Advisory Opinion on the Extraterritorial Application of Non-Refoulement Obligations under 1951 Convention relating to the Status of the Refugees and its 1967 Protocol* (January 26, 2007) <https://www.unhcr.org/media/advisory-opinion-extraterritorial-application-non-refoulement-obligations-under-1951-0> accessed September 30, 2024, 4–5.

547 Cf. Łachacz O., "Zasada non-refoulement w międzynarodowym prawie uchodźczym: zwyczaj międzynarodowy czy też peremptoryjna norma prawa międzynarodowego?" (2017) XV *Problemy Współczesnego Prawa Międzynarodowego, Europejskiego i Porównawczego*, 137, 139–140.

of *non-refoulement* as a peremptory norm of international law (*ius cogens*).[548] Currently, adherence to this principle requires states to balance refugee law, human rights and humanitarian law with the legitimate interests of the state to protect borders and stem the mass influx of migrants. In this context, the *refoulement* ban should be considered in a broad sense, taking into account the complementarity of the international human rights protection regime and refugee law. It should only be borne in mind that while in the case of human rights, crisis situations are part of the circumstances that justify their limitation and, in strictly defined circumstances, also the derogation of individual rights, the essence of refugee law is its operation in crisis and its construction as a response to crisis.[549]

1.5.4 Guarantees of migrants' rights in the European Convention on Human Rights

The European Convention on Human Rights, as is apparent from its Article 1, applies to all persons under the jurisdiction of States Parties to the agreement, whether or not they hold the nationality of that state. The freedoms and rights guaranteed by the ECHR, as enjoyed by everyone (*erga omnes*), therefore also apply to foreigners, including nationals of non-parties or stateless persons. This is confirmed by the ECtHR's jurisprudence, following individual complaints brought by migrant aliens against States Parties to the Convention. On the other hand, some provisions of the ECHR and its Additional Protocols refer explicitly or almost explicitly to aliens, such as Articles 5(1)(f), 6(3)(e) and 16 ECHR, Articles 2 and 4 of Protocol No. 4 and Article 1 of Protocol No. 7. In addition, Article 14 ECHR prohibits discrimination in the enjoyment of the rights guaranteed by the Convention on the basis of, *inter alia*, national origin, which is also a guarantee that applies to aliens. What remains to be considered is, firstly, whether the provisions of the ECHR provide for the possibility or necessity of special treatment for persons who are not nationals of a State Party. This is relevant in the context of migration caused by war or other extraordinary circumstances, such as the recent COVID-19 pandemic.

---

548 See Allain J., "The IUs Cogens Nature of Non-refoulement" (2001) 13 *International Journal of Refugee Law*, 533–558; cf. Łachacz O., *Zasada non-refoulement …*, 141–142.

549 See Łachacz O., *Zasada non-refoulement …*, 142; cf. Dauvergne C., "Refugee Law as Perpetual Crisis," in C. Harvey, and S. S. Juss (eds), *Contemporary Issues in Refugee Law* (Edward Elgar 2013) 14.

Indeed, these are exceptional situations, often emergencies in the case of mass migration, which may involve violations of fundamental rights justifying an individual complaint under Article 34 ECHR to the ECtHR. On the other hand, the possibility provided for in Article 15 ECHR to suspend (abrogate) the application of the obligations under the Convention in the event of war or other public danger threatening the life of the people of a State Party is analyzed later in the monograph.[550] Secondly, the question can be raised of whether, through *erga omnes* regulations, the Convention allows aliens a wider range of protection against unauthorized expulsion or return than the principle of *non-refoulement*.

Some of the rights guaranteed by the ECHR are of a specific nature, deriving from the need to protect values such as life or liberty and therefore linked most closely to human dignity. They are of an absolute nature, not subject to exceptions, limitations or derogations. These are the right to life (Article 2), the prohibition on torture and inhuman or degrading treatment (Article 3), the prohibition of slavery and forced labor (Article 4), and the right to liberty and security of person (Article 5).

The right to life is guaranteed as a fundamental right and its observance is an essential condition for the enjoyment of all other rights and freedoms. It requires special protection, which the Convention links to both negative and positive obligations for States Parties. Firstly, states are obliged to refrain from the intentional deprivation of life (an exception is set out in Article 2(2) ECHR and relates to situations where the use of force is absolutely necessary). Secondly, states are obliged to take appropriate measures to protect the lives of persons under their jurisdiction. They should adopt appropriate regulations for the protection of life and at the same time ensure their effective application. Under Article 15(2) ECHR, a state may not evade its obligations under Article 2 ECHR except in cases of death resulting from lawful acts of war. The Convention guarantee of the right to life is complemented by Additional Protocols: Protocol No. 6 concerning the abolition of the death

550 See Chapter 1.6: Chlebny J., "Derogations in Time of Emergency," in *Legal Restrictions on Third-Country Nationals in EU Emergencies* (Peter Lang 2026). See also: Braithwaite B., Harby C., and Miletić G. (eds), *The Protection of Human Rights during Times of Emergency: An Analysis of the Relevant Jurisprudence of the European Court of Human Rights through the Lens of the Covid-19 Pandemic* (London: AIRE Centre 2022) 198–215.

penalty (1983)[551] and Protocol No. 13 concerning the abolition of the death penalty in all circumstances (2002).[552] The provisions contained therein are neither subject to derogation under Article 15 ECHR, nor can states raise any reservations to them under Article 57 ECHR.

Another fundamental right subject to protection in all circumstances derives from Article 3 ECHR, which prohibits torture and inhuman or degrading treatment. This is an absolute right, not subject to exceptions, limitations or derogations. It belongs to the core values of a democratic society. States therefore have an obligation to ensure that anyone under their jurisdiction is effectively protected against violations of this prohibition. The guarantees under Article 3 ECHR apply to foreign nationals, e.g., those apprehended after crossing a border or held in detention. States are obliged to provide such persons with conditions respecting human dignity. It is a matter of ensuring that such persons are not subjected to hardship and suffering beyond the level of inconvenience inherent in deprivation of liberty and that their health and well-being are adequately safeguarded.

Another right that protects against arbitrary, unlawful deprivation of liberty is guaranteed by Article 5 ECHR. This is the right to liberty and security of person. In strictly defined situations, this right is subject to limitations, i.e., the state may deprive of liberty persons who threaten or violate public order or when they should suffer punishment for their actions. Article 5 ECHR enumerates exhaustively the cases in which deprivation of liberty is possible "in the manner prescribed by law." A legitimate reason for deprivation of liberty is to prevent the spread of infectious diseases (Article 5(1)(e)), which is relevant in situations similar to those like the recent COVID-19 pandemic. The lawful detention or arrest of a person to prevent his or her unlawful entry into the territory of a state, or of a person against whom expulsion or extradition proceedings are pending, is also permissible (Article 5(1)(f)).

---

551 See <https://www.coe.int/en/web/conventions/-/council-of-europe-protocol-no-6-to-the-convention-for-the-protection-of-human-rights-and-fundamental-freedoms-concerning-the-abolition-of-the-death-1> accessed September 30, 2024.

552 See <https://www.coe.int/en/web/conventions/-/council-of-europe-protocol-no-13-to-the-convention-for-the-protection-of-human-rights-and-fundamental-freedoms-concerning-the-abolition-of-the-death-1> accessed September 30, 2024.

The application of this provision is usually justified by the need to protect state security and public order.

Fundamental to the protection of individual rights is the principle of non-discrimination, which underpins the ECHR, as does the rule of law and values such as tolerance and social peace, as confirmed by the ECtHR in its jurisprudence.[553] The Convention contains in Article 14 the prohibition of discrimination in the enjoyment of the rights and freedoms guaranteed therein on various grounds, including race, color or national origin. This prohibition is not absolute and does not protect against every different treatment, but treatment that is different in similar situations. This means that the state does not have an absolute obligation to treat foreigners in the same way as its own citizens, but differences in treatment based on any criterion must be justified. The catalog of impermissible grounds for discrimination is open, and it cannot be excluded that a person's immigration status will fall within the category of "other grounds." The prohibition of discrimination is also not autonomous, as it applies only to situations of exercise of Convention rights.[554] In contrast, the general prohibition of discrimination derives from Protocol No. 12,[555] which, however, has not been ratified by all the ECHR States Parties.

The procedural guarantees that are relevant to ensure the effectiveness of the protection of fundamental rights are contained in Article 6 ECHR. This provision guarantees the right to a court and a fair trial, which is an expression of the rule of law. It also reaffirms the fundamental importance of the judiciary in the administration of justice. The exercise of the right to a court may be subject to certain limitations, which relate to the openness of court proceedings. These are permissible, *inter alia*, for reasons of morality, for reasons of public order or state security in a democratic society, when it serves to protect the private lives of the parties, or in special circumstances where publicity would be detrimental to the interests of justice.

---

553 See, notably, the judgment [Grand Chamber] of July 1, 2014, S.A.S. v. France, No. 43835/11, § 149.

554 Mousmouti M., "Aliens' Right Not to Be Discriminated Against (Article 14 and Protocol 12 ECHR)," in D. Moya, and G. Milios (eds), *Aliens before the European Court of Human Rights. Ensuring Minimum Standards of Human Rights Protection* (Leiden: Brill 2021) 211–234.

555 See <https://rm.coe.int/1680080622> accessed September 30, 2024.

The guarantees of the right to a court and a fair trial are particularly relevant in view of Article 13 ECHR. According to this provision, anyone whose rights and freedoms enshrined in the Convention have been violated has the right to an effective remedy before a competent state authority, and thus also before a court meeting the requirements under Article 6 ECHR. The right to a tribunal and the right to an effective remedy are universal, so everyone, including foreigners, should have access to effective legal protection under national law when their rights or freedoms are violated.

The provisions of the ECHR that can be applied to foreigners as a specific group of addressees of the rights guaranteed therein are Articles 5(1)(f) and 6(3)(e). As already indicated, Article 5 ECHR ensures everyone the right to liberty and security of person, linked to the prohibition of deprivation of liberty, apart from certain exceptions. One of the exceptions concerns foreign nationals: Article 5(1)(f) provides for the possibility of deprivation of liberty in the event of the lawful arrest or detention aimed at preventing unlawful entry into the territory of the state, or when deportation or extradition proceedings are pending. The detention of migrants is therefore permissible if it is to prevent their illegal entry into the state's territory or to carry out deportation proceedings. Of course, it must not be arbitrary and must have a basis in national law, in which judicial review should also be ensured (Article 5(4) ECHR).

An important guarantee under the Convention for foreign complainants who have been charged with a criminal offense is the right to the free assistance of an interpreter if they do not understand or speak the language used in court. The procedural guarantee under Article 6(3)(e) ECHR is important for the effective defense of rights before the court and, more broadly, for the fairness and justice of the judicial process. The obligation to provide the free assistance of an interpreter is incumbent on the state and is linked to the broader obligation to organize the criminal justice system in a manner consistent with the requirements of Article 6 ECHR.

The provision of the Convention that explicitly refers to foreigners is Article 16. It allows States Parties to restrict their political activities. According to this provision, the provisions of Articles 10, 11 and 14 ECHR (freedom of expression, freedom of assembly and association and prohibition of discrimination, respectively) cannot be considered to exclude the right of States Parties to restrict the political activities of aliens. In practice, this provision does not apply,[556] as European countries, due to the integration and institutional development of the European Union, have moved away from a restrictive approach in international law toward the political activities of foreigners.[557]

The Convention system of human rights protection also includes guarantees under the Additional Protocols to the ECHR that apply to foreigners. In Article 2 of Protocol No. 4, every person is guaranteed the right to freedom of movement and freedom to choose his or her place of residence within the territory of the state in which he or she lawfully resides and, in addition, the right to leave any country, including his or her own. Aliens may therefore exercise this right, but subject to the sovereign power of the state to control their entry into its territory. The right of a foreigner to enter, reside or remain in a particular state is not general in nature. The right to freedom of movement and to choose one's place of residence exists if the person concerned enters and resides legally in the territory of the state. A breach of the conditions of entry into or residence on the territory of a particular state precludes the exercise of the rights set out in Article 2(1) of Protocol No. 4. In addition, Article 2(3) and (4) of Protocol No. 4 set out the grounds for restrictions on the right to freedom of movement and freedom of choice of residence. The exercise of these rights may be subject to limitations which are necessary in a democratic society for reasons of national and public security, the maintenance of public order, the prevention of crime, the protection of health or morals, or the protection of the rights and freedoms of others. They may also be subject "in specific regions" to statutory restrictions justified by the public interest in a democratic society. Such a region may be, for example, a border zone.

In turn, Article 4 of Protocol No. 4 prohibits the collective expulsion of aliens. Any forcible removal of a group of aliens from the territory of a state, irrespective of the lawfulness and length of their stay, their place of detention,

---

556 See *Piermont v. France*, Nos. 15773/89 and 15774/89 (ECtHR April 27, 1995); see also *Perincek v. Switzerland*, No. 27510/08 (ECtHR October 15, 2015).

557 Durán Alba J. F., "Restrictions on the Political Activity of Aliens under Article 16 ECHR," in J. García Roca, and P. Santolaya (eds), *Europe of Rights: A Compendium on the European Convention of Human Rights* (Leiden: Brill, 2012) 497–501; Ziegler R., "Political Rights of Aliens: Articles 10, 11 and 16 of the ECHR and Article 3 of Additional Protocol I," in *Aliens* ..., 175–182.

their status as migrants or asylum seekers and their behavior when crossing the border, is prohibited. There need not be a violation of this prohibition if the collective expulsion is based on a reasonable and objective examination of the individual case of each foreigner belonging to the group, as confirmed by ECtHR case law.[558]

The procedural guarantees for the expulsion of aliens are set out in Article 1 of Protocol No. 7. They apply in individual cases and only to aliens lawfully present on the territory of the state. First and foremost, the expulsion of an alien is only permitted on the basis of a decision taken in accordance with the law, so such a decision must have a basis in national law. In the expulsion proceedings, the foreigner should, firstly, have the opportunity to present his or her case against the expulsion, which means that he or she must be given the opportunity to participate in the proceedings and be heard. Secondly, the foreigner should be provided with the right to lodge an appeal, which enables the (substantive and formal) review of the expulsion decision. Thirdly, the foreigner should be able to be represented before the competent authority conducting the expulsion proceedings, which means that there is no need for the foreigner to have direct contact with that authority. The expulsion of an alien without regard to the guarantees under Article 1(1)(a-c) of Protocol No. 7 is permissible if it is necessary on grounds of public order or justified on grounds of public security. An exception to the general rule establishing the prohibition of such expulsion is provided for in Article 1(2) of Protocol No. 7. The provisions require that aliens be informed of the factual circumstances that led the national authorities to consider that they pose a threat to national security, and that they be given access to the content of the documents and information in the case file on which the national authorities based the decision to expel them.

---

558 See, notably, [Grand Chamber] *Georgia v. Russia (No. 1)*, No. 13255/07, 167 (ECtHR July 3, 2014); *Čonka v. Belgium*, No. 51564/99 (ECtHR February 5, 2002), § 59. See also Scuto F., "Expulsion and Prohibition of Collective Expulsion of Migrants and Asylum Seekers. The Level of the ECtHR's Protection," in *Aliens* ..., 235–248.

1.5.5 The permissibility of restrictions on human rights in the light of acts of international law

It is the duty of states to respect and guarantee adequate human rights standards under international human rights instruments at all times. Also in situations of emergency, such as in recent decades, armed conflict, terror or persecution (on ethnic, religious, racial, political and cultural grounds) resulting in mass migrations, or the COVID-19 pandemic, states have an obligation to ensure compliance with international human rights law, humanitarian law and refugee regulations. International human rights law—including the UDHR, the ICCPR, the ICESCR and the ECHR—allows for interference with human freedoms and rights on the grounds of the need to protect certain values or other freedoms or human rights (so-called limitation clauses).[559] In the UDHR, the clause is of a general nature—Article 29(2) provides that in the exercise of his or her rights and freedoms, every person shall be subject only to such limitations as are prescribed by law for the sole purpose of securing due recognition and respect for the rights and freedoms of others and to meet the legitimate requirements of morality, public order and the general welfare of a democratic society. Similarly, the ICESCR contains a general clause that the enjoyment of rights, provided by the state in accordance with the Covenant, may be subjected by the state only to such limitations as are provided by law, and only to the extent that this is consistent with the essence of those rights, and only for the purpose of promoting the general welfare in a democratic society (Article 4). In the other human rights instruments listed, limitation clauses are individual in nature, as they are linked to specific rights or freedoms.

Interference with rights or freedoms is permitted both under normal functioning of the state and in circumstances involving specific threats that may justify declaring a state of emergency, as seen recently during the COVID-19 pandemic.[560] The measures introduced by states during the COVID-19 pandemic, resulting in the restriction of certain freedoms or rights, were

---

559 Tabaszewski R., "The Permissibility of Limiting Rights and Freedoms in the European and National Legal System Due to Health Protection" (2020) 3 *Review of European and Comparative Law*, 54–57.

560 See, *inter alia*, Florczak-Wątor M., Gárdos-Orosz F., Malíř J., and Steuer M., *States of Emergency and Human Rights Protection. The Theory and Practice of the Visegrad Countries* (Routledge 2024).

aimed at preventing and combating a global threat to human health and life.[561] Exceptional situations (war or other public danger threatening the existence of a nation) also justify, on the basis of both the ICCPR (Article 4) and the ECHR (Article 15), the derogation of certain freedoms and rights guaranteed by these acts. European countries used the derogation mechanism during the COVID-19 pandemic, considering it an exceptional circumstance justifying the temporary suspension of the obligation to respect certain human rights.[562]

The ECHR's limitation clauses allow for restrictions on the following rights or freedoms: the right to respect for private and family life (Article 8); freedom of thought, conscience and religion (Article 9); freedom of expression (Article 10); and freedom of assembly and association (Article 11). Restrictions on rights are also permitted by certain additional protocols to the Convention, such as Protocol No. 4 in the case of the right to freedom of movement and to freedom of choice of residence within the territory of a State (Article 2). Restrictions, conditions or other forms of interference with the right or freedom in question, permissible under the indicated provisions of the Convention, may apply to a specific exercise of that right or freedom, but interference with its essence is prohibited. And, in accordance with Article 17 ECHR, nothing in the ECHR may be interpreted as conferring on any state, group or individual the right to take action or perform an act aimed at nullifying or restricting the rights and freedoms set out in the Convention to a greater extent than is provided for in the Convention (prohibition of abuse of rights).

The ECHR's limitation clauses differ slightly in content, but are based on a scheme of a three-stage test that determines the permissibility of interference. In the ECHR system, the admissibility of restrictions is assessed *ad casum* by the ECtHR.[563]

---

561 See Kolendowska-Matejczuk M., and Mrowicki M., "Ochrona praw człowieka w stanach globalnego zagrożenia—analiza na przykładzie pandemii COVID-19" (2021) 2 *Krakowskie Studia Międzynarodowe*, 54–60; Tabaszewski R., *The Permissibility …*, 61–72; Smith R. K. M., *International Human Rights Law* (Oxford University Press 2022) 432–448; Radajewski M., *Prawa i wolności człowieka i obywatela w dobie pandemii*, in T. Gardocka, and D. Jagiełło (eds), *Pandemia COVID-19 a prawa i wolności obywatela* (Warszawa 2020) 77–92.

562 Lebret A., "COVID-19 Pandemic and Derogation to Human Rights" (2020) 7 *Journal of Law and the Biosciences*, 1–15 <https://doi.org/10.1093/jlb/lsaa015>.

563 Cf. *inter alia* Tabaszewski R., *The Permissibility …*, 67–72.

Firstly, the interference must be provided for by law. International law therefore requires states to comply with the principle of legality. Any restriction of rights or freedoms introduced without a legal basis is grounds for state responsibility for their violation.

Secondly, the interference must serve a legitimate objective—in other words, it must be necessary to protect certain interests or values, or the rights or freedoms of others. Individual provisions of the ECHR list such interests or values that may justify a restriction on a particular right or freedom. For example, restrictions on the right to privacy may be justified by the following values: state security, public safety or the economic well-being of the country, the protection of order and the prevention of crime, the protection of health and morals or the protection of the rights and freedoms of others (Article 8(2)). In the case of freedom of expression, these are: state security, territorial integrity, public security on the grounds that it is necessary to prevent disorder or crime, to protect health and morals, to protect the reputation and rights of others and to prevent the disclosure of confidential information or to safeguard the solemnity and impartiality of the judiciary (Article 10(2)). The common interests or values that allow for the restriction of the rights and freedoms guaranteed by Articles 8–11 ECHR and Article 2 of Protocol No. 4 include state/public security, public safety/public order, the protection of health or morals, or the protection of the rights and freedoms of others. This confirms that restrictions on human rights are exceptional in nature.

Thirdly, interference with rights or freedoms is permissible provided it is necessary in a democratic society. The restriction must result from *a pressing social need*, consistent with those values and interests that legitimize state action by interfering with the right or freedom in question. This "necessity" also entails an obligation to keep the restriction proportionate to the intended purpose, which is justified by those relevant values or interests. In assessing "necessity," states enjoy a *margin of appreciation*,[564] particularly

[564] Cf. Reynolds J., "The Margin of Appreciation Doctrine: Colonial Origins," in *Empire, Emergency and International Law* (Cambridge University Press 2017) 170–192. For the margin of appreciation in migration cases, see Mac Crorie B., and Santomauro G., "The Margin of Appreciation of States in the European Convention on Human Rights and Additional Protocol No. *15*," in *Aliens* ..., 249–276.

when choosing to restrict the exercise of a right or freedom in a situation of urgent, exceptional need. The degree of such discretion depends on the nature of the right to be protected, which is subject to review by the courts or tribunals.[565] In the light of Article 17 ECHR, the interference must not affect the essence of the right or freedom in question.

In the case of the ICCPR, restrictions are permissible in relation to: freedom of movement and freedom of choice of residence (Article 12), freedom to manifest religion or belief (Article 18), right to freedom of expression, freedom to seek, receive and impart information and ideas (Article 19), freedom of assembly (Article 21), and freedom of association (Article 22). The interests or values justifying interference with the rights and freedoms indicated are essentially the same. For example, the freedom of movement expressed in Article 12 ICCPR may be subject to restrictions that are provided for by law, are necessary for the protection of state security, public order, public health or morals, or the rights and freedoms of others, and are consistent with other rights recognized in the Covenant. In enacting legislation providing for restrictions permissible under Article 12(3) ICCPR, states should always be guided by the principle that restrictions must not impair the essence of the right to freedom of movement, which follows from Article 5(1) ICCPR. It is not sufficient for restrictions to serve a permissible purpose, they must also be necessary for their protection. Restrictive measures must comply with the principle of proportionality, which must be respected not only in the law defining the restrictions, but also by administrative and judicial authorities in the application of the law.[566]

1.5.6 Standards of protection of migrants' rights in the case law of the European Court of Human Rights

The European Court of Human Rights has developed—and is continuing to develop—in case law standards for the protection of human rights in migration and refugee cases. Initially, migration cases mainly concerned compliance with the principle of *non-refoulement* under Article 3 ECHR or

---

565 Cf. Tabaszewski R., *The Permissibility* …, 61–72.

566 See CCPR General Comment No. 27: Article 12 (Freedom of Movement). Adopted at the Sixty-Seventh Session of the Human Rights Committee on November 2, 1999, CCPR/C/21/Rev.1/Add.9, Points 11–15 <https://digitallibrary.un.org/record/366604?v=pdf#files> accessed September 30, 2024.

the right to family life under Article 8 ECHR,[567] but over time the Court has developed extensive jurisprudence on migration and asylum in relation to almost all Convention rights.[568] In recent years, the migration crisis has contributed to an increase in ECtHR judgments on violations of the principle of *non-refoulement* in relation to the return of foreign nationals to countries without effective asylum systems or systems that provide adequate standards of refugee protection and compliance.[569] In turn, the exceptional circumstances of the COVID-19 pandemic became a justification in ECtHR jurisprudence for limiting the exercise of most freedoms and human rights, both on the grounds of the general interest of public health, but also the need to protect the freedoms and rights of others, with a particular focus on vulnerable groups, including refugees and migrant children.[570] The state of public health emergency was also the basis for the derogation under Article 15 ECHR, which requires an appropriate approach by the Court to assess respect for human rights in such specific circumstances.[571]

For complaints based on allegations of violations of Article 2 ECHR (right to life), the Court analyses, from the perspective of the positive and negative obligations of ECHR States Parties, the various situations in which the lives of migrants and refugees may be at risk, both in the country of origin and

---

567 Cf. Furramani E., and Bushati R., *The Principle …*, 112–114.

568 Cf: European Court of Human Rights, *Guide on the case-law of the European Convention on Human Rights: Immigration* (February 29, 2024) <https://ks.echr.coe.int/documents/d/echr-ks/guide_immigration_eng> accessed September 30, 2024.

569 Cf. Domagała P., "The Migration Crisis in the Case Law of the ECHR—Some Remarks on the Obligations of Countries to Refugees and Immigrants" (2020) 7(2) *Polish Review of International and European Law*, 173–192 <https://doi.org/10.21697/priel.2018.7.2.04>.

570 Cf. *inter alia* Ćorić V., and Knežević Bojović A., "European Court of Human Rights and COVID-19: What are Standards for Health Emergencies?," in *New Legal Reality: Challenges and Perspectives* (University of Latvia Press, Riga) 380–398 <https://doi.org/10.22364/iscflul.8.2.26>; Jaskiernia J., "Challenges Posed by the COVID-19 Pandemic to the Protection of Human Rights" (2020) 4 *Stosunki Międzynarodowe—International Relations*, 65–78 <https://10.7366/020909614202004>; Braithwaite B., Harby C., and Miletić G. (eds), *The Protection …*, 61–66.

571 Cf. Kapelańska-Pręgowska J., "The (Still) Unresolved Question of COVID-19 Passes Compatibility with the ECHR. Comments on the ECtHR Decision of 7 October 2021 in Zembrano v. France (Application No. 41994/21)" (2022) 11 *Polish Review of International and European Law*, 169–182 <https://doi.org/10.21697/2022.11.1.07>.

during movement around Europe and in the host states.[572] The risk of loss of life in the foreigner's country of origin is an element of assessment in expulsion cases based on allegations of violations of Article 3 ECHR, which prohibits torture and inhuman and degrading treatment.[573] An alien's expulsion, extradition or obligation to return may result in a violation of Article 2 or Article 3 ECHR if there is a "real risk" that he or she may be subjected to treatment contrary to these provisions. These provisions form the basis of the principle of *non-refoulement*, which is developed in ECtHR jurisprudence affirming the Convention's protective function. In the Convention, the principle of *non-refoulement* is absolute, independent of the status of the person concerned and his or her action justifying the referral. In practice, this means that in cases of *refoulement*, the scope of protection under Articles 2 and 3 ECHR also extends to particularly dangerous persons.[574]

In the light of Article 3 ECHR, the Court decides numerous cases concerning migratory detention and the conditions of the stay of aliens on the territory of ECHR States Parties, especially in the case of persons who are seeking international protection.[575] In cases concerning the expulsion of foreign nationals with a real risk of re-trafficking in their country of origin, the Court analyses both the negative and positive obligations of states under Article 4 ECHR, which prohibits slavery and forced labor, with particular reference to cases of trafficking.[576] Equally relevant is the prohibition of arbitrary detention under Article 5 ECHR, which is subject to ECtHR analysis in cases of detention of migrants to prevent unauthorized entry or made with a view to deportation.[577] It follows from the case law, *inter alia*, that

---

572 See *inter alia Safi and Others v. Greece*, No. 5418/15 (ECtHR July 7, 2022), HUDOC; *Alkhatib and Others v. Greece*, No. 3566/16 (HUDOC January 16, 2024).

573 Cf. Ruiz Ramos J., "The Right to Life of Migrants and Refugees under Article 2 ECHR. Outside, Inside and Along the Way," in *Aliens* ..., 16–45.

574 Cf. Domagała P., *The Migration Crisis* ..., 185–188 and cited ECtHR's case law.

575 See judgments cited in: European Court of Human Rights, *Guide* ..., 14–16, 18, 19–20, 21–22, 24, 27–34; cf. Ineli-Ciger M., "Protecting Aliens with Article 3 of the ECHR. An Analysis with a Focus on Refugees and Migrants," in *Aliens* ..., 46–75; Domagała P., *The Migration Crisis* ..., 188–189 and cited ECtHR's case law.

576 Cf. Díaz Morgado C., "Prohibition of Slavery and Forced Labour (Article 4). Human Trafficking," in *Aliens* ..., 76–96.

577 Cf. Pinto Oliveira A. S., "Aliens' Protection against Arbitrary Detention (Article 5 ECHR)," in *Aliens* ..., 97–117; Domagała P., *The Migration Crisis* ..., 189–190 and cited ECtHR's case law.

under Article 5(2) ECHR, any person who is detained must be informed, in plain, intelligible language, of the relevant legal and factual grounds for his or her deprivation of liberty so that he or she may approach a court to challenge the lawfulness of such detention under Article 5(4) ECHR.[578] Indeed, it follows from Article 5(4) ECHR that a detained person has the right to initiate proceedings to have a court examine the procedural and substantive conditions which are necessary for the "lawfulness," within the meaning of Article 5(1) ECHR, of his or her deprivation of liberty.[579] For example, the Court considered that the requirements of Article 5(4) ECHR were met in a case where the applicant was not heard in person or by tele- or videoconference in the appeal proceedings concerning his immigration detention due to infrastructure problems in the first weeks of the COVID-19 pandemic-related lockdown. The Court took into account the fact that the applicant's lawyer had submitted written statements and was heard by telephone, and the difficult and unforeseen practical problems in the initial phase of the COVID-19 pandemic.[580]

The migrant cases examined by the ECtHR very often concern the right to family and private life. The jurisprudence based on Article 8 of the ECHR examines, in particular, issues related to family reunification, regularization of status, and the expulsion of the foreigner. In these three categories of migration cases, the notion of family life is central, although the Court's approach is not always uniform.[581] Foreigners' complaints brought before the ECtHR also relate to political and social rights. Freedom of expression (Article 10 ECHR) and freedom of association (Article 11 ECHR) extend to foreigners. Furthermore, the ECtHR takes into account in its jurisprudence the permissibility of imposing restrictions on the political activities

578 *Khlaifia and Others v. Italy*, No. 16483/12 (ECtHR December 15, 2016), § 115, HUDOC.

579 See, notably, *A.M. v. France*, No. 56324/13) (ECtHR July 12, 2016), §§ 40–41, HUDOC.

580 *Bah v. the Netherlands*, No. 35751/20 (ECtHR decision of June 22, 2021), HUDOC.

581 See the judgments cited in: European Court of Human Rights, *Guide* …, 7–10, 22, 40–43; cf. Milios G., "The Right to Family and Private Life in Migration and Asylum Cases (Article 8)," in *Aliens* …, 141–171; Domagała P., *The Migration Crisis* …, 190–191 and cited ECtHR's case law.

of foreigners under Article 16 ECHR.[582] The doctrine is critical of justifying interference with migrants' social rights on economic grounds and of treating economic contribution as a criterion that puts migrants on an equal footing with nationals.[583]

The prohibition of discrimination set out in Article 14 ECHR is relevant in migration cases. The Court has heard complaints of discrimination based on a person's immigration status, including migrants, asylum seekers, refugees, and others. In addition, the Court has analyzed cases in which the allegation of discrimination was raised on different grounds, but in the context of migration. The issue of discrimination in relation to foreigners has most often arisen in areas such as freedom of movement, the right to marry, or the right to family life.[584]

It follows from the case law that although immigration status is conferred by law and is not intrinsically linked to a person, it cannot be excluded from being considered an "other ground" within the meaning of Article 14 ECHR.[585] In particular, this applies to refugee status, which does not involve an element of choice.[586] The nature of the immigration status on which differential treatment is based is of great importance in determining the extent of the margin of appreciation to be accorded to a State Party to the Convention. Differential treatment based on this ground must always be objectively and reasonably justified. In turn, certain legal and other consequences flow from a person's immigration status.[587] The Court emphasizes that an assessment of the specific circumstances of each case, with particular regard to the law,

---

582 Cf. Ziegler R., "Political Rights of Aliens. Articles 10, 11 and 16 of the ECHR and Article 3 of Additional Protocol I," in *Aliens* ..., 172–190.

583 Cf. Caicedo Camacho N., "Social Rights and Migrants before the European Court of Human Rights," in *Aliens* ..., 191–210.

584 See *inter alia* The ECHR judgments of: May 25, 1985, *Abdulaziz, Cabales, and Balkandali v. the United Kingdom*, Nos. 9214/80, 9473/81, 9474/81, HUDOC; November 6, 2012, *Hode and Abdi v. the United Kingdom*, No. 22341/09, HUDOC; May 24, 2016, *Biao v. Denmark*, No. 38590/10, HUDOC.

585 See e.g., *M.T. and Others v. Sweden*, No. 22105/18 (ECtHR October 20, 2022), § 96, HUDOC.

586 See e.g., *Hode and Abdi v. the United Kingdom*, No. 22341/09 (ECtHR November 6, 2012), § 47, HUDOC.

587 See e.g., *Bah v. the United Kingdom*, No. 56328/07 (ECtHR September 27, 2011), §§ 46, 47 and 52, HUDOC.

is required in each case for the purposes of applying Article 14 ECHR. This includes cases where the situation of persons fleeing general conditions in their country of origin (qualifying for subsidiary protection status) are not analogous or substantially similar to those of persons fleeing due to an individualized risk of persecution or ill-treatment (qualifying for refugee status).[588]

Allegations of violations of Article 14 ECHR are often considered by the ECtHR in conjunction with Article 8 ECHR in cases that concern family reunification or the maintenance of ties between adult children and their parents. The Court has repeatedly emphasized that the Convention does not guarantee the right of an alien to enter or settle in a particular country.[589] However, although Article 8 does not impose a general obligation on states with regard to family reunification,[590] a migration control measure in accordance with this provision may constitute discrimination and a violation of Article 14 ECHR.[591] It follows from the case law that foreigners cannot rely on the existence of "family life" in relation to adults who are not part of his immediate family and have not been shown to be or have been dependent on them. However, the bond between adult children and their parents falls within the scope of "private life" within the meaning of Article 8 ECHR and in such cases Article 14 in conjunction with Article 8 ECHR may apply.[592] It follows from well-established ECtHR jurisprudence that there must be very compelling reasons for a difference in treatment based on national origin to be considered compatible with the Convention.[593]

588 See e.g., *M.T. and Others v. Sweden* (ECtHR October 20, 2022), §§ 97–111.

589 See e.g., *Ibrogimov v. Russia*, No. 32248/12 (ECtHR May 15, 2018), § 18, HUDOC; *Pajić v. Croatia*, No. 68453/13 (February 23, 2016), §§ 58 and 79, HUDOC; *Novruk and Others v. Russia*, nos. 31039/11 and 4 others (March 15, 2016), § 83, HUDOC.

590 See e.g., *Jeunesse v. the Netherlands*, No. 12738/10 (ECtHR October 3, 2014), § 107, HUDOC.

591 See e.g., *Abdulaziz, Cabales and Balkandali v. the United Kingdom*, Nos. 9214/80, 9473/81, 9474/81 (ECtHR May 28, 1985), § 71, HUDOC; May 24, 2016, *Biao v. Denmark*, § 118.

592 See e.g., *Novruk and Others v. Russia* (ECtHR March 15, 2016), §§ 88–89.

593 See e.g., *Gaygusuz v. Austria*, No. 17371/90 (ECtHR September 16, 1996), § 42, HUDOC; *Koua Poirrez v. France*, No. 40892/98 (September 30, 2003), § 46, HUDOC; February 18, 2009, *Andrejeva v. Latvia* [GC], No. 55707/00, § 87, HUDOC; *Savickis and Others v. Latvia*, No. 49270/11 (June 9, 2022), HUDOC.

In recent years, probably influenced by the migration crisis, there has been an increase in the number of ECtHR judgments on violations of the principle of *non-refoulement*.[594] The Court reaffirms the sovereign right of States Parties to the Convention to control the entry and stay of aliens on their territory.[595] In contrast, the expulsion or return of aliens is closely linked to the obligation to comply with the principle of *non-refoulement*. In assessing compliance with various provisions of the ECHR, the Court has dealt with ad hoc returns of (groups of) persons on the high seas, at land borders and shortly after entry into the territory of the state concerned. Cases heard by the ECtHR concerned the return of foreign nationals to countries that were ostensibly safe but did not necessarily have effective asylum systems or systems that maintained adequate standards of protection of migrants' rights and respect for human rights. The Court has affirmed in case law that the state must not send back persons, e.g., asylum seekers, to a country where they are at risk of inhuman and degrading treatment or torture, as this would violate Article 3 ECHR.[596] The case law shows that the right to seek asylum (international protection) and the principle of *non-refoulement* should also be respected in emergency situations.

In addition, the Court elaborates on the standards for the protection of aliens from impermissible collective expulsion under Article 4 of Protocol No. 4, also reaffirming the importance of the principle of *non-refoulement* in international human rights law. In *Hirsi Jamaa and Others v. Italy*,[597] the Court found a violation of Article 4 of Protocol No. 4 in relation to the collective expulsion ("push-back") of migrants, including asylum seekers, without any pre-deportation procedure to establish their identities, the reasons for their migration, or to issue individual expulsion decisions. Subsequent ECtHR jurisprudence shows that a violation of Article 4 of Protocol No. 4 occurs

---

594 Jakulevičienė L., "Principle of Non-refoulement in the Context of Recent ECtHR Caselaw and the EU Migration and Asylum Pact" (2023) 24(3) *ERA Forum*, 379–396.

595 See *inter alia Paposhvili v. Belgium*, No. 41738/10 (ECtHR December 13, 2016), HUDOC.

596 See e.g., *Sharifi and Others v. Italy and Greece*, No. 16643/09 (ECtHR October 21, 2014), HUDOC; *M.A. and Others v. Lithuania*, No. 59793/17 (December 11, 2018), HUDOC; *Ilias and Ahmed v. Hungary*, No. 47287/15 (November 21, 2019), HUDOC; *S.S. and Others v. Hungary*, Nos. 56417/19 and 44245/20 (October 12, 2023), HUDOC; *Sherov and Others v. Poland*, Nos. 54029/17 and 3 others (April 4, 2024), HUDOC.

597 Judgment of February 23, 2012, No. 27765/09, HUDOC.

when foreigners are not provided with the opportunity to present arguments against their expulsion to the competent authorities on an individual basis.[598] Furthermore, a violation of the prohibition of collective expulsion may also consist in a failure to take into account the individual circumstances of aliens when individual administrative decisions on expulsion are issued.[599]

Controversy in recent years has been sparked by the case of *N.D. and N.T. v. Spain*. In 2017, the Chamber ruled unanimously that the respondent State had violated Article 4 of Protocol No. 4 by immediately turning back migrants seeking to cross the border (*hot returns*).[600] By contrast, in 2020, the Grand Chamber ruled unanimously that the Spanish authorities had not violated Article 4 of Protocol No. 4 and Article 13 ECHR.[601] The Court held that it is permissible to turn back foreign nationals without individual proceedings if they cross the border at a place not intended for that purpose and they have the possibility to use legal border crossings. The Court put forward the concept of a two-stage test,[602] whereby once it has been established that the foreigner's entry was not in accordance with the entry regulations, it is necessary to examine whether the State has provided the individual with the opportunity to use lawful means to enter its territory and, subsequently, whether they had had a realistic opportunity to argue against his expulsion. This judgment constitutes a jurisprudential precedent.[603] The departure in the present case from the ECtHR's established line of jurisprudence has been the subject of numerous comments, many of them critical.[604] The criticism

598 Judgment of December 15, 2016, *Khlaifia and Others v. Italy*; see also judgment of July 23, 2013, *M.A. v. Cyprus*, No. 41872/10, HUDOC.

599 See *M.K. and Others v. Poland*, Nos. 40503/17 (ECtHR July 23, 2020), 42902/17 and 43643/17, HUDOC; *D.A. and Others v. Poland*, No. 51246/17 (July 8, 2021), HUDOC.

600 Judgment of October 3, 2017, Nos. 8675/15 and 8697/15, HUDOC.

601 Judgment of February 13, 2020, HUDOC.

602 ECtHR judgment in case *N.D. and N.T. v. Spain*, §§ 201, 209–211.

603 See Raimondo G., *N.D. and N.T. v. Spain. A Slippery Slope for the Protection of Irregular Migrants* (April 20, 2020) <https://www.law.ox.ac.uk/research-subject-groups/centre-criminology/centreborder-criminologies/blog/2020/04/nd-and-nt-v-spain> accessed September 30, 2024.

604 See, *inter alia*, Pichl M., and Schmalz D., *"Unlawful" may not mean rightless. The shocking ECtHR Grand Chamber judgment in case N.D. and N.T.*, Verfassungsblog, February 14, 2020 <https://ver-fassungsblog.de/unlawful-may-not-mean-rightless/> accessed September 30, 2024 <https://doi.org/10.17176/20200214-164325-0>; Oviedo Moreno C., *A Painful Slap from the ECtHR and an Urgent Opportunity for Spain*,

relates, in particular, to the concept of "the applicants' own behaviour," which authorizes states to carry out collective expulsions of migrants at external borders under certain conditions without first examining the personal situation of each participant and, consequently, without allowing them to seek asylum.[605] Subsequent ECtHR jurisprudence, however, seems to confirm that the solution adopted in *N.D. and N.T. v. Spain* does not automatically apply in every case in which a violation of Article 4 of Protocol No. 4 to the ECHR is alleged, but is subject to an ad hoc assessment.

For example, in *Asady and Others v. Slovakia*,[606] the Court referred to the illegal nature of the applicants' entry, but limited its assessment only to verifying whether, in the circumstances, the State had enabled the applicants to present arguments against their expulsion. However, the Court did not link the unlawful nature of the entry to the negative conditions that would preclude the possibility of invoking the rights under Article 4 of Protocol No. 4 to the ECHR. In *Shahzad v. Hungary*,[607] the Court developed the notion of lawful entry routes and their availability. It found that the State had failed to provide the applicant with an effective means of lawful entry because access to the lawful entry procedure in the transit zones was significantly limited due to distance and the daily limit of persons entitled to apply. Therefore, the absence of an individual expulsion decision could not be justified by the conduct of the foreigner. An analysis of the ECtHR case law leads to the conclusion that the Court maintains its previous position regarding

---

Verfassungsblog, February 14, 2020 <https://verfassungsblog.de/a-painful-slap-from-the-ecthr-and-an-urgent-opportunity-for-spain/> accessed September 30, 2024 <https://doi.org/10.17176/20200214-164222-0>; Thym D., "The End of Human Rights Dynamism? Judgments of the ECtHR on "Hot Returns" and Humanitarian visas as a Focal Point of Contemporary European Asylum Law and Policy" (2020) 32(4) *International Journal of Refugee Law*, 569–596.

605 See, inter alia, Carrera S., The Strasbourg court judgement "N.D. and N.T. v Spain": a "carte blanche" to push backs at EU external borders?, EUI Working Paper RSCAS 2020/21, 21; Wissing R., *Push Backs of "Badly Behaving" Migrants at Spanish Border Are Not Collective Expulsions (But Might Still be Illegal Refoulements)* (Ghent: Human Rights Centre 2020) 4.

606 *Asady and Others v. Slovakia*, No. 24917/15 (ECtHR March 24, 2020), § 62, HUDOC.

607 *Shahzad v. Hungary*, No. 12625/17 (ECtHR judgment of July 8, 2021), §§ 64–66, HUDOC.

the prohibition of collective expulsions and the application of the procedural guarantees contained in Article 4 of Protocol No. 4 to the ECHR, but extends the scope of the assessment—as in the aftermath of *N.D. and N.T. v. Spain*—to include elements such as the lawful means of access to the territory or the applicants' personal conduct, which needs to be examined in the light of the circumstances of the particular case.

The ECtHR's jurisprudence on migrants and refugees attaches considerable importance to procedural guarantees. The Convention guarantees the right to a fair trial (Article 6) and the right to an effective remedy (Article 13). Adjudication in migration cases *ad casum* requires assessing whether measures applied to migrants fall within the scope of Article 6 ECHR. For example, in *M.K. and Others v. France*,[608] the Court held that the French authorities' failure to provide a place of residence for migrants who had sought asylum, despite an administrative court's issuance of a protective measure to that effect, constituted a violation of the right to a fair trial in terms of access to a court and the effectiveness of enforcement proceedings. In the ECtHR's view, the applicants' right to obtain housing in such emergency circumstances derives directly from French law and, as such, can be treated as a right of a civil nature within the meaning of Article 6(1) ECHR.

In contrast, Article 6 ECHR does not apply to the procedure for the expulsion of aliens, as in this case the relevant procedural guarantees are set out in Article 1 of Protocol No. 7.[609] They concern the procedure for the expulsion of "aliens lawfully resident on the territory of the State." In *Muhammad and Muhammad v. Romania*, the Court summarized its case law on this provision.[610] The Court held that the deportation of the applicants, Pakistani nationals living in Romania on student visas, on grounds of national security, violated Article 1 of Protocol No. 7, as they did not have access to the classified documents on which the deportation decision

608 *M.K. and Others v. France*, Nos. 34349/18 and 2 others (ECtHR December 8, 2022), HUDOC; see also *amara v. Belgium*, No. 49255/22 (ECtHR July 18, 2023), HUDOC.

609 Cf. *Regner v. The Czech Republic*, No. 35289/11 (ECtHR September 19, 2017), HUDOC.

610 *Muhammad and Muhammad v. Romania*, No. 80982/12 (ECtHR October 15, 2020), §§ 114–157, HUDOC.

was based, nor were they provided with any specific information regarding the facts and grounds for deportation. In this judgment, the Court confirmed that the determination of the legitimacy of the exclusion of access to the content of classified documents requires a proper comparison (balancing) by the national court between the interests of state security and the procedural rights of the foreigner, which are closely related to the right to defense.[611]

Important in migration cases are the Court's findings on the subsidiary nature of Article 13 ECHR and the definition of the term "effective remedy."[612] Allegations of violations of Article 4 of Protocol No. 4 are most often linked precisely to Article 13 ECHR in the absence of an effective remedy in national law that foreigners could use to protect themselves against expulsion.[613] In the cases of aliens, the Court also makes use of so-called *interim measures*.[614] Most often it asks the respondent state to refrain from expelling persons to countries where they are in danger of death, torture or other ill-treatment, but also to accept and process the asylum applications of persons presenting themselves at a border crossing.[615] In practice, the Court only identifies provisional measures where there is a real and imminent risk of serious and irreparable harm. On the other hand, the state's failure to comply with a measure indicated by the Court is tantamount to a violation of Article 34 ECHR.[616]

For example, where an alien's complaint is on the grounds that expulsion would expose him or her to treatment contrary to Articles 2 or 3 ECHR, there must be an effective remedy in domestic law and practice under Article 13

---

611 See also *Poklikayew v. Poland*, No. 1103/16 (ECtHR June 22, 2023), HUDOC.

612 Cf. Boza Martínez D., "Procedural Rights Protecting Immigrants. Right to a Fair Trial (Article 6) and Right to an Effective Remedy (Article 13)," in *Aliens* …, 118–140; Karska E., Morawska E. H., Czepek J., Dąbrowski Ł. D., Oręziak B., and Gałka K., *Human* …, 227–236.

613 See ECtHR judgments in cases *Hirsi Jamaa and Others v. Italy*, § 194 and *Khlaifia and Others v. Italy*, § 166.

614 Rule 39 of the Rules of Court <https://www.echr.coe.int/documents/d/echr/rules_court_eng> accessed September 30, 2024.

615 *M.K. and Others v. Poland* (ECtHR July 23, 2020), § 235.

616 See *M.K. and Others v. Poland* (ECtHR July 23, 2020); July 8, 2021, *D.A. and Others v. Poland*, No. 51246/17, HUDOC; September 15, 2022, *O.M. and D.S. v. Ukraine*, No. 18603/12, HUDOC.

ECHR. This provision absolutely requires both an independent and detailed review at the national level of whether there is a reasonable risk of treatment of a foreigner contrary to the Convention, as well as the automatic suspensive effect of a remedy against a decision ordering departure.[617] With regard to Article 13 read in conjunction with Article 4 of Protocol No. 4, the Court made a distinction according to whether a complaint based on an allegation of a violation of Articles 2 or 3 of the ECHR was justified because of the risks to which aliens were exposed after expulsion. The Court found a violation of the Convention when the alien complainants' allegations were well-founded and they were effectively prevented from seeking asylum and did not have access to a remedy with automatic suspensive effect.[618] In contrast, the lack of suspensive effect of an expulsion decision does not in itself constitute a violation of Article 13 in conjunction with Article 4 of Protocol No. 4 if, in the view of the alien, there is no real risk of a violation of his or her rights guaranteed under Articles 2 or 3 ECHR in the country of destination.[619] In such a situation, the Convention does not impose an absolute obligation on the State Party to guarantee an automatic suspensive remedy, but requires that the person concerned has an effective opportunity to challenge the expulsion decision through a sufficiently thorough examination of his or her complaints by an independent and impartial national authority.[620]

1.5.7 Conclusions

In an era of dynamic social, economic and cultural phenomena, and threats arising from armed conflicts, terrorism, climate change or pandemics, respecting and protecting human rights are major challenges in the modern world. International human rights law, based on the principle of respect for human dignity, sets out basic guarantees for various categories of rights (personal, political, social, economic and cultural). Human rights are also subject to

617 See *M.S.S. v. Belgium and Greece*, No. 30696/09 (ECtHR January 21, 2011), § 293, HUDOC; July 23, 2020, *M.K. and Others v. Poland*, §§ 142–148 and 212–220.

618 See *M.K. and Others v. Poland* (ECtHR July 23, 2020), §§ 219–220; *D.A. and Others v. Poland* (July 8, 2021), §§ 89–90; *Hirsi Jamaa and Others v. Italy* (February 23, 2012), §§ 201–207; *Sharifi and Others v. Italy and Greece* (October 21, 2014), §§ 240–243.

619 *Khlaifia and Others v. Italy* (Judgment of December 15, 2016), § 281.

620 See *Khlaifia and Others v. Italy* (ECtHR December 15, 2016), § 279; *Moustahi v. France*, No. 9347/14 (June 25, 2020), §§ 156–164, HUDOC.

development, which is evidenced by the creation of successive generations of these rights (third-generation rights as a result of progressive globalization or the currently emerging fourth-generation rights linked to further civilizational development). It is important to note that, according to the provisions contained in international human rights instruments, human rights belong to all people and are not linked to nationality or citizenship. This means that states have an obligation to respect the freedoms and rights of everyone under their jurisdiction. The very presence of migrants in a state's jurisdiction imposes an obligation on the state to enable them to assert their human rights. However, in view of the increasing migration processes in the twenty-first century, including illegal immigration, the implementation of obligations to respect and protect human rights is closely linked to the problem of ensuring state security. The *ad casum* assessment of the implementation of these obligations by bodies applying international human rights instruments, such as the ECtHR, contributes not only to the development of human rights standards, but also to the shaping of the model of conduct of European countries toward foreigners.

Acts of international human rights law provide grounds for a broad approach to the protection of foreigners' rights. The rights guarantees contained therein apply to everyone, regardless of citizenship or nationality, although the regulation of the status of certain groups of foreigners is not excluded, an example of which is the Geneva Convention Relating to the Status of Refugees. In addition, the standards of human rights protection developed in the legal system of the United Nations (UDHR, ICCPR, ICESCR) and the Council of Europe (ECHR) are consistent and coherent with the guarantees in force in the legal system of the European Union. The jurisprudence of the ECtHR, which also refers to universal or EU human rights standards in migration matters, demonstrates that the standards of protection of foreigners' rights under the legal regimes of different international organizations are complementary. In the perspective of the entry into force of the EU Pact on Migration and Asylum, it should be expected that the validity and application of the new EU migration law regulations will contribute to strengthening the protection of migrants' rights and security (by excluding e.g., pushbacks), while preserving the right of states to control the entry and stay of foreigners on their territory.

The European Court of Human Rights reaffirms the sovereign right to control the entry and stay of aliens on the territory of States Parties to the Convention, nor does it question the power of States to expel aliens from their territory. States may take measures to prevent the illegal entry of aliens into their territory, but they are obliged to ensure that they are able to avail themselves of existing procedures and guarantees protecting, in particular, against arbitrariness. Also the Court of Justice of the EU confirms in its case law that any third-country national or stateless person has the right to apply for international protection on the territory of a Member State, including at its borders or in transit zones, even if he or she is illegally present on that territory.[621] In the case of refugees or those seeking this status, states must also respect their obligations under the Geneva Convention Relating to the Status of Refugees. In view of the contemporary threats posed by the increasing influx of third-country migrants into the EU, it is therefore necessary to have a reliable and efficient border procedure that guarantees respect for the fundamental rights of the individual. In turn, the right to seek international protection (asylum, refugee status) should also be respected in emergency situations. The particular need to provide rapid and effective protection to migrants has emerged clearly recently in connection with the armed conflict between Russia and Ukraine, which has resulted in Ukrainian citizens migrating en masse to EU Member States, especially to Poland. In this case, it was necessary to enable refugees not only to safely enter and stay on the territory of EU Member States, but also to enjoy fundamental rights (e.g., health care, education, social security).

In the context of the fight against terrorism or illegal immigration, contemporary issues of state security require special attention. Regardless of the circumstances, the protection of borders and state security must be carried out in a manner consistent with the rights set out in the ECHR. Of particular importance is the principle of *non-refoulement*. The Court develops this principle under Article 3 ECHR as a de facto construction of European human rights law that protects foreigners to a greater extent than its predecessor in

621 See CJEU judgments of: November 16, 2021, C-821/19, European Commission v. Hungary, ECLI:EU:C:2021:930, § 136; June 30, 2022, C-72/22 PPU, M.A., ECLI:EU:C:2022:505, § 58.

international refugee law. The protection under Article 3 ECHR is absolute, and therefore an expulsion order that would create a risk of torture and inhuman or degrading treatment is inadmissible. On the other hand, the expulsion of an alien does not exempt the State from complying with the requirements of the ECHR and providing him/her with genuine protection, both in the context of judicial cooperation measures and the implementation of immigration policy.[622] The principle of *non-refoulement* requires absolute compliance even in emergency situations. It is clear from the Convention that the prohibition of torture and inhuman or degrading treatment, as well as the right to life, are not subject to derogation in the event of war or other public danger threatening the life of the nation (Article 15).

With regard to migrants arriving or already present on the territory of EU Member States in situations of particular risk, such as the recent COVID-19 pandemic, states face the need to balance their responsibility to respond quickly and effectively to such situations and to protect the rights and freedoms that may be affected by the countermeasures. During the COVID-19 pandemic, States had to take measures to contain the spread of the SARS-CoV-2 virus and to protect the life and health not only of their citizens, but of every person under their jurisdiction. The urgent measures taken by EU governments to contain the spread of the virus, including border controls in the Schengen area, temporary travel restrictions, the introduction of sanitary measures, have not been without impact on mobility and migration. Restrictive measures have affected migrants' right to access relevant procedures, their residence status in EU Member States, and the enjoyment of other rights, notably access to health care services. Asylum procedures also required rapid adaptation to pandemic conditions. The situation of foreign nationals in detention centers required special attention, not least for the sake of Article 5 ECHR. Indeed, during the pandemic, the risk increased that certain measures adopted by States to protect health might violate Article 3 ECHR. On the other hand, Article 5(1)(e) ECHR allows for the lawful detention of persons to prevent the spread of communicable diseases, and Article 2(3) of

[622] See, notably, Delas O., "La création du principe de non-refoulement en droit international des droits de la personne par la Cour européenne des droits de l'homme : un chef-d'oeuvre à protéger" (2020) (Special Issue) *Revue québécoise de droit international/ Quebec Journal of International Law / Revista quebequense de derecho internacional*, 395–416 <https://doi.org/10.7202/1078546ar>.

Protocol No. 4 allows for restrictions on the exercise of the right to freedom of movement on health grounds. The Convention thus contains mechanisms to respond to emergencies such as a pandemic. Of course, exceptional measures taken by States to protect life and health must comply with the principles of legality and proportionality, i.e., they must not interfere with Convention rights to a greater extent than is strictly necessary in an emergency situation. They should be subject to effective and independent judicial review. There is no doubt that human rights must remain at the heart of any state response in emergency situations.

1.6 Derogations in time of emergency (Jacek Chlebny)

1.6.1 Derogating from the application of obligations in a state of public emergency in the ECHR

1.6.1.1 Application of the derogation clause

According to Article 15(1) of the ECHR,[623] the taking of measures by a State to abrogate the application of its Convention obligations is possible in a state of public emergency, to the extent strictly consistent with the requirements of the situation and provided that other obligations under international law are not violated. This provision provides a basis for a State Party to the Convention to exempt itself temporarily and to a certain extent from its obligation to comply with the ECHR. This exemption may also apply to rights enjoyed by aliens. It is incumbent on the State to inform the Secretary-General of the Council of Europe of the measures taken, the reasons for them, and when the measures taken will cease to operate (Article 15(3) ECHR). However, this is not a formal condition for the application of the derogation clause, as the notification of the measures taken to the Secretary General of the Council of Europe may even take place at a later but reasonable date. According to the jurisprudence, while Article 15(3) does not stipulate a timeframe for informing the Secretary-General, the ECtHR and the former European Commission of Human Rights require notification "without any

623 Convention for the Protection of Human Rights and Fundamental Freedoms drawn up in Rome on November 4, 1950, subsequently amended by Protocols Nos. 3, 5 and 8 and supplemented by Protocol No. 2 (Journal of Laws of 1993, No. 61, item 284, as amended), hereinafter: "ECHR."

unavoidable delay," and delays of three and four months have been found to be excessive, but 12 days to be acceptable.[624] The Secretary-General has no independent competence to assess the substantive reasonableness of the emergency measures taken. However, the ECtHR makes such an assessment in the context of its consideration of an individual complaint.[625] When hearing individual complaints, the Court has the power to assess the fulfillment of the substantive and procedural conditions for the suspension of rights under Article 15 ECHR.[626] Past experience shows that Member States have communicated to the Secretary-General the suspension of rights protected in the ECHR under Article 15(3) ECHR on the grounds of terrorist threat, international armed conflict, political upheaval, internal disturbances and civil war, and pandemics.[627]

Derogation of rights under Article 15 ECHR should be distinguished from specific limitation clauses. Indeed, many of the rights and freedoms guaranteed in the ECHR are subject to individual limitations due to a public policy clause, e.g., the right to respect for private and family life under Article 8(2) ECHR. Generally speaking, a derogation clause allows a State to exempt

---

624 *Greece v. United Kingdom*, App. No. 176/56, European Commission of Human Rights, September 26, 1958, § 158; "*Greek case*," App. No. 3321/67 et al., European Commission of Human Rights, November 5, 1969, §81; *Lawless v. Ireland (No. 3)*, App. No. 332/57, judgment of July 1, 1961, § 47.

625 Garlicki L., in L. Garlicki (ed), *Konwencja o Ochronie Praw Człowieka i Podstawowych Wolności. Komentarz do artykułów 1–18* (Warszawa 2010), 807–808. Pointing to the controversy concerning the issuance of formal notification, in particular, whether it is possible to make it *ex post*, L. Garlicki also draws attention to the obligation to comply with the national provisions of States whose constitutions provide for the introduction of a state of emergency.

626 The basic theses of the Strasbourg jurisprudence are summarized in official documents produced, updated and made available by the European Court of Human Rights: Guide on Article 15 of the European Convention on Human Rights (document prepared by the ECtHR Registry), updated August 31, 2023 <https://ks.echr.coe.int/documents/d/echr-ks/guide_art_15_eng>, hereafter ECtHR Guide and Derogation in time of emergency (Factsheet) published in February 2022 <https://www.echr.coe.int/documents/d/echr/FS_Derogation_ENG>.

627 The classification and data given are contained in §§ 47–52 of the Draft Report of the Steering Committee on Human Rights (CDDH) on Member States' practice in relation to derogations from the European Convention on Human Rights in situations of crisis, CDDH-SCR(2022)R2 Addendum March 10, 2023 <https://rm.coe.int/steering-committee-for-human-rights-cddh-drafting-group-on-human-right/1680a8cf03>.

itself, within a certain scope of time and subject matter, from the obligation to respect the rights and freedoms guaranteed by the ECHR, regardless of the existence of individual grounds restricting those rights. The individual limitation clauses of the rights and freedoms listed in Articles 8 to 11 of the ECHR refer to specific rights and provide grounds for their limitation due to the grounds indicated in these provisions.[628]

Whenever a derogation clause is applied, it is subject to an assessment of compliance with (1) the principle of margin of appreciation, (2) the principle of proportionality, and (3) the prohibition of undue exercise (abuse) of the rights listed in the ECHR.[629] The margin of discretion left to a Member State in connection with the application of a derogation clause is wide.[630] Under the principle of subsidiarity, the primary responsibility for ensuring the rights and freedoms protected by the Convention lies with the State Party. In turn, Article 18 ECHR does not allow a State to restrict rights and freedoms for purposes other than those for which they were introduced. The assessment of proportionality requires an evaluation of the measures adopted in relation to the type and nature of the threat to the nation posed by the emergency.[631] The prohibition of abuse of rights formulated in Article 17

---

628 E.g., under Article 8(2) ECHR, interference by a public authority with the exercise of the right to private and family life is permissible if it finds a legal basis in the law and is necessary in a democratic society for reasons of national security, public safety or the economic well-being of the country, the protection of order and the prevention of crime, the protection of health and morals or the protection of the rights and freedoms of others. For more on the differences, cf. Garlicki L., in L. Garlicki (ed), *Convention for the Protection of Human Rights and Fundamental Freedoms. Commentary to Articles 1–18* (Warszawa 2010), 798–799.

629 The above principles with regard to the application of the derogation clause are described e.g., by Latos B., *Derogation and Limitation Clause in the European Convention for the Protection of Human Rights and Fundamental Freedoms* (Warszawa 2006), 28–59.

630 E.g., A. and Others v. The United Kingdom (ECtHR February 19, 2009) § 184, in which the Court stated that "When the Court comes to consider a derogation under Article 15, it allows the national authorities a wide margin of appreciation to decide on the nature and scope of the derogating measures necessary to avert the emergency."

631 E.g., A. and Others v. The United Kingdom (ECtHR February 19, 2009), § 185: "approach under Article 15 is necessarily focused on the general situation pertaining in the country concerned, in the sense that the court—whether national or international—is required to examine the measures that have been adopted in derogation

ECHR encompasses such measures that seek to nullify or restrict the rights and freedoms enumerated in the Convention to a greater extent than the Convention provides. The application of the provisions of the Convention must be guided by the principle of the protection of human rights recognized by the State (Article 53 ECHR), which does not allow the provisions of the Convention to be interpreted to limit or exclude human rights or fundamental freedoms covered by a statutory guarantee or agreement to which the State is a Party.

1.6.1.2 A state of public danger threatening the life of the nation

A general derogation of rights is only possible due to a state of public danger threatening the nation's life. This state is not defined in the ECHR. The indication *expressis verbis* in the text of Article 15(1) ECHR of war as a state of public danger threatening the nation's life may be considered an interpretative guideline. The recognition of war as a state of public danger is not irrelevant to the interpretation of the concept. Indeed, a state of war must be regarded as an example of a state of public danger threatening the life of a nation. Other states of public danger must, therefore, be characterized—similar to war—by the scale and seriousness of the threat to the life of the nation. In countries that distinguish between a state of war and a state of martial law, the latter is not the same as a state of war under Article 15 ECHR.[632] The definition of the concept of another state of public danger appeared in the Strasbourg jurisprudence for the first time in the *Lawless* case.[633] The definition formulated in that case was developed in subsequent judgments. Additional

of the Convention rights in question and to weigh them against the nature of the threat to the nation posed by the emergency."

632 Garlicki L., in *Konwencja o Ochronie Praw Człowieka i Podstawowych Wolności. Komentarz do artykułów 1–18* (Warszawa 2010), 800.

633 According to the judgment in the "Lawless" Case, "in the general context of Article 15 of the Convention, the natural and customary meaning of the words 'other public emergency threatening the life of the nation' is sufficiently clear; whereas they refer to an exceptional situation of crisis or emergency which affects the whole population and constitutes a threat to the organized life of the community of which the State is composed"; Lawless v. Ireland (ECtHR 1.07.1961), § 28.

criteria were added: the immediacy and actuality of the danger.[634] In the light of the ECtHR case law to date, the concept of a state of public danger threatening the life of the nation corresponds to a natural and customary meaning. The public danger referred to in Article 15(1) ECHR is (1) present and directly threatening the life of the nation, (2) has effects relating to the whole nation (3), threatens the further organized life of society, and (4) is exceptional, i.e., requiring extraordinary measures.[635] The causes of the threat may not only be political in nature. Indeed, their source may also be natural or economic factors.[636] The criterion of the "life of the nation," on the other hand, means both its physical existence and survival, as well as its "normal functioning—necessary for the existence and operation of the state as a democratic community under the supreme authority of the people, acting and developing through the exercise by the citizens of their political rights."[637] In light of the ECtHR's writings and jurisprudence, the sources of threats to the nation's life are not homogeneous. They may arise from large-scale terrorist activities, a natural disaster, an epidemic, or an industrial disaster of great proportions, and perhaps even the collapse of the economic system's foundations. They also tend to be unpredictable.[638] The aforementioned causes do not preclude a pandemic, such as the recent COVID-19 pandemic,

---

634 In the so-called "Greek case" (Ruling of the European Commission of Human Rights, applications nos.: 3321/67 (*Denmark v. Greece*) 3322/67 (*Norway v. Greece*) 3323/67 (*Sweden v. Greece*) 3344/67 (*Netherlands v. Greece*), the requirement of "actual and imminent" danger was added). On the development of the jurisprudence on the concept of "other state of public danger threatening the life of the nation," cf. Latos B., *Klauzula derogacyjna i limitacyjna w Europejskiej Konwencji o ochronie praw człowieka i podstawowych wolności* (Warszawa 2006), 69 et seq.

635 The case law cited in §§ 9–10 of the ECtHR Guide and Latos B., *Klauzula derogacyjna i limitacyjna w Europejskiej Konwencji o ochronie praw człowieka i podstawowych wolności* (Warszawa 2006), 74–75.

636 Latos B., *Klauzula derogacyjna i limitacyjna w Europejskiej Konwencji o ochronie praw człowieka i podstawowych wolności* (Warszawa 2006) 83.

637 Jasudowicz T., "Zagrożenie życia narodu jako przesłanka wstępna derogacji zobowiązań w dziedzinie praw człowieka" (2020) 4(33) *Studia Prawa Publicznego*, 10.

638 Garlicki L., in L. Garlicki (ed), *Konwencja o Ochronie Praw Człowieka i Podstawowych Wolności. Komentarz do artykułów 1–18* (Warszawa 2010) 800; Latos B., *Klauzula derogacyjna i limitacyjna w Europejskiej Konwencji o ochronie praw człowieka i podstawowych wolności* (Warszawa 2006) 62, 67–68.

from being considered a state of public emergency threatening the nation's life.[639] In each case, however, the individual situation at the particular time in which the affected country finds itself must be assessed. In the preamble to the Draft Recommendation of the Committee of Ministers on the Effective Protection of Human Rights in Situations of Crisis and Its Draft Explanatory Memorandum prepared in 2024, the Covid-19 pandemic and Russia's aggression against Ukraine were identified as crisis situations that require assessment as a state of public danger threatening the life of the nation.[640] The literature has also suggested that the COVID-19 pandemic could be considered a state of public emergency that threatened the nation's life.[641] Similarly, European Parliament documents consider the COVID-19 pandemic to have met the criteria for a derogation of rights under Article 15 ECHR.[642] The legitimacy

639 In relation to the COVID-19 pandemic, ten countries—Albania, Armenia, Estonia, Georgia, Latvia, North Macedonia, Moldova, Romania, San Marino, and Serbia—have made declarations under Article 15(3) of the ECHR to the Secretary General of the Council of Europe, list <https://www.coe.int/en/web/conventions/derogations-covid-19>.

640 (Draft) Recommendation CM/Rec(2024) of the Committee of Ministers to member States on the effective protection of human rights in situations of crisis, hereafter Draft Recommendation CM/Rec(2024): "The Committee of Ministers of the Council of Europe (…) Expressing its concern at the impact on human rights of recent crises that have affected or continue to affect member States, such as the Covid-19 pandemic and Russia's war of aggression against Ukraine; (…) Reaffirming that derogation under Article 15 of the Convention is intended to be an exceptional procedure that is only permissible in times of war or other public emergency threatening the life of the nation and that certain rights are non-derogable, even in the most challenging circumstances; Recommends that the governments of member States: 1. ensure that human rights are respected and effectively protected during situations of crisis; 2. to this end, ensure that the principles set out in the appendix to this recommendation are implemented in practice and, as appropriate, in domestic law; 3. examine, within the Committee of Ministers, the implementation of this recommendation no later than five years after its adoption" <https://rm.coe.int/draft-recommendation-of-the-committee-of-ministers-on-the-effective-pr/1680ae67a2>.

641 Gil A. R., "Derogation Clauses of International Human Rights Instruments: Protecting Rights at the Maximum Possible Extent in Times of Crisis" (2021) V(1) *Catolica Law Review*, 17.

642 "Previously, Article 15 has mainly been applied in the context of terrorism or political violence (e.g., terrorism in Northern Ireland). However, the coronavirus outbreak seems to satisfy the conditions under Article 15 equally. The pandemic has posed an imminent threat to entire states, so it may well amount to a situation of

of recourse under Article 15(1) ECHR to the derogation clause due to the COVID-19 pandemic was not assessed in *Terhes v. Romania*.[643] However, it appears that the ECtHR may take a position on this issue in relation to the subsequent complaints that have been lodged and are pending.[644]

1.6.1.3 Measures taken on the basis of a derogation clause

Measures under Article 15(1) ECHR may not violate other obligations of the State under international law. This prohibition includes provisions of humanitarian law and absolute norms of international law beyond the list of non-derogable obligations set out in Article 4(2) of the International Covenant on Civil and Political Rights (ICCPR).[645]

State action must also respond to the requirements of the situation and comply with the principles of proportionality and temporariness.[646] The margin of discretion is exercised by the national authorities under the supervision of the ECtHR. The Court takes into account the nature of the derogated rights, the reasons for the state of public emergency and its duration.[647]

'public emergency'"—European Parliament document "Upholding human rights in Europe during the pandemic," <https://www.europarl.europa.eu/RegData/etudes/BRIE/2020/652085/EPRS_BRI(2020)652085_EN.pdf>.

643 In Terhes v. Romania (Application No. 49933/20), by a decision of April 13, 2021, the ECtHR declared the complaint inadmissible under Article 35(3)(a) ECHR and held that the allegation of a violation of Article 5(1) ECHR in relation to the lockdown imposed by the Romanian authorities was not substantiated. The level of restrictions on the applicant's freedom of movement was not such as to allow the general lockdown ordered by the authorities to be considered as constituting a deprivation of liberty. In the Court's view, the applicant could not, therefore, be considered a deprivation of liberty within the meaning of Article 5(1) (right to liberty and security of person) of the Convention.

644 The complaints in Pešić and Others v. Serbia (Applications nos. 48973/20, 54565/20 and 54676/20) communicated to Serbia on January 5, 2023 <https://hudoc.echr.coe.int/eng#{%22appno%22:[%2248973/20%22]}>.

645 Office of the High Commissioner for Human Rights, General Comment No. 29: Article 4: Derogations during a State of Emergency, adopted 2001, CCPR/C/21/Rev.1/Add.11, § 11,hereafter CCPR General Comment.

646 Latos B., *Klauzula derogacyjna i limitacyjna w Europejskiej Konwencji o ochronie praw człowieka i podstawowych wolności* (Warszawa 2006) 86, 89.

647 Brannigan and McBride v. The United Kingdom Applications nos. 14553/89, 14554/89 (ECtHR May 25, 1993), § 43.

The creation of a state of public emergency does not constitute an opportunity to restrict individual rights but is intended to protect the democratic order in the State.[648] The purpose of the restrictions introduced should, therefore, be assessed in view of the origins of the crisis. They should aim to mitigate its effects and protect the public. Measures introduced during the COVID-19 pandemic should have guaranteed equal access to medical care and protection of the most vulnerable social groups, e.g., children and the elderly. If their application resulted in a restriction of human rights, e.g., in terms of the right to freedom of movement, they should not have been discriminatory, applying only to foreigners or refugees. The measures applied are admissible if (a) it is not possible to prevent the danger by ordinary measures taken within the limits of the applicable legal order, (b) they are proportionate, and (c) they are accompanied by guarantees to prevent their abuse, in particular in the form of judicial review of their application.[649] The above requirements formulated in ECtHR jurisprudence for the adoption of legal measures in a state of emergency are also found in the Draft Recommendation of the Committee of Ministers on the Effective Protection of Human Rights in Situations of Crisis and Its Draft Explanatory Memorandum of 2024, which requires respect for the principles of legality, necessity, proportionality, temporariness and foreseeability in their application.[650]

1.6.1.4 Effects of the derogation on the rights of refugees and immigrants

Certain rights, enumerated in full in the Convention, are absolute and cannot be subject to any limitation, even in the circumstances referred to in Article 15(1) ECHR. The absolute protection of these rights is the most important limitation on the application of the derogation clause. According to Article 15(2) ECHR, the derogation clause cannot exclude: (1) the protection of the right to life (Article 2 ECHR) except in cases of death resulting

648 § 22 Guide ECtHR.

649 § 24 Guide ECtHR.

650 Article 1 § 3 Appendix to Draft Recommendation CM/Rec (2024): Member States should ensure that the legal framework regulating emergency powers respects the overarching principle of the rule of law and ensures that the exercise of such powers is governed by the principles of legality, necessity, proportionality, temporariness, and foreseeability.

from lawful acts of war, (2) the prohibition of torture (Article 3 ECHR), (3) the prohibition of detention in slavery or servitude (Article 4(1) ECHR), and (4) the prohibition of punishment without legal basis (Article 7 ECHR). A further limitation of the application of the derogation clause was made in the Additional Protocols to the ECHR. On the basis of Article 3 in conjunction with Article 1 and Article 2 of Protocol No. 6 to the ECHR,[651] the possibility of adopting measures revoking the prohibition of the death penalty and its execution was excluded (Article 1 of Protocol No. 6 to the ECHR), with the exception of the death penalty for acts committed in time of war or imminent threat of war. In contrast, more far-reaching protection is provided for by Article 2 of Protocol No. 13 ECHR,[652] which excludes the possibility of derogating from the prohibition of the death penalty conviction and execution on the basis of Article 15 ECHR.[653] This means the derogation of this prohibition is excluded even in a state of war. On the basis of Article 4 of Protocol No. 7 to the ECHR,[654] it is not permissible to apply Article 15 ECHR to suspend the prohibition of re-conviction or punishment in proceedings before a court of the same State for an offense for which he has previously been convicted with final judgment or acquitted in accordance with the law and rules of criminal procedure of that State.

It is difficult to prioritize the rights subject to derogation, but from the perspective of migrants and refugees, it is possible to identify those rights that shape their legal situation as either a refugee or an immigrant more

---

651 Protocol No. 6 to the Convention for the Protection of Human Rights and Fundamental Freedoms, concerning the abolition of the death penalty, done at Strasbourg on April 28, 1983 (OJ 2001, No. 23, item 266), hereinafter "Protocol No. 6 to the ECHR."

652 Protocol No. 13 to the Convention for the Protection of Human Rights and Fundamental Freedoms concerning the abolition of the death penalty in all circumstances, done at Vilnius on May 3, 2002 (OJ 2014, item 1155).

653 A deprivation of the right to life does not constitute a violation of the ECHR only under the conditions referred to in Article 2(2) ECHR and, therefore, if it occurs as a result of the absolutely necessary use of force: (a) in defense of any person from unlawful violence; (b) to effect lawful detention or to prevent the escape of a person lawfully deprived of his liberty; (c) in action lawfully taken to quell a riot or insurrection.

654 Protocol No. 7 to the Convention for the Protection of Human Rights and Fundamental Freedoms, drawn up on November 22, 1984 in Strasbourg (OJ 2003, No. 42, item 364), hereinafter: "Protocol No. 7 to the ECHR."

than others, e.g., the right to freedom of movement and freedom to choose one's place of residence (Article 2 of ECHR Protocol 4).[655] Due to the movement restrictions imposed during the COVID-19 pandemic, this right was subject to a number of restrictions. Compulsory quarantine may also have threatened the right to liberty and security of the person (ECHR Article 5). Of less practical significance may be the derogation of rights enabling participation in social or political life, e.g., the exercise of freedom of assembly and association (Article 11 ECHR).

Due to the Covid-19 pandemic, on the basis of Article 15(3) ECHR, States notified the Secretary General of the Council of Europe that they were taking measures relating to the right to liberty and security of person (Article 5 ECHR)—Armenia, Estonia, Georgia, the right to a fair trial (Article 6 ECHR)—Estonia, the right to respect for family and private life (Article 8 ECHR)—Latvia, Estonia, Romania, freedom of assembly and association (Article 11 ECHR)—Latvia, Romania, Armenia, Moldova, Estonia, Georgia, Albania, North Macedonia, rights to respect for property and prohibition of deprivation of property (Article 1 Additional Protocol No. 1 to ECHR)—Romania, Armenia, Estonia, Georgia, Albania, rights to education (Article 2 ECHR Additional Protocol No. 1)—Latvia, Romania, Moldova, Estonia, Georgia, Albania, North Macedonia, and the right to freedom of movement (Article 2 ECHR Protocol No. 4)—Latvia, Romania, Armenia, Moldova, Estonia, Georgia, Albania, North Macedonia.

1.6.2 Suspension of obligations under the ICCPR due to exceptional public danger threatening the existence of the nation

1.6.2.1 Principles governing the suspension of rights and freedoms guaranteed in the ICCPR

Under Article 4(1) of the International Covenant on Civil and Political Rights,[656] in cases of exceptional public danger threatening the existence of a nation, States Parties to the Covenant may take measures to suspend the

---

655 Protocol No. 4 to the Convention for the Protection of Human Rights and Fundamental Freedoms. Strasbourg.1963.09.16 (Journal of Laws of 1995 No. 36, item 175/2, as amended).

656 International Covenant on Civil and Political Rights Pact opened for signature in New York on December 19, 1966 (OJ 1977, No. 38, item 167), hereinafter: "ICCPR."

application of their obligations under the Covenant to the extent strictly appropriate to the requirements of the situation, provided that the measures taken do not conflict with their other obligations under international law and do not entail discrimination solely on the basis of race, color, sex, language, religion or social origin. It follows, therefore, from the wording of Article 4(1) of the ICCPR that the derogation to suspend "the application of obligations under the Covenant" is temporary and may occur within a strictly defined scope. Certain exhaustively identified rights of the Covenant are absolute and not subject to suspension. A further limitation involves the prohibition of measures that would conflict with other obligations under international law. Suspension of rights must be proportionate and meet the "exigencies of the situation." The measures applied must also not be discriminatory on grounds of race, color, sex, language, religion or social origin.

Article 4(2) of the ICCPR excludes the suspension of the right to life and restrictions relating to the death penalty (Article 6 ICCPR), the prohibition of torture and inhuman treatment (Article 7 ICCPR), the prohibition of slavery and servitude (Articles 8(1) and (2) of the ICCPR), the prohibition of deprivation of liberty on the grounds of inability to perform contractual obligations (Article 11 ICCPR), the prohibition of retroactivity in criminal law (Article 15 ICCPR), the right to legal subjectivity (Article 16 ICCPR) and freedom of thought, conscience and religion (Article 18 ICCPR). As with derogations under Article 15 ECHR, it is necessary for the suspension of the implementation of obligations under the ICCPR to immediately inform, through the Secretary-General of the United Nations, the other States Parties to the Covenant as to which provisions of the Covenant have been suspended and the reasons for doing so. The States Parties must also provide notification of the date on which the suspension ceases to have effect (Article 4(3) ICCPR) in the same manner.

Suspension of obligations under Article 4 of the ICCPR, and in particular the determination of the conditions for its admissibility, requires consideration of the fundamental principles of application and interpretation of the provisions of the Covenant set out in Article 5 ICCPR. Implicit in this provision is the prohibition of such an interpretation which would have the effect of nullifying the rights or freedoms recognized in the Covenant or of restricting them more broadly than is provided for in the Covenant (Article 5(1) ICCPR) and the prohibition of restricting or suspending fundamental human rights recognized or existing in any State Party to the Covenant under laws, conventions, ordinances or custom on the pretext that the Covenant does not recognize such rights or that it recognizes them more narrowly (Article 5(2) ICCPR). The purpose of the prohibition on abuse of the Covenant is to prevent States, by invoking the provisions of the Covenant, from bringing about a greater restriction of the rights contained therein than is permissible. The restrictions on rights envisaged for reasons such as the protection of national security or health cannot be an end in themselves. This also applies to restrictions introduced in connection with the proclamation of a state of emergency.[657] The significance of the "most favoured nation clause" lies in the protection of rights or freedoms guaranteed to a greater extent—either by other treaties, customary law, or domestic law—than is provided for in the Covenant. This means that even if a State complies with the standards of the Covenant, it can claim a breach of the Covenant by violating the provisions of other treaties or domestic law.[658]

1.6.2.2 Conditions for the suspension of obligations under the Covenant pursuant to Article 4 of the ICCPR

Suspension of obligations under Article 4 ICCPR has been linked to a formal condition: an official declaration of an exceptional public danger threatening the nation's existence.[659] This requirement is intended to ensure the implementation of the principles of legalism and the rule of law while emphasizing the exceptionality and temporariness of measures taken on the basis of Article 4 ICCPR. The concept of exceptional public danger includes, within the meaning of the provision in question, both internal or external conflicts (but these are not mentioned in the provision, unlike Article 15 ECHR), as well as various natural disasters, e.g., floods or earthquakes.[660] The willingness to invoke the provisions of Article 4 ICCPR in situations other than armed conflict

---

657 Wieruszewski R., in R. Wieruszewski (ed), *Międzynarodowy Pakt Praw Obywatelskich (Osobistych) i Politycznych* (Warszawa 2012) 94.

658 Wieruszewski R., in R. Wieruszewski (ed), *Międzynarodowy Pakt Praw Obywatelskich (Osobistych) i Politycznych* (Warszawa 2012) 96–97.

659 Wieruszewski R., in R. Wieruszewski (ed), *Międzynarodowy Pakt Praw Obywatelskich (Osobistych) i Politycznych* (Warszawa 2012), 80.

660 Wieruszewski R., in R. Wieruszewski (ed), *Międzynarodowy Pakt Praw Obywatelskich (Osobistych) i Politycznych* (Warszawa 2012) 78.

should, however, be treated with great caution by States Parties. Irrespective of the nature of the danger, the suspension of the application of obligations under the Covenant is permitted to States Parties only in situations and to the extent that the circumstance poses a threat to the existence of the nation.[661] This applies, in particular, to the duration, geographical scope, material scope and type of derogatory measures taken during the state of emergency. This means that even in extraordinary circumstances, States Parties are obliged to be guided by the principle of proportionality. The requirement formulated in Article 4(1) ICCPR to impose restrictions only in a manner that strictly corresponds to the requirements of the situation should thus be interpreted narrowly. Indeed, the possibility provided by the ICCPR to restrict certain rights in ordinary situations—e.g., freedom of movement (Article 12) or freedom of assembly (Article 21)—may be sufficient in given circumstances. This applies, *inter alia*, to situations such as a natural disaster, a major industrial accident or mass demonstrations involving incidents of violence.[662]

The separate nature of the limitations on rights provided for in the various provisions of the Covenant from the issue of suspension of their application (Article 4 ICCPR) is indicated, *inter alia*, by the regulation of Article 18 ICCPR. Although freedom of thought, conscience and religion is one of the rights covered by the absolute prohibition of derogation under Article 4(2) of the ICCPR, under Article 18(3) ICCPR, this right "may be subject [...] to such limitations as are prescribed by law and are necessary for the protection of public security, public order, health or morals or the fundamental rights and freedoms of others."[663] In doing so, it should be emphasized that the catalog of rights covered by the absolute prohibition of derogation, listed in Article 4(2) ICCPR, should not be regarded as fully exhaustive. Indeed, there are a number of regulations related to the prohibition of discrimination (e.g., Articles 26, 2, 3, 14(1), 23(4), 24(1) or 25), the elements or dimensions of which cannot be restricted in any case, despite the absence of their explicit mention in the text of Article 4(2) ICCPR. Indeed, the prohibition of discriminatory measures on the basis of race, color, sex, language, religion or social origin expressed in Article 4(1) ICCPR means that the application of

661 § 3 General Comment CCPR.

662 § 4 and 5 General Comment CCPR.

663 § 7 General Comment CCPR.

measures derogating from the provisions of the Covenant may not lead to different treatment of persons on the basis of the said characteristics.[664] Nor may it violate the principles of international humanitarian law. Indeed, the provisions of Article 4(1) ICCPR do not provide a basis for excluding States Parties' obligations under treaties or general international law. This is also indicated by the wording of Article 5(2) ICCPR, according to which "none of the fundamental human rights recognized or existing in any State Party to the present Covenant by law, convention, ordinance or custom shall be restricted or suspended on the pretext that the present Covenant does not recognize such rights or that it recognizes them to a narrower extent." On the other hand, the category of peremptory norms includes, inter alia, the prohibition of hostage-taking, the prohibition of collective punishment, the prohibition of arbitrary deprivation of liberty or the injunction to respect due process, and the presumption of innocence.[665]

The provisions of Article 4 ICCPR, in particular, cannot be used to justify human rights violations that constitute crimes against humanity. In the view of the Human Rights Committee, this implies an absolute prohibition of restrictions on certain rights—not listed in Article 4(2) ICCPR—as norms of general international law. This includes inter alia, provisions such as (1) the injunction to treat persons deprived of their liberty humanely and without violating their dignity; (2) the prohibition of hostage-taking, abduction or detention; (3) the prohibition of genocide; (4) the prohibition of deportation and forced displacement; (5) the prohibition of discrimination, including the protection of the rights of persons belonging to minorities; and (6) the prohibition of war propaganda and the advocacy of national, racial or religious hatred amounting to incitement to discrimination, hostility or rape.[666]

One of the conditions for the suspension of obligations under the Covenant is also the provision by States Parties of effective remedies under Article 2(3) ICCPR. Indeed, rights expressly declared non-derogable must be covered by procedural guarantees, including a guarantee of judicial redress. Such a requirement is justified by the principles of legalism and the rule of law underlying the Covenant as a whole. In this sense, State Parties must ensure

664 § 8 General Comment CCPR.
665 § 9 and 11 General Comment CCPR.
666 § 12 and 13 General Comment CCPR.

the basic requirements of a fair and just trial, even in a state of exceptional public danger threatening the nation's existence.[667]

In any event, when exercising their right of derogation under Article 4 ICCPR, States Parties are required to promptly inform the other States Parties, through the Secretary-General of the United Nations, both of the provisions from which they have derogated and of the reasons and scope of the measures taken. This requirement also applies to the notification of the termination of the derogation.

1.6.3 Restriction of the rights and freedoms guaranteed in the Charter of Fundamental Rights of the European Union

The possibility of introducing restrictions on the exercise of the rights and freedoms recognized by the Charter of Fundamental Rights of the European Union[668] has been linked, under Article 52(1) CFR, to the need to fulfill two conditions. First, the possibility of doing so must be provided for by statute. Secondly, any restrictions "may be imposed only if they are necessary and genuinely meet objectives of general interest recognized by the Union or the need to protect the rights and freedoms of others." In this sense, they are to give effect to the principle of proportionality while preserving the essence of individual rights and freedoms.

It is noteworthy that the CFR refers to the ECHR in interpreting its provisions. Indeed, as it follows from Article 52(3) of the CFR, the rights contained therein, corresponding to those guaranteed by the ECHR, should be interpreted in accordance with the latter. This also applies, it seems, to the absolute nature of some of its provisions. This understanding of the regulation in question is also indicated by the content of Article 53 CFR. Indeed, it introduces a prohibition on interpreting the provisions of the CFR in a way that restricts or violates human rights and fundamental freedoms as recognized by international law and the constitutions of the Member States.

By contrast, the very possibility of imposing a limitation on the exercise of rights and freedoms should be treated as an exception. Indeed, as is clear

---

667 §§ 14–16 General Comment CCPR.

668 Charter of Fundamental Rights of the European Union (OJ EU. C. 2007 No. 303, 1 as amended); hereinafter: "CFR."

from Article 54 CFR, nothing in the CFR may be understood as conferring the right to take measures to nullify the rights and freedoms recognized in the Charter or to restrict them to a greater extent than is provided for in the Charter. This also applies to exceptional situations that threaten public security. It is worth noting here the position of the jurisprudence of the Court of Justice of the European Union (CJEU) on Article 18 CFR (right to asylum). The CJEU excluded the possibility of depriving a foreigner of an effective right to apply for international protection due to a massive influx of migrants even if a Member State declares a state of war, a state of emergency or a situation of exception for this reason.[669]

1.6.4 Conclusions

Suspension of the application of obligations under the ECHR, the ICCPR, and the CFR in a state of public emergency is a procedure separate from the procedure for the restriction of rights by law to protect public security, public order, public health or morals, or the fundamental rights and freedoms of others. As a special solution to protect the democratic order of the state in a situation of exceptional public danger threatening the existence of the nation, it is linked to the need to meet a number of formal conditions.

Firstly, it is only applicable in a situation where the life of the nation is at risk, i.e., in the event of internal or external armed conflict, large-scale terrorist activities, natural disasters, epidemics or industrial disasters of major proportions. This condition was also fulfilled, as indicated by an analysis of ECtHR jurisprudence and the literature, by the Covid-19 pandemic. In each case, however, it requires an assessment of the individual situation of the State Party resulting from the pandemic cycle in which it is located and, therefore, the degree of public health emergency prevailing in its territory.

Secondly, the measures applied must be proportionate. There is, therefore, no scope for an expansive interpretation of derogation clauses. This observation applies in particular to so-called peremptory rights, including the prohibition of discrimination based on race, color, sex, language, religion or social origin. States Parties are obliged to make use of derogations by way

---

669 CJEU judgment of June 30, 2022, Valstybės sienos apsaugos tarnyba et al., C-72/22 PPU, ECLI:EU:2022:505, especially §§ 61–63.

of exception, reaching in the first instance for legal solutions provided for in "normal" situations—the possibility of statutory limitations of particular rights for the protection of public security, order, health or public morals or the fundamental rights and freedoms of others.

Thirdly, the suspension of the application of obligations under the ECHR, the ICCPR and the CFR entails the obligation to immediately notify the competent authorities and officially declare an exceptional public emergency threatening the existence of the nation. On the other hand, the notification must clearly indicate the provisions from which the State has derogated, the reasons for the derogation, the extent of the measures taken and their duration. The termination of the derogation is also subject to the obligation to notify.

Substantive and procedural law perspective: human rights of migrants in times of emergency in selected countries

2.1 Belgium (Geert Debersaques, Anke Meskens)

2.1.1 Substantive law perspective: human rights of migrants in times of emergency in Belgium

The present contribution aims to critically navigate through the vast framework of human rights protection and how they are safeguarded toward third-country nationals in the Belgian legal landscape. We will traverse a selection of these fundamental rights, recognizing that our exploration is not exhaustive. Rather, our chapter illuminates fundamental rights that underpin the treatment and protection of migrants and therefore serves as a selective examination of key rights that are pivotal to the Belgian discourse of human rights related to migration.

In doing so, we will refer to Belgian legislation, mainly the law on foreign nationals,[670] and will highlight pertinent Belgian case law—primarily case law by entities involved in the asylum procedure—i.e., the Council for asylum

[670] I.e., Law on entry to the territory, residence, establishment and removal of foreign nationals of December 15, 1980, *Moniteur Belge* December 31, 1980. This legal Act is often referred to as "the Aliens Act." However, the authors have chosen to adhere to the abbreviation ("the Law on foreign nationals") utilized by the CJEU, *inter alia* in case C-302/18 X v Belgian State [2018] ECLI:EU:C:2019:830.

and immigration proceedings of Belgium[671] and the Council of State of Belgium—which acts as a court of last resort.[672]

2.1.1.1 The state of emergency in Belgium

2.1.1.1.1 Article 187 of the Constitution

The Belgian Constitution[673] does not mention the notion of "state of emergency," nor does it provide for a comprehensive framework to set aside certain constitutional rules regarding fundamental rights during crisis. Notably, while select constitutional provisions refer to specific emergency situations, particularly pertaining to situations of armed conflict, broader provisions on the state of emergency are lacking in Belgian constitutional law. In this regard, Article 187 of the Constitution acts as a principal safeguard against nearly any form of state emergency prerogatives.

Pursuant to Article 187 of the Constitution, it is not possible to *suspend* the Constitution in whole or in part, i.e., whereby a constitutionally guaranteed right is temporarily formally, or *de facto*, set aside.[674] However, the prohibition on suspending constitutionally guaranteed rights does not preclude their "restriction," wherein the respective fundamental right remains applicable but is subject to a measure seemingly incompatible with it. Such restrictions are generally deemed acceptable, as fundamental rights are not always absolute.

---

671 "Raad voor Vreemdelingenbetwistingen" in Dutch ("RvV") or "Conseil du Contentieux des Etrangers" in French ("CCE"). This is also commonly referred to as "the Council for Alien Law Litigation." For the purpose of this contribution, the authors have chosen to adhere to the legal glossary adopted by the CJEU. Henceforth, we will refer to the "Council for asylum and immigration proceedings" (see, *inter alia* in case C-302/18 X v Belgian State [2018] ECLI:EU:C:2019:830).
It should be noted that the European Court of Human Rights refers to the Council for asylum and immigration proceedings as "Aliens Appeals Board," e.g., in case *Paposhvili v Belgium* [GC] [2016] App No. 41738/10 (ECtHR, December 13, 2016).

672 For more information, please refer to: Kingdom of Belgium, Federal Public Service Foreign Affairs, Foreign trade and development cooperation, "Asylum and migration" <https://diplomatie.belgium.be/en/policy/policy-areas/striving-global-solidarity/asylum>.

673 Hereinafter: "the Constitution."

674 Article 187 of the Belgian Constitution states: "The Constitution cannot be suspended in whole or in part."

The Constitution establishes a system of formal restrictions on fundamental rights, while human rights treaties impose substantive restriction criteria[675]: Article 187 of the Constitution states that it is not possible to suspend the Constitution in whole or in part, and, pursuant to Article 53 of the European Convention on Human Rights,[676] it is likewise not possible to deviate from the fundamental rights guaranteed in the ECHR under Article 15 ECHR.[677]

The Constitution mandates that most restrictions can only be adopted by formal law.

Additionally, regulatory, and punitive measures are always permissible, whereas preventive restrictions, which entail prior authorization to exercise the fundamental right, are prohibited for most fundamental rights.[678] If a fundamental right is at issue that is guaranteed both in the Constitution and in a human rights treaty, the Constitutional Court requires that a restriction must cumulatively satisfy both types of restriction criteria.[679]

A mere restriction of a fundamental right is therefore not problematic in itself in light of Article 187 of the Constitution. However, it is argued that a set of very extensive restrictions on various fundamental rights simultaneously, which cannot be justified according to the mentioned criteria, may effectively amount to a suspension and therefore may be at loggerheads with Article 187 of the Constitution.[680]

---

675 Alen A., and Muylle K., *Handboek van het Belgisch Staatsrecht* (Wolters Kluwer 2011) 78–78.

676 Hereinafter: "ECHR."

677 Council of State, Legislative Section, Advise concerning A preliminary draft of law "concerning measures of administrative policing during an epidemic emergency" [2021] 68.936/AV <http://www.raadvst-consetat.be/dbx/adviezen/68936.pdf#search=68.936>, §8.

678 Van Haegenborgh G., and Verrijdt W., "De noodtoestand in het Belgische Publiekrecht" [2016] 1 Preadviezen Vereniging voor de vergelijkende studie van het recht <https://www.bjutijdschriften.nl/tijdschrift/PVVR/2016/1/PVVR_2666-7126_2016_010_001_001.pdf>.

679 Constitutional Court of Belgium [2004] 202/2004.

680 Van Haegenborgh G., and Verrijdt W., "De noodtoestand in het Belgische Publiekrecht" [2016] 1 Preadviezen Vereniging voor de vergelijkende studie van het recht <https://www.bjutijdschriften.nl/tijdschrift/PVVR/2016/1/PVVR_2666-7126_2016_010_001_001.pdf> 15.

2.1.1.2 Human rights related to migration

2.1.1.2.1 Introduction: the legal framework in Belgium

The Law on foreign nationals along with subsequent amendments, serves as the cornerstone delineating the rights and responsibilities accorded to third-country nationals residing within its borders.

Within the Belgian legal framework governing extended residence of third-country nationals, two main distinct categories are delineated in the Law on foreign nationals.

The first category, laid down in Article 10 of the Law on foreign nationals, pertains to specific foreigners who were granted permission to reside in the Kingdom of Belgium. Typically, this category encompasses individuals granted residence status based on well-defined criteria, notably those associated with family reunification.

Conversely, the second category, addressed in Articles 9, *9bis*, and *9ter* of the Law on foreign nationals, pertains to third-country nationals who are merely "authorized" to stay in Belgium. Unlike the more prescriptive criteria applicable to the first category, the authorization under Article 9, *9bis* and *9ter* of the Law on foreign nationals involves a discretionary decision, affording the Immigration Office the flexibility to consider various factors beyond strict legal requirements. As the Council of State has held, however, this does not mean that the Immigration Office enjoys unfettered discretion. The margin of assessment conferred on the administration under Article 9bis of the Law on Foreign Nationals is not arbitrary, since that power must be exercised in compliance with the provision itself and with the legal notion of "exceptional circumstances" as interpreted in the case law.[681] This means, however, that the discretionary assessment enjoyed by the Immigration Office allows for a more nuanced evaluation of individual circumstances when considering the authorization to stay in Belgium stemming from Articles 9, 9bis and 9ter of the Law on foreign nationals.

Moreover, in order to be permitted to extend their stay in Belgium for a duration exceeding 90 days, foreigners are normally required to secure permission via the Belgian embassy or consular post of their place of residence or stay abroad, prior to arrival in the state. However, Article 9bis of the Law on foreign nationals stipulates that individuals (whose residency status in

---

681 Council of State of Belgium [2025] 261982.

Belgium is unlawful or precarious), who wish to obtain long-term residency without the necessity of returning to their country of origin, may lodge an application directly in Belgium, provided they are able to substantiate exceptional circumstances. It is for the Immigration office to assess the circumstances through an individual assessment. Article 9ter of the Law on foreign nationals provides for the possibility of granting leave to remain on medical grounds. Articles 9, *9bis*, and *9ter* of the Law on foreign nationals therefore constitute pivotal legal provisions specifically designed to address unique situations related to residence and migration in Belgium. These provisions play a pivotal role in accommodating individuals facing exceptional circumstances, providing legal pathways for their continued stay in the country.

This differentiation underscores the nuanced nature of immigration regulations in Belgium, where certain individuals are "allowed" to stay based on predefined criteria, while others may be "authorized" to stay through a more personalized and discretionary assessment process.

The focus of our contribution is primarily directed toward the latter category. Indeed, a comprehensive examination of all legal pathways for residence of third-country nationals and their connection to human rights exceeds the scope of this contribution.

2.1.1.2.2 The right to private and family life under Article 8 ECHR

2.1.1.2.2.1 Introduction

The European Convention on Human Rights takes precedence as a higher standard over national immigration law.[682]

Article 8 of the European Convention on Human Rights safeguards the right to respect for private and family life. Article 8 protects a wide range of personal and family relationships, encompassing not only familial bonds but also other close relationships. The right is not absolute, and limitations are permitted when necessary. Hence, Article 8 of the European Convention on Human Rights does not prevent states from establishing conditions for the entry and residence of foreigners on their territory, nor from taking removal measures against foreigners who do not meet the conditions.[683,684]

---

682 Council of State of Belgium [2009] 193552.

683 Council of State of Belgium [2009] 193380.

684 Notably, in earlier case law, the Council of State of Belgium argued (in contradiction with the Court of Cassation) that the principle of respecting private and family life

In the Belgian legal landscape, Article 8 of the European Convention on Human Rights has materialized as a protective measure against *refoulement* or involuntary deportation. This development is inherently logical, given that the familial relationships of an individual subjected to denied entry or deportation are inherently more profound, intimate, and extensive than those of a foreign national on a temporary visit.

The interference with family life under Article 8 of the European Convention on Human Rights arises solely when the foreigner establishes that family life in their country of origin is exceptionally challenging, and the denial of a settlement application or a residence permit, in adherence to the prevailing regulations, would consequently represent such interference.

Henceforth, under this section, we shall first delve into an examination of the diverse modalities of long residence as stipulated within Belgian legislation, concurrently considering their intersection with the provisions outlined in Article 8 of the European Convention on Human Rights. Afterwards, we will explore Article 8 ECHR considering expulsion decisions of foreigners.

2.1.1.2.2.2 The right to residence in the context of Article 8 ECHR

2.1.1.2.2.2.1 Authorization to stay due to exceptional circumstances on the basis of Article 9bis of the Law on foreign nationals

The exceptional residence permit procedure is an essential aspect of Belgium's commitment to upholding human rights and ensuring that vulnerable individuals are not left without legal recourse.

Article *9bis* § 1 of the Law on foreign nationals, stipulates the following: "In extraordinary circumstances and provided that the foreigner possesses an identity document, the residence permit can be requested from the mayor of the place where he resides. The mayor forwards it to the minister or his authorized representative. If the minister or his authorized representative grants the residence permit, the residence permit in Belgium will be issued."

Therefore, Article *9bis* of the Law on foreign nationals provides a basis for, i.e., humanitarian regularization, allowing individuals facing exceptional circumstances to apply for residence in Belgium. It provides a legal framework

is entirely unrelated to measures of removal taken by the government to safeguard society from those who disturb public order. Cfr.: Council of State of Belgium [2009] 193552, Court of Cassation of Belgium [1981] RW 1981–82, [1982] 721.

for individuals who find themselves in exceptional circumstances, making it difficult for them to return to their country of origin.

Humanitarian considerations, such as serious health issues, family ties, or other compelling reasons, are considered under this provision. Hence, the procedure under Article *9bis* allows individuals to apply for an exceptional residence permit based on humanitarian grounds. The decision to grant or deny a stay is made by the Immigration Office,[685] taking into consideration the specific circumstances presented by the applicant. The Immigration Office is granted broad discretion in appreciating the exceptional circumstances.

There are two conditions for an application ex Article 9bis to be granted. Firstly, an examination is conducted to determine if there are "extraordinary circumstances" justifying the submission of the request in Belgium. This concerns the admissibility of the application.

Only when the answer to this question is in the affirmative, secondly, an assessment is made to determine if the invoked reasons to obtain the residence permit (the substance of the matter) are sufficient. The extraordinary circumstances should not be confused with the substantive arguments invoked to obtain the residence permit. Accepting a specific situation as an extraordinary circumstance to declare an application admissible under Article 9 bis of the Law on foreign nationals does not necessarily mean that the application should also be declared well-founded.[686] Extraordinary circumstances within the meaning of Article 9, paragraph 3, of the Law on foreign nationals are circumstances that make it impossible or particularly difficult to submit the application in accordance with the appropriate procedure from the country of origin or the place of residence abroad. These extraordinary circumstances must not be confused with the substantive arguments invoked to obtain the authorization to reside.[687]

Extraordinary circumstances must pertain to the conditions that prevented the foreigner, before leaving for Belgium, from applying for the residence

---

685 "Dienst Vreemdelingenzaken" in Dutch (DVZ), Office des étrangers (OE) in French. As a federal public entity, the Immigration Office is tasked with enforcing the provisions of the Law on foreign nationals and the Royal Decree of October 8, 1981 on access to the territory, residence, settlement and removal of foreign nationals (hereafter: "Decree on foreign nationals").

686 Council of State of Belgium [2009] 196.179.

687 Council of State of Belgium [2009] 196179.

permit at a Belgian diplomatic or consular post, or if the foreigner is already in Belgium, returning to the country of origin for such application.[688]

In the realm of immigration and residence permit applications based on Article *9bis*, the term "extraordinary" does not go as far as to require that it must be "impossible" for the foreigner to apply for a residence permit abroad. It is necessary, but sufficient that it is "particularly difficult" to do so. There is no requirement for an insurmountable obstacle or force majeure. In assessing whether the circumstances are "extraordinary," a proportionality test is applied. The extraordinary circumstances are examined in relation to the country of which the foreigner holds nationality or in relation to the country of his habitual residence when he has resided there for an extended period of time.[689] Already accepted as "extraordinary circumstances" include the risk of blood revenge,[690] recognition as stateless,[691] discrimination against homosexuals in the country of origin and the right to private and family life of the applicant.[692]

Not accepted as extraordinary circumstances include the extended duration of stay in Belgium, integration in Belgium,[693] language proficiency,[694] and the high cost of the round trip to the country of origin.[695] These reasons can be invoked, however, as grounds for justification (and add to the substance of the application), but they are not sufficient to meet the aforementioned condition of admissibility of "extraordinary circumstances." Moreover, extraordinary circumstances must indicate that it is impossible or particularly difficult to return to the country of origin to submit the application there.

As a rule, a challenging situation in the country of origin is insufficient on its own to invoke it as an extraordinary circumstance. However, the foreigner can demonstrate in what way specifically this situation is exceptional for him and prevents their return to their country.

As mentioned before, the right to family or private life, recognized by Article 8 European Convention on Human Rights, can constitute an

---

688 Council of State of Belgium [2016] 235.719.
689 Council of State of Belgium [2017] 188561.
690 Council of State of Belgium [2015] 148318.
691 Council of State of Belgium [2017] 185933, Council of State of Belgium [2018] 12969.
692 Council for asylum and immigration proceedings [2009] 197916, Council for asylum and immigration proceedings [2018] 200767.
693 Council for asylum and immigration proceedings [2016] 178496.
694 Council of State of Belgium [1998] 73.000.
695 Council of State of Belgium [2014] 117448.

extraordinary circumstance in application of Article 9bis of the Law on foreign nationals.[696]

Article 8 of the European Convention on Human Rights mandates a specific and detailed balancing of interests. This requirement extends beyond cases involving removal measures and necessitates the Immigration Office to provide reasoned justifications addressing all circumstances presented by the applicant as extraordinary.[697] The obligation to respect the right to private and family life, as enshrined in Article 8 of the European Convention on Human Rights, underscores the need for a thorough and individualized assessment of each case.

Moreover, the invocation of respect for the right to private and family life can serve as a substantive reason for seeking a residence permit under Article 9bis of the Law on foreign nationals. This dual role emphasizes the multifaceted nature of Article 8 of the European Convention on Human Rights within the Belgian immigration context, encompassing both procedural considerations in the evaluation of removal measures and substantive grounds for obtaining a residence permit.[698]

In return, the onus is on the foreigner to delineate the exceptional circumstances mandated by law.

A foreigner must clearly indicate which information he considers as extraordinary circumstances and which he considers as the underlying reasons of his application. A government decision cannot be annulled due to a lack of justification concerning elements that were not presented as extraordinary circumstances in the application.[699] If the circumstances that the foreigner invokes as extraordinary already existed before his arrival in Belgium, he must explain why he could not submit the application abroad.[700]

In the context of an application on the basis of Article 9bis of the Law on foreign nationals, the competent authorities, such as the Immigration Office or the competent minister, are obligated to provide the reasons behind their decision. This must ensure transparency and accountability in the

---

696 Council for asylum and immigration proceedings [2018] 197916, Council for asylum and immigration proceedings [2018] 200767.

697 Council for asylum and immigration proceedings [2018] 200767. Council of State of Belgium [2025] 262532.

698 Council for asylum and immigration proceedings [2015] 137693.

699 Council for asylum and immigration proceedings [2018] 241270.

700 Council for asylum and immigration proceedings [2010] 44408.

decision-making process, providing applicants with clear reasons for the acceptance or rejection of their application.

A standard formulation or a reference to the policy decision to impose an immigration stop is not a sufficient justification for the authority to deny an application ex Article 9bis of the Law on foreign nationals, as, in accordance with Article 9 of the Law on foreign nationals, the Immigration Office has the authority to deviate from such immigration stop. The rejection of a request for international protection also does not automatically entail the rejection of a residence permit, as the scope of application is different.

A refusal must address the circumstances that the foreigner presents as extraordinary. If such circumstances are considered, the substantive reasons for obtaining the residence permit must be addressed. Through the reasoning, the foreigner must clearly understand why their application was rejected—that is, why their reasons were not considered extraordinary or, even if the presented circumstances were recognized as extraordinary, the underlying reasons for his application are not considered valid.

When the right to private and family life, as articulated in Article 8 of the European Convention on Human Rights, is invoked as an exceptional circumstance within the context of an application under Article 9bis of the Law on foreign nationals, the Immigration Office is obliged to undertake a more comprehensive case-by-case analysis. Merely asserting that Article 8 is inapplicable due to the entire family being required to leave the territory, thus avoiding family separation, does not suffice.

2.1.1.2.2.3 Expulsion of migrants under Belgian legislation in the context of Article 8 ECHR

The intricacies of family life in the context of expulsion decisions underscore the judiciary's recognition of the heightened significance and potential vulnerabilities associated with the disruption of familial bonds in cases involving denied entry or deportation.

Article 74/13 of the Law on foreign nationals stipulates: "When making a decision regarding removal, the minister or their authorized representative takes into account the best interests of the child, family and private life, and the health condition of the concerned third-country national". Furthermore, Article 7 § 1 of the Law on foreign nationals provides the obligation to issue an order to leave the territory only "without prejudice to more favourable provisions contained in an international treaty," including the right to respect for private and family life protected by Article 8 European Convention on Human Rights. In any case, Article 8 of the European Convention on Human Rights takes precedence as a higher standard over national immigration law.[701]

The discretionary power of the competent authority in this case to issue an order to leave the territory, therefore, is not absolute.[702]

The respect for the right to family life in the expulsion of foreigners has been addressed several times in the case law of the European Court of Human Rights. Article 8 ECHR doesn't grant an automatic right to individuals to enter or stay in a country where they are not nationals.

As a rule, when the situation does not involve an existing residency being terminated, but rather an initial admission, the decision cannot constitute an interference with family or private life to which Article 8, paragraph 2 of the ECHR applies.[703] Pursuant to the case law European Court of Human Rights, in case of initial admission, the assessment pivots on whether there is a positive state obligation to uphold and foster the right to private and/ or family life protected in Article 8 ECHR.[704]

The extent of the positive obligations on the state depend on the merits of the case. Following a comprehensive assessment, a "fair balance" must be struck between the interests of the foreigner and their family on the one hand, and of society (in this case the general interest of Belgian society) in conducting migration policy and maintaining public order on the other.[705]

States exceed their margin of appreciation when they fail to conduct a fair balancing of interests, leading to a violation of Article 8, paragraph 1, of the ECHR.[706]

This balancing of interests should also occur when there is either no residence right or it has ceased to exist.[707]

---

701 Council of State of Belgium [2009] 193552.

702 Council of State of Belgium [2018] 240917.

703 Council for asylum and immigration proceedings [2024] 302585.

704 *Ahmut v The Netherlands* [1996] App No. 21702/93 (ECtHR, November 28, 1996), § 63; *Rodriguez Da Silva and Hoogkamer v The Netherlands* [2006] App No. 50435/99 (ECtHR, January 31, 2006), § 38; *Jeunesse v The Netherlands* [GC] [2014] App No. 12738/10 (ECtHR, October 3, 2014), § 108.

705 Council of State of Belgium [2015] 231356.

706 *Nuñez v Norway* [2011] App No. 55597/09 (ECtHR June 28, 2011), § 84; Council for asylum and immigration proceedings [2024] 302424.

707 Council of State of Belgium [2015] 231356.

In Belgium, the Council for asylum and immigration proceedings only exercises legality control over the contested decision, verifying whether the Immigration Office has considered all relevant facts and circumstances in their balancing of interests and, in so doing, has not unreasonably concluded that such balance resulted in a "fair balance."[708]

According to the European Court of Human Rights, pivotal to ensuring a right to respect for private or family life is the very existence of a private or family life worthy of protection under Article 8 ECHR.

Central to the determination of the positive obligation of the state in case of initial admission is determining whether family ties were formed at the time when the individuals were aware of immigration regulations in the host country posing immediate precarity to such ties. In the latter case, only in highly exceptional circumstances would the expulsion of the family member who is not a national of the host country amount to a breach of Article 8 ECHR.[709] In this instance, it is incumbent on the claimant to specifically demonstrate that they have built social ties with the community they reside in that are so intense that they form part of their social identity, thus falling under the notion "private life" in Article 8 ECHR, and cannot be classified as "ordinary" social relationships.[710] The Council for asylum and immigration proceedings follows this line of reasoning, upholding *inter alia* that the mere fact that the claimant has built a network of friends is insufficient to demonstrate this.[711]

Moreover, in ascertaining the positive obligations stemming from Article 8 ECHR, scrutiny extends to identifying obstacles to sustaining family life elsewhere. For instance, according to the Council of State, regarding a decision to refuse residence and order to leave the territory, the family life of the applicant is not affected if he is not separated from his family.[712]

Absent such impediments, there can be no infringement of Article 8 ECHR. It is for the claimant to demonstrate tangible barriers hindering

---

708 Council for asylum and immigration proceedings [2024] 302424.

709 *Mitchell v United Kingdom* [1998] App No. 40447/98 (ECtHR, November 24, 1998); *Ajayi and Others v United Kingdom* [1999] App No. 27663/95 (ECtHR, June 22, 1999); *Butt v Norway* [2012] App No. 47017/09 (ECtHR, December 4, 2012), § 79; Council for asylum and immigration proceedings [2024] 302410.

710 Council for asylum and immigration proceedings [2024] 300900.

711 Council for asylum and immigration proceedings [2024] 300900; 302410.

712 Council of State of Belgium [2018] 240621.

the continuation of family life abroad. Mere existence of family life within one jurisdiction is insufficient. The European Court of Human Rights even suggests that contemporary communication methods, or periodic visits, may facilitate the maintenance of family ties.[713]

Examinations on the existence of private or family life by the Courts ruling on an appeal against a removal decision should be made *ex nunc* to fully safeguard Article 8 ECHR. Before, this was already possible in summary proceedings for extremely urgent necessity, but given recent evolvements in the European Court of Human Rights case law, Belgian judicial bodies are now also obliged to carry out this assessment during regular annulment appeals (before the Council for asylum and immigration proceedings) and during appeals in cassation (before the Council of State).

Moreover, in the recent *Makdoudi* case,[714] the Belgian state argued that it could not take into account family life because the applicants' parental status became official only after the ministerial decision of expulsion was made.

Therefore, according to the government, family life did not exist at the time of the expulsion decision.[715]

The Council of State of Belgium was confronted with the fact that, during the course of proceedings before the Council of State, the applicant was recognized as the father of a child. However, initially, the Council of State refused to take this acknowledgment into consideration, asserting that the applicant could not retrospectively assert the establishment of paternity for the first time the appeal in cassation before the Council of State. However, the European Court of Human Rights did not follow this line of reasoning and ruled that there was indeed family life in this case within the meaning of Article 8 of the European Convention on Human Rights. According to the Court, the existence of family or private life is scrutinized when the removal decision becomes final, which is the date of the Council of State's cassation judgment. At that time, the applicant had already acknowledged his daughter two months prior.

---

713 *ME v Sweden* [2014] App No. 71398/12 (ECtHR June 26, 2014).

714 *Makdoudi v Belgium* [2020] App No. 12848/15 (ECtHR February 18, 2020).

715 Vandennieuwenhuysen E., "Belgische beoordelingsmomenten in uitwijzingsprocedures geviseerd door het EHRM: het arrest-Makdoudi en de artikelen 5 en 8 EVRM (noot onder EHRM 18 februari 2020, nr. 12848/15, Makdoudi t. België)" [2020] *TVreemd* 277, 289.

2.1.1.2.3 *The prohibition of torture, inhumane or degrading treatment or punishment under Article 3 ECHR*

2.1.1.2.3.1 *Introduction*

Article 3 of the European Convention on Human Rights prohibits torture, inhumane, or degrading treatment or punishment. According to the Strasbourg case law, it is an absolute right, which means that no circumstances or exceptions can justify any form of mistreatment. The European Court of Human Rights has consistently emphasized Article 3 European Convention on Human Rights as a fundamental safeguard against any form of physical or mental harm.

On multiple occasions, the European Court of Human Rights has affirmed that extradition to a requesting state can raise issues under Article 3 ECHR, thus potentially holding the extraditing state responsible, when there are serious and proven grounds to believe that the individual faces a genuine risk of being subjected to treatment contrary to Article 3 ECHR.[716] Hence, according to European Court of Human Rights case law, consideration must be given to the general situation in the country of destination and to the individual circumstances of the person concerned.[717] In assessing the general situation in a country, the European Court of Human Rights often attaches importance to information contained in recent reports from independent international human rights organizations.

In the same vein, the Council of State of Belgium ruled that, given the burden of proof lying on the applicant, a mere reference to the general situation in the requesting country or the mere possibility of inhuman treatment contrary to Article 3 ECHR does not suffice to establish a violation of the latter provision. The individual must also demonstrate the circumstances specific to their case that suggest treatment contrary to Article 3 ECHR.[718]

2.1.1.2.3.2 *The right to residence in the context of Article 3 ECHR*

2.1.1.2.3.2.1 *Introduction*

In the landmark *Paposhvili* case, the European Court of Human Rights held that a person with serious medical conditions facing deportation could rely on Article 3 European Convention on Human Rights based on his or her medical

---

716 *Soering v United Kingdom* [1989] App No. 14038/88 (ECtHR July 7, 1989), §§ 88 and 91; *Zarmayev v Belgium* [2014] App No. 35/10 (ECtHR May 27, 2014), § 87.

717 *Zarmayev v Belgium* [2014] App No. 35/10 (ECtHR May 27, 2014), § 89.

718 Council of State of Belgium [2022] 252800, § 18.

conditions.[719] The landmark ruling significantly expanded the interpretation of Article 3 ECHR. The case concerned an applicant who had lodged a request before Belgian authorities for regularization on medical grounds based on Article *9ter* of the Law on foreign nationals.[720] In addition to his deteriorating health conditions, the applicant referred to the fact that he had been continuously resident in Belgium for 11 years and had lasting social ties in that country, and to his family situation. The applicant also argued that if he was sent back, he would be left to fend for himself while ill in a country in which he no longer had any family ties and where the medical facilities were unsuitable and expensive.

Notably, in Belgium, the regulation of residence of seriously ill foreigners is covered by Article 9ter of the Law on foreign nationals and is also (partially) covered by Article 48/4 of the same law.

2.1.1.2.3.2.2 Article 9ter of the Law on foreign nationals concerning the possibility of granting a residence permit on medical grounds

2.1.1.2.3.2.2.1 Article 9ter of the Law on foreign nationals: a provision of domestic law sui generis?

Article *9ter* of the Law on foreign nationals pertains to the regulation of the stay of seriously ill foreigners for whom appropriate treatment is lacking in the country of origin or residence. Returning them would pose a real risk to the life or physical integrity of the individual or expose them to a real risk of inhuman or degrading treatment.

Although Article 9ter was presented by the Belgian legislator as partially transposing Article 15 (b) of Council Directive 2004/83/EC of

---

719 *Paposhvili v Belgium* [GC] [2016] App No. 41738/10 (ECtHR, December 13, 2016).

720 Notably, Belgian Judge Lemmens at the European Court of Human Rights provided a concurring opinion, emphasizing that the previous case, N v UK (*N v United Kingdom* [GC] [2008] App No. 26565/05 (ECtHR May 27, 2008) had not adequately addressed the protection of seriously ill individuals who were not on the brink of death. Judge Lemmens noted that Belgian case law already provided broader protection than the strict stance taken by the ECtHR in N v UK by taking the view that a residence permit on medical grounds for individuals at risk of inhuman or degrading treatment should be provided if there is no appropriate medical care in the receiving country. The GC approach in the *Paposhvili case* thus aligned (more or less) with Belgium's approach, affirming the need to consider the potential harm to seriously ill individuals facing deportation (see: Concurring Opinion of Judge Lemmens, *Paposhvili v Belgium* [GC] [2016] App No. 41738/10 (ECtHR, December 13, 2016) 53 et seq).

April 29, 2004,[721] concerning "seriously ill" foreigners and was depicted as providing the opportunity for these individuals to be granted permission to stay in Belgian territory under the status of subsidiary international protection,[722] the Court of Justice of the European Union, in two cases, namely the case *Mohamed M'Bodj v Belgian State*[723] and case *Centre public d'action sociale d'Ottignies-Louvain-La-Neuve v Moussa Abdida*,[724] explained that a residence permit based on Article 9ter of the Law on foreign nationals, is not a "form of subsidiary international protection," nor is it a "more favourable standard" within the meaning of Article 3 of the directive since it is not compatible with its terms and purpose. Instead, it falls under the terms of Article 2, g), in fine, of Directive 2004/83/EC, as an "other type of protection outside the scope of this directive."

Furthermore, in the *M'Bodj ca*se, the Court of Justice of the European Union (hereinafter: "CJEU") determined that the grant of residence on medical grounds to individuals not meeting the essential criteria for subsidiary protection under the Qualification Directive could not be considered a higher standard within the meaning of the Qualification Directive. Therefore, such cases fell outside the scope of the Directive. Even considering the precedent set by the European Court of Human Rights in *N. v. the United Kingdom*, which allowed humanitarian grounds to be invoked in exceptional cases involving the expulsion o f a seriously ill foreigner, the CJEU maintained that the risk of health deterioration due to the absence of appropriate treatment in the receiving country did not warrant subsidiary protection unless the harm was inflicted by a State or non-State third party.

In the *Abdida case*, the CJEU clarified that while residence on medical grounds did not fall under the Qualification Directive, decisions rejecting such residence were governed by Directive 2008/115/EC on common standards and procedures for returning illegally staying third-country nationals

---

721 Council Directive 2004/83/EC of April 29, 2004 on Minimum Standards for the Qualification and Status of Third Country Nationals or Stateless Persons as Refugees or as Persons Who Otherwise Need International Protection and the Content of the Protection Granted [2004] OJ L 304/12. Hereinafter: "Directive 2004/83/EC."

722 Parliamentary Doc. Chamber, session 2005–06, No. 2478/1, 187–189.

723 C542/13 M'Bodj [2014] ECLI:EU:C:2014:2452.

724 C562/13 Abdida [2014] ECLI:EU:C:2014:2453.

(the "Return Directive").[725,726] As a return decision, refusals of medical residence were subject to the safeguards outlined in the Return Directive and the Charter of Fundamental Rights of the EU.[727] Article 19 § 2 of the Charter of Fundamental Rights emphasizes that individuals should not be removed to a state where there was a serious risk of torture or other inhuman or degrading treatment.[728]

Drawing from the *N. v. the United Kingdom* case law,[729] the CJEU concluded that the removal of a foreigner with a serious illness to a country with inferior treatment facilities might exceptionally raise Article 3 concerns in cases where compelling humanitarian grounds against removal exist. The CJEU asserted that remedies for decisions refusing medical residence must have a suspensive effect, aligning with the Strasbourg Court's jurisprudence, necessitating the provision for meeting the applicant's basic needs pending an appeal ruling in accordance with the Return Directive.

The line of reasoning articulated by the Court of Justice of the European Union is inherently logical: in order to qualify for subsidiary protection, it does not suffice for the foreign national to prove that he runs the risk of being subjected to inhuman or degrading treatment when he returns to his country of origin, he must also prove that the risk is caused by factors which are directly or indirectly attributable to the authorities in his country. This is not the case with a person whose health condition requires medical treatment, and in whose country of origin adequate treatment is not available, as humanitarian situations do not fall within the scope of the directive. The situation is different if the foreign national is deliberately denied medical treatment.[730]

From the above, it can be reasonably be deduced that Article 9ter of the Law on foreign nationals, mentioned above, does not constitute a transposition

---

725 C562/13 Abdida [2014] ECLI:EU:C:2014:2453, §§ 33 and 38–63.

726 Directive 2008/115/EC on common standards and procedures for returning illegally staying third-country nationals [2008] OJ L 348/98. Hereinafter: "Return Directive."

727 Charter of Fundamental Rights of the European Union [2010] OJ C 83.

728 This provision reads as follows: "No one may be removed, expelled or extradited to a State where there is a serious risk that he or she would be subjected to the death penalty, torture or other inhuman or degrading treatment or punishment."

729 *N* v United Kingdom [GC] [2008] App No. 26565/05 (ECtHR May 27, 2008).

730 C542/13 M'Bodj [2014] ECLI:EU:C:2014:2452.

of a norm of derived European law but must be understood as a simple norm of domestic law. Both the Constitutional Court of Belgium[731] and the Council of State of Belgium[732] have since supported this view, ruling that the scope of Directive 2004/83/EC does not extend to individuals authorized to stay in Belgian territory for health reasons, unless it involves intentionally refusing medical care in the country of residence or habitual residence. Consequently, it should be interpreted in the current situation solely with reference to domestic law, autonomously—of course bearing in mind the ECHR, especially Articles 3 and 8.

With the introduction of Article *9ter* in the Law on foreign nationals, the Belgian legislator in 2006 intended to reserve the benefits of this provision for foreigners who are "seriously ill" to the extent that their removal would constitute a violation of Article 3 of the European Convention on Human Rights, a treaty provision whose wording Article 9ter of the Law on foreign nationals indeed mirrors. The requirement for a certain threshold of severity of the illness is evident from the very terms of Article 9ter, § 1, where the legislator refers to "such an illness"—meaning to this extent severe—that it poses a "real risk" to life or physical integrity or a "real risk" of inhuman or degrading treatment. The case law of the Council of State confirms this approach.[733]

---

731 Constitutional Court of Belgium [2015] 59/2015.

732 Council of State of Belgium [2015] 232141.

733 Council of State of Belgium [2015] 232141, § 8, where the Council of State held that: "The applicant refers to two French-language judgments of the Council of State of 19 November 2013, from which it deduces that also with regard to the [scenario of a real risk of inhuman or degrading treatment due to a lack of adequate treatment in the country of origin], Article 9ter of the Law on foreign nationals could only be applied under the same strict conditions of Article 3 of the ECHR could be applied." However, as the Council of State in subsequent French rulings No. 228,778 of October 16, 2014 and 229,073 of November 5, 2014, the illness must be a ruled, the disease does have to reach a minimum threshold of severity to fall under the cases provided for in Article 9b of the Law on foreign nationals, but neither the legislative text nor the relevant preparatory works show that the legislator intended that the authorisation to stay under Article 9ter merely resembles a "permit to die." The contention that the scope of application of Article 9b coincides with that of Article 3 of the ECHR, as it is currently interpreted by the ECtHR, would however amount to that since the ECtHR considers that suffering because of "a naturally occurring disease" only "in very exceptional cases" links it to the condition protected by Article 3 of

The preparatory works of both the laws of December 29, 2010,[734] and January 8, 2012,[735] which twice amended the Article 9ter of the Law on foreign nationals toward a tightening of the procedure, confirm the legislator's intention to target only "foreigners truly suffering from a serious illness" and, consequently, to curb the enthusiasm of foreigners for this avenue of residence in cases of a "manifest lack of severity" of the illness. It aims to address the "improper use" that may have occurred, or even abuses of medical regularization.[736]

2.1.1.2.3.2.2.2 Material scope of application of Article 9ter of the Law on foreign nationals

Article 9ter § 1 of the Law on foreign nationals unequivocally presents two scenarios that may lead to the granting of a residence permit for a seriously ill individual: the illness poses a real risk to their life or physical integrity, or it poses a real risk of inhuman or degrading treatment due to a lack of adequate treatment in the country of origin. The two possibilities juxtaposed in this provision are to be asserted independently from one another.[737]

A first scenario pertains to the situation where the illness is such that it poses a real risk to the life or physical integrity of the foreign applicant. It is required that the invoked risk of death or certain harm to the person's physical integrity, which must be "real" at the time of the application, has,

---

ECHR. [...] It therefore is no violation of the cited provision by further considering in the judgment under appeal that considering that "nor can it be inferred from Article 9b(1) of the Law on foreign nationals that only illnesses which cause a critical state of health be inferred that only diseases which produce a critical state of health or which are advanced can lead to an authorization for residence in application of section 9ter of the Law on foreign nationals."

734 Act of December 29, 2010 on miscellaneous provisions, *Moniteur Belge* December 31, 2010.

735 Act of January 8, 2012 "amending Article 9ter of the Act of December 15, 1980 on access to the territory, residence, establishment and removal of foreigners," *Moniteur Belge* February 6, 2012.

736 Parliamentary Doc. Chamber, session 2010–2011, No. 0771/001, 146–147; Parliamentary Doc. Chamber, session 2011–2012, No. 1824/001, 4; Parliamentary Doc. Chamber, session 2011–2012, No. 1824/006, 3–4.

737 Council of State of Belgium [2015] 232141.

if not immediate, a certain degree of actuality, meaning its occurrence is certain in the relatively short term. This scenario pertains to "deathbed cases."

A second scenario envisages the situation where the illness is "such" that it poses a real risk of inhuman or degrading treatment for the foreign applicant, "when there is no adequate treatment in their country of origin or the country where they reside." In this case, although the illness has a certain degree of severity, it does not *a priori* rule out removal to the country of origin. The adequacy of treatment is assessed regarding availability and accessibility of the medical treatment in the country of origin, considering, among other things, the financial means of the applicant.

The adequacy of treatment is not limited to the current treatment but must also consider potential complications that may arise in the medical condition.

The assessment of the medical condition and medical support in the country of origin is conducted on an individual basis, taking into account the specific situation of the applicant. It is crucial to determine whether, in the absence of adequate treatment, meaning untreated, the patient would face a real risk of being subject to treatment contrary to Article 3 of the European Convention on Human Rights upon return.[738]

2.1.1.2.3.2.2.3 Application of Article 9ter of the Law on foreign nationals

For an application ex Article 9ter of the Law on foreign nationals, an applicant must be able to present an identity document as well as a medical certificate. Following the request, and based on the information provided in the medical certificate, the Immigration Office will first examine the admissibility of the request. Regarding the identity document, it should be noted that initially, the concept was interpreted in the same manner as the identity document required under Article 9bis of the Law on foreign nationals. However, the Constitutional Court of Belgium deemed this interpretation, particularly in the context of the right to residence for medical reasons under Article 8 ECHR, to be inconsistent with the principle of equality enshrined in Articles 10 and 11 of the Constitution, read in conjunction with Article 3 ECHR. This requirement was not imposed on an applicant seeking subsidiary protection under Article 48/4 of the Law on foreign nationals (see infra for more details).

---

738 Council of State of Belgium [2014] 229072.

If it is reasonable to demand that the applicant proves their identity under Article 9ter, proof of identity should suffice with "any document whose authenticity cannot be disputed. An identity document does not need to be submitted if identity can be demonstrated in another way."[739]

These individuals, provided they can prove their identity, can also submit a residence application to the minister or his authorized representative. The explanatory memorandum specifies in this regard that a foreigner who does not present an identity document and fails to demonstrate that he is unable to obtain such a document in Belgium will nonetheless not be removed if his medical condition is so severe that deportation would constitute a violation of Article 3 of the European Convention on Human Rights.[740]

The medical certificate must, upon submission of the application, specify the illness, degree of severity, and treatment, under penalty of inadmissibility.

After the first stage regarding the admissibility is concluded by the Immigration Office, a comprehensive review is carried out by the Immigration Office, on the basis of a medical examination.

If the request on the basis of Article 9ter is deemed substantiated, the individual concerned receives a one-year residence permit, which is renewable on an annual basis. Following five years subsequent to the submission of the request, permanent residence status, implying unrestricted duration, is bestowed upon the individual.

2.1.1.2.3.2.2.4 Connection between Article 9ter of the Law on foreign nationals and Article 3 ECHR: severity of the illness as a distinguishing feature?

As articulated earlier, in order to invoke Article 9ter of the Law on foreign nationals, the illness of the individual concerned must pose a genuine risk either to their life or physical integrity, or to exposure to inhuman or degrading treatment due to a lack of adequate treatment in the country of origin. Hence, while the invoked illness must have reached a minimum threshold of severity to fall within the provisions of Article 9ter,[741] neither the text of the legal provision nor did the relevant parliamentary works indicate that the

---

739 Constitutional Court of Belgium [2009] 193/2009.

740 Parliamentary Doc. Chamber, session 2005–06, No. 2478/001, 35.

741 Council of State of Belgium [2014] 229073.

Belgian legislator intended to reserve the residence permit provided for in Article 9ter to ultimately resemble a mere "permit to die" on Belgian territory.

This is also apparent from the Belgian case law, which explicitly adopted a (non-restrictive) stance. Notably, following the implementation of an admissibility screening practice for Article 9ter requests by the Immigration Office—which restricted Article 9ter requests to situations falling within the scope of Article 3 ECHR, prompted by the ruling *N v United Kingdom*.[742] Rather, the Council for asylum and immigration proceedings highlighted that Article 9ter of the Law on foreign nationals does not solely mandate the existence of a threat to life, yet also encompasses situations involving a genuine risk to physical well-being or the potential for inhuman or degrading treatment. Thus, a threat to life is not a critical prerequisite, as per the Council for asylum and immigration proceedings' case law, for a violation of Article 3 ECHR. Rather, other "exceptional" circumstances, as defined in the ECtHR decision in *D v United Kingdom*,[743] could prevent expulsion. Therefore, the Immigration Office needs to undertake a comprehensive assessment of all relevant factors, which requires a comprehensive case-by-case assessment.[744] However, as a cassation judge,[745] the Council of State later found that the Council for asylum and immigration proceedings had made an error in its (broad) assessment that Article 3 ECHR also encompasses cases where there

---

742 *N v United Kingdom* [GC] [2008] App No. 26565/05 (ECtHR May 27, 2008).

743 *D v United Kingdom* [1997] App No. 30240/96 (ECtHR May 2, 1997).

744 Council for asylum and immigration proceedings [2012] 92393; Council for asylum and immigration proceedings [2012] 93227; Council for asylum and immigration proceedings [2012] 92258. For a full overview of the evolution in Belgian case law, see: *Paposhvili v Belgium* [GC] [2016] App No. 41738/10 (ECtHR, December 13, 2016).

745 It should be remarked that the Council of State, when adjudicating appeals in cassation, does not serve as an appellate body. Rather, the Council of State examines errors of law and procedure (in common law countries referred to as an appeal on a point of law). As such, the Council of State, as a cassation judge, lacks authority to replace its evaluation with that of the Council for asylum and immigration proceedings, nor can it determine on behalf of the latter whether e.g., psychological and medical certificates presented by the applicant would validate the events claimed in support of the request, or establish psychological sequelae of a nature and gravity such as to imply a presumption of treatment contrary to Article 3 ECHR. See, to that effect, concerning a request for international protection: Council of State of Belgium [2023] 255855.

is a mere, genuine risk of inhuman or degrading treatment.[746,747] Nonetheless, the Council of State clarified that the interpretation of Article 9ter was not incorrect, since this proviso goes further than Article 3 ECHR, covering cases where there exists a real risk of inhuman or degrading treatment.[748]

Therefore, for an extended period of time, the scope of Article 9ter of the Law on foreign nationals did not entirely align with the parameters of Article 3 of the European Convention on Human Rights, as elucidated in the *N. v. UK* case law,[749] and appears to extend beyond the confines of Article 3 of the ECHR.

Indeed, in earlier case law, the European Court of Human Rights, in its assessment, linked the experience of distress arising from a "naturally occurring" illness with the circumstances protected by Article 3 only in "very exceptional cases," often referred to as "deathbed" cases. This application of an exceptionally high threshold in Article 3 ECHR indicates that the application of Article 9ter of the Law on foreign nationals encompasses a (much) broader range of situations than those traditionally delineated by the "very exceptional circumstances" standard set in the *N. v UK* case law.[750] In fact, the standard as set in *N v UK* was so high that it was near impossible to pass it.[751]

Nevertheless, given recent jurisprudential developments concerning Article 3 ECHR, especially in the case *Paposhvili v Belgium*, the scopes of Article 9ter and Article 3 ECHR are as converging as ever, as the ECtHR has recently reshaped its case law and, seemingly influenced by Belgian case law,[752] lifted its previous restrictive approach for the assessment of medical conditions. The landmark *Paposhvili* case prompted consideration of whether strict application of the criterion established in *N v United Kingdom*, which

746 Council of State of Belgium [2013] 225632 and 225633.

747 For a recent state of the case law, see judgment Council of State of Belgium [2023] 255855, as regards the application of Article 3 ECHR.

748 Council of State of Belgium [2013] 225632 and 225633.

749 *N v United Kingdom* [GC] [2008] App No. 26565/05 (ECtHR May 27, 2008).

750 *N v United Kingdom* [GC] [2008] App No. 26565/05 (ECtHR May 27, 2008).

751 Except in the case *D v United Kingdom* [1997] App No. 30240/96 (ECtHR May 2, 1997). Human Rights Center of Ghent University, "European Court of Human Rights: Paposhvili v Belgium (Application No. 41738/10 Third Party Intervention" (2019) <https://hrc.ugent.be/wp-content/uploads/2019/10/Paposhvili.pdf>.

752 Concurring Opinion of Judge Lemmens, *Paposhvili v Belgium* [GC] [2016] App No. 41738/10 (ECtHR, December 13, 2016) 53 et seq.

strictly considered the proximity to death of the individual concerned, created a gap in the protection against inhuman treatment. The Grand Chamber recognized the existence of such gap and broadened the material scope of Article 3 ECHR while at the same time maintaining a high threshold for application of Article 3 of the ECHR.

Moreover, in the landmark case of *Paposhvili v. Belgium*, the European Court of Human Rights (EHRM) asserts that authorities, when assessing the aforementioned accessibility, must take into account the cost of medication and treatment, the presence of a social and family network, and the distance to be covered.[753] In so doing, the Court accepted that not only expulsion of "deathbed" applicants could amount to a breach of Article 3 ECHR, but that the threshold of "very exceptional circumstances" was lowered for the purpose of Article 3 to cases where there is a risk of decline which results in intense suffering or a significant reduction in life expectancy.

In the case, according to the court, there would have been a violation of Article 3 if Belgium had expelled Mr. Paposhvili to Georgia without having assessed "*the risk faced by him in the light of the information concerning his state of health and the existence of appropriate treatment in Georgia*." Similarly, expulsion of Mr. Paposhvili would amount to a breach of Article 8 ECHR if Belgium would not have had assessed the impact of his return on his "right to respect for his family life in view of his state of health."

2.1.1.2.3.2.3 Subsidiary protection in case of illness under Article 48/4 of the Law on foreign nationals

Individuals who do not qualify for refugee status and who cannot invoke residency on serious medical grounds (Article 9ter of the Law on foreign nationals) and in respect of whom there are substantial grounds for believing that, if they return to their country of origin,[754] they would face a real risk of serious harm and who cannot or, because of that risk, do not wish to avail themselves of the protection of that country and do not fall under the

[753] Council of State of Belgium [2017] 12573.

[754] Or in the case of a stateless person, to the country where he used to reside habitually.

grounds for exclusion[755] are granted subsidiary protection status (Article 48/4, § 1, of the Law on foreign nationals).[756]

The risk of serious harm, consists of the following: death penalty or execution, torture or inhuman or degrading treatment or punishment of an applicant in their country of origin, or serious threat to the life or person of a civilian due to arbitrary violence in the case of an international or domestic armed conflict.[757]

In this regard, the material scope of Article 48/4 of the Law on foreign nationals coincides with Article 3 ECHR. Hence, refusal of subsidiary protection implies that removal does not constitute a violation of Article 3 ECHR, unless when an exception clause was used to deny the residence permit based on Art 48/3 of the Law on foreign nationals, Article 48/4 of the Law on foreign nationals or Article 9ter of the Law on foreign nationals.

2.1.1.2.3.3 Expulsion of migrants under Belgian legislation in the context of Article 3 ECHR

A risk of violating Article 3 of the European Convention on Human Rights arises when a foreigner's right of residence is terminated, or when the foreigner is denied residency in Belgium, necessitating a return to their country of origin where they face a treatment carrying a serious and substantial risk of breaching Article 3 of the ECHR.

However, for a considerable period, there was ambiguity within Belgian legal practice regarding the specific point in time at which the risk of violating Article 3 of the ECHR should be assessed: whether the correct reference point is the issuance of the removal measure or its forced implementation. The jurisprudence within the Belgian legal framework exhibited some divergence on this matter.

Some earlier jurisprudence purported the view that the mere imposition of a removal measure does not *ipso facto* mandate the repatriation of a foreign national to their country of origin.[758] According to this line of case law, only

---

755 As provided for in § 55/4 of the Law on foreign nationals.

756 This is the transposition of (now) Article 2(f) of the *Qualification Directive*.

757 Article 48/4, § 2 of the Law on foreign nationals.

758 Council for asylum and immigration proceedings [2011] 213233.

in cases involving forced removal, a breach of Article 3 of the ECHR can be implicated, necessitating an examination solely at that moment to ascertain the existence of a risk of breaching that article. A removal measure could only be contested on the grounds of an Article 3 ECHR violation if it was accompanied by deprivation of liberty.

However, recent jurisprudential developments have charted a divergent path, culminating in the determination that, as a general principle, removal measures in general should refrain from breaching Article 3 ECHR.[759] Therefore, an inquiry is imperative to ascertain the potential violation of Article 3 ECHR when implementing a removal measure.[760] This legal evolution in Belgian jurisprudence is consistent with both the jurisprudence of the ECtHR[761] and with Article 74/13 of the Law on foreign nationals, which asserts the necessity to consider, inter alia, the health status of the foreign national in the execution of measures regarding removal.[762] Consequently, it can now be posited that a comprehensive investigation into the potential violation of Article 3 ECHR becomes imperative in the issuance of such an order.

2.1.1.3 Personal rights for third-country nationals

2.1.1.3.1 Article 10, 11 and 191 Constitution

Article 191 of the Belgian Constitution states: "Every foreigner present on the territory of Belgium is entitled to the protection afforded to individuals, except as provided by law." In essence, the status of a Belgian citizen and a foreigner is identical. This doesn't equate to "every foreigner legally residing on the territory." It merely requires being a foreigner, regardless of the legality of one's stay. Whether someone is legally present on the territory is entirely

---

759 Council for asylum and immigration proceedings [2019] 218564.

760 See i.a. Council for asylum and immigration proceedings [2023] 285531, which stresses that in the context of an expulsion measure a careful examination in the light of Article 3 of the ECHR must take place.

761 *SJ v Belgium* [GC] [2015] App No. 70055/10 (ECtHR March 19, 2015); Verrijdt W., "Bespreking van EHRM, 27 februari 2014, S.J.t./ België" (2016) 15 *Rechtskundig Weekblad* 757–758.

762 Article 74/13 of the Law on foreign nationals stipulates the following (translation): "When making a decision regarding removal, the minister or his authorized representative takes into account the paramount interests of the child, family and personal life, and the health condition of the concerned third-country national."

irrelevant from a constitutional standpoint when invoking the protection of, for instance, Articles 10 and 11 of the Constitution. Hence, there exists a fundamental equality. Furthermore, in accordance with Article 191, foreigners may invoke the principle of equality before the Constitutional Court, subject to the dual condition that they are physically present on Belgian territory and that the Constitution or the law does not impose any legally valid deviations or restrictions regarding the enjoyment of the relevant rights and freedoms. This provision underscores that the protection of constitutional rights is not limited to Belgian nationals: the principle of equality applies to all individuals present in Belgium, including foreigners.

Based on Article 191 of the Belgian Constitution, differential treatment disadvantaging a foreigner can only be introduced through a legal (or constitutional) norm. The purpose of this provision is not to empower the legislator, when creating such differentiation, to disregard the fundamental principles enshrined in the Constitution. Article 191 does not imply that the legislator, when introducing differential treatment to the detriment of foreigners, is exempt from ensuring that this difference is not discriminatory, irrespective of the nature of the principles at stake.[763]

The Constitutional Court of Belgium has accepted that a violation of Article 191 of the Constitution can only occur if the contested provisions establish differential treatment between certain foreigners and Belgians. If, for instance, a provision creates differential treatment between two categories of foreigners, depending on whether or not they are nationals of a EU Member State, only a violation of Articles 10 and 11 of the Constitution can be asserted.[764] In practice, this means that foreigners can rely on Articles 10 and 11 of the Belgian Constitution whenever their rights are affected. Article 191 of the Constitution thus reinforces a constitutional framework of substantive equality, ensuring that foreign nationals are not excluded from the protection of fundamental rights and freedoms enjoyed by Belgian citizens.

---

763 Constitutional Court of Belgium [1993] 20/93.

764 Constitutional Court of Belgium [2007] 81/2008, B.33.1.

2.1.1.4 Political rights for third-country nationals

2.1.1.4.1 The right to civil service

Article 10, second paragraph, of the Belgian Constitution establishes the principle that Belgian nationality is required for appointment to civil and military posts.

A brief historical perspective helps to contextualise the constitutional nationality requirement. At the time of the drafting of the Belgian Constitution, the principle that only Belgians could be appointed to civil and military posts was considered self-evident. In the uncertain period following the Belgian Revolution, the primary concern of the National Congress was the consolidation of the newly acquired national independence. As a result, the principle itself was not meaningfully contested.

Debates within the Belgium-founding Congress instead focused on the scope of possible exceptions. Some members expressed concern that allowing legislative derogations might enable the executive to appoint foreign loyalists to key positions, thereby undermining national sovereignty. Others, however, emphasized the practical necessity of recruiting foreigners for specific roles, such as professors, translators, or military specialists. The compromise ultimately adopted retained the nationality requirement as a rule, while allowing exceptions to be established by law for "particular cases".

This compromise is reflected in the original wording of what is now Article 10 of the Constitution, which has remained substantively unchanged since 1831. Early interpretations already suggested that the requirement applied broadly to public functions financed by the public treasury, while excluding positions in the private sector or religious institutions.[765]

The Council of State has consistently interpreted this requirement broadly: it applies not only to positions within the central federal administration, but to all public functions in the wide sense, including posts within decentralized or autonomous public bodies, irrespective of the nature of the employment relationship.[766] Exceptions to this nationalities requirement may only be introduced by a *formal act of the legislature*. Since Belgium's transformation into

---

765 Weekers B 'De toegang van niet-Belgen tot de Belgische publieke sector' [2005] 1 T.Gem. 5.

766 See Goedertier G, Vande Lanotte J, De Pelsmaeker T and Goossens J, *Belgisch Publiekrecht* (Die Keure 2015) 310; Weekers B, 'De toegang van niet-Belgen tot de Belgische publieke sector' [2005] 1 T.Gem. 6.

a federal state, the term "law" in this context must be understood to encompass decrees and ordinances enacted by the competent Communities and Regions. Consequently, only the legislative authority – federal, regional, or community-may validly derogate from the constitutional nationality requirement.[767]

However, importantly, these constitutional provisions must be interpreted in light of Article 45(4) of the Treaty on the Functioning of the European Union (TFEU), which excludes "employment in the public service" from the scope of the free movement of workers.[768] The Court of Justice of the European Union (CJEU) has consistently held that this exception must be interpreted restrictively. It applies only to posts involving direct or indirect participation in the exercise of public authority and duties designed to safeguard the general interests of the State or other public entities.[769] This includes, for example, functions with coercive powers, authority to make binding decisions, or positions central to the core prerogatives of the State. In the case law of the EU, no distinction is made between statutory or contractual functions.

Belgian administrative jurisprudence has progressively aligned itself with this European interpretation. Initially, the Council of State approached the relationship between Article 10, second paragraph, of the Constitution and EU law as a genuine conflict, to be resolved through the primacy of EU law. Relying on Article 34 of the Constitution and the principle of the precedence of directly effective international law, it held that EU law required access for EU nationals to public posts not involving the exercise of public authority, regardless of the constitutional nationality requirement. In this perspective, national implementing measures were merely declaratory of an obligation already existing under EU law.[770]

Subsequently, however, both the legislative section and the administrative litigation section of the Council of State moved towards an interpretation

---

767 Council of State of Belgium [2014] 226980; Weekers B, 'De toegang van niet-Belgen tot de Belgische publieke sector' [2005] 1 T.Gem. 5-16

768 Consolidated versions of the Treaty on European Union and the Treaty on the Functioning of the European Union [2016] OJ C202/1. Hereinafter: 'TFEU'.

769 C-149/79 Commission v Belgium [1980] ECR I-03881; C-173/94 Commission v Belgium [1996]. In order to justify the derogation provided for in Article 45(4) TFEU, it is also necessary that these public authority powers are effectively exercised on a regular basis by the persons concerned and do not represent a very minor part of their activities C-405/01 Colegio de Oficilaes de la Marina Mercanto Española [2003]

770 Council of State of Belgium [1996] 62922; Council of State of Belgium [2014] 226980

based on EU-conformity rather than conflict. Article 10, second paragraph, of the Constitution is now read in light of Article 45(4) TFEU, such that the notion of "civil and military posts" must be understood as referring only to positions involving the exercise of public authority or the protection of the general interests of the State. This implies that it is for the competent legislature to identify those posts that may legitimately remain subject to a nationality requirement.[771]

This EU-conform interpretation was explicitly confirmed in the Council of State's judgment of 31 March 2014, no. 226.980, which held that national courts must interpret constitutional provisions, as far as possible, in conformity with EU law, in particular to ensure compliance with the free movement of workers.[772] A similar approach has been adopted by the Constitutional Court, which has likewise interpreted Article 10, second paragraph, of the Constitution in light of Article 45(4) TFEU and the case law of the CJEU.[773]

In practical terms, the constitutional nationality requirement can no longer be invoked to exclude EU citizens from posts that do not fall within the narrow category of "public authority" functions as defined by the CJEU. Accordingly, nationals of EU Member States and of the European Economic Area (EEA) may access both statutory and contractual posts within Belgian public administrations insofar as the functions involved do not entail direct or indirect participation in the exercise of public authority or tasks central to safeguarding the essential interests of the public administration.[774] Belgian administrative practice has gradually reflected this requirement, opening a wide range of public-sector positions to EU citizens while reserving a limited core of authority-bearing functions to Belgian nationals.

For third-country nationals, however – including persons holding long-term resident status in Belgium under Directive 2003/109/EC – the situation remains fundamentally different. The constitutional rule in Article 10 continues to prevent them from holding public posts unless the legislature expressly provides otherwise.[775] While long-term residents enjoy an enhanced

---

771 Velaers, J, *De Grondwet, een artikelsgewijze commentaar*, I (Die Keure 2019) 186

772 Velaers, J, *De Grondwet, een artikelsgewijze commentaar*, I (Die Keure 2019) 186; Council of State of Belgium [2014] 226980

773 Constitutional Court [2017] 53/2017

774 Article 28 of the EEA Agreement; C-104/06 Commission v Sweden [2007], § 32.

775 Council of State of Belgium [2014] 226980

status under EU and Belgian immigration law, that status does not confer a general right of access to public-service employment.

In sum, Article 10, second paragraph, of the Belgian Constitution establishes a threefold regime governing access to public office: Belgian nationals enjoy unrestricted access; nationals of EU Member States may access positions that do not entail participation in the exercise of public authority, subject to legislative derogations in specific cases and third-country nationals may access public employment only where such access has been expressly conferred by law.[776]

2.1.1.5 Economic, social, and cultural rights for third-country nationals

2.1.1.5.1 Introduction

As the Constitutional Court of Belgium has repeatedly established, for instance in judgment no. 32/2006, when the legislator aims to implement an immigration policy and, for that purpose, imposes rules that must be adhered to for lawful residence on the territory, he employs an objective and pertinent criterion of distinction if consequences are attached to compliance or non-compliance when granting social services.[777] The policy regarding access to the territory and the residence of foreigners would be undermined if it were assumed that the same social services must be provided to foreigners residing illegally in Belgium as to those legally residing. The distinction between these two categories of foreigners justifies that the State does not bear the same obligations toward them.

The intention not to undermine federal immigration policy can also justify that the decree legislator, in his exercise of his powers, does not bear the same obligations toward the category of foreigners residing illegally on the territory.[778]

The underlying principle in the jurisprudence of the Constitutional Court is that ultimately, it is the legislator (either the decree legislator or federal legislator) who determines who is in lawful residence and falls under that notion. Each government authority has the discretion to define a target group.

[776] Velaers, J, *De Grondwet, een artikelsgewijze commentaar*, I (Die Keure 2019) 187

[777] Constitutional Court of Belgium [2006] 32/2006.

[778] Constitutional Court of Belgium [2013] 37/2013, B.7.

Notably, it was not until the early 2000s that Belgium established a comprehensive reception policy. Originally, asylum seekers in Belgium received financial assistance from the Public Service for Social Welfare ("OCMW") according to the generic provisions of the OCMW law.[779] However, the significant influx of asylum seekers in 2000 prompted the Belgian legislature to quickly restrict financial support for individuals in the asylum process. This led to the replacement of financial aid with material assistance provided in reception centers.[780] More recent case law indicates that this legislative discretion is not without limits. In its judgment no. 23/2026, the Constitutional Court of Belgium confirmed that asylum seekers, in principle, are entitled to reception, generally in the form of material assistance, which may be necessary to ensure a standard of living consistent with human dignity. The Court observed that restricting or denying such reception may result in serious harm, particularly where no alternative support is available. It also raised doubts as to the compatibility with EU law of excluding applicants who have already obtained protection in another Member State, and referred a question to the Court of Justice of the European Union. While recognising the legislator's margin of appreciation, the Court held that excluding financial assistance in exceptional circumstances may reduce the protection of fundamental rights, especially where no adequate accommodation is available. Such measures may affect the rights to human dignity, social assistance, adequate housing, and, in certain cases, private and family life. The contested provisions were therefore suspended pending a decision on the merits.[781]

2.1.1.5.2 The right to education

According to the Constitutional Court of Belgium, it is not unreasonable for the legislator to, in principle, reserve specific efforts and resources intended to promote personal development, social functioning, continued participation in education, professional engagement, or language proficiency for individuals who, due to their administrative status, are

---

779 Act of July 8, 1976 on public centers for social welfare, *Moniteur Belge* August 5, 1976. Hereafter: "OCMW law" (Openbare Centra voor Maatschappelijk Welzijn "OCMW" in Dutch/Centres Publics d'Action Sociale "CPAS" in French).

780 Article 57ter of the "OCMWlaw."

781 Constitutional Court of Belgium [2026] 23/2026.

presumed to be permanently or at least for a significant duration established in Belgium.[782]

Article 24, § 3, of the Belgian Constitution, Article 2 of the First Additional Protocol to the European Convention on Human Rights and Article 13 of the International Convention on Economic, Social and Cultural Rights, pertain to the right to education. The right to education applies for foreigners, albeit with specific exemptions within the realm of adult education.

In the context of adult education, the Flemish legislator establishes a distinction between those in illegal and legal residence.[783] Individuals legally residing in the Flemish Community can access adult education, while those in illegal residence cannot. The same differentiation applies to integration requirements and the acquisition of nationality.

From the parliamentary preparation, it is evident that the decree legislator, by introducing the condition of lawful residence, aimed to align the Flemish policy regarding access to adult education with federal residency policies: "The main reason remains the coherence of federal and community policies. The Flemish Government does not want to undermine migration policy by allowing undocumented individuals to attend a course that they can use as motivation for a new regularization application."[784] This was accepted by the Constitutional Court of Belgium. The Constitutional Court argued that the right to education guaranteed by Article 24, § 3, of the Constitution does not preclude the regulation of access to education, particularly post-compulsory education, based on the needs and capabilities of both the community and the individual. In his judgment, explicit reference is made to the jurisprudence of the European Court of Human Rights, including the *Case relating to certain aspects of the laws on the use of languages in education in Belgium*[785] and case *Ponomaryovi v. Bulgaria*, § 49.[786] According to the court, neither Article 2 of the First Additional Protocol to the European Convention on Human Rights nor the right to education guaranteed by Article 24, § 3, of the Constitution

---

782 Constitutional Court of Belgium [2013] 37/2013, B.7.

783 ibid.

784 Parliamentary Doc. Chamber, session 2010–11, No. 1082/9, 42.

785 *Case "Relating to Certain Aspects of the Laws on the Use of Languages in Education in Belgium"* [1968] App Nos. 1474/62; 1677/62; 1691/62; 1769/63; 1994/63; 2126/64 (ECtHR July 23, 1968), § 49.

786 *Ponomaryovi v. Bulgaria* [2011] App No. 5335/05 (ECtHR June 21, 2011), § 49.

impedes the imposition of conditions on access to post-compulsory education, provided that the principle of equality is respected.[787]

In sum, the Court concludes that parties to the Article 2 of the First Additional Protocol to the European Convention on Human Rights have an obligation regarding individuals who have not received (complete) primary education to make efforts to maximize the accessibility of basic education, taking into account economic possibilities and the state of public finances. However, the right to access education can be subject to limitations, as long as these limitations adhere to the principle of equality.

According to the Constitutional Court, the competent legislator is empowered to make a distinction between foreigners residing legally and those residing illegally in Belgium. Consequently, it cannot be reproached to the legislator, considering the discretionary power mentioned above, for excluding individuals residing illegally on Belgian territory from enrollment in adult education.[788]

What was not accepted by the Constitutional Court, however, was a decree which stipulated that, starting from September 1, 2023, newcomers in Flanders were required to pay for a Dutch as a Second Language (NT2) course and the new NT2 test, as well as for civic orientation (MO) lessons and the MO test. The regulations governing adult education and integration provide certain exemptions, reductions, and reimbursements for eligible newcomers with a socio-economic vulnerable profile, but mandatory newcomers were excluded from these benefits.[789]

Moreover, Article 113novies, §4bis and §6bis of the Adult Education Decree[790] excluded adult mandatory newcomers from certain social corrections (such as fee exemptions or reductions applicable to, among others, recipients of social welfare, job seekers, and asylum seekers with material support) if they enroll in a course to achieve the required language level at a Centre for Adult Education or a Centre for Basic Education. For voluntary newcomers, these social corrections still apply.

787 Constitutional Court of Belgium [2013] 37/2013, § B.11.

788 Constitutional Court of Belgium [2013] 37/2013, §§ B.11 and B.12.1 and 12.2.

789 Constitutional Court of Belgium [2023] 115/2023.

790 Decree of the Flemish Parliament of June 15, 2007 concerning adult education, as amended by Decree of the Flemish Parliament of June 24, 2022 (August 31, 2007) *Moniteur Belge*.

The legislative intent behind this new measure, as evident from the parliamentary preparations, was for the decree legislator to ensure that newcomers would value the language training more and perceive it as less discretionary.[791]

Previously, the 2007 Decree of the Flemish Parliament had already provided for exemptions, reductions, and reimbursements of registration fees, primarily considering the socio-economic situation of specific participants to eliminate financial barriers. On the other hand, by introducing registration fees, the decree legislator aimed to emphasize the non-discretionary nature of the course and install a sense of responsibility among participants.

Article 113novies, §4bis and §6bis of the Adult Education Decree was challenged by a group of social organizations before the Constitutional Court of Belgium.

In its judgment, the Constitutional Court noted that the group of adult mandatory newcomers is predominantly composed of non-Belgians, while the group of other individuals, including voluntary newcomers taking language courses, can include Belgian citizens. According to the Constitutional Court, the differential treatment is based on an objective criterion, namely whether one is a mandatory newcomer or not. The Constitutional Court observes that the aforementioned treatments result in certain foreigners receiving less favorable treatment. The disadvantaged group consists of a much higher percentage of non-Belgians than Belgians. These individuals experience a specific disadvantage indirectly based on their nationality. The difference in treatment must be supported by very strong considerations in such a case.[792]

In his judgment, the Constitutional Court stresses the fact that non-Belgians are treated less favorably without reasonable justification.[793] While the Constitutional Court acknowledges that the objective of making mandatory newcomers more responsible can be a reasonable justification for imposing registration fees on those not in a precarious socio-economic situation, it finds no justification in the present arrangement for treating individuals in identical precarious socio-economic situations differently based on whether or not they are mandatory newcomers. The Constitutional Court determines

---

791 Parliamentary Doc. Flemish Parliament, session 2021–22, No. 1269/3, 4.

792 Constitutional Court of Belgium [2023] 115/2023, § B.41.2.

793 Constitutional Court of Belgium [2023] 115/2023, § B.46.2.

a violation of the principles of equality and non-discrimination as per Articles 10 and 11 of the Constitution and the "norm of foreigner protection" in Article 191 of the Constitution. Consequently, it annuls the aforementioned Article 113, §4bis, and §6bis of the Adult Education Decree. As a result, even mandatory newcomers in challenging socio-economic situations can now avail themselves of exemptions, reductions, and reimbursement of registration fees for NT2 language education.[794]

2.1.1.5.3 The right to social allowances

Article 23 of the Constitution stipulates that everyone has the right to lead a life in keeping with human dignity. To ensure this, the respective legislators, considering corresponding duties, guarantee economic, social, and cultural rights, the conditions for the exercise of which they determine. These rights include, among others, the right to social assistance. Article 23 of the Constitution does not specify the implications of these rights, expressing only their principles. It is the responsibility of each legislator to ensure these rights, in accordance with the second paragraph of that article, taking into account the corresponding duties.

From the parliamentary preparation of Article 23, it is evident that by ensuring the right to social assistance, the constitutional legislator aimed at the right guaranteed in the organic law concerning public centers for social welfare.[795]

It falls within the discretionary power of the legislator to determine the measures which it deems adequate and appropriate to achieve the aim of Article 23 of the Constitution.[796] Although not explicitly mentioned in Article 23 of the Constitution, it stems from the parliamentary preparation that Article 23 of the Constitution imposes a *standstill obligation*, preventing the competent legislature from "significantly" reducing the level of protection provided by the applicable legislation "without valid reasons related to the general interest." However, this obligation does not mandate every legislator, within their powers, to leave the modalities of social assistance

---

794 Constitutional Court of Belgium [2023] 115/2023.

795 Parliamentary Doc. Senate, special session 1991–92, No. 100-2/4, 99 and 100.

796 Constitutional Court of Belgium [2019] 198/2019, § B.19.2; Constitutional Court of Belgium [2019] 129/2019, § B.9.3; Constitutional Court of Belgium [2019] 6/2019, § B.6.1.

unchanged. It prohibits them from adopting measures that would substantially degrade the right guaranteed in Article 23, first and third paragraphs, 2° of the Constitution, unless there are valid reasons related to the general interest. Nevertheless, the standstill principle does not deny them the authority to assess how to best ensure that right.

The core of the standstill principle lies in the evaluation of changes in legal protection between legislation at different times, specifically between the former and current legislation. This principle allows for a comparison of legal protection under two regulations or laws that are temporally separated.[797]

As regards the right to social allowances for foreigners, in 2013, with the intention of preventing fraud in social services to preserve the inherently limited resources allocated to such services for those who genuinely need them, the legislator sought to exclude a category of legally residing foreigners from the right to social services if their residence permit was granted under Article 9bis, and only when issued to individuals due to the existence of a work permit B or a professional card.[798]

By excluding a category of legally residing foreigners from the right to social services, Article 57sexies of the Law of July 8, 1976, significantly reduces the level of protection in this matter for individuals belonging to that category of foreigners. To be consistent with Article 23 of the Constitution, such a substantial reduction must be justified by reasons of general interest.

Adjudicating a preliminary question posed by the Labor Court of Liège (section Verviers), the Constitutional Court of Belgium argued that it is not justified to exclude an abstractly defined category of legally residing foreigners from the right to social services, especially since The issuance of a work permit B or a professional card is already subject to several strict conditions. Specifically, those authorized to legally reside in the territory based on Article 9bis of the law of December 15, 1980, with a work permit B or a professional card, should not be excluded from the right to social services without reasonable justification for the right to lead a dignified life. Moreover, according to the Constitutional Court, the measure is disproportionate to the objectives pursued, especially because it has significant negative

797 Parliamentary Doc. Senate, special session 100-2/3, 13.

798 Article 57 sexies of OCMW law, inserted by Article 20 of the Program Law of June 28, 2013, *Moniteur Belge* July 1, 2013.

consequences for the right to social services, as guaranteed by Article 23 of the Constitution, without being justified by any general interest.[799]

In its judgment no. 80/99 of June 30, 1999 (ECLI:BE:GHCC:1999:ARR.080) and judgment No. 194/2005 of December 21, 2005, the Constitutional Court of Belgium determined that applying a measure which terminates social services for any foreigner subject to an order to leave the territory, regardless of whether they are medically incapable of leaving Belgium, constitutes unreasonable discrimination. Such approach fails to recognize the fundamental differences that exist between individuals who can comply with the order to leave territory and individuals who, due to medical reasons, cannot be removed. Consequently, foreign nationals who are medically incapable of leaving the territory should have access to social services.[800,801] Furthermore, against the backdrop of Article 23 of the Constitution, the Constitutional Court of Belgium examined a legislative amendment that excluded asylum seekers from eligibility for a child-related tax credit during the pendency of their asylum procedure. The Court ruled that this amendment did not violate the standstill principle regarding the right to social assistance. In this case, the Constitutional Court held that the temporary exclusion of asylum seekers from the child tax credit did not infringe Article 23 because it did not remove their access to core social assistance or compromise their minimum subsistence. The judgment illustrates that legislative measures affecting certain groups must be carefully assessed against the Constitution, but that not every limitation constitutes a violation, particularly when the measure does not undermine the essential content of the rights guaranteed by Article 23 of the Constitution[802]

---

799 Constitutional Court of Belgium [2015] 133/2015.

800 Constitutional Court of Belgium [2023] 106/2023.

801 Article 57 § 2 (1) 1 of the OCMW law stipulates that the mission of the OCMW/CPAS (= Public Centre for Social Welfare) regarding an individual illegally residing on the territory is limited to providing urgent medical assistance. However, given the mentioned case law, the aforementioned provision should be interpreted—as per the constitutional court's case law—as meaning that it does not apply to a foreigner who is medically incapacitated to be removed. See, to that effect: Constitutional Court of Belgium [2023] 106/2023, § B.7.

802 Constitutional Court of Belgium [2019] 3/2019, para B.13.3.

2.1.1.6 Solidarity rights for third-country nationals

2.1.1.6.1 The right to live in peace

2.1.1.6.1.1 The inviolability of the home

Article 15 of the Belgian Constitution underscores the inviolability of the home. According to this provision, no house search may take place except in the cases provided for by the law and in the form prescribed by the law.

Article 22 of the Constitution guarantees the right to respect for private and family life.

The concept of a "home" under the scope of Article 15 of the Constitution is expansively interpreted. Likewise, the Constitutional Court of Belgium upholds a non-restrictive and functional view to the concept of residence.[803] Thus, for a third-country national residing in a reception center, their "home" could be considered the reception center, within the framework for accommodation.

The inviolability of the home is, therefore, closely linked to the right to family and private life enshrined in Article 8 ECHR. Therefore, the entry of a home under Belgian law must not only meet the constitutional requirements mentioned in Article 15 of the Constitution, but also necessitates compliance with the conditions for interference with the right to respect for the home provided in Article 8 ECHR. According to the Court of Cassation of Belgium, the waiver of this right is only valid if given unequivocally, with knowledge, and without coercion, based on informed consent.[804]

Hence, in the absence of procedural safeguards for illegally staying third-country nationals in the law to facilitate legally sound entry into residences,[805] a violation of Article 15 of the Constitution and of Article 8 ECHR is apparent when the entry into the residence of the foreigner and the subsequent detention, lacks any authorization and in the absence of clear implicit or explicit consent from the foreigner who actually enjoys the use of the

---

803 Constitutional Court of Belgium [2010] 91/2010, § B.53, see also: *Prokopovitch v Russia* [2013] App No. 58255/00 (ECtHR November 18, 2004).

804 *Gutsanovi v Bulgaria* [2013] App No. 34529/10 (ECtHR October 15, 2013), § 220; Court of Cassation [2022] P.22.1200.F.

805 Velaers J., *De Grondwet, een artikelsgewijze commentaar*, I (Die Keure 2019) 284.

non-public place.[806] This underscores the importance of consent and legal procedures when entering a non-public place by government authorities.

The need for a legislative intervention in Belgium is especially illustrated by the recent case of the ECtHR, *Sabani v. Belgium*.[807] In the case at hand, the applicant had been subject to an order to leave the territory, accompanied by a decision to be held in a specific location. She was arrested and handcuffed by the police inside her residence.

Subsequently to the facts of the present case, the court of first instance rejected the argument that Article 8 of the ECHR had been breached on grounds of unlawful interference with her home.

Upon appeal, the Indictments Division noted that the applicant's arrest followed Article 8 of the Convention since it fell within the scope of the police services' missions as provided by Article 21 of the Law on the Police Service.[808] This Article authorizes police services to apprehend foreigners who do not possess the required identification documents and to take the prescribed measures against them under the law or by competent authority.

The European Court of Human Rights did not endorse the stance taken by the Belgian courts: insofar as interference with the applicant's right to respect for her home has been established under Article 8, it must be based on a clear and precise legal foundation.[809] However, Article 21 of the Police Service Act cannot constitute such a basis since it does not empower police officers to enter a foreigner's home. The Court observes that this provision applies only in the case of a serious and imminent danger of calamities, disasters, or emergencies, or when the life or physical integrity of individuals is seriously threatened. Furthermore, in the instant case, it has not been established that the applicant gave her consent to the police entry into her home.[810] A mere opening of the door when the

---

806 Court of Cassation [2022] P.22.1200.F.Court of Cassation [2017] P.17.05.0517.F; Rk. Ghent [2016] GE.56. ET.48/2016; Court of Cassation [2015] 2015/VE/190, [2016] 2 TVreemd, 244.

807 *Sabani v Belgium* [2022] App No. 53069/15 (ECtHR March 8, 2022); Vandrooghenbroeck S., and Herinckx A., "Quelle base légale pour l'arrestation d'étrangers en séjour irrégulier?" (2023) 5 *JLMB*, 208–216.

808 Act of August 5, 1992 on the Police Service, *Moniteur Belge* (December 22, 1992).

809 *Lekić v. Slovenia* [GC] [2018], App No. 36480/07 (ECtHR December 11, 2018), § 95.

810 *Sabani v Belgium* [2022] App No. 53069/15 (ECtHR March 8, 2022), §§ 55–58.

police presented themselves to her, cannot suffice to infer authorization to enter the residence.[811]

The above-mentioned case illustrates the regulatory conundrum in the Belgian legal order that stems from the absence of a legal framework for access of residence. In the absence of such framework, and bearing in mind the obligations stemming from Article 8 ECHR and Article 15 of the Constitution, in several instances, the foreigner, after appealing against his detention, is released due to the absence of any authorization and the lack of clear implicit or explicit consent from the foreigner. In the absence of a legal framework for entry of residence, forced expulsion, in practice, is only feasible for foreigners who consent to residence entry or can be coincidentally apprehended outside their residence.[812]

The legislative proposal of December 7, 2017, amending the Law on foreign nationals, aimed to ensure the implementation of a legal framework for entry of residence and providing for prior authorization from the investigative courts to enter a residence.[813]

However, to date, this proposal didn't become law, resulting in a legislative gap and a situation where, in several instances, the foreigner, after appealing against his detention, was released due to the absence of any authorization and the lack of clear implicit or explicit consent from the foreigner. Without a legal framework for entry of residence, forced expulsion, in practice, is only feasible for foreigners who consent to residence entry or can be coincidentally apprehended outside their residence. Consequently, in practice, many third-country nationals facing expulsion continue to reside in Belgium in illegally staying status for years, even though this remains a criminal offense.

This regulatory void in the Belgian legal order, therefore, has the potential to undermine the European Return Directive which obliges the Member States of the European Union to take measures to remove irregularly staying foreigners who do not voluntarily return.

This broader structural deficiency in ensuring effective and rights-compliant state intervention is also reflected in the field of reception conditions.

---

811 *Sabani v Belgium* [2022] App No. 53069/15 (ECtHR March 8, 2022), § 46.

812 Vandromme S., "België veroordeeld wegens woonstbetreding bij illegale vreemdeling" (2022) 449 *De Juristenkrant*, 2.

813 Parliamentary Doc. Chamber, session 2017–18, No. 2798/001.

In its judgment no. 23/2026 of 26 February 2026, the Constitutional Court of Belgium suspended several legislative provisions reforming the reception of asylum seekers. The Court emphasised that denying material assistance may cause a serious and irreparable harm to asylum seekers, as reception is often essential to guarantee a life in human dignity. It further considered that abolishing the possibility of financial aid in exceptional circumstances and restricting access to material assistance may infringe fundamental rights, including the right to human dignity (Article 23 of the Belgian Constitution) and the right to respect for private and family life (Article 22 of the Belgian Constitution).

The Court also noted uncertainty regarding the compatibility of these measures with EU law and referred a preliminary question to the CJEU on the interpretation of the relevant EU instruments, in particular as to whether an application for international protection lodged in a second Member State after protection has already been granted elsewhere may be treated as a "subsequent application", thereby allowing limitations to material reception conditions under Directive 2013/33/EU.[814] Subsequently, the same practice was also examined by the Council of State of Belgium, which suspended its implementation on the grounds that it risked causing serious and irreparable harm , notably homelessness and extreme material deprivation.[815]

These developments reflect a broader trend towards increasingly restrictive migration governance, prompting renewed legislative intervention. A new attempt by the federal legislature regarding access of residence is imminent. Notably, in 2025, the 2025–2029 Belgian Government coalition agreement provides that the federal immigration office (Dienst Vreemdelingenzaken, "DVZ") will be granted the possibility, in cooperation with the police and upon authorization from an investigative judge, to access the residence of third-country nationals who remain in Belgium after a final rejection of their application and who refuse entry.[816]

---

814 Constitutional Court of Belgium [2026] 23/2026.

815 Council of State of Belgium [2026] 266219.

816 Federaal regeerakkoord: Regeerakkoord van de federale regering Bart De Wever ('Federaal regeerakkoord 2025-2029') <https://www.belgium.be/sites/default/files/resources/publication/files/Regeerakkoord-Bart_De_Wever_nl.pdf> accessed 10 November 2025, 175.

This legislative initiative has now been concretised, as the federal government has approved the draft law on home entry ("woonstbetreding") in second reading.[817] The proposed framework explicitly enables the police, together with the federal immigration office ('Dienst voor Vreemdelingenzaken' or 'DVZ'), to enter a private residence in order to carry out an administrative arrest, provided prior authorization is granted by an investigative judge. The measure is designed to address practical enforcement obstacles, as authorities are currently unable to act when individuals refuse to open the door or actively evade contact by remaining inside their residence.

This measure is explicitly framed as an *ultimum remedium*, intended as a necessary step to enforce return decisions in the broad sense.[818] It may only be requested from the investigative judge where no voluntary compliance has been given to an enforceable return, removal, or transfer order, and where there are reasonable grounds to believe that the person is present at the specified address. Moreover, the measure is targeted at individuals in irregular stay who systematically refuse to cooperate with their return and who pose a threat to public order or national security.

Once located, the individual may be administratively detained and, under the instructions of the Immigration Office, immediately transferred to a closed reception centre or detention unit pending removal. The government emphasizes that this aims to ensure that return decisions are effectively enforced and do not remain a "dead letter" in practice.

While the federal government underscores both the requirement of prior judicial authorization and the exceptional, last-resort nature of such interventions, the Flanders Bar Association (Orde van Vlaamse Balies, "OVB") stresses the need for comprehensive safeguards to protect fundamental rights. These include the inviolability of the home and private life (Article 8 ECHR), the right to an effective remedy and fair trial, and judicial oversight comparable to the safeguards provided for searches under the Belgian penal code.

---

817 Ministerraad geeft groen licht voor woonstbetreding bij illegale criminelen' <https://verlinden.belgium.be/nl/nieuws/ministerraad-geeft-groen-licht-voor-woonstbetreding-bij-illegale-criminelen> accessed 7 April 2026.

818 'Federaal regeerakkoord 2025-2029') <https://www.belgium.be/sites/default/files/resources/publication/files/Regeerakkoord-Bart_De_Wever_nl.pdf> accessed 10 November 2025, 175.

Furthermore, guarantees must be ensured regarding humane treatment following detention and during transfer to closed centres, alongside clarity on which independent authority is responsible for monitoring compliance with these rights.[819]

The planned home entry measures under the 2025–2029 coalition agreement thus highlight the persistent tension between the effective enforcement of immigration law and the protection of fundamental rights. Although the government frames the measure as necessary, proportionate, and respectful of the rule of law, there remains a critical need for clear procedural safeguards, independent oversight, and strict conditions governing its application to ensure compliance with Articles 15 and 22 of the Belgian Constitution and Article 8 ECHR. Without such safeguards, forced residence entry risks giving rise to constitutional and European human rights violations. This concern is illustrated by cases such as *Sabani v. Belgium*, where the absence of a clear legal framework and explicit consent led to scrutiny by the European Court of Human Rights, demonstrating the legal risks associated with entering a residence without adequate safeguards.[820]

In this sense, it remains to be seen whether the proposed new framework introducing this type of measure sufficiently addresses the concerns that had previously been raised in relation to earlier, unsuccessful proposals, namely the absence of specific safeguards to protect third parties, in particular minor children, living in the home, the lack of clear limitations on the hours during which home entry may be carried out (including the possibility of execution from as early as 5 a.m.), the insufficiently defined operational framework governing the execution of the measure, such as the absence of a requirement that the home entry take place in the presence of, or under the supervision of, a magistrate, and the lack of any effective a *posteriori* judicial review of the authorization for home entry.

In previous proposals, the Legislative Section of the Council of State noted in particular that the authorization appeared to escape any form of a posteriori judicial review. Although the foreign national received a copy of

---

[819] Orde van Vlaamse Balies, *Asiel en Migratie — Federaal Regeerakkoord 2025-2029* (12 March 2025) https://www.advocaat.be/nl/fetch-asset?path=ovb/Documenten/Nieuws/20250312_Asiel-en-Migratie_Federaal-Regeerakkoord-DEF.pdf accessed 26 November 2025.

[820] *Sabani v Belgium* [2022] App No 53069/15 (ECtHR 8 March 2022).

the authorization at the time of execution, no appeal was provided against the decision of the investigative judge with a view to having it annulled. While the individual concerned could raise irregularities in the context of an appeal against their detention before the *pre-trial chamber (raadkamer)* under Article 71 of the Law on foreign nationals of 15 December 1980, this safeguard was limited in scope and did not extend to other persons residing in the home. As a result, it did not adequately protect the rights to the inviolability of the home and to respect for private and family life of third parties living in the residence where the home entry was carried out.[821]

Another practice that raises concerns in regard of the inviolability of the home, is the proactive collaboration between the director of a reception center offering "return places" and police services executing orders of the Immigration office within the reception center. Notably, the Labor Court of Liège (Namur division), ruled that the inviolability of the home is not ensured in the reception structure and that there is violation of Article 3 ECHR which arises from the circumstance where asylum seekers find themselves compelled to decide between the fundamental right to freedom and the entitlement to accommodation.

Within the context of the Dublin convention's monitoring process, asylum seekers are apprised of the possibility of transfer to a closed center for forced relocation in the event of their refusal of voluntary return. This informational disclosure raises concerns about the imposition of undue pressure on individuals seeking asylum. Moreover, the labor court underscored the infringement upon the right to an effective appeal when asylum seekers are coerced into leaving the center to secure their freedom.[822]

---

821 Council of State, Legislative Section 'Advise on an act amending the Law of 15 December 1980 on access to the territory, residence, establishment and removal of foreign nationals, with a view to ensuring the enforcement of removal measures' [2020] 68.144/4, https://www.raadvst-consetat.be/dbx/adviezen/68144.pdf#search=woonstbetreding, §5). Since the current legislative proposal is still at an early stage, it remains to be seen whether it will adequately address these previously identified concerns.

822 Labour Court of Liège, Namur Division [2021] AR 21/12/K, <www.agii.be/sites/default/files/202100419_arbrb_luik.pdf>.

2.1.2 Procedural law perspective: human rights of migrants in times of emergency in Belgium

2.1.2.1 Special procedures on entry and residence of the third-country nationals

2.1.2.1.1 Legal framework in Belgium

Belgian migration law does not have special procedures regarding entry and residence, even in *times of emergency*, neither in the Law on foreign nationals nor in the Constitution. Belgium does not—not even during the COVID-19 pandemic—make use of the possibility provided for in Article 15 of the ECHR to derogate from the *non-suspendable* fundamental rights in enshrined in that treaty. Moreover, the Belgian Constitution provides that the Constitution cannot be suspended in whole or in part[823] (Article 187 of the Constitution). According to the prevailing legal doctrine, this prevents the Belgian government from applying Article 15 ECHR or Article 4 ICCPR to suspend the effect of certain fundamental rights. This follows from the observation that constitutional and treaty fundamental rights form an "indivisible whole" and from the principle of the broadest legal protection, which is enshrined in Article 53 ECHR. Only restrictions on fundamental rights are possible in a state of emergency and only on the basis of the usual criteria provided for in the Constitution and international treaties.[824]

---

823 See *supra*. However, these rights can be restricted, meaning that a fundamental right remains applicable without alteration, but a measure is taken that appears incompatible with it at first glance (although the courts will be able to assess whether that restriction is justified, for example, in times of COVID-19). The essential difference between *suspending* and *restricting* parts of the Constitution thus boils down to whether certain actions of the legislative and executive branches are subject to judicial review. A suspension thus touches upon an essential characteristic of the rule of law (see for more details regarding the possibility of declaring a state of emergency in Belgium: Van Haegenborgh G., and Verrijdt W., "De noodtoestand in het Belgische Publiekrecht" (2016) 1 *Preadviezen Vereniging voor de vergelijkende studie van het recht* <https://www.bjutijdschriften.nl/tijdschrift/PVVR/2016/1/PVVR_2666-7126_2016_010_001_001.pdf>.

824 Moreover, the impossibility of suspending fundamental rights implies that any government action, even when it aims to remedy an emergency situation, can be submitted to an independent and impartial judge for review. Indeed, the Belgian authorities also cannot suspend the right of access to justice as guaranteed by the analogous fundamental rights enshrined in Article 13 of the Constitution and Article 6 ECHR.

As regards the rights and freedoms protected in the Belgian Constitution,[825] the application of the "state of emergency" made possible under Article 15 ECHR (and Article 4 ICCPR) means that it will have no effect in Belgium as far as those rights are concerned.

However, Article 83 of the Law on foreign nationals specifies that during wartime,[826] the minister's powers remain governed by the Law Decree of October 12, 1918 on the residence in Belgium of aliens and persons of foreign origin.[827] According to this Law Decree, during wartime, foreigners and Belgians who have obtained naturalization are required to declare their identity to the municipal administration of their place of residence within eight days of the proclamation of wartime. They are only permitted to stay in Belgium if authorized by the competent minister and may be compelled to relocate to a specified location, or can even be interned.[828] Although this regulation is still formally in force, since the end of the Second World War it has neither been implemented nor adjusted to the significantly altered human rights framework in which the rights of detained individuals (under national and international law) must now be accommodated.[829]

---

825 These apply to foreigners as well as Belgians, subject to the exceptions provided by law (Article 191 of the Constitution).

826 Under Belgian law, this concept has a very limited meaning: it refers to the period of time between the moment the King establishes the state of war and declares the end of hostilities (Article 167 § 1, second paragraph, Constitution). See Alen A., and Muylle K., *Handboek van het Belgisch Staatsrecht* (Wolters Kluwer 2011) 234.

827 Law Decree of October 12, 1918 regarding the residence in Belgium of foreigners and persons of foreign origin, *Moniteur Belge* October 13, 1918. This law was implemented by the Ministerial Decree of September 28, 1945 on the application of the Law Decree of October 12, 1918, *Moniteur Belge*, October 5 1945.

828 It concerns internment as a security measure of foreigners who are on Belgian territory.

829 The summary drafting of the 1918 Law Decree authorizing internment—and thus detention or imprisonment—without formal conditions appears to be legally insufficient in the present circumstances of the time (CIDH, "Werkdocument 34 Internering van burgers" <https://cidh.be/sites/default/files/34N.pdf> accessed April 2024). In addition, the need for compliance with the international rules on the internment of civilians, as specified in the Geneva Convention relating to the Protection of Civilian Persons in Time of War of August 12, 1949 and Additional Protocol I to the Geneva Conventions of August 12, 1949 relating to the Protection of Victims of International Armed Conflict, should be noted. Both are incorporated into Belgian domestic law (see the Act of September 3, 1952 adopting the four Geneva Conventions

From the above, it is evident that even in a situation that might be deemed a state of emergency (as per Article 15 of the ECHR) in other countries, there are no special regulations concerning entry and residence. Consequently, the standard legal provisions continue to be in effect.

2.1.2.1.2 The (general) procedure on entry and residence

Border control is carried out by (federal) police.[830] They exercise the control at the external borders[831] in accordance with the provisions of the Schengen Borders Code (e.g., Article 7). A foreigner who does not meet the entry conditions defined in Article 3 of the Law on foreign nationals[832] is returned by the authorities responsible for border control to the place from which they departed (Article 3, §4, of the Law on foreign nationals).[833]

---

of 1949 (*Moniteur belge* of November 7, 1986 and the Act of April 16, 1986 adopting Additional Protocols I and II of 1977 (*Moniteur belge* November 7, 1986).

830 As such, the standing corps of Frontex does not carry out missions on the mainland in Belgium. However, in the framework of the *sea operation channel*, Frontex is active in the sense that it deploys a plane to the Channel and North Sea coastal region in response to the increased migratory pressure in the area. The aim of the operation on the coastline is to prevent the rising number of sea crossings. The plane streams live video and other data directly to the agency's HQ of Frontex and relevant authorities (<https://www.frontex.europa.eu/what-we-do/operations/operations/>). However, this aspect remains outside the present discussion.

831 Belgium only has a limited number of external borders through which a foreigner can directly enter the EU. In practice, these are the international air connections outside the Schengen area and the international train connection to the UK and the seaports. Control therefore takes place only in the international airports, the seaports and the terminal of the international train to the UK.

832 These essentially correspond to the grounds for refusal of entry stipulated in Article 14 of the Schengen Borders Code, read in conjunction with its Article 6 (Parliamentary Doc. Chamber, session 2016–17, No. 2215/001, pp 11–12). It further expressly provides that the possibility of refusing entry to an alien, in the cases, is not intended to prejudice the application of treaty provisions or international provisions. Therefore, that internal provision does not allow for the refusal of an alien's entry into the territory without complying, in particular, with Article 3 of the European Convention on Human Rights and the principle of non-refoulement, contained in Article 33 of the International Covenant of July 28, 1951 on the status of refugees (Constitutional Court of Belgium [2019] 112/2019, § B.11.1).

833 This will, if the expulsion occurs as a result of the control at an international airport, be the responsibility of the carrier (Article 74/4 of the Law on foreign nationals) This

An appeal for annulment against the decision of return is possible before the Council for asylum and immigration proceedings, either alone or combined with an application for interim relief to suspend that decision. This removal can also be "temporarily" postponed if the decision to return the third-country national to the borders exposes them to a violation of the non-refoulement principle (Article 74/17, § 1, read in conjunction with Article 74/10 Law on foreign nationals)

Once a foreigner sets foot on Belgian soil, the foreigner in illegally staying status may be the subject of an order to leave the territory—i.e., the Schengen territory—and this on one of the grounds provided for in the Law on foreign nationals.[834]

2.1.2.1.3 Deprivation of liberty, restriction of liberty and use of coercion

2.1.2.1.3.1 Deprivation of liberty and restriction of liberty

Firstly, the police may administratively detain a foreigner who is not in possession of the legally required (identity) documents for a maximum period of 24 hours pending a decision from the Immigration Office (Article 74/7 of the Law on foreign nationals and Article 21 of the Law of August 5, 1992 on the police service[835]).

This administrative detention, with a maximum duration of 24 hours, aims to extend the permissible deprivation of liberty of up to 12 hours for identity verification purposes in accordance with Article 34 of the Police Service Act, by an additional 12 hours to enable the competent authorities to decide on the removal of these foreigners if the identity verification leads to the determination of an irregular situation.[836]

---

does not impose obligations on the foreigners themselves but on the companies transporting them Constitutional Court of Belgium [1998] 43/98, § B.3.1).

834 It concerns the "return decision" provided for in the Return Directive. It concerns third-country nationals in illegal residence or whose residence has become illegal (e.g., of a student whose residence is terminated by the minister (Article 61 § 1 of the Law on foreign nationals), or whose residence is terminated for reasons of public order or national security (Articles 21–22 of the Law on foreign nationals).

835 Act of August 5, 1992 on the Police Service, *Moniteur Belge* December 22, 1992 (hereafter: "police service act").

836 Constitutional Court of Belgium [1998] 43/98, § B.27.1.

To maintain public safety or ensure compliance with legal provisions regarding access to the territory, residence, establishment, and removal of foreigners, the administrative police authorities may, within the limits of their powers, prescribe identity verification to be carried out by the police services under the conditions determined by these authorities. The identity documents handed over to the police officer may only be retained for the time necessary for verifying the identity and must then be immediately returned to the person concerned. If the person refuses or is unable to provide proof of their identity, or if their identity is doubtful, they may be detained for the time necessary for verifying their identity. The person must be given the opportunity to prove their identity by any means. Under no circumstances shall the person be detained for this purpose for longer than 12 hours (Article 34, paragraphs 3 and 4 of the Police Service Act).

Pursuant to conditions stipulated in the Law on foreign nationals, a foreigner can be detained for the duration as stipulated in the law on foreign nationals. This detention constitutes an administrative deprivation of liberty rather than a judicial deprivation of liberty due to committing or being convicted of a crime.

Firstly, pending removal from the territory, a foreigner[837] may be detained in a specific place located at the border for a period of two months, which

837 A foreigner may not be detained for the sole reason that he has made an application for international protection (Article 74/5 § 1 of the Law on foreign nationals cf. Article 8 § 1 of the Directive 2013/33/EU of the European Parliament and the Council of June 26, 2013 laying down standards for the reception of applicants for international protection (recast)). With regard to these foreigners, a border procedure is provided for as regards the processing of applications for international protection (Article 57/6/4 of the Law on foreign nationals). That provision allows the Commissioner General for refugees and stateless persons (CGRS) to declare inadmissible or deal with an application for international protection submitted at the border or in a transit zone through an accelerated procedure. If the conditions for this are not met, the CGRS decides that further investigation is necessary and the applicant is admitted to the territory in accordance with Article 74/5 § 4 4° of the Law on foreign nationals. If the CGRS, within four weeks of receiving the application for international protection has not taken a decision, the foreigner shall also be admitted to the territory in accordance with Article 74/5 § 4 5° of the same Act. Pending the decision of the CGRS or until the aforementioned four-week period has expired, the foreigner in question shall not have permission to stay in the territory and may be detained at

is extendable (Article 74/5 of the Law on foreign nationals).[838] Furthermore, Article 71 of the law on foreign nationals allows the foreign national detained in a specific place located at the border under Article 74/5 of the same Act to appeal against the detention measure before the council chamber of the territorially competent criminal court. This led the Constitutional Court to conclude that the right to access to justice is guaranteed.[839]

---

the border in accordance with Article 74/5, § 1 (Constitutional Court of Belgium [2021] 23/2021, § B.122.1).
Where no decision has been taken in respect of an applicant detained at the border within four weeks, that applicant shall be granted access to the territory of the Member State for the purpose of examining his/her application for international protection. That right of access means, in principle, that the measure of detention at a specified place taken in respect of the applicant for the purpose of ruling on his/her right to enter the territory come under Article 74/5 of the Law on foreign nationals, lapses. However, it does not prevent the competent authority from taking a new decision to detain the alien at a well-defined place, based on new grounds, pursuant to Article 74/6 of the same Law (Court of Cassation of Belgium [2020] P.20.0481.F). In the aforementioned judgment, the Constitutional Court held that this was in accordance with Article 43(2) of the Directive 2013/32/EU of the European Parliament and of the Council of 26 June 2013 on common procedures for granting and withdrawing international protection ("Procedural Directive") (Constitutional Court of Belgium [2021] 23/2021, § B.124.2). The detention at the border in the context of Article 43 of the Procedural Directive does not occur because the foreigner concerned has lodged an application for international protection, but to allow the competent authorities, subject to the conditions laid down in that article, to carry out an initial examination of that application, before the person concerned is granted admission to the territory. The Constitutional Court considered that, as the European Court of Human Rights has held in its judgments (i.a. Saadi v UK [2008] App No. 13229/03 (ECtHR January 29, 2008, § 66 and Ilias and Ahmed v Hungary [2017] App No. 47287/15, March 14, 2017 §§ 213 and 225) such an examination must be possible in the context of efficient immigration control, and it cannot be assumed that the mere fact of lodging an application for international protection at the border or in a transit zone has the effect of making the person regularly resident in the territory, so that as long as the person has not been admitted to the territory, his stay is irregular (ibid., § B.122.8).

838 As long as a person has not been turned back, they are not considered to have entered the country, even though in practice this is a fiction. This is the case because all closed detention centers within the Kingdom are deemed equivalent to a location situated in the border area.

839 Constitutional Court of Belgium [2021] 23/2001, § B.123.2.

The law on foreign nationals provides also provides for the possibility of forcibly returning to the external border the foreigner[840] against whom a removal measure has been taken and has not complied with it within the specific period. The foreigner can be forcibly led to the border of his choice, in principle, in principle excluding[841] States with which Belgium shares internal borders as referred to in the Schengen Borders Code, or embarked for a destination of his choice, excluding these states (Article 27 § 1 Law on foreign nationals).[842]

Unless other effective, yet less coercive measures can be applied, these foreigners may be detained for the purpose of removal, especially when there is a risk of absconding or when the foreigner avoids or obstructs the preparation of return or removal procedure during het period strictly necessary for the execution of the removal measure.[843]

The Law on foreign nationals also provides for the possibility of less coercive measures than detention. For instance, during the time limit to voluntarily execute the order to leave the territory, the foreigner can be obliged to fulfill preventive measures in order to avoid the risk of absconding

---

840 As long as a person has not been driven back, he does not enter the country and is locked up in a "border area. In practice, this is a fiction: All detention centers within the kingdom are equivalent to a place located in the border area. Cfr Article 74/5 § 2 of the Law on foreign nationals, an alien detained in such a place is not considered authorized to enter the kingdom. Furthermore, foreigners are no longer detained in the transit zone at the international airport. Which, incidentally, is part of the Belgian territory (*Shamsa v Poland* [2003] App No. 45355/99 and 4357/99 (ECtHR November 27, 2013; Council of State of Belgium [2002] 102722; Council for asylum and immigration proceedings [2010] TVreemd, 148).

841 Unless the foreigner possesses the nationality of a State with which Belgium has an internal border, or has a valid residence permit or a temporary residence permit from a Contracting State, he may be returned to the border of this State or embarked with this State as destination.

842 Removal is at the expense of a foreign national (Article 27 § 3 of the Law on foreign nationals). Sometimes a third party may be called upon, such as the guarantor if there is an obligation to cover costs within the meaning of Article 3bis of the Law on foreign nationals.

843 This is apparent rom several provisions: Article 7, § 3, Article 8bis § 4, Article 27 § 3 of the Law on foreign nationals. The general rule is laid down in Article 74/8 § 1 of the Law on foreign nationals, which confirms the principle that the necessary measures may be taken so that the alien does not leave the place where he is detained in accordance with the articles listed in that provision without the required consent.

(Article 74/14 § 2 of the Law on foreign nationals).[844] These may include reporting regularly,[845] depositing an appropriate financial guarantee or handing over a copy of the documents that allow to establish identity.[846] Furthermore, under certain conditions, house arrest is possible,[847] and biometric data can be collected[848] from several categories of foreigners, including the foreign national subject to a removal or expulsion measure.

2.1.2.1.3.2 Use of coercion

The use of coercion is defined by law both in terms of the cases in which coercion may be used and the conditions to which such use is subject.

---

844 As long as the period for voluntary departure is running, the third-country national is protected against forced removal (Article 74/14 § 2 of the Law on foreign nationals).

845 It was ruled that the obligation to report twice daily to the local police, being limited in his mobility and contact with certain individuals, and having no income, is not contrary to Article 3 of the European Convention on Human Rights (Council for asylum and immigration proceedings [2009] 32402).

846 Article 110, quaterdecies of the Royal Decree on foreign nationals.

847 For example, a foreigner who undermines public order or the security of the country can be compelled by the minister to leave certain places, refrain from entering them, or stay in a specific location (Article 26 of the Law on foreign nationals). The parliamentary preparatory work indicates that this measure is intended to be more flexible than expulsion or deportation, "allowing the foreigner to be compelled to leave or stay in a specific place, for example, to avoid being expelled while still completing their studies" (Parliamentary Doc. Chamber, session 1977–78, No. 144/7, 37). This measure does not involve deprivation of liberty through arrest or detention, so it was ruled that Article 5 of the European Convention on Human Rights (ECHR) is not applicable (Constitutional Court of Belgium [2019] 112/2019, B.38.3, which also ruled that this arrangement is compatible with the non-discrimination principle contained in Articles 10 and 11 of the Constitution, read in conjunction with the freedom of movement guaranteed by Article 2 of Protocol 4 to the ECHR, and with the right to an effective remedy to ensure respect for that freedom, guaranteed by Article 13 of the same Convention (Idem point B.38.9). For other cases, please refer to: Denys L, *Overzicht van het vreemdelingenrecht* (Inni Publishers 2019) 872–873.

848 Article 30bis and 51/3 of the Law on foreign nationals. The Constitutional Court ruled that this interference with the right to respect for private life, as guaranteed by Article 22 of the Constitution, Article 7 of the Charter, and Article 8 of the ECHR, is justified and does not entail disproportionate consequences regarding the rights of the affected foreigners, given the objectives pursued (Constitutional Court of Belgium [2021] 23/2021, § B.7 et seq).

The minister's authorized representative may use coercion in relation to the foreigner who has been administratively deprived of his freedom, and in the context of his transfer (by the security officer-driver of the Immigration Department.[849]

This use of coercion is subject to the conditions stipulated by Article 37 of the Police Service Act. This implies that considering the risks involved, force may be used to pursue a lawful objective that cannot be achieved by other means. Any use of force must be reasonable and proportionate to the objective pursued and any use of force is preceded by a warning unless such use would render it ineffective.

During these transfers, security drivers may use force against the foreigner to gain control over them if the behavior of the foreigner poses a danger to their own physical integrity or that of others, or if the foreigner disrupts order. Force may also be used to ensure the successful completion of the transfer if, based on the behaviors of the foreigner, material indications, or circumstances, the security driver has reasonable grounds to believe that

---

849 In any case, the conditions of Article 37 of Police Service Act (Report to the King accompanying the royal decree on foreign nationals). For the specific provisions regarding transfer, refer to the Royal Decree of December 8, 2008, establishing the regime and rules applicable to the transfer, carried out by security drivers of the Immigration Office, of foreigners referred to in Article 74/8 § 1 of the law on foreign nationals).
Under this regulation, it is stipulated (Article 8) that prior to boarding the vehicle, the foreigner shall undergo a security search, in accordance with Article 74/8 § 5 of the Law on foreign nationals. This search is conducted by a security driver of the same gender as the foreigner or by another staff member of the Immigration Office of the same gender, in which case the search is conducted under the supervision of the security driver. In the case of departure from a center, this search may also be conducted in accordance with Articles 111/1 to 111/2 of the Royal Decree of August 2, 2002, establishing the regime and operational measures applicable to the places located on Belgian territory, managed by the Immigration Office, where a foreigner is detained, made available to the government, or held, in accordance with the provisions set forth in Article 74/8, § 1, of the Law on foreign nationals. Any prohibited or dangerous items shall be confiscated by the director of the center where the foreigner is or will be staying. In the case of transfer to a border in the context of the removal procedure from the Kingdom, the dangerous items shall be handed over to the federal police.

the foreigner will pose a danger[850] to their own physical integrity or that of others, that the foreigner will disrupt order, or that there is a risk of escape. The permitted means of force include physical encouragement, restraint, and handcuffs (Article 21 of the royal decree of December 8, 2008 on foreign nationals).[851]

If the third-country national resists their removal or poses a risk of danger, forced return is carried out, if necessary, under escort. Coercive measures against the foreigner may be used, but in compliance with Article 1 and 37 of the Law on the Police Service. This violence must therefore pursue a legitimate purpose that cannot be achieved in another way. It must be reasonable and proportionate to the intended aim.

If the removal is conducted by air, measures are taken in accordance with the common guidelines for air removal set out in Decision 2004/573/EC[852] (Article 74/15 of the Law on foreign nationals). The internal regulations expressly stipulate that only coercive measures of a model listed and approved by the Director-General upon the proposal of the Minister of the Interior may be used on board. Furthermore, the use of coercive measures must remain strictly exceptional, particularly during take-off and landing of the aircraft. Their use is decided by the aircraft commander as a precautionary measure on an exceptional basis, and he may request the assistance of passengers or authorize them to provide assistance in accordance with Article 6 of the Tokyo Convention[853] to carry out this measure. During the

---

850 This implies that coercion can also be imposed preventively, in order to ensure the successful completion of the transfer (Report to the King on the Royal Decree of December 8, 2008 on foreign nationals).

851 If a foreigner attempts to escape during departure, transport or arrival, the security officer-driver must prevent the escape, without endangering the physical integrity of himself, the alien or third parties, and provided sufficient security officers-drivers remain available to guard the other aliens (Article 21 of the Royal Decree of December 8, 2008 on foreign nationals).

852 Council Decision 2004/573/EC of April 29, 2004 on the organization of joint flights for removals from the territory of two or more Member States, of third-country nationals who are subjects of individual removal orders, OJ L 261/28.

853 Article 6 of the Convention on Offenses and Certain Other Acts Committed on Board Aircraft, drawn up in Tokyo on September 14, 1963 and approved by the Act of July 15, 1970 (*Moniteur Belge* October 30, 1970) shows that only the captain is authorized to use a coercive measure against a person who is on board the aircraft in full flight. The passengers—including escort members—may not themselves decide to take

flight, any passenger—including members of the escort—may, however, take reasonable precautions without such prior authorization if they have reasonable grounds to believe that such action is immediately necessary for the safety of the aircraft or the persons and property aboard the flight.[854] In no case may the passenger be fastened to a fixed object in the aircraft using coercive measures, and the use of coercive measures that could jeopardize the safety of the aircraft, crew, or passengers, including the foreigner being removed, is prohibited, in particular 1) total or partial obstruction of the airways and 2) the administration of sedatives or any drug aimed at subduing the person against their will.[855]

2.1.2.2 Identification of standards for proper organization of administrative authorities and courts

2.1.2.2.1 Basic standards for proper functioning administrative authorities and courts

The basic standards regarding the entry and stay of foreigners in general and third-country nationals in particular allow the foreigner to enforce their rights as mentioned in the immigration legislation. The procedure(s) concerning entry and stay must adhere to the guarantees in this regard. Some are explicitly mentioned in the immigration law, while others arise from common law.

---

such a measure, except in mutual agreement with the captain (in this sense, Council of State, Legislative Section "Advise concerning a preliminary draft of ministerial decree regulating the conditions for the transportation on board civil aircraft of passengers with specific security risks" [1999] 29756 <http://www.raadvst-consetat.be/dbx/avis/29756>).

854 For the purposes of this decree, the aircraft shall be deemed to have commenced its flight when it is at the beginning of the runway and starts the take-off procedure.

855 Articles 5 and 6 of the Ministerial Decree of April 11, 2000 regulating the conditions of carriage on board civil aircraft, of inadmissible passengers and persons to be removed, *Moniteur Belge* (April 14, 2000). This special regulation was introduced following the high-profile death of Semira Adamu on September 22, 1998, which led, among other things, to a strict regulation on the use of coercive measures on board: see Foblets M. C., "Wat als verwijderingsmaatregelen mislukken- verwijdering of de keerzijde van migratie," in *Migratie en migrantenrecht. Recente ontwikkelingen* (Die Keure 2011) 582.

As far as common law guarantees are concerned, it is important to highlight the application of the general principles of good administration.[856] Consistent with common law, every decision regarding entry and stay must be based on grounds supported by reasons, the factual existence of which has been duly proven and can be considered in court to justify that action. Additionally, the administration must always arrive at its decision in a careful manner. The principle of carefulness implies that the administration must prepare its decision carefully. This entails that the decision must be based on genuinely existing and concrete facts that have been determined with the required care. The government is obliged, among other things, to proceed with due care in preparing the decision and to thoroughly examine the factual and legal aspects of the dossier so that it can decide with knowledge.

Among the general safeguards provided in a normative text, mention must be made of the law on formal justification[857] (i.e., the external or formal legality of the decision). According to this general regulation, applicable throughout the Kingdom, all administrative authorities—including those competent to make decisions in migration matters—must include in the act the legal and factual considerations underlying the decision, and this in an "adequate" manner. The adequacy of the justification means that the justification must be pertinent, meaning that it must clearly relate to the decision, and it must be forceful, meaning that the reasons cited must suffice to support the decision.[858] In addition to this general formal justification obligation, the Law on foreign nationals provides for its own

---

856 On the application in immigration law, see Milojkwowic M., et al., "De algemene beginselen van behoorlijk bestuur in het vreemdelingenconcentieux," in C. Bamps et al., *10 jaar Raad voor Vreemdelingenbewistingen: daadwerkelijke rechtsbescherming* (Die Keure 2017) 143–161. In the hierarchy of norms, general principles of good administration take a position superior to the decisions made by lower authorities such as the King, ministers or other subordinate entities. They fulfill a vital role in overseeing administrative action, serving as a safeguard mechanism to rectify imbalances stemming from the privileged position of the administration vis-à-vis the governed populace (Mast A., et al., *Overzicht van het Belgisch administratief recht* (Mechelen 2021) 59).

857 Act of July 29, 1991 *on formal grounds of administrative decisions*, *Moniteur Belge* September 30, 1991.

858 Consistent jurisprudence in administrative litigation: see e.g., Council of State of Belgium [2024] 258437.

justification obligation of the same scope (Article 62 § 2, first paragraph, law on foreign nationals). The general formal justification obligation includes some exceptions to the obligation to include the reasons in the contested decision, including the hypothesis that this could endanger the external security of the state. Furthermore, the law on foreign nationals provides for an exception specific to immigration law: the facts justifying decisions regarding migration are mentioned in the relevant decision (e.g., refusal of entry), unless reasons of state security prevent this.[859]

Importantly, the right to be heard (*audi et alteram partem*) can also be invoked as a general principle of good administration, as a safeguard regarding entry and residence.[860]

The right to be heard increasingly gained wider application in Belgian case law, in the sense that no serious measure of a nature to seriously affect one's interests can be taken against anyone without first giving him the opportunity to make his point of view known in a useful way.[861] This principle also

---

859 For an analysis and how to apply the ZZ doctrine to that in judicial review, see Debersaques G., and Ryckaseys, "De formele motiveringsplicht en de redenen van staatsveiligheid (noot onder HvJ 4 juni 2013, nr. C-300/11, ZZ/secretary of state)' [2013] *TVreemd*, 349–350. See also: Intervention by G. Debersaques during the ACA-Europe Seminar "Public order, national security and the rights of the third-country nationals in immigration and citizenship cases," *Cracow*, September 18, 2017 <https://www.aca-europe.eu/index.php/en/library>.

860 However, the principle is not characterized as a principle of public order, which means that it cannot be raised before the immigration court of its own motion and cannot be raised for the first time in cassation before the Council of State (Council of State of Belgium [2017] 238474; Council of State of Belgium [2017] 237502). The Court of Cassation applies the ruling of the Court of Justice of the European Union in its judgment of March 17, 2016, in case C-161/15, namely "that Union law must be interpreted as meaning that when the applicable national law provides that a plea alleging infringement of national law, raised for the first time before the national court ruling in cassation, is admissible only if it concerns a matter of public policy, a plea alleging infringement of the right to be heard as guaranteed by Union law, raised for the first time before that same court, must be declared admissible if that right, as guaranteed by national law, meets the requirements for classification as a matter of public policy laid down in that law, which is for the referring court to ascertain."

861 See for example: Council of State of Belgium [2021] 252014; Council of State of Belgium [2020] 246623.

applies in principle in immigration cases, such as expulsion decisions.[862] This principle is, however, subject to two caveats.

First, the obligation to hear a concerned party as a principle of good administration applies only in the absence of an explicit norm, but a normative regulation does not preclude the supplementary application of the general principle of good administration of the obligation to hear.[863] This is the case to the extent that the normative regulation does not (sufficiently) guarantee that the individual is given the opportunity to present relevant elements in support of their position.[864] Article 62 § 1 of the law on foreign nationals stipulates that when considering terminating or revoking the residence of a foreign national authorized or admitted to stay in Belgium for more than three months, the foreign national must be informed in writing and given the opportunity to present relevant elements that could prevent or influence the decision. There are several statutory exceptions to this obligation to hear.[865] For instance, this obligation to hear does not apply if reasons of national security oppose it.[866]

---

862 For a foreign national who is being removed and who is subject to a return obligation, the country of return for the foreign national is generally their country of origin. However, if reasonable doubt exists in a particular case, the administrative authority, taking into account the principles of good administration, must hear the concerned foreign national before taking any measures that may harm them. The measure can be contested before the Council for asylum and immigration proceedings. The same applies to any subsequent decision to forcibly return a foreign national to the border (Constitutional Court of Belgium [2019] 112/2019, § B.45.5).

863 E.g., Council of State of Belgium [2023] 256506.

864 When the legislator incorporates the fundamental right to be heard before making a decision that could be subject to legal challenge, he is not obliged to regulate the details of the procedure introduced in order to ensure compliance with that right. It is the availability of a remedy against the decision that enables the concerned foreign national to raise, as a ground, the failure of the administration to comply with the right to be heard.

865 Article 62 § 1 § 3 of the Law on foreign nationals.

866 In three instances, an exception can be made to the right to be heard: (1) when reasons of state security oppose it, (2) when special circumstances peculiar to the case prevent it due to their nature or severity, and (3) when the individual cannot be reached. It is up to the competent court, to whom an appeal has been lodged against a decision to terminate the residence of a foreign national taken after the conclusion of an administrative procedure, during which the individual did not have the opportunity to assert the elements deemed relevant by him, to ascertain

A second consideration concerns the fact that in the vast majority of cases, decisions regarding the access, stay, and removal of foreigners implement EU law.[867] Therefore, the right to be heard applies as a general principle of EU law to these decisions.[868] Although the Council of State currently states in its case law that the principle of "audi et alteram partem" has the same content as the right to be heard as a European principle of good administration,[869] some modalities may differ.

---

in a concrete manner whether the motive put forward by the administration for not respecting the right to be heard pursues a public interest objective and whether that right has not been disproportionately infringed upon (Constitutional Court of Belgium [2019] 112/2019, § B.77.3).

867 An order to leave the territory can be considered as an adverse decision that may adversely affect the interests of the foreign national concerned. Therefore, the right to be heard, as a general principle of EU law, applies in this case (see, for example, Council for asylum and immigration proceedings [2024] 300752).

868 The Court of Justice of the European Union has repeatedly stated that the right to be heard is an integral part of the right of defense, which is a general principle of EU law (C-249/13 Boudjilida [2014]; C-166/13 Mukarubega [2014] ECLI:EU:C:2014:2336; C-141/12 and C-372/12 Ys and others [2014]ECLI:EU:C:2014:2081).
The Belgian national court rigorously applies this case law (see, for example, Council of State of Belgium [2017] 237502; Council of State of Belgium [2017] 238292; Council of State of Belgium [2017] 238293; Council of State of Belgium [2017] 238373; Council of State of Belgium [2017] 238474). The right to be heard ensures that everyone is able to properly and effectively express their views in the context of an administrative procedure and before a decision is made that may adversely affect their interests. This rule aims, in particular, to ensure the effective protection of the individual concerned by informing them to correct any mistakes or to present individual circumstances that argue for the decision to be made, not to be made, or to be made in a certain way. This viewpoint is supported in the national case law of both the Council of State, acting as a cassation court and by the Council for asylum and immigration proceedings (see, for example, Council of State of Belgium [2022] 255200; Council of State of Belgium [2018] 240622).

869 Council of State of Belgium [2016] 236329; Council of State of Belgium [2016] 178727. Both the EU right to be heard (C-584/10 P, C-539/10 P and C-595/10P Kadi [2013], § 98 et seq; C-141/12 and C-372/12 YS and others [2014], §§ 66–68) and the right to be heard in the Belgian legal order (see for instance: Constitutional Court of Belgium [2011] 44/2011; Council of State of Belgium [1989] 31712; Council of State of Belgium [1991] 36751; Council of State of Belgium [1992] 39951; Council of State of Belgium [1992] 41367 Council of State of Belgium [1994] 50005; Council of State of Belgium [2008] 188391; Council of State of Belgium [2009] 189380; Council of State of Belgium [2009] 189381; Council of State of Belgium [2009] 193640; Council of State

The Court of Justice of the European Union has repeatedly noted that a breach of the rights of defense, in particular the right to be heard, under EU law leads to the annulment of the decision taken after the administrative procedure only if this procedure could have had a different outcome without this irregularity.

It follows from this that not every irregularity in the exercise of the rights of defense during an administrative procedure constitutes a breach of those rights. Furthermore, not every failure to respect, in particular, the right to be heard systematically leads to the unlawfulness of the decision taken. In order to establish such unlawfulness, it is for the national court to examine, in light of the specific factual and legal circumstances of the case, whether, if it considers that there has been an irregularity affecting the right to be heard, the administrative procedure in question could have had a different outcome because the individual could have put forward elements to justify their position.

To demonstrate a breach of the right to be heard, the foreign national must therefore demonstrate that, if they had been heard, a different decision could have been made. It is the Council for asylum and immigration proceedings' task to examine, based on the specific factual and legal circumstances of the case, whether there is an irregularity affecting the right to be heard to such an extent that the decision-making process could have had a different outcome.[870] In light of the cited case law of the Court of Justice of the European Union, the Council for asylum and immigration proceedings does not add a condition to the right to be heard. Although Belgian law does not explicitly provide for such an exception, it does have an exception to the obligation to hear if the facts to be heard about are not subject to dispute.[871] The Court of

of Belgium [2009] 194764; Council of State of Belgium [2009] 197310; Council of State of Belgium [2010] 203094; Council of State of Belgium [2019] 245584; Council of State of Belgium [2021250636; Council of State of Belgium [2021] 252080; Council of State of Belgium [2023] 256424; Council of State of Belgium [2023] 257690) the right to access the case file at a convenient time.

870 Settled case law: C-383/13 M.G and N.R. [2013] ECLI:EU:C:2013:533 and case law referred to. Belgian case law applies this modality in migration cases where the EU law obligation of the right to be heard applies, as evidenced by, for instances cases: Council of State of Belgium [2018] 240621 and 240622; Council of State of Belgium [2017] 238373; Council of State of Belgium [2016] 233719.

871 Council of State of Belgium [1997] 64234; Council of State of Belgium [2010] 203565.

Cassation, on the other hand, rules that the right to be heard may be waived if the hearing would not have allowed for a different decision.[872]

The protection of third-country nationals is also guaranteed by the fundamental rights enshrined in the Belgian Constitution—according to Article 191 thereof, foreigners enjoy the same rights as Belgians, except for the exceptions provided by law—and in international standards such as the ECHR, the Charter, the Convention on the Rights of the Child, and so forth.

Regarding the provided safeguards, the *non-refoulement* principle[873] is also noteworthy, which is an integral part of Belgian positive law. Thus, Article 74/17[874] of the law on foreign nationals provides that the removal shall be temporarily postponed if the decision to return or remove to the borders of the territory exposes the third-country national to a violation of the non-refoulement principle. In its judgment No. 112/2019 of July 18, 2019,[875] the Constitutional Court ruled that in cases where a significant time has elapsed between the decision to remove in the form of an order to leave the territory and the actual execution of that order, the minister or his authorized representative shall, at the time of the execution of the order to leave the territory, conduct a new examination of the risk of violation of Articles 3 and 8 of the European Convention on Human Rights.

---

872 Court of Cassation of Belgium [2019], No. AR F.18.0062.N, 2 APT 2020, 356.

873 As protected by Article 3 of the Convention against Torture and Other Cruel, Inhuman or Degrading Treatment or Punishment and Article 33 of the 1951 Convention relating to the Status of Refugees, and as also arising from Article 3 of the European Convention on Human Rights and Article 19(2) of the Charter.

874 See also Article 22 § 1 of the Law on foreign nationals which includes settled nationals and third-country nationals who enjoy long-term resident status in the Kingdom.

875 § B.7.5. Furthermore, the Constitutional Court ruled that from Articles 12(1) and 13(1) and (2) of the Return Directive, it follows that the decision on actual removal, whether or not it coincides with the issuance of an order to leave the territory or whether it is taken after an order to leave the territory has been issued previously, must be issued in writing, must be reasoned, and must be subject to appeal (point 7.6).
Council for asylum and immigration proceedings [GC] [2018] 199329, which requires that the aforementioned provisions of the Return Directive stipulate that there must be an effective remedy against a decision to return to the border, regardless of whether that decision is taken simultaneously with an order to leave the territory or not, and that the decision to return to the border is thus a separate decision against which an appeal can be lodged with the Council.

Against all individual decisions that are administrative acts, taken concerning the access, residence, and removal of foreigners,[876] there is a jurisdictional appeal available to the Council for asylum and immigration proceedings (Articles 39/1 and 39/2 of the law on foreign nationals). The Council for asylum and immigration proceedings is an administrative court.[877] Article 39/2 of the law on foreign nationals is the key provision that determines the scope of the Council's jurisdiction. According to paragraph 1 of this provision, the Council rules on appeals brought against decisions of the Commissioner General for Refugees and Stateless Persons. It may "confirm or reform" these decisions, or, in limited cases, "annul" them. This concerns, on the one hand, a reforming jurisdiction of decisions of the Commissioner General for Refugees and Stateless Persons concerning international protection, where the ruling of the Council, with devolutive effect, replaces the decision of the Commissioner General,[878] and, on the other hand, an annulment jurisdiction regarding other decisions falling under the jurisdiction of the Council.[879] The latter concerns a legality review of the decision of the immigration administration.[880] It was ruled that such an appeal for annulment before the Council for asylum and

---

876 With the exception of deprivation of liberty measures, against which an appeal can be lodged with the council chamber pursuant to Article 71 of the Law on foreign nationals. The constitutional division of powers between administrative bodies and courts (Articles 144–145 of the Constitution) does not allow the Council for asylum and immigration proceedings to rule on this matter.

877 As exemplified by Council of State of Belgium [2023] 256142: "An appeal for annulment before the Council for asylum and immigration proceedings, with the possibility, if desired and in case of extreme urgency, to request a suspension, constitutes an effective remedy." Furthermore, the principle of *non-refoulement* is legally established both regarding appeals concerning decisions on requests for international protection (see Article 39/70 of the Law on foreign nationals and Constitutional Court of Belgium [2016] 13/2016, § B.39.1 et seq, legally defined exceptions based on Article 41(1) of the recast asylum procedures directive), and concerning other decisions regarding the alien subject to a removal or return measure (Article 39/85 of the Law on foreign nationals).

878 This implies that any irregularity committed in the administrative procedure before the commissioner general cannot affect the legality of the decision of the Council for Asylum and Immigration Proceedings. To that effect, see: Council of State of Belgium [2019] 244696.

879 This includes decisions on entry, residence and expulsion of foreigners, as well as decisions on the application of Dublin III.

880 Constitutional Court of Belgium [2016] 13/2016, § B.37.1.

immigration proceedings, with the possibility, if desired, of filing a suspension action in case of extreme urgency, constitutes an effective remedy in law.[881] Furthermore, the *non-refoulement* principle is legally established both in appeals concerning decisions on requests for international protection (see Article 39/70 of the law on foreign nationals and Constitutional Court case 13/2016 of January 27, 2016, paragraphs B.39.1 et seq., legally determined exceptions in this regard supported by Article 41(1) of the recast procedural directive) as well as concerning other decisions regarding the foreigner that are the subject of a removal or repatriation measure (Article 39/85 of the law on foreign nationals).

2.1.2.2.2 The effect of times of emergency on the standards for proper organization of administrative authorities and courts

In times of emergency, it is not permissible to suspend or reduce these standards in any way, whether temporarily or otherwise. Regarding the obligation for formal justification, it is explicitly stated that the urgency of the situation does not exempt the administration from the duty to provide explicit justifications for its actions.[882]

Exceptions (in theory) are decisions where neither the normative regulation of the right to be heard contained in Article 62 § 1 of the Law on foreign nationals nor the EU principle of the right to be heard applies, and

---

881 See, for example, Council of State of Belgium [256142] 256142. In the context of such a referral, the Council for asylum and immigration proceedings assesses the legality of the contested decision based on the information available to the authority at the time it rendered its decision. The Council cannot consider any new evidence submitted by the applicant, nor can it examine the current situation of the applicant at the time it decides on a potential violation of Articles 2 and 3 of ECHR in the event that the concerned foreigner would be returned to their country of origin. Such an appeal itself does not constitute an effective remedy within the meaning of Article 13 of the European Convention on Human Rights. However, considering all appeals available to the foreigner, including appeals that allow them to contest the implementation of a removal measure to a country where, according to their argument, there is a risk of a violation of Article 2 or Article 3 of the ECHR, this is indeed the case. This is evident in appeals lodged against decisions refusing a residence permit under Article 9 ter of the Law on foreign nationals: see Constitutional Court of Belgium [2019] 186/2019; Constitutional Court of Belgium [2019] 206/2019.

882 Act of July 29, 1991 *on formal grounds of administrative decisions*, *Moniteur Belge* September 30, 1991, Art. 5.

where only the Belgian interpretation of the right to be heard applies. Case law from the Council of State indicates that, for decisions where the right to be heard as a principle of good administration applies, this right can be waived if the decision is urgent.[883] In such cases, the right to be heard may be set aside, but, as mentioned earlier, these are exceptional cases, and the correct application of this principle is subject to oversight by the Council for Alien Law Litigation.

2.1.2.2.3 How do public authorities and courts cope with the amount of applications for international protection?

To address the influx of asylum requests, the legislator has implemented several managerial techniques[884]:

A first approach is a systemic approach of avoiding or processing backlogs that have arisen by intervening in the exercise of the responsible authority's mandate. For instance, the Commissioner General for Refugees and Stateless Persons is required to develop a plan outlining the necessary measures to eliminate or prevent the backlog in the processing of cases. This plan must be submitted for approval to the Council of Ministers (Article 57/24 of the Law on foreign nationals). Similarly, the Chief of Police of the Council for asylum and immigration proceedings is tasked with drafting a policy plan (Article 39/6 § 1 of the Law on foreign nationals.). Additionally, an annual activity report is prepared and published annually upon the initiative of the Chief of Police of the Council for asylum and immigration proceedings (Article 39/3 of the Law on foreign nationals), and the Commissioner General

---

883 Council of State of Belgium [1985] 25373; Council of State of Belgium [1988] 31091; Council of State of Belgium [1989] 32752; Council of State of Belgium [1990] 34130; Council of State of Belgium [2004] 128424; Council of State of Belgium [2015] 230037; Council of State of Belgium [2021] 251451; Council of State of Belgium [2022] 254056; Council of State of Belgium [2022] 255146; Council of State of Belgium [2023] 257030; Council of State of Belgium [2023] 257356.

884 Abstraction is made of the case of a mass influx or imminent mass influx of displaced persons, to which the special situation of temporary protection applies on the basis of Council Directive 2001/55/EC Council Directive 2001/55/EC of July 20, 2001 on minimum standards for giving temporary protection in the event of a mass influx of displaced persons and on measures promoting a balance of efforts between Member States in receiving such persons and bearing the consequences thereof, OJ L 212 (Article 57/29 et seq of the Law on foreign nationals).

reports to the minister annually on his mission (Article 57/28 of the Law on foreign nationals). In case of backlog, the Chief may instruct one or more chambers to hold additional sessions every 15 days or as he determines, outside of regular sessions (Article 39/6 of the Law on foreign nationals).

A second technique consists of prioritization by the legislator of certain requests for international protection. The Constitutional Court has accepted that the specificity, increase and urgency of disputes arising from the application of the Law of December 15, 1980 justify the adoption of special rules suitable for expediting the processing of appeals before the Council for asylum and immigration proceedings.[885]

As such, the Commissioner General for Refugees and Stateless Persons treats requests for international protection with priority if:

1° the applicant is detained or subject to a security measure,
2° the applicant is in a penal institution,
3° the minister or his representative requests the Commissioner General to prioritize the request for international protection, or
4° the request is likely to be well-founded (Article 57/6, § 2 of the Law on foreign nationals).

If the Council for asylum and immigration proceedings has prioritized the appeal of such a case, it will also be handled with priority by the Council for asylum and immigration proceedings (Article 39/76 of the Law on foreign nationals).

Finally, a third technique used is the legislator's shortening of the processing deadlines for the Commissioner General for Refugees and Stateless Persons.

The Council for asylum and immigration proceedings must decide within two months of receiving an appeal against decisions of inadmissibility by the Commissioner General. The Commissioner General can decide that the application for international protection is inadmissible under certain circumstances, such as when the applicant already enjoys real protection in a first country of asylum or comes from a third country that can be considered a safe third country, among others. Thus, the

[885] Constitutional Court of Belgium [2016] 13/2016, § B.17.5.

Council of State takes a decision within two months of receiving the appeal against the inadmissibility decisions taken by the Commissioner General for Refugees and Stateless Persons. Indeed, the latter can decide that the application for international protection is inadmissible if, under circumstances, it appears, for example, that the applicant already enjoys real protection in a first country of asylum, or comes from a third country that can be considered a safe third country for the applicant, or where the applicant already enjoys international protection in another Member State of the European Union, or if the applicant is a national of a Member State of the European Union or of a State party to a Treaty of Accession to the European Union that has not yet entered into force (Article 57/6, § 3 of the Law on foreign nationals).

These decisions of inadmissibility must be made within short deadlines, ranging from two working days to 15 working days depending on the case.[886]

Other techniques aimed at limiting the influx of requests for international protection are non-existent. For instance, the decision by the competent Secretary of State for Asylum and Migration to limit the number of asylum requests that can be submitted to the administration to 50 per day was suspended by the Council of State. It was deemed that this decision excessively hinders certain foreigners who wish to apply for international protection from exercising one of their fundamental rights, namely the actual possibility to use the procedure to be recognized as a refugee or to obtain subsidiary protection.[887] Similarly, the Council of State suspended the decision of the Secretary of State for Asylum and Migration, which disqualified single men who have applied for asylum from qualifying for reception measures. The Council of State concluded that this decision is not in line with the right to reception granted to all asylum seekers under the law of January 12, 2007, concerning the reception of asylum seekers and certain other categories of foreigners.[888]

---

886 See in particular Article 57/6 § 3 of the Law on foreign nationals, where different deadlines apply depending on the nature of the decision to be taken on the request for international protection.

887 Council of State of Belgium [2018] 243306.

888 Council of State of Belgium [2023] 257300.

2.1.2.3 Application of new technologies into administrative and court proceedings

53. The Commissioner General for Refugees and Stateless Persons has the authority to conduct the personal interview of the applicant for international protection "remotely."[889] Remote hearing refers to the situation "in which at least the official or interpreter is physically located in a different room from the applicant, and, if applicable, the lawyer, the confidant, and/or the guardian, and participates in the personal interview through the use of communication means that allow a remote hearing in real time, for example, through a direct audiovisual connection or the use of video conferencing technology."[890]

The procedure before the Council of Alien Law Litigation does not provide for such a possibility of holding a hearing remotely.

2.2 Czech Republic (Ivo Pospíšil)

2.2.1 Constitutional definition of states of emergency in the Czech Republic

2.2.1.1 General background

The Constitution (Constitutional Act No. 1/1993 Coll.) defines the Czech Republic as a sovereign, unitary and democratic state governed by the rule of law and based on respect for the rights and freedoms of man and of the citizen (Article 1(1)). However, there are situations in which these values, upon which the state is founded and which it must respect, are threatened, necessitating extraordinary measures. In such situations, these principles may be curtailed or negated in order to maintain the "viability" of the State. In legal or political theory, we talk about the security doctrine, which in the last 20 years (at least since the attack on the World Trade Center in New York

---

[889] Article 12/1 of the Royal Decree of July 11, 2003 regulating the operation and procedure before the Commissioner General for Refugees and Stateless Persons, published in the *Moniteur Belge* on January 27, 2004. Refer to the appeal against certain modalities concerning remote hearings, especially see ruling: Council of State of Belgium [2022] 254655.

[890] Report to the King on the Royal Decree of November 26, 2021 amending the royal decree of July 11, 2003 regulating the operation and procedure before the Commissioner General for Refugees and Stateless Persons, published in the *Moniteur Belge* on September 9, 2022.

on September 11, 2001) has adopted a broader concept. It no longer focuses solely on situations of international or domestic armed conflicts (i.e., war in the traditional sense), but extends to broader threats (including terrorism, public unrest, migration, disruption of social peace) that may not necessarily originate from human activity (as in the case of natural disasters, health epidemics and pandemics).[891]

States of emergency, along with the associated changes in the ordinary powers of the authorities and the possibility of more radical restrictions on fundamental rights and freedoms, are also reflected in the concept of a defensive (or militant) democracy.[892] This concept is based on the assumption that the democratic rule of law has the legitimacy to restrict certain manifestations of freedom and the exercise of rights when necessary to preserve the democratic system itself. In doing so, the system is therefore endowed with the power to temporarily deny the principles and premises on which it is based in order to protect itself from destruction.[893] However, we are always confronted with the dilemma of whether to protect sovereignty, security and other general values at the cost of temporarily restricting fundamental rights, as well as limiting the principles of the separation of powers, democratic legitimacy, predictability or judicial control.

Like other countries, the Czech Republic gained valuable experience during the so-called coronavirus pandemic, i.e., the Covid-19 outbreak. This period served as an unprecedented test of the entire constitutional system and all the above-mentioned principles. Indeed, it was the first time in the history of the independent Czech Republic that the national rules for states of emergency were applied to such an extent.

---

891 Waisová Š., "Od národní bezpečnosti k mezinárodní bezpečnosti. Kodaňská škola na křižovatce strukturálního realismu, anglické školy a sociálního konstruktivismu" (2004) 39(3) *Mezinárodní vztahy*, Ústav mezinárodních vztahů.

892 Uhl P., "Obecně k ústavnímu zákonu o bezpečnosti České republiky," in P. Rychetský, T. Langášek, T. Herc, and P. Mlsna (eds) a kol., Ústava České republiky. *Ústavní zákon o bezpečnosti ČR. Komentář* (Praha: Wolters Kluwer 2015) 1140.

893 In the Czech environment, see for example Mareš M., and Výborný Š., *Militantní demokracie ve Střední Evropě* (Brno: Centrum pro studium demokracie a kultury 2013).

2.2.1.2 The constitutional and sub-constitutional regulation of states of emergency

At the constitutional level, states of emergency are not regulated in the Constitution, but in a separate constitutional Act No. 110/1998 Coll., on the security of the Czech Republic. While the 1992 Constitution was based on the traditional concept of security and regulated only the situation of a state of war, this separate law was a response to discussions within the security community and the recognized need to define other emergency situations. Such scenarios would necessitate extending the executive's powers to issue orders and permitting limitations on the protection of fundamental rights and freedoms beyond the scope that would be inadmissible under normal circumstances. Undoubtedly, this constitutional act was also inspired by the Czech Republic's integration into new security structures, such as preparations for joining NATO in 1999.

The constitutional act regulates three types of states of emergency: a state of emergency, a state of national emergency, and a state of war. Each of them is linked to specific conditions under which it may be declared, involves different procedures for activation and termination, and has varying consequences, particularly in terms of restrictions on fundamental rights and freedoms.

What they have in common is their primary aim: to protect sovereignty, territorial integrity, democratic order, internal order and security, the life and health of persons, property, or the environment (see Article 2 of the Act).

A state of emergency is reserved for situations where the state as a whole or any part of its territory are facing a natural disaster, an ecological or industrial accident, or another similar danger that significantly threatens life, health, property, or internal order and security (Article 5(1) of the Act). The grounds for the declaration are thus conditions that are neither deliberate nor social in nature. The authority empowered to declare such a state of emergency is the Government; in very exceptional circumstances, if there is a risk of delay, the Prime Minister may make the declaration (however, the Government must confirm or revoke their decision within 24 hours). It is the duty of the Government to inform the Chamber of Deputies (the lower house of Parliament) without delay, and the Chamber may revoke the declaration of a state of emergency. Thus, the declaration is based on a certain cascade of powers: the declaration is entrusted to the government for reasons of speed and efficiency, but it is subject to control by the Chamber of Deputies. This principle is also reflected in the time limitation of the state of emergency—it can be declared for a maximum period of 30 days and can only be extended with the prior consent of the Chamber of Deputies, which can also decide to end it at any time.

This state can be declared for the whole country or only for a specific part of it. The territorial scope must be precisely defined in the decision (government resolution), as well as the reason for its declaration.

From the point of view of the protection of fundamental rights and freedoms, it is essential that the government define which rights are restricted and to what extent, in accordance with the Charter of Fundamental Rights and Freedoms,[894] as well as which obligations are imposed and to what extent. The drafters of the Constitution probably had in mind that the government, either directly in the resolution declaring the state of emergency or in a separate resolution issued at the same time as the declaration, would provide a list of all the rights to be restricted and specify the nature of the restrictions.

The Constitutional Security Act thus requires the government to explicitly define the rights that are restricted. In doing so, reference is made to a specific law: Act No 240/2000 Coll., on crisis management and on amending certain acts (the Crisis Act).

Before the coronavirus pandemic, a state of emergency was declared in the Czech Republic during the floods in 2002, 2006, 2007 and 2013. However, these declarations did not result in any constitutional or judicial disputes. This was not the case during the coronavirus pandemic. During this period, the state of emergency was declared repeatedly and became a source of political disputes, escalating to the level of a constitutional crisis.[895] The declaration

---

894 This is a national catalog of constitutionally guaranteed rights and freedoms, which is also not part of the Constitution, but was promulgated separately as a resolution of the Presidium of the Czech National Council under No. 2/1993 Coll.

895 It was declared for the first time by Government Resolution No. 69/2020 of March 12, 2020, it was extended twice with the consent of the Chamber of Deputies and lasted until May 17, 2020; the next one was declared on October 5, 2020 and extended by the Chamber of Deputies a total of five times, its further extension was rejected by the Chamber of Deputies on February 11, 2021 and another (new) state of emergency was abolished on February 27, 2021 (later declared in the obiter dicti of Resolution Pl. ÚS 20/21 of the Constitutional Court as unconstitutional), and accepted later, including its double extension until April 11, 2021. The last state of emergency lasted from November 26 to December 5, 2021.

of a state of emergency itself is not subject to judicial review in the Czech Republic, not even by the Constitutional Court. In resolution Pl. ÚS 8/20 the Constitutional Court stated that it does not have the authority to review the declaration of a state of emergency, but "the act of declaring a state of emergency could be annulled by the Constitutional Court if it contradicts the fundamental principles of the democratic rule of law and if it would mean a change in the essential elements of the democratic rule of law."[896]

Another type of state of emergency is the so-called state of national emergency, which is declared by Parliament as a whole (i.e., both chambers—the Chamber of Deputies and the Senate), upon the proposal of the Government. The reason for this is a threat to the sovereignty, territorial integrity or democratic foundations of the state, although the constitutional law does not specify which specific events may be the source of the threat. Such threats may include natural disasters, which could also justify a state of emergency, but more typically they will involve social and political reasons, such as social unrest, migration waves, etc. To declare such a state of emergency requires a relatively low quorum (considering the consequences of such a decision), namely a majority of all Members of Parliament and all Senators. Unlike a state of emergency, the declaration of such a state does not need to be substantiated, nor is it limited in time and can therefore be declared for an unlimited period. The regulation is deficient in that it does not specify which body is responsible for revoking the state of national emergency or the procedure for doing so (it can be logically assumed that it must be the body that declared it). Nor is it the duty of Parliament to specify the scope of the rights that can be derogated from under this state. Once again, this is regulated only by the Crisis Act, which gives the government the same scope of powers as in the case of a state of emergency, while also granting it the

---

896 The Constitution of the Czech Republic, following the German model, contains the so-called eternity clause (Ewigkeitsklausel), which defines the material core of the Constitution. This cannot be changed even by amending the Constitution or by a posterior constitutional act. According to Article 9(2) of the Constitution, it is impermissible to change the essential elements of a democratic state governed by the rule of law. For more details, see Rychetský P., "Změna ústavy," in P. Rychetský, T. Langášek, T. Herc, and P. Mlsna (eds) a kol., Ústava České republiky. Ústavní zákon o bezpečnosti ČR. Komentář (Praha: Wolters Kluwer 2015) 97.

additional power to restrict the entry of foreigners into the territory of the Czech Republic (on this issue, see the following chapters for greater detail).

Finally, the last state of emergency is a state of war, which is the only one directly regulated in the Constitution (Article 43). It is declared by Parliament as a whole (again, both chambers) and, unlike a national emergency, does not require a proposal from the government. Parliament is therefore the absolute sovereign in this case. Restrictions on rights and obligations are regulated by a number of laws, starting with Act No. 585/2004 Coll., on conscription and its provisions (the Defense Act) and ending with Act No. 40/2009 Coll., the Criminal Code.

As already mentioned, the Czech Republic has so far had practical experience with declaring states of emergency, whereas the other two types have neither been declared nor required implementation.

2.2.2 Substantive law perspective: the human rights of migrants in the Czech Republic

2.2.2.1 Institutional framework of protection

As a member of the European Union, the Czech Republic is naturally bound by a number of obligations arising from both international law and EU law. With regard to the rights of migrants, the Czech Republic is primarily bound by the 1951 Refugee Convention[897] and its 1967 Protocol.[898] However, these only protect persons in a specific situation who have lost the protection of their country and are seeking international protection in one of the contracting parties. The most important obligation is the principle of non-refoulement, which prohibits a state from expelling a foreigner to a country where their life or personal freedom would be threatened (Article 33 of the Convention).

A whole range of rights of foreigners then derives from other international legal obligations, in particular the International Covenant on Civil and Political Rights and the European Convention on Human Rights. Above all, this convention and the case law of the ECtHR fundamentally complement

---

897 Convention Relating to the Status of Refugees, United Nations, Treaty Series, vol. 189, July 28, 1951.

898 Protocol Relating to the Status of Refugees, United Nations, Treaty Series, vol. 606, January 31, 1967.

and regulate the rules concerning the entry, residence, and, where applicable, the expulsion of migrant foreigners. Although the Convention itself, or rather its Protocol No. 4 (Article 4), expressly regulates only the prohibition of collective expulsion of foreigners, the case law of the ECtHR has interpreted a number of other rights protected by the Convention so broadly that they may also apply to issues of entry and residence of individual foreigners in the territory. This concerns, in particular, the right not to be subjected to torture or degrading and inhuman treatment (Article 3 of the Convention), which the ECtHR has interpreted as meaning that, in the case of expulsion or transfer of a foreigner to another state, a potential violation of the Convention is sufficient. The essential question is whether there are substantial grounds for the conclusion that the foreigner is at risk of torture or degrading or inhuman treatment in another state.[899]

The right of a foreigner to private and family life under Article 8 of the Convention is interpreted in a similarly broad manner, which represents a fundamental corrective both when deciding on the expulsion of a foreigner from the territory of a state and when deciding on his or her residence permit. If a decision on a foreigner's residence would constitute a disproportionate interference with their right to private and family life, then the state has a duty not to expel the foreigner, to allow them to remain in the territory, and to grant them a residence permit.[900]

The Czech Republic is naturally also bound by EU law standards that exist within the framework of the EU's common migration and asylum policy (in particular the Qualification and Asylum Procedure Directives and the Dublin III Regulation).

With regard to the legal framework at the national level, it is necessary to mention first and foremost the provisions of Article 43 of the Charter of Fundamental Rights and Freedoms, which guarantees the right to asylum to foreigners persecuted for exercising their political rights and freedoms.

---

[899] See for example the judgments in Soering against the United Kingdom, July 7, 1989, or Ahmed against Austria, May 17, 1996.

[900] See for example the judgment in Khachatryan and Konovalova against Russia, July 13, 2021. The case law of the ECtHR in the field of Article 8 goes even so far as to say that the right to private and family life may even be a corrective factor in decisions on the deprivation of an individual's citizenship (case of Ramadan against Malta, June 21, 2016).

However, this constitutional definition is more of a supplement to the rules arising from the aforementioned 1951 Refugee Convention, as it covers only one of the reasons for granting protection to foreigners. After the collapse of communism, this constitutional provision thus reflected previous historical experience, when it was the citizens of the former Czechoslovakia who were forced to seek asylum in other countries.

The Charter of Fundamental Rights and Freedoms, which is not a part of the Constitution but represents a component of the broader concept of "constitutional order" (see Article 112 of the Constitution) and has legal force similar to that of a constitutional law, contains a whole catalog of rights and freedoms. Most of them apply to individuals regardless of whether they are citizens of the Czech Republic or foreigners. Moreover, its Article 42 par. 2 expressly stipulates that foreigners enjoy these rights and freedoms unless they are granted exclusively to citizens. According to Article 42 par. 3, where all existing regulations use the term "citizen," this means every person in relation to the fundamental rights and freedoms granted by the Charter, regardless of citizenship. The Act No. 83/1990 Coll., on the Association of Citizens, might serve as an example. The act, after the fall of the communist regime, expressly guaranteed the right of association only to citizens. In light of this provision of the Charter, however, it had to be interpreted as applying to any individual, including foreigners.[901]

The Charter guarantees, above all, the right of free movement and residence (Article 14). It expressly states that everyone who is lawfully present in the territory of the state has the freedom of movement and the right to leave the territory freely. However, only citizens are also guaranteed the right to enter the territory of the state freely and may not be forced to leave it. The Charter does not guarantee foreigners the right to enter the territory of the Czech Republic. The right of entry may therefore derive from EU law or be guaranteed only at the level of ordinary law. The Charter then guarantees foreigners that they may only be expelled in cases specified by law.

At the level of legal regulation, the basic sources are Act No. 326/1999 Coll., on the Residence of Foreigners in the Czech Republic and on Amendments

---

901 Compare with Bobek M., "Čl. 42. Osobní působnost Listiny a jiných předpisů," in E. Wagnerová, V. Šimíček, T. Langášek, and I. Pospíšil (eds), *Listina základních práv a svobod. Komentář* (Prague: Wolters Kluwer 2012), 850.

to Certain Acts, and Act No. 325/1999 Coll., on Asylum. Some of the partial rights of foreigners or persons granted international protection under the Asylum Act are then regulated in other legal regulations. For example, issues of school education are governed by Act No. 561/2004 Coll., on preschool, primary, secondary, higher vocational and other education (education act), while participation in public health insurance is regulated by Act No. 48/1997 Coll., on public health insurance and on amendments to certain related laws.

The Ministry of the Interior plays a key role in migration policy, deciding on matters relating to the residence of foreigners and international protection. While the ministry decides on matters of international protection in a single instance, the Commission for Deciding on the Residence of Foreigners is the appeal body for residence issues. However, it is part of the ministry's organizational structure. Their decisions are subject to review by the administrative courts, which, however, are based on the principle of cassation, meaning that the courts cannot decide on merits (for example to grant international protection), but only overturn the decisions of administrative authorities.[902]

The Act on the Residence of Foreigners in its current form essentially implements EU legislation, in particular Regulation 2016/399, on a Union Code on the rules governing the movement of persons across borders (Schengen Borders Code). It thus regulates issues of entry and refusal of entry into the territory, residence status, and finally the obligation to leave the territory and expulsion. The Act essentially distinguishes between three types of residence status: temporary residence, long-term residence, and permanent residence. A long-term residence permit may be granted for the purpose of family reunification, study, scientific research, employment (the so-called employee card, or, in the case of specially qualified professions, the so-called blue card) or business (investment).

---

902 An exception would be a case similar to that dealt with by the ECJ in its judgment of July 29, 2019, Alekszij Torubarov v. Bevándorlási és Menekültügyi Hivatal, C-556/17. If the ministry repeatedly failed to respect the binding legal opinion of the administrative court, the court would be directly obliged to decide on the application itself (on merits). However, this has never happened in the Czech Republic, although the Supreme Administrative Court has already acknowledged this situation in its decisions (see judgment of January 31, 2020, No. 5 Azs 105/2018-46, §§ 84 and 85).

In practice, the very system of applying for a long-term residence permit has proved problematic. Since the end of the last century, the Czech Republic has been transforming from a pure transit country to an immigration country—its economic potential has attracted foreigners from many countries (especially from the former Soviet Union, but also from Vietnam) to immigrate, but the system was not prepared for such an influx of applications or able to cope with various forms of abuse. Residence permits were thus associated with images of endless queues of applicants waiting at Czech embassies in these countries, with suspicions of corruption and lack of transparency. The state addressed this, for example, through digitization—the so-called Visapoint system allowed foreigners to register in advance to submit their applications in person, electronically, which was also supposed to determine the order of applicants. However, this system also failed and was abused (by people who registered most of the appointments in advance and sold them on for considerable sums of money).[903]

A separate but very sensitive issue is the detention of foreigners, i.e., the restriction of their personal freedom for the duration of proceedings. This is only possible for the purpose of ensuring expulsion, departure, or transfer to another country. This is only possible if the intended purpose cannot be achieved by other, less severe means (e.g., the foreigner's obligation to stay at an address provided to the police and report to the police at regular intervals, or to deposit in advance funds corresponding to the costs of expulsion, the so-called special measures).

The Asylum Act is essentially only an implementation of EU regulations or obligations arising from international law. It regulates several types of protection, which it subsumes under the general term of international protection. First and foremost, it concerns the granting of asylum to persons who are persecuted for exercising their political rights and freedoms, or who have a well-founded fear of persecution on grounds of race, gender, religion, nationality, membership of a particular social group, or for holding certain political opinions in the country of which they are a citizen, or, in the case of a stateless person, in the country of his or her last permanent residence.

---

903 This system has been strongly criticized by administrative courts—see, for example, the Supreme Administrative Court judgment of May 30, 2017, No. 10 Azs 153/2016-52.

In addition, subsidiary protection may be granted to a foreigner who does not meet the grounds for asylum but who is found to have a well-founded fear that, if returned to the country of his or her nationality or, in the case of a stateless person, to the country of their last permanent residence, they would face a real risk of serious harm. This includes the threat of the death penalty or execution, torture or inhuman or degrading treatment or punishment of the applicant, or a serious threat to the life of a civilian or their human dignity due to indiscriminate violence in a situation of international or internal armed conflict. Finally, the last type of international protection until mid-2025 was the so-called national humanitarian asylum, which could be granted to a person who did not qualify for asylum or subsidiary protection. In most cases, humanitarian reasons were the serious health conditions of the applicant or family reasons.

2.2.2.2 Selected issues of human rights of migrants

As mentioned above, foreigners who are legally present on the territory of the Czech Republic are guaranteed freedom of movement within its territory, just like citizens. This freedom may be restricted by law if it is necessary to ensure state security, maintain public order, protect health, or protect the rights of others (Article 14 par. 1 and 2 of the Charter). In the case of foreigners, not only may their freedom of movement be restricted, but they may also be deprived of their personal liberty where their free movement would made impossible any further decisions in their case. As mentioned above, this is achieved through the detention of foreigners, which can be realized in accordance with both the Foreigners Residence Act and the Asylum Act. The conditions under which a foreigner may be detained are similar in both cases.

In times of state emergencies, freedom of movement may be restricted even more significantly, and as the following subchapter shows, during the Covid-19 pandemic, the state did indeed restrict movement between different parts of the country; however, this affected both foreigners and citizens.

Foreigners residing legally in the Czech Republic are guaranteed all fundamental rights in the same way as citizens. The exception is the guarantee of property rights: Article 11 par. 2 of the Charter stipulates that the law may in certain cases regulate that certain things may only be owned by citizens or legal entities based in the Czech Republic. In the past, this legal restriction was actually used: foreigners could not acquire real estate in the Czech

Republic by purchase, which was justified by concerns about the "buying up" of real estate at low prices caused by differences in currency values and economic performance. However, foreigners practically circumvented this restriction by establishing legal entities based in the Czech Republic, to which this restriction did not apply. A similar restriction then applied to property restitution, which was limited to Czech citizens only (i.e., only a citizen was an eligible person to acquire property in restitutions).[904]

As already mentioned, specific attention is paid to the right to private and family life of foreigners. In view of the case law of the ECtHR, this may be a factor in assessing applications for residence permits or their revocation, as well as the obligation to leave the country or expulsion orders. This aspect is expressly regulated by Section 174a of the Foreigners Residence Act. According to this section, when assessing the proportionality of the effects of a decision, the administrative authority shall take into account, in particular, the seriousness or type of the foreigner's unlawful conduct, the length of the foreigner's stay in the territory, his or her age, state of health, the nature and strength of family relations, economic circumstances, social and cultural ties established in the territory, and the intensity of ties to the state of which the foreigner is a citizen. However, these aspects shall only apply where expressly provided for by law. This provision has been criticized as insufficient by administrative courts' case-law, which requires that interference with the private and family life of a foreign national always must be examined if the foreigner raises such an objection in the proceedings. This is because it involves the implementation of obligations arising from Article 8 of the Convention, which, according to Article 10 of the Constitution, take precedence over the text of the domestic law.[905]

A specific issue in this regard is the consideration of the best interests of the child under Article 3 par. 1 of the 1989 Convention on the Rights of the

---

904 The Constitutional Court found this regulation to be in conformity with the constitutional order (decision Pl. ÚS 33/96), but the Human Rights Committee in Geneva deemed it to be in violation of Article 26 of the International Covenant. For more details, see Šimáčková K., "Čl. 11. Ochrana vlastnictví," in E. Wagnerová, V. Šimíček, T. Langášek, and I. Pospíšil (eds), *Listina základních práv a svobod. Komentář* (Prague: Wolters Kluwer 2012) 306–308.

905 See for example the judgment of the Supreme Administrative Court of February 14, 2020, No. 5 Azs 383/2019-40.

Child. This stipulates that the interests of the child must be a primary consideration in any action concerning children, whether undertaken by public or private social welfare institutions, courts, administrative authorities, or legislative bodies. However, this does not mean that the best interests of the child represent an absolute precedence in all circumstances. On the contrary, both the case-law of the ECtHR and the Czech Constitutional Court perceive it only as a mandate to balance various conflicting interests.[906]

The case law of the Constitutional Court has introduced a certain categorization of various proceedings according to the intensity of the best interests of the child. These range from proceedings in which decisions are made directly on the rights and obligations of the child as a child (proceedings on children care and contact), to proceedings the purpose of which is to regulate the rights and obligations of the child without affecting the status of the child (proceedings on private law obligations), to proceedings the aim of which is not to directly interfere with the legal status of the child, but which have an indirect legal impact on the child. In these categories, the best interests of the child are reflected with varying intensity, from the primary and decisive criterion to "simple" weighing (balancing) with other values and interests. The administrative courts in the Czech Republic have concluded that decisions in matters concerning foreigners fall into the latter category.[907]

The concept of vulnerable persons also has its place in decisions on the rights of foreigners. It is not explicitly addressed in the Act on the Residence of Foreigners, but only in the Asylum Act. The latter defines such a person as an unaccompanied minor, a parent or family with a minor child, or a parent or family with an adult child with a disability, a person over 65 years of age, a person with a disability or serious illness, a pregnant woman, a victim of human trafficking, or a person who has been tortured, raped, or subjected to other serious forms of psychological, physical, or sexual violence. However, when deciding on matters concerning foreigners, it is necessary to take this status into account, based on the direct application of EU regulations that work with this concept (see for example Article 3 par. 9 of Directive 2008/115/EC

906 Decision of April 14, 2020, No. IV. ÚS 950/19.

907 See for example the Supreme Administrative Court judgment of August 17, 2020, No. 1 Azs 260/2020-27.

on common standards and procedures in Member States for returning illegally staying third-country nationals).[908]

Foreigners in the Czech Republic are also guaranteed many of the political rights (the right of assembly, the right of association, the right to information). The exception is the right to associate in political parties and movements, which is restricted to Czech citizens only (Article 20 par. 2 of the Charter). However, the ECJ has ruled that this provision is contrary to EU law as regards citizens of other Member States who are established in the Czech Republic. They are guaranteed the right to vote and stand for election in municipal elections and elections to the European Parliament, and one of the institutional instruments for this is precisely the membership in political parties.[909]

In cases involving these rights, more significant restrictions may also be imposed in states of emergency. The state did so during the Covid-19 pandemic, when it restricted gatherings of people, regardless of whether they were citizens or foreigners.

As regards the guarantee of social rights, these mainly concern the right to healthcare covered by public health insurance and the right to various forms of social benefits and assistance. Here, it mainly depends on the specific status of the foreigner—the scope and content of these rights vary depending on whether the foreigner has been granted some form of international protection or what type of residence permit they have.

However, the Charter of Fundamental Rights and Freedoms guarantees the right to free healthcare based on public health insurance only to citizens (Article 31). Act No. 48/1997 Coll., on public health insurance, is more benevolent and regulates participation in public health insurance much more broadly: it covers all persons who have a permanent residence permit, employees of employers based in the Czech Republic (i.e., all employed foreigners), beneficiaries of international protection (asylum holders), and minors with a long-term residence permit. Other foreigners have the right to health protection and healthcare, but this is fully paid from their own resources. In

---

908 See the Supreme Administrative Court judgment of August 18, 2022, No. 1 Azs 218/2021-71.

909 ECJ judgment of November 19, 2024, Commission v. Czech Republic, C-808/21, similarly also Šimíček, V. Čl. 20. "Sdružovací právo," in E. Wagnerová, V. Šimíček, T. Langášek, and I. Pospíšil (eds), *Listina základních práv a svobod. Komentář. 2. doplněné a aktualizované vydání* (Prague: Wolters Kluwer 2023) 514.

the case of long-term residence permits, the law requires the submission of proof of commercial insurance with one of the insurance companies based in the Czech Republic.[910]

As far as social rights are concerned, the Charter of Fundamental Rights and Freedoms guarantees the right to adequate material security again only to citizens. Other persons have the right, if they are in material need, to have their basic living conditions secured (Article 30). In this case, too, the implementing laws are more lenient. Act No. 117/1995 Coll., on State Social Support, extends the range of persons entitled to social benefits to foreigners with permanent residence permits, long-term residence permits for the purpose of employment or scientific research, and their family members with long-term residence permits, provided that they actually reside in the Czech Republic. Holders of international protection (asylum, subsidiary protection) are also entitled to these benefits.

2.2.3 Restrictions on human rights in states of emergency and the status of aliens

2.2.3.1 Limitation of rights in general

It has already been stated that in the case of states of emergency, the Constitutional Security Act requires the government to define the rights that are restricted. Reference is made to a specific law, namely Act No 240/2000 Coll., on crisis management and amending certain acts (the Crisis Act). The latter allows for restrictions on the following rights:

(a) the right to inviolability of the person and inviolability of the dwelling when evacuating a person from a place where he or she is in imminent danger to life or health,
(b) the ownership and use rights of legal and natural persons to property, if the right of the owner or user is compulsorily restricted for reasons of protection of life, health, property or the environment, which are threatened by an emergency situation, and adequate compensation is provided for such restriction,

---

910 This model was found consistent with the constitutional order by the Constitutional Court in its decision of May 3, 2017, No. Pl. ÚS 2/15.

(c) freedom of movement and residence within the defined area of the territory threatened or affected by the crisis situation,
(d) the right to assemble peacefully in a defined area of territory threatened or affected by a crisis situation,
(e) the right to engage in business activities that would jeopardize the crisis measures being implemented or disrupt or prevent their implementation,
(f) the right to strike if such a strike would lead to disruption of or prevent rescue and recovery work.

Specifically, in times of emergency, the government is authorized to order

(a) evacuation of persons and property from the defined area,
(b) the prohibition of entry, stay and movement of persons in specified places or areas,
(c) a duty to work, to assist at work or to provide material resources,
(d) the immediate implementation of construction, construction work, landscaping or removal of structures or vegetation to mitigate or avert the threat resulting from the emergency situation,
(e) to the employer, service authority or official, the obligation to telework or to perform service from another location,
(f) mandatory reporting of temporary change of residence of persons,
(g) measures to protect national borders and the residence of aliens or stateless persons,
(h) transfer persons in custody or serving a prison sentence to another prison or exclude the free movement of such persons outside the prison,
(i) deployment of soldiers on active service and fire protection units to carry out crisis measures,
(j) the use of economic measures for states of crisis in preparation for a state of national emergency,
(k) the provision of care for children and young people if the parents or other legal representative cannot provide such care in a crisis situation,
(l) priority supply of critical infrastructure elements to children's, health or social facilities, the armed forces, security forces and integrated

rescue system units, if they are involved in the implementation of crisis measures, to the extent necessary,
(m) an alternative method of deciding on social security benefits and their payment.

Finally, the government is entitled to impose prohibitions in the area of fiscal, monetary and banking policy, such as prohibiting the acquisition of funds in foreign currency, the making of all payments from the Czech Republic abroad, or the deposit of funds in foreign accounts, among other measures.

Unfortunately, during the states of emergency declared at the time of the coronavirus pandemic, the government adopted a practice of not specifying any concrete measures in the decree of the declaration, nor did it define the fundamental rights it was interfering with, leaving everything to other so-called crisis measures adopted under the Crisis Act.

It is only these specific crisis measures that are subject to judicial review (not the declaration of a state of emergency itself). The Constitutional Court has identified these measures as a type of legal regulation with the force of a sub-legislative regulation (see resolution Pl. ÚS 8/20).

Theoretically, this concept has the advantage that the measures are reviewable, like other sub-legislative legislation, in the norm review proceedings before the Constitutional Court, which is entitled to formally annul them. Moreover, according to Article 95(1) of the Constitution, the judges of ordinary courts are not bound by such measures and, if they find them to be inconsistent with the law or the Constitution, they have the authority to disregard them when deciding a case. On the other hand, however, this concept raises the question of whether it is consistent with other provisions of the Charter of Fundamental Rights and Freedoms, in particular Article 4(2), according to which the limits of fundamental rights may be regulated only by law.

In practice, however, this concept has proven to be severely limited and inappropriate—the Constitutional Court formally annulled only one crisis measure adopted by the government during the entire pandemic, because the government adopted them in such a rushed and disorganized manner that the proceedings before the Constitutional Court were not able to accommodate them at all. Therefore, in the future, it would be advisable for the Czech Republic to provide for a special procedure before the Constitutional Court to review crisis measures in emergency situations. At the very least, this procedure should have an accelerated regime, with the Constitutional Court having to complete the review procedure even after the measure has expired.[911] There was also a view expressed in the expert community as to whether it would be appropriate to modify the procedure to allow Parliament or the Chamber of Deputies to intervene, and, in a similar way to the Constitutional Act on Security, to allow the annulment of a declaration of a state of emergency or of individual government measures.[912]

This is also why the so-called Pandemic Act (No. 94/2021 Coll., on emergency measures during the epidemic of the Covid-19 disease) was later adopted. This act empowered the Ministry of Health to adopt measures, not in the form of legal regulations, but in the form of so-called "measures of a general nature," the review of which was entrusted to the Supreme Administrative Court at one level.

Prior to its adoption and at the time when the state of emergency was not declared, restrictive measures were ordered by the Ministry of Health in the form of measures of a general nature pursuant to Act No. 258/2000 Coll., on the Protection of Public Health and Amendments to Certain Related Acts.

Conversely, in the event of a declared state of national emergency, it is not the duty of Parliament to specify the scope of the rights that can *be derogated from* in such a state. This matter is, again, regulated by the Crisis Act, which grants the government the same scope of powers as in the case of a state of emergency. Additionally, the government has the authority to regulate the entry of persons into the territory of the State and to restrict the entry of persons who are not citizens of the state, and to conduct increased security measures for stored nuclear materials, sources of ionizing radiation, dangerous chemicals, biological agents and genetically modified organisms. In a state of national emergency, conscription and enlistment under the Defense Act may also be implemented.

---

911 According to Act No. 182/1993 Coll., on the Constitutional Court, the court shall discontinue the norm review proceedings once the challenged law or other legal regulation has ceased to be valid. An exception to this rule are motions filed by ordinary courts in proceedings concerning a concrete review of norms—in this case, the Constitutional Court has stated in the past that it shall not terminate the proceedings, as the assessment of constitutionality is necessary for the ordinary court to be able to decide on its case (see judgments Pl. ÚS 33/2000 and Pl. ÚS 38/06).

912 Wintr J., "Úvaha nad vhodným nastavením nouzového stavu v českém právním řádu," in V. Šimíček (ed), *Dělba moci* (Prague: Leges, 2022) 127.

2.2.3.2 Restrictions on the rights of foreigners in states of emergency

With regard to the specific status of foreigners, it is regulated at the national level by Act No. 326/1999 Coll., on the residence of foreigners in the Czech Republic and on amendments to certain acts, and Act No. 325/1999 Coll., on asylum. Certain other aspects are regulated in a number of special acts, such as Act No. 48/1997 Coll., on public health insurance, or Act No. 561/2004 Coll., on preschool, primary, secondary, higher vocational and other education (Education Act), etc.

The Act on the residence of foreigners regulates the basic issues of entry, residence and possible departure from the territory of the Czech Republic and implements provisions under EU law. However, it does not contain any provisions regulating restrictions on the rights of foreigners in the event of declared states of emergency. These are only very generally regulated in the Crisis Act, or in Act No 258/2000 Coll., on the protection of public health and on amending certain related acts. During the COVID-19 pandemic, they were further addressed in the so-called Pandemic Act.

Any substantive or procedural restrictions on the rights of foreigners are thus left to the discretion of the government in a state of emergency and, outside such a state, for example in the case of health epidemics, to the decisions of the Ministry of Health.

As already mentioned, the Crisis Act allows the government to implement measures to protect the national borders and regulate the residence of foreigners or stateless persons during a state of emergency. During the COVID-19 epidemic in 2020–2022, the government used this competence in an unprecedented way: by Resolution No. 76/2020 Coll. of March 13, 2020, it prohibited the entry of all foreigners except those who had been granted temporary or permanent residence on the territory of the Czech Republic. Similarly, it prohibited all its citizens and foreigners with temporary or permanent residence from leaving the country. This measure was not subject to review before the Constitutional Court, but it can reasonably be concluded it was unconstitutional.

Other legal instruments employed by the executive outside of declared states of emergency, but which imposed similar restrictions on the rights of foreigners, were protective measures issued by the Ministry of Health under the Public Health Protection Act. This Act regulates both measures to prevent the introduction of an infectious disease from abroad (§ 80) and measures to control the spread of an epidemic (§ 69).

As regards the first power, the judicial case law has limited its application to cases of diseases that have not yet appeared in the Czech Republic; it can no longer be used to address the further spread of a disease that has already been introduced into the Czech Republic (see the judgment of the Municipal Court in Prague, Case No. 18 A 16/2021). Naturally, this power applies not only to foreigners, but also to nationals entering the territory of the State.

With regard to measures aimed at preventing the spread of an epidemic, the Act also allows the Ministry to restrict the movement and contact of persons and groups of persons. Additionally, it contains a residual clause under which the Ministry has the power to prohibit or mandate certain other activities deemed necessary to eradicate the epidemic or the mitigate risk of its occurrence (section 69).

However, the case law has appropriately curtailed the scope of this general clause. The Supreme Administrative Court has already found that, under this provision, the Ministry may, in light of the *eiusdem generis* (same kind) rule of interpretation, be granted "the power to prohibit or order only such "other specified" activities as are similar in type to the more specific definition of activities listed in the preceding items of the list of emergency measures. Of course, the activities will not be the same, but at the same time they cannot be any conceivable human activity. The degree of similarity must be assessed both in terms of the nature of such activities and their relationship to the purpose of the legislation, i.e., the control or prevention of an epidemic (e.g., the risk of such activities for the spread of the epidemic, etc.), but also in terms of the intensity of the interference with the rights of the addressees of the measures, in particular the fundamental rights guaranteed by the constitutional order of the Czech Republic" (judgment No 6 As 114/2020-63, paragraphs 143 and 144).

Thus, during the pandemic period, the Ministry of Health significantly restricted the entry and movement of foreigners into the territory of the Czech Republic on the basis of these provisions. An example is the protection measure of September 18, 2020, which imposed a ban on the entry into the Czech Republic of all third-country nationals, with the exception of, for example

a) foreigners with long-term or permanent residence permits in countries at low risk of contracting COVID-19,
b) holders of a valid long-term visa, long-term, temporary or permanent residence permit issued by the Czech Republic,
c) foreigners with a long-term or permanent residence permit in the European Union who transit the Czech Republic within 12 hours,
d) family members of EU nationals,
e) international transport workers, if the reason for entry is supported by an appropriate document,
f) diplomats and officials of international organizations registered with the Ministry of Foreign Affairs.

Entities hosting foreigners for the purpose of economic or educational activities were obliged to provide them with accommodation and health care for the entire duration of their stay and to return them to their country of origin if the purpose of their stay was terminated.

The competent state authorities were required not to accept applications for visas and permits for temporary or permanent residence, except for short-term visas for seasonal employment, scientific purposes, or study. Additionally, all pending proceedings were suspended.

This example shows that the scale of the restrictions was enormous and quite unprecedented.

2.2.3.3 Procedural guarantees for the protection of rights in states of emergency

In times of states of emergency, procedural rights, including the right to a fair trial, can theoretically also be restricted. This may involve both access to remedies, including judicial protection, and restrictions on certain "sub-rights" guaranteed under the right to a fair trial (for example, the right to a personal hearing).[913] However, the core of these rights must always be preserved.

---

913 On the right to a fair trial in the Czech Republic, see, for example, Pospíšil I., "Právo na soudní a jinou právní ochranu," in E. Wagnerová, V. Šimíček, T. Langášek, and I. Pospíšil (eds), a kol, *Listina základních práv a svobod. Komentář. 2. doplněné a aktualizované vydání* (Praha: Wolters Kluwer, 2023) 759–832.

In the case of the coronavirus pandemic in the Czech Republic, there was no significant impact on the availability of legal remedies. On the contrary, very soon after its outbreak, the legislator adopted Act No. 191/2020 Coll., on certain measures to mitigate the impact of the SARS-CoV-2 coronavirus epidemic on persons involved in legal proceedings. For cases in which a party to court proceedings, including administrative court proceedings, missed a deadline for performing an act (e.g., filing a lawsuit or cassation complaint, filing a plea of bias, making a statement, etc.) for an excusable reason due to pandemic-related limitations that made performing the act impossible or significantly more difficult, the law introduced a special provision for maintaining the deadline. Thus, procedural rights were not restricted in this respect; rather, they were strengthened to protect the party to the proceedings who might have been disadvantaged by the pandemic or measures taken to prevent its spread.

The pandemic and the measures against its spread also affected the conduct of proceedings before (administrative) courts and basically accelerated the use of electronic resources and instruments in justice in the Czech Republic. Oral hearings did not have to be adjourned, but could be held via videoconferencing equipment. According to Section 102a of Act No. 99/1963 Coll., Civil Procedure Code, the court may "at the request of a party or if it is expedient, [...] carry out an act using videoconferencing equipment, in particular to arrange for the presence of a party or an interpreter at the hearing or to conduct the examination of a witness, an expert or a party."

The case law has established that in exceptional situations, an online hearing by videoconference does not constitute an unreasonable and disproportionate restriction on the right to a hearing in the presence of the parties.[914] Participation in a hearing by videoconferencing equipment may even offer certain advantages for a party (particularly in terms of time savings and economy of proceedings), but it also entails certain limitations regarding direct contact with the court and the other parties. At the same time, allowing only one of the parties to participate online, in a situation where the other

914 It is guaranteed in the Czech Republic by Article 38(2) of the Charter of Fundamental Rights and Freedoms.

party had the same opportunity but chose not to take advantage of it, does not constitute a violation of equality of arms (Supreme Administrative Court judgment No 1 Afs 316/2020-71).

On the other hand, the Supreme Administrative Court has held that a pandemic and these measures cannot justify dispensing with oral hearings in court where the law requires courts to decide after hearing the parties (Supreme Administrative Court judgment No. 1 As 150/2020-107).

The case law has also enabled the courts to respond to the situation with flexibility and speed. For example, according to the judgment of the Regional Court in Prague No. 43 A 9/2021-140, judges or presidents of chambers were required to take measures to protect the health of the parties. If they considered that the spread of the COVID-19 virus could occur in the courtroom, taking into account the specific circumstances (e.g., the size of the room, the number of persons present, the presence of persons showing symptoms of the disease or, on the contrary, persons from risk groups, etc.), they were entitled to order the participants to put on face masks or respirators. This applied even if the law or a measure of the Ministry of Health related to the pandemic provided for an exemption from mandatory face protection during court proceedings, or even if no such obligation was provided for at all.

This power derives from the general competence conferred on judges and presiding judges by the Rules of Procedure to conduct hearings in an orderly, dignified and undisturbed manner. In cases involving foreigners, this effectively meant that all court proceedings continued during the emergency, and the courts had a duty to hear them without undue delay.[915] It also became common for oral hearings to be held entirely remotely by videoconference.

---

915 Pursuant to Act No. 150/2002 Coll., the Administrative Procedure Code, a number of foreigners' cases (e.g., international protection, administrative expulsion of a foreigner, obligation to leave the territory, detention of a foreigner) are heard in priority to the other judicial agenda.

2.3 France (Fanny Jacquelot)

2.3.1 Substantive law perspective: emergency standards in France

2.3.1.1 Introduction

In France, there are several mechanisms that can be used to declare a state of emergency. Two are provided for in the Constitution (Articles 16 and 36) but are used very rarely, if at all. What is more common is the state of emergency provided by the 1955 law, which has already been used on several occasions in France, and a new measure linked to the COVID-19 epidemic, known as a "state of health emergency." On the fringes, there is also a system based on the case law of the *Conseil d'Etat*, known as "exceptional circumstances," which allows the administration, under the control of the judge, to disregard ordinary legality when events so require and to ensure the continuity of public services.[916]

2.3.1.2 The state of emergency provided in the Constitution

The Constitution of October 4, 1958 provides for two crisis regimes. The first is the state of siege (Article 36 C.): decreed by the Council of Ministers, it is introduced in the event of imminent danger and the need to deal with a conflict (serious internal disturbances), for a period of 12 days, which may be extended. Police powers are exercised by the military authorities, who then have extended powers.

The second crisis regime is that provided for in Article 16 of the Constitution, which allows the President of the Republic to grant himself full powers in the event of a serious and immediate threat to the independence of the Nation and when the regular functioning of the public authorities is interrupted (this regime was used only once, in 1961).

---

916 This was confirmed by the *Conseil d'Etat* during the First World War: CE decision of February 28, 1919, *Dames Dol et Laurent*, No. 61593; CE decision of June 28, 1918, *Heyriès*, No. 63412. The *Conseil d'Etat* subsequently recognized the existence of "exceptional circumstances" following a serious natural disaster (CE, decision of May 18, 1983, *Rodes*, req. No. 25308: the eruption of the Soufrière volcano in Guadeloupe).

2.3.1.3 The state of emergency provided by law

The first state of emergency was introduced by Law no. 55-385 of April 3, 1955. It is decided by the Council of Ministers either in the event of imminent danger resulting from serious attacks on public order, or in the event of a public calamity (exceptional natural disaster). It makes it possible to review the framework of legality to allow the administrative authorities in particular to have more latitude in their actions than they would normally have. This law has been amended several times. But the most significant of these came in the wake of the deadly attacks of November 13, 2015, for which a state of emergency was declared in 2015 until 2017. Since 1958, the state of emergency has been declared seven times: 1955, 1958, 1961, 1984, 2005 and 2015–2017. It was recently reintroduced in New Caledonia by decree no. 2024-436 of May 15, 2024 for 12 days. Law no. 2015-1501 of November 20, 2015 on the state of emergency extended the possibilities offered by the state of emergency situation: in particular, it provides for rules on house arrest; authorizes the dissolution of associations involved in acts that seriously undermine public order; and allows the competent administrative authorities to conduct day and night searches.

During the COVID-19 crisis, another exceptional regime was created by Law no. 2020-290 of March 23, 2020: the state of health emergency. This allowed the government and administrative authorities to take measures that derogate from ordinary law, such as lockdowns and requisitions, in health matters, given the seriousness of the situation in terms of public health. The provisions of the Public Health Code authorizing a state of health emergency expired on August 1, 2022. As the law currently stands, it is therefore no longer possible to declare a state of health emergency without passing a new law.

2.3.2 Human rights related to migration: the right to asylum

2.3.2.1 Introduction

Third-country nationals have conditional freedom to come and go on national territory, which may extend to the use of derogations provided for the treaties during a state of emergency. However, a certain number of protection measures are available, such as temporary protection or asylum,[917] which allow reception with associated rights such as family reunification. However, here

[917] Alland, D., and Teitgen-colly C., *Traité du droit de l'asile* (P.U.F., 2002).

again, the periods of emergency have led not only to derogations but also to malfunctions that have significantly altered the guarantees previously offered.

2.3.2.2 The right to migrate

In France, the entry and residence of third-country nationals are subject to the will of the State.[918] This may relate to the requirement that residence be legal, but not exclusively, since other considerations may also be taken into account, such as family reunification, freedom to marry and, to a certain extent, the right to health.[919] However, as the Constitutional Council points out, "no principle or rule of constitutional value guarantees foreigners general and absolute rights of access to and residence on national territory."[920]

As part of the state of emergency decreed in 2015 and then extended several times, France reinstated controls at the Schengen area's external borders due to the "risk of terrorist attack that remains high on French territory." While these measures were not supposed to exceed two years, the *Conseil d'Etat*, in a decision of December 28, 2017,[921] approved a further extension, considering that maintaining controls was proportionate to the seriousness of the threat.

During the state of health emergency, under the terms of an instruction issued by the Prime Minister on March 18, 2020, all foreign nationals (with some exceptions) were refused entry to France.

2.3.2.3 Temporary protection

Temporary protection is the result of European Directive 2001/55/EC of July 20, 2001 on "mass influxes of displaced persons." It was transposed into French

---

918 Duvingnau J., *Le droit fondamental au séjour des étrangers*, thesis, Pau (2010); De Reydet de Vurpillieres C., *Les portes de la loi : souveraineté, droits de l'homme, hospitalité : quel(s) droit(s) pour les étrangers?* Thesis, Paris X (2019); Robert L., "Discrétion de l'Etat vs. Droits fondamentaux : les juridictions européennes face aux politiques *migratoires*," in H. Fulchiron (ed), *La famille du migrant* (LexisNexis 2020) 189–202.

919 Lecucq O., *Le statut constitutionnel des étrangers en situation irrégulière*, thesis, Aix-en-Provence, 1999; Tchen, V., "Le droits fondamentaux des étrangers" (May 22, 1995) 61 *Les Petites Affiches*, 4–13.

920 C.C., decision no. 93-325 DC of August 13, 1993, *Loi relative à la maîtrise de l'immigration et aux conditions d'entrée, d'accueil et de séjour des étrangers en France*.

921 CE, decision of December 28, 2017, *Anafé et autres*, No. 415291. On this decision, see Cassia P., "Le *Conseil d'Etat* décode Schengen" <https://blogs.mediapart.fr/paul-cassia/blog/291217/le-conseil-d-etat-decode-schengen>.

law by Law no. 2003-1119 of November 26, 2023 (Article 44). This directive is a direct response to a problem connected with the war in the former Yugoslavia. At the time, it was noted that most displaced persons had been received by a very small number of states, with little coordination. The aim of the 2001 directive was therefore to rationalize the reception of displaced persons by asking Member States to pool their material and financial resources. The planned process is simple: the Council of the European Union takes a decision to define, in the event of a humanitarian crisis, the groups of people likely to benefit from temporary protection (with an indication of the start and end dates). The protection granted is therefore limited in time. It is granted for a minimum period of six months, renewable up to a maximum of three years. During this period, the group of individuals concerned has the right of residence. In order to differentiate this special regime from asylum or subsidiary protection, temporary protection does not apply in cases of crimes against peace, war crimes, crimes against humanity, serious non-political crimes, acts contrary to the aims and principles of the United Nations or threats to public order, public security or State security. On expiry of the temporary protection, the individuals concerned must leave French territory.

The 2001 directive was first applied to the conflict in Ukraine. On March 3, 2022, the countries of the European Union granted "temporary protection" status to Ukrainians seeking to leave the country in the midst of the fighting. They were granted a temporary residence permit with the possibility of working. Under this scheme, Ukrainian nationals and people who actually live in Ukraine, as well as members of their families, are entitled to protection throughout the EU. This temporary protection has already been extended and is due to end in March 2025. For the time being, it entitles the people concerned to: the right of residence, access to the labor market, access to housing, social assistance, medical assistance and support for unaccompanied minors, as well as access to education.

Temporary protection does not, however, grant a limited right of residence. It is granted not to an individual because of his or her personal situation, but to a group of individuals affected by a crisis that is limited in time and that should end with the return of the individual to his or her country of origin.

2.3.2.4 Sources of the right to asylum in France

2.3.2.4.1 Domestic sources of asylum law

Since 2005, the internal legislative and regulatory sources of the right of asylum have been contained in the Code on the Entry and Residence of Foreigners and the Right of Asylum (CESEDA). Previously, the relevant texts were scattered and difficult to read. Since May 1, 2021, a new version of the CESEDA has been in force.[922]

From 2021 onwards, all applications to the authorities, administrative acts and court decisions must refer to the new provisions of the CESEDA, as the previous provisions have been repealed. The structure of the new code has been streamlined compared with the previous version. It is now divided into eight books. Book I concerns general provisions. The second book deals with European Union citizens. The third book contains the rules applicable to "entry into France," the fourth concerns "residence in France," and the fifth relates to "the right of asylum and other international protection." Book VI deals with "Removal decisions" and Book VII completes it with provisions on the "Enforcement of removal decisions." Finally, Book VIII deals with "controls and sanctions." The introductory part of the code contains specific provisions relating to the structures involved in immigration and asylum policy in France, such as the French Office for Immigration and Integration (OFPRA), the French Office for the Protection of Refugees and Stateless Persons (OFPPIR) and the National Court for the Right of Asylum (CNDA). This section also includes provisions relating to interpreters, legal rules on the processing of personal data, and provisions on the transportation of foreign nationals in waiting zones or administrative detention centers. This rewriting of the CESEDA has made it possible to unify the law on French territory: the rules on the right of asylum now apply not only in mainland

---

922 Under the Enabling Act No. 2018-778 of September 10, 2018, the legislature effectively authorized the government to rewrite the legislative part of the Code by ordinance, "in order to reorganize its layout, clarify its wording and include the provisions of other codes or non-codified provisions falling within the scope of the law and directly concerning the entry and residence of foreign nationals in France." See Ordinance No. 2020-1733 of December 16, 2020 rewriting the Code on the Entry and Residence of Foreigners in France and the Right of Asylum in its legislative part, and Decree No. 2020-1734 of December 16, 2020 for the regulatory part.

France but also in the overseas territories[923] (unlike the law governing the stay and departure of foreign nationals in France).

2.3.2.4.2 External sources of asylum law

The Geneva Convention of July 28, 1951, as amended by the New York Protocol of January 31, 1987, is the primary source of the right to asylum. It is not rivaled in domestic law by the European Convention on Human Rights insofar as the European Court has made it clear that the right to asylum is not a right guaranteed by the Convention system.

The European Union has also had a common asylum policy since the Treaty of Amsterdam of October 2, 1997, which was followed by a number of initiatives to define a common framework for European Asylum, focusing in particular on the unification of processing conditions and statuses, including the principle of a one-stop shop for asylum.

2.3.2.5 The different types of protection granted for asylum applications

2.3.2.5.1 Introduction

All third-country nationals may apply for asylum in France if they are subject to persecution in their country of origin and their safety, freedom and life are threatened. Two forms of protection may then be granted: refugee status or subsidiary protection. In both cases, the French Office for the Protection of Refugees and Stateless Persons (OFPRA) has jurisdiction. OFPRA's decision may be appealed to the National Court of Asylum (CNDA).

The asylum application procedure is a one-stop shop, but it can lead to several outcomes. The competent bodies mentioned above can grant the applicant three types of protection: the first under asylum, the second under refugee status and the third under subsidiary protection. Each of these systems is subject to specific criteria. If the applicant does not meet any of these criteria, their application will be rejected.

An asylum seeker is someone who has applied for asylum protection and is awaiting a response from the relevant authorities. A refugee, on the other

---

923 The CESEDA therefore also applies to the French overseas departments, as well as to Saint-Pierre-et-Miquelon, New Caledonia, the French Southern and Antarctic Territories, French Polynesia and Wallis and Futuna.

hand, is someone who has already received a positive response to their asylum application and has been recognized as a refugee by OFPRA or the CNDA. Finally, there may also be people who are beneficiaries of subsidiary protection: in this case, it is the individual who has received a positive response to their asylum application but who, on the other hand, does not have refugee status but is a beneficiary of subsidiary protection.

More specifically, refugee status can be granted on the basis of several different texts. Firstly, there is the Geneva Convention of July 28, 1951 relating to the Status of Refugees. Secondly, refugee status may be granted if the individual has been placed under the mandate of the Office of the United Nations High Commissioner for Refugees.[924] Finally, the Preamble to the 1946 French Constitution is the last basis for refugee status, although it is less frequently used.

If refugee status cannot be granted, the French authorities will look into the possibility of placing the applicant under subsidiary protection. This specifically concerns individuals who cannot be returned to their country of origin if they risk being exposed to a danger of death or inhuman or degrading treatment. Pending a decision on their case, France has a duty to house non-EU foreign nationals in dignified conditions. This is clear from a decision by the European Court of Human Rights on July 2, 2020, which

---

[924] The UNHCR has offices in over 130 countries, including France. It can deal with applications for refugee status. In these circumstances, it can either declare a return to the country of origin if the conditions are favorable, pronounce integration in the country of asylum, or finally, decide on resettlement in a third country. However, if an individual, notwithstanding the UNHCR's decision, considers that the measure of which he or she is the beneficiary does not afford him or her sufficient protection, he or she may leave the country in question and request that France confer refugee status on him or her.
Under Articles 6 and 7 of its Statute, the UNHCR can issue two types of mandate: the "strict" mandate and the "broad" mandate. As stated in Article L. 511-1 2° of the CESEDA (the French Code on the Entry and Residence of Foreigners and the Right of Asylum), the issue of a "strict" mandate automatically leads to recognition of refugee status in France. Prior to this, however, OFPRA must check the authenticity of the warrant. On the other hand, in the case of a "broad" mandate, i.e., where the UNHCR guarantees protection to the individual outside the cases provided for in the aforementioned articles, OFPRA is not bound and refugee status is not necessarily granted.

condemned France for violating Article 3 of the ECHR by leaving asylum seekers without accommodation for several months.[925]

2.3.2.5.2 Constitutional asylum

For many years, French institutions relied mainly on the five types of persecution referred to in the Geneva Convention (Article 1, A, 2°). Then, in 1993, the right of asylum was incorporated into the French Constitution of 1958, opening up the possibility of granting refugee status to people who declared that they were "fighting for freedom."[926] This added a new ground for protection to the 1951 Convention.[927] This will be referred to as "constitutional asylum." In its decision no. 93-352 DC of August 13, 1993,[928] the Constitutional Council established, on the basis of paragraph 4 of the Preamble to the 1946 Constitution,[929] the obligation for "the French administrative and judicial authorities to examine the situation of asylum seekers who fall within the scope of this paragraph," with the consequence that they may benefit from a temporary right of residence while their application is being examined.

In ordinance to qualify, four conditions must be met, which have been highlighted by OFPRA:

- The applicant must be the victim of "effective persecution." Mere fears are therefore not admissible.

---

925 European Court of Human Rights, decision of July 2, 2020, req. no. 28820/13.

926 There is no specific definition of what constitutes an "action in favour of freedom." However, case law has clarified some of its contours. It includes, for example, "exceptional action in favour of freedom of expression and of the press" (CNDA, decision no. 12036401 and no. 12036400 of September 27, 2013), such as helping "the mission of foreign journalists who had gone clandestinely to Chechnya to report on the conflict there" (CNDA, decision no. 08010080 of July 2, 2009). It may also involve actions to promote women's rights (CNDA decision no. 17049253 of February 17, 2020).

927 Since Ordinance No. 2020-1733 of December 16, 2020, constitutional asylum has also been mentioned in Article L. 511-1 of the *CESEDA*.

928 C.C., decision no. 93-325 DC of August 13, 1993, *Loi relative à la maîtrise de l'immigration et aux conditions d'entrée, d'accueil et de séjour des étrangers en France*.

929 § 4 of the Preamble to the 1946 Constitution states that "anyone persecuted for his action in favour of freedom has the right to asylum in the territory of the Republic."

- The perpetrators of persecution may or may not be clearly identified or institutionalized.
- Applicants must have demonstrated their commitment to democracy.
- The applicant's commitment to democracy must be based on considerations relating to the general interest and not his or her own self-interest.

However, it should be emphasized that constitutional asylum only concerns a small proportion of refugees in France each year. A report by the CNDA in 2021 states that only one person benefited from it in 2020. Conventional asylum (i.e., asylum applied for on the basis of the Geneva Convention) is the most widely used form of asylum in France.

2.3.2.5.3 Conventional asylum

Any person in the situation defined in Article 1, A, 2° of the Geneva Convention of July 28, 1951 relating to the Status of Refugees may apply for asylum in France. Under the terms of this provision, refugee status may be granted to any person who "owing to well-founded fear of being persecuted for reasons of race, religion, nationality, membership of a particular social group or political opinion, is outside the country of his nationality and is unable or, owing to such fear, is unwilling to avail himself of the protection of that country." These different grounds may be invoked alone or in combination, bearing in mind that the EU Member States have agreed to extend the scope of the existing grounds and add others, such as that relating to sexual orientation.[930]

The protection here is individual. The French courts are careful to ensure compliance with this requirement, which derives from the aforementioned provision of the Geneva Convention. For example, in a 1993 decision, the *Conseil d'Etat* held that a general policy of forced sterilization did not necessarily require proof of personal persecution.[931] In all cases, the burden of

---

930 European Directive 2011/95/EU of December 13, 2011 on the assessment of acts of persecution and the grounds for persecution. On this point, see also Article L. 511-2 of the CESEDA.

931 CE, decision no. 103545 of December 29, 1993: in this case, the *Conseil d'Etat* ruled that "the policy of limiting births practiced in China was not sufficient to justify granting the person concerned refugee status, in the absence of a well-founded individual

proof lies with the person claiming to be the victim of persecution. Unlike constitutional asylum, where it is necessary to prove actual persecution, in this case the Geneva Convention does not require proof of persecution that has already occurred. It can also be a well-founded but merely potential fear. This was taken up by Law no. 2015-925 of July 29, 2015, which refers to fear of persecution.[932] On the other hand, the persecution must be of a certain degree of seriousness, even if the Geneva Convention is not entirely explicit on this point. Generally speaking, the reason for the persecution must be related to the wording of Article 1 of the Geneva Convention, otherwise it will be rejected by the *CNDA*, as was the case, for example, for economic reasons.[933]

It should also be noted that the Geneva Convention contains an exclusion clause in Article 1, F which excludes from its scope persons who, even if they are the object of persecution mentioned in the Convention, are at the same time guilty of acts deemed incompatible with refugee status (crimes against peace, war, humanity; serious non-political crimes committed outside the host country before being admitted as a refugee; acts contrary to the purposes and principles of the United Nations). This clause is applied by the French national courts and must, if necessary, be raised ex officio by the CNDA.[934] In this case, all protection is therefore excluded. Moreover, the French legislator has extended the principle to persons applying for subsidiary protection.[935] In addition, the Law of July 29, 2015 transposing the aforementioned Directive 2011/95/EU of December 13, 2011 added a further element to the exclusion clause concerning those responsible for terrorist acts.[936]

2.3.2.5.4 Subsidiary protection

Subsidiary protection may be granted to individuals who do not qualify for refugee status, even though they face the following risks in their own country:

---

fear of being persecuted for reasons of race, religion, nationality, membership of a particular social group or political opinion."

932 CESEDA, Articles L. 511-5, L. 513-4 (fear of persecution following departure from the country of origin) and L. 531-6 (fear of persecution due to persecution already suffered).

933 CNDA, decision no. 05039947 of July 10, 2013.

934 CE, decision no. 396261 of June 7, 2017.

935 Article L. 512-2 CESEDA.

936 Article L. 511-7. This ground for exclusion also constitutes grounds for the revocation of refugee status.

the death penalty, torture or inhuman or degrading treatment or punishment; serious and individual threats to life or person as a result of violence which may be directed against persons irrespective of their personal situation and which results from a situation of internal or international armed conflict.[937] This was established by Directive 2002/90/EC of 28 and December 29, 2002 (subsequently replaced by Directive 2011/95/EU of December 13, 2011). It was transposed into French law by Law no. 2003-1176 of December 10, 2003. Subsidiary protection thus replaced the territorial asylum system. In order to avoid creating parallel or even competing processes, subsidiary protection can only be applied only if the application for conventional asylum has been rejected.[938]

2.3.2.6 The malfunctioning of the asylum system during the state of health emergency

The procedure for making an asylum application, based on the one-stop shop system, has been subject to major malfunctions. In spring 2020, the decision to close establishments open to the public also affected the institutions responsible for receiving asylum applications. The French Office for Immigration and Integration completely suspended its activities, neutralizing a whole part of the current system.

A number of appeals have been lodged. In particular, the Paris Administrative Tribunal, in a summary ordinance dated April 21, 2020[939] was called upon to rule on the paralysis of the asylum application system. It noted that Article 4 of law no. 2020-290 of March 23, 2020 declared a state of emergency in France. Article L. 3131-15 of the Public Health Code, resulting from this same law, authorized the Prime Minister to restrict certain fundamental rights such as freedom of movement and freedom of assembly. It was against this backdrop that the French Office

---

937 Article L. 512-1 CESEDA. Subsidiary protection has the same exclusion clause as conventional asylum.

938 In this sense, CE, decision of December 10, 2008 *OFPRA v Pogossyan*, req. no. 278227: "the right to benefit from subsidiary protection can only be examined after it has been established that the applicant cannot be recognized as a refugee; thus, by granting the benefit of subsidiary protection to Mr A without having first investigated whether he could be recognized as a refugee, the Commission erred in law."

939 Paris Administrative Tribunal, ordinance of April 21, 2020, No. 2006359/9.

for Immigration and Integration suspended all public reception procedures other than asylum procedures. However, following the closure of the one-stop shops for asylum seekers, particularly in the northern departments of France, the multilingual platform that all asylum seekers must contact was also closed due to the coronavirus epidemic. As a result, appointments at the one-stop shops for asylum seekers were purely and simply blocked. As the Tribunal points out, this closure of the one-stop shops and of the reception platform made it impossible to register an asylum application, even though Article L. 741-1 of the CESEDA requires that an application be processed within a maximum of ten days. The Administrative Tribunal therefore stated that "none of the provisions of the Law of March 23, 2020, nor any of the regulations issued for its application, has the purpose or effect of authorizing the competent administrative authorities to no longer register asylum applications." By making it impossible to register and process asylum applications, the administration has therefore seriously and manifestly unlawfully infringed the right to asylum. For this reason, the Paris Administrative Tribunal ruled that the Prefect of Police and the Prefects of the departments in the Ile-de-France region should be ordered to re-establish, within five days and until the end of the state of health emergency, the system for registering asylum applications, by adapting it to the flow of applications, and to reopen, "under the health conditions imposed by Covid-19, the one-stop shops in ordinance to manage this flow." The Administrative Tribunal also instructed the OFII to reopen the platform in question without delay. The OFII platform was reopened on May 7, 2020 and registrations resumed on May 5, 2020.

Other institutions have had their operations impacted. OFPRA, for example, continued to register only asylum applications received by post. Additional time was allowed for those who were unable to send in their applications on time. As for the CNDA, hearings have been completely suspended. In a press release dated March 15, 2020, the CNDA announced that it would continue to register the appeals, documents and pleadings sent to it, regardless of the method of transmission, and that it would also continue to process applications for legal aid. In accordance with the Emergency Health Law no. 2020-290 of March 23, 2020, it indicated that the time limits for appeals would be adapted to the circumstances. Two ordinances dated

March 25, 2020[940] were therefore adopted to extend the time limits for appeals before the CNDA. In addition, in order to speed up proceedings and make up for the delays incurred during the COVID-19 pandemic, ordinance no. 2020-558 of May 13, 2020 provided for the removal of the CNDA's ordinary law panel (comprising a president, a judge appointed by the HCR and a judge appointed by the *Conseil d'Etat*) in favor of a single judge. This measure was referred to the *Conseil d'Etat* in the context of a "*référé-liberté*" (emergency procedure) and it granted the applicants' request for suspension.[941] However, it did not find fault with the possibility of the judge using videoconferencing.

All this explains why the new law no. 2024-42 of January 26, 2024 to control immigration and improve integration has reformed certain administrative procedures for applying for asylum. It provides for the gradual creation of territorial centers called "France Asylum." These centers will be rolled out across the country after three pilot sites have been set up. The aim is to eventually replace the one-stop shop system for asylum seekers (GUDA). These centers will enable asylum seekers to register with the prefecture, open their rights with OFII and submit their asylum application to OFPRA. In the same spirit, the CNDA has been reformed. Territorial chambers of the CNDA will be set up to hear applications as closely as possible, using the single-judge procedure.

2.3.2.7 Restrictions on fundamental rights during a state of health emergency

2.3.2.7.1 Restrictions on freedom of movement

Statutory refugees and beneficiaries of subsidiary protection may travel freely[942] in France and abroad, excluding the country of persecution. They must provide a travel document.

During the COVID-19 period, France, like other European countries, limited freedom of movement. France "closed" its borders from March 17,

---

[940] Ordinance No. 2020-305 of March 25, 2020 adapting the rules applicable before the administrative courts; Ordinance No. 2020-306 of March 25, 2020 on the extension of deadlines during the health emergency period and the adaptation of procedures during this same period.

[941] CE, ordinances *Association ELENA France et autres, GISTI et autre, Conseil national des barreaux*, June 8, 2020, No. 440717, No. 440812, No. 440867.

[942] Article L. 321-1 of the CESEDA.

2020. Only people residing in France could enter, as well as those working in certain priority sectors.

2.3.2.7.2 *Restrictions on family reunification*

The right to family reunification for relatives of refugees was not recognized until 1994. Law no. 2015-925 of July 29, 2015 established a general framework in this area. On this basis, people who have been recognized as refugees can apply to be joined by their spouse and minor children.[943] The reform of September 10, 2018 extended the right to family reunification to beneficiaries of subsidiary protection.[944] As a result, from March 1, 2019, the spouse or partner is automatically entitled to a four-year residence permit. The same applies to minor children. The entry into France of family members of refugees or beneficiaries of subsidiary protection is subject to compliance with the conditions set out in Articles L. 434-1 (procedures for submitting applications for residence permits), L. 434-3 to L. 434-5 (temporary residence permit regime) and the first paragraph of Article L. 434-9 of the Aliens Code (rejection of applications submitted by polygamous families).

Family members must therefore obtain a long-stay visa to enter the country. There may be exemptions depending on nationality. In principle, such applications must be processed more quickly than others, as family reunification is an "essential refugee right" designed to enable "persons who have fled persecution to resume a normal life."[945] This is why France was condemned by the European Court of Human Rights for not having made special provisions for dealing specifically with these applications.[946]

As part of the COVID-19 health crisis, the government stopped issuing family reunification visas to the spouses and children of non-European foreign nationals residing in France from March 18, 2020, in order to limit the movement of people from abroad. The effect of this measure was to limit or even freeze the prospects of family reunification in France. An application for suspension of this government decision was lodged with the *Conseil d'Etat*.

---

[943] Article L. 424-3 of the CESEDA.

[944] Article L. 424-11 of the CESEDA.

[945] Court of Human Rights, decision of July 10, 2014, *Tanga-Muzinga v. France*, Application No. 2260/10.

[946] Court of Human Rights, decision of July 10, 2014, Tanga-Muzinga v. France, Application No. 2260/10.

In an ordinance dated January 21, 2021,[947] the *Conseil d'Etat* found that the contested measure seriously infringed the right to a normal family life of the persons concerned and the best interests of the child. For this reason, it suspended the measure in question on the grounds that there were serious doubts as to its legality.[948]

2.3.3 Personal rights for third-country nationals

2.3.3.1 Introduction

The fundamental personal rights of third-country nationals are guaranteed by the French State, including the right to health protection,[949] individual freedom, privacy and data protection. However, certain arrangements are made to guarantee public order. During the state of health emergency, certain substantial arrangements were made, in particular with regard to the right to health and personal freedom.

2.3.3.2 Health

In principle, all foreign nationals working in France and legally resident in the country have access to healthcare.[950] They are therefore covered by the universal health protection scheme. In particular, they can benefit from the "Protection Universelle Maladie" (PUMA).

Since 2020, State Medical Aid (*aide médicale d'Etat*[951]) has enabled people of all nationalities to access emergency care. In particular, this aid mainly benefits illegal foreign nationals whose resources do not exceed a certain ceiling. The *Conseil d'Etat* has stated that "the irregular situation of a foreigner (cannot) be an obstacle to his or her right to benefit from hospital

947 CE, ordinance of January 21, 2021, No. 447878.

948 On these aspects, see in particular, Odasso L., and Fogel F., ""Vie privée et familiale" en temps de pandémie. Continuités et ruptures d'une politique discriminatoire : le cas de la France" (2022) 38(1 and 2) *European Journal of International Migration* <https://journals.openedition.org/remi/20140>.

949 See in particular: Défenseur des droits, *Personnes malades étrangères : des droits fragilisés, des protections à renforcer* (2019).

950 Law No. 2015-1702 of December 21, 2015. See also Article L. 111-2-1 of the Social Security Code, which specifically states that social protection is guaranteed to "everyone."

951 Law No. 99-641 of July 27, 1999, which introduced State Medical Aid on January 1, 2000.

medical assistance, once the insufficiency of his or her resources has been established."[952] This right also applies to the beneficiary's spouse and minor children. It also applies to foreign nationals held in administrative detention.

During the state of health emergency linked to COVID-19, the health rights of legal foreign nationals were extended by ordinance no. 2020-312 of March 25, 2020 on the extension of social rights. The same applies to State Medical Aid. Rights that expired between March 12, and July 31, 2020 were extended for three months.

In times of health emergency, certain specific questions have also arisen, in particular that of putting an end to the detention of illegal immigrants for health reasons. For example, in an ordinance issued on April 15, 2020,[953] the Paris Administrative Tribunal prohibited, on the grounds of public health, the placement of new detainees in certain detention centers because they constituted hotbeds of contagion. It also ordered the administrative authorities to lift the detention of COVID-19-positive foreign nationals. However, the *Conseil d'Etat* overturned the latter measure, deciding that the health conditions of those detained were sufficient.[954]

2.3.3.3 Individual freedom

In France, third-country nationals may be subject to restrictions on their personal freedom. In particular, they may be held in administrative detention or placed under house arrest.

2.3.3.3.1 Administrative detention

It is aimed at foreign nationals who have been ordered to leave French territory but cannot leave immediately. However, it must be a solution of last resort, i.e., when no alternative is possible.

Placement in administrative detention is subject to compliance with Article 66 of the 1958 French Constitution, which guarantees the protection of individual freedom by the judicial authority.[955] However, the decision

---

952 CE, decision of October 18, 2002, *El Mjidi*, No. 232543.

953 Paris Administrative Tribunal, ordinance of April 15, 2020, No. 2006287/9, 2006288/9, 2006289/9.

954 CE, ordinance of May 7, 2020, No. 440255.

955 <https://www.conseil-constitutionnel.fr/sites/default/files/as/root/bank_mm/anglais/constiution_anglais_oct2009.pdf>.

to detain a person is taken solely by the prefect. The duration of detention has been modified several times since 1980 (seven times). It is currently set out in Law no. 2018-778 of September 10, 2018: the initial detention period is 48 hours. Then 28 days are added in the event of non-enforcement of the removal ordinance in the absence of travel documents or means of transport. A further 15 days are then added, followed by a further 15 days and then 30 days in the event of obstruction of the enforcement of the removal ordinance.

2.3.3.3.2 House arrest

House arrest stems from the 2008 Return Directive (Article 15). It was recently reorganized in France, in particular by Law no. 2016-274 of March 7, 2016. It is a complex system because it is governed by several distinct legal regimes.

The first is judicial house arrest. Under the terms of Article L. 743-13 of the Foreign Nationals Code, the judicial authority (the liberty and detention judge) may place a foreign national already in detention under house arrest, provided that he or she has "effective representation guarantees": the existence of a known place of residence and possession of an identity document allowing admission to the country of return.

The second measure, which is used more frequently, is administrative house arrest. It is intended for foreign nationals who are unable to leave the country immediately. The decision here rests with the prefect, who must, in particular, take into account the risk of the person concerned absconding before deciding to place him or her there.

In the first case, house arrest may be imposed for six months, renewable once.[956] Since 2016, house arrest may be imposed for an unlimited period in the case of a person subject to a judicial ban on entry, or an administrative ban on entry or deportation.[957] In this case, the law does not provide for a periodic review of the decision or a specific appeal. In a 2017 decision, the French Constitutional Council approved this measure on the grounds that it "prevents a person who not only has no right of residence but who has also committed an offense or whose presence constitutes a serious threat to

---

956 Article L. 732-4 of the CESEDA.

957 Article L. 732-5 of the CESEDA.

public order" from moving freely within the country.[958] However, it asked the legislature to allow foreign nationals to request a review of their situation and not to require them to be detained for more than 12 hours a day, failing which the measure would be a deprivation of liberty contrary to the requirements of Article 66 of the Constitution. In the second case, house arrest is imposed for 45 days, renewable once.[959] This refers to situations where foreign nationals are forced to leave the country (expulsion, judicial ban on entry, etc.). There is a third possibility: this concerns people involved in acts of terrorism.[960] Law no. 2011-467 of March 14, 2011 even provides for the person concerned to be placed under electronic surveillance for a period of three months, renewable for up to two years.

2.3.3.3.3 Personal freedom of foreign nationals during a state of emergency

2.3.3.3.3.1 Problems during states of emergency under the 1955 law

Declared on several occasions since 1955, the state of emergency has given rise to litigation, in particular for failure to comply with the legal conditions required when the personal liberty of a non-European national is infringed. For example, in judgment no. 15/03928 of November 26, 2015, the *Tribunal de Grande Instance* of Paris noted that the prefect had simply invoked the state of emergency to request an extension of administrative detention, without providing any supporting documentation.

In another case, the judge upheld the refusal to release foreign nationals held in administrative detention on the grounds of the state of emergency. He considered that "the argument based on the state of emergency in force since November 13, 2015, to which must be added that of the reinforced *vigipirate* plan already in place, constitutes a set of insurmountable circumstances for the administration, which effectively do not allow it to have the necessary manpower to provide the necessary escorts."[961]

958 C.C., decision No. 2017-674 QPC of November 30, 2017, *Kamel D.*
959 Article L. 731-1 of the CESEDA.
960 Article L. 733-15 of the CESEDA.
961 *Tribunal de Grande Instance* of Meaux, January 15, 2016, No. 16/00175.

2.3.3.3.3.2 Problems during the state of health emergency

As part of the state of health emergency, measures derogating from ordinary law have been validated or adopted. For example, in an ordinance dated May 4, 2020,[962] the *Conseil d'Etat* approved the retention of foreign nationals suffering from COVID-19 in administrative detention centers.

Another point that attracted attention during this period was the possibility of placing foreign nationals in isolation. Outside a state of emergency, Articles L. 3131-5 and L. 3131-17 of the Public Health Code allow people arriving from abroad to be isolated for health reasons. Article L. 3115-10 of the Public Health Code authorizes the Prefect to take "by reasoned ordinance, any individual measure to combat the international spread of disease, in particular the isolation or quarantine of persons suffering from a contagious infection or likely to suffer from such an infection." However, such measures are only applicable when borders are crossed. However, Article L. 3131-1 of the same code authorizes the Minister for Health, in the event of a serious health threat requiring emergency measures (particularly in the event of a threatened epidemic), to take any measure to respond to the risks incurred. It was on this basis that, as part of the COVID-19 pandemic, the Prime Minister decided to quarantine people who had stayed in the Wuhan region of China. But this was not enough to curb the pandemic. Law no. 2020-290 of March 23, 2020 declaring a state of health emergency therefore introduced two new provisions into the Public Health Code (Articles L. 3131-15 and L. 3131-17) allowing any person, French or foreign, from abroad to be placed in quarantine or isolation.

2.3.3.4 Privacy

The *Conseil d'Etat* has consistently held[963] that "it follows from the general principles of law and, in particular, from the Preamble to the Constitution of October 27, 1946, to which the Constitution of October 4, 1958 refers, that foreign nationals residing lawfully in France have, like nationals, the right to lead a normal family life." The families of foreign nationals settled in France

---

962 CE, ordinance of May 4, 2020, *Minister of the Interior v. Associations des avocats pour la défense des droits des étrangers et al.*, No. 440255.

963 CE, decision of December 8, 1978, *GISTI and others*, No. 10097.

are therefore entitled to family reunification, subject to compliance with the relevant procedures.[964]

However, during the period of the health emergency, Prime Ministerial Instruction no. 6268-SG of May 19, 2021 specified the conditions for entry into France in the light of the regulations enacted to combat the COVID-19 pandemic. Some of these measures infringed privacy rights. In an ordinance dated June 17, 2021,[965] the *Conseil d'Etat* ordered the Prime Minister to amend the text of the circular to include marriage among the compelling reasons for granting a visa. It also instructed the Minister of the Interior to amend the international travel certificate along the same lines so that "the issue of visas for marriage in France is no longer subject to the production of an authorization from the country of residence."

In a decision handed down on June 29, 2021, the *Conseil d'Etat* ruled on an instruction issued by the Prime Minister on December 29, 2020, which suspended the issue of vaccines throughout the health crisis, without providing for any derogation. The administrative judge emphasized that the health situation at the time of the events, "marked by the continuing high level of strain on the hospital system and the appearance of new, more contagious variants of the virus in different geographical areas," explains why restrictions on access to French territory had been maintained. However, he added that, on the date the Prime Minister's instruction was adopted, the procedure for issuing visas and allowing the families of foreign nationals benefiting from family reunification to enter French territory had already been interrupted for more than nine months. The *Conseil d'Etat* therefore considered that the Prime Minister's instruction "disproportionately infringed the right to respect for private and family life guaranteed by Article 8 of the European Convention for the Protection of Human Rights and Fundamental Freedoms, insofar as it does not provide for any derogation for beneficiaries of family reunification procedures." Taking the view that private life must be respected even in times of crisis, he annulled the instruction in question on the grounds of ultra vires.

---

964 CE, decision of December 28, 2009, *Mme A, épouse B*, No. 308231.
965 CE, ordinance of June 17, 2021, No. 453113.

2.3.3.5 Data protection

In order to guarantee the right of legal residence for foreign nationals and to combat illegal entry and residence in France, Article L. 142-1 of the CESEDA provides that certain personal data may be collected, such as fingerprints and a photograph. This applies in particular to non-European nationals applying for a visa to stay in France, but also to foreign nationals residing illegally in France who are the subject of a decision to expel them from French territory.

Under the terms of Article R. 142-11 of the CESEDA, this automated processing of personal data is called "Application de Gestion des dossiers des ressortissants étrangers en France" (AGDEF2). An appendix lists all the data likely to be collected in this context. The data is kept for at least five years and is deleted if it has not been updated, except in certain limited cases listed.[966] The protection of this personal data is guaranteed by European regulation no. 2016-679 and by the French Data Protection Act no. 78-17 of January 6, 1978.

2.3.4 Political rights for third-country nationals

Foreign nationals from countries outside the European Union do not enjoy full political rights. In particular, they do not have the right to vote and are not eligible to stand in national elections. Only nationals of European Union countries residing in France have the right to vote and stand for election in municipal and European elections. Previously, they enjoyed freedom of association only with ministerial authorization. Since Law no. 81-908 of October 9, 1981, which repealed this system, foreign nationals have been free to set up associations.

2.3.5 Economic, social, and cultural rights for third-country nationals

2.3.5.1 Introduction

Third-country nationals who are legally resident in France are entitled to social security benefits,[967] giving them access to the public health service,

[966] Article R. 142-21 of the CESEDA.

[967] See Clergerie J.-L., "L'application du principe de non-discrimination en matière de sécurité sociale à des ressortissants de pays tiers à la communauté" (1998) 93 *Les Petites*

housing assistance and childcare.[968] They can also obtain a work permit to join the universal social security system. Certain rights are also provided for foreign nationals in an irregular situation or seeking protection as asylum seekers. Certain adaptations were necessary during the state of health emergency, particularly with regard to the right to work.

2.3.5.2 Right to work

2.3.5.2.1 General law

In order to work, third-country nationals must obtain a work permit[969] and hold a residence permit. In principle, the application for a work permit is made by the employer. The prefect of the department is responsible for taking all decisions relating to residence and work. Asylum seekers have a special status in this context. Since 1991, they have had no right to work. They can obtain a work permit if OFPRA has not ruled on the application for protection for more than six months and if the employer so requests. It should be noted that, generally speaking, there are certain professions that are not open to foreign nationals, such as the civil service, but also professions in the private sector, such as lawyers, pharmacists, doctors, etc.

Immigration law no. 2024-42 of January 26, 2024 contains additional provisions concerning the employment of foreign nationals. Undocumented workers in occupations where there is a shortage of staff (catering, public works, etc.) may exceptionally be granted a "temporary worker" or "employee" residence permit. This measure will be tested until 2026. In addition, to meet the needs of hospitals, which were keenly felt during the COVID-19 health emergency, a new 4-year "talent-medical and pharmacy professions" residence permit has been introduced.

Affiches, 25.

968 Article L. 111-1 of the French Social Security Code establishes the principle of universal social security benefits. This operates according to a "principle of national solidarity." The preamble to the 1946 Constitution states that this principle guarantees "all persons working or residing in France on a stable and regular basis coverage of sickness, maternity, paternity and family expenses."

969 Article R. 5221-1 of the French Labour Code.

2.3.5.2.2 *Adaptations during emergency periods*

Law no. 2020-734 of June 17, 2020 on various provisions relating to the health crisis and other urgent measures introduced measures that depart from ordinary law in terms of foreigners' right to work. In particular, Article 8 of the law stipulates that until classes resume at universities and higher education establishments (which had been suspended), foreign nationals present in France on March 16, 2020 and holding a temporary residence permit bearing the word "student" may, exceptionally, engage in paid employment up to a limit of 80 % of the annual working time.

As part of the crisis arising from Russia's invasion of Ukraine, France provided that Ukrainians arriving in France could obtain temporary protection and thus be authorized to work.[970] A "businesses get involved" portal was set up on which businesses could offer jobs to displaced persons in France. In this context, Decree no. 2022-468 of April 1, 2022 relating to the terms and conditions of the work permit granted to beneficiaries of temporary protection was adopted, exempting them from any need to apply for a work permit in France, with effect from April 2, 2022.

2.3.6 Human rights of the specific vulnerable groups: unaccompanied minors

On French territory, unaccompanied minors benefit from special protection from the moment they arrive, based in particular on the constitutional principle of respect for the best interests of the child.[971] They are given shelter and must undergo an age assessment to prove their minority.[972] If this is verified, they are taken into care by the child welfare services at departmental

---

970 See: Instruction on the implementation of the decision of the Council of the European Union of March 5, 2022, taken in application of Article 5 of Council Directive 2001/55/EC of July 20, 2001.

971 C.C., decision no. 2018-768 QPC of March 21, 2019, M. Adama S.; See Jacquelot F., "La radiographie osseuse pratiquée sur les jeunes migrants non accompagnés et l'alinéa 11 du Préambule de la Constitution de 1946 : perspectives d'une protection en devenir," (8/2019) Constitutions, 252–261. The International Convention on the Rights of the Child of January 26, 1990, to which France is a party, also enshrines this principle.

972 Jacquelot F. (ed), *Repenser la détermination de l'âge du mineur non accompagné. Perspectives empiriques et comparées* (September 2023) <https://gip-ierdj.fr/fr/publications/repenser-l-age-du-mineur-etranger/>.

level. Depending on their age, they will either be sent to school or placed in apprenticeships. They are therefore entitled to education and instruction,[973] vocational training and health care.[974] Thus, a *Conseil d'Etat* decision on February 15, 2017 was able to rule that the refusal to give an unaccompanied minor a provisional work permit, pending his residence permit, was illegal. In fact, it held that the minors in question are presumed to be authorized to reside legally in France.[975]

Since Law no. 2015-925 of July 29, 2015, unaccompanied minors have benefited from specific asylum rights. In particular, OFPRA is entitled to examine their applications as a matter of priority in accordance with special examination procedures. Immigration law no. 2024-42 of January 26, 2024 reinforced the status of unaccompanied minors in France, confirming the ban on expelling foreign minors from France and expressly prohibiting the holding of unaccompanied minors in administrative detention.

Unaccompanied minors arriving in France as a result of the conflict in Ukraine are dealt with in detail in two instructions issued by the Minister of Justice on 1 and April 7, 2022 on the situation of minors from Ukraine.[976]

2.3.7 Procedural law perspective

2.3.7.1 Special procedures on the entry and residence of third-country nationals

2.3.7.1.1 Introduction

The rules governing admission to France are set out in the Aliens Code (books 3 and 4) in coordination with the rules of the European Union and the Schengen area, with a view to joint management of external borders. However, France provides for removal measures that can be coercive and, since the state of emergency declared in 2015, it has maintained controls at its internal borders.

---

973 Article L. 111-2 of the Education Code, read in conjunction with § 13 of the Preamble to the 1946 Constitution: "every child has the right to a school education which, complementing the action of his family, contributes to his education."

974 They also enjoy a number of subjective rights, such as freedom of expression and the right to respect for private and family life.

975 CE, decision December 27, 2017, No. 415436.

976 Instruction of April 1, 2022 on the situation of minors from Ukraine; Instruction of April 7, 2022 on dealing with the situation of minors from Ukraine.

2.3.7.1.2 The standard entry and residence procedure for third-country nationals in France

2.3.7.1.2.1 Entering France

Residence in France, whether for a short or long period, is in principle subject to legal entry into the country. Regular entry is generally justified by the presentation of a visa. The visa has become not only a condition of entry but also of residence in the country: if a foreigner is not in possession of the visa required by law, he or she will generally not be able to obtain a residence permit.[977]

Border controls are regulated by both the Aliens Code and the Schengen Borders Code (Regulation 2016/399 of March 9, 2016). This regulation lays down measures common to all States regarding the crossing of the EU's external borders. Thus, entry to French territory may be refused in any of the following cases, if the individual:

- Is not in possession of the documents required by law (passport, visa, etc.);
- Is subject to a judicial ban on entering France, a deportation order or a ban on returning to French territory;
- Has been signed by one of the States in the Schengen area for the purpose of refusing entry or is likely to jeopardize public order and internal security.

2.3.7.1.2.2 Removal from French territory

A removal order is issued when a foreign national can no longer be kept in France. There are several types of deportation, depending on the circumstances:

- Administrative deportation measures: these are taken either when a residence permit is refused or when an application for renewal is made, or when a residence permit is withdrawn, or when an illegal residence status is discovered during an identity check. In such cases, two measures may be adopted: either an obligation to leave French territory (OQTF)[978] or expul-

977 Article L. 311-1 (Documents required for entry and residence in France), L. 312-2 to L. 312-4 (Long-stay visa) of the CESEDA. And art. R 311-1 to R 311-3 (Conditions for admission to France), R 312-1 to R 312-2 (Submission of visa application) of the CESEDA.

978 Articles L 611-1 to L 611-3 of the CESEDA. An OQTF is a decision adopted by the Prefect declaring that a third-country national is residing illegally and imposing

sion.[979] Pending enforcement of the removal order, surveillance measures may be taken against the foreign national (house arrest or placement in a detention center).

- Ban on leaving French territory: this is a criminal sanction imposed by a judicial judge. This measure entails deportation to the border and a ban on re-entering French territory for the duration of the measure.[980]
- There may also be measures decided on within the EU and the Schengen area, in particular surrender to the competent authorities of an EU Member State or the Schengen area (cf. in particular the Dublin II Regulation); automatic deportation as a result of an alert for refusal of entry in the SIS file; enforcement of a removal order issued by one of the other EU Member States.

2.3.7.1.3 *Special entry and residence procedures in times of emergency*

Once in the Schengen area, foreign nationals have the right to free movement. However, there are possible derogations provided for in Article 25 of Regulation (EU) 2016/399 of the European Parliament and of the Council of March 9, 2016. This allows controls to be reintroduced temporarily "in the event of a serious threat to public policy or the internal security of a Member State." It was on this basis that, following the declaration of the state of emergency in 2015, France notified the European Commission of a list of crossing points subject to systematic checks. The same applies from March 17, 2020 in the context of the COVID-19 pandemic.

---

an obligation to return, in principle to his or her country of origin or to another country. The imposed departure may be voluntary or involuntary.

979 Articles L 630-1 to L 632-7 of the CESEDA. This measure is taken by the Prefect or the Minister of the Interior against a legally resident foreign national who is likely to pose a serious threat to public order. In this case, the foreign national may be forcibly returned to his or her country of origin or to another country. The deportation order can take two forms: immediate deportation or house arrest. In the case of immediate deportation (appeals do not suspend enforcement), the foreign national may be forced to board a means of transport (plane, train, boat) under police escort for the duration of the travel. The individual's residence permit is also withdrawn.

980 Articles L 641-1 to L 641-4 of the CESEDA.

Since then, France has continued to be one of the States that rely on the aforementioned Article 25 to maintain border controls, citing the fight against terrorism in particular. The *Conseil d'Etat* has been called upon several times to address France's increasing number of requests for derogations. While it does not question the principle of maintaining internal border controls,[981] in a recent decision of February 2, 2024,[982] it stressed that such controls must respect the fundamental rights of foreigners refused entry to French territory.

2.3.7.2 Identification of standards for proper organization of administrative authorities and courts

2.3.7.2.1 Introduction

A number of principles of good administration govern relations between third-country nationals and the authorities in France. However, this remains rather summary. This is why the practical details of these relationships have had to be clarified or even redefined by the administrative courts.

2.3.7.2.2 Relations between third-country nationals and the authorities

Third-country nationals are constantly having to deal with the authorities, whether it's to obtain a visa, a residence permit or its renewal, or a work permit. The same applies to all aspects of social security, in order to receive social benefits and health cover. In France, all government departments are "public services" and as such are subject to compliance with a number of principles. These include the principles of continuity, adaptability, accessibility and neutrality. These guarantee transparent operating conditions and procedures for processing requests in the forms and within the timescales laid down by law. In particular, the provisions contained in the 2015 Code of Relations between the Public and the Administration (CRPA) apply. For example, Article L. 211-2 of the CRPA requires that all individuals have the right to be informed of the reasons for unfavorable administrative decisions that concern them. In particular, the administration must give reasons for decisions restricting the exercise of public freedoms, imposing a penalty or refusing an authorization.

---

981 CE, decision of December 28, 2017, No. 415291.

982 CE, decision of February 2, 2024, No. 450285.

Since 2013, one government department has been dealing specifically with relations with foreign nationals. This is the Directorate-General for Foreigners in France (DGEF). It is responsible, within the Ministry of the Interior, for immigration, asylum, integration and access to French nationality policy. Its remit covers all aspects of foreign nationals' stay in France: entry, residence, work, combating illegal immigration, asylum, integration and naturalization. It is responsible for implementing the guidelines set by the Minister, with two programs in particular: "Integration and access to French nationality" and "Immigration and asylum." It also manages the European Asylum, Migration and Integration and Internal Security funds in France. It therefore acts at international, European and national levels. Internally, it has links with OFPRA and OFII. In addition, a number of appeals are available to ensure that administrations comply with the principles set out above.

2.3.7.2.3 The right to a judge for third-country nationals

Generally speaking, the court with jurisdiction to hear disputes relating to foreign nationals is the administrative court. It therefore has jurisdiction in cases where consular authorities refuse to issue a visa. However, the *Conseil d'Etat* has recognized that diplomatic and consular authorities have a wide margin of discretion when issuing visas.[983] For this reason, it limits itself in this regard to a review of the manifest error of assessment.[984] However, it may tighten its control over decisions regarding the assessment of whether an applicant's professional qualifications meet the legal requirements in cases where a visa has been refused.[985]

The administrative court also checks that the administration respects the right of foreign nationals to lead a normal family life within the meaning of Article 8 of the European Convention on Human Rights.[986] The *Conseil d'Etat* ruled that the administration's enforcement of a judgment annulling a decision to refuse a residence permit, on the grounds that this refusal infringes the right to family life of the person concerned, implies the issue of

983 CE, decision of February 28, 1986, No. 41550.
984 CE, decision of April 22, 1992, No. 118336.
985 CE, decision of December 30, 2010, No. 335170.
986 CE, decision of April 10, 1992, No. 75006; CE, decision of December 17, 1997, *Préfet de l'Isère c/ Y*, No. 171201.

a temporary residence permit bearing the words "private and family life."[987] In addition, it considered that a foreign national could invoke Article 8 of the ECHR against an OQTF.[988] This is what led the administrative judge to consider that when the administrative authority plans to take such a measure, it must ensure, by taking into account all the factors relating to the foreign national's private and family life, that the measure is not likely to cause disproportionate harm to that life.[989]

For example, it has ruled that consulates may not refuse to issue visas to the spouse and minor children of a statutory refugee, except on grounds relating to the protection of public order.[990] For some years now, however, the administrative courts have also been checking whether the foreigner's presence in France actually constitutes a threat to public order.[991]

With regard to residence permits, the *Conseil d'Etat* has consistently ruled that foreign nationals have the right to apply for residence and work permits. Under these conditions, it specifies, the administration must process this application as part of an individual examination.[992]

The administrative judge has also laid down the principles that apply to the administration in the context of expulsion measures such as an OQTF. In particular, the *Conseil d'Etat* has specified that this type of measure is a police measure for which reasons must be given,[993] just like an expulsion order.[994] It also ruled that the right to be heard, enshrined in Article 41 of the Charter of Fundamental Rights of the European Union, implies that the prefect, before

987 CE, decision of November 30, 1998, No. 188350.

988 CE, decision of October 19, 2007, B and A, No. 306821.

989 For example, the *Conseil d'Etat* ruled that it was illegal to expel a foreign national who had committed numerous offenses for which he had been sentenced to more than ten years in prison, but whose mother and siblings, most of whom were French nationals, had lived in France for a long time and he himself was married to a French national and had a child with her (CE, decision of March 26, 2004, No. 242238).

990 CE, decision of February 3, 2012, *Ministre de l'intérieur, de l'outre-mer, des collectivités territoriales et de l'immigration*, No. 353952. On the other hand, it validated the refusal of a visa to a spouse insofar as its acceptance would have led to the creation of a situation of polygamy in France (CE, April 16, 2010, A, No. 318726).

991 CE, decision of October 17, 2003, *M. X*, No. 249183.

992 CE, decision of February 24, 1982, *Minister of the Interior v X*, No. 25289.

993 CE, decision of October 19, 2007, *B and A*, No. 306821.

994 CE, decision of July 24, 1981, No. 31488. This is the case even if the decision is taken as a matter of urgency: CE, decision of January 13, 1988, No. 65856.

taking a decision on the obligation to leave French territory, must allow the person concerned to present his or her written and oral observations.

As part of the various appeals available to third-country nationals, it is always possible to apply for legal aid. And if a foreign national subject to a deportation order is held in administrative detention, he or she is entitled to the assistance of a lawyer, with whom he or she must be able to confer confidentially.[995]

2.3.7.2.4 Adaptations during a state of health emergency

2.3.7.2.4.1 Administrative authorities

As mentioned above, prefectures were closed to the public during the state of health emergency, with significant consequences for the situation of third-country nationals. In particular, all residence procedures at prefectures were suspended. Ordinance no. 2020-328 of March 25, 2020 extended the validity of residence permits by 90 days. A new Ordinance no. 2020-460 of April 22, 2020 again extended the period for the same length of time. Similarly, the validity of asylum application certificates that expired between March 16 and May 15, 2020 was extended by 90 days (automatic extension).

2.3.7.2.4.2 Administrative justice

Law no. 2020-290 of March 23, 2020, an emergency law to deal with the COVID-19 pandemic, enabled the Prime Minister to take measures by ordinance to combat the spread of the COVID-19 pandemic, including adaptations to the administrative litigation procedure. In particular, this involved extending certain time limits for appeals and judgments[996] which had expired during the state of emergency.[997]

---

995 CE, decision of July 30, 2003, *Syndicat des avocats de France*, No. 236016.

996 Ordinance No. 2020-305 of March 25, 2020, adapting the rules applicable before the administrative courts.

997 Where the legally prescribed time limit for appeals expired between March 12, 2020 and the expiry of a period of one month after the end of the state of emergency, it would start running again from the latter date—i.e., June 24 (unless the state of health emergency was modified)—for its initial duration, calculated as a clear time limit, up to a maximum of two months. In the case of an appeal subject to the ordinary two-month time limit, if the time limit for appeal expired on March 30, the application was admissible up to and including August 24, 2020. These procedures also applied to appeals against decisions handed down by legal aid offices.

In addition, during the state of health emergency, the judge could decide that hearings would be held without the public, or even by videoconference or telephone. This issue was the subject of a dispute before the administrative judge. However, the system was endorsed, especially as the Constitutional Council had already ruled on the constitutionality of the videoconferencing system with regard to the right to an effective remedy.[998]

2.3.7.3 Application of new technologies in administrative and courts proceedings

2.3.7.3.1 Introduction

For many years now, the French administration has been entering an era of modernization through new technologies, which is also accompanied by a quest for simplification and transparency of procedures. The same is true of the courts, which are dematerializing certain aspects of procedure in order to speed up timeframes and make justice more accessible.

2.3.7.3.2 New technologies in administrative and legal proceedings

Since the late 1990s, the public sector has been strategically seeking to use new digital technologies in its day-to-day operations.[999] The electronic regis-

In the case of applications against ordinances imposing an obligation to leave French territory, ordinances transferring asylum seekers and appeals to the National Court of Asylum, the time limits for appeals expiring between March 12, 2020 and the end of the state of health emergency began to run again at the end of this period—i.e., on May 24—for their initial duration.
However, when a foreign national subject to an ordinance requiring him or her to leave French territory was placed in administrative detention or when a refusal to enter the country on asylum grounds was challenged, the time limits for appeals set out in the French Code on the Entry and Residence of Foreigners and the Right of Asylum were not amended by the ordinances of March 25, 2020.

998 C.C., decision no. 2018–770 DC of September 6, 2018, *Law for controlled immigration, an effective right of asylum and successful integration*. For the constitutional judge, videoconferencing is not contrary to the right to an effective judicial remedy, or to the rights of the defense, or to the right to a fair trial insofar as it makes it possible to guarantee the proper administration of justice.

999 Government Action Programme for the Information Society (PAGSI) in 1998; ADELE (Electronic Administration) project for the period 2004–2007. More recently, the digital transition has become a central plank of the State's reform policy, whether through the General Review of Public Policies, the Modernization of Public Action, or the Public Action 2022 program.

tered letter (LRE) is a turning point for administrative procedures, making public services more accessible. The administration is also making increasing use of artificial intelligence in its decision-making, based on predictive analyses. 2019 saw the launch of ALICEM, a public security solution that enables citizens to prove their identity online, giving them access to more than 500 online services.

The justice system is following a converging dynamic. In 2023, France unveiled its plan for the digital transformation of the Ministry of Justice by 2027. The aim is to overhaul digital working methods, including the complete dematerialization of civil and criminal proceedings, and the reform of information systems for the prison service and the judicial protection of young people. As a result, it will be possible to apply for legal aid and go to court online. Alongside the Ministry's main projects, other legal players such as court officers and public officials (lawyers, notaries, bailiffs, court-appointed agents, etc.) and various private companies (legaltechs) are developing other innovative services (predictive justice or access to legal information). These projects all use new tools, whether open data or artificial intelligence.

2.3.7.3.3 New technologies specifically for third-country nationals

In 2014, the Ministry of the Interior opened a digital administration for foreign nationals in France: *ANEF*. The ultimate aim is to dematerialize all procedures concerning foreign nationals in France, including residence and access to nationality. To date, the following operations can be carried out online:

- Validation of a long-stay visa valid as a residence permit;
- Certain residence permit applications or renewals (student, talent passport, visitor, beneficiary of international protection);
- Applications for or renewal of residence permits issued to foreign nationals who are ill;
- Residence permits for private and family life;
- Work permit application;
- Declaration of change of situation;
- Application for or renewal of a travel document for foreign nationals or a movement document for foreign minors;

This system speeds up and simplifies procedures for third-country nationals residing in France. It is available 24 hours a day, every day. Certain difficulties have been noted, in particular the fact that the platform is periodically blocked, which prevents third-country nationals from making any applications. For this reason, the administrative judge ruled that the "useful measures" summary application[1000] could be brought to enjoin the administration to take action, such as asking it to make an appointment directly with the prefecture. It will also be possible to ask the authorities to unblock or update the ANEF account in order to relaunch the application and speed up its processing. Following the decision of the interim relief judge, the authorities have 15 days to comply. In the context of this procedure, the *Conseil d'Etat* considered that there was a presumption of urgency in the context of a residence permit renewal. It also ruled that there was a presumption of urgency in the event of a malfunction in the teleservice.[1001]

2.4 Italy (Paola Pannia)

2.4.1 Introduction

This chapter aims to explore the pregnancy of the concept "emergency" when looking at the legislative, political and social landscape surrounding life experiences and trajectories of migrants, in Italy.

Before getting in *medias res*, some preliminary methodological considerations are needed. First, migration is a complex phenomenon. As every complex phenomena, migration lacks a uniform and universally accepted

---

[1000] Article L. 521-3 of the Code of Administrative Justice: "In urgent cases and on a simple request, which will be admissible even in the absence of a prior administrative decision, the interim relief judge may ordinance any other useful measures without obstructing the execution of any administrative decision."

[1001] CE, decision of June 9, 2022, No. 4533915 and decision of June 22, 2022, No. 461563. In these cases, it ruled that "when the appointment can only be requested after prior formalities have been carried out online, it follows from what has just been said that if the foreign national establishes that he or she was unable to complete these formalities, in particular when the website does not allow selection of the category of permit to which the application should be attached [...] The condition of urgency is thus in principle established in the case of an application to renew a residence permit."

definition. One of the reason is that migration intersects many different fields of studies, and, thus, many different perspectives, all of them claiming priority over the others. For the ends of this contribution, the definition of "migrants" provided by IOM will be used. Migrant is "An umbrella term, not defined under international law, reflecting the common lay understanding of a person who moves away from his or her place of usual residence, whether within a country or across an international border, temporarily or permanently, and for a variety of reasons. The term includes a number of well-defined legal categories of people, such as migrant workers; persons whose particular types of movements are legally defined, such as smuggled migrants; as well as those whose status or means of movement are not specifically defined under international law, such as international students" and as further specified "those who flee wars or persecution."[1002] In the light of the overall framework of this book, the analysis will give prevalence to the legal dimension of migration. Nonetheless, the cultural and social aspects of it won't be disregarded.

As migration, also emergency is a complex concept, involving both a factual and a normative dimension. In the common sense, emergency refers to "something dangerous or serious, such as an accident, that happens suddenly or unexpectedly and needs fast action in order to avoid harmful results."[1003] Beyond this, the word "emergency" conveys a very precise normative meaning, where its common sense becomes relevant for the relationship between citizens and public power. Even in this case, there is no widely accepted definition. However, some common features arise when speaking of "emergency" as a legal term: it is a "significant departure from a state of normalcy" that is a) highly disrupting of the status quo; b) temporary; c) geographically circumscribed.[1004] Finally, there is another important aspect characterizing the legal meaning of emergencies (regardless of it being real or only perceived): they "threaten rule of law values most directly by serving as a pretext for governments to ignore or circumvent constraints that ordinarily prevent or

---

1002 Key Migration Terms, Migration Glossary | IOM, UN Migration <https://www.iom.int/key-migration-terms>.

1003 <https://dictionary.cambridge.org/dictionary/english/emergency>.

1004 Fatovic C., "Emergencies and the Rule of Law," in *Oxford Research Encyclopedia of Politics* (2019) <https://oxfordre.com/politics/view/10.1093/acrefore/9780190228637.001.0001/acrefore-9780190228637-e-93>.

minimize arbitrary exercises of power."[1005] All democratic countries codify emergency powers and, above all, their limits, in the Constitutional Chart and/or in the law. Nonetheless, the governmental use of extraordinary powers linked to emergency is becoming a structural part of the legal order.[1006] This particularly applies to the migration domain, as this contribution will show in relation to the Italian context through an analysis of the legal framework on migration supplemented by academic articles, parliamentary studies and third sector research reports.[1007]

The first part of this contribution is dedicated to the Italian legislative framework on migration. Here, the analysis first offers some background information about the wider Italian normative and social context directly related to migration (par. 2.1.). Next, the main constitutional provisions and pieces of law regulating the legal status of migrants will be illustrated, adopting a longitudinal view (2.2. and 2.3.). The analysis of the rights of migrants in times of emergency occupies the core of this contribution (par. 3). Adopting both a procedural and substantial perspective, this section retraces the main stages of the Italian legislation in times of emergency, exploring if and to what extend the rights of migrants have been respected. In its final part, section 4 attempts to capture the most relevant trends of migration governance in time of emergency in Italy, and their implications on the rights of foreigners.

2.4.2 A diachronic overview on the legislative framework regulating the rights of migrants in Italy: emergency as an overarching keyword[1008]

2.4.2.1 A (quite) recent history of immigration

According to the recent figures released by ISTAT (the Italian institute of statistics), on January 1, 2023, the foreign population (including both

---

1005 ibid.

1006 ibid. There are numerous authors claiming a downgrading of democracy everywhere in the world. See on this, among many others: Graber M. A., Levinson S., and Tushnet M. (eds), *Constitutional Democracy in Crisis?* (New York: Oxford University Press 2018); Ginsburg T., and Huq A. Z., *How to Save a Constitutional Democracy*, (Chicago: University of Chicago Press 2018).

1007 All websites pages have been retrieved on December 16, 2024.

1008 This chapter draws upon the research carried out in the frame of an EU funded research (Respond—<https://www.respondmigration.com/>), further adjourned and integrated.

communitarian and non-communitarian foreigners) is 5 million and 50 thousand units, increasing by 20 thousand individuals (+3.9‰) over the previous year. The proportion of foreign residents in the total population is 8.7 %, slightly increasing from 2022.[1009] The number of third-country citizens is about 3 million and 727 thousand. Of those, 60 % have a EU long-term residence permit. In 2022, nearly 449 thousand residence permits were issued to non-EU citizens, with a significant increase compared with 2021 (+ 86 %), largely due to refugees fleeing from Ukraine. For this reason, in 2022, more than 200 thousand migrants entered Italy to claim international protection (45.1 %) while in 2021 asylum applicants were just 31 thousand. Family reunification represents the second main reason for new entries in Italy (28.1 %), followed by work reasons (15.0 %) which increased significantly compared to 2021 (+32.2 %). Among these new arrivals to Italy, a significant component is represented by unaccompanied foreign children.

From January to December 2023, the number of migrant who approached the Italian coast is around 157,000 thousand. During the timeframe 2014–2023, the number of migrants who arrived in Italy by sea reached its peak in 2016 with 181,000 individuals, who dropped to only 11,400 in 2019.[1010] Harsh immigration law enacted by the right-wing government, together with the cooperation agreement with Libia, may explain this decrease.

Obviously, these data are only part of a broader picture, but still suffice to show how migration has become a structural phenomenon in Italy. At the same time, the incidence of foreigners residing in Italy is lower than in other countries, such as Germany and Spain, which also detain a larger share of residents with a migratory background who may have acquired citizenship. In Italy, instead, the history of immigration has more recent roots. Indeed, Italy has been for a long time an emigration country. Since its unification in 1861 until the post-World War II millions of Italians migrated to North and South America, Australia and to a number of European Country (mainly

---

1009 Noi Italia 2024—home (istat.it) <https://noi-italia.istat.it/pagina.php?id=3&categoria=4&action=show&L=0>.

1010 Italy: immigrants' sea arrivals 2014-2023 | Statista <https://www.statista.com/statistics/623514/migrant-arrivals-to-italy/>.

Belgium, Switzerland and Germany), accounting for the largest voluntary migration in recorded history.[1011]

This trend slowly started to slightly reverse during the post-war economic boom, in 1960, when Italy witnessed a first wave of migration, which mainly concerned seasonal workers and female domestic workers especially from Eastern Africa (such as Somalia, Eritrea and Ethiopia, which were former Italian colonies), the Philippines and former Portuguese territories.[1012] Another shift occurred in mid 1970s, with the oil crisis which, among its consequences, reduced the capacity of Northern EU countries' labor market to attract migrant workers.[1013] Interestingly enough, from the beginning, undocumented migrants have represented a relevant part of migration in Italy: in 1970s and 1980s, peaks in the number of residence permits coincide with regularization measures adopted by the Italian government to respond to the need of workforce.[1014] Despite numbers of migrants setting foots in the country kept growing, it is only in 1998 that the first legislative text regulating migration makes its appearance (the so-called Consolidated Law on Migration).

With specific reference to asylum, until 1990, only European citizens could apply, due to the "geographical limitation," with which Italy ratified the Geneva Convention. The main impetus to the construction of the national protection system arrived from local reactions to historical events (the flows of Albanians in 1991 and in 1997) and, more incisively, from the European Union, the Schengen process and the legislative instruments of the Common European Asylum System, established since 1999.[1015]

1011 Hom S., and Ben-Ghiat R., *Introduction to Italian Mobilities* (Routledge 2015).

1012 Colombo A., and Sciortino G., "Italian Immigration: the Origins, Nature and Evolution of Italy's Migratory Systems" (2004) 9 *Journal of Modern Italian Studies*, 49–70.

1013 Sciortino G., *L'ambizione della frontiera. Le politiche di controllo migratorio in Europa* (FrancoAngeli 2000).

1014 Colombo A., and Sciortino G., *Italian immigration…*, 54.

1015 Common European Asylum System—European Commission (europa.eu) <https://home-affairs.ec.europa.eu/policies/migration-and-asylum/common-european-asylum-system_en>.

2.4.2.2 The Italian constitutional framework on third-country nationals and their rights

Coherently with the picture outlined above, the Italian Constitution of 1948[1016] dedicates only few and generic rules directly addressing asylum, migration and the legal status of foreigners, whereas directly refers to the rights of emigrants, stating that "every citizen is free to leave the territory of the Republic and return to it except for obligations defined by law" (Article 16(2)) and recognizing "the freedom to emigrate, except for legal limitations for the common good," protecting at the same time "the Italian labour abroad" (Article 35(4).

With specific reference to migrants, the most relevant normative provision is Article 10, which states that "(2) legal regulation of the status of foreigners conforms to international rules and treaties; [and] (3) foreigners who are, in their own country, denied the actual exercise of the democratic freedoms guaranteed by the Italian Constitution, are entitled to the right to asylum under those conditions provided by law." Although the constitutional right to asylum has never been fully transposed into law, according to solid jurisprudence, it has found its implementation in the refugee status, the subsidiary protection and the humanitarian protection.[1017] Beyond Article 10, other constitutional provisions that secure foreigners' rights, even when undocumented, are: a) the "personalist principle" of Article 2 enshrining the "inviolable rights of human beings,"[1018] b) the equality clause

1016 For the official English version of the Italian Constitution, see <https://www.senato.it/documenti/repository/istituzione/costituzione_inglese.pdf>.

1017 In its decision no. 4455/2018, the Court of Cassation clarified that the humanitarian protection represents "one of the forms of implementation of constitutional asylum, precisely by virtue of its open nature and the fact that the conditions for its recognition are not wholly precisely definable, consistently with the broad scope of the right of asylum contained in the constitutional provision, which expressly refers to denial of the exercise of democratic liberties."

1018 Article 2 of the Italian Constitution states: "the Republic recognizes and guarantees the inviolable human rights, be it as an individual or in social groups expressing their personality, and it ensures the performance of the unalterable duty to political, economic, and social solidarity."

of Article 3[1019]; c) Article 24 on the right to legal defense,[1020] d) Article 111 on the right to a fair trial regulated by law[1021] and e) Article 117, which, by subjecting the legislative power to the obligations deriving from the Constitution, EU legislation and international treaties,[1022] strongly contributes enhancing the legal guarantees provided to foreigners and the protection of their rights.

Article 117 is key to migration governance also because distributes legislative powers between the State and the Regions. The legislation on

---

1019 Article 3 of the Italian Constitution states: "(1) All citizens have equal social status and are equal before the law, without regard to their sex, race, language, religion, political opinions, and personal or social conditions. (2) It is the duty of the Republic to remove all economic and social obstacles that, by limiting the freedom and equality of citizens, prevent full individual development and the participation of all workers in the political, economic, and social organization of the country."

1020 Article 24(2) of the Constitution says: "Defense is an inviolable right at every stage and instance of legal proceedings. The poor are entitled by law to proper means for action or defense in all courts." In decision No. 198/2000, the Constitutional Court clarified that the effective exercise of the right of defense "implies that the recipient of a provision of restriction of the self-determination freedom, be enabled to understand its content and meaning." As a consequence, "under the hypothesis of ignorance without fault of the expulsion order—in particular for non-compliance with the obligation of translation of the legal act—the deadline for proposing an appeal should not be considered" (No. 198/2000).

1021 It is worth mentioning §§ 1, 2 and 3 of Article 111 of the Italian Constitution according to which "Jurisdiction is implemented through due process regulated by law."

"All court trials are conducted with adversary proceedings and the parties are entitled to equal conditions before an impartial judge in third party position. The law provides for the reasonable duration of trials.In criminal law trials, the law provides that the alleged offender shall be promptly informed confidentially of the nature and reasons for the charges that are brought and shall have adequate time and conditions to prepare a defense. The defendant shall have the right to cross-examine or to have cross-examined before a judge the persons making accusations and to summon and examine persons for the defense in the same conditions as the prosecution, as well as the right to produce all other evidence in favor of the defense. The defendant is entitled to the assistance of an interpreter in the case that he or she does not speak or understand the language in which the court proceedings are conducted."

1022 Article 117(1) of the Italian Constitution proclaims that "Legislative powers shall be vested in the State and the Regions in compliance with the Constitution and with the constraints deriving from EU legislation and international obligations."

immigration, right of asylum and legal status of non-EU citizens is subjected to the exclusive legislative competence of the State, while other policy area affecting the management of migration and the legal status of foreigners, such as housing, healthcare, education, are assigned to the concurrent (i.e., education and health care) or exclusive regional legislative competence.[1023] Meant to inject in the Italian system a stronger decentralization, the enforcement of Article 117 did not result in cutting out the Regions from the governance of migration. Instead, thanks to the interpretation of the Constitutional Court, it represented the basis to build a multilevel model of migration management. This model, though, still struggles to be established in an efficient and orderly way, also in the lack of sufficient and efficient systems of coordination and monitoring. Central government and regions, together with their bureaucracy, are not the only actors involved in the migration governance. Their competing, often conflicting interests have to cohabit with the claims coming from other important voices, such as the ones of supranational organizations on the one hand and non-governmental organizations, industry-lobbies and labor unions on the other. Furthermore, also national and supranational courts play a relevant role. Nonetheless, this contributed to create further instability and uncertainty that, in a vicious circle, further fuels the criticalities that will be illustrated below.

2.4.2.3 The most relevant legislative provisions: an overview on the legal status of third-country nationals

The Legislative Decree No. 286/1998, the Consolidated Law on Immigration represented the first attempt to regulate migration in a coherent and systematic way. Its adoption was influenced by the European Union, which has represented a key driving force also later, particularly with reference to asylum (in the light of the Common European Asylum System). Indeed, in Italy, the regulation of asylum is scattered among many different legislative decrees which were adopted to transpose the relevant EU Directives on asylum into the Italian legal system., whereas an organic law still lacks.

Concerning the main provisions on entry and stay, as many other countries, Italy does not provide a visa for asylum. Asylum seekers can submit

1023 Article 117(3) of the Italian Constitution.

their claims only at the border or once in the Italian territory. Yet, Italian authorities have the duty to allow asylum applicants to enter the country, in the light of the Geneva Convention, the principle of non-refoulement and other crucial principles enshrined in the European Convention on Human Rights (i.e., the right to be protected from inhuman or degrading treatments).

Differently from asylum applicants, third-country nationals do not have a right but only a legitimate expectation to enter the Italian State, vis-à-vis the discretionary decision of Italian authorities.[1024] They must hold a valid passport, a visa and adequate economic resources and should not represent a danger for public order. Visa may be temporary, i.e., lasting up to 90 days (for visits, business and tourism)—in these cases the rules of the common EU Visa Code[1025] apply—or "long-stay." These latter visas, subjected to each specific national legislation, are the prerequisite to obtain a permit to stay related to the same reasons mentioned in the visa (i.e., work, study, family, religious reasons, etc.). The permit to stay, which should be asked to the Police Headquarter or the Prefecture within 8 days from the entry, grants to third-country nationals the right to stay in the Italian territory.[1026] There are some exceptions to this general rule when fundamental principles are at stake (such as the protection of children rights, the right to family unity or the prohibition of torture). Thus, in specific situations, third-country nationals (e.g., unaccompanied children, pregnant women, or women up to 6 months from the childbirth, and foreigners cohabiting with an Italian first-degree relative or spouse) cannot be expelled or returned, even if they do not own a visa or a regular permit to stay.[1027]

Since 2002, a system of quota (whose number is annually established by the so-called Decreto Flussi) regulates the entry of migrants for employment, self-employment and seasonal work. It is based on the idea that third-country nationals who want to enter Italy for employment must have a pre-existing job offer from an Italian employer. Indeed, it is the Italian employer who, after

1024 See among the others, Corte Cass., S.U., decision no. 1417/2004.

1025 Regulation (EC) No. 810/2009 of the European Parliament and of the Council of July 13, 2009 establishing a Community Code on Visas (Visa Code), with amendments introduced by Regulation (EU) 2021/1134.

1026 Article 5 of the Consolidated Law on Immigration.

1027 Article 19 of the Consolidated Law on Immigration.

having verified that no employee already residing in Italy is available, has to submit the online application to request the *nulla osta* (authorization document) for the foreign employer to enter Italy for work reason, together with documents proving the employees' accommodation and the commitment to pay the foreigner's travel costs to return to his/her country of origin.[1028] This system has proven highly ineffective to respond to the labor demand in Italy: numbers of entry quota are far from meeting the internal labor demand. Furthermore, the procedure is too complex and full of bureaucratic hurdles.[1029] Finally, severe irregularities have been detected in the practice of Italian embassies competent to issue the work visa.[1030]

Beyond these criticalities, for the aim of this chapter, it is important to mention that from 2011, entry quota has been dramatically reduced by the government, due to the economic crisis and the reduced possibility to find a job in Italy.[1031] Opportunities to regularly enter the country were limited to high-qualified workers, rich entrepreneurs and "seasonal workers" in the field of agriculture and tourism. Recently, this trend has been partially reversed with an increase in the number of foreign workers admitted in the country, although controversially featured by a sectorialization and ethnicization tendency.

Concerning foreigners' rights, different legal treatments apply to different legal status, unless fundamental rights are at stake. Indeed, in the

---

1028 Article 22 of the Consolidated Law on Immigration.

1029 Cappiali T., "An Italian "Integration Crisis": The Role of the State and Political Actors in Excluding Immigrants and Ethnic Minorities," in M. A. Evangelista (ed) *Italy from Crisis to Crisis: Political Economy, Security, and Society in the Twenty-first Century* (Routledge, 2018); Zanfrini L., Il lavoro. Fondazione ISMU, Dodicesimo rapporto sulle migrazioni 2006. Franco Angeli, 2007; Corte dei Conti, Programma controllo 2006—L'attività di gestione integrata dei flussi di immigrazione (2008) <www.corteconti.it/Ultimi-doc/Attivit--23/index.asp>; Ferraris V., "Migrant's Offside Trap: A Strategy for Dealing with Misleading Rules and Hostile Playing Field," in J. Shapland, and P. Ponsaers (eds), *The Informal Economy and Connections with Organized Crime: The Impact of National Social and Economic Policies* (The Hague 2009).

1030 Gherardi S., *Immigration Flow Decree (Decreto flussi): Illegitimate Practices by Italian Embassies Abroad*, (August 9, 2024) <https://openmigration.org/en/analyses/immigration-flow-decree-decreto-flussi-illegitimate-practices-by-italian-embassies-abroad/>; Ferlisi M., *L'irrazionalità sistemica dei decreti flussi. Perché non è solo una questione criminale* (June 12, 2024) <https://altreconomia.it/lirrazionalita-sistemica-dei-decreti-flussi-perche-non-e-solo-una-questione-criminale/>.

1031 <https://www.gazzettaufficiale.it/eli/id/2012/11/22/12A12384/sg>.

latter case, as also the Italian Constitutional Court has often highlighted, the regular presence in the country is the only requirement to be fulfilled. The Court took this reasoning even further, by declaring that there is an "inalienable core of the right to health" guaranteed by the Constitution as an "inviolable part of the human dignity" that obliges its protection also in favor of undocumented migrants.[1032] Against this solidaristic logic, different approaches govern the domain of social rights, realizing a sort of post-entry, internal migration control.[1033] Here, the selection of beneficiaries of social measures is often based on the specific legal status owned by the foreigner. Indeed, while an "equivalence clause," established by Article 29 of Directive 2011/95, guarantees to beneficiaries of international protection the same rights as Italian citizens, for third-country citizens holding a short-term residence permit the access to social rights is more complicated. Criteria such as the duration of stay are often used by the national (as well as regional) legislator to exclude foreigners from the enjoyment of social services and benefits.

Finally, a blanket exclusion from political rights (both at local and national level) apply to all foreigners, regardless their legal status.

2.4.2.4 The evolution of the Italian Immigration law

The main stages of the evolution of the Italian legislation on migration can be summarized as follows:

- Italy as a country of emigration (1861–1980): From the national unification (1861) until the 1970s Italy was a country of emigration. At that time, the law regulating migration was the "Public Security Consolidated Law

1032 Corte cost, decision no. 329/2011. For further details see: Pannia P., "Questioning the Frontiers of Rights: the Case Law of the Italian Constitutional Court on Non-European Union Citizens Social Rights" (2022) 14(SI) *European Journal of Legal Studies*, 133.

1033 Geddes A., "Migration and the Welfare State in Europe" (2003) *The Political Quarterly*, 150; Corsi C., *Lo Stato e lo Straniero* (Cedam, 2001); Biondi dal Monte F., *Dai Diritti Sociali alla Cittadinanza. La Condizione Giuridica dello Straniero tra Ordinamento Italiano e Prospettive Sovranazionali* (Giappichelli, 2013); Pannia P., "Questioning the Frontiers of Rights: the Case Law of the Italian Constitutional Court on Non-European Union Citizens Social Rights" (2022) 14(SI) *European Journal of Legal Studies*, 133.

No. 773/1931, which looked at foreigners" entry and stay essentially as an issue of public order.[1034]

- First attempts to regulate migration (1980–1997): After the ratification of the OIM International Convention of 1975, in 1986, Law No. 943/1986 (the so-called "Foschi Law"), approved by a large, multiparty centrist coalition, addressed specific area of migration, essentially related to the legal status of migrant workers. In the same year, around 118.000 undocumented migrants were regularized.[1035] After few years, the same centrist political coalition approved the Law No. 39/1990 (the so-called "Martelli Law"), which, among the other things, as required by the Schengen process, removed the so-called "geographical limitations" extending the right to apply for international protection also to non-EU nationals.[1036] Furthermore, it provided new procedures for determining refugee status and set up the Central Commission for the Recognition of International Protection composed by officials from the central government and UNHCR experts. It introduced entry quota for migrant workers together with new entry visa and regulated expulsions for undocumented migrants. Finally, it approved a new regularization program.[1037] In 1992, the Parliament approved a new citizenship law (Law No. 91/92), mainly based on the so-called *jus sanguinis* criterion, favoring Italian descendants. In 1995, around 250.000 irregular migrants benefited from another regularization process.
- First relevant normative changes (1998–2013): The Law No. 40/1998 (the so-called "Turco-Napolitano Law") approved by a center-left coalition and soon incorporated into the Legislative Decree No. 286/1998 (the so-called "Consolidated Law"), introduced a comprehensive normative framework on migration and the legal status of foreigners. The Consolidated Law

---

1034 Nascimbene B., *Diritto degli stranieri* (Cedam: Padova, 2004).

1035 Abbondanza G., "Italy's Migration Policies Combating Irregular Immigration: from the Early Days to the Present Times" (2017) 52(4) *The International Spectator*, 76–92.

1036 Finotelli C., and Sciortino G., "The Importance of Being Southern: The Making of Policies of Immigration Control in Italy" (2009) 11 *European Journal of Migration and Law*, 119–138; Hein C. (ed), *Rifugiati. Vent'anni di storia del diritto d'asilo in Italia* (Donzelli Editore, 2010).

1037 Castellazzi S., "Le implicazioni legislative del fenomeno sociale migratorio. L'evoluzione normativa in Italia," in G. Cordini, and V. Gasparini Casari (eds), *Il diritto dell'immigrazione* (Mucchi Editore: Modena 2010) 93–140.

proclaimed a fundamental set of principles on foreigners' legal status (such as the right to non-discrimination) while guaranteeing essential social rights (such as the right to health, education and social integration). The Consolidated Law also provided an organic regulation on conditions of entry (through the "programmatic document" and the establishment of yearly entry quotas for migrants for work reasons)[1038] and stay. A system of "sponsorship" allowed migrants to enter the country "to search for a job," under the guarantee of an Italian citizen or a legally resident foreigner. Also to comply with the requests of other EU Member States following the Schengen process,[1039] more stringent controls at the borders were provided along with a broader recourse to pushbacks and deportation and the creation of temporary detention centers for migrants waiting to be deported (the so-called *Centri di permanenza e assistenza*). In 1999, around 250.000 undocumented migrants were regularized by a new regularization program. After a few years, the Consolidated Law was partially amended by the new center-right government through the Law No. 189/2002, the (so-called "Bossi-Fini Law"). The Bossi-Fini Law substituted the previous system of sponsorship with a complicated mechanism where migrants willing to enter the country for work reasons had to demonstrate there was an employer in Italy already committed to hire them. The Law also introduced more restrictive provisions on expulsion and detention. It also provided for the largest regularization process ever approved in Italy, involving the regularization of 646.000 foreign workers.[1040] The center-right coalition further stressed the security approach to migration using the criminal law to fight against illegal entry and residence (the so-called "clandestinity"). Laws No. 125/2008 and No. 94/2009, named "Security Packages" (*Pacchetto Sicurezza*) introduced the crime of "clandestinity" and the "aggravating circumstance of clandestinity," later declared unconstitutional,[1041] under which the punishment for a crime committed by an undocumented

1038 For further details, see Chapter 3.

1039 Ponzo I., "Looking into Policy Change: How the Italian Asylum Regime Came of Age," in C. Finotelli, and I. Ponzo (eds) *Migration Control Logics and Strategies in Europe. IMISCOE Research Series* (Cham: Springer 2023).

1040 McMahon, *Immigration and Citizenship in an Enlarged European Union: The Political Dynamics of Intra-EU Mobility* (London: Palgrave Macmillan, 2015) 48.

1041 Italian Constitutional Court, decision no. 249/2010.

foreigner could be increased up to one third compared with the same crime committed by an Italian citizen or a regularly resident foreigner. Meanwhile, the Decree-Law No. 78/2009 established the regularization of foreign workers in the domestic labor and in the care sector. Finally, as far as asylum is concerned, important legislative acts were approved in order to comply with the EU obligations and the construction of a "Common European Asylum System": the Legislative Decrees No. 85/2003; No. 140/2005; No. 251/2007; No. 25/2008, that respectively transposed the EU Directives on "temporary protection," "reception conditions," "qualification," "asylum procedures." In 2011, Italy experienced a high increase in the number of asylum applications, following the so-called "Arab Spring," which put under pressure the still underdeveloped national asylum system. Meanwhile, in 2012, under the Monti government that succeeded the center-right coalition, the L.D. No. 109 enforcing the EU directive 2009/52/CE to counteract illegal employment, provided a new regularization process.

- The reformist phase[1042] (2014–2017): The arrival of an unprecedented mixed migration flow pushed the Italian government to approve a number of radical reforms. New tools of migration governance made their appearance, triggered by the EU (i.e., the creation of "hotspots" and the relocation program). Meanwhile, the procedure of refugee determination and the national system of reception underwent significant changes with D. Lgs. No. 142/2015 and the Law Decree No. 46/2017.
- The entropic phase (2018–2023): During this timeframe, the political salience of migration reached its peak. The politicization of migration coupled with the alternation in power of political parties with opposite ideologies resulted in a trend of continuous and schizophrenic reforms. The rapid evolution of the national protection status based on humanitarian reasons is quite paradigmatic of the "back-and-forths" movements featuring national immigration laws in the last years. Article 5, section 6 of the Consolidated Law on Immigration provided the right to apply for a residence permit for humanitarian reasons when there were "serious reasons, in particular of humanitarian nature or resulting from constitutional or international obligations of the Italian State." This normative

1042 This last phase will be here just synthetically presented. For a more detailed analysis, please see the next chapter.

> provision was first eliminated by the center-right coalition with the Law Decree No. 113/2018. Then, with the Law Decree No. 130/2020, the residence permit for humanitarian reasons was reintroduced by the center-left coalition which expanded its scope to include claims of protection from the risk of harm to private and family life in the event of removal from the territory of the State. Finally, the Law Decree No. 20/2023 adopted by the far-right coalition intervened again on Article 5, section 6 of the Consolidated Law on Immigration, restricting the possibility to obtain a residence permit for humanitarian reasons only when the foreigner's repatriation was contrary to "constitutional or international obligations of the Italian State."

Similarly, in 2018, the government undertook a policy of "closed port" coupled with the approval of normative provisions aimed at limiting the activity of ONGs involved in search and rescue operations at sea. In 2019, a second Salvini Decree imposed hefty fines on ships involved in search and rescue which entered the Italian ports without the ministerial permission. This policy was resumed with the Law Decree No. 1/2023 containing "urgent provisions for the management of migratory flows."

Finally, the same oscillating trend featuring Italian immigration law can be observed regarding the possibility to convert residence permits. The possibility to apply for the conversion of the residence permit, initially limited by the Consolidated Law to a few typologies of residence permits (e.g., residence permit for family reasons), was extended to include further residence permits by Law No. 173/2020. This reform was subsequently cancelled by Law Decree No. 20/2023, which reduced again the possibility for conversion of the residence permit (art. 7). Recently, a new Law Decree, No. 145/2024, brough further changes to the Consolidated Law on Immigration, providing that those holding a residence permit for seasonal work can convert it into a residence permit for work reasons, even out of quota (art.1 (1) f).

The picture outlined above offers relevant insights on the "Italian way" of governing migration while offering many starting points to reflect about the salience of the emergency approach surrounding the Italian normative framework on migration. The next section will illustrate how these pieces of law, and particularly those enacted in times of emergency, affect the rights of migrants on both a substantial and procedural level.

2.4.3 The Italian legislation on foreigners' rights in time of emergency: a substantial and procedural perspective

The word "emergency" appears only once in the Consolidated Law on Immigration: Article 35 refers to emergency to secure undocumented foreigners the access to urgent or essential healthcare, even when they lack economic resources to cover the related cost.[1043] However, the relevance of "emergency" in the Italian Immigration Law goes well beyond this isolated explicit mention. As this section will illustrate, emergency is a concept that covertly surrounds the entire national normative framework on immigration, displaying a noxious incidence on foreigners' rights. As already highlighted in the section above, for instance, the systematic use of the Law Decree[1044] together with ample use of emergency narratives are quite eloquent example of this approach of permanent, latent emergency.

Which are the mechanisms through which, in the name of emergency (implicitly or explicitly mentioned), the Italian legislation has affected the substantial and procedural guarantees of migrants?

This section requires to shift the focus adopted thus far to analyze, beyond the governance of migration, also its implications on foreigners' rights. The purpose, here, is not to provide an exhaustive and detailed illustration of all legislative amendments approved by the Italian legislator in times of emergency. Rather, the objective is to shed light on the most

---

1043 Article 35(6) "Withstanding the financing of urgent hospital services or however essential at the expense of the Ministry of Interior, the charges caused by the remaining services provided for by § 3, toward foreign citizens lacking sufficient economic resources, are covered within the ambit of the availability of the national health fund with relevant reduction of the programmes referred to emergency interventions."

1044 The Law Decree is an act having force of law and an act of primary legislation. According to art. 77 of the Constitution "1. The government may not issue decrees with the force of law unless empowered by a proper delegation of the chambers. 2. As an exception by necessity and urgency, government may issue provisional measures with the force of law and submits them on the same day to the chambers for confirmation; if the chambers are not in session, they have to be summoned for that purpose within five days.
(3) Legal decrees lose effect at the date of issue if they are not confirmed within 60 days of their publication. However, chambers may sanction rights and obligations arising out of decrees are not confirmed." For further details see Ferrari G. F., Introduction to Italian public Law (Giuffrè 2008).

recurrent and relevant legislative tools, strategies and discourses enacted under the pressure of (real or assumed) emergencies, and to illustrate how these measures have affected the rights of third-country nationals, both on a substantial and procedural perspective. The decision to simultaneously adopt a substantial and procedural perspective on foreigners' rights relies upon two main reasons. First, these two dimensions are strictly interrelated, especially when law is concretely implemented: the same legislative measure can have an impact both on substantial and procedural rights. Furthermore, often, the infringement of a procedural right has indirect consequences also upon the respect of a substantial right, and vice-versa. Second, instead of providing a double list of procedural and substantial violations of migrants' rights in time of emergency, this section prefers to contextualize each legislative measure under scrutiny within a broader picture.

2.4.3.1 The Balkan "emergencies"

The first migration-related emergency occurred in 1992, when a high influx of migrants fleeing from the conflict in ex-Jugoslavia arrived in the Italian territory. The Law Decree 24.07.1992 No. 350[1045] was adopted to deal with the "needs of first aid, accommodation, assistance of displaced persons." In a context where the national system of reception was still poorly developed and equipped, both ex lege and de facto, the vast majority of migrants had to provide for all necessities by their own, while only few people were accommodated in governmental reception centers established by the Ministry of Interior. Even in the latter case, migrants were often channeled to big, crowded centers for prolonged period of time,[1046] where the access to basic rights and integration perspectives proved to be difficult. Beyond this, the management of migration was hindered by the lack of a structural plan and coordination system. As a result, the responsibility to provide assistance and reception to people displaced from ex-Jugoslavia was not equally distributed throughout the Italian territory but disproportionately burdened frontlines regions, such as Friuli Venezia Giulia and the Adriatic Coast. To this end,

1045 Decreto-legge 24 luglio 1992, No. 350—Normattiva.
1046 <https://documenti.camera.it/_dati/leg17/lavori/documentiparlamentari/IndiceETesti/022bis/021/00000003.pdf>.

it is worth mentioning the so-called Apulia Law, No. 563/1995 that created centers for the first assistance and identification of migrants in view of their possible repatriation.[1047]

Although the Law No. 39/1990 already provided some procedures for recognizing refugee status, people fleeing from Albania were granted a temporary protection status.[1048] Reasons to prefer an emergency approach over the enforcement of "ordinary" law comprehend not only the risk that the Geneva Convention could not be applied (in this case there was a situation of general danger rather than individual persecution) but also the need to fasten the procedures and avoid the more stringent assistance duties that would have followed the possible recognition of refugee status.[1049]

The temporary protection measure was the Italian response also to the Somali conflict: on September 9, 1992 the Ministerial Decree[1050] was adopted to manage the situation of Somali citizens who were present in Italy and were not entitled to obtain the refugee status, but still unable to return to their country. Also, in consideration of "the traditional ties existing between Italy and Somalia," those Somali citizens were given the right to apply for a temporary residence permit for reasons of work or study, for a maximum duration of one year, renewable upon expiration.

Much more intense were the interventions required to ensure the access to protection and accommodation to people fleeing from the social and political storm which affected Albania in 1997, and, thereafter, Kosovo. The Law

---

1047 These centers were renamed First Aid Centres and Assistance (CPSA) in 2006. As highlighted this law represented the basis for the activity subsequently carried out in Hotpots. Giannetto L., Ponzo I. and Roman E., "National Report on the Governance of the Asylum Reception System in Italy," in *Ceseaval Research on the Common European Asylum System* (2019) <https://www.fieri.it/wp-content/uploads/2019/06/WP3_Italy.pdf>.

1048 Article 2 Law Decree No. 350/1992.

1049 Ponzo I., *Looking into Policy Change: How the Italian Asylum Regime Came of Age*, cit., who also mentions F. Campomori, Le Politiche per i rifugiati in Italia: dall'accoglienza all'integrazione. Missione impossibile?, Social Cohesion Paper 2/2016, OCIS; Bona M., and Marchetti S., "Il diritto d'asilo in Italia: sviluppi normativi e nel sistema di accoglienza a partire dagli anni Novanta," in L. Gorgolini (ed), *Le migrazioni forzate nella astoria d'Italia del XX secolo* (Il Mulino 2017) 219–250.

1050 Gazzetta Ufficiale Serie Generale No. 252, October 26, 1992 <https://www.gazzettaufficiale.it/atto/serie_generale/caricaDettaglioAtto/originario?atto.dataPubblicazioneGazzetta=1992-10-26&atto.codiceRedazionale=092A4844>.

Decree n. 60/1997[1051] adopted to face the "exceptional influx of Albanians," guaranteed measures of first assistance and reception. Meanwhile, in March 1997 Italy signed an agreement with Albania. The Decree No. 60/1997 also provided for Albanians arriving in Italy a "nulla-osta" to enter the country and a temporary residence permit. However, in September of the same year, a Directive of the of the President of the Council of Ministers of 29 november 1997 declared the end of the humanitarian provisional measures, providing for the repatriation of those Albanians who had entered Italy after March 1 and were not entitled to remain in the country.

Officially meant to control "irregular migration," the agreement allowed Italian authorities to conduct naval patrols in the Adriatic Sea, which, de facto, resulted in operations of collective pushbacks and, in some cases, led to sea tragedies, such as the sinking of the Kater I Rades, when at least 58 Albanians died.[1052]

The year after, another conflict exploded in the region: the war in Kosovo. From 1998 on, a high number of migrants landed on the Italian shores. However, only with the Decree of May 12, 1999, the Italian government triggered, for the first time of the President of the Council of Ministers, Article 20 of the just adopted Consolidated Law on Immigration, which provided the power to adopt measures of temporary protection when conflicts, natural disasters or other serious events occur in non-European countries. Migrants fleeing from the war in Kosovo were issued a temporary permit of stay, valid for 6 months, renewable until a safe return to Kosovo could have taken place. The decree also provided for temporary special measures of assistance and accommodation that would have been granted until December 31, 1999, then further prorogued until June 2000.[1053] Nonetheless, the delay of the Italian response created, at least at the beginning, a disparity of treatment between Kosovars arrived before and after March 26, 1999. Indeed, only the latter

1051 <https://www.gazzettaufficiale.it/atto/serie_generale/caricaDettaglioAtto/originario?atto.dataPubblicazioneGazzetta=1997-03-20&atto.codiceRedazionale=097G0103&elenco30giorni=false>.

1052 Chaloff J., Albania and Italy. Migration policies and their development relevance. A Survey of Innovative and "Development-Friendly" Practices in Albania and Italy, working paper, CeSPI, 51/2008.

1053 Decree December 30, 1999.

were granted the temporary protection status, while the asylum application submitted by the formers was often dismissed.

Concerning reception, thanks to the financial aid provided by the EU Commission, and under the pressures posed by the entry into force of the 1997 Dublin Convention, the so-called Shared Action (Azione Comune) was launched. Drawn upon some local virtuous experiences, Shared Action was a network led by the third sector, with the collaboration, sometimes, of local municipalities (i.e., those in Trieste, Ivrea and Forlì), aimed at setting up a structured reception system with more harmonized services. Shared Action soon developed into the National Asylum Plan and, with Law No. 189/2002 became the so-called SPRAR (Protection System for Asylum Seekers and Refugees). This system was conceived as the national ordinary system of reception, with a spread network of facilities (often apartment-based) mainly run by local NGOs involved in the social sector, in cooperation with local municipalities, funded at the central level. Founded upon the protection of rights and integration, a clear set of provisions requires the provision of high-standard services, clearly defined, harmonized throughout the country and periodically monitored.

These intentions nevertheless, when Italy transposed the Reception Directive 2003/9/CE a binary logic prevailed: an extraordinary reception system was introduced next to the ordinary one of the SPRAR, revealing an approach that mainly looked at refugees as a temporary phenomenon.

2.4.3.2 The "Arab Spring"

As a result of the political (and social) turmoil that affected many North African countries in early 2011, a significantly high number of migrants (by historical standards) landed on the Italian shores with the aim to apply for asylum. On February 12, 2011, the Italian government responded to these consistent arrivals and the dramatic increase of asylum applications declaring the "state of emergency" until December 31, 2011, with a special decree of the President of the Council. The state of emergency was prorogued many times until its conclusion on January 31, 2013.[1054]

The competence to manage migrants' reception was given to the "National Civil Protection Service," an entity which, in principle, intervenes in cases

---

1054 Order of the Prime Minister, February 12, 2011, No. 3933/2011.

of "natural disasters, catastrophes or other events that, due to their intensity and extent, must be faced with extraordinary means and powers."[1055] Despite Italy already had a national protection system for asylum applicants and refugee (surrounded by specific laws, standards, and funds),[1056] an extraordinary reception plan was set up. Regions and local municipalities were required to actively collaborate to accommodate Tunisian migrants who had reached the Italian shores since January 2011. With this aim, relevant economic resources were allocated to the National Civil Protection Fund.[1057] At that time, the national protection system for asylum seekers and refugees did not have sufficient places to accommodate the high number of migrants coming from North Africa. Nonetheless, the decision to create an extraordinary system, diverting human and economic resources from the ordinary one (the SPRAR), ended up creating a fuzzy picture. Very different standards of accommodation were experienced by migrants across the country.[1058] Those who were not channeled into the SPRAR reception system were mostly accommodated in large-size facilities, with very scarce or completely absent integration measure. Their access to very basic rights was severely undermined.[1059] Furthermore, as highlighted by the same Italian government, the

---

1055 Law No. 225/1992, art. 5.

1056 There was a specific fund established with Law No. 189/2002: the National Fund for Asylum Policies and Services.

1057 Decree of the Presidency of the Council of Ministries, September 21, 2011, "Ulteriori disposizioni urgente dirette a fronteggiare lo stato di emergenza umanitaria nel territorio nazionale in relazione all'eccezionale afflusso di cittadini appartenenti ai paesi del Nord Africa Gazzetta."

1058 Nascimbene B., and Di Pascale A., "The Arab Spring and the Extraordinary Influx of People Who Arrived in Italy from North Africa" (2011) 13(4) *European Journal of Migration and Law*, 341–360.

1059 Ponzo I., Giannetto L., and Roman E., "The Variance in Multilevel Governance of Asylum Seekers' Reception in Italy: the Key Roles of Policy Legacy, Politics and Civil Society," in T. Caponio, and I. Ponzo (eds), *Coping with Migrants and Refugees: Multilevel Governance Across the EU* (Routledge 2022) 90 ss. See also Amnesty International, *Italy: Amnesty International Findings and Recommendations to the Italian Authorities Following the Research Visit to Lampedusa and Mineo* (2011) <http://www.amnesty.org/en/library/info/EUR30/007/2011/en>; ASGI, *Grave preoccupazione per le ripetute violazioni del diritto nei riguardi degli stranieri respinti, espulsi o trattenuti nei CIE, dei richiedenti asilo e dei lavoratori stranieri* (2011) <http://www.asgi.it/public/parser..download/save/1-asgicomunicati.12811.pdf>.

decision to elect the Civil Protection Service as the responsible entity, with ample extraordinary powers, "hindered the attainment of an overall and structured vision that would stably address an activity so closely linked to the complex issue of migration flows," i.e., reception.[1060]

Extraordinary measures were implemented also to assess and determine the legal status of migrants coming from North Africa. The Italian request to trigger the procedure laid down in Directive 2001/55/EC,[1061] which would have provided those migrants a temporary protection status, was rejected by the European Council. A decision of the Council of Minister, and, subsequently, a Decree of the presidente of the council of ministers resorted to Article 20 of the Consolidated Law on Immigration, and the temporary protection measures there provided.[1062] As a result, on an automatic basis, about 25000 Tunisian citizens who had reached Italy between January 1 and April 5, 2011 were granted a residence permit on humanitarian grounds. In October, the temporary permit duration was extended for further 6 months.[1063]

Meanwhile, in April 2011, Italy signed an informal agreement with Tunisia (a so-called "exchange of notes").[1064] While the details of this agreement remained secret, the objective of the collaboration was clear: staunching the flow of irregular migrants and facilitating the repatriation of Tunisian that had illegally entered Italy after the entry into force of the Decree of April 5. Far from representing an isolated action, the agreement between Italy and Tunisia fitted a broader context: a bilateral practice of migration control by sea, that already countered other initiatives of this kind, such as a previous readmission

---

1060 <http://www.libertaciviliimmigrazione.dlci.interno.gov.it/it/governance-dellaccoglienza> (traduzione mia).

1061 Council Directive 2001/55/EC of July 20, 2001 on minimum standards for giving temporary protection in the event of a mass influx of displaced persons and on measures promoting a balance of efforts between Member States in receiving such persons and bearing the consequences thereof.

1062 Decree of the President of the Council, April 5, 2011, *Misure di protezione temporanea per i cittadini stranieri affluiti dai Paesi nordafricani.*

1063 Decree of the President of the Council of Ministries, October 6, 2011, *Proroga dei permessi di soggiorno rilasciati per motivi umanitari* <http://www.protezionecivile.gov.it/resources/cms/documents/DPCM_proroga_permessi_di_soggiorno.pdf>.

1064 Ministry of Foreign Affairs, Press Release, *Emergenza Immigrazione: Accordo Italia-Tunisia su sbarchi e rimpatri, April* 6, 2011 <http://www.esteri.it/MAE/IT/Sala.Stampa/ArchivioNotizie/ Approfondimenti/2011/04/20110406_AccordoItaliaTunisia.htm>.

agreement with Tunisia dating back 1998 and the "Treaty on Friendship, Cooperation and Partnership" signed with Libya in 2008, completed in 2009 with the Memorandum of Implementation, and confirmed in its contents by the he National Transitional Council of Libya (NTC) in June 2011.[1065]

The legal status of migrants was thus decided according to a temporal and geographical fracture. Having landed to Italy before or after April 5 became a legally relevant criteria to identify migrants coming from Tunisia as, respectively, in need of protection or illegal (when lacking the necessary requirements to remain in Italy). The very same simplified procedure also affected the peculiar situations of migrants coming from Sub-Saharan Africa or Asia who were working in Lybia and reached Italy after the Lybian conflict. Those people whose asylum application was often rejected, were not entitled to receive the temporary protection neither (because non-Tunisian citizens). Thus, they often ended up receiving an order of expulsion.[1066]

2.4.3.3 The EU "refugee crisis" of 2015

In 2015, as effect of various wars in the Middle East, Italy experienced a significantly increased arrival of migrants. Soon afterwards and in the years immediately following, a number of radical reforms were adopted to deal with the record numbers of asylum seekers. Even in this case, the EU impulse was crucial.[1067] These reforms mainly concerned the management of arrivals, the national system of reception and the procedure of international protection.

2.4.3.3.1 The management of arrivals and the hotspots approach

To comply with the European Council's Decisions of September 2015, hotspots were set up, close to the main area of arrivals[1068]. Here, immediately

---

1065 Press release, Ministry of Foreign Affairs of June 17, 2011 <http://www.esteri.it/MAE/IT/SalaStampa/ArchivioNotizie/Approfondimenti/2011/06/20110617_FrattiniCntLibico.htm>.

1066 <https://net.cisl.it/migrantinrete/FOV3-00057A0A/FOV3-00057A0B/I11069883B/__OpenNdx>.

1067 Caponio T., and Cappiali T., "Italian Migration Policy in Times of Multiple Crises: Social and Political Implications" (2018) 23(1) *South European Society and Politics*, 115–132; UN Human Rights Council, Report by the Special Rapporteur on the human rights of migrants, Addendum: Follow-up mission to Italy (December 2–6, 2014) 2015 <http://www.refworld.org/docid/5576e8404.html>.

1068 see footnotes 106 and 107 in this volume.

after the disembarkation, migrants were subjected to procedures of medical screening, pre-identification, registration, photo-identification and fingerprinting by Italian authorities, together with EU agencies (i.e., Frontex, EASO, Europol).[1069]

The system of hotspots succeeded in injecting greater order into migration management (in 2016, the fingerprinting rate reached the 97 %).[1070] However, this result occurred at the price of migrants' rights. Indeed, being obliged to remain available to authorities until the conclusion of the identification procedures, migrants often experienced a "de facto" detention.[1071] Furthermore, hotspots lacked (and still lack) of transparent and harmonized procedures, also because of the absence of appropriate monitoring. As a consequence, migrants in hotspots were often in condition of overcrowding, deprived of basic rights, such as access to healthcare, adequate hygienic standards, information concerning asylum, and, with specific reference to unaccompanied minors, a prompt guardian appointment, as well as dedicated spaces and access to leisure and educational activities. Illegitimate practices such as the

1069 European Commission, Progress report on the European Agenda on Migration, COM(2017) 669, November 15, 2017 <https://ec.europa.eu/home-affairs/sites/home-affairs/files/what-we-do/policies/european-agenda-migration/20171114_progress_report_on_the_european_agenda_on_migration_en.pdf>.

1070 European Court of Auditors, Special report No. 06/2017: EU response to the refugee crisis: the "hotspot" approach <https://www.eca.europa.eu/en/Pages/DocItem.aspx?did=41222>.

1071 Since a law regulating hotspots' activities still lacks, this practice violates Article 13 of the Constitution that reads: "No one may be detained, inspected, or searched nor otherwise subjected to any restriction of personal liberty except by order of the Judiciary stating a reason and only in such cases and in such manner as provided by the law. In exceptional circumstances and under such conditions of necessity and urgency as shall conclusively be defined by the law, the police may take provisional measures that shall be referred within 48 hours to the Judiciary for validation and which, in default of such validation in the following 48 hours, shall be revoked and considered null and void." See on this: Superior Council of the Judiciary (CSM), Advisory opinion required by the Ministry of Justice on the Law Decree No. 13/2017 <https://www.csm.it//documents/21768/41479/parere+sul+dl+13+del+2017+relativo+ai+procedimenti+in+materia+di+protezione+internazionale+(delibera+del+15+marzo+2017)/d5c25710-1d74-a9d4-6fdf-07b2e8c3d06d>, Chamber Inquiry Committee on the system of reception, identification and expulsion, on the condition of detention and on pledged financial resources, Final Report, 2016 <http://www.camera.it/_dati/leg17/lavori/documentiparlamentari/IndiceETesti/022bis/006/INTERO.pdf>.

use of force in obtaining fingerprints and the issuing of orders to leave the country without any proper hearing or access to the asylum procedure were, and still are, time to time, alleged by many organizations.[1072]

Recently, a fierce condemnation of these practices came from the European Court of Human Rights, in the decision held on March 30, 2023[1073] where violation of Articles 3, 5 and 13 of the Convention, as well as Article 4 of the Protocol No. 4 to the Convention, has been ascertained in relation to the situation suffered by four Tunisian citizens who, in October 2017, had been rescued at sea and transferred to the hotspot on the island of Lampedusa. Furthermore, Italy was condemned again in two rulings concerning some unaccompanied foreign minors who suffered inhuman and degrading treatments.[1074]

2.4.3.3.2 Reforms meant to restructure the national reception system

The second most important reform addressed the national asylum system, that in 2015 resulted unprepared and underequipped to ensure protection and accommodation to a considerably increased number of asylum seekers. With the aim to restructure the national reception system, while transposing the EU Reception Directive, the Legislative Decree No. 142/2015 was published. Its purpose was to assign centrality to the SPRAR system, that is the "Italian model of decentralized and integrated reception."[1075] To this end, a two tyer system was set up, entailing: a) a first phase, in governmental first-line reception facilities, where asylum seeker were subject to operations of

---

1072 Senate extraordinary Committee on human rights, Report on centers of identification and expulsion, 2017 <https://www.senato.it/application/xmanager/projects/leg17/file/repository/commissioni/dirittiumaniXVII/allegati/Cie_rapporto_aggiornato_2_gennaio_2017.pdf>; Cild, Asgi and Indiewatch, *Hotspot e Centri di Permanenza per i Rimpatri Violazioni dei diritti umani e dei diritti di difesa dei migranti* (2018) <https://cild.eu/wp-content/uploads/2018/04/Dossier-Lampedusa.pdf>; Mangiaracina A., Una «nuova» forma di detenzione per l'identificazione dei migranti. Note a margine del d.l. n. 13/2017, Materiali per una storia della cultura giuridica (2017) 589–606.

1073 European Court of Human Rights, *J.A. and Others v. Italy*, March 30, 2023, case No. 21329/18.

1074 European Court of Human Rights, *Darboe and Camara v. Italy*, July 21, 2022, case No. 5797/17; European Court of Human Rights, *A.T. and others v. Italy*, November 23, 2023, case No. 47287/17.

1075 <https://www.retesai.it/wp-content/uploads/2016/07/sprar_description.pdf>.

identification, registration of the asylum application and assessment of the health conditions art. 8, 9 and 10) and b) a second phase, in reception centers belonging to the so-called SPRAR network, where asylum applicants and refugees could gain access to further services and integration projects (art. 14).

Nonetheless, the implementation of the model designed by law fell short of expectations. In the lack of available places in the "ordinary system" of the SPRAR network, many asylum applicants were accommodated in large-scale buildings (CARA) or in extraordinary reception centers (CAS) (art. 11). The latter, firstly conceived by the law as an extraordinary measure of last resort, has more and more become the backbone of the national protection system. In September 2016, out of 162.000 available places in reception facilities, only 26.000 were provided within the SPRAR network, against 136.000 in CAS or CARA.[1076] In December 2017, 80.9 % of asylum seekers were accommodated in CAS or other temporary reception facilities (Chamber Inquiry Committee 2017:98). Still, in 2022, places in CAS covered the 60 % of the entire reception system in Italy.[1077] Differently from SPRAR, CAS reception facilities are not subject to monitoring and control from the central government. There are no uniform procedures and standards as well as clear requirements of competence for the staff working therein. When CAS are involved, procedures of selection sometimes lack transparency and accountability, with cases of direct assignment instead of open public tender procedures. This resulted, and still results, in a high heterogeneity of the standard of services provided, not always in line with international and constitutional principles protecting migrants' fundamental rights.[1078]

1076 Facchini D., "Il sistema di protezione e accoglienza che ancora non c'è. Le proposte del Tavolo asilo" (June 24, 2022) *Altraeconomia* <https://altreconomia.it/il-sistema-di-protezione-e-accoglienza-che-ancora-non-ce-le-proposte-del-tavolo-asilo/>.

1077 Centriditalia, Un fallimento annunciato, 2023 <https://www.openpolis.it/il-fallimento-annunciato-dellaccoglienza-dei-migranti-in-italia/#e-online-il-nuovo-rapporto-centri-ditalia-un-fallimento-annunciato>. For further details see also par. 3.5.

1078 Banca d'Italia, I rifugiati e i richiedenti asilo in Italia, nel confronto europeo, 2017 <https://www.bancaditalia.it/pubblicazioni/qef/2017-0377/QEF_377_17.pdf>; Oxfam, La lotteria dell'accoglienza. Il Sistema dell'emergenza permanente, 2017 <https://www.oxfamitalia.org/wp-content/uploads/2017/11/La-Lotteria-Italia-dellaccoglienza_Report-Oxfam_8_11_2017_Final.pdf>. Furthermore, this led to system of corruption and mafia infiltration. See among the others Nadeau B. L., *Roadmap to Hell: Sex, Drugs and Guns on the Mafia Coast* (London: Oneworld

Furthermore, an additional layer of uncertainty also came from the legal reforms that were approved in the framework 2018–2023, by different political forces, with opposed aims. Indeed, in 2018, the so-called Salvini Decree excluded asylum seekers from the SPRAR system (renamed in SIPROIMI and reserved only to refugees and unaccompanied minors), while curtailing public funds and, thus, the number and quality of services provided therein (art. 12). The national protection status based on humanitarian grounds was eliminated,[1079] thus enlarging the number of undocumented migrants (art. 1).[1080] For asylum applicants, accommodated in extraordinary centers, services were dramatically reduced to a minimum standard: shelter, food, essential legal and linguistic support.

In late October 2020, the Law Decree No. 130/2020 was approved with a different aim: reinforcing the national ordinary system of reception and widening the pool of its potential beneficiaries. According to the Decree, also asylum seekers had the right to be accommodated in the new "System of reception and integration (the so called SAI)," to receive an ample range of services, such as sanitary assistance, social and psychological support, cultural and linguistic mediation, course of Italian language and legal assistance (Article 4(3) b). Furthermore, it introduced a new form of "special protection" (Article 1 (1) e) to grant protection to those who were not eligible for international protection but had nonetheless the right to be protected against removal under the obligations derived by international refugee or human rights instruments.

Publications, 2018). For instance, in large-scale buildings, such as CARA of Mineo and the Sant'Anna reception centre in the Isola di Capo Rizzuto in Calabria, asylum seekers not only faced inhuman conditions, but they were also subjected to constant threats of sexual and labor exploitation, or even human trafficking.

1079 The "humanitarian protection" was a national protection status granted to those who were not eligible for international protection but endangered by "serious reasons of humanitarian nature" (Article 5, Legislative Decree No. 286/1998). The Salvini Decree replaced the humanitarian protection (which had a quite broad spectrum of application) with a set of temporary, more restrictive, legal statuses: a) "special protection" grounded on the principle of *non-refoulement*; b) severe medical issues; c) environmental disasters; d) acts of particular civil value; e) "special cases" targeting victims of trafficking, labor exploitation and domestic violence.

1080 According to the estimate of ISMU and ISPI, migrants who found themselves "outside the law" increased from 562.000 to almost 700.000 in 2020. See Cesareo V., "The Challenges of the Pandemic," in V. Cesareo (ed), *The 26 Italian Report on Migrations* (ISMU Foundation, 2020) 9.

The new law clearly mentions those who would face a risk of torture or inhuman or degrading treatment if returned to their country of origin and those who would face a violation of their right to family and private life if removed from the Italian territory.

As it will be further illustrated (3.5.2.), this frame was reversed again in 2023, when the access to the national system of reception was curtailed again for asylum seekers, together with the range and standard of services provided for them.

2.4.3.3.3 Reforms aimed at speeding up the international protection procedure

On a different side, another important reform was approved in 2017, aimed at boosting and fastening the international protection procedure. The Law Decree No. 13/2017 (converted into Law No. 46/2017) increased the number of Territorial Commission, the administrative entities competent to determine the refugee status in Italy, and changed its composition, now made of highly qualified officers depending on the Ministry of Interior.[1081] Reforms also addressed the judicial procedure occurring in case of appeal against the rejection of asylum application from the Territorial Commission. The law introduced 26 specialized court sections within the ordinary jurisdiction, competent to exclusively deal with issued related to asylum and immigration law (Article 8). Besides this, the Law Decree No. 13/2017 removed one stage of appeal from the procedure for international protection (Article 6(13)). Hence, in case of a first rejection of the asylum application, the asylum seeker could only appeal before the Court of Cassation, which, however, cannot inquire into the essence of the case, but only ensure the correct application of the law. Moreover, this law excluded that the appeal could automatically suspend the effects of the decision, required instead the request for a formal suspension. Finally, the Law Decree provided that judges had to base their decision upon the video recording of the asylum applicant interview at the Territorial Commission, without cross-examination, while the hearing of the asylum applicant was admitted only in exceptional cases, such as when the videotaping is not available or if the personal interview is considered essential

[1081] It was previously composed by a representative of: UNHCR, the Ministry of the Interior, the competent Police Headquarter and the local municipality.

to clarify some aspects (Article 6). These reforms curtailed fundamental procedural guarantees for asylum seekers.[1082]

2.4.3.4 The covid emergency and the regularization

To respond to the rapid rise of infections and deaths provoked by the Covid-19 pandemic, the Italian government declared the state of emergency[1083] and approved several measures to limit the circulation of persons, with blanket curfew for long period of time upon the entire population.[1084] These limitations did not hit all citizens in the same way: undocumented migrants, due to their vulnerable (legal) conditions were among the most affected by the pandemic crisis. Living on the street or in overcrowded occupied buildings, they were often excluded from any public housing support. Furthermore, fearing to be stopped by the police and returned home, undocumented migrants also experienced difficulties to access the health service whose standards and addressees, in the lack of a national minimum standard, were heterogeneously regulated from region to region.

The restrictionist approach of the Salvini Decree, coupled with a securitization narrative, showed some of its most negative implications when the pandemic crisis exploded. As mentioned, as effect of the Salvini Decree, not only the number of undocumented migrants increased (mainly due to the elimination of the humanitarian residence permit), but also the condition of asylum seekers worsened. Only admitted to extraordinary reception centers, they were often accommodated in large and overcrowded facilities where covid hotbed could easily spread.[1085] The same applied for repatriations centers (the so-called CPR), where migrants were detained in the absence of the

---

1082 ASGI and Magistratura democratica, Decreto-legge 17 febbraio 2017, n. 13 (Disposizioni urgenti per l'accelerazione dei procedimenti in materia di protezione internazionale, nonché per il contrasto dell'immigrazione illegale) (2017) <http://www.magistraturademocratica.it/mdem/upy/farticolo/md_asgi_dl_13_2017.pdf>.

1083 Delibera del consiglio dei ministri 31 gennaio 2020, Dichiarazione dello stato di emergenza in conseguenza del rischio sanitario connesso all'insorgenza di patologie derivanti da agenti virali trasmissibili.

1084 Decreto-legge 25 marzo 2020, n. 19, Misure urgenti per fronteggiare l'emergenza epidemiologica da COVID-19, art. 2 a.

1085 Carlotti S., "Migration Policy and Health Insecurity Italy's Response to COVID-19 and the Impact of the Security Decree," (2/2020) *Rivista Trimestrale di Scienza dell'Amministrazione*.

necessary medical assistance and, more in general, the basic equipment to deal with covid infections.[1086]

Meanwhile, on April 7, 2020, the government adopted a decree which classified Italian harbors as unsafe places for persons rescued outside the Italian SAR by ships flying a foreign flag, for the entire duration of the emergency. A new practice was inaugurated to deal with these cases, that of the "quarantine ships." Based on Decree no. 1287/2020 of the Head of the Civil Protection Department, the Department for Civil Liberties and Immigration of the Ministry of the Interior together with the Italian Red Cross had the power to isolate ships and impose a "health surveillance" period.[1087] Soon the use of Quarantine ships was extended also to migrants arriving to the national territory independently. Also their functions were widened to comprehend operations of migrants' identification and registration. The legitimacy of these conducts, and particularly migrants' isolation and monitoring limitations, was contested by many organizations. Quarantine ships became a sort of "floating hotspots," i.e., "spaces of temporary confinement while decisions were made on whether arriving migrants were eligible to apply for asylum or should be deported before their applications were processed."[1088]

Meanwhile, the general limitation of the freedom of movement also had implications on the labor market of UE countries, particularly in sectors that heavily relied on migrant labor supply, such as agriculture.[1089] Italy responded to this crisis of migrant labor forces adopting a large-scale regularization with the Law Decree No. 34/2020 (the "Relaunch Decree"), converted into Law No. 77/2020. Two further aims were proclaimed by the Law Decree No. 34/2020:

1086 ASGI, Coronavirus, avvocati e associazioni al Ministero dell'Interno: sospendere gli ingressi e chiudere i CPR. *ASGI*, March 14, 2020 <https://www.asgi.it/notizie/coronavirus-cpr/> (May 30, 2020).

1087 In April 2020, 183 migrants were transferred to the cruise ferry, *Rubattino*, where they were quarantined for nearly 20 days. In May 2020, the ship Moby Zazà substituted the *Rubattino* and other ships were added afterwards. Montagna N., "Quarantine Ships as Spaces of Bordering: The Securitization of Migration Policy in Italy During the COVID-19 Pandemic" (2024) 58(2) *International Migration Review*, 499–521 <https://doi.org/10.1177/01979183231154560>.

1088 ibid.

1089 Sommaribas A., and Nienaber B., "Migration and Mobility of Third-Country National Labor Workers to an Inside Europe During the Covid-19 Pandemic—A Legal Analysis" (2021) 9(22) *Comparative Migration Studies*.

by reducing the number of migrants who were more exposed to the virus, i.e., undocumented migrants, the measure would have increased both the protection of the general public health as well as migrant's human rights.

The law provided two paths for the regularization of undocumented workers. The first was a work permit granted to those undocumented who were working without a regular contract, upon their employers' application. The second provided the possibility to obtain a 6-months temporary permit to find a new job to those unemployed migrants who could demonstrate to have previously lawfully worked in the country. Based on a political compromise, the regularization soon showed the loopholes of its conceptualization and implementation. First and foremost, the measure did not allow for a generalized regularization but focused only on some specific categories of workers: agricultural, domestic and care, leaving aside crucial sectors, such as tourism and construction. The regularization measure also contained bureaucratic constraints, such as, among others, a requirement to prove the presence in Italy prior to March 8, 2020 or the employment in the listed sectors before October 31, 2019. Those working without a regular contract could only turn to the first regularization path, which put everything in the hands of employers, thus exposing migrants to possible abusive practices, such as requests of money or blackmail.

At the end of June 2024, only 74 % of applications has been examined,[1090] leaving many migrants (and their employees) in a legal limbo.

2.4.3.5 The current "state of emergency": the Ukraine war and beyond

2.4.3.5.1 The state of emergency declared after the Ukraine war

Immediately after the beginning of the war in Ukraine, on February 28, 2022 the government declared the state of emergency "to ensure assistance to the Ukrainian population on national territory as a consequence of the current serious international crisis.[1091] On this normative basis, the head of

---

1090 Ero straniero, La sanatoria senza fine (2024) <https://erostraniero.it/sanatoria-senza-fine/>.

1091 Delibera del Consiglio dei Ministri del 28 febbraio 2022—Dichiarazione dello stato di emergenza in relazione all'esigenza di assicurare soccorso ed assistenza alla popolazione ucraina sul territorio nazionale in conseguenza della grave crisi internazionale in atto <https://www.protezionecivile.gov.it/it/normativa/delibera-cdm-del-28-febbraio-2022-emergenza-ucraina-0/>.

the civil protection[1092] issued a series of decrees aimed at establishing an emergency system of reception, also in derogations from the current legislation.[1093] New facilities (almost three thousand) dedicated to Ukrainians were rapidly opened in the ordinary system of reception (the so-called SAI), without complying with the rule of the open public tender. Meanwhile, new ordinances broadened and boosted services offered in extraordinary centers (the so-called CAS) to make them more adequate to accommodate Ukraine citizens fleeing from the war.

To supplement the network of SAI and CAS centers, Decree-Law No. 21 of March 21, 2022 identified an additional reception model to be implemented with the support of municipalities and third sector and social private entities: the so-called "widespread reception." A call was issued on April 11, 2022 to identify suitable facilities for the reception of Ukrainians (co-housing measures with families or accommodation made available by private entities, including hotels), up to a maximum of 15,000 places. Subsequently, Decree-Law No. 50 of May 17, 2022 provided for the possibility of increasing this network of widespread reception for an additional 15,000 places. In line with this approach, an economic contribution has been provided to municipalities that hosted Ukrainian citizens to strengthen their offer of social services. This contribution was provided by the Civil Protection Ordinance 927/2022, which also defined the criteria for territorial distribution based on the number of Ukrainian residents in relation to the number of residents. This model of "widespread reception" represented the main Italian response to the Ukraine crisis together with the "subsistence contribution," that is a contribution of 300 euros per month for each Ukrainian citizen holding temporary protection who has found independent accommodation. In short time, thus, a structured reception based on a clear "Plan for the reception and assistance to the population

1092 As already said, the civil protection is the entity competent to manage emergency situations.

1093 For a detailed list of the normative provisions issued by the civil protection, see <https://emergenze.protezionecivile.gov.it/it/pagina-base/il-sistema-di-accoglienza-e-assistenza-alla-popolazione-ucraina/>.

from Ukraine" was set up, while ensuring transparency, with a precise dashboard on reception, constantly updated.[1094]

The relevance of these measures was partly overshadowed by their "ethnicization," since migrants coming from other countries experiencing the same need for protection were not entitled to the same legal treatment. Furthermore, some loopholes were reported, especially concerning the accommodation in families who soon suffered from the lack of equipment and support from the local municipalities in terms, for instance, of cultural mediators, interpreters and psychological assistance.[1095]

Meanwhile, following the decision of the EU Council to trigger the Directive 2001/55/EC on temporary protection, the Italian government published the Decree of the President of the Council of Ministers of March 28, 2022 on "temporary protection measures for persons from Ukraine as a consequence of the ongoing events of war." The temporary protection was reserved only to Ukrainian citizens and third-country nationals who in Ukraine were holders of residence permits for international protection or EU long-term residence permits. Furthermore, only people who fled Ukraine after February 24, 2022 could obtain a temporary protection, thus excluding those who had already left the country before. Furthermore, the temporary protection measures, proclaimed by the Eu Council, will end on March 5, 2025. The Decree that transposed the Directive does not regulate the legal status of Ukrainians after that date. Thus, Ukrainians holding a residence permit for temporary protection risk entering in a legal limbo after March 5. Currently the only option is applying for the international protection, with the danger to congestion the Italian system of protection, already in difficulty.

These limitations nevertheless, since the adoption of the Decree of March 28, 2022, police headquarters (competent to issue residence permits) received guidance to establish a dedicated desk with direct access for Ukrainians only. Through ad hoc provisions, thus, Ukrainians could obtain a quick issuance of the residence permit for temporary protection.

1094 <https://mappe.protezionecivile.gov.it/it/mappe-e-dashboards-emergenze/mappe-e-dashboards-ucraina/>.

1095 Oxfam, Protetti o no? (2023) <https://www.oxfamitalia.org/wp-content/uploads/2023/11/PROTETTI_ONO_OXFAM_3_11_23-1.pdf>.

2.4.3.5.2 *The rapid succession of reforms and the declaration of a new "state of emergency"*

Since its election, the far-right-wing government currently in power approved numerous reforms on immigration and international protection. The Law Decree No. 1/23 of January 2, 2023, on "Urgent provisions for the management of migration flows," was approved to regulate the activities of NGOs carrying out search and rescue operations in the Mediterranean Sea. The law confirmed the power of the Minister of the Interior (in agreement with the Minister of Defence and the Minister of Infrastructure and Transport, after having informed the President of the Council of Ministers) to restrict or prohibit the transit and stopover of ships in the Italian territorial sea, unless they are military or on non-commercial government service. By subjecting the NGOs activities of search and rescue to a number of conditions and requirements, the law ended up making extremely difficult and limiting the saving of migrants live.[1096]

Some months later, the Decree-Law No. 20/2023 of March 10, 2023, on "Urgent provisions on the subject of legal entry flows of foreign workers and the prevention of and fight against irregular immigration" modified ample parts of the Consolidated Law on Immigration, the Qualification Decree, the Procedures Decree and the Reception Decree, in a restrictive sense. Paradoxically, this law was triggered by a sea tragedy that occurred at the Italian coast in 2023, during the night between February 25 and 26, where about 180 migrants lost their lives.[1097]

Among the main changes, the requirements to obtain the residence permit for special protection (grounded on humanitarian reasons) were severely restricted, eliminating the explicit reference to the right to private and family life enshrined in the European Convention of Human Rights (at least in theory, because Italy still abides by those constitutional and international principles on which this form of protection relies on). Furthermore, the possibility to convert the residence permit for special protection was eliminated,

---

1096 See for further details <https://www.asgi.it/asilo-e-protezione-internazionale/decreto-legge-1-2023/>.

1097 Giuffrida A., ""The Beach Is Like a Cemetery": Italian Village Grapples with Shipwreck Aftermath" (February 27, 2023) *The Guardian* <https://www.theguardian.com/world/2023/feb/27/italy-shipwreck-calabria-migration>.

thus making the system more rigid and legal routes to maintain a regular legal status less accessible and stable.[1098]

Most of the reforms approved with the Decree concerned the national reception system, which received a strong twist toward an "extraordinary" regime. First, the Decree amended the rules on the reception of asylum seekers, excluding them (again) from the national ordinary reception and integration system, (with the sole exception of vulnerable migrants and those who have entered Italy through humanitarian corridors). Services to be provide in first-line reception centers were reduced: here, migrants are not guaranteed psychological support, legal information and language courses which becomes only optional. Furthermore, new exceptions were provided to the maximum capacity of reception facilities for asylum seekers in extraordinary reception centers, to activate in urgent cases. On the same vein, a new type of reception facility was created: the so-called temporary centers, which can be activated by the prefectures in case no places are available in extraordinary reception centers (CAS). The legal nature of these centers poses many challenges. Since the insufficiency of places is at the basis also for the activation of CAS, it has become difficult to detect the difference between the two centers (extraordinary or temporary). The generic wording of the law is coupled with scarcely transparent procedures. For instance, the general rule that requires open public tenders to determine the contractors of reception centers can be derogated when extraordinary centers are at stake. All this inevitably reduces guarantees and increases the risk of infringements of migrants' rights. For instance, in few months, among the more than 1,500 temporary centers that have been opened, there are hotels, former vaccination hubs, gyms, tents that are hardly suitable to guarantee adequate reception.[1099]

Contextually, the Law Decree introduced new hypothesis of detentions (for those asylum seekers subjected to border procedure in hotspots),[1100] extended maximum terms of detention and further shortened the procedural

---

1098 The possibility to convert the residence permit has been eliminated also in the case of residence permit for natural calamities and healthcare.

1099 Centriditalia, Un fallimento annunciato, 2023.

1100 The Decree introduces the possibility to subject asylum seekers to detention when they have not presented a valid passport or other equivalent document, or do not provide for suitable financial guarantee. The Court of Cassation has recently questioned the compatibility of this provision with the Reception Conditions Directive

deadlines for the expulsion of foreigners from the territory of the State. By enlarging the situations that can led to detention as well as the potential recipients of this measure, progressively transforming detention centers into reception facilities.[1101]

This approach was further promoted with the declaration of the six-month state of emergency made by the government on April 11, 2023.[1102] Even if numbers of arrivals through the Mediterranean routes were similar to those of 2018, in the words of the Prime Minister, the state of emergency was presented as necessary to "provide more effective and timely responses to the management of flows." Extended three times for further six months, in force of the decision of the Council of Ministers of October 10, 2024, the state of emergency will expire on April 10, 2025.[1103] Under the umbrella of the state of emergency, extraordinary fundings and powers were envisaged further worsening the lack of transparency surrounding this area. Thereafter, a new law qualified hotspot, centers and ordinary and extraordinary reception centers as "works for defence and national security," thus allowing for derogations from general rules on public tenders, construction, landscape, city planning.[1104] Very recently, the European Committee for the prevention of torture, after having visited numerous CPR, highlighted "several shortcomings, such as the absence of any rigorous and independent monitoring of such interventions and the lack of an accurate recording of injuries sustained by detained persons or of

---

(art. 8 and 9) by referring the case to the CJEU (interlocutory order of February 8, 2024, decision n. 3562/2024, R.G. 20674/2023).

1101 Campesi G., "Seeking Asylum in Times of Crisis" (March 2018) 37(1) *Refugee Survey Quarterly*, 44.

1102 Delibera del Consiglio dei Ministri 11 aprile 2023, Dichiarazione dello stato di emergenza in conseguenza dell'eccezionale incremento dei flussi di persone migranti in ingresso sul territorio nazionale attraverso le rotte migratorie del Mediterraneo <https://www.gazzettaufficiale.it/eli/id/2023/05/08/23A02609/sg>.

1103 Delibera del Consiglio dei Ministri 10 ottobre 2024, Proroga dello stato di emergenza in conseguenza dell'eccezionale incremento dei flussi di persone migranti in ingresso sul territorio nazionale attraverso le rotte migratorie del Mediterraneo <https://www.gazzettaufficiale.it/eli/gu/2024/11/11/264/sg/pdf>.

1104 Camera dei Deputati, servizio studi, Politiche di coesione, rilancio dell'economia del Mezzogiorno e Immigrazione, D.L. 124/2023 / A.C. 1416, Dossier No. 60—Elementi per la valutazione degli aspetti di legittimità costituzionale 24 ottobre 2023 <https://documenti.camera.it/leg19/dossier/Pdf/Cost060.pdf>.

any assessment as to their origin."[1105] Finally, in October, a new normative provision, introduced with Law Decree No. 133 of 2023, allowed, albeit for limited periods, the reception of unaccompanied foreign minors aged 16 years or over, in conditions of promiscuity with adults. The mass arrival of migrants in a reduced period of time is now the basis to allow authorities to conduct age assessment procedures with "anthropometric surveys or other health assessments, including radiographic ones," in derogation from the general rule providing to adopt socio-health assessments, carried out by multidisciplinary and multi-professional teams. These amendments[1106] are in open conflict with international rules and neglect the condemnations that Italy recently received from the European Court of Human Rights for its illegitimate practices concerning unaccompanied minors.[1107]

2.4.3.5.3 The Agreement Italy-Albania and the issue of the "safe third countries of origin"

In November 2023, the Italian government signed an agreement (hereinafter also "protocol") with Albania, with the objective to "reinforce the collaboration in migration."[1108] According to the Protocol, ratified by Law No. 14/2024, the access and stay of migrants in the centers in Albania are allowed only "for the purpose of carrying out border or return procedures provided for by Italian and European legislation" (Article 4, sect. 3). Thus, those procedures will be assessed on Albanian territory, but under Italian jurisdiction. The Italian legislation allows for an accelerated procedure[1109] for the examination

1105 The European Committee for the Prevention of Torture and Inhuman or Degrading Treatment or Punishment, Report to the Italian government on the visit to Italy, December 13, 2024 <https://rm.coe.int/1680b2c7e7>.

1106 The amendments have been introduced by Law Decree No. 133 of October 5, 2023 to Article 19 (3 bis) and Article 19 bis (6) of Law Decree No. 142/2015.

1107 Darboe and Camara v. Italy, No. 5797/17, ECtHR (First Section), July 21, 2022 <https://hudoc.echr.coe.int/fre#{%22itemid%22:[%22001-218424%22]}>.

1108 Protocollo tra il Governo della Repubblica italiana e il Consiglio dei ministri della Repubblica di Albania per il rafforzamento della collaborazione in materia migratoria <https://www.esteri.it/wp-content/uploads/2023/12/PROTOCOLLO-ITALIA-ALBANIA-in-materia-migratoria.pdf>.

1109 The accelerated procedure (together with the border procedure that can be carried out immediately upon disembarkation or tracing of the asylum seeker) provides for reduced deadlines for examining the application for international protection. The

of asylum applications directly in the border or transit zones in two specific cases identified by Article 28-bis of Legislative Decree 25/2008, paragraph 2: letter b) when the migrant makes its application for international protection, after having been apprehended for evading or attempting to evade the relevant controls; letter b bis): when the application for international protection is made by an applicant from a country designated as a safe country of origin.[1110]

Beyond the high costs required by the construction and management of the two centers activated in Albania, in Shengjin and in Gjader, the Italy-Albania Protocol had raised many doubts for its compatibility with EU law and national constitutional principles. These concerns triggered the reactions of judges competent to examine and validate the detention of migrants held in Albania. Their decisions, which also brought to a preliminary reference to the EU Court of Justice,[1111] halted the implementation of the Italy-Albania Protocol, currently suspended.

---

decision that rejects the asylum application can be challenged before the Court in terms reduced by half compared to ordinary applications (15 days instead of 30 days) and without the automatic suspension of the effects of the challenged decision.

1110 The law Decree No. 113/2018, had added to Article 2 of DLgs 25/2008, Article 2-bis "Safe countries of origin," providing that "by decree of the Minister of Foreign Affairs and International Cooperation, in agreement with the Ministers of the Interior and of Justice, the list of safe countries of origin shall be adopted on the basis of the criteria set out in § 2. The list of safe countries of origin shall be updated periodically and notified to the European Commission." By a decree of the Minister of Foreign Affairs and International Cooperation (MAECI) adopted on October 4, 2019, the first list of safe third countries was issued, which was subsequently updated by a decree of the MAECI dated March 17, 2023 and by a decree of the MAECI dated May 7, 2024. The list of "safe country of origins" has been incorporated by Decree-Law No. 158/2024, containing "urgent provisions on the subject of procedures for the recognition of international protection." The application for international protection submitted by a third-country citizen coming from one of the countries included in the list is subject to the so-called accelerated procedure. It is worth to highlight that the institution of the list of safe countries of origin comes from the UE law (art. 29, 30, 31 of Directive 2005/85/EC and art. 37 of Directive 2013/32/EU).

1111 Tribunal of Rome, interlocutory order, November 11, 2024.

2.4.4 Conclusive remarks: tools, reasons and implications surrounding the construction of a regime of permanent emergency

In a recent declaration, the Ministry of Interior of the current far-right government said that "in the last years, at least since the Arab Spring onwards, the migration issue has appeared to the public opinion and government alike, essentially, indeed almost exclusively, as a situation of crisis to which respond in an emergency."[1112] Interestingly enough, this statement crystallizes the link between migration and emergency, while migration as a phenomenon to a phenomenon the deficiencies of its management. At the same time, though, the Ministry's words also sound as an explicit acknowledgment of the way in which migration has been "essentially, indeed almost exclusively" framed and addressed in the last years by the national legal discourses, normative provisions and practices related to it.

This conclusion is fully supported by evidence emerged in this contribution, which show how the Italian policy on migration is structurally affected by deficient and ineffective tools of planning, coordination, management and monitoring. What often lacks is a "national control room," able to ensure an orderly, safe and efficient governance of migration. The high governmental instability that has traditionally featured the Italian political landscape may certainly contribute explaining this data. Another relevant element is related to the multiplicity of actors involved in it, composing what has been named "a battleground field."[1113] For instance, the EU-driven reforms on asylum are paradigmatic of this trend, as well as the role of political negotiations between Italy and other EU Member States about the management of migration. Similarly, numerous institutional entities populates the domestic migration domain. Each entity (with its own mandate and mission) is competent and

---

[1112] Informativa urgente del governo in ordine all'eccezionale incremento del fenomeno migratorio, con particolare riguardo alla situazione presso l'isola di Lampedusa (my translation) 17 novembre 2023 <https://www.interno.gov.it/it/stampa-e-comunicazione/sindacato-ispettivo-parlamentare/informativa-urgente-governo-ordine-alleccezionale-incremento-fenomeno-migratorio-particolare-riguardo-alla-situazione-presso-lisola-lampedusa>.

[1113] Campomori F., Ambrosini M., "Multilevel Governance in Trouble: The Implementation of Asylum Seekers" Reception in Italy as a Battleground" (2020) 8(22) *Comparative Migration Studies*, 1–19.

responsible for single apparatus of the complex migration machine. The compresence between the Ministry of the Interior and the Ministry of Labour, which share key aspects of migration policies, clearly exemplifies this. At the same time, as seen, Regions detain important competences on the governance of migration, while a big role is played also by local municipalities and the third sector. To further complicate (and fragmentate) the context, even the action of the judiciary cannot be underestimated.

In the lack of a sound and coherent coordination, management and monitoring at the central level, a condition of pervasive and structural uncertainty surrounds the legal status of migrants throughout the country, both on a substantial and procedural level.

It would be simplistic to read this uncertainty as the unintended consequence of the inherent complexity of governing migrations. Indeed, this chapter on the Italian management of migration in times of emergency show that this uncertainty is also favored, alimented, and sometimes, even created, by the very same institutions that should work to eliminate it. Again, the words of the current Ministry of Interior resonate, when in Parliament he acknowledges the limited compliance of the Italian migration policy with the crucial principle of legal certainty. He explains this breach with the failure of past national migration policies to tackle irregular migration and promote legal migration channels. Nonetheless, these policy gaps have not been closed, but rather exacerbated by recent policies.

From the analysis conducted thus far it is possible to detect the most relevant legal mechanisms through which the emergency logic is put forward.

First, the Law Decree is the main instrument used by the Italian legislator to regulate migration. In the current legislature (which started on October 22, 2022), 9 Law Decrees concerning migration have been adopted, often covering very different aspects of migration, with a random approach. These continuous reforms, coupled with the structural lack of an organic and clear legal framework, hinders a sound and coherent interpretation and application of the laws, subjecting migrants to broad authorities' discretion. Furthermore, beyond reinforcing the idea of migration as an "emergency" issue (Law Decrees may only be adopted by the government in case of necessity and urgency[1114]) the abuse of Law Decrees ends up marginalizing the role

[1114] Article 77 of the Italian Constitution.

of the Parliament, thus curtailing the democratic control and procedural guarantees provided by it.

Secondly, in migration issues, the Italian Parliament is more and more deprived of its central role also as effect of the ample recourse to acts of secondary legislation (by-laws, regulations, ministerial circulars, administrative rules, etc.) and informal acts, such as informal agreements, communications, standard operational procedures (see recently the Italy-Albania Protocol).[1115] This trend has another result: it neutralizes the judicial scrutiny. Other attempt to circumvent the judicial control have been recently put in place by the current government. Against the opinion of the organization representing judges and magistrates in Italy,[1116] the competence to confirm whether or not a migrant can be detained in the Albanian centers has been transferred from judges of the specialized sections on immigration to judges of the Court of Appeal. The fracture between the legislative and judiciary powers on migration issues is more and more open.

An emergency approach also surrounds the national reception system. Despite an "ordinary" system of reception, well elaborated, structured, regulated and monitored, has been set up, the majority of migrants are accommodated in the so-called extraordinary reception centers (recently complemented by the "temporary reception centres"). Here, the possibility

---

1115 Among the others, Nascimbene B., *Diritto degli stranieri*, cit, 140; Bucci G., *Una Circolare per circolare. A proposito delle politiche sull'immigrazione* (2004) <http://www.costituzionalismo.it/articoli/145/>; Gjergji I., "La cittadinanza degli stranieri: una trama scaturita dai 'laboratori segreti' della pubblica amministrazione," in Andreozzi, D., and Tonolo, S. (eds), *La cittadinanza molteplice. Ipotesi e comparazioni, Trieste, EUT Edizioni Università di Trieste* (2016) 25–37; Siccardi C., *I diritti costituzionali dei migranti in viaggio. Sulle rotte del Mediterraneo* (Napoli 2021); Algostino A., "L'esternalizzazione soft delle frontiere e il naufragio della Costituzione" (2017) 1 *Costituzionalismo.it*, 139–182.

1116 According to its Secretary, Salvatore Casciaro, the law will make the "definition of the status of asylum seekers slower, with the risk of prolonging the time these persons stay in Italy even for those who are not entitled to it." Furthermore, he added, the Court of Appeals would be likely to experience bottlenecks and they are "already swamped with work." See ANSA, Italy: Government issues decree amendment in attempt to strengthen Albania plan, November 15, 2024 <https://www.infomigrants.net/en/post/61202/italy-government-issues-decree-amendment-in-attempt-to-strengthen-albania-plan>.

to derogate from the general law (i.e., in matter of public tender) and the low level of transparency result in a very fragmented picture where standards of care and assistance for asylum seekers and refugees vary a lot between the different centers of accommodation and the enjoyment of basic rights becomes "a matter of luck."[1117]

Besides this, the frequent resort to "ex post regularization shemes" show that even a crucial issue such as the creation of legal paths for migration has been addressed by the Italian government through an emergency logic. Indeed, despite their loopholes, these "extraordinary measures" represent the only possibility for numerous migrants that already have an informal job in Italy to regularize their legal status and build a more stable life in the country. The system of annual quota (the so-called Decreto Flussi) has proven unrealistic and unable to ensure a regular stay and job of migrants in the country, as well as respond to the pressing needs of the Italian labor market. Nonetheless, although some little—good but insufficient—reforms recently approved,[1118] it remains the only legal route to reach Italy for work reason.

Finally, the contribution highlights the ambiguities of the emergency lexicon. On the one hand, harsh policy discourses on migration often deflated when moving to the practice,[1119] also due to the social and economic costs and difficulties of the entire system of stopping, detection, deportation and expulsion. On the other hand, evidence denounces how emergency can be detached by "factual" conditions. The government may aptly use the

---

1117 Oxfam, La lotteria dell'accoglienza. Il Sistema dell'emergenza permanente, cit.

1118 See par. 3.5.2 With Legislative Decree 145/2024, entitled "Urgent provisions on the entry into Italy of foreign workers, on the protection and assistance to victims of caporalato, on the management of migration flows and international protection, as well as on the related jurisdictional proceedings," the government introduced specific protection for foreign workers who are victims of particularly exploitative crimes. A new residence permit for special cases has been introduced, to be issued to foreigners who are victims of illicit labor exploitation, pursuant to the new Article 18-ter (which is in addition to the better-known forms of protection under Article 18 and 18-bis of Legislative Decree 286/98 for victims of trafficking and domestic violence).

1119 Ambrosini M., "Surviving Underground: Irregular Migrants, Italian Families, Invisible Welfare" (2012) 21 *International Journal of Social welfare*, 361–371.

emergency legal frame to circumvent international and constitutional obligations and, thus, create and reinforce a “special legal status” of migrants, where basic human rights and procedural guarantees are increasingly replaced by a system of contingent measures and exceptions.[1120]

2.5 Poland

2.5.1 Substantive law (Michał Kowalski)

2.5.1.1 Introductory remarks

The primary objective of this part of the study is to present the system of material and legal guarantees for protecting the rights of foreigners currently in force in the Polish legal order. It is important in this respect to analyze the constitutional standard of protection of foreigners’ rights in the light of the extensive catalog of human rights provided for in the second chapter of the Constitution of the Republic of Poland of April 2, 1997.[1121] Additionally, the analysis should consider how the protection of these fundamental constitutional rights is affected when one of the three states of emergency is declared. The examination and evaluation of these elements will allow for the reconstruction of the substantive legal standard of protection of foreigners’ rights at the constitutional level.

The starting point for these considerations will be the basic constitutional assumptions by which the Republic of Poland ensures the freedoms and rights of a human being and citizen (Article 5), and by which the inherent and inalienable dignity of a human being is recognized to constitute

1120 Pannia P., ““Institutional Uncertainty” as a Technique of Migration Governance: A Comparative Legal Perspective” (2020) 45(4) *DPCE Online* <http://www.dpceonline.it/index.php/dpceonline/article/view/1205>; Pannia P., “Excluded from Guarantees, Excluded from the Community: “Institutional Uncertainty” in the Migration Domain as a Symptom of “Constitutional Degradation,”” in T. Groppi, G. Milani, and V. Carlino (eds), *Framing and Diagnosis Constitutional Degradation. A Comparative Perspective* (Consulta online, 2022).

1121 The Constitution of the Republic of Poland of April 2, 1997 (Dz. U. [Journal of Laws] No. 78, item 483, as amended—hereinafter referred to as the “Constitution of the Republic of Poland,” “the Polish Constitution,” or “the Constitution RP”).

a source of freedoms and rights of a human being and citizen. This dignity is inviolable and its respect and protection is the duty of public authorities (Article 30). The currently binding Polish Constitution, following in the footsteps of many constitutions of former Eastern Bloc countries, contains a very extensive catalog of subjective rights. Some of these rights concern all people, including foreigners, such as the right to life (Article 38), or the prohibition of torture or cruel, inhuman or degrading treatment and punishment (Article 40). Other constitutional subjective rights concern Polish citizens, and mostly pertain to political rights such as the active electoral right (Article 62), membership of a political party (Article 11) or access to the public service (Article 60), including professional military service. The constitutional ground also establishes some specific subjective rights relating exclusively to foreigners, such as the right of asylum and obtaining the status of a foreigner, as it is indicated that foreigners may exercise the right of asylum in the Republic of Poland in accordance with principles specified by statute (Article 56), and a foreigner who seeks protection from persecution in Poland may be granted refugee status in accordance with international agreements binding on the Republic of Poland (Article 57).

In turn, it is stipulated under Article 37 of the Constitution that whoever is under the authority of the Republic of Poland enjoys the freedoms and rights provided for in the Constitution. Exceptions to this principle, relating to foreigners, are defined by law. Two legal acts of statutory rank, namely the Law on foreigners[1122] and the Law on granting protection to foreigners within the territory of the Republic of Poland,[1123] are generally applicable in this respect. The analysis of their selected elements will allow for the presentation of substantive legal guarantees of statutory rank and outlining their implementation of constitutional requirements.

The conclusion of the study will present basic information and statistical data on the current migration situation of Ukrainian citizens due to the war in their country. Indeed, this is an unprecedented situation in the post-war history of Europe. Governmental data from the Office for Foreigners[1124] shows

---

1122 Law of December 12, 2013 on foreigners (Journal of Laws of 2024, item 769).

1123 Law of June 13, 2003 on granting protection to foreigners within the territory of the Republic of Poland (Journal of Laws of 2023, item 1504, as amended).

1124 <https://www.gov.pl/web/udsc/obywatele-ukrainy-w-polsce--aktualne-dane-migracyjne2>.

that one year after the Russian aggression against Ukraine, almost 1 million Ukrainian citizens, mainly women and children, were receiving temporary protection in Poland. A total of 1.4 million people at that time had valid residence permits in the country. Since February 24, 2022, the migration situation in Poland has been dominated by an increased influx of Ukrainian citizens. They are the most numerous group of foreigners in Poland, accounting for more than 80 % of all foreigners settling in the country. Most Ukrainians stay in Poland under temporary protection, which is confirmed by obtaining a PESEL number on the basis of the Law on assistance to citizens of Ukraine in connection with the armed conflict on the territory of that country,[1125] which defines specific principles of legalizing the stay of Ukrainian citizens who arrived in Poland in these circumstances, as well as citizens of Ukraine holding the Pole's Card, who, together with their immediate family, arrived on the territory of the Republic of Poland due to these military actions. According to data from the Office for Foreigners, women and children make up about 87 % of this group. Children and adolescents account for approximately 43 % of Ukrainian citizens with PESEL numbers. Among adults, on the other hand, women account for 77 % of persons.

The government figures indicate that 360,000 Ukrainian citizens hold valid temporary residence permits. The vast majority of these are issued in connection with taking up employment. Slightly more than 65,000, on the other hand, have permanent residence permits or long-term EU resident permits. The territorial distribution of Ukrainian citizens settling in Poland is characterized by a concentration in provinces with large urban agglomerations. The most popular regions are the Mazowieckie voivodeship—21 % of persons (mainly Warsaw), the Dolnośląskie voivodeship—11 % (mainly Wrocław), the Wielkopolskie voivodeship—11 % (mainly Poznań), the Małopolskie voivodeship—10 % (mainly Cracow) and the Śląskie voivodeship—9 %.[1126]

1125 Law of March 12, 2022 on assistance to Ukrainian citizens in connection with the armed conflict on the territory of that country (OJ 2024, item 167 as amended).

1126 Figures do not include persons staying in Poland under a visa-free regime or on the basis of visas (<www.gov.pl>).

2.5.1.2 Constitutional standard

The Constitution provides for the principle of universality of constitutional rights and freedoms, at the same time indicating the possibility of limiting this principle with regard to foreigners.[1127] Pursuant to Article 37(1) Constitution RP, whoever is under the jurisdiction of the Republic of Poland enjoys the freedoms and rights ensured in the Constitution. Admittedly, in accordance with paragraph 2 of this provision, exceptions to this principle relating to foreigners are defined by the Law on foreigners and the Law on the on granting protection to aliens on the territory of the Republic of Poland, thus it may be assumed, in principle, that all human rights provided for in the in the second chapter of the Polish Constitution, which are not civil rights, are enjoyed by foreigners.

In the Polish Constitution, direct or implicit reference to foreigners is made in Articles 55(4) and (5), 56(1) and (2) and 79(2). A foreigner who has been granted asylum may exercise the rights to which foreigners residing on the territory of the Republic of Poland are entitled on the basis of a permit. He/she may then take up employment, study, conduct business activities and apply for social assistance benefits on the same principles as Polish citizens.[1128]

The starting point for presenting the rights to which foreigners are entitled under constitutional regulation is the concept of human dignity. This can already be found in the in the Preamble to the Constitution of the Republic of Poland, where it is indicated that all those who will apply this Constitution for the benefit of the Third Republic are called upon to do so with care for the preservation of the inherent dignity of the person, his or her right to freedom and duty of solidarity with others, and to consider respect for these principles as the unshakable foundation of the Republic of Poland. The normative character of human dignity was granted on the basis of Article 30 of the Constitution, according to which the inherent and inalienable dignity of the person constitutes a source of freedoms and rights of persons and citizens. It is inviolable and its respect and protection is the duty of public authorities. The essence of human dignity is human

---

1127 Tuleja P., in P. Tuleja (ed), *Konstytucja Rzeczpospolitej polskiej. Komentarz* (Warszawa 2023) 137–138.

1128 Laaroussi M., *Prawo cudzoziemców do równego traktowania i niedyskryminacji. Standard konstytucyjny i międzynarodowy oraz jego realizacja na przykładzie Belgii, Maroka i Polski*, unpublished doctoral thesis, 124.

subjectivity (autonomy), and therefore the freedom to act according to one's own will, internal self-determination and worldview, taking into account the autonomy, subjectivity and dignity of others. This also implies the prohibition of subjecting a person to situations or treatment that may undermine that dignity, the prohibition of persecution or discrimination, the prohibition of violating bodily integrity, and the prohibition of interfering with freedom of thought and belief.[1129]

In addition to dignity, which is the starting point for the analysis of the constitutional system for the protection of human rights, including the rights of foreigners, human freedom is mentioned among the general principles. The human right to freedom is already provided for in the Preamble to the Constitution, and its normative development is found in Article 31(1) and (2), according to which human freedom is subject to legal protection and everyone is obliged to respect the freedom and rights of others. No one may be forced to do what the law does not require him or her to do. Human freedom is therefore a value that is subject to legal protection, hence everyone is obliged to respect the freedom and rights of others. From this follows the prohibition of forcing anyone to do what the law, as the basic regulator of social relations, does not prescribe. In essence, this means freedom of human action wherever the law does not impose prohibitions. This is the complete opposite of the situation existing in relation to the state and its organs. An organ of the state acts where and insofar as it has been authorized to do so by the law and acts on a legal basis. Any action of the organs of the state that lacks a legal basis is illegal, for in accordance with Article 7 Constitution RP, the organs of public authority act on the basis and within the limits of the law. In turn, any person may act wherever the law does not prohibit or prohibit a particular action. It may therefore be assumed that such an understanding of the principle of human freedom implies a prohibition on forcing anyone to do what the law does not prescribe and guarantees that human freedom is subject to legal protection. In doing so, however, freedom is of a limited nature, for the freedom of human action must take into account the imperatives of the public interest as well as the need to respect the freedom of others.[1130]

1129 Garlicki L., *Polskie prawo konstytucyjne. Zarys wykładu* (Warszawa 2022) 109.

1130 Garlicki L., *Polskie prawo konstytucyjne* ..., 111.

The last of the general principles provided for under the Constitution relating to human rights, including the rights of foreigners, is the principle of equality. Based on Article 32(1) and (2) of the Polish Constitution, everyone is equal before the law. Everyone has the right to equal treatment by public authorities. No one may be discriminated against in political, social or economic life for any reason. The principle of equality prescribes equal treatment of the subjects of freedoms and rights in the process of applying the law by public authorities (equality before the law), consideration of the principle of equality in the creation of the law (equality under the law) and observance of the primary rule of non-discrimination in political, social and economic life for any reason. It should be noted here that the principle of equality relates to the legal situation and does not therefore include an order to eliminate inequalities of economic, social or cultural origin. This principle should not be seen as precluding the use of compensatory favoritism or positive discrimination for groups in weaker positions (e.g., persons with disabilities, women, or children) aimed at achieving actual equality or so-called positive discrimination toward certain groups of subjects in a weaker position (e.g., persons with disabilities, women or children), which serves the purpose of actual equality. In this connection, the Constitution provides for a number of specific levels that further strengthen the functioning of the general principle of equality and prohibition of discrimination. Thus, it separately formulates the principle of equality between women and men, stipulating on the grounds of Article 33(1) and (2) that a woman and a man in the Republic of Poland have equal rights in family, political, social and economic life. In particular, a woman and a man have an equal right to education, employment and promotion, to equal remuneration for work of equal value, and to social security, as well as to occupy positions, perform functions and obtain public dignities and distinctions. In addition, the Constitution enshrines the principle of equality of the right to property, indicating on the basis of Article 64, paragraphs 1 and 2 that everyone has the right to property, other property rights, and the right of inheritance. Property, other property rights and the right of inheritance shall be subject to equal legal protection for all.[1131]

1131 Garlicki L., *Polskie Prawo konstytucyjne ...*, 113–114.

It should be recalled that with regard to the status of persons who do not have Polish citizenship, i.e., foreigners, the Constitution stipulates that they are the subjects of all rights and freedoms, as well as duties that have not been reserved for citizens by constitutional provisions. Apart from the formulation of basic principles relating to the entire constitutional system of human rights protection, i.e., human dignity, freedom, equality and prohibition of discrimination, the Constitution grants a special status to certain categories of natural persons, particularly to children.[1132] The Polish state is committed to protecting the rights of the child, as mandated by Article 72 of the Constitution, which ensures such protection. Everyone has the right to demand from public authorities the protection of the child against violence, cruelty, exploitation and actions which undermine their moral sense. A child deprived of parental care has the right to care and assistance from public authorities. In the course of establishing the rights of the child, public authorities and those responsible for the child are obliged to listen to and, as far as possible, give priority to the views of the child. The competence and the method of appointment of the Ombudsman for the Rights of the Child are specified by statute.[1133]

In addition, the Constitution provides for the establishment of compulsory education, as Article 70(1) states that everyone has the right to education. Education up to the age of 18 is compulsory. The manner in which compulsory education obligations are fulfilled is determined by law. Most children and young people receive their education in public schools. However, schools other than public schools (private, community) have also been established and developed for some time. The Constitution, while mandating compulsory education until the age of 18, leaves parents free to choose either a public or other school. In addition, the Constitution also prohibits the permanent employment of children under the age of 16, on the basis of Article 65(3). The types and nature of permissible employment are specified by statute.[1134]

The extensive system of rights and freedoms established under the current Polish Constitution provides for three categories: 1) personal, 2) political and

---

1132 Garlicki L., *Polskie Prawo konstytucyjne ...*, 116.

1133 This is the Law of January 6, 2000 on the Ombudsman for Children (Journal of Laws of 2023, item 292).

1134 This is the Law of June 26, 1974 of the Labour Code (Journal of Laws of 2023, item 1465, as amended).

economic, and 3) social and cultural. The first category consists of the most basic rights to which—as a rule—all people under the jurisdiction of Polish law are entitled, thus also foreigners. They include 16 rights, which pertain to the most personal sphere of an individual's functioning in the state, such as:

1. the right to life—in accordance with Article 38 of the Constitution, the Republic of Poland guarantees to every human being the legal protection of life;
2. the prohibition of scientific experiments on human beings without their consent—under Article 39 of the Constitution, no one may be subjected to scientific experiments, including medical experiments, without freely given consent;
3. the prohibition of torture, inhuman or degrading treatment and punishment—under Article 40 of the Constitution, no one shall be subjected to torture or cruel, inhuman or degrading treatment or punishment. Corporal punishment is prohibited;
4. inviolability, personal freedom and humane treatment—under Article 41 of the Constitution, everyone shall be guaranteed personal inviolability and personal freedom. Deprivation or restriction of liberty may take place only on the terms and in the manner specified by statute.[1135] Anyone deprived of his or her liberty not on the basis of a court judgment shall have the right to appeal to a court for an immediate determination of the legality of that deprivation. The deprivation of liberty shall be notified without delay to the family or person designated by the deprived person. Any detainee should be informed immediately and in a manner that he or she understands of the reasons for his or her detention. He or she should be placed at the disposal of the court within 48 hours of detention. A detainee should be released if, within 24 hours of being placed at the disposal of the court, he or she is not served with a court order for pre-trial detention together with the charges. Everyone deprived of liberty should be treated humanely. Everyone unlawfully deprived of his or her liberty is entitled to compensation;

1135 Article 394 of the Law on foreigners, which regulates proceedings for the detention of a foreigner, his or her placement in a guarded center or the use of a detention center for foreigners, is applicable to foreigners in this respect.

5. criminal responsibility, right to defense, presumption of innocence—Article 42 of the Constitution stipulates that only the person who has committed an act prohibited by the law in force at the time of its Commission is subject to criminal responsibility. This principle does not preclude punishment for an act which, at the time it was committed, constituted an offense under international law. Everyone against whom criminal proceedings are brought has the right to a defense at all stages of the proceedings. He or she may, in particular, choose a defense counsel or, under the conditions laid down by law, have a defense counsel of his or her own motion. Everyone shall be presumed innocent until his or her guilt is established by a final court judgment;
6. the right to a court—under Article 45(1) of the Constitution, everyone has the right to a fair and public hearing without undue delay by a competent, independent, impartial and independent court;
7. the right to privacy—Article 47 of the Constitution stipulates that everyone has the right to the legal protection of his or her private life, family life, honor and good name and to decide on his or her personal life;
8. the right to protection of personal data—in line with Article 51 of the Constitution, no one may be obliged otherwise than by law to disclose information concerning his or her person. Public authorities may not obtain, collect and make available information about citizens other than that necessary in a democratic state under the rule of law. Everyone has the right of access to official documents and data collections concerning him or her. Restrictions on this right may be laid down by law. Everyone has the right to demand the rectification and removal of information that is false, incomplete or collected contrary to the law. The principles and procedures for collecting and making information available shall be specified by statute;
9. parental rights, limitation or termination of parental rights—under Article 48, parents have the right to bring up their children according to their own convictions. This upbringing shall take into account the child's degree of maturity, as well as his/her freedom of conscience and religion and his/her convictions. Parental rights may be limited or terminated only in cases specified by statute and only on the basis of a final court judgment;

10. secrecy of communications—under Article 49 of the Constitution, the freedom and protection of secrecy of communications shall be guaranteed. These may be restricted only in the cases specified by law and in the manner prescribed therein;
11. inviolability of the dwelling—according to Article 50 of the Constitution, the inviolability of the dwelling shall be guaranteed. A search of a dwelling, a room or a vehicle may only take place in the cases specified by law and in the manner prescribed therein;
12. freedom of movement—in the light of Article 52 of the Constitution, everyone shall be guaranteed the freedom to move within the territory of the Republic of Poland and to choose his place of residence and stay. Everyone may freely leave the territory of the Republic of Poland. The freedoms referred to in paragraphs (1) and (2) may be subject to limitations specified by law. A person whose Polish origin has been established in accordance with the Law of November 9, 2000 on repatriation,[1136] may settle permanently in the territory of the Republic of Poland;
13. freedom of conscience and religion—under Article 53 of the Constitution, everyone is guaranteed freedom of conscience and religion. Freedom of religion includes the freedom to profess or embrace a religion of one's choice and to manifest one's religion individually or with others, publicly or privately, through worship, prayer, participation in rituals, practice and teaching. Freedom of religion also includes having temples and other places of worship according to the needs of the believers and the right of persons to receive religious assistance where they are. Parents have the right to ensure their children a moral and religious upbringing and teaching in accordance with their convictions. The religion of a regulated church or other religious association may be taught at school without violating the freedom of conscience and religion of others. The freedom to publicly express one's religion may be restricted only by law and only if this is necessary to protect state security, public order, health, morals or the freedoms and rights of others. No one may be compelled to participate or not to participate in religious practices. No one may be compelled by public authorities to disclose his or her philosophy of life, religious convictions or belief;

1136 Journal of Laws of 2022, item 1105.

14. freedom of expression—under Article 54 of the Constitution, everyone is guaranteed the freedom to express his or her opinions and to obtain and disseminate information;
15. prohibition of extradition—under Article 55(4) and (5), extradition is prohibited if it concerns a person suspected of committing a non-violent offense for political reasons or if its execution will violate human and civil liberties and rights. The admissibility of extradition shall be decided by a court. For foreigners, the aforementioned extradition bans are an exception to the rule that extradition of such persons under Polish law is permissible. Restrictions on the extradition of persons who do not have Polish citizenship also result from Article 56, which guarantees foreigners the right to asylum and to apply for refugee status[1137];
16. right of asylum and refugee status—pursuant to Article 56 of the Constitution, foreigners may exercise the right of asylum in the Republic of Poland on the principles specified by statute.[1138] A foreigner who seeks protection from persecution in the Republic of Poland may be granted refugee status in accordance with international agreements binding the Republic of Poland. Thus, the State has the right to grant refuge on its territory to a person prosecuted in his/her own country for political activities. Such a person may apply for asylum while already in Poland or through the Polish diplomatic service while in another country. The right to asylum is a specific human right, as it is granted only to foreigners. It is not granted to a citizen of the Republic of Poland, as, in accordance with Article 36 of the Constitution, he/she always enjoys the right to protection by the Polish state, even if he/she stays outside its borders. A foreigner may apply for asylum and refugee status at the same time, and the refusal to grant one of these rights does not exclude the possibility to apply for the other status. It is generally assumed that asylum is a refuge granted to a foreigner on the territory of Poland, which includes the right to enter and legally stay on this territory and a guarantee of non-refoulement to another state. Having the status of an asylum seeker entitles the person to settle in Poland, whereas refugee

---

1137 Tuleja P., in P. Tuleja (ed), *Konstytucja Rzeczpospolitej Polskiej* ..., 206.

1138 Law of June 13, 2003 on granting protection to foreigners within the territory of the Republic of Poland (Journal of Laws of 2023, item 1504, as amended).

status only allows the person to reside on the territory of the Republic of Poland for a specified period of time. A person with refugee status, unlike an asylum seeker, does not enjoy protection against extradition. Refugee status may be obtained by a foreigner who seeks protection in Poland against persecution.[1139] In the light of Article 79(2) of the Constitution, the right to asylum and refugee status are not protected by an appeal to the Constitutional Tribunal.

The second category of rights provided for in the second chapter of the Constitution is freedom and political rights, i.e., those related to participation in public life. Most often, these rights are enjoyed only by citizens of the Republic of Poland, i.e., persons holding Polish citizenship. They are therefore excluded from the circle of rights to which foreigners are entitled. Examples include: the right to vote in elections and referenda, i.e., the active electoral right, the right of popular legislative initiative, or the right of access to public service, including professional military service. However, it appears that certain rights of freedom and political rights are also enjoyed by foreigners. In this regard, the following may be identified:

17. freedom of assembly—under Article 57 of the Constitution, everyone is guaranteed the freedom to organize and participate in peaceful assemblies. The limitation of this freedom may be imposed by statute;
18. freedom of association—under Article 58 of the Constitution, everyone is guaranteed freedom of association. Associations whose purpose or activities are contrary to the Constitution or the law shall be prohibited. The refusal to permit an association or the prohibition of the activities of such an association shall be decided by the courts. The law specifies the types of associations subject to court registration, the procedure for such registration and the forms of supervision of such associations;
19. associations and their rights; the right to strike—under Article 59 of the Constitution, freedom of association in trade unions, farmers' socio-occupational organizations and employers' organizations is guaranteed. Trade unions and employers and their organizations have the right to bargain, in particular with a view to resolving collective disputes, and

1139 Florczak-Wątor M., in P. Tuleja (ed), *Konstytucja Rzeczypospolitej Polskiej. Komentarz* (Warszawa 2023) 207–208.

to conclude collective bargaining agreements and other agreements. Trade unions have the right to organize labor strikes and other forms of protest within the limits specified by statute. For protection of the public interest, the law may restrict the conduct of strikes or prohibit them in respect of certain categories of workers or in certain areas. The scope of freedom of association in trade unions and employers' organizations and other trade union freedoms may be subject only to such statutory limitations as are permitted by international agreements binding on the Republic of Poland.

20. the right to petitions, proposals and complaints—based on Article 63 of the Constitution, everyone has the right to submit petitions, motions and complaints in the public interest, his own or another person's interest, with his consent, to public authorities and to social organizations and institutions in connection with the performance of their prescribed duties within the field of public administration. The procedure for the consideration of petitions, motions and complaints is specified by statute.

The last category of rights provided for in the second chapter of the Constitution are economic, social and cultural freedoms and rights. Some of them are only provided for citizens of the Republic of Poland, such as the right to social security, and access to health care services, although the right to health care is granted to everyone regardless of citizenship, as is the right to information on the state and protection of the environment. In addition, at the constitutional level, foreigners are entitled to:

21. the right to ownership, other property rights, right of inheritance—under Article 64 of the Constitution, everyone has the right to ownership, other property rights and the right of inheritance. Ownership, other property rights and the right of inheritance shall be subject to equal legal protection for all. Ownership may be restricted only by statute and only to the extent that it does not violate the substance of this right;
22. freedom to choose and pursue an occupation and place of work—under Article 65 of the Constitution, everyone is guaranteed the freedom to choose and pursue his or her occupation and to choose his/her place of work;

23. the right to safe and hygienic working conditions; right to leave—based on Article 66 of the Constitution, everyone has the right to safe and hygienic working conditions. An employee has the right to days free from work and paid annual leave; the maximum permissible hours of work shall be specified by statute.
24. the right to education—Article 70 of the Constitution states that everyone has the right to education. Education up to the age of 18 is compulsory. The manner in which compulsory education is carried out is specified by statute. Education in public schools shall be free of charge. The law may allow certain educational services to be provided by public schools for a fee. Parents are free to choose schools other than public schools for their children. Citizens and institutions have the right to establish primary and secondary schools, as well as institutions of higher education and educational establishments. The conditions for the establishment and operation of non-public schools and the participation of public authorities in their financing, as well as the principles of pedagogical supervision of schools and educational establishments, are specified by statute;
25. the freedom of artistic creation and scientific research, the freedom to teach and enjoy cultural goods—under Article 73 of the Constitution, everyone shall be guaranteed freedom of artistic creation and scientific research and the dissemination of its results, as well as the freedom to teach and to enjoy cultural goods.

In addition to the broadly guaranteed constitutional freedoms and rights, as well as the specific rights to which foreigners are entitled, they also have certain obligations. Admittedly, some duties apply only to citizens, such as loyalty to the Republic of Poland and concern for the common good (Article 82 of the Constitution), and defense of the Fatherland (Article 85 of the Constitution). However, foreigners have the following duties:

26. duty to observe the law of the Republic of Poland—under Article 83 of the Constitution, everyone has a duty to observe the law of the Republic of Poland.
27. obligation to pay public burdens and benefits—under Article 84, everyone shall comply with his responsibilities and public duties, including the payment of taxes, as specified by statute.

28. duty to take care of the quality of the environment—based on Article 86 of the Constitution, everyone is obliged to take care of the quality of the environment and is liable for the deterioration caused by him or her. The principles of this responsibility are specified by statute.

It should be emphasized that the rights and freedoms very broadly proclaimed under the second chapter of the Constitution are not absolute in nature. There are certain limitations in this respect. The Constitution provides for two regimes of functioning of the human rights system. First, in the normal functioning of the state, when the possibility of limiting these rights is provided for on the grounds of Article 31(3) of the Constitution, which stipulates that limitations to the exercise of constitutional freedoms and rights may be established only by statute, and only when they are necessary in a democratic state for its security or public order, or for the protection of the environment, health and public morals, or the freedoms and rights of other persons. Such limitations may not impair the essence of the freedoms and rights. In a formal sense, the principle of limiting constitutional subjective rights only in the law applies, i.e., the principle of the exclusivity of the law for regulating the legal situation of the individual in the state, which also applies to the legal situation of foreigners.

In addition to the formal statutory requirement, the Constitution provides for the possibility of restrictions on the exercise of constitutional freedoms and rights only if they are necessary in a democratic state for its security or public order, or for the protection of the environment, public health and morals, or the freedoms and rights of others. Thus, any law introducing restrictions on the rights and freedoms of an individual, including foreigners, must serve the protection of the public interest by referring to one of the six specific areas, while the absence of such a substantive legal relationship with the constitutional value in question prejudges the lack of grounds for the establishment of limitations. In other words, in addition to the presented formal reservation concerning the statutory form, with regard to the right to encroach upon the sphere of individual freedoms and rights, the Constitution introduces further restrictions. These limitations on the exercise of rights and freedoms may be introduced by statute only if they are necessary in a democratic state in order to ensure its security. In addition, these restrictions must not affect the essence of freedoms and rights, so there are *limits* to the *restrictions*. The general principle in this respect, therefore, explicitly emphasized by the Constitution, is that the said limitations may not infringe on the essence of freedoms and rights. The Constitution, while establishing this important principle concerning freedom, at the same time defines its guarantees and limits, as well as the conditions for the application of its necessary limitations. The essence of the principle of proportionality is the idea that excessive interference should be prohibited, i.e., if any limitations of rights and freedoms must be established, this can only be to the extent that is necessary (the minimum necessary). This is because a balance must be struck between the public interest and the protection of individual rights and freedoms, including those of foreigners.[1140]

Outside the normal functioning of the state, restrictions on the rights and freedoms of the individual are possible if a state of emergency is introduced. The Constitution provides for three types of state of emergency: martial law, state of emergency and state of natural disaster. Martial law, which may be introduced in the event of an external threat to the state, including those caused by acts of a terrorist nature or acts in cyberspace, an armed attack on the territory of the Republic of Poland, or when an international agreement imposes an obligation of joint defense against aggression.[1141] A state of emergency may be introduced when there is a threat to the constitutional system of the state, the security of citizens or public order, including those caused by acts of a terrorist nature or acts in cyberspace, which cannot be removed by the use of ordinary constitutional means.[1142] A state of natural disaster, on the other hand, may be imposed to prevent the consequences of natural disasters or technical failures bearing the hallmarks of a natural disaster and to remove them. The concept of a natural disaster is understood as a natural disaster or technical failure, the consequences of which threaten the life or health of a large number of people, property of great magnitude, or the environment over large areas, and aid and protection can only be effectively

---

1140 Garlicki L., *Polskie prawo konstytucyjne* ..., p. 121.

1141 Article 2(1) of the Law of August 29, 2002 on martial law and the competences of the Supreme Commander of the Armed Forces and the principles of his subordination to the constitutional organs of the Republic of Poland (i.e., Journal of Laws of 2022, item 2091).

1142 Article 2(1) of the Law of June 21, 2002 on the state of emergency (Journal of Laws of 2017, item 1928).

undertaken with extraordinary measures, in cooperation between various bodies and institutions and specialized services and formations acting under unified leadership. A natural disaster is understood to be an event related to natural forces, in particular lightning, seismic shocks, strong winds, intense precipitation, prolonged occurrence of extreme temperatures, landslides, fires, droughts, floods, ice phenomena on rivers and the sea, as well as on lakes and reservoirs, mass occurrence of pests, plant or animal diseases, infectious diseases of humans, or the action of another element. In turn, a technical breakdown is understood as a sudden, unforeseen damage or destruction of a building, technical facility or a system of technical facilities causing an interruption in their use or loss of their properties. A natural catastrophe or technical failure can also be triggered by events in cyberspace and acts of a terrorist nature.[1143]

One of the fundamental consequences of the introduction of the state of emergency is the restriction of the sphere of individual freedoms and rights, including the rights of foreigners. This is an issue of great importance from the point of view of human rights, therefore the Constitution does not leave the public authorities any discretion in determining which freedoms and rights may be subject to limitations. By referring to the detailed definitions in the statutes relating to particular states of emergency, the Constitution clearly indicates which constitutional freedoms and rights may be subject to limitations (Article 233, paragraph 2), and which are not subject to limitations under any circumstances (Article 233, paragraph 1).

Pursuant to Article 233(1) of the Constitution, a law defining the scope of restrictions on human and civil liberties and rights during martial law and states of emergency may not restrict the freedoms and rights set out in Articles 30 (human dignity), 34 and 36 (citizenship), Article 38 (protection of life), Articles 39, 40 and 41(4) (humane treatment), Article 42 (bearing criminal responsibility), Article 45 (access to court), Article 47 (personal rights), Article 53 (conscience and religion), Article 63 (petitions) and Articles 48 and 72 (family and child). For obvious reasons, the prohibition of restrictions on rights derived from nationality does not apply to foreigners.

1143 Articles 2 and 3 of the Law of April 18, 2002 on the state of natural disaster (Journal of Laws of 2017, item 1897).

In turn, on the basis of, Article 233(3) of the Constitution, a law defining the scope of restrictions on human and civil liberties and rights in a state of disaster may restrict the freedoms and rights set out in Article 22 (freedom of economic activity), Article 41(1), (3) and (5) (personal freedom), Article 50 (inviolability of the dwelling), Article 52(1) (freedom of movement and residence in the territory of the Republic of Poland), Article 59(3) (right to strike), Article 64 (right to property), Article 65(1) (freedom of work), Article 66(1) (right to safe and hygienic working conditions) and Article 66(2) (right to rest).

The prohibition of restrictions under martial law and states of emergency covers 14 articles of the Constitution relating to the freedoms and rights of the individual and, in addition, there is an additional prohibition of discrimination against the individual on the grounds of race, sex, language, religion, social origin, birth and property. Provision is also made for the principle of compensating property losses resulting from restrictions on individual freedoms and rights during a state of emergency (Article 228(4)).

2.5.1.3 Statutory guarantees

The rules and conditions for foreigners' entry into, transit through, stay in and departure from the territory of the Republic of Poland, and the procedure and authorities competent in these matters, are provided for in the Law on foreigners.[1144] Excluded from its scope of application are members of diplomatic missions and consular posts of foreign countries and other persons equal to them, pursuant to laws, agreements or commonly established international customs, on condition of reciprocity and possession by these persons of documents confirming their functions entitling them to enter the territory of the Republic of Poland and to stay therein. The exemption also applies to citizens of the Member States of the European Union, the Member States of the European Free Trade Association (EFTA)—parties to the Agreement on the European Economic Area or the Swiss Confederation and members of their families who join them or reside with them, as well as family members of citizens of the Republic of Poland[1145] who join them

1144 Kumela-Romańska M., *Administracyjnoprawny status cudzoziemca w Polsce* (Warszawa 2017) 160 et seq.

1145 Within the meaning of Article 2(4)(b) (<https://sip.lex.pl/#/document/17294228?unitId=art(2)pkt(4)lit(b)&cm=DOCUMENT>) of the Act of July 14, 2006 on entry into the territory of the Republic of Poland, residence and departure from this territory or reside with them, and citizens of the United Kingdom of Great Britain and Northern Ireland.[1146]

According to Article 3(2) of this Act, anyone who does not have Polish citizenship is considered a foreigner.[1147] Natural persons who are citizens of foreign countries, persons who do not have any citizenship and persons of undetermined citizenship may be considered foreigners.[1148]

It follows from the provisions of statutory rank that restrictions on the rights of foreigners may be absolute or relative. Absolute limitations on the rights of foreigners occur with regard to access to the performance of certain offices and functions and, as mentioned earlier, refer to certain political rights of constitutional rank. For example, a foreigner may not be the President of Poland, a professional soldier, a member of the State Tribunal, an Ombudsman, a judge, a prosecutor, a notary public, a police officer, a public official or an employee of a local government. On the other hand, some restrictions are relative in nature, which means that certain professions or functions may be performed by foreigners after fulfilling certain statutory conditions or obtaining the relevant consent or permission of a specific state authority.[1149]

Another distinction between categories of foreigners and, in essence, the rights to which they are entitled was introduced in connection with Poland's accession to the European Union. Certain rights are in fact granted to citizens of the European Union, members of their families who are not EU citizens,

---

of citizens of the Member States of the European Union and members of their families (Journal of Laws of 2021, item 1697 and of 2023, item 547).

1146 In accordance with Article 10(1)(b) (<https://sip.lex.pl/#/document/69283165?unitId=art(10)ust(1)lit(b)&cm=DOCUMENT>) and (d) (<https://sip.lex.pl/#/document/69283165?unitId=art(10)ust(1)lit(b)&cm=DOCUMENT>) of the Agreement on the withdrawal of the United Kingdom of Great Britain and Northern Ireland from the European Union and the European Atomic Energy Community (Official Journal of the EU L 29 31.01.2020, 7), and their family members referred to in Article 10(1)(e) (<https://sip.lex.pl/#/document/69283165?unitId=art(10)ust(1)lit(e)&cm=DOCUMENT>) and (f) <https://sip.lex.pl/#/document/69283165?unitId=art(10)ust(1)lit(f)&cm=DOCUMENT> of the Agreement.

1147 Chlebny J. (ed), *Prawo o cudzoziemcach. Komentarz* (Warszawa 2020) 32.

1148 Lewicki M., "Cudzoziemcy," in Z. Duniewska, B. Jaworska-Dębska, E. Olejniczak-Szałowska, and M. Stahl (eds), *Prawo administracyjne materialne* (Warszawa 2020), 74.

1149 Lewicki M., "Cudzoziemcy" …, 76.

as well as citizens of third countries who, by virtue of international agreements or arrangements, enjoy rights under EU law. For example, pursuant to Article 10 § 1(3)(a) and (4) of the Election Code,[1150] the right to vote (active voting right) in elections to the governing bodies of local government units, i.e., to the council of a municipality, is vested in Polish citizens, citizens of the European Union who are not Polish citizens, and citizens of the United Kingdom of Great Britain and Northern Ireland, who are 18 years of age or older on the voting day at the latest, and are permanently resident in the area of that municipality. In the election of a mayor in a given municipality, on the other hand, an individual has the right to be elected to the council of that municipality. The Polish legal system thus refers to certain categories of rights to which citizens of the Member States of the European Union and their family members are entitled, as well as a separate category of rights to which other foreigners are entitled.[1151]

A foreigner who crosses the border is obliged to have a valid travel document; a valid visa or other valid document authorizing him/her to enter the territory of the Republic of Poland and to stay therein, if required; a permit to enter another country or a residence permit in another country, if such permits are required in the case of transit (Article 23 of the Law on foreigners).

A foreigner entering the territory of Poland is obliged to justify the purpose and conditions of the planned stay; as well as to possess and present, upon request, a document confirming the possession of health insurance or possession of travel medical insurance with a minimum sum insured of EUR 30,000, valid for the duration of the foreigner's planned stay on the territory of Poland, covering any expenses which may arise during his/her stay on that territory in connection with the need to return for medical reasons, the need for urgent medical assistance, emergency hospital treatment or death, in which the insurer undertakes to pay the costs of the medical services provided to the insured person directly to the entity providing such services, on the basis of a bill issued by this entity—in the case of entry on the basis of a national visa, and funds sufficient to cover the costs of the planned stay and the return journey to the country of origin or residence, or the costs of

1150 Law of January 5, 2011—Electoral Code (Journal of Laws of 2023, item 2408, as amended).

1151 Lewicki M., "Cudzoziemcy"..., 76.

transit to a third country which will grant an entry permit, or a document confirming the possibility of obtaining such funds in accordance with the law (Article 25(1) of the Law on foreigners).

Furthermore, a foreigner may be granted protection on the territory of Poland pursuant to the provisions of the Law on granting protection to foreigners.[1152] Pursuant to Article 13 of this act, a foreigner is granted refugee status if, due to justified fear of persecution in the country of origin on the grounds of race, religion, nationality, political opinion or membership of a particular social group, he/she cannot or does not want to benefit from the protection of that country. A minor child born in the Republic of Poland to a foreigner who has been granted refugee status is also eligible for refugee status.

The aforementioned persecution must, by its nature or repetition, constitute a serious violation of human rights, in particular rights whose abrogation is inadmissible under Article 15(2) of the Convention for the Protection of Human Rights and Fundamental Freedoms,[1153] or must be an accumulation of various acts or omissions, including those constituting a violation of human rights, whose impact is as severe as the persecution. In particular, persecution may involve the use of physical or psychological violence, including sexual violence; the application of legal, administrative, police or judicial measures in a discriminatory or discriminatory manner; the initiation or conduct of criminal proceedings or punishment, in a manner that is disproportionate or discriminatory; the absence of the right to appeal to a court against a punishment that is disproportionate or discriminatory; the initiation or conduct of criminal proceedings or punishment for refusal to perform military service during a conflict if performing military service would constitute a crime or acts falling within the scope of the grounds for exclusion; or acts directed against persons on the basis of their sex or minority.[1154]

A foreigner who does not fulfill the conditions for refugee status shall be granted subsidiary protection where return to his or her country of origin would expose him or her to a real risk of suffering serious harm through capital punishment or execution, torture, inhuman or degrading treatment

1152 Chlebny J., *Postępowanie w sprawie nadania statusu uchodźcy* (Warszawa 2011) 3 et seq.

1153 Convention drawn up in Rome on November 4, 1950 (OJ 1993, item 284, as amended).

1154 Chlebny J., *Postępowanie w sprawie …*, 169 et seq.

or punishment, a serious and individualized threat to life or health arising from the widespread use of violence against the civilian population in a situation of international or internal armed conflict, and because of this risk he or she is unable or unwilling to avail himself or herself of the protection of the country of origin.[1155]

The authority conducting the proceedings on granting international protection shall first rule on granting or refusing to grant the foreigner refugee status, and in the event of refusal to grant refugee status it shall rule on granting or refusing to grant subsidiary protection. The authority conducting the proceedings on granting international protection shall issue a single decision relating to the applicant and other persons on behalf of whom the applicant is acting, unless issuing a single decision would lead to disclosure of the specific situation of the applicant or the person on behalf of whom the applicant is acting, which could jeopardize their interests, in particular in cases involving persecution on grounds of sex, sexual orientation, gender identity or age.[1156]

In the course of proceedings, a foreigner may plead a well-founded fear of persecution or a real risk of suffering serious harm caused by events occurring after leaving the country of origin. In such a case, a well-founded fear of persecution or a real risk of suffering serious harm may be caused by the foreigner's actions after leaving the country of origin, in particular if they were an expression and continuation of beliefs or sexual orientations held in the country of origin.[1157]

Pursuant to the content of Article 30 para. 1 of the Law on granting protection to foreigners, the Border Guard authority competent to accept the application for international protection establishes the identity of the person to whom the application relates; obtains data and information to the extent necessary to complete the application form; photographs the person to whom the application relates and takes fingerprints from him/her using fingerprint cards or an electronic fingerprint collection device; determines whether the person to whom the application relates has documents authorizing

1155 Article 15 of the Law on granting protection to foreigners.
1156 Article 47(1) and (2) of the Law on granting protection to foreigners.
1157 Article 17 of the Law on granting protection to foreigners.

him/her to cross the border or whether he/she is legally staying on the territory of the Republic of Poland.

The Border Guard authority also provides the applicant in writing in a language he/she understands with information on the following: the rules and procedures for granting international protection; the rights to which the applicant is entitled, the obligations incumbent on him/her and the consequences of their non-fulfillment as well as the consequences of the explicit and implicit withdrawal of the application for international protection; the possibility to consent to providing the representative of the Office of the United Nations High Commissioner for Refugees with information on the course of the procedure for granting international protection, and to reviewing the case files and making notes and copies of them; the organizations providing assistance to foreigners; the scope of social assistance and medical care, the period of their entitlement, the possibility to apply for assistance in the form of a financial benefit and the rules of admission to the center for foreigners; the mode and principles of providing free legal assistance and the entities providing such assistance; and the address of the reception center where he/she is to appear within two days from the date of submitting the application—if an applicant has not indicated in the application a different address where he/she is to stay, or is not staying in a guarded center or custody for foreigners.

The Border Guard authority is also obliged to provide the assistance of an interpreter when submitting the application; ensures medical examination and necessary sanitary treatment of the body and clothes of the person to whom the application pertains; provides disabled persons, elderly persons, single parents and pregnant women to whom the application pertains with transport to the reception center and, in justified cases, food during that transport; sends, through the Chief of Police, fingerprints of the person to whom the application pertains to the central system and, within 48 hours from the submission of the application, forwards it to the Head of the Office for Foreigners.

According to Article 32 of the Law on granting protection to foreigners, the Border Guard authority which, on the basis of statements made by an applicant claiming to be an unaccompanied minor or on the basis of other circumstances, has doubts as to the age of the applicant, shall ensure that a medical examination is carried out in order to establish the actual age of the applicant. The performance of such a medical examination shall require the consent of the applicant claiming to be an unaccompanied minor or his/her legal representative. Before the medical examination referred to above is commenced, the Border Guard authority which has accepted the application for international protection shall inform the applicant claiming to be an unaccompanied minor in a language which he/she understands of the possibility of having his/her age established through medical examination; the manner in which the medical examination shall be carried out; the relevance of the result of the medical examination to the proceedings for granting international protection; and the consequences of refusing to undergo the medical examination. The medical examination shall be performed in a manner that respects the dignity of the applicant, using the least invasive examination technique possible. The result of the medical examination shall indicate whether the applicant under examination is an adult. Where no conclusive result of the medical examination can be obtained, the applicant shall be considered to be a minor. In the absence of consent to medical examination, an applicant claiming to be a minor shall be considered to be an adult.[1158]

Article 34 of the Law on granting protection to foreigners stipulates that the examination of the application for international protection shall take place within 6 months from the date of submission of the application for international protection on the form. This time limit may be extended to 15 months when the case is particularly complicated; if a large number of foreigners apply for international protection at short intervals and this makes it impossible to examine the application for international protection within 6 months; or, in conjunction with Article 41, when the applicant does not provide information necessary to establish the facts of the case, in particular with respect to his/her age, past experiences relevant to the case, identity, nationality, relatives, country and places of previous residence, previous applications for international protection, travel route and reasons for lodging the application for international protection, does not make available the evidence at his/her disposal substantiating the circumstances indicated in the grounds of the application for international protection, and does not appear for the examination of the application for international protection, and fails

---

[1158] Article 32 of the Law on granting protection to foreigners.

to appear at the summons of the authority conducting the proceedings for questioning or explanations.[1159]

In addition to the general legal mechanisms provided for under the Law on foreigners and the Law on granting protection to foreigners, which have been outlined above, a special Law on assistance to Ukrainian citizens in connection with the armed conflict on the territory of that State, also referred to as the Ukrainian Special Law, has been in force in Poland since March 12, 2022, providing for special solutions for this numerous group representing more than 80 % of all foreigners residing in Poland. As previously mentioned, it sets out special rules for legalizing the stay of Ukrainian citizens who arrived on the territory of the Republic of Poland from the territory of Ukraine in connection with the hostilities conducted on the territory of that country, as well as Ukrainian citizens holding the Pole's Card who, together with their immediate families, arrived on the territory of the Republic of Poland because of the armed conflict.

The Act provides for a broad scope of subjects, indicating that whenever the Act refers to a citizen of Ukraine, this shall also be understood as covering a non-citizen spouse of a citizen of Ukraine, a minor child of a citizen of Ukraine, or a minor child of a spouse of a citizen of Ukraine, if they have arrived on the territory of the Republic of Poland from the territory of Ukraine in connection with the armed conflict conducted on the territory of that country and are not Polish citizens or citizens of EU Member States other than the Republic of Poland.

This special legal act also stipulates specific rules for the following: the entrustment of work to citizens of Ukraine legally residing in the territory of the Republic of Poland; assistance provided by provincial governors, local government units and other entities to citizens of Ukraine; the creation of an Assistance Fund to finance or subsidize the implementation of tasks to assist citizens of Ukraine; certain entitlements of citizens of Ukraine whose stay in the territory of the Republic of Poland is recognized as legal; specific rules for extending the periods of legal stay of citizens of Ukraine and documents issued to them by the Polish authorities concerning their entitlements to enter and stay in the territory of the Republic of Poland; certain entitlements of

1159 Article 34 in conjunction with Article 41 of the Law on granting protection to foreigners.

Polish citizens and citizens of Ukraine who are students, academic teachers or research workers entering from the territory of Ukraine; specific regulations concerning education, upbringing and care of children and pupils who are citizens of Ukraine, including support of local self-government units in the implementation of additional educational tasks in this respect; special rules for the organization and functioning of higher education institutions in connection with the provision of university places for citizens of Ukraine; special rules for taking up and carrying out economic activity by citizens of Ukraine legally residing in the territory of the Republic of Poland; and special rules for the distribution of medicinal products and medical devices intended for humanitarian aid in the territory of Ukraine by the Government Strategic Reserve Agency.

If a citizen of Ukraine arrived legally on the territory of Poland in the period from February 24, 2022 and declares his/her intention to stay on the territory of the country, his/her stay on the territory of the country shall be deemed legal until September 30, 2025. The stay of a child born on the territory of Poland by a mother who is a person referred to in the previous sentence during the period concerned, the mother shall also be deemed legal, provided that the child is not a Polish citizen or a citizen of a EU Member State other than the Republic of Poland. In addition, if a citizen of Ukraine holding a Pole's Card has left Ukraine in the period from February 24, 2022 and has subsequently arrived legally on the territory of the Republic of Poland and declares his/her intention to remain on the territory of the Republic of Poland, his/her stay on that territory shall be deemed legal until September 30, 2025.

Ukrainian citizens whose stay in the territory of Poland is considered legal may undertake and perform economic activity in the territory of the Republic of Poland on the same principles as Polish citizens. This entitlement is granted on the condition that the Ukrainian citizen obtains a PESEL number.[1160] In addition, citizens of Ukraine legally residing on the territory of

1160 The provision of Article 23(1) and (2) of the Law on assistance to Ukrainian citizens in connection with the armed conflict on the territory of that country.

the Republic of Poland may be employed in auxiliary and service positions in local government units and state offices.[1161]

A special regulation has been formulated with regard to minors. A minor Ukrainian citizen who is staying in the territory of Poland unaccompanied by an adult responsible for him/her according to the law shall be represented by a temporary guardian who shall exercise custody over his/her person and property. A temporary guardian, unless the scope of his/her rights and obligations has been specified otherwise upon his/her appointment, shall be entitled to represent the minor and exercise custody over his/her person and property. The temporary guardian should obtain the permission of the guardianship court in all major matters that concern the minor's person or property. Ukrainian children deprived of parental care and upbringing have been provided with foster care, and the requirements for the operation of crèches, children's clubs and day care providers have been relaxed.[1162]

In order to provide education, upbringing and care for children and pupils who are citizens of Ukraine, whose stay in the territory of the Republic of Poland is recognized as legal, or who are legally residing in the territory of the Republic of Poland, if they arrived in the territory of the Republic of Poland from the territory of Ukraine as of February 24, 2022, in connection with the armed conflict on the territory of that state, other locations of teaching, upbringing and caring activities subordinated organizationally to schools or kindergartens may be created.[1163]

Furthermore, Ukrainian citizens residing in Poland are entitled to family benefits, the 800+ benefit, the family benefit, the good start benefit and subsidized reduction of the parent's fee for the child's stay in a crèche,[1164] i.e., the same benefits as Polish citizens.

In addition to the above, Ukrainian citizens legally residing on the territory of Poland and with a PESEL number may be granted cash and non-cash

---

1161 The provision of Article 23a of the Law on assistance to Ukrainian citizens in connection with the armed conflict on the territory of that country.

1162 The provision of Article 27 of the Law on assistance to Ukrainian citizens in connection with the armed conflict on the territory of that country.

1163 The provision of Article 51(1) of the Law on assistance to Ukrainian citizens in connection with the armed conflict on the territory of that country.

1164 The provision of Article 26 of the Law on assistance to Ukrainian citizens in connection with the armed conflict on the territory of that country.

benefits and non-monetary benefits, under the principles and in the mode of the Law of March 12, 2004 on social assistance.[1165]

2.5.1.4 Conclusions

Poland is currently in an exceptional situation with regard to the large number of foreigners residing on the territory of the country, who have found refuge here from the threats of a full-scale war triggered by the Russian military aggression against Ukraine. In addition, hybrid actions are being conducted against Poland by Russia and Belarus on the Polish-Belarusian border, aimed at the illegal crossing of this border by citizens of countries mainly from the Middle East. It seems that both the actions of the Polish authorities, including state administration bodies, and the construction of the legal system, have so far met these challenges. First and foremost, high standards of respecting the human rights of foreigners are provided for in the Polish Constitution.

Of primary importance from the point of view of other legal regulations of both constitutional and statutory rank are undoubtedly the normative general principles relating to the constitutional catalog of rights and freedoms—personal, political and economic, social and cultural—such as human dignity, freedom, equality and prohibition of discrimination. These values are fundamental to the understanding of human rights, including those of subjects such as foreigners, women, children and persons with disabilities. Most of the rights and freedoms provided for in the Constitution are enjoyed by foreigners. These are presented in the study in 28 points.

It should be emphasized that the Constitution stipulates that whoever is under the authority of the Republic of Poland enjoys the freedoms and rights provided for in the Constitution. Exceptions to this principle relating to foreigners are defined by law. Two legal acts of statutory rank are generally applicable in this respect, namely the Law on Foreigners and the Law on granting protection to foreigners within the territory of the Republic of Poland. The analysis of these statutory provisions leads to the conclusion that they correspond closely to the constitutional standard, with due diligence protecting human dignity, respecting the subjectivity of foreigners, and prohibiting their discrimination. As always, much depends on the sensitivity of

1165 The provision of Article 29 of the Law on assistance to Ukrainian citizens in connection with the armed conflict on the territory of that country.

persons applying these norms, nevertheless the legal regulations themselves set high standards for the protection of foreigners, and the state's activities in this respect are subject to the control of administrative courts.[1166]

Special norms apply to citizens of war-torn Ukraine, whose population constitutes more than 80 % of all foreigners residing in Poland. Their legal status and the benefits to which they are entitled from the Polish state have in fact been made equal to the status and benefits of Polish citizens. Special protection is afforded to children, war orphans, soldiers and civilians wounded in combat, as well as women and persons with disabilities.

According to data from the Central Statistical Office, as of March 31, 2023, there were 997,737 Ukrainian residents in Poland, of which a significant proportion, over 81 %, were living in cities. More than half (64.8 %) of this almost one million-strong community were women, with a ratio of 184 women per 100 men arriving from Ukraine due to the armed conflict on Ukrainian territory. The age structure of Ukraine's residents under temporary protection is significantly differentiated by gender. Among those aged 0–19 years, boys predominate slightly. They account for more than two-thirds of the incoming Ukrainian residents (66.2 %). Among those aged 20 and over, women clearly predominate. Their share in particular age groups is 3–4 times higher, and in the case of persons in the 55–59 age group, it is more than six times higher (nearly 23,000 women and less than 4,000 men). Among the Ukrainian population under temporary protection, people of working age predominated (51.8 %). Nearly 40 % were people of mobile age. People of pre-working age (41.9 %) were also a numerous group, while those of post-working age were only 6.3 %. This means that mainly mothers with children came to Poland. The majority of Ukrainian residents who arrived were persons with Ukrainian citizenship (99.7 %). A small percentage were persons with citizenship of another country. Among them, persons with Russian citizenship dominate (just over 1,000), followed by persons with Belarusian (427 persons), Georgian (291 persons) and Moldovan (270 persons) citizenship.[1167]

1166 Kowalski M., *Prawo do sądu administracyjnego. Standard międzynarodowy i konstytucyjny oraz jego realizacja* (Warszawa 2019) 13 et seq.

1167 Data publicly available on the website of the Central Statistical Office—stat.gov.pl.

2.5.2 Procedural law perspective

2.5.2.1 Special procedures on the entry and residence of third-country nationals (Paweł Dańczak)

2.5.2.1.1 General overview

The legislation in force in Poland until recently did not contain any specific solutions relating directly to the issue of foreigners' entry and stay on the territory of the Republic of Poland, which would constitute a form of response to the possible occurrence of various crisis situations.

This does not mean, however, that Polish law lacks provisions for responding to exceptional situations causing a serious threat to security or public order or the existence of the nation or the state, which the Constitution of the Republic of Poland defines in Chapter XI jointly as states of emergency. At the same time, Article 228(1) of the Constitution distinguishes three types of such states, i.e., martial law, a state of emergency and a state of natural disaster, the introduction of which should be justified by the emergence of a situation of particular internal threat in the State, as well as by the ineffectiveness of the actions of the organs of its authority within the framework of standard systemic solutions, i.e., cases when ordinary constitutional measures prove ineffective. Their proclamation is associated with a periodic modification of the competencies of the subjects of public authority, usually by strengthening the position of the executive at the expense of the competencies of other types of authorities, as well as by limiting the guarantees of individual freedoms and rights, or by simplifying the lawmaking procedures. Article 233 of the Constitution refers to this, indicating which specific freedoms and rights of the individual are subject to restriction in the case of a specific type of state of emergency.[1168]

It should be remembered that a state of emergency should be exceptional and temporary, i.e., applied very rarely and for a short time. In the Polish reality, this is confirmed by the fact that in the period of the current Constitution of the Republic of Poland, the regulation related to such states was applied only once, in connection with the migration crisis on the Polish-Belarusian border, when on September 2, 2021 a state

---

1168 Radziewicz P., in P. Tuleja (ed), *Konstytucja Rzeczypospolitej Polskiej. Komentarz* (Warszawa 2023) 703–711, 717–721; Tuleja P., *Pandemia COVID-19 a konstytucyjne stany nadzwyczajne* (Palestra 2020), No. 9, 5.

of emergency was introduced on the territory of a part of Podlaskie and Lubelskie Voivodeships. However, constitutional practice shows that public authorities are reluctant to use constitutional solutions related to the declaration of states of emergency, even if the factual situation would indicate such a need, instead resorting to extra-constitutional solutions, such as the instruments from the COVID-19 pandemic period—as covered in the next section.[1169]

2.5.2.1.2 The COVID-19 pandemic

Although the COVID-19 pandemic had a significant impact on the daily functioning of both individuals and institutions, including those from the public administration sphere, the Polish authorities, throughout its duration, did not establish specific procedures comprehensively regulating the issue of entry and stay of foreigners on the territory of Poland in connection with the spread of the virus. This does not mean, however, that this issue was ignored in the Polish legislation. The reaction of the Polish authorities to the occurrence of life and health-threatening conditions due to the coronavirus was, however, of a limited character, as the norms introduced at that time were mainly aimed at creating a legal framework for solutions aimed at limiting direct contacts of individuals, including foreigners, with officials of the administrative apparatus. This was reflected, for instance, in the extension by the Law of March 2, 2020 on special solutions related to preventing, counteracting and combating COVID-19, other infectious diseases and crisis situations caused by them,[1170] which affected the legal status of foreigners

1169 Florczak-Wątor M., "Konstytucyjna regulacja stanów nadzwyczajnych w świetle dotychczasowej praktyki jej (nie)stosowania" (2022) 10 *Państwo i Prawo*, 333–334. Extra-constitutional regulation of states of emergency was also written in: Paśnik J., *Pozakonstytucyjne ustawodawstwo stanów nadzwyczajnych* (Przegląd Prawa Publicznego 2023), No. 4, 31–47.

1170 Journal of Laws item 374 with amendments (hereinafter: "the COVID-19 Act"). The aforementioned act introduced, in the provisions of Articles 15z-15zd, various solutions related to the status of foreigners and their residence on the territory of the Republic of Poland, consisting, inter alia, in the extension of the validity period of national visas and temporary residence permits, waiving the requirement to submit documents required when applying for a visa in person, extension of the validity period of residence cards, documents confirming the right of permanent residence, Polish identity documents for foreigners, permits for tolerated stay,

residing in Poland. At the same time, this Act introduced mechanisms that modified administrative procedure and court-administrative proceedings, enabling cases to be conducted while minimizing the risk of virus transmission and the spread of the pandemic on the country's territory.[1171] However, it should be noted again that the procedural solutions introduced at that time and modifications of the instruments already in place did not strictly concern the cases of foreigners and their status but, in principle, referred to all addressees of the actions of the public administration and the judiciary, i.e., also foreigners.

One of the consequences of the pandemic was the legislator's introduction of certain restrictions, including those related to entry, stay, and movement in Poland (e.g., the obligation to register the place of stay, to undergo quarantine or home isolation). However, as before, their addressees were not only foreigners but all persons who found themselves in the factual situations defined by law.

From a legal point of view, it was not the restrictions themselves that were assessed as controversial, but rather the legal basis for their introduction. This was constituted primarily by the provisions of the ordinance introducing the

temporary identity certificates for foreigners. It needs to be emphasized, however, that although these solutions were systemic in nature and constituted the State's response to the crisis situation in the form of the coronavirus pandemic, they did not create a specific type of procedures related to the entry and stay of foreigners on the territory of the Republic of Poland, but only introduced certain solutions interfering with the course of standard procedures in order to limit the transmission of the virus.

1171 For example, Article 15zzs of the COVID-19 Act regulated numerous issues relating to the running of procedural and judicial time limits, including with regard to the suspension of their commencement and suspension, or the non-application of provisions on the inaction of administrative authorities, or the obligation of these authorities to notify the party of the failure to deal with the case in time. On the other hand, Articles 15zzs[1] and 15zzs[4] introduced the possibility of conducting hearings in courts using technical devices allowing them to be conducted at a distance with simultaneous direct transmission of image and sound (so-called remote hearings) and extended the possibility for the court to hear cases in closed session if their hearing was deemed necessary and the hearing required by the Act could cause undue risk to the health of the persons participating in it and could not be conducted at a distance with simultaneous direct transmission of image and sound. In closed session in these cases, the court was required to decide in a panel of three judges.

state of epidemic,[1172] and later the state of epidemic threat, issued based on the Law of December 5, 2008 on preventing and combating infections and infectious diseases in humans.[1173] This, in turn, gave rise to constitutional doubts because, in the light of the Polish Constitution, all limitations on human rights and freedoms must have a direct basis in statute.[1174] At the same time, this form of response to the pandemic outbreak, which in its features corresponded to a state of natural disaster, was rightly regarded as an attempt by the executive power to circumvent constitutional regulations concerning states of emergency.[1175]

1172 Regulation of the Minister of Health of March 20, 2020 on the declaration of an epidemic state in the territory of the Republic of Poland, Journal of Laws of 2020, item 491 as amended; Regulation of the Minister of Health of May 12, 2022 on the declaration of a state of epidemic emergency on the territory of the Republic of Poland, Journal of Laws of 2022, item 1028. § 2 of the first of the above-mentioned acts provided, inter alia, that during the period of the state of epidemic emergency, the movement of passengers in rail transport performed with crossing the border of the Republic of Poland shall be suspended (§ 1). In addition, a person crossing the state border, in order to go to his or her place of residence or stay in the territory of the Republic of Poland, was obliged to provide an officer of the Border Guard with information on: the address of the place of residence or stay where he or she will undergo compulsory quarantine; the telephone number for contacting that person; and he or she had to undergo, after crossing the state border, a compulsory quarantine lasting 14 days, counting from the day following the crossing of that border.

1173 Journal of Laws of 2019, item 1239 as amended—Text of the Law in force on the date of introduction of the epidemic state in Poland.

1174 Judgment of the Supreme Court of December 7, 2021, II KK 342/21, LEX No. 3271454, as well as the judgment of the Supreme Administrative Court of March 4, 2022, II GSK 38/22 with gloss by Jakubowski A., and Roszkiewicz J. (2023) 5 *Orzecznictwo Sądów Polskich*, 98–122. In the cited case law and the gloss, it was emphasized, inter alia, in the context of the introduction of the state of epidemics, that interference in the sphere of rights and freedoms in the state of epidemics must fully meet constitutional standards. At the same time, it was pointed out that in a situation in which none of the states of emergency listed in the Constitution of the Republic of Poland has been introduced, constitutional rights and freedoms cannot be completely suspended by a sub-statutory act based on a general statutory authorization, and legislative intervention in this respect may only take place by way of statute.

1175 More extensively on this topic: Czarnow S., "Próba refleksji nad reakcją państwa na pandemię COVID-19—uwagi o porządku prawnym czasu epidemii i jego wpływie na prawa i wolności człowieka" (2023) 1 *Radca Prawny. Zeszyty Naukowe* 99–125;

2.5.2.1.3 Inflow of Ukrainian nationals in connection with the invasion of Ukraine by the Russian Federation

The aggression of the Russian Federation against Ukraine, while causing a sudden mass influx of Ukrainian citizens to Poland and prompting a response from the Polish authorities, did not serve as the impetus for introducing special procedures related to the entry and residence of foreigners into Polish law. Despite the urgency of the situation, it did not result in the creation of solutions of an exceptional nature.

The most important legal act enacted in connection with the influx of Ukrainian citizens fleeing the consequences of the ongoing war in their country was the Law of March 12, 2022 on Assistance to Ukrainian Citizens in Connection with the Armed Conflict on the Territory of that State,[1176] which regulates, inter alia, certain rights of citizens of that state whose stay on the territory of Poland is recognized as legal,[1177] as well as the principles of extending the periods of their legal stay and the documents issued to them by the Polish authorities concerning the rights of entry and stay on the territory of Poland.[1178] The prerequisites for

---

Czarnow S., "Między stanem epidemii a stanem klęski żywiołowej—COVID-19 a niektóre prawa człowieka" (2021) 3 *Radca Prawny Zeszyty Naukowe*, 11–42; Florczak-Wątor M., "Niekonstytucyjność ograniczeń praw i wolności jednostki wprowadzonych w związku z epidemią COVID-19 jako przesłanka odpowiedzialności odszkodowawczej państwa" (2020) 12 *Państwo i Prawo*, 5–22; Kurzępa E., "Stan epidemii a stan klęski żywiołowej—rozważania w kontekście bezpieczeństwa państwa" (2021) 5 *Przegląd Prawa Publicznego*, 5–21.

1176 Original text: *Journal of Laws* (2022), item 583, as amended—Hereinafter also referred to as the "Ukrainian Special Law."

1177 For a more extensive discussion of this law, see Chapter 2 in Kowalski M., "Substantive Law," in *Legal Restrictions on Third-Country Nationals in EU Emergencies* (Peter Lang 2026).

1178 For example, in Article 42(1) and (2) of the Ukrainian Special Law it is established that: If the last day of the period of stay of a citizen of Ukraine in the territory of the Republic of Poland on the basis of a national visa falls within the period from February 24, 2022, the period of stay on the basis of this visa and the period of validity of this visa shall be extended by law until December 31, 2022. In such a case, a new visa sticker shall not be affixed to the travel document of the Ukrainian citizen. On the other hand, Article 44 of the Ukrainian Special Law indicates that: "The stay of a citizen of Ukraine who has been allowed to enter the territory of the Republic of Poland on the section of the border between the Republic of Poland and Ukraine by the commander of the Border Guard post on the section of the

depriving a Ukrainian citizen of the right of residence are also regulated by indicating the circumstances under which their stay is no longer be recognized as legal.[1179]

The law mentioned above adopts the general principle that a Ukrainian citizen who entered Poland after February 24, 2022 in connection with the hostilities in his/her country is deemed to enjoy temporary protection in Poland[1180] and may enjoy the rights provided by this law.

The Ukrainian Special Law did not introduce specific procedures concerning the entry and stay of Ukrainian citizens and foreigners from other countries in the territory of Poland. The legislator mainly adopted the principle that the extension of the legality of stay and relevant documents would not require additional procedural steps to be taken by the foreigners to whom the provisions of the particular act were addressed, but such an effect would occur by operation of law.[1181]

---

border between the Republic of Poland and Ukraine pursuant to Article 32(1) of the Law of December 12, 2013 on foreigners (Permission to enter the territory of the Republic of Poland for special reasons) shall be considered legal for a period of 18 months."

1179 Pursuant to Article 11 of the Ukrainian Special Law, in its most up-to-date wording, it was established that: the departure of a citizen of Ukraine from the territory of the Republic of Poland for a period exceeding 30 days deprives him/her of the right to recognize his/her stay as legal with the exception of persons directed to perform work or services outside the territory of the Republic of Poland by entities conducting activities on the territory of the Republic of Poland. Also, the use by a citizen of Ukraine of temporary protection on the territory of a European Union Member State other than the Republic of Poland granted due to warfare conducted on the territory of Ukraine deprives him/her of the right to recognize his/her stay on the territory of Poland as legal.

1180 The understanding of "temporary protection" was linked to the content of Article 106(1) of the Law of June 13, 2003 on granting protection to foreigners within the territory of the Republic of Poland, according to which: "Foreigners arriving in large numbers in the Republic of Poland, who have left their country of origin or a specific geographical area, due to foreign invasion, war, civil war, ethnic conflicts or gross violations of human rights, may be granted temporary protection on the territory of the Republic of Poland regardless of whether their arrival was spontaneous or resulted from assistance provided to them by the Republic of Poland or the international community."

1181 Grześkowiak M., "Specustawa ukraińska jako szczególny przypadek formalizacji tzw. tymczasowego schronienia dla osób przymusowo migrujących" (2023) 8 *Europejski Przegląd Sądowy*, 4–10.

By means of the Ukrainian Special Law, the legislator also wanted to counteract the negative effects of the mass influx of third-country nationals and the related increase in the number of the aforementioned cases. This was intended to address allegations of inaction and delays in administrative proceedings conducted in this respect by the public administration bodies responsible for handling cases concerning the granting, modification and revocation of residence permits for foreigners. To this end, the Act introduced a provision stating that, from the date of initiation of proceedings until the date specified in the Act, the course of time limits for handling the aforementioned types of cases does not commence, and any time limits already in progress are suspended for this period.[1182] This solution has been

---

[1182] In accordance with Article 100d(1) of the Special Law:
During the period up to September 30, 2025, the time limits for dealing with:
1) grant the foreigner:
(a) temporary residence permits,
(b) permanent residence permits,
(c) residence permits for long-term residents of the European Union,
2) Amendments:
(a) temporary residence and work permits,
(b) a temporary residence permit for the purpose of highly qualified employment,
3) revocation of the foreigner:
(a) temporary residence permits,
(b) permanent residence permits,
(c) residence permits for long-term residents of the European Union—in proceedings conducted by the provincial governor shall not be commenced or commenced shall be suspended for that period.
At the same time, § 3 and 4 provide that:
(3) During the period referred to in § 1:
(1) The provisions on the inaction of the authority and on the obligation of the authority conducting the proceedings in the cases referred to in § 1 to notify a party or a participant in the proceedings of the failure to deal with the case in time shall not apply;
(2) the body conducting the proceedings in the cases referred to in § 1 shall not be fined or ordered to pay sums of money to the complainants for failing to issue decisions within the time limits prescribed by law.
(4) The cessation of actions by the body conducting the proceedings in the cases referred to in § (1), or their delay, within the period referred to in § (1), may not be the basis for raising legal remedies concerning inaction, protraction or violation of the right of a party to have the case heard without undue delay.

critically assessed,[1183] inter alia, due to its incompatibility with constitutional and convention standards related to the right to a court and the right to have

1183 Judgment of the Voivodship Administrative Court in Łódź of April 9, 2024, III SAB/Łd 7/24; judgment of the Voivodship Administrative Court in Poznań of June 30, 2023, II SAB/Po 43/23; judgment of the Voivodship Administrative Court of October 12, 2023, III SAB/Łd 148/23; judgment of the Voivodship Administrative Court in Poznań of November 9, 2023, IV SAB/Po 130/23—<https://orzeczenia.nsa.gov.pl/> accessed August 30, 2024. The jurisprudence pointed out that acceptance of the view that by an incidental law, even concerning an important issue, it is possible to suspend the running of all time limits in all proceedings initiated by foreigners' applications for residence permits would not only be incompatible with the right to a court guaranteed by Article 45 of the Polish Constitution, standing directly in contradiction with Article 77(2) of the Basic Law, according to which "The law may not close off the judicial path for anyone to pursue violated freedoms or rights." Moreover, acceptance of such a solution would also violate Article 47 of the Charter of Fundamental Rights of the European Union, which provides in its first sentence that "Everyone whose rights and freedoms guaranteed by the law of the Union are violated shall have the right to an effective remedy before a tribunal in accordance with the conditions laid down in this Article." However, a general (erga omnes) suspension of time limits in residence permit cases would have the effect of precluding any judicial review in view of the passivity of the public administrations adjudicating in this regard. It was stressed that the reference to Article 47 of the Charter of Fundamental Rights is justified by the fact that this provision is applicable to those matters regulated in the national order which have as their component rights and freedoms guaranteed by the law of the European Union, and the issue of granting residence permits is the subject of numerous regulations contained in EU directives, so the national norms constitute their implementation. It was also pointed out that under Article 6(1), first sentence, of the Convention for the Protection of Human Rights and Fundamental Freedoms, everyone is entitled to a fair and public hearing within a reasonable time by an independent and impartial tribunal established by law, to decide on his civil rights and obligations or on the merits of any criminal charge brought against him. It was emphasized at the same time that the notion of "civil rights and obligations" used in this provision is an autonomous notion of the Convention, understood on the grounds of this provision broadly, and in practice encompassing many types of cases which in the Polish legal system are classified as administrative cases (cf. Hofmański P., Wróbel A., in L. Garlicki (ed), *Konwencja o Ochronie Praw Człowieka i Podstawowych Wolności. Komentarz* (vol. I, Warszawa 2010), art. 6 Nb 27 and 223), including some concerning foreigners. For more detailed analysis, see: Commentary to Article 100c, Jaźwińska M., Mickiewicz P., and Słubik K., in W. Klaus (ed), *Ustawa o pomocy obywatelom Ukrainy w związku z konfliktem zbrojnym na terytorium tego państwa oraz niektórych innych ustaw. Komentarz* (Warszawa 2022), LEX/el 2023.

a case heard within a reasonable time. These standard arise from Articles 45(1) and 77(2) of the Constitution of the Republic of Poland,[1184] Article 47 of the Charter of Fundamental Rights,[1185] Article 6(1) of the Convention for the Protection of Human Rights and Fundamental Freedoms[1186] and due to its contradiction with the provisions of Article 5(2), and (4) of Directive 2011/98/EU of the European Parliament and of the Council of December 13, 2011. This Directive specifies a single application procedure for a single permit for third-country nationals to reside and work in the territory of a Member State and establishes a standard set of rights for third-country workers legally residing in a Member State.[1187]

2.5.2.1.4 General procedure

Polish legislation lists several entities responsible for protecting the state border.[1188] In practice, the main burden of this task rests with the Border

---

1184 According to Article 45(1) of the Polish Constitution, "Everyone has the right to a fair and public hearing without undue delay by a competent, independent, impartial and independent court."

1185 OJ EU.C.2007.303.1 of December 14, 2007.

1186 Convention for the Protection of Human Rights and Fundamental Freedoms drawn up in Rome on November 4, 1950, subsequently amended by Protocols Nos. 3, 5 and 8 and supplemented by Protocol No. 2—*Journal of Laws* 1993, No. 61, item 284. According to Article 6(1) of this Act, "Everyone is entitled to a fair and public hearing within a reasonable time by an independent and impartial tribunal established by law, to decide on his civil rights and obligations or on the merits of any criminal charge against him. The proceedings before the court shall be open to the public, but the press and the public may be excluded from all or part of the trial on moral grounds, for reasons of public order or national security in a democratic society, when the welfare of minors so requires or when it serves to protect the private life of the parties, or in special circumstances, within the limits deemed absolutely necessary by the court, when publicity would prejudice the interests of justice."

1187 OJ EU. L 2011.343.1—The provisions of the Directive referred to establish, inter alia, a maximum period within which the competent authority should give a decision on a complete application to grant a foreigner a permit to reside in an EU Member State, providing that this should be done as soon as possible, but in any event within four months of the date on which the application was submitted.

1188 Pursuant to Article 7 of the Law of October 12, 1990 on the protection of the state border (Journal of Laws of 2024, item 388, as amended), the minister in charge of internal affairs is responsible for the protection of the state border on land and at sea and for the control of border traffic, within the scope defined in separate regulations. The Minister of National Defense is responsible for the protection of the

Guard (BG), i.e., a uniformed formation designed both to guard the border and to control border traffic and prevent illegal migration (Article 1(1) of the Law on the Border Guard).[1189] The performance of tasks under the latter aspect consists of controlling the observance of regulations on foreigners' entry into and stay on the territory of Poland, identifying and analyzing migration threats and counteracting them, including crimes related to illegal migration. Within the scope mentioned earlier, the Border Guard is obliged to cooperate with the authorities and other entities competent in matters related to granting entry or residence permits to foreigners on the territory of Poland, including performing activities upon the request of these authorities and entities, following the principles resulting from relevant provisions (Article 1(2a) of the Law on the Border Guard), including in particular the Law on foreigners and the Law on granting protection to foreigners within the territory of the Republic of Poland.

Border control is carried out by Border Guard officers.[1190] They are obliged to respect the regulations stemming from the provisions of the Schengen

---

state border in the airspace of the Republic of Poland. At the same time, the tasks of the minister in charge of internal affairs are performed by the Commander-in-Chief of the Border Guard, while the tasks of the Minister of National Defense in the area of protection of the state border in the airspace of the Republic of Poland are performed by the Operational Commander of the Armed Forces with the assistance of the Duty Commander of the Air Defense. The On-Call Air Defense Commander is an officer of the Armed Forces of the Republic of Poland designated to serve in the air defense system of the Republic of Poland and to perform the function of the national representative of state authorities in the North Atlantic Treaty Organisation Integrated Air Defence System.

1189 OJ 2024, item 915, as amended.

1190 The operations of the Border Guard at the eastern land external borders of Poland, which are also the external borders of the EU, are supported by officers of the FRONTEX Agency, inter alia within the framework of the TERRA operation. In 2021, the entire length of the EU's eastern land borders saw a significant increase in irregular migration flows. In response, the aforementioned joint operation Terra was launched along these borders and covers 11 EU countries, from Finland to Greece, including Poland. A total of more than 700 permanent service officers support national authorities in border management and the fight against cross-border crime, focusing mainly on border protection, border checks and assistance in detecting false documents. They also support host countries in gathering information on smuggling networks and migratory phenomena and identify vulnerable groups. In addition to personnel, Frontex also deploys patrol cars and thermal imaging vehicles (after

Borders Code (Articles 7–13) and, in addition, from the regulations contained in the Law on foreigners, i.e., Section III—Crossing the border.[1191] In the course of their official activities, they are obliged to respect dignity and observe human and civil liberties and rights (Article 9(5) of the Border Guard Act).[1192]

A foreigner who does not fulfill the conditions for entry into the territory of Poland[1193] shall be refused such entry by way of an administrative decision

---

<https://www.frontex.europa.eu/what-we-do/operations/operations/?etrans=pl> accessed September 30, 2024).

1191 In the Polish literature on the subject, it is noted that the relationship between the regulation contained in the Schengen Borders Code and the Law on foreigners is not fully clear and creates problems in defining clear boundaries, i.e., when only the Borders Code is applicable and when the national regulation is appropriate in a given case—vide: judgment of the Supreme Administrative Court of September 20, 20218, II OSK 1025/18 with gloss by Dąbrowski P. (2019) 3 *Orzecznictwo Sądów Polskich*, 125–153; Dąbrowski P., *Cudzoziemiec niepożądany w polskim prawie o cudzoziemcach* (Warszawa 2011) 144–146; Rogala R., in J. (ed), *Prawo o cudzoziemcach Komentarz* (Warszawa 2020) 118–120 and 133–134.

1192 This provision constitutes a kind of supplement, under national law, to the regulation contained in Article 7 of the Schengen Borders Code, according to which "1. Border guards shall, in the performance of their duties, fully respect human dignity, in particular when dealing with vulnerable persons. Any measures taken in the performance of their duties shall be proportionate to the objectives pursued by such measures. (2) When carrying out border checks, border guards shall not discriminate against persons on grounds of sex, racial or ethnic origin, religion or belief, disability, age or sexual orientation."

1193 The grounds for refusal of entry set out in Article 28 of the Law on foreigners largely duplicate the grounds for refusal of entry set out in Article 14 in conjunction with Article 6 of the Schengen Borders Code, which makes it difficult to correctly identify which of the above-mentioned legal acts should apply in a specific individual case. According to Article 28(1) of the Law on foreigners: A foreigner shall be refused entry into the territory of the Republic of Poland if: 1) does not possess a valid travel document, a valid visa or other valid documents authorizing entry into and stay on the territory of the Republic of Poland, or 2) does not possess the document referred to in Article 25(1)(2) lit. a, or 3) has used up the permitted period of stay in the territory of the Schengen States of 90 days in each period of 180 days, unless international agreements provide otherwise, or 4) has not presented sufficient documents to confirm the purpose and conditions of the intended stay, or 5) does not possess sufficient financial means in an amount depending on the duration and purpose of the intended stay or financial means for the return journey to the country of origin or residence or for the transit through the territory of the Republic of Poland to a third country

(Article 28 and Article 33 of the Law on foreigners), as a consequence of which the foreigner is handed over to the third country from which he/she has arrived, except in situations provided for in the Act.[1194] The commanding officer of the Border Guard post is competent to issue a decision on refusal of entry. A foreigner has the right to appeal against this decision to the Commander-in-Chief of the Border Guard, but submitting such an appeal does not give the foreigner the right to stay on the territory of Poland, as the decision to refuse entry is, by virtue of law, immediately enforceable (Article 33 of the Law on foreigners).

When the basis for refusal of entry is the relevant provisions of the Law on foreigners and not the Schengen Borders Code, the investigation procedure is limited to interviewing the foreigner, inspecting the documents in his/her possession, interviewing the persons indicated by the foreigner who is accompanying him/her on the journey, carrying out checks in the available registers, records and lists in matters of foreigners, as well as obtaining the necessary information from state institutions, governmental and local government authorities, economic units carrying out activities in the field of public utility, other economic units and social organizations or natural

---

which will grant an entry permit, or a document confirming the possibility of obtaining such means in accordance with the law, or 6) possesses a forged or counterfeited travel document, visa or any other document entitling him/her to enter and stay in the territory of the Republic of Poland, or 7) his/her entry is made during the period of validity of the entry on the list of aliens whose stay in the territory of the Republic of Poland is undesirable, or 8) his/her data is in the Schengen Information System for the purpose of refusing entry and stay, or 9) his/her entry into or stay on the territory of the Republic of Poland may constitute a threat to public health, or 10) it is required for reasons of defense or state security or the protection of public security and order or the international relations of the Republic of Poland or another EU Member State.

1194 Pursuant to Article 31(1) of the Law on foreigners, "A foreigner who has been refused entry to the territory of the Republic of Poland may—in particularly justified cases, due to his/her state of health—not be transferred to a third country. Such a foreigner shall be provided with medical care in the event of a threat to life or health." In addition, it follows from Article 32 of the Law on foreigners that "In the case referred to in Article 6(5)(c) of the Schengen Borders Code, the commanding officer of the Border Guard post, after obtaining the consent of the Chief Commandant of the Border Guard, may allow a foreigner to enter the territory of the Republic of Poland for a period of stay not exceeding 15 days."

persons. However, the activities undertaken in the investigation procedure may be limited only to the inspection of the documents in the foreigner's possession if the circumstances of the foreigner's failure to fulfill the conditions necessary to cross the border do not raise any doubts (Article 34 of the Law on foreigners).[1195]

The Polish Law on foreigners (Article 35) also regulates the possibility of bringing a foreigner to the border without delay. This may occur only if the conditions stipulated in the Act are met, i.e., when the border was unintentionally crossed in violation of the law, and the foreigner was apprehended immediately after crossing the border in the border zone.[1196] In practice, such a situation mainly concerns third-country nationals apprehended by the competent authorities at the time of illegal crossing of the external border or in the vicinity of the border after it has already been crossed. However, the use of the above-mentioned solution must take place immediately after the apprehension, and there must be no doubts concerning the country from

---

1195 The case-law of the Supreme Administrative Court emphasizes that in order to conclude that the prerequisite set out in Article 34(2) of the Law on foreigners is fulfilled, i.e., the existence of unquestionable circumstances as to the non-fulfillment by the foreigner of the conditions necessary to cross the border, the authority is obliged, in the absence of other evidence, to carry out at least an interview (questioning) with the foreigner as to the purpose of crossing the border, from which a protocol should be drawn up in accordance with the rigors set out in Article 67 §§ 1 and 2 of the Code of Administrative Proceedings and Article 68 § 1 of the Code of Administrative Proceedings. Such an action shall also constitute the fulfillment of the obligation to conduct proceedings in a manner inspiring the confidence of its participants in public authorities, i.e., the principle set out in Article 8 of the Code of Administrative Proceedings—vide: judgments of the Supreme Administrative Court: of July 18, 2019, II OSK 414/19; of January 11, 2019, II OSK 2270/18 and II OSK 2868/18; of November 20, 2018, II OSK 1713/18; of July 26, 2018, II OSK 1752/18 <https://orzeczenia.nsa.gov.pl>.

1196 The concept of the border area is regulated in Article 12(1) of the Law of October 12, 1990 on the protection of the state border (Journal of Laws of 2024, item 388). According to it, the border zone comprises the entire area of municipalities adjacent to the state border and, in the maritime section, to the seashore. If the width of the border zone thus defined does not reach 15 km, the area of the municipalities directly adjacent to the municipalities adjacent to the state border or the seashore shall also be included in the border zone.

which the foreigner came inadvertently. Thus, it will usually be an accidental border crossing.[1197]

A foreigner whose entry or stay on the territory of Poland is considered illegal, in the light of the general provisions of the Law on foreigners, must take into account the fact that a decision on the obligation to return will be issued and subsequently executed against him/her, which may also include a ruling prohibiting re-entry into the territory of Poland and other Schengen States. Such a decision, based on one of the grounds listed in Article 302 of the Law on foreigners,[1198] is issued by the commanding officer of the Border

---

1197 See judgment of 07.06.2016, C-47/15, Sélina Affum v. Préfet du Pas-Calais and Procureur général de la Cour d'appel Douai, ECLI:EU:C:2016:408, § 72; Rogala R., in J. Chlebny (ed), *Prawo o cudzoziemcach Komentarz*, (Warszawa 2020) 143.

1198 Article 302 (1) of the Law on foreigners provides that: A decision to oblige a foreigner to return shall be issued to a foreigner when:
1) is or has been in the territory of the Republic of Poland without a valid visa or other valid document authorizing him/her to enter and stay in that territory, if a visa or other document is or was required, or
2) has not left the territory of the Republic of Poland after having used up the permitted period of his/her stay in the territory of all or some of the Schengen States to which he/she was entitled without a visa, within any period of 180 days, unless international agreements provide otherwise, or
3) has not left the territory of the Republic of Poland after having used up the permitted period of his/her stay indicated in the Schengen visa within any period of 180 days, or after having used up the permitted period of his/her stay on the basis of a national visa, or
4) performs or, on the date of initiation of the control of legality of performance of work carried out by an authorized body, performed work without a relevant work permit or a declaration on entrusting work to a foreigner entered in the register of declarations, or
5) undertook economic activities in contravention of the relevant regulations in force in the territory of the Republic of Poland, or
6) does not have the financial means necessary to cover the costs of stay on the territory of the Republic of Poland, return journey to the country of origin or residence, or transit through the territory of the Republic of Poland to a third country which will grant an entry permit, and has not indicated reliable sources for obtaining such financial means, or
7) it is mandatory to enter the foreigner's data in the register of foreigners whose residence on the territory of the Republic of Poland is undesirable, or
8) the foreigner's data are in the Schengen Information System for the purposes of refusing entry and stay, if the foreigner is staying on the territory of the Republic

Guard division or the commanding officer of the Border Guard post, and the appeal authority is the Commander-in-Chief of the Border Guard (Article 310 of the Law on foreigners). An exception is provided in the case of a decision to require the foreigner to return who is feared to be involved in terrorist or espionage activities or suspected of committing one of these offenses. In such a case, the decision is issued by the minister in charge of internal affairs, acting on the application of the Chief Commandant of the Police, the Head of the

---

of Poland under the visa-free regime or on the basis of a Schengen visa, excluding a visa authorizing only entry into and stay on the territory of the Republic of Poland, or
9) is required for reasons of national defense or security or the protection of public safety and order or the interests of the Republic of Poland, or
10. has crossed or attempted to cross the border in breach of the law and the circumstances referred to in Article 303(1)(9a) do not apply, or
11) has been sentenced by a final judgment in the Republic of Poland to an enforceable sentence of imprisonment and there are grounds for conducting proceedings for his or her transfer abroad for the purpose of enforcing the sentence imposed on him or her, or
12. is outside the border area where he/she is allowed to stay pursuant to the local border traffic permit, unless otherwise provided for in international agreements, or
13) stays on the territory of the Republic of Poland after the expiry of the period of stay to which he/she was entitled under the local border traffic permit, unless international agreements provide otherwise, or
14) the further stay of the foreigner on the territory of the Republic of Poland will constitute a threat to public health, as confirmed by a medical examination, or to the international relations of another Member State of the European Union, or
15) the purpose and conditions of the foreigner's stay on the territory of the Republic of Poland are inconsistent with those declared, unless the provisions of the law allow them to be changed, or
16) a decision has been issued to refuse to grant refugee status or subsidiary protection, to declare the application for international protection inadmissible, to discontinue the proceedings on granting international protection or to deprive him/her of refugee status or subsidiary protection and the foreigner:
(a) has failed to leave the territory of the Republic of Poland within the period and in the case referred to in Article 299(6)(1)(b), or
(b) is in a guarded centre or in custody for foreigners.
It should be borne in mind that further provisions of the Law on foreigners provide for derogations when a decision on the obligation to return is not issued, proceedings in such a case are not initiated or the enforcement of the decision on the alien's obligation to return is abandoned.

Internal Security Agency or the Head of the Military Counterintelligence Service (Article 329a of the Law on foreigners).

2.5.2.1.5 Special procedures

2.5.2.1.5.1 Crisis at the EU external border—the Polish-Belarusian border

In the summer of 2021, an unprecedented situation occurred at the Polish-Belarusian border, which is at the same time a part of the external border of the EU, related to an unprecedented influx of tens of thousands of migrants from Belarus, coming mainly from the Middle East region.[1199] It is widely acknowledged that this procedure was inspired by the Lukashenko regime and was actively supported by Belarusian services, which transported foreigners who arrived thanks to the cooperation of Belarusian authorities with travel agencies and airlines from urban centers to the border, equipping them with tools to cross the border and with food in case they needed to camp on the Belarusian side of the border.[1200] According to statistics reported by the Border Guard, 39,670 attempts to illegally cross the Polish-Belarusian border were recorded in 2021, while a year earlier, there were only 129 similar cases.[1201]

1199 The characteristics of this procedure are described, inter alia, by Hetnarowicz-Sikora J., and Walentowicz, J., "Realistic Measures to Protect the Rights and Security of an Immigrant on the Belarus Border from the Perspective of the Law on Foreigners, the Law on the Protection of Foreigners and Acts of International Law" (2022) 3–4 *Journal of Criminal Law and Penal Studies*, 71–72.

1200 Bruneau C., Plucinska J., and Abi Nader Y., *How Minsk became a destination for migrants travelling as tourists* (<https://www.reuters.com/world/europe/how-minsk-became-mecca-migrants-travelling-tourists-2021-11-15/> accessed August 17, 2024); Jak migranci przygotowywali się do wyruszenia z Mińska na granicę. RAPORT WIDEO (<https://belsat.eu/pl/news/08-11-2021-jak-wygladaly-przygotowania-do-szturmu-granicy-przez-migrantow-raport-wideo/> accessed August 17, 2024); Porażające nagranie. Służby białoruskie rzucają w tłum migrantów produkty żywnościowe. Przepychanki o jedzenie (<https://www.pap.pl/aktualnosci/news%2C997464%2Cporazajace-nagranie-sluzby-bialoruskie-rzucaja-w-tlum-migrantow-produkty>; cited after: Grześkowiak M., "Od aktywizmu do "polityki przyzwolenia." Komisja Europejska wobec nieregularnej migracji w latach 2015–2021 ze szczególnym uwzględnieniem kryzysu humanitarnego na granicy polsko-białoruskiej" (2023) 3 *Państwo i Prawo*, 21–47.

1201 <https://twitter.com/Straz_Graniczna/status/1478327785903038469?t=k2VdF_GmykZQBEunvENA9g&s=19>.

In the public space, it was indicated that the exploitation of migrants by the Belarusian government was aimed at destabilizing the situation in the region by artificially creating migration pressure on the Polish-Belarusian border, which is also the external border of the EU.[1202] At the same time, the European Council condemned the instrumental treatment of migrants and refugees by the Belarusian authorities and the provocation of a humanitarian crisis,[1203] and the actions taken by the Belarusian regime became widely referred to as a "hybrid attack" or "hybrid war."[1204]

A consequence of the massive influx of migrants to the Polish-Belarusian border was the introduction into Polish legislation of norms limiting the rights of foreigners illegally crossing the border, consisting of equipping the Border Guard with the competence to turn back foreigners crossing the border outside the Polish-Belarusian border crossing points. This measure is commonly called the push-back procedure,[1205] which can be regarded as either

---

1202 Zdanowicz M., "The Migration Crisis on the Polish-Belarusian Border" (2023) 28(1) *Białostockie Studia Prawnicze—Bialystok Legal Studies* <https://doi.org/10.15290/bsp.2023.28.01.06>, 104 and 106. The issue of instrumentalization of migration was also referred to by the European Commission, which in December 2021 presented a proposal for a regulation on instrumentalization in the field of migration and asylum together with a proposal to amend the Schengen Borders Code in order to define the concept of instrumentalization of migrants—Proposal for a Regulation of the European Parliament and of the Council on the situation of instrumentalization in the field of migration and asylum, COM(2021) 890. It is worth noting that, according to the authors of "THE STRATEGIC RISK ANALYSIS REPORT 2024," commissioned by FRONTEX, Russia and Belarus will continue and probably expand their hybrid operations in the near future, and the instrumentalization of migration by Belarus itself is a precedent proving the capacity of hostile third countries to engage in this kind of hybrid interference, consisting, inter alia, in the creation of artificial migration routes, and thereby destabilizing the situation of a specific EU Member State and the EU as a whole—THE STRATEGIC RISK ANALYSIS REPORT 2024, 36 <https://www.frontex.europa.eu/assets/Publications/Risk_Analysis/Risk_Analysis/Strategic_Risk_Analysis_2024_Report.pdf> accessed September 30, 2024.

1203 European Council Meeting (December 16, 2021)—Conclusions, Brussels, December 16, 2021, EUCO 22/21, item 21.

1204 Bodnar A., and Grzelak A., "The Polish-Belarusian Border Crisis and the (Lack of) European Union Response" (2023) 28(1) *Białostockie Studia Prawnicze—Bialystok Legal Studies* <https://doi.org/10.15290/bsp.2023.28.01.04>, 76.

1205 Law of October 14, 2021 amending the act on foreigners and certain other acts (Journal of Laws 2021, item 1918).

a quasi-border procedure or a special (special) border procedure, although not within the meaning of Article 43(2) of Directive 2013/32/EU.[1206]

The first act regulating this issue was the Ordinance of the Minister of Interior and Administration of August 20, 2021, amending the Ordinance on temporary suspension or restriction of border traffic at certain border crossing points.[1207] Under § 3(2b) of the amended border ordinance, Border Guard officers were equipped with the power to turn back to the state border line foreigners who were detected outside the range of a border crossing

1206 Directive 2013/32/EU of the European Parliament and of the Council of June 26, 2013 on common procedures for granting and withdrawing international protection (recast), OJ EU.L.2013.180.60. As a supplementary note, it should be added that, in addition to the amendments to the regulations which sanctioned in the Polish legal order the institution of returning foreigners to the border line, the reaction of the Polish authorities was also the introduction, in the area of the highest concentration of migratory movements, along the line of the Polish-Belarusian border, first of all, of a temporary ban on staying in a specific area of the border zone covering the area of 183 municipalities from the Podlaskie and Lubelskie Voivodeships, and also of a state of emergency. See the regulations issued in this respect by the Minister of Internal Affairs and Administration on the introduction of a temporary ban on staying in a specified area in the border zone adjacent to the state border with the Republic of Belarus of: November 30, 2021, February 28, 2022, June 12, 2024, However, in the case of the regulation issued on the last of the aforementioned dates, the territorial scope of its validity was defined differently from the preceding acts, by designating zones of a specific width counted from the line of the state border into the territory of Poland along a 60.67 km long section of the Polish-Belarusian border (Journal of Laws of 2021, item 2193; Journal of Laws of 2022, item 488; Journal of Laws of 2024, item 861). See Matłacz A., and Robert Horbaczewki, *Od czwartku "stefa buforowa" przy granicy z Białorusią* <https://www.prawo.pl/samorzad/strefa-buforowa-przy-granicy-z-bialorusia,527405.html> accessed September 30, 2024. The state of emergency, on the other hand, was introduced by the ordinance of the President of the Republic of Poland of September 2, 2021 on the introduction of a state of emergency in the area of a part of the Podlaskie Voivodeship and a part of the Lubelskie Voivodeship (Journal of Laws, item 1612). A permanent fence has also been erected along the border with Belarus in order to limit the physical possibility of foreigners entering the territory of Poland through the so-called "green border."

1207 Journal of Laws of 2023, item 1536). This regulation amended the regulation of the Minister of Internal Affairs and Administration of March 13, 2020 on temporary suspension or restriction of border traffic at certain border crossing points (Journal of Laws of 2020, item 1403, hereinafter: "Border Guard Ordinance").

point or at a border crossing point where border traffic had been suspended or restricted.

The second act introducing the push-back mechanism was the amendment of the Law on foreigners, sometimes referred to as the "export act,"[1208] which introduced Article 303b into the Law on foreigners. Under it, the commanding officer of the Border Guard post became competent to issue a decision ordering a foreigner apprehended immediately after illegally crossing the border to leave the territory of Poland and, at the same time, forbidding him/her to re-enter the territory of the Republic of Poland and other Schengen States for a period from 6 months to 3 years. The amending act also introduced changes to the Law on granting protection to foreigners within the territory of the Republic of Poland by adding Article 33(1a). This amendment constituted a kind of supplement to the provision of Article 303b of the Law on foreigners, as it stipulated that an application for international protection submitted under the conditions specified in Article 303b of the Law on foreignersshall be left unprocessed unless the foreigner has arrived directly from the territory where his/her life was threatened by persecution or the risk of serious harm, has presented credible reasons for illegal entry and has applied for international protection immediately after crossing the border.

The Polish literature points out that crossing the border in places not intended for this purpose is a violation of the law in force and, in a given country, may be considered an offense or even a crime. Moreover, it was pointed out that under Article 5 of the Schengen Borders Code, the crossing of the external borders of the EU is allowed at border crossing points during their fixed opening hours, and foreigners intending to apply for international protection are not exempted from this rigor. In principle, therefore, a foreigner should make a request for such protection at a border crossing point and not at any place of his or her choice. Of course, this does not mean that by crossing the border at an unauthorized place, a foreigner a priori forfeits the right to exercise his/her Conventionally guaranteed rights, including the

---

1208 Sobczak K., *WSA umorzył skargę na "pushback," bo Straż Graniczna dostarczyła dokument o wycofaniu* <https://www.prawo.pl/prawo/pushback-wsa-umorzyl-skarge-rodziny-z-iraku,514119.html> accessed September 30, 2024.

guarantees arising from the principle of non-refoulement,[1209] the essence of which is that a foreigner whose fundamental rights are at risk should not be turned back from the border.[1210] Nevertheless, it should be borne in mind that this principle is not absolute, as it cannot be invoked by a foreigner who has grounds for being considered a threat to the security of the State in which he or she has been found or who has been convicted by a final judgment of severe crimes and constitutes a danger to the society of the state concerned.[1211] Furthermore, the very essence of state sovereignty includes the right to regulate the entry, residence, and expulsion of aliens. However, even in exercising this authority, States must adhere to the rights guaranteed by Article 3 of the European Convention on Human Rights and Fundamental Freedoms, which implies absolute protection of foreigners against expulsion if they would be subjected to torture, inhuman or degrading treatment or punishment.[1212] Moreover, the protection of foreigners' rights at the border also stems from the prohibition of their collective expulsion.[1213]

The occurrence of a new, hitherto unprecedented crisis situation on the Polish-Belarusian border, involving, inter alia, attempts by migrants to cross the border collectively (including even with the use of violence) as part of the so-called "hybrid war" organized by the Belarusian regime, raises doubts about the solutions introduced in Polish law sanctioning the push-back procedure. On the one hand, it raises concerns about the violation of the principle of non-refoulement; on the other hand, it prompts questions about the limits of the acceptable reaction of a country confronted with the instrumental use of migration by another state.

The solutions introduced into Polish law and synthetically described earlier have not gained wider acceptance among the institutions upholding human

---

1209 Respect for the principle of non-refoulement is required by Article 33(1) of the Convention relating to the Status of Refugees, drawn up in Geneva on July 28, 1951 (OJ 1991, item 515, hereinafter: "Geneva Convention").

1210 Chlebny J., "Zawrócenie cudzoziemca na granicy," (2023) 5 Zeszyty *Naukowe Sądownictwa Administracyjnego*, 9–13.

1211 Article 33(2) of the Geneva Convention.

1212 Convention for the Protection of Human Rights and Fundamental Freedoms drawn up in Rome on November 4, 1950, subsequently amended by Protocols Nos. 3, 5 and 8 and supplemented by Protocol No. 2 (Journal of Laws 1993, No. 61, item 284 as amended, hereinafter: "Convention").

1213 Article 4 of Protocol No. 4 to the Convention.

rights and freedoms, although it should be noted that their assessment in Polish society does not seem to be so unambiguously negative. Even during the implementation stage of these regulations, the Ombudsman signaled their inconsistency with the provisions of the Geneva Convention, Article 19 of the Charter of Fundamental Rights,[1214] with the European Convention for the Protection of Human Rights and Fundamental Freedoms, as well as with Article 56(2) of the Polish Constitution, which guarantees the right to seek protection in Poland and the right to an effective remedy referred to in Article 13(1) of Directive 2008/115/EC of the European Parliament and of the Council of December 16, 2008 on common standards and procedures in Member States for returning illegally staying third-country nationals, and Article 47 of the Charter of Fundamental Rights. In doing so, the Ombudsman pointed to the failure to provide an effective remedy in the case of a foreigner's return because although Article 303b of the Law on foreigners provides for the possibility to lodge a complaint against the decisions of the commanding officer of the Border Guard post issued in this case, this avenue of appeal is ineffective. This is because lodging a complaint does not stop the procedure of turning the foreigner back, and the mere drafting of such a complaint and sending it under the conditions where the foreigner is located (e.g., a forest on the Polish-Belarusian border) seems unrealistic.[1215]

1214 This provision stipulates that no one may be removed, expelled or extradited to a State where there is a serious risk that he or she may be subjected to the death penalty, torture or other inhuman or degrading treatment or punishment.

1215 Cited after: Skibińska R., *Choć pushbacki cudzoziemców są wątpliwe prawnie, to ciągle mają miejsce* <https://www.prawo.pl/samorzad/pushback-niezgody-z-prawem-wyroki-sadow,523677.html> accessed September 30, 2024; Opinion of the Ombudsman of October 3, 2021 submitted to the Senate of the Republic of Poland <https://bip.brpo.gov.pl/sites/default/files/2021-10/Opinia_RPO_cudzoziemcy_3.10.2021.pdf> accessed September 30, 2024; the literature points out that the need for a suspensive remedy stems from the jurisprudence of the Court of Justice of the European Union, from which it follows that such a remedy should have suspensive effect at least if the foreigner would be exposed to the risks set out in Article 18 of the Charter of Fundamental Rights in conjunction with Article 33 of the Geneva Convention or Article 19(2) of the Charter of Fundamental Rights. Otherwise, the right to an effective remedy provided for in Article 47 of the Charter of Fundamental Rights is violated—Judgment of the Court of Justice of the European Union of June 19, 2018, C-181/16, Sadikou v. État belge, EU:C:2018:465, § 54.

The practice of the push-back of foreigners has also failed to gain approval in the literature. It has been assessed as contrary to human rights standards and irreconcilable with the state's international obligations, including relevant EU law regulations.[1216] Even a definition of the term push-back has been formulated, which describes it is an unlawful international practice of actually returning persons to the country from whose territory they (usually illegally) crossed the border, without allowing them to apply for refugee status and without initiating other administrative proceedings against them, including return procedures.[1217] It was also highlighted that the practice of turning back foreigners had previously been used by Hungary, resulting in a finding by the Court of Justice of the European Union that this country had failed to fulfill its obligation to ensure effective access to the international protection procedure, and in similar situations relating to Poland, the European Court of Human Rights found that the European Convention on Human Rights had been violated when persons arriving from Belarus were refused applications for international protection by Border Guard officers.[1218]

[1216] Bodnar A., and Grzelak A., "The Polish-Belarusian Border Crisis and the (Lack of) European Union Response" (2023) 28(1) *Białostockie Studia Prawnicze—Bialystok Legal Studies* <https://doi.org/10.15290/bsp.2023.28.01.04>, 61; Baranowska G., "Pushbacks in Poland: Grounding the Practice in Domestic Law in 2021," *Polish Yearbook of International Law* (2023, vol. 41) 193–211; Klaus W. (ed), *Poza prawem. Prawna ocena działań państwa polskiego w reakcji na kryzys humanitarny na granicy polsko-białoruskiej* (Warszawa 2022); Grześkowiak M., "Od aktywizmu do "polityki przyzwolenia." Komisja Europejska wobec nieregularnej migracji w latach 2015–2021 ze szczególnym uwzględnieniem kryzysu humanitarnego na granicy polsko-białoruskiej" (2023) 3 *Państwo i Prawo*, 23.

[1217] Baranowska K., "Legalność i dopuszczalność procedury push-back (wywózek) i ocena prób ich legalizowania w Polsce," in W. Klaus (ed), *Poza prawem. Prawna ocena działań państwa polskiego w reakcji na kryzys humanitarny na granicy polsko-białoruskiej* (Warszawa 2022) 10. This author also notes that the practice of push-back violates the so-called procedural directive (2013/32/EU), according to which persons seeking international protection should be able to remain in a Member State of the European Union throughout the proceedings in their case.

[1218] Zdanowicz M., "The Migration Crisis on the Polish-Belarusian Border" (2023) 28(1) *Białostockie Studia Prawnicze—Bialystok Legal Studies* <https://doi.org/10.15290/bsp.2023.28.01.06>, 108; see also Judgment of the Court (Grand Chamber) of December 17, 2020 on the case of European Commission v. Hungary, C-808/18; M.K. and others v. Poland, applications nos. 40503/17, 42902/17, and 43643/17 (ECtHR

Also, the Helsinki Foundation for Human Rights report assessed that the practice in question violates international and EU law. If a foreigner reveals an illegal border crossing, a proper administrative procedure should be implemented to oblige him/her to return in accordance with all guarantees referred to in Directive 2008/115/EC.[1219]

Finally, one cannot overlook the fact that also in Polish court rulings, the assessment of the legality of turning foreigners back from the border turned out to be negative. The Voivodeship Administrative Court in Białystok challenged the legality of the Border Guard officers' actions in this respect, holding that § 3 section 2b of the Border Guard Ordinance was issued in breach of the boundaries of statutory authorization and, therefore, could not constitute a legal basis for the practice mentioned above. Thus, the Court declared the contested action ineffective, concurrently finding both a violation of the prohibition of collective expulsion and the principle of non-refoulement.[1220]

Despite the relatively short period during which the push-back mechanism has been in effect in Polish law, it can be said with certainty that it raises controversies from the point of view of its compliance with the standards of protection of individual rights derived not only from the Polish Constitution, but also from international and EU law. Although it cannot be unequivocally ruled out that push-back, understood as a "special border procedure," has fulfilled the function of an effective barrier limiting illegal crossing of the Polish-Belarusian border, doubts are raised as to the costs of such actions both in the human sphere, in the sense that protecting the state border is done at the expense of human life and the health of migrants, and in the sphere of image for the Polish state. It is difficult not to get the impression that the practice of returning foreigners has exposed the inadequacy of the existing

---

July 23, 2020); Also Case of D.A. and others v. Poland, Application No. 51246/17 Judgment of July 8, 2021.

1219 Czarnota K., and Górczyńska M., *Gdzie prawo nie sięga. Raport Helsińskiej Fundacji Praw Człowieka z monitoringu sytuacji na polsko-białoruskiej granicy* <https://www.hfhr.pl/wp-content/uploads/2022/06/Raport_Gdzie_Prawo_Nie_Siega-HFPC-30062022.pdf> accessed August 28, 2024, 33.

1220 See judgments of the Voivodship Administrative Court in Białystok of September 15, 2022, II SA/Bk 492/22; of April 4, 2023, II SA/Bk 145/23; of May 30, 2023, II SA/Bk 244/23 <https://orzeczenia.nsa.gov.pl>.

procedures and the institutions responsible for implementing them, as well as the limitations of states and their organizations in responding to crisis situations involving sudden mass migration waves. This is evident regardless of whether such waves are inspired by the actions of hostile neighboring states or arise from other circumstances, such as economic factors, social unrest, or armed conflicts.

There is no doubt that in view of the hostile actions of the Belarusian regime, which destabilized the situation not only on the border but also in the entire region, Poland was forced to take measures to protect the state border, which is, at the same time, the external border of the European Union. Some of the solutions adopted to this end raise significant concerns, particularly the Border Guard's push-back procedure. This practice risks violating the principle of non-refoulement and effectively prevents the individual assessment of a foreigner's circumstances, as well as the submission of an application for international protection. In the Polish legal literature, however, it is pointed out that foreigners do not have an unlimited right to choose the place of crossing the border, including for the purpose of applying for international protection, just as they do not have an absolute right to an individual decision specifying a ban on entry or an order to leave the territory of the state. It is argued that this position is supported by the case law of the European Court of Human Rights,[1221] without denying that the solutions adopted by the Polish authorities are debatable.

1221 Grand Chamber judgment of the European Court of Human Rights of February 13, 2020 in the case of N.D. and N.T v. Spain, applications nos. 8675/15 and 8697/15. This judgment established the conditions precluding State responsibility for turning back a foreigner at the border without individual proceedings in relation to an allegation of a violation of the prohibition on the collective expulsion of aliens, in the context of a complex allegation of a violation of Article 4 of Protocol No. 4 to the ECHR. The Court indicated that the assessment of this allegation requires a two-stage test (§§ 201, 209–211 of the grounds of the above-mentioned judgment). First, it is necessary to establish the foreigner's ability to benefit from an effective and lawful entry procedure, which involves the availability to foreigners of border crossings where they could apply for international protection. Next, it is necessary to examine whether the failure to use the available procedures is objectively justified. See: Chlebny J., "Wyzwania dla procedury uchodźczej w czasie kryzysu na granicy," in *Współczesne problemy orzecznicze sądów administracyjnych Polski i Czech. Materiały ze spotkania polsko-czeskiej grupy roboczej sędziów sądów administracyjnych*

Polish legislation does not provide for border procedures within the meaning of Article 43(2) of Directive 2013/32/EU.[1222] It is also unlikely that, if transposed into national legislation, the short timeframes outlined for examining an application for international protection would be an effective solution to a crisis arising from a hybrid war. For this reason, greater hopes are pinned on the solutions provided for in the provisions of the New Pact on Migration and Asylum, mainly those concerning the so-called screening of foreigners before they are allowed to enter the territory of a Member State. This process will enable actions to be taken with regard to a foreigner that will ultimately allow for the application of an appropriate procedure aimed at either granting or refusing entry and implementing a decision obliging the foreigner to return.[1223] Similar expectations are associated with the proposal for a Regulation of the European Parliament and of the Council on the situation of instrumentalization in the area of migration and asylum.[1224]

(Kraków, 11–13 czerwca 2023) (2024) 20 (Special issue) *Zeszyty Naukowe Sądownictwa Administracyjnego*, 15–16.

1222 Directive 2013/32/EU of the European Parliament and of the Council of June 26, 2013 on common procedures for granting and withdrawing international protection (recast), OJ EU.L.2013.180.60.

1223 Draft Regulation of the European Parliament and of the Council introducing screening of third-country nationals at the external borders and amending Regulation (EC) No. 767/2008, (EU) 2017/2226, (EU) 2018/1240 and (EU) 2019/817 (COM(2020) 612 final. According to the principles of this control, it would target, inter alia, persons crossing the external border in an unauthorized manner, or who have applied for international protection during border checks without fulfilling the entry conditions. The purpose of this screening is to identify persons who may pose a threat to internal security and, in certain cases, to determine the health status of foreign nationals. Importantly, the screening could also be carried out on the territory of a Member State if the third-country national has not been subjected to external border control (Articles 5 and 6). Moreover, during such a screening, third-country nationals should not be allowed to enter the territory of a Member State (Article 4).

1224 Draft Regulation of the Parliament and of the Council on the situation of instrumentalization in the areas of migration and asylum (COM (2021) 890). The draft defines the concept of instrumentalization as a situation where a third country or a non-state actor induces irregular migration to the Union by encouraging third-country nationals or stateless persons to move to or from its external borders, and then to those external borders or to the territory of one or more Member States, or by facilitating or even coercing such movements, where such actions indicate that the third country or non-state actor has the intention to destabilize the Union or a Member State, and where the nature of such actions is such as to jeopardize the

This proposal provides for the introduction of an emergency asylum and return procedure, as well as a derogation from the reception conditions for third-country nationals or stateless persons,[1225] subject to instrumentalization, apprehended in the vicinity of an external border in connection with an unauthorized border crossing (Article 1 of the above-mentioned draft Regulation). The purpose of this act would be to guarantee a state subjected to migratory pressure accurate control of foreigners at the border while respecting the principle of non-refoulement. The regulation would not legalize the turning back of aliens, including their collective turning back, and its application would require authorization by the Council based on a proposal from the Commission acting on a request from a Member State (Article 7 of the cited draft).

The crisis on the Polish-Belarusian border inspired by the Belarusian regime, resulting from the instrumental use of migration to destabilize the situation in neighboring countries and de facto the entire European Union, necessitates a revision of the way of looking at the standards to which foreigners are entitled, which were developed several decades ago. There is no doubt that a State subjected to migratory pressure must be equipped with instruments ensuring effective protection of its borders in a manner compatible with the foreigner's right to obtain international protection. At present, it seems difficult, to say the least, to strike a balance in this respect since, even in states of emergency, it is not possible to restrict access to the procedure for granting international protection.[1226] Member States should work together

essential functions of the State, including its territorial integrity, the maintenance of law and order or the safeguarding of national security (recital 1).

1225 These derogations mainly consist in extending the time limits foreseen for border procedures. For example, the extraordinary asylum procedure provides for longer deadlines for registering an application (3 weeks) and issuing a decision (up to 20 weeks, including the possibility of appeal, starting from the registration of the application). At the same time, in a situation of instrumentalization of migrants, the extraordinary return procedure consists of abandoning the application of the rules on return laid down in EU legislation in favor of the application of national law while respecting fundamental guarantees, including those under the Charter of Fundamental Rights of the European Union (recitals 12, 13 and Article 4 of the draft Regulation).

1226 See: Chlebny J., "Wyzwania dla procedury uchodźczej w czasie kryzysu na granicy," in *Współczesne problemy orzecznicze sądów administracyjnych Polski i Czech.*

to develop mechanisms to effectively counter migration crises, even if this is not an easy task. Perhaps effective border procedures should be one of them. However, it should be made clear that, at present, the countries directly exposed to such situations usually also bear the brunt of the consequences themselves. One of the recent initiatives of the Polish authorities, even if it is considered somewhat controversial, is therefore unsurprising: the adoption by the Council of Ministers of a resolution outlining what is described as a comprehensive and responsible Polish migration strategy for the years 2025–2030 titled "To regain control. Ensure Security."[1227] It lists eight areas of public policy intervention, including terms of access to national and international protection, emphasizing the need to amend international regulations and adapt them to the current migration situation so that current procedures are not used in hybrid actions. The document announces, among other things, further strengthening of border infrastructure (including through physical and electronic security of the Polish-Belarusian and Polish-Russian borders), the implementation of programs increasing security, and taking legislative measures at the national and European level in response to the instrumentalization of migration. At the same time, the Strategy underlines the critical attitude of the Polish authorities toward the adopted New Pact on Migration and Asylum, accusing it of presenting superficial regulatory solutions. It also emphasizes the need to establish a separate institution at the central (national) level with broad competences for the creation and implementation of migration policy, as well as the importance of developing a national return program to support an effective system of return of foreigners whose stay in Poland is unjustified or undesirable.

Materiały ze spotkania polsko-czeskiej grupy roboczej sędziów sądów administracyjnych (Kraków, 11–13 czerwca 2023) (2024) 20 (Special issue), *Zeszyty Naukowe Sądownictwa Administracyjnego*, 20–21. The author points out that, as the law currently stands, the provisions of the Procedural Directive 2013/32/EU, which is still in force, guarantee access to the procedure for granting international protection even in the event of a declaration of martial law, a state of emergency or an emergency situation caused by a mass influx of foreigners.

1227 Annex to Resolution No. 120 of the Council of Ministers of October 15, 2024, hereinafter: "strategy."

2.5.2.2 Deprivation of liberty, restriction of liberty and coercion (Paweł Dańczak)

2.5.2.2.1 Deprivation and restriction of liberty

The application of various measures restricting a foreigner's freedom depends on the person's current status.

In the case of an application for international protection, it is stipulated that until the decision on the granting of international protection becomes final, an applicant for international protection may be obliged to: 1) report at specified intervals to a designated authority, 2) pay a monetary security in a specified amount, not less than twice the minimum wage provided for in the provisions on the minimum wage, and 3) reside in a designated place.[1228] These measures are not of an isolating nature, but are an alternative to deprivation of liberty; moreover, they may be applied individually or jointly. The decision on the application of such measures is issued by the Border Guard authority, which has detained the foreigner. The decision may be appealed against to the district court (not administrative court) competent for the seat of the Border Guard authority, which issued the decision within 7 days from the date of its notification. The court shall consider the complaint within 7 days.[1229] If a foreigner does not comply with the obligations imposed on him/her, he/she may be detained, but only in cases specified in the Act.[1230]

1228 Article 88 (1) of the Law of June 13, 2003 on granting protection to foreigners within the territory of the Republic of Poland (Journal of Laws of 2023, item 1504, as amended).

1229 Article 88 (2) and (3) of the Law on granting protection to foreigners on the territory of the Republic of Poland. This regulation implements the standards of European law, as well as those arising from the European Convention on Human Rights and Fundamental Freedoms (judgment of the European Court of Human Rights of October 8, 2009, Mikolenko v. Estonia, application No. 10664/05, HUDOC).

1230 These cases are defined in Article 87 (1) of the Law on granting protection to foreigners on the territory of the Republic of Poland, and thus such detention is possible only in order to: 1) to establish or verify their identity; 2) to gather with their participation information on which the application for international protection is based and which would be impossible to obtain without detention—if there is a significant probability of their escape; 3) to issue or execute a decision on the foreigner's obligation to return, when proceedings on the obligation to return are pending against the applicant or the person on behalf of whom the applicant is applying, or when a decision on the obligation to return has been issued against the applicant or the person on behalf of whom the applicant is applying, and the

The Law on granting protection to foreigners within the territory of the Republic of Poland also permits the application of isolation measures to a foreigner seeking international protection, such as placement in a guarded center or a detention center for foreigners. The general basis for the application of both indicated detention measures is the lack of possibility to apply the aforementioned non-isolation measures. However, the placement of a foreigner in a detention center for foreigners, which is essentially a separate facility within a guarded center for foreigners or a Border Guard post,[1231] should be a measure of last resort, being applicable only to a foreigner who has not complied with the rules of stay in a guarded center or who runs the risk of not complying with those rules.[1232]

Placement in a guarded center or detention center for foreigners, according to Article 89 of the Law on granting protection to foreigners within the territory of the Republic of Poland, is decided by the district court (common court) upon the request of the Border Guard authority that has detained the foreigner. The period of stay in such a facility may not exceed 60 days, with the possibility of extending it to 90 days or for a specific period necessary to issue a decision on granting international protection. The district court's decision may be appealed against to the regional court.

Although a common court is competent in the case of placement in a guarded center or in a detention center for foreigners, release from such a facility takes place by way of a decision of an administrative authority, i.e., the Head of the Office for Foreigners. An appeal against such a decision is

---

applicant or the person on behalf of whom the applicant is applying have previously had the opportunity to submit an application for international protection and there is a reasonable suspicion that the application has been submitted only to delay the issuance of or to delay or prevent the execution of the decision on the foreigner's obligation to return; 4) when required for reasons of defense or state security or the protection of public security and order; 5) in accordance with Article 28 (<https://sip.lex.pl/#/document/68336766?unitId=art(28)&cm=DOCUMENT>) of Regulation 604/2013—where there is a substantial likelihood that the applicant or the person on whose behalf the applicant is applying will abscond and immediate transfer to another Member State is not possible.

1231 Liszewska A., in J. Chlebny, W (ed), *Prawo o cudzoziemcach Komentarz* (Warszawa 2020) 1191.

1232 Article 88a (2) of the Law on granting protection to foreigners on the territory of the Republic of Poland.

not examined under the administrative procedure, as control in this respect is still exercised by a common court.

Measures limiting the foreigner's freedom of movement are also a safeguard of the procedure for granting international protection before its completion. They are applied by way of a decision of the Head of the Office for Foreigners and consist in ordering the foreigner to stay in a specific place of residence or a specific locality until the decision on granting the refugee status becomes final. During this period, the foreigner may not leave the designated place without the permission of the Head of the Office for Foreigners and is obliged to report to this authority at intervals indicated in the decision.[1233] If the foreigner leaves the designated residence or locality without the relevant consent, the application for international protection shall be deemed implicitly withdrawn.[1234]

Extensive regulations concerning the restriction and deprivation of freedom of foreigners are also contained in the Law on foreigners (Articles 394–427). It should be pointed out at the outset that illegal crossing of the Polish border by a foreigner and illegal stay on the territory of Poland result in issuing a decision obliging the foreigner to return. Under Article 394 of the Law on foreigners, a foreigner who, inter alia, has circumstances justifying the issuance of such a decision or who evades the obligations set out in the decision (e.g., leaving the country within a set deadline) may be detained for a period not exceeding 48 hours.[1235] The detention is carried out by the Border Guard or the Police. However, the role of the Police is limited, as once the foreigner is detained, they hand him/her over to the Border Guard while simultaneously applying for a decision on the obligation to return.

1233 Article 89c of the Law on granting protection to foreigners on the territory of the Republic of Poland.

1234 § 40 (2) of the Law on granting protection to foreigners on the territory of the Republic of Poland.

1235 Pursuant to § 394 (1a) of the Law on foreigners, detention of a foreigner may also be based on: 1) the forced execution of a decision to oblige the foreigner to return, or 2) transfer on the basis of Regulation 604/2013, or 3) transfer to another Member State of the European Union, a Member State of the European Free Trade Association (EFTA)—a party to the Agreement on the European Economic Area or the Swiss Confederation on the basis of an international agreement on the transfer and reception of persons, or 4) transfer to a third country on the basis of an international agreement on the transfer and reception of persons.

A detained foreigner is released if he/she has not been placed at the disposal of a court within 48 hours and, at the same time, no application for placing him/her in a guarded center or for placing him/her in custody for foreigners has been submitted, or if a decision on placing him/her in a guarded center or for placing him/her in custody for foreigners has not been delivered to him/her within 24 hours from the time he/she was placed at the disposal of a court. The Border Guard applies to the court for placing a foreigner in one of the above-mentioned facilities. The Border Guard is also competent in issuing a decision on applying non-isolation measures referred to in Article 398 sec. 2 of the Law on foreigners, consisting in his/her obligation, until the decision on return obligation or transfer to another Member State is executed, to report at specified intervals to the Border Guard authority indicated in the decision; to pay a monetary security deposit; to hand over the travel document to the authority's depository; and to reside in a designated place.

The application of a detention measure serves the purpose of preparing the foreigner for his/her return or carrying out the process of his/her expulsion when less repressive measures cannot be applied in a given case. In particular, this measure is aimed at limiting the possibility of the foreigner fleeing, or is for situations when public security and order considerations are required. The basic measure used in this type of situation is placing a person in a guarded center for foreigners, and if there is a risk that the foreigner will not comply with the rules of staying in such a center, then he/she may be placed in a detention center for foreigners. However, the use of detention measures is out of the question if it would cause a danger to the life or health of the foreigner or if his/her psychophysical condition would justify the presumption that the foreigner has been subjected to violence. The basic maximum duration of a foreigner's stay in a guarded center or detention center is 3 months, but in the circumstances provided for by the Act, this period may be extended—up to a total of 18 months, excluding the period of the foreigner's stay in a guarded center or custody for foreigners in connection with his/her application for international protection. The solutions provided for in the Law on foreigners with regard to restricting or depriving a foreigner of freedom are in line with the content of Directive 2008/15/EC.[1236]

1236 This follows from Articles 398a, 399, 400 and 403 of the Law on foreigners. See also Liszewska A., in J. Chlebny (ed), *Prawo o cudzoziemcach* (Komentarz,

Neither on the basis of the provisions of the Law on foreigners nor of the Law on granting protection to foreigners within the territory of the Republic of Poland did the national authorities introduce specific solutions concerning the application to foreigners of measures leading to restriction or deprivation of freedom. Thus, the presented outline of such measures concerned the regulation applicable to all foreigners, regardless of the circumstances related to their crossing the border or staying on the territory of Poland. This does not mean, however, that the Polish authorities remained passive, if only in the face of the migration crisis on the Polish-Belarusian border. By introducing into the provisions of the Law on the protection of the state border the institution of a temporary ban on staying in a specific area in the border zone and deciding to erect a physical barrier (fence) along the land section of the border with Belarus, penal measures were also envisaged for violating the said ban or for destroying infrastructure intended to protect the state border. Illegal stay in the prohibited area is punishable by arrest or a fine, while a person committing destruction of border infrastructure is liable to imprisonment from 6 months to up to 5 years. The provisions of the Law on the protection of the state border do not limit the scope of criminal liability regulated in this way only to Polish citizens, which means that foreigners may also be subject to such liability, especially those attempting to cross the border in a place not intended for this purpose.[1237]

2.5.2.2.2 *Direct coercion*

Polish law regulates direct coercion in a detailed and comprehensive manner in the provisions of the Law of May 24, 2013 on means of direct coercion

---

Warszawa 2020) 769–783; Directive 2008/115/EC of the European Parliament and of the Council of December 16, 2008 on common standards and procedures in Member States for returning illegally staying third-country nationals, OJ EU.L.2008.348.98.

1237 This follows from Articles 10, 12, 12a–12c and Articles 18c and 18d of the Law on the protection of the state border. For more on the consequences of illegally staying in a prohibited area see: Tuleja P., "Temporary Ban on Border Zone and Humanitarian Crisis" (2022) 3–4 *Journal of Criminal Law and Penal Studies*, 121–127; Kurzępa B., "Karnoprawne aspekty ochrony polskiej granicy państwowej . Przestępstwa graniczne" (2023) 2 *Prokuratura i Prawo*, 87–93.

and firearms,[1238] which provides for the possibility of using such measures also against foreigners.

This law regulates, inter alia, the catalog of means of direct coercion, the cases and principles of their use and application, and the entities authorized to use them, including officers of numerous services, including the Police and the Border Guard.[1239]

According to the provisions of this Act, the use of means of direct coercion or the use of firearms should serve to achieve the purposes indicated in the Act and be within the scope of the tasks that the Act entrusts to the entity entitled to use these means. The justification for the use of direct coercive measures may be, inter alia, to enforce the behavior required by law in accordance with the order issued; to repel a direct, unlawful attack on the life, health or freedom of an officer or another person, as well as to counteract activities aimed at such an attack; to counteract a breach of public order or security; to counteract a direct attack on protected areas, objects or equipment (including those important for the security or defense of the state or the inviolability of the state border); to counteract an attack on the inviolability of the state border; and to apprehend or detain a person, as well as to thwart his/her escape.[1240]

The use of direct coercion is subject not only to the principle of expediency but also to the principle of proportionality, as the choice of a particular measure should be appropriate to the degree of danger posed, with the least possible inconvenience and scale of damage caused by its use. If the situation so requires, more than one measure of direct coercion may be used simultaneously. Measures other than incapacitation techniques (physical force) are prohibited at the same time for women with visible pregnancy, persons whose appearance indicates an age of 13 years or less, and persons with visible disabilities.[1241]

Some measures of direct coercion, i.e., the use of physical force in the form of transport techniques, as well as the use of handcuffs, a straitjacket, an incapacitating belt or a safety helmet, can be used preventively to prevent

---

1238 Journal of Laws of 2024, item 383.

1239 This follows from Articles 1 and 2 of the Law on means of direct coercion and firearms.

1240 Articles 5 and 11 of the Law on means of direct coercion and firearms.

1241 Articles 6–9 of the Law on means of direct coercion and firearms.

a person from escaping, including those placed in a guarded center or a detention center for foreigners.[1242]

A measure that is in a sense dedicated to foreigners is placement in an isolation room. Such a room is a separate room included in the living quarters of a guarded center for foreigners, in which a person is placed individually when his/her isolation is dictated by the necessity to protect the life, health or freedom of other persons, or the need to ensure order or security in the areas or facilities subject to protection or to counteract destruction of property and manifestations of self-aggression. The foreigner's stay in such a room may not last longer than 48 hours. The placement in the room should be preceded by checking the foreigner and depriving him/her of objects which may constitute a threat, as well as informing him/her, in a language he/she understands, about the reasons for their placement in the isolation room and the maximum permitted period of placement in this room.[1243]

Article 4 of the Law on means of direct coercion and firearms defines the term "bringing," which also appears in the provisions of the Law on foreigners in the context of the forced execution of a decision obliging an alien to return.[1244] Such enforcement is carried out precisely by bringing the foreigner to the border or to an airport or seaport of the country to which he/she is brought, whereby this term should be understood as any actions taken with regard to the foreigner, inter alia, in order to move him/her as a person detained, apprehended or forcibly brought to the competent authorities or institutions, as well as in order to move the foreigner from a guarded center or detention center for aliens; to the border or from that border to an airport or seaport of the State to which he/she is being expelled, or of the State in which the alien is being transferred to another Member State.

The possibility to use means of direct coercion is not limited exclusively to Border Guard officers in the course of enforcing the decision to oblige a foreigner to return. Such a possibility is also provided for in Article 372 of the Law on foreigners in the course of conducting the transit of a foreigner by

---

1242 Article 13 of the Law on means of direct coercion and firearms.

1243 The above follows from Article 29 of the Law on means of direct coercion and firearms and the provisions of the Regulation of the Minister of the Interior of June 3, 2013 on the isolation room, Journal of Laws of 2013, item 641.

1244 Articles 388 and 389 of the Law on foreigners.

air. Such a right applies to officers of another Member State of the European Union who are part of the foreigner's escort. However, the cases when it is possible to resort to means of direct coercion are limited to the necessity to protect the health, life and freedom of the escorting officer and to prevent the foreigner's escape, his/her self-mutilation or maiming of other persons, as well as the foreigner's destruction of property when there are no Border Guard or Police officers or in order to support them.[1245]

2.5.2.3 Cooperation with the European Border and Coast Guard Agency (Paweł Dańczak)

To ensure effective protection of state borders, which are at the same time external borders of the European Union, a mechanism for the creation of Rapid Border Intervention Teams has been established at the level of the EU law,[1246] under which the European Border and Coast Guard Agency (Frontex) can deploy, for a limited period, European teams of border guards to undertake a rapid intervention on the territory of a Member State.[1247] In light of Polish legislation, such secondment can be requested by the minister in charge of internal affairs, who acts at the request of the Commander-in-Chief of the Border Guard.[1248] The secondment of Rapid Border Intervention Teams to provide assistance should take place in exceptional and urgent situations. Such a situation, by recital 7 of Council Regulation (EC) No 2007/2004, would arise if a Member State faced with a mass influx of third-country nationals attempting to enter its territory illegally, which would require an

---

1245 Rogala R. observes that the general principle on the possibility of the use of direct coercive measures is the limitation of the escort's reaction to self-defense (Article 7 (1) of Directive 2003/110/EC), and the use of direct coercive measures for other purposes must be justified and proportionate. Rogala R., in J. Chlebny (ed), Prawo o cudzoziemcach. Komentarz (Warszawa 2020) 739–740.

1246 Regulation (EC) No. 863/2007 of July 11, 2007 establishing a mechanism for the creation of a rapid border intervention and amending Council Regulation (EC) No. 2007/2004 as regards that mechanism and regulating the powers and tasks of guest officers (OJ L 199, 31.07.2007, 30).

1247 The basis for the formation of such teams was created by Council Regulation (EC) No. 2007/2004 of October 26, 2004 establishing a European Agency for the Management of Operational Cooperation at the External Borders of the Member States of the European Union (Official Journal of the EU L 349 of November 25, 2004, 1).

1248 Article 17c of the Law on the protection of the state border.

immediate response, and in which case the deployment of a Rapid Border Intervention Team could contribute to providing an effective response. Rapid Border Intervention Teams are not designed to provide long-term support.

An assessment of Frontex's actual capacity to support Member States in crisis situations is difficult to formulate, not least because of the scant information on the forms and extent of this Agency's cooperation with individual Member States. In the past, especially during the period of increased migration flows in 2015, this Agency has been accused of inadequate response and failure to protect people in the face of human rights violations. As a result of this, Frontex has been strengthened and given broader border management powers, both operationally and in terms of monitoring and coordinating action to stop irregular migration along all its routes and to prevent irregular migrants from entering the European Union.[1249]

As far as cooperation with Poland is concerned, available media information, citing the Ministry of Interior and Administration and the Agency's office in Warsaw, shows that recently, in agreement with the Polish side, the Frontex Agency deployed officers to selected border crossings in Poland as part of their permanent service. These included experts specialized in detecting forged documents and stolen vehicles. In addition, Frontex supported Poland by deploying 20 officers as part of Operation Terra at the eastern external border, providing increased technical and operational assistance to EU Member States by coordinating operational activities at the external land borders to control illegal immigration flows and combat cross-border crime. Under this operation, for the Polish border, the Agency's officers in Poland were to support Polish officers only at border crossing points.[1250]

1249 Cited after: Bodnar A., and Grzelak A., "The Polish-Belarusian Border Crisis and the (Lack of) European Union Response" (2023) 28(1) *Białostockie Studia Prawnicze—Bialystok Legal Studies* <https://doi.org/10.15290/bsp.2023.28.01.04>, 84; Moreno-Lax V., EU External Migration Policy and the Protection of Human Rights, September 2020, EP/EXPO/DROI/FWC/2019-01/LOT6/1/C/06 EN September 2020—PE 603.512.

1250 <https://konkret24.tvn24.pl/polska/kryzys-na-granicy-frontex-dziala-tylko-wtedy-gdy-panstwo-sobie-nie-radzi-z-sytuacja-nie-tylko-st7967532> accessed September 30, 2024.

Frontex itself currently identifies, as one of its main objectives, the need to intensify operational and technical support in carrying out effective returns and to offer Member States a range of developed services in this regard.[1251] This aligns with the assumptions of the migration strategy for 2025–2030 adopted by the Polish government, which plans to create a national return program with two components: voluntary and forced. Its implementation is to be carried out using the competencies of the European Union, including precisely the Frontex Agency.[1252] It seems, however, that the Polish authorities do not intend to significantly increase this Agency's involvement in protecting the Polish borders, or at least they do not give tangible expression to such plans. Indeed, the aforementioned strategy suggests that the preferred approach to securing Poland's borders with Belarus and Russia, as well as addressing migration crises originating from these areas, lies in the development of physical and electronic barriers rather than in fostering institutional and personnel cooperation.

2.5.2.4 Identification of basic standards for public administration bodies and administrative courts adjudicating cases concerning entry and residence of third-country nationals in the territory of the Republic of Poland (Grzegorz Rząsa)

2.5.2.4.1 Introductory remarks

In the Member States of the European Union, it is a general rule that decisions on migration matters, i.e., on the entry and residence of third-country nationals, are issued in the first stage by public administrative authorities. Subsequently, after the exhaustion of possible legal remedies available under administrative procedures, these decisions may be subject to judicial review. In doing so, it is emphasized that currently, it is not possible to identify a single model, common to all Member States, for the organization of the judiciary in migration matters.[1253]

1251 The Strategic Risk Analysis Report 2024, 36, <https://www.frontex.europa.eu/assets/Publications/Risk_Analysis/Risk_Analysis/Strategic_Risk_Analysis_2024_Report.pdf> accessed September 30, 2024.

1252 Annex to Resolution No. 120 of the Council of Ministers of October 15, 2024.

1253 See Chlebny J., "Public Order, National Security and the Rights of Third-Country Nationals in Immigration Cases" (2018) 20 *European Journal of Migration and Law*, 117.

Also, in the Polish legal system, as a rule, the settlement of issues related to the entry and stay of third-country nationals in the territory of the Republic of Poland (hereinafter also "Poland") is entrusted to public administration bodies.[1254] In particular, the competence of common courts related to placing a foreigner in a guarded center or custody for foreigners in connection with proceedings for granting international protection or proceedings for obliging a foreigner to return,[1255] remain outside the scope of this study.

As regards the cases of issuing permits for crossing the border under the local border traffic regime and, above all, the questions of issuing visas or visa refusals, revocations, and cancellations, as well as the issues of cancelling visa stickers, the competence in those matters is vested in the consuls.[1256] The scope of affairs delegated to the competence of consuls under separate provisions is contained in Article 34 of the Law of June 25, 2015—Consular Law.[1257] On the other hand, in the territory of Poland, as a rule, the competence in matters concerning the entry and stay of third-country nationals in the territory of the Republic of Poland is exercised by the Border Guard authorities, i.e., the commanding officer of the Border Guard division or the commanding officer of the Border Guard post, voivodes, the Head of the Office for Foreigners and the Council for Refugees. The Border Guard authorities adjudicate *inter alia* the cases concerning the refusal of entry into the territory of the Republic of Poland,[1258] the obligation to return,[1259] as well as the cases concerning granting of residence permits for humanitarian reasons and granting permits for tolerated stay.[1260] In turn, voivodes and the

---

1254 For more on the principles of entry of foreigners into the territory of the Republic of Poland and the forms of their stay therein, see e.g., Krakała A., in B. Jaworska-Dębska (ed), *Kontrola legności pobytu cudzoziemców na terytorium RP*, in: *O prawie administracyjnym i administracji. Refleksje. Jubilee book dedicated to Professor Małgorzata Stahl* (Łódź 2017) 378–388.

1255 Article 88a of the Law of June 13, 2003 on granting protection to foreigners within the territory of the Republic of Poland (i.e., Journal of Laws of 2023, item 1504; hereinafter: "the Law on granting protection" or "the Protection Act") and Article 394 et seq of the Law of December 12, 2013 on foreigners (i.e., Dz. U. of 2023, item 519).

1256 Articles 42(1) and 66(1) of the Law on foreigners.

1257 Journal of Laws of 2023, item 1329; hereinafter: "Consular Law."

1258 Article 33(1) and (2) of the Law on foreigners.

1259 Articles 310 and 321(1) of the Law on foreigners.

1260 Article 356 of the Law on foreigners.

Head of the Office for Foreigners recognize, *inter alia*, the cases concerning granting temporary and permanent residence permits to foreigners.[1261] With regard to cases concerning the granting of international protection, on the other hand, competence is held by the Head of the Office for Foreigners and the Council for Refugees.[1262] The Head of the Office also adjudicates upon granting asylum.[1263]

Decisions issued by the above-mentioned public administration bodies may be subject to control by administrative courts.[1264] This control is exercised in terms of legality (compliance with the law) and the administrative court is, as a rule, not entitled to resolve an administrative case on the merits.[1265] In other words, the court does not take over the administrative case for final settlement, i.e., it cannot, in principle, replace the public administration body and issue a final decision on the case.[1266] Hence, judicial-administrative control is sometimes referred to as judicial supervision over the activities of public administration.[1267] If the contested decision or ruling is found to be unlawful, the administrative court, depending on the type of failure found, either repeals the contested act or declares it invalid.[1268] The public administration body, when re-examining a case, is bound by the indications as to the further

---

1261 Article 104(1) in conjunction with Article 16(1)(1) and Article 22(1)(1)(a) of the Law on foreigners.

1262 Article 16(1)(1) and (2) of the Law on foreigners and Article 89p(1) of the Law on granting protection.

1263 Article 94 of the Law on granting protection. The decision of the Head of the Office for Foreigners on asylum may be appealed against with a request for reconsideration (cf. Rogala R., in J. Chlebny (ed), Prawo o cudzoziemcach. Komentarz (Warszawa 2020) 1241).

1264 The issue of judicial and administrative review of decisions taken by consuls will be discussed in § 4 of this paper.

1265 Article 184 of the Constitution of the Republic of Poland in conjunction with Article 1 of the Law of July 25, 2002 on the system of administrative courts (i.e., Journal of Laws of 2022, item 2492).

1266 Cf. e.g., judgment of the SAC of November 15, 2022, II OSK 1953/21, CBOSA.

1267 See Drachal J., Jagielski J., and Gołaszewski P., in R. Hauser, and M. Wierzbowski (eds) *Prawo o postępowaniu przed sądami administracyjnymi. Commentary* (Warszawa 2023) 12–13.

1268 Article 145 of the Law of August 30, 2002 Law on proceedings before administrative courts (i.e., Journal of Laws of 2023, item 1634, as amended).

proceedings and legal assessments expressed in the final judgment of an administrative court.[1269]

2.5.2.4.2 *The principle of equal treatment of foreigners residing in the territory of Poland and Polish citizens*

According to Article 37(1) of the Polish Constitution, whoever is under the authority of the Republic of Poland enjoys the freedoms and rights provided for in the Constitution. In turn, pursuant to Article 37(2) of the Polish Constitution, exceptions to this principle, relating to foreigners, are determined by law. Based on Article 37(1) of the Constitution of the Republic of Poland, the principle of universality of enjoyment of the rights and freedoms provided for in the Constitution of the Republic of Poland is formulated,[1270] as well as the principle of equal treatment of foreigners residing in the territory of Poland and Polish citizens.[1271] One should share the view that from Article 37(1) of the Constitution of the Republic of Poland follows the presumption of enjoyment of the same freedoms and rights by foreigners and Polish citizens.[1272] Exceptions to this principle may be introduced only by statute and, moreover, they should meet the premise of proportionality, i.e., the limitations must be necessary in a democratic state for its security or public order, or for the protection of the environment, health, and public morals, or the freedoms and rights of other persons (Article 31(3) of the Constitution of the Republic of Poland). However, three caveats should be made here, closely related to Article 37(2) of the Constitution of the Republic of Poland. Firstly, the criterion of nationality may be a legitimate reason for differentiating the legal situation of the addressees of a given legal norm. In this sense, Article 37(2) of the Constitution of the Republic of Poland supplements the premises for limiting freedoms and rights indicated in Article 31(3)

1269 Article 153 of the Law on proceedings before administrative courts.

1270 See Florczak-Wątor M., in M. Safjan, and L. Bosek (eds), *Konstytucja RP.* Vol. I. *Komentarz do art. 1–86* (Warszawa 2016) 916.

1271 See Jagielski J., *Status prawny cudzoziemca w Polsce (problematyka administracyjno-prawna)* (Warszawa 1997) 112.

1272 See Chlebny J., "Konstytucyjny standard ochrony cudzoziemców w sprawach wjazd i pobytu w świetle orzecznictwa Naczelnego Sądu Administracyjnego," in J. Chlebny (ed), *Wolności i prawa człowieka i obywatela w orzecznictwie sądów administracyjnych. Jubilee book for the 100th anniversary of the establishment of the Supreme Administrative Court* (Warszawa 2022) 360.

of the Constitution of the Republic of Poland.[1273] Secondly, with regard to foreigners, limitations on the exercise of constitutional freedoms and rights may be more far-reaching than in the case of Polish citizens. In practice, this refers in particular to limitations motivated by the need to maintain public security and order. Thirdly, Article 37(2) of the Constitution of the Republic of Poland should be interpreted in such a way that it is possible, upon fulfillment of specific prerequisites, not only to limit by law but also to restrict completely the application of certain rights and freedoms to foreigners.[1274] Obviously, with respect to foreigners, the validity of such rights, which the Polish Constitution itself recognizes as inviolable, such as human dignity (Article 30 of the Polish Constitution), cannot be excluded by law. Similarly, regulations that would violate Poland's international obligations or the norms of EU law cannot be adopted with respect to foreigners either. At the same time, in the context of the obligation to comply with the law of the European Union, it has to be recalled that procedural regulations concerning cases of aliens in which EU law is applied are subject to the procedural autonomy of the Member States. These regulations, however, have to comply with the principles of equivalence (in other words: non-discrimination or equivalence) and effectiveness (in other words: efficiency).[1275] To rephrase it, national procedural rules, where European Union substantive law is applied, must not be less favorable than those for similar claims based on national law. Furthermore, those rules must not make the implementation of European Union law impossible or excessively difficult.[1276]

1273 Cf. Chlebny J., *Konstytucyjny standard …*, 361.

1274 See e.g., judgment of the Constitutional Tribunal of November 15, 2000, P 12/99, OTK 2000, No. 7, item 260; decisions of the Supreme Administrative Court: of August 30, 2022, II OSK 1435/22, CBOSA; of September 21, 2023, II OSK 1748/23, CBOSA; of January 17, 2024, II OSK 2504/23; decision of the SAC of February 7, 2024, II OSK 2598/23, CBOSA.

1275 See CJEU judgment of September 9, 2020, C-651/19, *JP vs. Commissaire Général Aux Réfugiés et Aux Apatrides*, § 34–35.

1276 Cf. e.g., Chlebny J., in G. Łaszczyca, and A. Matan (eds), *System Prawa Administracyjnego Procesowego. Vol. I …, . Zagadnienia ogólne* (Warszawa 2017) 404. For more on the principle of equivalence and effectiveness see, e.g., Wróbel A., in A. Wróbel, *Charter of Fundamental Rights of the European Union. Commentary* (Warszawa 2020) 1117–1126; Widdershoven R., "National Procedural Autonomy and General EU Law Limits" (2019) 2 *Review of European Administrative Law*, 5–15; Arnull A., "The Principle of

2.5.2.4.3 The standards applicable to proceedings before public administration authorities in cases concerning the entry and stay of a foreigner in the territory of Poland (in context of the right to good administration)

In administrative proceedings concerning the entry and stay of third-country nationals in the territory of the Republic of Poland, the provisions of the Law of June 14, 1960—CAP[1277]—are, as a rule, applicable. The provisions of the CAP are applied taking into account the procedural provisions contained in the individual acts regulating the issue of entry and stay of third-country nationals in the territory of the Republic of Poland.[1278] The relations between these provisions and the provisions of the CAP are resolved based on *lex specialis derogat legi generali* doctrine. It should be added that the provisions of the CAP are applied here directly and not appropriately, i.e., without any modifications within the scope not regulated in the respective substantive laws.[1279]

The assessment of whether the national procedural rules concerning the entry and residence of third-country nationals in the territory of the Republic of Poland meet the European standards of the right to good administration requires, first of all, the identification of the basic rights of the parties which constitute these standards. From the point of view of its place in the system of sources of law, Article 41(1) and (2) of the Charter of Fundamental Rights of the European Union CFR[1280] is of fundamental importance here. Although this provision refers to the institutions, bodies, organs, and organizational

---

Effective Judicial Protection in EU law: An Unruly Horse?" (2011) 1 *European Law Review*, 51–70.

1277 Journal of Laws of 2023, item 775; hereinafter: "CAP."

1278 See, *inter alia*, Article 4 of the Law on granting protection, Article 3(1) of the Law of July 14, 2006 on the entry into, residence in and exit from the territory of the Republic of Poland of nationals of the Member States of the European Union and their family members (i.e., Dz. U. of 2021, item 1697; hereinafter: "Act on the entry and stay of EU citizens") and Article 10 of the Law on foreigners.

1279 Cf. e.g., Chlebny J., in A. Matan (ed), *System Prawa Administracyjnego Procesowego. Vol. IV. Postępowania autonomiczne i szczególne. Postępowania niejurysdykcyjne* (Warszawa 2021) 571.

1280 Official Journal of the EU C of December 14, 2007. No. 303 s. 1, as amended; hereinafter: "CFR" (see e.g., Lenaerts K., "Exploring the Limits of the EU Charter of Fundamental Rights" (2012) 8 *European Constitutional Law Review*, 367.

units of the Union, it must be assumed that since the right to good administration is a general principle of European Union law, in the light of the principle of loyalty,[1281] the standards of the right to good administration must also be respected by national authorities applying this law.[1282] What is important here is that it is not only about the application of provisions that are the result of the technical implementation of the European legal norms but also of provisions that constitute a direct and necessary instrument for ensuring the desired effect of a European norm.[1283] The right to good administration, as a general principle of Union law, was also referred to by the CJEU in the case concerning the foreigner's obligation to return.[1284]

At the same time, it should be noted that the right to good administration is also the subject of normative acts of a *soft-law* nature. This refers in particular to the European Parliament resolution of September 6, 2001—the European Code of Good Administration[1285] and recommendations of the Committee of Ministers of the Council of Europe, including in particular Recommendation CM/Rec (2007)7 of July 20, 2007 on good administration.[1286] The aforementioned legal acts, although they do not have the character of sources of universally binding law, should nevertheless be taken into account by public administration bodies in the process of interpretation and application of administrative law. This is because they define certain basic standards which should be observed by the administration of a democratic law-governed state (Article 2 of the Constitution of the Republic

---

1281 Article 4(3) of the Treaty on European Union.

1282 Cf. e.g., Judgment of the NSA of May 16, 2018, II OSK 1589/16; CBOSA; Kowalik-Bańczyk K., in A. Wróbel (ed), *Charter of Fundamental Rights of the European Union. Commentary* (Warszawa 2020) 1054–1055.

1283 Cf. e.g., Chlebny J., in G. Łaszczyca, and A. Matan (eds), *System Prawa Administracyjnego Procesowego. Vol. I. Zagadnienia ogólne* (Warszawa 2017) 404; CJEU judgment of May 8, 2014, H.N. v Minister for Justice, Equality and Law Reform, Ireland, Attorney General, C-604/12, § 49–50 <https://curia.europa.eu>.

1284 See CJEU judgment of December 11, 2014, C-249/13, *Boudjlida vs. Préfet des Pyrénées-Atlantiques*, § 30–34 <https://curia.europa.eu>.

1285 Hereinafter: "EKDA." The text of this Code is contained, *inter alia*, in the work of J. Świątkiewicz," *Europejski Kodeks Dobrej Administracji. Introduction, text and commentary on the application of the code in the conditions of Polish administrative procedures* (Warszawa 2007).

1286 <https://rm.coe.int/16807096b9> accessed April 1, 2024; hereinafter: "Recommendation CM/Rec(2007)7."

of Poland).[1287] Similar importance can be attributed to the study entitled "Principles of administrative law concerning the relations between administrative authorities and private persons" prepared by a group of experts within the Council of Europe (hereinafter: "the Council of Europe Handbook").[1288] From the point of view of the implementation of the standards of good administration in cases concerning the obligation of a foreigner to return, an important *soft-law* act is the Commission Recommendation (EU) No 2017/2338 of November 16, 2017 establishing a common "Return Handbook" for use by the competent authorities of the Member States performing return-related tasks.[1289]

Drawing, *inter alia*, on the content of Article 41(1) and (2) of the CFR, the EKDA, Recommendation CM/Rec(2007)7, and the Council of Europe Handbook, as well as the doctrinal *acquis*,[1290] it can be assumed that this right includes, in its most general dimension, the right to an impartial and fair hearing of an administrative matter within a reasonable time. At the same time, it should be noted that the catalog of rights constituting the right to good administration, contained in the above-mentioned soft-law acts, is not closed.[1291] It can be supplemented by legislative changes, but doctrine and jurisprudence also play an important role in the development of this right. This includes not only the jurisprudence of national courts but also the jurisprudence of the Court of Justice of the EU and the jurisprudence of the European Court of Human Rights.

Turning to the assessment of the compliance of the Polish regulations with the European standards on the right to good administration, it should be stated that the national regulations take these standards into account to a large extent. The general principles of the CAP, contained in Articles 6–16 of the CAP, play

---

1287 Cf. e.g., Rząsa G., "The Principle of Legalism in General Administrative Proceedings" (selected issues) (2016) 13 *Monitor Prawniczy*, 710–711 and the case law cited therein.

1288 <https://rm.coe.int/1680700263> accessed April 9, 2024.

1289 OJ. EU. L. of 2017. No. 339, 83 as amended, see in particular § 12.1; cf. e.g., judgment of the SAC of December 12, 2023, II OSK 1655/23, CBOSA.

1290 See, for example, Chlebny J., in W. Piątek, J. P. Tarno (eds), *System Prawa Administracyjnego Procesowego. Vol. II. Part 2. Zasady ogólne postępowania administracyjnego* (Warszawa 2018) 211–246.

1291 Cf. della Cananea G., *The Common Core of European Administrative Laws; retrospective and prospective,* (Brill/Nijhoff 2023) 200.

a fundamental role in this respect.[1292] These principles are contained in the law of procedural character, but a part of these principles may be ascribed a substantive legal meaning at the same time.[1293] This applies in particular to the principles of legalism, the rule of law, and the principle of trust. This is so important that in Polish law there is still, despite legislative attempts and proposals made by the doctrine, no general part of administrative law.[1294] The principles of administrative proceedings should also include general principles of law stemming from the Constitution of the Republic of Poland and the principles of law originating from the centuries-old tradition (often dating back to Roman law), the validity of which in democratic legal orders is not in doubt.[1295]

Bearing in mind the above-mentioned catalog of rights constituting the European standard of the right to good administration, it may be pointed out that the principle of public administration bodies acting on the basis and within the limits of the law is explicitly expressed in Article 6 of the CAP. Moreover, it is, an indispensable element of the rule of law, the principle of which can be found in Article 7 of the CAP. As for the principle of equal treatment of the parties, it can be found, *inter alia*, in Article 8 § 1 of the CAP. The same provision indicates the obligation of a public administration body to remain impartial. Similarly, Article 8 § 1 of the CAP expresses the principle of proportionality. In turn, the principle of legal certainty and protection of acquired rights is an indispensable element of the rule of law (Article 7 of the CAP), the principle of trust (Article 8 § 1 of the CAP) and the principle of protecting the permanence of final administrative decisions (Article 16 of the CAP). The CAP also provides for the principle of speed of proceedings, obliging the authority to act in the case thoroughly and quickly,

---

1292 For more on these principles see, for example Piątek W., and Tarno J. P. (eds), *System Prawa Administracyjnego Procesowego. Vol. II. Part 2. Zasady ogólne postępowania administracyjnego* (Warszawa 2018), *passim*. As for studies in English see, e.g., Korzeniowski D., "General principles of the CAP as guidelines for public administration authorities" (2023) 2(80) *Ubezpieczenia w Rolnictwie—Materiały i Studia*, 209–230.

1293 See e.g., judgment of the SAC of June 4, 1982, I SA 258/82, ONSA 1982, No. 1, item 54, and judgment of the SAC of May 31, 2022, III OSK 4007/21, CBOSA.

1294 See, for example, Zimmermann J., *Prawo administracyjne* (Kraków 2006) 92.

1295 See e.g., Rząsa G., in M. Wierzbowski, and Wiktorowska A. (eds), *Kodeks postępowania administracyjnego. Komentarz* (31st edn, Legalis 2023), Nb 3 to Article 6; judgments of the SAC: of April 26, 2023, II OSK 1580/20; of January 17, 2024, II OSK 1596/23—CBOSA.

using the simplest possible means leading to its settlement (Article 12 § 1 of the CAP). In the CAP, the right of a party to active participation in the proceedings and the possibility to express one's standpoint before the decision is issued is expressed, *inter alia*, in Article 10 of the CAP. This right is specified in further provisions of the Code, including Article 79a of the CAP. The expression of the principle of openness of proceedings is, in particular, the right of the parties to have access to the case file (Articles 73–74 of the CAP), as well as the right of the parties to receive information from the public administration body about the factual and legal circumstances which may affect the determination of their rights and obligations which are the subject of administrative proceedings (Article 9 of the CAP). The protection of personal data is also ensured in administrative proceedings (Article 2a of the CAP). It should further be pointed out that a party to administrative proceedings has the right to be assisted by an attorney (Article 32 of the CAP). As far as the costs of the proceedings are concerned, as a rule, they are borne by the public administration body while the parties are usually obliged to pay fees related to obtaining a specific entitlement (Articles 261–267 of the CAP). The requirement of clarity of a decision is one of the elements of the principles of the rule of law, trust, and persuasion (Articles 7, 8, and 11 of the CAP). The CAP also regulates in detail the requirements to be met by the justification of an administrative decision, including instructions as to the legal remedies available to a party against such a decision (Article 107 § 3 of the CAP). A party has the right to lodge an appeal against a decision with an authority of the second instance or file a motion for reconsideration of the case (Article 127 of the CAP). Final administrative decisions may also be subject to judicial review (Article 16 § 2 of the CAP).

Examples of the application of the aforementioned standards of good administration, including the principles of the rule of law, trust, and proportionality in the cases concerning entry and stay in the territory of the Republic of Poland may be found in several judgments of the Supreme Administrative Court[1296] concerning the obligation of a foreigner to return due to crossing the border in violation of the law.[1297]

1296 Hereinafter, "SAC."

1297 See, e.g., Rząsa G., *Zastosowanie funkcji korygującej zasad ogólnych Kodeksu postępowania administracyjnego do sankcyjnych decyzji związanych—na przykładzie postępowania*

Another example of administrative courts resorting to the general principles of the CAP to ensure real protection of foreigners' rights can be found in the 2018 judgments of the SAC in the cases concerning decisions refusing entry into the territory of the Republic of Poland.[1298] It is worth adding that the above-described faulty practice of the Border Guard authorities in the matter of determining whether a foreigner had declared at a border crossing point an intention to submit an application for international protection resulted in the European Court of Human Rights (hereinafter: "ECtHR")[1299] finding that Poland violated, *inter alia*, Article 3 of the Convention on the Protection of Human Rights and Fundamental Freedoms (hereinafter: "ECHR")[1300] and Article 4 of Protocol No. 4.[1301] In this context, one has to agree with the thesis that the violation of the ECHR found by the ECtHR was a consequence not of faulty legislation, but of faulty interpretation and practice of application of national and the EU regulations by the Border Guard authorities which consequently prevented foreigners from submitting applications for international protection.[1302]

In the context of matters concerning the entry and stay of third-country nationals in the territory of the Republic of Poland, it should be further noted that certain rights of the parties constituting the standards of the right to good administration are subject to certain modifications. For example, with regard to foreigners, in order to strengthen their right to be heard, Article 7 of the Aliens Act modifies, with respect to the general principle of

---

w sprawie zobowiązania cudzoziemca do powrotu, in: *Determinanty prawa i postępowania administracyjnego oraz sądowoadministracyjnego. Księga Jubileuszowa dedykowana profesor Aleksandrze Wiktorowskiej* (Warszawa 2024) 159–170.

1298 See, e.g., judgments of the SAC: of May 17, 2018, II OSK 2766/17; of July 26, 2018, II OSK 1752/18; of November 20, 2018, II OSK 1627/18—CBOSA.

1299 See Joined Cases 40503/17, 42902/17 and 43643/17—LEX No. 3033298 (ECtHR July 23, 2020).

1300 Journal of Laws of 1993, No. 61, item 284, as amended.

1301 Protocol No. 4 to the Convention for the Protection of Human Rights and Fundamental Freedoms, drawn up in Paris on March 20, 1952 and drawn up in Strasbourg on September 16, 1963 (Journal of Laws of 1995, No. 36, item 175/2 as amended)—hereinafter: "Protocol No. 4."

1302 See Chlebny J., "Crossing the Border by an Alien Intending to Submit an Application for International Protection. Gloss to the Judgment of the ECtHR of 23 July 2020, Joined Cases 40503/17, 42902/17 and 43643/17" (2020) 12 *Europejski Przegląd Sądowy*, 51.

information in Article 9 of the CAP, the scope of instructions given to them. In particular, the scope of the obligation to inform under the former Act is very broad and also applies to circumstances that are not directly related to actions during the proceedings.[1303] These instructions should, as a rule, be formulated in writing,[1304] in a language the foreigner understands. The condition of instruction in an intelligible language is not identical to the obligation to instruct in the native language or the language chosen by the foreigner—it is sufficient to instruct in any language sufficiently understood by the foreigner.[1305] At the same time, there should be a factual presumption that the foreigner has a sufficient command of the official language of the country of origin. The burden of rebutting this presumption of fact lies with the foreigner concerned, being the party to the procedure.[1306] An exception to the principle of instructing the foreigner about his/her rights and obligations in writing is provided for, *inter alia*, in Article 327(2) of the Aliens Act and Article 12(2) of Directive 2008/115/EC. These provisions allow, in the case of a decision obliging the foreigner to return, for the foreigner to be orally instructed as to whether the decision is to be appealed, and, if so, under what procedure. Against the background of these provisions, the jurisprudence has expressed the view that the necessity to draw up a written instruction each time in a language understood by the foreigner, especially in a situation where the foreigner is apprehended immediately for the illegal crossing of the border, could lead to a significant prolongation of the proceedings on the obligation to return and thus undermine the fundamental

---

1303 Cf. e.g., Chlebny J., "Right to Information and Assistance of an Interpreter in the Case of Obliging a Foreigner to Leave the Territory of Poland," in J. Sługocki (ed), *Dziesięć lat polskich doświadczeń w Unii Europejskiej. Problemy prawnoadministracyjne*, vol. 2 (Wrocław 2014) 618–619; judgment of the SAC of May 10, 2023, II OSK 1544/22, CBOSA.

1304 See Article 327(2) of the Law on foreigners and Article 12(2) of Directive 2008/115/EC of the European Parliament and of the Council of December 16, 2008 on common standards and procedures in Member States for returning illegally staying third-country nationals (OJ. EU L of 2008. No. 348, 98 as amended, hereinafter: the "Return Directive" or "Directive 2008/115/EC"—see judgment of the SAC of January 17, 2024, II OSK 1596/23, CBOSA.

1305 See Chlebny J., in J. Chlebny (ed), *Prawo cudzoziemców. Komentarz* (Warszawa 2020) 54–55.

1306 See judgment of the SAC of March 1, 2023, II OSK 2841/21—CBOSA.

objective of the Return Directive, which is the fast and effective removal from the territory of the European Union of foreigners staying there illegally.[1307]

In practice, the issue of proper instruction of a foreigner about his/her rights often arises also in the context of the possibility of waiving the right to appeal against the decision obliging to return.[1308] The jurisprudence approves of the practice of the Border Guard authorities to use instruction forms in a language which a foreigner understands and to provide oral translations of procedural statements submitted by him or her.[1309] It is essential that instructions given to a foreigner meet the standards developed in court rulings on the grounds of Article 127a in conjunction with Article 9 of the CAP in conjunction with Article 7 of the A.C.C., including information not only about the inadmissibility of lodging an appeal in connection with a waiver of the right to appeal but also instruction about the inadmissibility of lodging a complaint with an administrative court in such a case.[1310]

From the point of view of the foreigner's right to active participation in administrative proceedings, including the right to be heard, the problem of the language barrier is an important limitation. With regard to this issue, it should be recalled that in proceedings involving foreigners, there is a general principle, closely related to the essence of state sovereignty, that the authorities of a given state conduct administrative and judicial proceedings in the official language of that state. In Poland, this principle is, moreover, directly anchored in the Constitution of the Republic of Poland.[1311] This principle also applies to proceedings for granting international protection.[1312] Therefore, it can be said that a foreigner applying for the right of entry or residence in the territory of the Republic of Poland, in the light of both national and EU regulations, as well as international regulations, cannot demand that the administrative proceedings be conducted in a language understood by the foreigner and not

1307 See judgment of the SAC of January 17, 2024, II OSK 1596/23, CBOSA.

1308 See Article 127a of the CAP.

1309 See e.g., the judgment of the SAC of December 19, 2022, II OSK 693/22, CBOSA.

1310 See e.g., the judgment of the SAC of December 12, 2023, II OSK 1765/23, CBOSA.

1311 See Article 27 of the Constitution of the Republic of Poland and Articles 4 and 5(1) of the Law of October 7, 1999 on the Polish language—Journal of Laws of 2021, item 672; cf. e.g., judgment of the WSA in Warsaw of April 19, 2021, IV SA/Wa 2446/20, CBOSA.

1312 See Chlebny J., *Postępowanie w sprawie o nadanie statusu uchodźcy* (Warszawa 2011) 265–266.

in Polish. With regard to administrative proceedings conducted under the Aliens Act, Article 8(1) of this Act confirms the general principle applicable in administrative proceedings that applications in matters regulated by this Act shall be drawn up in Polish. A party in these proceedings is also obliged to submit documents formulated in a foreign language, serving as evidence in the proceedings, together with their translation into Polish by a sworn translator (Article 8(2) of the Law on foreigners).[1313]

In this context, especially in terms of the implementation of the right to a hearing, the problem of providing the foreigner with the assistance of an interpreter is of fundamental importance. The Aliens Act provides for the general rule that the name of the interpreter shall be given in the minutes of the interrogation of foreigners, in matters regulated by the Act. The conclusion can be drawn from this provision that if the authority admits evidence of a foreigner's testimony, it is incumbent upon the authority to ensure the participation of an interpreter in such interrogation. The consequence of this position is, *inter alia*, that the authority bears the costs of the interpreter services in such a case. The rule in administrative proceedings is that the costs of the proceedings (expenses) shall be borne by the authority conducting the proceedings, which results from the evidentiary obligations of the authority[1314] and from strictly defined cases when the costs of the proceedings shall be borne by the party.[1315] On the other hand, the authority conducting the proceedings under the Aliens Act is not, as a rule, obliged to provide the party with the assistance of an interpreter during procedural actions other than the hearing. Exceptions to this rule concern, *inter alia*, proceedings on granting a foreigner a temporary residence permit for victims of trafficking in human beings[1316] and proceedings on issuing a decision to oblige a foreigner to return.[1317] Against the background of these regulations, a reasonable postulate has been put forward in the doctrine for the introduction of a comprehensive regulation concerning the participation of an interpreter in the proceedings conducted on the basis of the Aliens Act, the purpose of which would be, on the one hand, to extend the possibility of the interpreter's participation

1313 Cf. judgment of the SAC of October 28, 2021, II OSK 147/21, CBOSA.
1314 Articles 7, 75 § 1, 77 § 1 of the CAP.
1315 Article 262 § 1 of the CAP.
1316 Article 176 of the Law on foreigners.
1317 Article 327(1) of the Law on foreigners.

in these proceedings and, on the other hand, the possibility to charge the party, apart from certain exceptions, with the costs of the interpreter's participation.[1318] On similar principles, the legitimate participation of a translator in the proceedings on granting international protection has been defined, while in these proceedings the costs of translation into Polish of documents drawn up in a foreign language admitted as evidence in the proceedings shall be ensured, if necessary, by the authority before which the proceedings are conducted.[1319] Against the background of Article 11(2) of the Protection Act, it is assumed in case law that the administrative body is obliged to translate into Polish also those documents which the foreigner presents claiming that they constitute evidence of important circumstances in the case. This is because it is impossible to determine whether a document drawn up in a foreign language concerns circumstances which are relevant in the case and thus must be admitted as evidence without knowing its content.[1320] In proceedings for international protection, a party is also provided with the assistance of an interpreter in submitting an application for proceedings,[1321] and may also apply for free legal information and free legal aid.[1322]

Concluding the issue of translations, it is worth noting that the authority is obliged to translate certain elements of certain decisions issued in proceedings with the participation of foreigners. In particular, the authority which issued the decision on the foreigner's obligation to return shall provide, in a language which the foreigner understands, an oral or written translation of the legal basis of the decision, the decision as well as instructions as to

---

1318 See Chróścielewski W., and Chlebny J., "Z problematyki informacji udzielanej cudzoziemcom przez organy prowadzące postępowania administracyjne," in M. Cherka, P. Gołaszewski, J. Piech, and M. Wierzbowski (eds), *Kryzys, stagnacja, renesans? Prawo administracyjne przyszłości. Księga jubileuszowa profesora dr hab. Jacka Jagielskiego* (Warszawa 2021) 1020–1021.

1319 Article 11(2) of the Protection Act.

1320 See judgment of the SAC of April 13, 2023, II OSK 1131/22, CBOSA.

1321 Articles 29(1) and 30(1)(6) of the Protection Act.

1322 Articles 69c–69m of the Protection Act. This regulation implements the provisions of Directive 2013/32/EU of the European Parliament and of the Council of June 26, 2013 on common procedures for granting and withdrawing international protection—(OJ EU L 2013.180.60, hereinafter: "Procedural Directive")—cf. e.g., judgment of the SAC of August 22, 2023, II OSK 2766/22 and judgment of the SAC of January 4, 2023, II OSK 1686/22, CBOSA.

whether and how the decision may be appealed against.[1323] On the other hand, in the case of decisions concerning the granting or refusal of international protection, declaring the application for international protection inadmissible or discontinuing the proceedings in these cases or transferring the applicant to the Member State responsible for examining the application, the authority is obliged to provide a written translation into a language understood by the applicant of the legal basis of the decision, the decision and instructions.[1324]

The Aliens Act also provides for special provisions regarding the code principles which introduce limitations to the procedural rights of the parties under the CAP. For example, one can point to Article 6 sec. 1 of the Aliens Act, in the light of which, the authority issuing a decision or a decision in proceedings conducted pursuant to the provisions of this Act may refrain from drawing up their justification in the part concerning the factual justification if it is required by considerations of defense or state security or the protection of public security and order.[1325] An analogous solution is provided for, *inter alia*, in Article 5 of the Protection Act, Article 5 of the Law on the entry and residence of EU citizens, as well as in Article 11 of the Law of April 2, 2009 on Polish citizenship.[1326]

The possibility of limiting the foreigner's right to know the full reasons for the decision on the grounds of defense or state security or the protection of public security and order should not raise any doubts, both in the context of national law and EU law, as well as international law. It is, however,

1323 Article 327(2) of the Law on foreigners. This regulation is a manifestation of the implementation of Article 12(2) of the Return Directive. The translation of the legal basis of the decision, the determination and the instruction on remedies seems to fulfill the requirement to translate the "main elements of the return decision."

1324 Article 53(2) of the Protection Act.

1325 On the other hand, it is unacceptable not to draw up a statement of reasons for the decision in the part concerning the determination of the condition of Polish origin of the foreigner (art. 6 § 2 of the Law on foreigners). This provision is a manifestation of the position taken by the Constitutional Tribunal in the judgment of May 13, 2003, SK 21/02 (OTK-A 2003, No. 5, item 39), in which the Tribunal stated that art. 77 in connection with art. 23 § 1 clause 2 of the Law on foreigners of June 25, 1997 (Journal of Laws of 2001, No. 127, item 1400), to the extent in which it allows waiving the justification of a decision in the part concerning the Polish origin of a foreigner is inconsistent with art. 52 § 5 and art. 51 § 3 in connection with art. 2 and art. 31 § 3 of the Constitution of the Republic of Poland.

1326 OJ 2023, item 1989.

a separate question whether the principle of proportionality has been observed in the introduction of certain restrictions, given their scope. In each case, the balance between the public interest and the interest of the foreigner should be made here (Article 7 in connection with Article 8 § 1 of the CAP). It is worth adding that such notions as, *inter alia*, security and public order are elements of many regulations concerning the right of entry or stay of a foreigner in the territory of the Republic of Poland,[1327] but they have not been defined by the legislator. The doctrine emphasizes, moreover, that neither in EU law nor in the jurisprudence of the CJEU or the ECtHR do we find an unambiguous definition of such concepts as public order, and national security (possibly internal or external security of the state).[1328] These concepts fall under the category of public (social) interest and are legal concepts that are subject to interpretation. Meaning-wise, being undefined phrases, they leave administrative bodies, as well as the administrative court, with a natural discretion.[1329] It is generally accepted that public security is such a state in which the general public, as well as other entities, including the state and other public institutions, are not threatened by any danger (threat to certain goods) and are not threatened by the disruption of the normal course of social life and the functioning of public institutions and facilities, and this regardless of the source.[1330] The concept of public order, in turn, is broader than the concept of legal order, as it encompasses the factual state within the state, regulated by legal and extra-legal norms, the observance of which enables the normal coexistence of individuals within the state organization, in a specific place and time.[1331] In order to assess whether a given foreigner

---

1327 Instead of many see, for example, the following provisions of the Law on foreigners: § 28(1)(10), § 65(1)(5), § 100(1)(4), § 197(1)(4), § 215(1)(2).

1328 See Chlebny J., *Public Order …*, 119.

1329 See Chlebny J., "Protection of public interest and a foreigner's right to stay in Poland" (2007), no. 10 *Europejski Przegląd Sądowy*, 18; judgment of the SAC of October 12, 2023, II OSK 2217/21, CBOSA.

1330 See, e.g., Ura E., Pieprzny S., and Pado T., "Pojęcie bezpieczeństwa publicznego w prawie administracyjnym," in J. Zimmermann (ed), *Koncepcja systemu prawa administracyjnego* (Warszawa 2007) 161–177; Jagielski J., in *Obywatelstwo polskie. Komentarz do ustawy* (Warszawa 2016) 106; Chlebny J., in *Prawo cudzoziemców …*, 50–51; judgment of the SAC of November 22, 2023, II OSK 1434/22, CBOSA.

1331 See judgment of the SAC of May 15, 2018, II OSK 2765/17 and judgment of the SAC of October 12, 2023, II OSK 2217/21—CBOSA.

may constitute a threat to the protection of public security and order, it is also important whether the subject of the proceedings is the imposition of an administrative sanction on a party (e.g., obligation to return, deprivation of residence title) or whether it is the granting of entitlement to a party (e.g., in the form of granting a residence title or recognition as a Polish citizen). In a case concerning the granting of entitlement to a party, the aforementioned discretionary leeway on the part of the public administration bodies is more far-reaching than it is in the case concerning the application of administrative sanctions against a foreigner.[1332] In particular, the level of threat posed by the foreigner to public safety and order justifying the refusal to grant an entitlement may be lower than in cases concerning the application of sanctions against such a foreigner. Such an approach is justified, *inter alia*, by the principle of proportionality.

As far as domestic law is concerned, the basis for limiting and in certain cases even excluding the validity of the foreigner's right to know the full reasons for the decision is Article 37(2) in conjunction with Article 31(3) of the Polish Constitution. In particular, Article 31(3) of the Polish Constitution refers to the premise of limiting rights and freedoms on grounds of state security or public order. With regard to European Union law, categories such as defense or state security or public safety and order fall within the concept of general interest recognized by the European Union, as referred to, *inter alia*, in Article 52(1) of the CFR, and thus constitute a legitimate reason for limiting the rights provided for in the CFR, including the right to good administration. It should be added that, in the case of European Union law on aliens, some of the directives that make up this law contain specific regulations on the justification of decisions. For example, in the light of Article 12(1) of Directive 2008/115/EC, the factual justification of a return decision may be limited if national law allows for the right to information to be restricted, in particular, to protect national security, defense, public security and for the prevention, investigation, detection and prosecution of criminal offenses. As far as international law relating to foreigners is concerned, on the other hand, in the context of restrictions on a foreigner's right to know the full reasons for adjudication, one can point to cases of recourse

1332 Cf. judgment of the SAC of April 9, 2024, II OSK 417/23, CBOSA.

to the security or public order clause in the provisions of the ECHR.[1333] From the point of view of the issue of interest, attention should also be drawn to Article 1(2) of Protocol No. 7 of November 22, 1984 to the Convention for the Protection of Human Rights and Fundamental Freedoms.[1334] In the light of this provision, an alien may be expelled, without first exercising, *inter alia*, the right to present reasons against expulsion, if this is necessary for reasons of public order or justified on grounds of state security. The solution provided for in Article 1(2) of Protocol No. 7 is similar in content to Article 32(2) of the Convention relating to the Status of Refugees, drawn up in Geneva on July 28, 1951.[1335] In particular, also in the light of the Geneva Convention, the expulsion of a refugee may take place without giving him or her an opportunity to present evidence of his or her justification if compelling reasons of state security militate against it.

The issue of restricting a foreigner's access to a case file on the grounds of a threat to public safety or order is often considered in jurisprudential practice through the prism of up to an effective remedy before a court, and will therefore be discussed in more detail in the next chapter of this paper.

2.5.2.4.4 *Standards applicable to proceedings before an administrative court in cases concerning the entry and stay of a foreigner in the territory (in the context of the right to an effective remedy before a court)*

In the domestic legal order, the right to a court is expressed primarily in Article 45 of the Polish Constitution. According to paragraph 1 of this provision, everyone has the right to a fair and public hearing without undue delay by a competent, independent, impartial and independent court. The provisions of Article 45 of the Constitution of the Republic of Poland should be interpreted and applied taking into account, *inter alia*, Article 77(2) of the Constitution, according to which law may not close off a judicial path for anyone to pursue violated freedoms or rights. *Lege non distinguente*, Articles 45 and 77(2) of the Constitution of the Republic of Poland apply to the cases adjudication of which has been entrusted to administrative courts. The competence of these courts, at the

---

1333 See, for example, Articles 6(1) 8(2) ECHR and Article 2(3) and 2(4) of Protocol No. 4.
1334 Journal of Laws of 2003, No. 42, item 36.
1335 Journal of Laws of 1991, No. 119, item 517; hereinafter: "Geneva Convention."

constitutional level, is generally defined in Article 184 of the Polish Constitution. The constitutional standard of administrative judiciary is also set, *inter alia*, by Article 10 of the Constitution of the Republic of Poland (the principle of the division and balance of legislative, executive and judicial powers), Article 176(1) of the Constitution (the principle of two-instance court proceedings) and also by the constitutional guarantees of independence and autonomy of judges (Articles 178–181 of the Constitution of the Republic of Poland).[1336]

The content of the constitutional right to a court has a well-established meaning as a result of numerous judgments of the Constitutional Court.[1337] This jurisprudence points to four essential structural elements of the right to a court: 1) the right of access to court, i.e., the activation of the procedure before a competent, independent, impartial and independent court; 2) the right to appropriate shaping of the court procedure in accordance with the requirements of justice and openness, in particular in accordance with the principles of the so-called procedural justice; 3) the right to obtain a binding court decision; 4) the right to appropriate shaping of the system and position of the bodies adjudicating the cases. Therefore, it may be assumed that Article 45 of the Constitution of the Republic of Poland encompasses the right to a court in the formal (availability of court proceedings in general) and substantive (possibility of legally effective protection of rights through court proceedings).[1338] As far as the court in terms of the Constitution is concerned, it is understood as an organ of judicial power with a specific systemic position and characteristics, separate and independent from the legislature and the executive (Article 173 of the Constitution), and, moreover, competent to hear a case and independent and impartial in its adjudication.[1339] In this context, attention should be drawn to the key guarantee role, which, with regard to the systemic prerequisite of the independence of administrative judiciary from the executive power, is played by the entrustment of administrative supervision over

---

1336 Cf. e.g., Kmieciak Z., "Constitutional standard of administrative judiciary" (2022) 10 *Państwo i Prawo*, 120.

1337 Instead of many see e.g., the Constitutional Court judgment of May 12, 2017, SK 49/13, OTK-A 2017/4.

1338 See, e.g., the Constitutional Tribunal judgment of October 3, 2017, SK 31/15, OTK-A 2017/62.

1339 Judgment of the Constitutional Tribunal of January 13, 2015, SK 34/12, OTK-A 2015, No. 1, item 1.

administrative courts to the President of the Supreme Administrative Court,[1340] appointed by the President of the Republic of Poland for a six-year term from among candidates presented by the General Assembly of Judges of the Supreme Administrative Court.[1341] With regard to administrative courts in particular, it would be inadmissible, in the light of the constitutional standard of the right to a court, to entrust this supervision to the Minister of Justice, i.e., a member of the Council of Ministers, i.e., a representative of the executive power, i.e., the power whose legality of actions is precisely to control the administrative judiciary under Article 184 of the Constitution of the Republic of Poland. An equally important guarantee of the independence of the administrative judiciary is a system of disciplinary responsibility separate from that of the ordinary judiciary. That is, disciplinary cases of administrative court judges and court assessors are examined by the NSA.[1342] Finally, it should be pointed out that in the light of the wording of Article 45(1) of the Constitution (*verba legis*: "Everyone has the right"), as well as the above considerations concerning the principle of equal treatment of a foreigner residing in the territory of Poland and a Polish citizen, there is no doubt that the constitutional right to a court may also be exercised by foreigners.

The above-described elements of the constitutional right to a court, in connection with the systemic guarantees of independence of the Polish administrative judiciary (including the independence of this judiciary from the executive power, including, above all, the Minister of Justice), fully correspond to the standards of the right to a court in administrative cases developed in the ECtHR case law on the grounds of Article 6 ECHR. A compilation of these standards can be found, *inter alia*, in the Council of Europe Handbook,[1343] and, above all, in the Recommendation of the Committee of Ministers of the Council of Europe No. Rec (2004) 20 of December 15, 2004 on Judicial Review of Administrative Acts[1344] and in the explanatory memorandum for

---

1340 Articles 34–35 p.u.s.a.

1341 Article 185 of the Polish Constitution.

1342 Article 9 of the Law on the system of administrative courts.

1343 Council of Europe Handbook, 37–42.

1344 <https://rm.coe.int/09000016805db3f4> accessed April 17, 2024; hereinafter: "Recommendation Rec (2004) 20."

this recommendation.[1345] Reference has been made here in particular to the judgment of the ECtHR of October 4, 2001. ECHR of October 4, 2001 in the case of Potocka v. Poland (Application no. 33776/96).[1346] In the light of this judgment of the ECtHR and Article 134 § 1 of the Law on proceedings before administrative courts, the thesis that the cassation model of administrative judicature adopted in the Polish system, based on the control of administrative acts from the point of view of their compliance with the law (understood very broadly, and therefore also with the procedural rules concerning findings of fact and assessment of evidence), meets the standards set by Article 6 of the ECHR is legitimate.[1347] From the point of view of the effectiveness of judicial protection granted by administrative courts, it is also important that the ECHR requires that all administrative acts may be subjected to judicial review, either directly or indirectly, i.e., when reviewing another administrative act.[1348] This condition is also fulfilled in the Polish model of administrative justice. In particular, in the light of Article 135 of the Law on proceedings before administrative courts, the court shall apply the measures provided for by the law in order to remove the violation of the law in relation to acts or actions issued or undertaken in all proceedings conducted within the limits of the case to which the complaint relates, if this is necessary for its final settlement.

As regards the right to effective judicial protection, provided for in Article 47 of the CFR, it is a general principle of European Union law. This principle has been developed through the jurisprudence of the EU courts, which have referred to the common constitutional traditions of the Member States and the provisions of international agreements, in particular the ECHR.[1349] The

---

1345 <https://search.coe.int/cm/Pages/result_details.aspx?ObjectID=09000016805dba26> accessed April 17, 2024; hereinafter: "Explanatory Memorandum.'"

1346 See Nowicki M. A., "Potocka and Others v. Poland—ECHR judgment of 4 October 2001, Application No. 33776/96," in M. A. Nowicki (ed), *Nowy Europejski Trybunał Praw Człowieka. Wybór orzeczeń 1999–2004* (Kraków 2005) 573.

1347 Cf. e.g., Chlebny J., and Piątek W., *"Ewolucja ustrojowa i kompetencyjna sądownictwa administracyjnego"* (2021) 1–2, *Zeszyty Naukowe Sądownictwa Administracyjnego*, 32; Rząsa G., *Nieważność postępowania sądowoadministracyjnego jako podstawa skargi kasacyjnej* (Warszawa 2011) 99.

1348 See § B.1.a of Recommendation Rec (2004)2 and § 29 of the Explanatory Memorandum.

1349 See Półtorak N., in A. Wróbel (ed), in *Karta Praw Podstawowych Unii Europejskiej. Komentarz* (Warszawa 2019), Nb 3 to Article 47.

power provided for in Article 47 of the CFR is closely linked to the general principle of the rule of law, as expressed in Article 2 of the Treaty on European Union, as well as the second subparagraph of Article 19(1) of the Treaty on European Union, which expresses the obligation of Member States to provide for the legal remedies necessary to ensure effective judicial protection in the areas covered by the law of European Union.[1350]

In the context of the subject matter of this study, it should be assumed that, in general terms, the basic components that make up the right to effective judicial protection referred to in Article 47 of the CFR correspond to those elements that make up the constitutional right to a court and the right to a court under Article 6 of the ECHR. These are therefore, first and foremost, the right of access to a court, the right to a court that is independent, impartial and established by law, the right to a fair and public hearing, and the right to have a case heard within a reasonable time. The final part of Article 47 of the CPP also indicates the right to obtain legal advice, to be assisted by an attorney and the right to assistance. Although these rights are not explicitly indicated in Article 45 of the Polish Constitution, it is assumed that they are part of the right to effective judicial protection under the Polish Constitution.[1351] It should be added at this point that the principles of judicial protection are sometimes directly regulated in EU secondary law, including by specifying the competence of a national court or the guarantees to which a party is entitled in proceedings before a court.[1352]

It can therefore be said that, in principle, the standards determining the effective right to a court provided for in Article 47 of the CFR are reflected in national law. However, in the context of cases concerning foreigners, the jurisprudence of administrative courts has revealed certain inconsistencies

---

1350 See CJEU judgment of July 15, 2021, C-791/19, Commission v Poland, § 50–54 <https://curia.europa.eu>.

1351 See e.g., Wegner J., Wróblewski B., “Prawo jednostki do nieodpłatnej pomocy prawnej” (2021) 6 *Przegląd Prawa Publicznego*, 5; Trociuk S., “Legal Aid for the Poor as a Form of Ensuring Effective Access to National and European Justice, in H. Izdebski and H. Machińska (eds), *Access of citizens to European justice* (Warszawa 2005) 14; Rząsa G., “Konstytucyjne aspekty pomocy prawnej udzielanej osób ubogim” (2005) 3–4 *Przegląd Legislacyjny*, 40–41; the Constitutional Court judgment of August 29, 2006, SK 23/05, OTK-A 2006, No. 8, item 94.

1352 See Chlebny J., “Sądownictwo administracyjne w Polsce z perspektywy art. 47 KPP” (2022) 10 *Europejski Przegląd Sądowy*, p. 30.

of national law with the EU standard of the right to effective judicial review. First and foremost, the problem of the possibility of challenging decisions concerning the refusal to issue a visa before an administrative court should be pointed out here. That is, Article 5(4) of the Law on proceedings before administrative courts provides for a general exclusion of the judicial route in cases of visas issued by consuls, with the exception of visas issued to a foreigner who is a family member of a citizen of a Member State of the European Union, a Member State of the European Free Trade Association (EFTA). As a result of a preliminary question from the Supreme Administrative Court,[1353] followed by the CJEU judgment of December 3, 2017, C-403/16, *El Hassani v Minister of Foreign Affairs*,[1354] Article 5(4) of the Law on proceedings before administrative courts was amended in such a way that judicial review was additionally allowed in cases concerning the issuance of Schengen visas. In turn, from the CJEU judgment of March 10, 2021, C-949/19, *M.A. v Consul of the Republic of Poland*,[1355] it follows that an action before a court against a decision to refuse to issue a national visa should be admissible when the application for a national visa realizes certain rights provided for under EU law, such as those arising from Article 34 para. 5 of Directive 2016/801 of the European Parliament and of the Council of the EU of May 11, 2016 on the conditions of entry and residence of third-country nationals for the purposes of scientific research, study, training, voluntary service, pupil exchange schemes or educational projects and au pair work.[1356] However, such cases do not include the consul's refusal to issue a national visa for the purpose of a work permit—in those cases, a complaint to the administrative court is not available.[1357]

1353 See the decision of the SAC of June 28, 2016, II OSK 1346/16, CBOSA.

1354 <https://curia.europa.eu>. For more on this case, see, for example, Dorosz-Kruczyński J., "Case of El-Hassani v. Polish Minister of Foreign Affairs and judicial control of public administration activities in Poland" (2021) 1 *Krytyka Prawa*, 191–208.

1355 <https://curia.europa.eu>.

1356 OJ EU L 2016.132.21.

1357 See decisions of the SAC: of August 30, 2022, II OSK 1435/22, ONSAiWSA 2023, No. 2, item 29; of January 17, 2024, II OSK 2504/23; NSA of February 7, 2024, II OSK 2598/23—CBOSA. Fully sharing this position of the NSA, it may be added that it also remains in conformity with the ECHR. In particular, it follows from § 13 of the Explanatory Memorandum that Recommendation Rec (2004) 20 which does not prevent States from taking over very limited exceptions to the principle that every

The problem of compliance of national regulations with the European standard of the right to a court, against the background of cases concerning foreigners, also arose, *inter alia*, against the background of cases in which the applicant did not have access to classified materials on the basis of which it was established that he or she constitutes a threat to state security or public order. In the jurisprudence of the administrative courts, the view has become established that, in such a case, a sufficient guarantee of the foreigner's right of defense is that he or she will be informed of the essential reasons for the determination in a manner that takes due account of the necessary secrecy of the evidence and that the courts hearing the case are provided with full and unrestricted access to the classified material based on which the determination was made, their jurisdiction having to cover all the facts of the case and not being limited to the examination of the reasons indicated by the applicant.[1358] This position is strongly supported by, *inter alia*, the CJEU judgment of June 4, 2013, C-300/11, *ZZ v Secretary of State for the Home Department*[1359] and the ECtHR Grand Chamber judgment of September 19, 2017 in *Regner v Czech Republic.*[1360] This approach appears to have struck the right balance between the foreigner's right to defense and the need to protect the public interest, including the state's obligation to take effective measures to ensure public security and order. However, the ECtHR in its judgment of June 22, 2023 in *Poklikayew v. Poland*,[1361] referring extensively to the ECtHR judgment of October 5, 2020 in *Muhammad and Muhammad v. Romania*,[1362] held that the fact that the final decision had been made by an independent court was not sufficient to offset the restrictions on the rights of the defense associated with the total deprivation of access to the documents that formed the essential factual basis of the decision.[1363] The *Muhammad and Muhammad* and *Poklikayew*

administrative act is subject to judicial review, including that this may apply to, *inter alia*, foreign affairs, international agreements and defense or national security.

1358 See, e.g., judgment of the SAC of December 5, 2022, II OSK 2295/21 and judgment of the SAC of October 21, 2020, II OSK 1637/20, CBOSA.

1359 <https://curia.europa.eu>.

1360 Application No. 35289/11, LEX No. 2355186.

1361 Application No. 1103/16 <https://hudoc.echr.coe.int>.

1362 Application No. 80982/12 <https://hudoc.echr.coe.int>. For more on this judgment, see Chlebny J., "Glosa to the ECHR Judgment of 15 October 2020, 80982/12" (2020) 6 *Zeszyty Nuakowe Sądownictwa Administracyjnego*, 163–174.

1363 Cf. judgment of the SAC of June 29, 2023, II OSK 1854/22, CBOSA.

judgments cited above update the urgent need for appropriate changes in domestic law aimed at broadening the foreigner's right to defense, while at the same time preserving the protection of an important public interest, such as the protection of classified information. It seems that the optimal solution to this situation may be to allow the court to appoint an attorney for the foreigner from among the lawyers who have the right to access classified information.[1364]

2.5.2.4.5 Selected cases of restrictions on foreigners' rights due to crisis situations

When talking about crisis situations, one should first refer to the concept of "crisis," the central element of which is a clear deterioration of the situation in a given area.[1365] Furthermore, it should be noted that the issue of preventing and combating crises is the subject of research conducted by specialists in various fields of knowledge, including economics, public safety, public administration, psychology and medicine. Hence, a distinction is made between economic crises, social crises, political crises, military crises, ecological crises, and physiological crises, among others.[1366] For the purposes of this study, it is worth recalling the general definition of "crisis situation" proposed by R. Wroblewski.[1367] According to this definition, a "crisis situation" is a set of circumstances, both external and internal, which affect a given system in such a way that a process of change begins and continues in the system, resulting in an imbalance and then an attempt to restore it by taking appropriate regulatory measures, if any. This definition is broader than the one contained in Article 3(1) of the Law of April 26, 2007 on crisis management,[1368] where the term "crisis situation" is understood as a situation adversely affecting the level of security of people, property of significant size or the environment, causing significant limitations in the operation

1364 See Chlebny J., "Refusal of Access to the File in an Administrative Case" (2014) 10 *Państwo i Prawo*, 107–108.

1365 See Dubisz S. (ed), *Słownik języka polskiego* (Warszawa 2006) 332.

1366 See Otwinowski W., "Crisis and Crisis Situation" (2010) 2 *Scientific and Methodical Review. Education for Security*, 86.

1367 See Wróblewski R., *Zarys teorii kryzysu. Zagadnienia prewencji i zarządzania kryzysami* (Warszawa 1996) 10—quoted by Idrian P., "Zarządzanie kryzysowe a system bezpieczeństwa narodowego" (2015) 3 Obronność—*Zeszyty Naukowe Wydziału Zarządzania i Dowodzenia Akademii Obrony Narodowej*, 21.

1368 Official Journal 2023, item 122.

of the competent public administration bodies due to the inadequacy of their forces and resources.

Crisis situations, posing a serious threat to values such as life or health, e.g., in the form of the COVID-19 pandemic, or related to a massive, uncontrolled influx of foreigners, resulting in destabilization of the work of migration services, as well as those that may pose a threat to public order and security, including the risk of causing social unrest, undoubtedly constitute a legitimate reason for limiting certain rights to which foreigners are entitled. Obviously, however, these restrictions must meet the condition of proportionality, both in its formal aspect (they may be introduced by means of a law) and its material aspect (fulfill the criterion of usefulness, necessity and proportionality *sensu stricto*).[1369]

With regard to the restrictions related to the COVID-19 pandemic, including restrictions on the right to a court, foreigners residing in Poland were, in principle, subject to the same restrictions as Polish citizens. In particular, it should be pointed out here to the resulting from the various versions of the Law of March 2, 2020 on special solutions related to the prevention, prevention and combating of COVID-19, other infectious diseases and crisis situations caused by them,[1370] extension of the possibility for administrative courts to adjudicate in closed sessions. In particular, against the background of Article 15zzs4 of the Covid Law, the NSA of seven judges indicated,[1371] that the introduction of a derogation from the principle of hearing administrative court cases[1372] was justified by the protection of human life and health. The NSA stressed that from the perspective of preserving the right to a fair trial, the most important thing is to preserve the right of a party to present its position in the case (guarantee of the right to defense). The point is that the participants in the proceedings should be notified of the date of the closed hearing and have the opportunity to take a position on the case. Also in the doctrine, the aforementioned solutions provided by the Covid Law have been assessed as not violating the constitutional and European standard of

1369 Article 31(3) of the Polish Constitution and Article 52 of the CFR.
1370 OJ 2024, item 340; hereinafter: "COVID Law."
1371 See the resolution of seven judges of the SAC of November 30, 2020, II OPS 6/19, ONSAiWSA 2021/3/35.
1372 Article 90(1) of the Law on proceedings before administrative courts.

the right to a court.[1373] In my opinion, this assessment should be fully shared. The experience gained in the course of application of the solutions included in the Covid Law and concerning the extension of the possibility to hear administrative court cases in a closed session allows the formulation of the thesis that such a mode of work of administrative courts has significantly contributed to the improvement of the efficiency of proceedings without lowering the quality of jurisprudence. Since in administrative court proceedings in principle, there are no evidentiary proceedings, and the decision of the administrative court is made based on the documents collected in the case file, including above all the administrative case file, it should, in my opinion, be introduced as a principle that these cases should be heard in closed session by a panel of three judges.[1374] It should therefore be postulated that a hearing before an administrative court (both of first and second instance) should be scheduled only if such a request is made by a party or the court deems it necessary for the clarification of the case. However, such a request would only be binding on the court of first instance. In addition, the administrative court should be equipped with the possibility to request the parties to submit written explanations, along the lines of the power provided for in Article 514, sentence 2, of the Code of Civil Procedure. Nevertheless, the right to request a hearing should not be granted to the body whose action, inaction or protracted conduct of the proceedings is the subject of the complaint. This is because this entity does not benefit from the constitutional guarantees related to the right to a public hearing. Clearly, the parties should be notified well in advance of the date of the public hearing and informed of the possibility of submitting their views in writing within a certain time limit. The proposed solution would strengthen the party's right to have the case heard without undue delay and would reduce the costs of justice without significantly limiting the party's right to fair and open (in the internal aspect) administrative court proceedings. It should be emphasized that, with regard to the external openness aspect in the case of administrative courts, the principle of publishing the decisions of these courts in a publicly

---

1373 See e.g., Kowalski M., "Between Openness and Efficiency of Administrative Court Proceedings (Some Reflections Related to the Pandemic and Its End" 2023) 12, *Państwo i Prawo,* 128.

1374 See e.g., Rząsa G., *Invalidity of Proceedings* ..., 345–346.

accessible database of decisions is also an important guarantee. The acceleration of administrative court proceedings, at the expense of limiting external openness, may also contribute to the strengthening of citizens' trust in the administration of justice. It should be noted that it is the lengthiness of court proceedings, and not the possible lack of their transparency, that has been indicated for years in public opinion surveys as the most significant problem of the Polish justice system.[1375] Concluding this thread, it should be pointed out that the proposed solution also does not interfere with the European standard of the right to an open hearing of an administrative court case. In particular, it follows from the ECtHR judgment of March 13, 2018 in *Mirovni Inštitut v Slovenia*[1376] that in administrative court cases, the requirement of a public hearing applies only to the court of first instance and, moreover, it is not an absolute requirement. In particular, the position of the parties on the issue is important, as well as whether the case involves legal or highly technical issues, and if there are issues concerning the credibility of evidence or contested facts, whether these can be fairly resolved on the basis of the parties' submissions and other written material.

The possibility of more extensive adjudication of judicial-administrative cases in closed sessions is particularly important in cases concerning foreigners if one takes into account the systemic problems of public administration bodies in the timely handling of these cases, including especially those concerning temporary residence permits,[1377] which have been going on for several years. This situation has been exacerbated by the COVID-19 pandemic. The massive influx of Ukrainian citizens to Poland following the outbreak

---

[1375] See Rząsa G., "Skarga na bezczynność wniesiona po zakończeniu postępowania administracyjnego. Glosa to the resolution of the SAC of 22 June 2020" (2021) 1, *Orzecznictwo Sądów Polskich*, 157–158. Current public opinion polls confirm this state of affairs, with concerns about the apolitical nature of judges being the second most prominent (see *Social assessments of the judiciary. Research Communication No. 95/2022*, Public Opinion Research Centre Foundation 2022, 10).

[1376] Application No. 32303/13, LEX 2456380.

[1377] See, e.g., the Ombudsman's speech of June 27, 2023 to the Minister of the Interior and Administration, reference XI.541.31.2021.KM <https://bip.brpo.gov.pl/sites/default/files/202306/Do_MSWiA_cudzoziemcy_wojewodowie_przewleklosc_27.06.2023.pdf> accessed April 27, 2024.

of war on February 24, 2022 with the Russian Federation[1378] has created a serious threat to the functioning of the already overburdened and inefficient administrative apparatus handling foreigners' cases. It is worth noting that of the Ukrainian citizens who arrived in Poland due to the war, almost 1,800,000 persons applied for a PESEL number with the addition of UKR,[1379] thus at least that many persons enjoy temporary protection in Poland.[1380] In addition, the possibility to apply for, *inter alia*, a temporary residence and work permit has been introduced for beneficiaries of this protection from April 2023,[1381] thus significantly broadening the derogation from the principle that a person benefiting from temporary protection cannot

---

1378 In the first half of 2022 alone. The Border Guard recorded more than 5,000,000 border crossings by Ukrainian nationals, an increase of 172% compared to the first half of 2021 (see <https://www.strazgraniczna.pl/pl/granica/statystyki-sg/2206,Statystyki-SG.html> accessed April 27, 2024).

1379 See <https://dane.gov.pl/pl/dataset/2715,zarejestrowane-wnioski-o-nadanie-statusu-ukr/resource/55530/table?page=12&per_page=50&q=&sort=> accessed April 27, 2024.

1380 See Articles 2(7) and 4 of the Law of March 12, 2022 on Assistance to Citizens of Ukraine in Connection with the Armed Conflict on the Territory of Ukraine (Journal of Laws of 2024, item 167; hereinafter: "Law on Assistance to Citizens of Ukraine"). The institution of temporary protection was introduced due to the necessity to ensure compliance with the principle of *non-refoulement* in emergency situations, when there is a real need for protection—while there is no possibility to make quick individual decisions or such a possibility is reduced to the minimum (see Chrostowska-Malak K., "Institutions of International Protection of Foreigners in Poland—Political and Legal Solutions," *Nowa Polityka Wschodnia* (2023, No. 1) 91). The basic legal act at the EU level concerning temporary protection is Council Directive 2001/55/EC of July 20, 2001 on minimum standards for giving temporary protection in the event of a mass influx of displaced persons and on measures promoting a balance of efforts between Member States in receiving such persons and bearing the consequences thereof (Official Journal of the EU.L No. 212, 12; hereinafter: "Directive 2001/55/EC"). In national law, on the other hand, the framework provisions on temporary protection are regulated in Articles 106–118a of the Law on Assistance. For displaced persons from Ukraine, temporary protection has been extended until March 4, 2025—see Council Implementing Decision 2023/2409 of October 19, 2023 on the extension of temporary protection introduced by Implementing Decision (EU) 2022/382 (OJ EU.L.2023.2409).

1381 See Article 42(13) of the Law on Assistance to Citizens of Ukraine.

simultaneously apply for a temporary residence permit.[1382] Bearing in mind the crisis situation described above in the form of a massive influx of Ukrainian citizens in connection with the war on the territory of that country, the legislator decided to introduce exceptional, time-limited regulations concerning the suspension of the deadlines for the consideration of certain types of migration cases (*inter alia*, concerning the granting of temporary residence permits, permanent residence permits and residence permits for long-term residents of the European Union).[1383] Consequently, a regulation was also introduced, according to which the cessation of actions by the authority conducting proceedings in these cases or their delayed performance, during the period of suspension of the deadlines, may not be the basis for raising legal remedies concerning inaction, protraction or violation of the right of a party to have the case heard without undue delay.[1384] These provisions significantly interfere with the procedural rights of foreigners.[1385] Therefore, the SAC assumed that they do not apply to states of inaction or protraction that occurred before the entry into force of those special regulations, i.e., April 15, 2022.[1386] It seems that at present, in connection with the stabilization of the migration situation on the Polish-Ukrainian border, there are significant doubts as to whether there are still good reasons for the further extension of these exceptional, by their very nature episodic, regulations. In other words, it is necessary to consider whether the reason justifying the introduction of the aforementioned restrictions on the procedural rights of foreigners has already fallen away. In the case of another possible extension

---

1382 See Article 99(1)(4) of the Law on foreigners. The purpose of this provision is, *inter alia*, to fulfill one of the functions of temporary protection provided for in Council Directive 2001/55/EC, which is to relieve the broader asylum services of Member States from the obligation to individually examine mass applications submitted by displaced persons (cf. e.g., judgment of the SAC of November 22, 2023, II OSK 1038/23, CBOSA).

1383 See Articles 100c (1)–(3) and 100d (1)–(3) of the Law on Assistance to Citizens of Ukraine.

1384 See Articles 100c(4) and 100d(4) of the Law on Assistance to Citizens of Ukraine.

1385 In the case law of the SAC, it is assumed that Articles 100c and 100d apply to all foreigners and not only to citizens of Ukraine (see e.g., judgment of the SAC of June 5, 2023, II OSK 2059/22 and of February 13, 2024, II OSK 2362/23, CBOSA).

1386 See, e.g., judgment of the SAC of March 21, 2023, II OSK 2342/22 and judgment of the SAC of February 13, 2024, II OSK 660/23, CBOSA.

of Article 100d of the Law on assistance to citizens of Ukraine, with the migration situation on the Polish-Ukrainian border substantially unchanged, the problem of compliance of such a regulation with the principle of proportionality (Article 31(3) of the Constitution of the Republic of Poland and Article 52 of the CFR) becomes relevant, including in particular the problem of the continued existence of the premise for the necessity of introducing such limitations. It should be emphasized that exceptional regulations introducing limitations on rights and freedoms due to a specific crisis situation should remain in force only until such time as those special circumstances justifying the introduction of the derogation from general principles are present—*cessante ratione legis, cessat lex ipsa.*[1387]

A mass influx of migrants to the Polish-Belarusian border, initiated and organized by the authorities of the Republic of Belarus,[1388] is another example of circumstances justifying the introduction in the national law of exceptional regulations on the rules of entry and residence of third-country nationals. Recently, the Russian Federation has been undertaking similar actions on the border with Finland.[1389] In fact, we are dealing here with the instrumentalization of migration as a part of a hostile action taken by a foreign state to destabilize the internal security situation in a EU Member State.[1390] These actions are one of the manifestations of conducting, *inter alia*, against Poland (and indirectly against the entire European Union) the

---

1387 "When the cause for which a law was passed ceases to exist, the law itself also ceases to be in force" (see e.g., judgment of the SAC of November 18, 2024, II OSK 926/24, CBOSA).

1388 See, for example, *Asylum and Return: Commission Proposes Temporary Legal and Practical Measures to Address the Emergency Situation at the EU's External Border with Belarus* <https://ec.europa.eu/commission/presscorner/detail/en/IP_21_6447> accessed April 28, 2024.

1389 See e.g., Graca J., and Rodkiewicz W., *Russia Is Putting Migration Pressure on the Border with Finland, Analysis* of the Centre for Eastern Studies (November 17, 2023) <https://www.osw.waw.pl/en/publikacje/analyses/2023-11-17/russia-putting-migration-pressure-border-finland> accessed April 28, 2024.

1390 See e.g., *Communication from the Commission to the European Parliament and the Council on Countering Hybrid Threats from the Weaponisation of Migration and Strengthening Security at the EU's External Borders*, (Brussels December 11, 2024), COM(2024) 570 final.

so-called hybrid war.[1391] The use of mass migration as a means to achieve specific political goals is, by the way, not a new phenomenon.[1392]

As regards the regulations introduced in Poland in response to the mass influx of migrants on the Polish-Belarusian border, in the first stage, by means of the Ordinance of the Minister of Internal Affairs and Administration of August 20, 2021 amending the Ordinance on temporary suspension or restriction of border traffic at certain border crossing points,[1393] a solution was introduced according to which persons disclosed at the border crossing point where border traffic has been suspended or restricted and outside the territorial scope of the border crossing point shall be returned to the state border line. This regulation has already been challenged by the administrative courts on grounds that it legislates in a regulation a matter that should be contained in a law, with reference also to the need to respect the principle of *non-refoulement*.[1394] In the next stage, the Alien Act was amended in such a way to introduce the possibility of issuing an immediately enforceable order by the Border Guard authority to leave the territory of Poland to a person who has been apprehended immediately after crossing the border in violation of the law regulating external borders within the meaning of Article 2(2) of the Schengen Borders Code.[1395] Against the background of these provisions, the jurisprudence has expressed the view that the circumstance that the 2021 migration crisis on the border with Belarus was triggered by deliberate actions of states hostile to Poland cannot exclude, as it were *in genere*, the application of the principle of *non-refoulement* to all foreigners illegally crossing the border of the Republic of Poland with Belarus. It is

1391 Cf. Chlebny J., *Turning Back a Foreigner at the Border* (ZNSA 2023), No. 5, 13.

1392 See Dov Bachmann S.-D., and Paphiti A., "Mass Migration as a Hybrid Threat?—A Legal Perspective" (2021) 50(1) *Polish Political Science Yearbook*, 125–129.

1393 Journal of Laws of 2021, item 1536.

1394 See, e.g., The judgment of the WSA of September 15, 2022, II SA/Bk 492/22, CBOSA (the cassation appeal of the public prosecutor against this judgment was dismissed by the SAC in the judgment of January 9, 2024, II OSK 2749/22). For more on the principle of *non-refoulement* see, e.g., Chlebny J., *Postepowanie w sprawie ...*, 115–128 and Rogala R., *Prawo cudzoziemca do ubiegania na granicy o udzielenie ochrony międzynarodowej*, (EPS 2021), No. 11, 13–14.

1395 See Article 303b in conjunction with Article 303(1)(9a) of the Law on foreigners added by the Law of October 14, 2021 amending the law on foreigners and certain other acts (*Journal of Laws*, item 1918).

necessary here to maintain certain balance between border protection and the protection of fundamental rights. In particular, it is a question of the need to examine whether Belarus is a safe country for such a person, where he or she will not be exposed to the dangers referred to in Article 19(2) of the CFR. For the assessment of the legality of the order to command a foreigner to leave the territory of Poland, it is also important whether the place and time at which the foreigner was turned back (the order was executed) do not pose a direct and real threat to the life or health of such a person.[1396] The obligation to check whether the issuance and execution of the order referred to in Article 303b(1) of the Law on foreigners would not lead to a violation of the principle of *non-refoulement* was also pointed out in the judgment of the SAC of May 10, 2023.[1397]

The fundamental problem of a mass influx of migrants supported by a third country with the aim of destabilizing the situation in a neighboring country boils down to the question of properly balancing the obvious need to protect the public interest with the individual interest of individual persons crossing the border illegally. It must be accepted that a democratic state cannot be a state powerless in the face of hostile actions by a neighboring state, including when hostile actions are undertaken using migrants. Failure to act effectively in such a case would undermine confidence in the public authorities (Article 2 of the Polish Constitution) and would also undermine the duty to maintain the inviolability of borders and to guard the security of citizens (Article 5 of the Polish Constitution). On the other hand, the actions taken by the public authorities of a democratic state should take into account the principle of *non-refoulement.* In particular, the procedure for the return of migrants disclosed immediately after illegally crossing the border (i.e., the so-called "push-back") must not lead to the exposure of such migrants to loss of life or health, as well as result in subjecting such migrants to torture or inhuman or degrading treatment or punishment.[1398] The postulate of the necessity to respect, within the framework of combating the migration crisis on the Polish-Belarusian border, the principle of *non-refoulement*, is strongly

---

1396 See judgment of the WSA in Warsaw of May 26, 2022, IV SA/Wa 386/22, CBOSA.

1397 II OSK 1735/22, CBOSA.

1398 Articles 2 and 3 of the ECHR and Articles 2 and 4 of the CFR and Article 4(4)(b) of Directive 2008/115/EC.

emphasized not only in the jurisprudence of administrative courts but also in the Polish science of law.[1399] This position of the Polish administrative courts and the science of law here seems to correspond fully with the standard set in the ECtHR judgment of February 13, 2020, *N.D. and N.T. v. Spain*,[1400] where it was stated that the implementation of the universally recognized obligation and necessity for Contracting States to protect their borders should be carried out in a manner consistent with the guarantees of the Convention, and in particular with the obligation of *non-refoulement*.

2.5.2.4.6 Conclusions

The analysis made it possible to formulate the following conclusions. Firstly, Polish law applies the principle of equal treatment of foreigners residing in the territory of Poland and Polish citizens. Secondly, national law broadly implements the standards arising from the European right to good administration. However, in the light of recent ECtHR judgments, it seems necessary to introduce specific regulations reinforcing the foreigner's right to defense in cases where the decision is based on considerations of security or public order and where the basic evidence constitutes classified information. The possible extension of these rights of aliens must not, however, significantly impede public authorities from performing their primary function of ensuring public security and order. Thirdly, crisis situations such as a pandemic or a massive influx of refugees in connection with the Russian-Ukrainian war may also justify the introduction of certain restrictions on the right to a court, but these restrictions must be proportionate, including not lasting longer than the crisis situation actually lasts. Lastly, the restrictions on certain rights of foreigners for reasons of public interest are justified particularly in the case of crisis situations such as a massive influx of migrants organized by third countries in order to destabilize a Member State. These restrictions, which have their justification, *inter alia*, in the duty of public authorities to maintain the inviolability of borders and to guard the security of citizens,

---

1399 See Chlebny J., *Turning back a foreigner* ..., 28; Bodnar A., and Grzelak A., "The Polish-Belarusian Border Crisis and the (Lack of) European Union Response" (2023) 28 *Białostockie Studia Prawnicze—Bialystok Legal Studies*, 83.

1400 Applications Nos. 8675/15 and 8697/15, § 232, LEX No. 2854807.

also have to be adequate to the risks involved and, moreover, cannot result in the exclusion of the duty to observe the principle of *non-refoulement*.

2.6 Slovakia (Lilla Garayova)

2.6.1 Introduction

In recent years, the European Union (EU) and its Member States have faced unprecedented challenges related to the governance of migration during times of emergency. As outlined in the preceding chapters, emergencies—be they public health crises like the COVID-19 pandemic, geopolitical conflicts such as the Russian invasion of Ukraine, or hybrid threats targeting EU borders—have necessitated the reevaluation and adaptation of legal frameworks governing the entry and residence of third-country nationals (TCNs). This chapter builds on that broader EU perspective, focusing on the Slovak Republic's legal responses and the interplay between national, European, and international obligations.

Emergencies often place legal systems under immense strain, compelling governments to introduce restrictive measures aimed at safeguarding public health, national security and social stability. However, such measures inevitably raise fundamental questions: To what extent can states lawfully restrict the right to migrate? How can the balance between public interests and individual human rights be maintained? In Slovakia, as in other EU Member States, these questions have come to the forefront during key moments of crisis.

This chapter examines how Slovakia's legal framework has evolved in response to migration-related emergencies, with a particular focus on the protection of human rights. The discussion begins by exploring the substantive rights of TCNs—such as the right to leave and return, the right to seek asylum, and the right to family reunification. It explores how these rights are safeguarded or restricted during emergencies, drawing on examples such as travel restrictions, health mandates and the use of temporary border controls.

Equally important are the procedural safeguards designed to uphold fairness, transparency and accountability in migration-related proceedings. These include access to legal remedies, procedural fairness and the right to good administration. The chapter critically examines whether Slovakia's institutional responses have upheld these standards or introduced disparities in treatment, particularly for vulnerable groups such as unaccompanied minors and persons with disabilities.

A significant part of the analysis focuses on the impact of digitalization in administrative and court processes. While digital tools have the potential to improve efficiency, they also present challenges related to accessibility, data privacy and the digital divide. The chapter evaluates whether these innovations have created more inclusive procedures or reinforced existing inequalities. By situating Slovakia's legal measures within the context of European legal standards and international commitments, this chapter provides a comprehensive understanding of the legal tensions that arise in times of emergency. It underscores the importance of ensuring that restrictions remain proportionate, necessary and temporary in nature, reinforcing the principle of human dignity even in the most challenging circumstances.

2.6.2 Substantive law perspective: the human rights of migrants in times of emergency in Slovakia

Migration is an essential part of today's world. While many people migrate for work, family reunification, or education, others do so for religious or political reasons. Slovakia is bound by a range of international agreements that shape its obligations toward migrants and asylum seekers. The country is a signatory to the 1951 Refugee Convention[1401] and the 1967 Protocol,[1402] which enshrine the principle of non-refoulement, prohibiting the return of individuals to places where they face persecution or harm. Additionally, Slovakia adheres to the International Covenant on Civil and Political Rights (ICCPR)[1403] and the European Convention on Human Rights (ECHR),[1404] both of which protect the right to seek asylum, freedom of movement, and family reunification. As an EU Member State, Slovakia also follows directives

1401 UN General Assembly, Convention Relating to the Status of Refugees, United Nations, Treaty Series, vol. 189, 137, July 28, 1951.

1402 UN General Assembly, Protocol Relating to the Status of Refugees, United Nations, Treaty Series, vol. 606, 267, January 31, 1967.

1403 UN General Assembly, International Covenant on Civil and Political Rights, United Nations, Treaty Series, vol. 999, 171, December 16, 1966.

1404 Council of Europe, European Convention on Human Rights, as amended by Protocols Nos. 11, 14 and 15, ETS No. 005, November 4, 1950.

and regulations such as the Dublin III Regulation,[1405] which outlines the responsibility of Member States in processing asylum claims.

Slovakia's national legal framework governing migration and asylum is built upon a combination of constitutional provisions, national laws and administrative regulations. The Constitution of the Slovak Republic[1406] guarantees fundamental rights and freedoms, including protection against discrimination and the right to seek asylum. Act No. 480/2002 Coll. on asylum[1407] is the cornerstone of national asylum legislation, detailing the process for granting asylum, temporary refuge, and subsidiary protection. This Act is complemented by Act No. 404/2011 Coll. on the Stay of Foreigners,[1408] which regulates entry, residence permits and deportation procedures.

The Migration Office of the Ministry of Interior plays a key role in implementing these legal provisions, managing reception centers, and overseeing asylum processing. Special procedures are applied during emergencies, such as health screenings and mandatory quarantine upon entry, as mandated during the COVID-19 pandemic. Moreover, the legal framework specifies the rights and obligations of asylum seekers, including access to legal representation and the right to appeal administrative decisions. Administrative courts serve as a safeguard, providing oversight and ensuring that the principles of fairness, proportionality, and due process are respected. Slovakia's legal system incorporates international and EU obligations, ensuring that national regulations align with broader human rights frameworks and non-refoulement principles. However, challenges remain in maintaining procedural efficiency during times of crisis, as seen in delays in asylum processing and the handling of appeals.

The significance of international migration as a historical and societal phenomenon cannot be overstated, as it influences the political landscape of

---

[1405] European Union: Council of the European Union, Regulation (EU) No. 604/2013 of the European Parliament and of the Council of June 26, 2013 establishing the criteria and mechanisms for determining the Member State responsible for examining an application for international protection lodged in one of the Member States by a third-country national or a stateless person (recast), OJ L. 180/31-180/59; June 29, 2013, (EU)No. 604/2013, June 29, 2013.

[1406] Constitution of the Slovak Republic (No. 460/1992 Coll. as amended).

[1407] Act No. 480/2002 Coll. on Asylum, as amended.

[1408] Act No. 404/2011 Coll. on the Stay of Foreigners, as amended.

nations and has both short-term and long-term potential to reshape demographic structures. Migration, therefore, necessitates a systematic and sustainable approach that involves close collaboration between domestic and international actors. The current level of global mobility is unprecedented and continues to rise sharply, making migration one of the defining global issues of the twenty-first century. Almost all of the world's approximately 196 countries function as either origin, transit zones, or destinations for migrants. Recognizing this complexity, Slovakia's approach to migration management is both flexible and accountable. As a member of the European Union, Slovakia cannot pursue migration policy in isolation. In an integrated Europe without internal borders, there is an increasing emphasis on aligning migration policies with other key sectors, such as security, defense, sustainable development, demographic policy, and employment strategies. The permanent incorporation of migration issues into the EU's external relations further reinforces the need for a coordinated and multi-layered strategy.

Slovakia's Migration Policy Framework up to 2025[1409] outlines the government's vision for a modern, comprehensive, and effective migration policy, covering all aspects of migration. The aim of migration policy, in accordance with national interests and the international commitments of the Slovak Republic, is to create conditions for legal migration, taking into account the priorities, needs, and capacities for accepting foreigners, including their integration into society. The migration policy advocates for a regulated dimension of labor mobility that could prevent social, economic, and environmental tensions while emphasizing the preservation of the security of the Slovak Republic and the rights of its citizens, as well as the rights of foreigners residing in its territory. In the field of international protection, the goal of the migration policy is to provide effective protection to those in need while simultaneously preventing abuse of the asylum system, including through the reform of the Common European Asylum System.

Other objectives of the Slovak Republic's migration policy include the effective fight against illegal migration and related negative phenomena, such as human trafficking, smuggling, and the exploitation of foreigners, as well as strengthening the protection of the external Schengen border

---

1409 Ministry of Interior of the Slovak Republic, Slovakia's Migration Policy Framework up to 2025.

and implementing return policies for individuals unlawfully residing in the territory of the Slovak Republic. An additional goal of migration policy is to strengthen the link between migration and development, with a focus on building global partnerships with countries of origin and transit, in cooperation with EU and UN partners. The migration policy also aims to assess the possibility of centralizing migration, integration and asylum agendas under a single centralized office.

The migration policy also emphasizes the need to be prepared to address new challenges related to the prevention and resolution of emergencies, as exemplified by the migration crisis of 2015 and the COVID-19 pandemic. The impact of these events was particularly felt in the shortages across various professions, including healthcare professionals, which highlighted the need to secure adequate mobility of human resources and the workforce. It is highly likely that such situations will reoccur. Suitable solutions, including specific proposals, should therefore be incorporated into relevant crisis plans.

The various areas of migration policy are managed by the respective state administration bodies within their competencies. However, its implementation follows a coordinated approach that involves not only the relevant state authorities but also local state administration bodies and self-governments. In addition, it anticipates the broad involvement of international organizations, civil society, the private sector, the academic sector, and migrant communities, taking into account national, regional and international contexts.

Slovakia is a member of several international organizations and groupings that devote focused attention to migration issues. In relation to migration policy, the EU's political and legal framework is therefore decisive for Slovakia. Within the EU, migration and asylum constitute a dynamic policy area characterized by increasing harmonization, yet their impact on the societies of individual EU Member States remains uncertain. The EU has had common policies related to asylum and migration since 1999. In recent years, especially in connection with the migration situation since 2015, the EU has adopted several strategic documents, which have often been accompanied by legislative proposals. At the same time, it is necessary for Slovakia to remain proactive in implementing its political commitments. The EU's comprehensive cooperation with countries of origin and transit, using a broader spectrum of available tools (such as trade, visa and development policies, as well as investments), has become a strategic approach to controlling migration flows. The primary interest of both the EU and Slovakia remains securing the full cooperation of third countries in the readmission of illegal migrants. In the past few years, continued cooperation with Turkey and a new framework for relations with African countries following the expiration of the Cotonou Agreement were of key importance. From a geographical perspective, Ukraine and the Western Balkans remain priority countries for Slovakia's cooperation on migration.

This area is also significantly influenced by internal EU migration management processes, which will, in turn, impact Slovakia's migration policy. This includes strengthening the mandate of the Frontex agency, the proposed transformation of EASO into the European Union Agency for Asylum, and the reform of the Common European Asylum System based on the package of legislative proposals presented in September 2020 (the New Pact on Migration and Asylum).

Legal migration is primarily understood as entry into the country with valid documents, a visa, or an appropriate residence permit. In recent years, Slovakia has focused its legal migration efforts mainly on managed economic migration, labor mobility, residence for the purpose of employment, entrepreneurship, studies, and family reunification related to these purposes. Managed economic migration is primarily influenced by so-called megatrends, such as geopolitical factors, changes in the labor market, demographic trends—particularly population aging—changes in educational systems, technological advancements, digitalization, and the transition to a climate-neutral economy. The management of economic migration must also address the challenges of the global competition for talent and skilled labor by actively recruiting and creating favorable conditions for their arrival and integration. In this process, it is crucial to foster an attractive environment for foreigners who are essential to the development of the economy and society. Labor mobility thus becomes a significant component of legal migration to Slovakia.

These megatrends are reflected in the Foreign Nationals' Labour Mobility Strategy,[1410] which aims to streamline, expedite, and enhance the flexibility of the system governing the entry and residence of third-country nationals for

---

1410 Ministry of Labour, Social Affairs and Family of the Slovak Republic, *Foreign Nationals' Labour Mobility Strategy* (2023).

employment and entrepreneurship, especially in professions where there is an identified labor shortage. This goal is also presented in Slovakia's Economic Policy Strategy until 2030[1411] and elaborated in more detail in the Action Plan for Smart Industry.[1412]

The newly established European Labour Authority, headquartered in Bratislava, also has a positive impact on the cooperation and coordination of EU Member States in the management of economic migration. Its role is to oversee the proper application of European labor and social security laws in cross-border situations.

Slovakia has outlined several key priorities to enhance its management of economic migration. These priorities aim to ensure that the process of integrating foreign workers is efficient, secure, and aligned with the country's absorption capacities and labor market demands.

A primary focus is on deploying all available resources to handle the arrival of foreign workers effectively. This includes ensuring that migration flows are managed in line with Slovakia's economic needs and societal absorption capacities. To this end, streamlining procedures and improving infrastructure for managing foreign labor play a crucial role in maintaining efficiency while addressing labor shortages.

Strengthening security measures is another key pillar of Slovakia's economic migration strategy. The government places significant emphasis on verifying the authenticity of submitted documents and detecting forgeries. This also involves uncovering any misuse of legal documents for exploitative purposes. By implementing stricter checks, Slovakia aims to uphold the integrity of its migration system and prevent fraud.

In addition to security, improving inter-institutional cooperation is essential. Linking information systems and enhancing communication between relevant institutions can reduce bureaucratic inefficiencies and improve the overall management of migration cases. A related priority is ensuring that foreign nationals have access to accurate and comprehensive information in multiple languages. The development of a dedicated information portal offering key updates in major world languages is intended to facilitate this.

1411 Ministry of Finance of the Slovak Republic, *Slovakia's Economic Policy Strategy until 2030* (2022).

1412 Ministry of Economy of the Slovak Republic, *Action Plan for Smart Industry* (2019).

To ensure compliance with labor laws, Slovakia prioritizes swift interventions by control units in cases of legal violations or instances of illegal employment. This is complemented by efforts to streamline and digitize the residence permit application process, thereby reducing processing times and enhancing transparency.

Recognizing the importance of international collaboration, Slovakia aims to strengthen cooperation with control authorities at the national and cross-border levels.

Finally, to ensure that public administration can effectively support migration processes, there is an ongoing effort to optimize staffing levels at key institutions, particularly those handling high volumes of migration-related cases.

The general effects of globalization and developments in Slovak society, particularly in connection with Slovakia's membership in the EU and the Schengen area, have brought both positive aspects and certain negative consequences. One of the main negative impacts has been the increased emigration of Slovak citizens, with a notable outflow of qualified workers, both in the category of university-educated individuals and in professions experiencing labor shortages, as well as the permanent departure of university students. As a result, Slovakia faces a weakening labor market, a decline in educational potential, a reduction in the population of reproductive and productive age, and an aging population, along with certain social challenges exacerbated by the lack of high-quality reintegration programs aimed at motivating Slovak citizens to return home. Slovakia recognizes the challenges posed by emigration, particularly the outflow of highly skilled professionals, and has set strategic priorities aimed at mitigating its negative impacts while fostering the reintegration of returning citizens. These efforts focus on understanding emigration trends, addressing underlying causes, and creating supportive conditions for reintegration into Slovak society.

A key aspect of this strategy is the monitoring and analysis of emigration flows. This involves tracking the movement of Slovak citizens, as well as qualified foreign workers, students, and academics who have successfully integrated abroad. By examining the forms, causes and consequences of emigration, Slovakia aims to identify patterns and understand the factors driving skilled individuals to leave.

To address the root causes of emigration, Slovakia plans to develop a comprehensive strategy aimed at reducing economic, social, and demographic pressures that contribute to the emigration of skilled workers, especially in professions facing labor shortages. A particular focus is placed on university graduates who seek permanent opportunities abroad. By implementing measures to improve domestic opportunities, the government seeks to reduce the "brain drain."

Recognizing the importance of engaging with its diaspora, the government aims to create an information and consultation platform for Slovak citizens living abroad. This platform could provide resources, guidance and information to maintain connections with expatriates and support their potential return. Based on these insights, Slovakia plans to implement improvements to make these programs more appealing and effective. These measures are intended not only to counter the negative impacts of emigration but also to harness the potential of Slovak citizens who choose to return, contributing their skills and experiences to the country's development.

Slovakia's migration policy adheres to the traditional pillars of asylum policy while also embracing new forms of international protection in response to the emerging challenges faced by the international community. The future development of international protection in Slovakia will be determined primarily by the outcomes of the ongoing implementation on the reform of the Common European Asylum System. Since its establishment, Slovakia has committed to protecting individuals who, due to the threat of serious injustice or persecution in their countries of origin for reasons such as political beliefs, nationality, race, religion, or membership in a particular social group, cannot or do not wish to return to their home countries. In accordance with its international obligations, as well as European and national legislation, Slovakia provides various forms of protection, including granting asylum or subsidiary protection, family reunification, or granting asylum on humanitarian grounds.

Additionally, based on its capacities and as an expression of solidarity with the most affected countries, Slovakia actively and voluntarily participates in other humanitarian solutions, such as humanitarian transfers, resettlement of endangered individuals from third countries, or relocations from other EU Member States. A fundamental priority is the granting of asylum in accordance with international commitments, particularly the 1951 Geneva

Convention on the Status of Refugees[1413] and its 1967 New York Protocol.[1414] Each application for asylum is subject to an individualized assessment to ensure that decisions are fair, transparent, and in line with legal standards. Alongside asylum, subsidiary protection is provided to individuals who may not qualify as refugees but face serious risks if returned to their home countries, in compliance with European and Slovak legislation.

Slovakia also places significant emphasis on its role within the European Union and has actively participated in negotiations on the reform of the Common European Asylum System (CEAS). A critical element of Slovakia's position in these discussions was its opposition to the adoption of mandatory relocation quotas for asylum seekers. This stance was notably demonstrated in 2015 when Slovakia, alongside Hungary, contested the EU's provisional mechanism for the mandatory relocation of asylum seekers.[1415] The country maintains that any reform must respect its sovereignty and national interests, insisting that proposed legislative packages be viewed as a comprehensive whole, with agreement contingent on an outcome that aligns with Slovakia's priorities.

Another key aspect of Slovakia's international protection strategy is its commitment to preserving national decision-making authority while incorporating lessons learned from the practical experiences of other EU Member States. This enables Slovakia to remain responsive to evolving migration dynamics while upholding its autonomy in decision-making processes related to asylum and protection.

Slovakia also recognizes the importance of solidarity in international burden-sharing, particularly in response to forced migration. However, it emphasizes that participation in such efforts must be voluntary and consider the country's capacities. In addition to providing protection, Slovakia prioritizes the systematic integration of individuals granted international protection. This includes ensuring that those who receive protection can

---

1413 UN General Assembly, Convention Relating to the Status of Refugees, United Nations, Treaty Series, vol. 189, 137, July 28, 1951.

1414 UN General Assembly, Protocol Relating to the Status of Refugees, United Nations, Treaty Series, vol. 606, 267, January 31, 1967.

1415 Court of Justice of the European Union, Judgment in Joined Cases C-643/15 and C-647/15, Slovakia and Hungary v Council (ECLI:EU:C:2017:631).

access essential services, such as housing, education and employment, to support their long-term integration into Slovak society.

Finally, Slovakia contributes to EU-wide efforts by deploying experts through the European Union Agency for Asylum (EASO) to assist countries experiencing significant migration pressures. By sharing expertise and resources, Slovakia supports the stabilization of asylum systems in frontline states, thereby contributing to the broader goal of managing migration at the European level. In 2024, experts from the Migration Office of the Slovak Ministry of Interior were deployed to these asylum support teams to assist in managing migration pressure. During 2024, we deployed 12 experts, to the Netherlands, Italy and Cyprus. The Slovak experts were dedicated to providing information to asylum seekers, registering asylum applications and identifying the Member State responsible for the asylum procedure. In terms of both quantity and quality, the Slovak contribution is assessed very positively. In terms of the number of deployments, our country is among the top contributing EU Member States. The experts deployed by the Migration Office are assessed as very knowledgeable and practically proficient, with the ability to adapt quickly to the new system and to react to situations as they arise. They thus contribute to reducing the burden on the asylum and reception system of the Member State concerned. In this way, Slovakia has long expressed its solidarity with Member States under migration pressure, and in 2018–2024 the Migration Office of the Ministry of the Interior of the Slovak Republic has already deployed 70 of its experts in this way.[1416]

The integration of foreigners who legally reside in Slovakia and wish to settle permanently is a key instrument of successful migration policy. Integration is a continuous, long-term, and dynamic mutual process of respect and reciprocal acknowledgment of the rights and obligations of all residents. Slovakia adopts an integration model based not only on adherence to Slovak legislation but also on foreigners' respect for Slovak cultural norms, language and traditions. It is expected that integration measures will result in coordinated and interconnected tools and actions that enable foreigners to participate in the labor market, acquire proficiency in the Slovak language, and access education, healthcare, social services, and housing. These measures

1416 Data provided by the Slovak Ministry of Interior.

should also facilitate their participation in civic and political life and, where applicable, lead to the granting of Slovak citizenship.

The primary goal of Slovakia's integration policy within migration policy is to ensure long-term harmonious coexistence among all residents of Slovakia. Targeted integration measures aim to provide foreigners with dignified living conditions, thereby preventing the emergence of potential negative social phenomena. Another goal is to strengthen and expand the means, methods and forms of financing integration measures, with a focus on systematic funding and the effective use of EU funds and other alternative non-budgetary resources. Slovakia's integration strategy focuses on strengthening integration efforts at regional, municipal and local levels to ensure that communities are equipped to support foreigners in their new environment.

One of the key priorities is to provide quality education for the children of foreigners, including Slovak language instruction tailored as a foreign language to facilitate linguistic integration. Access to adequate housing is also recognized as essential for promoting stability and enabling newcomers to build their lives within Slovakia.

In addition to addressing practical needs, Slovakia emphasizes the cultural and social integration of foreigners. This includes fostering community engagement and participation in cultural and social life.

The integration strategy also aims to enhance the academic preparation of social workers by introducing specialized courses on social work methods and policies focused on foreigner integration. This ensures that professionals working in this field are equipped with the necessary skills to provide effective support.

Efforts to strengthen social inclusion and cohesion are complemented by plans to introduce a mechanism for language and cultural orientation. This mechanism helps foreigners navigate their new environment by providing essential knowledge about the Slovak language, cultural norms and public services.

To address the healthcare needs of foreigners, Slovakia plans to streamline and digitize health-related data collection through an interconnected "e-Health Migration" system linking the Ministry of Interior and the Ministry of Health. This initiative will improve the monitoring of health services and ensure that evidence-based preventive and healthcare services are provided in accordance with recommended procedures for diagnostics and treatment.

Additionally, the government plans to track health indicators and healthcare needs to tailor services effectively and promote the well-being of foreigners residing in the country.

After this brief introduction to the current substantive legislative framework and migration policy of Slovakia, the following pages will cover specific areas of interest related to migration. Migrants, particularly those fleeing persecution, conflict, or economic hardship, encounter legal frameworks that determine their access to fundamental freedoms, protections and services. The interplay between national sovereignty, international obligations, and humanitarian principles often shapes these legal frameworks, resulting in significant variations across jurisdictions. The next sections will provide an in-depth analysis of various rights, beginning with the human rights directly associated with migration itself.

2.6.2.1 Human rights related to migration

Slovak legislation incorporates human rights obligations into its domestic laws through the Constitution[1417] and key acts regulating migration, such as Act No. 480/2002 Coll. on Asylum[1418] and Act No. 404/2011 Coll. on the Stay of Foreigners.[1419] These laws detail the rights of migrants to legal representation, access to health care, and procedural fairness. The Migration Office plays a key role in ensuring that these rights are upheld, including during health crises or security emergencies.

Article 23 of the Slovak Constitution guarantees the right of individuals to leave their country and return, a principle reinforced by international instruments like Article 12 of the ICCPR.[1420] Article 23 of the Constitution states:

> "(1) Freedom of movement and residence shall be guaranteed.
> (2) Everyone residing legally on the territory of the Slovak Republic has the right to leave its territory freely.
> (3) Freedoms defined in paragraphs 1 and 2 may be restricted by a law if it is necessary for national security, maintenance of public order, for

1417 Constitution of the Slovak Republic (No. 460/1992 Coll. as amended).
1418 Act No. 480/2002 Coll. on Asylum, as amended.
1419 Act No. 404/2011 Coll. on the Stay of Foreigners, as amended.
1420 UN General Assembly, International Covenant on Civil and Political Rights, United Nations, Treaty Series, vol. 999, 171, December 16, 1966.

the health protection or the protection of the rights and freedoms of others, and in the interest of the environment protection in specified territories.
(4) A citizen must not be forced to emigrate or to be expelled from his or her homeland.
(5) An alien may be expelled only in cases provided by a law."

This right is integral to personal freedom and is often invoked by both citizens and migrants. Article 23 of the Slovak Constitution guarantees the freedom of movement and residence while also outlining clear exceptions and restrictions. Paragraph 3 specifies that these freedoms may be limited by law if necessary for national security, public order, health protection, the rights and freedoms of others, or environmental protection in specific territories. The interpretation of terms such as "necessary for national security" or "maintenance of public order" is subject to judicial review, and courts often assess whether the restrictions meet the criteria of proportionality and necessity. Legal scholars highlight that these exceptions must be narrowly defined to prevent undue limitations on fundamental freedoms. The balance between legitimate state interests and individual rights is frequently revisited in case law, particularly during emergencies, when such restrictions are more likely to be applied. During emergencies, this right may be subject to conditions aimed at safeguarding public health and security. For example, during the COVID-19 pandemic, travelers faced exit and entry bans unless they met specific criteria, such as presenting negative COVID-19 tests or proof of vaccination.[1421] Slovak legal doctrine often addresses the balance between such public health measures and individual freedoms, emphasizing the need for proportionality and judicial oversight. European case law, such as key rulings by the European Court of Human Rights, provides further guidance by establishing that restrictions must be necessary, clearly defined, and temporary.[1422] This context reinforces the importance of maintaining

[1421] Henčeková, S., and Drugda, Š., *Slovakia: Change of Government under COVID-19 Emergency*. (Verfassungsblog 2020, May 22).

[1422] Trykhlib K., "The Principle of Proportionality in the Jurisprudence of the European Court of Human Rights." (2020) 4 *EU and Comparative Law Issues and Challenges Series*, 128–154.

procedural safeguards to ensure that public health interventions do not disproportionately restrict freedom of movement.

In addition to health-related restrictions, Slovakia has implemented temporary travel bans and imposed specific entry protocols during security crises. These measures triggered legal debates about their proportionality and compliance with human rights obligations. While exceptions were made for humanitarian cases and the reunification of immediate family members, procedural delays often led to prolonged separations.

The legal framework also includes provisions for special exceptions in cases involving vulnerable groups, distinguishing between citizens and non-citizens in terms of emigration, expulsion, and legal protections. Paragraph 4 of Article 23 prohibits forcing citizens to emigrate or be expelled from their homeland, reflecting the constitutional principle of protecting the connection between citizens and their state. By contrast, paragraph 5 permits the expulsion of non-citizens only under conditions established by law, ensuring due process but reinforcing the state's discretion over the residency of foreign nationals. Legal debates often focus on the justification and proportionality of these distinctions, questioning whether the different treatment of citizens and non-citizens aligns with international human rights norms and whether procedural safeguards sufficiently prevent arbitrary decisions. Slovak authorities can grant exemptions to ensure the return of unaccompanied minors or persons with severe health conditions. However, civil society organizations have highlighted the need for clearer guidelines and greater transparency in granting such exceptions.

Slovakia's approach to ensuring the right to leave and return demonstrates the challenge of balancing national security and public safety with respect for individual freedoms. Continuous judicial oversight remains crucial for upholding the principle of proportionality and preventing the undue limitation of this fundamental right.

The right to asylum is a cornerstone of international protection, enshrined in both international treaties and national legislation. Slovakia's asylum system, governed by Act No. 480/2002 Coll.,[1423] ensures protection for individuals fleeing persecution due to race, religion, nationality, political opinion, or membership in a particular social group, in line with the 1951 Refugee

1423 Act No. 480/2002 Coll. on Asylum, as amended.

Convention and its 1967 Protocol. This legal framework incorporates the principle of non-refoulement, meaning that no person may be returned to a country where their life or freedom would be threatened. In practice, however, accessing asylum during emergencies can be fraught with challenges. Restrictions at border points, limitations on in-person submissions, and bureaucratic hurdles have been reported, particularly during the COVID-19 pandemic and the Ukrainian refugee crisis. Digital application systems were introduced to mitigate access issues, but this highlighted disparities in digital literacy and technological resources among applicants.

Slovakia also adheres to the Dublin III Regulation, which mandates that the first EU country where an asylum application is lodged is responsible for processing the claim. This regulation aims to prevent "asylum shopping" but can place disproportionate pressure on border countries. Slovakia has participated in discussions about reforming this system to ensure more equitable responsibility-sharing within the EU.

Legal scholars have noted that while the legal framework provides safeguards, the effectiveness of these protections depends on timely and fair procedures. Judicial review plays a key role in ensuring that administrative decisions adhere to legal standards and that applicants have access to an effective remedy. Nonetheless, concerns persist regarding the consistency of decisions, the treatment of vulnerable groups, and the adequacy of legal representation for asylum seekers.

The right to asylum thus remains a critical area where national interests must be balanced with human rights obligations. Slovakia's continued participation in EU-wide initiatives and reforms aims to address systemic issues and strengthen the capacity to respond effectively to future crises. The Slovak Asylum Act outlines the criteria for granting protection to individuals fleeing persecution and serious harm, and it establishes procedural standards to ensure fair and humane treatment throughout the asylum process. The Act is divided into multiple sections, each addressing a specific aspect of the asylum process, providing a legal pathway for protection and ensuring compliance with both national and international legal standards.

Grounds for Asylum—This section defines the eligibility criteria for asylum and aligns with the 1951 Refugee Convention and the 1967 Protocol. The Act specifies that asylum can be granted to individuals who fear persecution due to their race, religion, nationality, political opinion, or membership in a particular social group. The language used in this section underscores Slovakia's commitment to international conventions by providing protection from discrimination and targeting persecution rooted in identity and beliefs. The two main groups of grounds for asylum are persecution and membership in a social group. The Act adopts a broad interpretation of persecution, consistent with international standards, covering harm inflicted by both state and non-state actors. This includes threats to life, arbitrary imprisonment, and systemic discrimination. The definition of "social group" remains one of the more contested grounds for asylum. Slovak jurisprudence has interpreted this category to include groups defined by characteristics such as gender identity, sexual orientation, and family or kinship ties. However, the lack of uniform guidelines has resulted in varying interpretations by courts, highlighting the need for a more consistent application to strengthen legal certainty.

Subsidiary protection serves as an additional safeguard for individuals who do not meet the strict legal definition of a refugee but who nonetheless face a serious risk of harm if returned to their country of origin. This category typically applies to individuals at risk of torture, inhuman or degrading treatment, or indiscriminate violence due to armed conflict.

The Act provides specific criteria for determining whether an applicant faces serious harm, taking into account factors such as widespread violence, systemic instability, and documented abuses in the applicant's country of origin. This ensures that decisions are grounded in an objective analysis of credible evidence.

The inclusion of subsidiary protection underscores Slovakia's acknowledgment of its broader humanitarian obligations. The Act's provisions ensure that individuals who fall outside the narrow definition of a refugee are still protected from life-threatening conditions.

The procedural framework for submitting asylum claims is another critical element of the Act. Applications must be filed at designated locations, including border checkpoints, police units, or reception centers. By centralizing the submission process, the Act aims to enhance accountability and minimize the risk of informal or undocumented claims. However, this centralized system can create logistical challenges during periods of high migration inflows, potentially leading to delays and inefficiencies. The Act mandates that all applicants be informed of their rights and the asylum process in a language they understand. The requirement to provide information in an applicant's preferred language demonstrates a commitment to procedural fairness and due process. However, the practical implementation of this obligation has faced challenges, particularly in cases involving rare languages and dialects. Some applicants have had to rely on informal translations, which can lead to misunderstandings about their legal rights and responsibilities.

The Act guarantees asylum seekers access to adequate living conditions while their claims are being processed. This includes temporary accommodation, access to food and healthcare, and social support services. Specific facilities are designated to house asylum seekers during the adjudication process. These centers are tasked with providing humane and secure living environments in accordance with international standards for the treatment of displaced persons. The Act explicitly provides for access to medical care and psychological assistance, recognizing the vulnerability of many asylum seekers who have experienced trauma. Despite these provisions, reports of overcrowding during migration surges have raised concerns about the quality of living conditions and the adequacy of the available services.

Applicants whose asylum claims are denied have the right to appeal. The appeal process begins at district courts, with the Supreme Court serving as the final authority for disputed cases. This multi-tiered system provides a safeguard against procedural errors and ensures that applicants have the opportunity to seek redress. District courts serve as the first level of judicial oversight, reviewing the legality and fairness of administrative decisions. One notable challenge in the appeals process is the inconsistency in rulings across different courts. Legal scholars have criticized the absence of standardized interpretations of key legal concepts, which can result in unpredictable outcomes.

The way the Asylum Act is structured ensures that the legal framework for international protection in Slovakia is comprehensive and transparent. Each section addresses critical stages in the asylum process, reinforcing procedural fairness and aligning national policies with international human rights standards.

The principle of non-refoulement, as enshrined in Section 6 of the Act, prohibits the expulsion or return of individuals to territories where they may face persecution or serious harm. This provision mirrors the obligations set out in Article 33 of the 1951 Refugee Convention[1424] and Article 3 of the European Convention on Human Rights.[1425] The provision's application has been scrutinized during periods of crisis, such as the 2015 migration wave and the Ukrainian refugee influx, where delays and inconsistencies in processing claims have been noted. Instances of prolonged detentions at borders have raised concerns about procedural safeguards.

In recent years, Slovakia has introduced digital submission options, particularly during the COVID-19 pandemic. However, these systems have been criticized for accessibility issues, especially for those with limited digital literacy.

The Act mandates that the Migration Office issue a decision on asylum applications within 60 days. As of July 2024, the Slovak government implemented amendments to immigration laws, reducing the processing time for asylum applications from 90 to 60 days. Extensions are permitted in complex cases, but delays must be justified. Reports from civil society organizations indicate that the statutory timeframe is often exceeded, particularly during periods of high demand.[1426]

Despite the comprehensive legal framework, Slovakia faces numerous practical challenges. Resource limitations, coordination issues, and the need for enhanced support for vulnerable groups are among the key areas requiring attention. A significant obstacle for Slovakia's asylum system is the scarcity of resources, particularly during periods of increased migration flows. Reception centers often operate with constrained budgets, leading to delays and bottlenecks in claim processing and reduced capacity to accommodate asylum seekers adequately. Although the legal framework provides protections for vulnerable groups, such as unaccompanied minors, victims of trafficking, and persons with disabilities, implementation remains inconsistent. There is a pressing need for enhanced training of case officers in trauma-informed practices and for expanded access to psychological and legal support services to address the complex needs of these groups. Slovakia's asylum system

---

1424 UN General Assembly, Convention Relating to the Status of Refugees, United Nations, Treaty Series, vol. 189, 137, July 28, 1951.

1425 Council of Europe, European Convention on Human Rights, as amended by Protocols Nos. 11, 14 and 15, ETS No. 005, November 4, 1950.

1426 Human Rights League, *Observations on Asylum Procedures in Slovakia. European Union Agency for Asylum* (2022).

operates within the broader EU framework, including adherence to the Dublin III Regulation, which mandates that asylum claims be processed in the first EU country of entry. This requirement can create procedural delays and additional burdens, especially when other Member States reject responsibility for applicants, shifting the pressure onto Slovakia's system.

To address persistent challenges in the asylum process, Act No. 480/2002 Coll. on Asylum underwent substantial revisions in 2024 through Act No. 144/2024 Coll.[1427] These amendments were introduced to respond to rising migration flows, align national regulations with EU directives, and address systemic shortcomings in the asylum framework. One of the primary drivers behind the amendment was the increased migration flows stemming from geopolitical instability in Eastern Europe, particularly the war in Ukraine. The influx of asylum seekers placed significant pressure on Slovakia's asylum system, necessitating faster processing times and strengthened support services to manage the growing demand.

The amendment also aimed to harmonize Slovakia's asylum laws with EU legislation, including the evolving EU Pact on Migration and Asylum and Regulation on the European Border and Coast Guard (Frontex). This alignment was essential to maintain Slovakia's compliance with EU standards and improve its cooperation within the European Asylum framework. Reports from civil society organizations and international bodies revealed procedural gaps in the system, such as delays in decision-making, overcrowded reception centers, and inconsistent application of non-refoulement principles. These reports highlighted the need for reforms to enhance procedural efficiency and uphold international protection standards. The amendment also focused on the protection of vulnerable groups, such as unaccompanied minors, victims of trafficking, and individuals with disabilities. Strengthening these protections was crucial for fulfilling Slovakia's obligations under international human rights agreements, including the UN Convention on the Rights of the Child[1428] and EU anti-trafficking directives. Finally, the amendment sought to implement digital modernization to address inefficiencies in outdated case

[1427] Act No. 144/2024 Coll. on Asylum.

[1428] UN General Assembly, Convention on the Rights of the Child, United Nations, Treaty Series, vol. 1577, 3, November 20, 1989.

management systems. By introducing electronic solutions, the legislative changes aimed to improve communication with applicants and streamline the handling of asylum claims.

To ensure more timely and equitable asylum decisions, the amendment implemented several procedural reforms. The maximum timeframe for the Migration Office to issue decisions on standard asylum applications was reduced from 90 days to 60 days, with extensions allowed only in particularly complex cases. This adjustment aims to address delays and provide applicants with quicker resolutions. Additionally, applicants now have access to free legal assistance at an earlier stage of the process, ensuring that they receive adequate representation during the initial application phase.

The amendment also introduced measures to expand and upgrade reception facilities. Additional funding was allocated to increase the capacity of existing reception centers and construct new temporary housing units to prevent overcrowding, particularly during periods of high migration inflows. On-site healthcare teams were deployed in larger reception centers to provide essential medical services, including mental health support, recognizing the need to address the psychological well-being of asylum seekers.

Furthermore, specialized family support units were established to accommodate families and vulnerable individuals, such as children, with services informed by trauma-sensitive care principles.

To modernize the asylum process and enhance administrative efficiency, the amendment launched the e-Asylum Portal, a comprehensive digital platform designed to increase transparency and accessibility. This platform allows applicants to track the status of their claims in real time, upload necessary documents, and receive notifications regarding their case progress. Importantly, the system provides multilingual support to accommodate non-Slovak speakers and improve communication with applicants throughout the process.

The amendment also strengthened protections for vulnerable applicants by introducing tailored procedures for groups such as unaccompanied minors and trafficking survivors. These procedures include mandatory psychological assessments and the creation of individualized care plans to ensure that applicants receive support tailored to their specific needs. Additionally, new specialized units within the Migration Office were established to handle cases involving vulnerable individuals, ensuring consistency in decision-making and adherence to international protection standards.

The amendment also sought to strengthen Slovakia's cooperation with EU partners in managing migration. Provisions were introduced to enhance Slovakia's participation in EU relocation schemes designed to balance the distribution of asylum seekers across Member States. This approach aims to alleviate the pressures faced by individual Member States and promote solidarity within the EU. Additionally, Slovakia increased its contribution to the European Border and Coast Guard (Frontex) by implementing new training programs for border officers in collaboration with the agency.

The 2024 amendment to Act No. 480/2002 Coll. on asylum marks a significant step in addressing the legal and practical challenges facing Slovakia's asylum system. However, the success of these reforms will depend on sustained funding, effective interagency cooperation, and continuous monitoring.

The right to enter a safe country represents a critical aspect of international protection, especially for refugees and asylum seekers fleeing persecution or conflict. This right is closely tied to the broader principle of non-refoulement, which prohibits returning individuals to places where they face a credible risk of serious harm. In Slovakia, this principle is implemented through Act No. 480/2002 Coll. on Asylum, as well as adherence to the Dublin III Regulation, which governs the allocation of responsibility for processing asylum claims within the European Union.

Under the Dublin system, Slovakia is generally required to process asylum applications submitted by individuals who first enter the EU through Slovak territory. This framework aims to prevent "asylum shopping" but can create significant logistical challenges during periods of mass migration. In some instances, exceptions are made to allow for family reunification or to provide humanitarian relief, particularly when vulnerable groups such as unaccompanied minors or individuals with disabilities are involved.

During the Ukrainian refugee crisis, Slovakia introduced temporary humanitarian corridors to facilitate the safe transit of individuals escaping active conflict zones. These corridors were widely regarded as a necessary measure to uphold the right to safety while managing border security. However, reports highlighted disparities in how entry protocols were applied, with some asylum seekers facing extended waiting times and inconsistent information.[1429]

Legal scholars have noted that Slovakia's commitment to the principle of providing safe access must be balanced with its national security interests. This tension became especially evident during the COVID-19 pandemic, when public health concerns led to temporary closures of border crossings and the implementation of stricter entry requirements. While these measures aimed to protect public health, they also raised concerns about proportionality and the accessibility of asylum procedures for those in urgent need of protection.

In practice, ensuring the right to enter a safe country requires a coordinated effort between government agencies, NGOs, and international organizations. The Migration Office of the Ministry of Interior plays a central role in assessing and processing asylum applications, but capacity constraints have sometimes led to delays in handling large influxes of refugees. Cooperation with EU partners and adherence to shared legal standards are critical in mitigating these challenges.

While legal frameworks in Slovakia provide a foundation for protecting the right to enter a safe country, continued reforms and resource allocation are essential to address gaps in implementation and to ensure that those seeking refuge receive timely and fair access to protection.

The right to freedom of movement is a fundamental principle enshrined in the Slovak Constitution and protected under EU and international law. This right includes the ability to move freely within the country, cross borders, and reside in any part of the state. However, in the context of migration, this right often faces restrictions during times of emergency. For third-country nationals (TCNs), especially asylum seekers and individuals with temporary protection, the right to freedom of movement can be curtailed to address public health concerns, security issues, or logistical constraints.

During the COVID-19 pandemic, Slovakia implemented nationwide curfews, regional lockdowns, and restrictions on interregional travel. While these measures were designed to prevent the spread of the virus, they significantly

---

1429 Human Rights League, *Observations on Asylum Procedures in Slovakia* (European Union Agency for Asylum 2022).

affected TCNs awaiting decisions on asylum claims or seeking family reunification. Many were restricted to reception centers or specific regions, with limited permissions to leave for essential reasons. Legal scholars have debated the proportionality of these measures, pointing out that prolonged restrictions can lead to isolation, delays in legal processes, and a negative impact on mental well-being.

Moreover, the Schengen Borders Code allows for the temporary reintroduction of internal border controls during exceptional circumstances. Slovakia has invoked these provisions during migration surges and security threats. In such cases, TCNs have faced longer wait times, increased document checks, and, in some instances, detentions if they did not meet entry requirements. This raises concerns about potential breaches of the principle of non-discrimination and the need for consistent application of EU-wide guidelines.

To mitigate these impacts, Slovakia's legal framework includes certain safeguards. For example, TCNs placed under travel restrictions have the right to legal recourse and can request exemptions for humanitarian reasons, such as attending urgent medical appointments or reuniting with family members. However, the practical accessibility of these remedies remains a challenge, particularly for individuals lacking legal assistance.

The digitalization of administrative processes, such as online applications for travel exemptions and status updates, has partially eased mobility restrictions for some TCNs. Nevertheless, digital inequality remains an issue, as not all applicants have reliable internet access or digital literacy.

Recent reports by NGOs highlight the importance of maintaining a balance between legitimate public safety concerns and the fundamental right to freedom of movement. Continuous judicial oversight, clear communication of restrictions, and fair processing of exemption requests are necessary to prevent the disproportionate impact of emergency measures on vulnerable populations. As Slovakia continues to adapt its migration policies, ensuring that restrictions are time-bound, justified, and respectful of human dignity will be essential for compliance with national and international human rights standards.

The Slovak legal framework requires applicants to undergo a thorough review of their residency status, financial stability, and housing conditions to ensure they meet the necessary criteria for family reunification.

Under Slovak law, TCNs applying for family reunification must hold a valid residence permit and demonstrate that they can provide adequate living conditions and financial support for their family members. This process, regulated by Act No. 404/2011 Coll. on the Stay of Foreigners,[1430] aims to prevent economic dependency while supporting integration. However, during emergencies, the additional burden of proving financial and housing stability becomes more challenging due to job losses, restricted mobility, and administrative backlogs.

The COVID-19 pandemic and the Ukrainian refugee crisis exemplified how public health emergencies and geopolitical conflicts can exacerbate the challenges of family reunification. Temporary travel bans, quarantine requirements, and the closure of administrative offices led to significant delays in processing reunification requests. In some cases, families were separated for extended periods, causing emotional distress and raising concerns about the protection of the right to family life as enshrined in Article 8 of the European Convention on Human Rights.

Applicants facing delays or denials can seek judicial review to challenge administrative decisions. However, courts have often struggled with increased caseloads during crises, leading to prolonged proceedings. Some rulings have emphasized the state's obligation to act expeditiously in family reunification cases, particularly when minors are involved, to prevent undue harm.

Special considerations are made for vulnerable individuals, such as unaccompanied minors and refugees fleeing active conflict zones. These cases often qualify for expedited procedures and exemptions from standard requirements.

Special Provisions for Vulnerable Groups: Slovakia's legal framework recognizes the need for special protections for vulnerable groups, including unaccompanied minors, victims of trafficking, women, older adults, and persons with disabilities. The country's commitment to the UN Convention on the Rights of the Child (UNCRC)[1431] affirms the principle of prioritizing the best interests of the child in all proceedings. This has led to specific measures such as appointing legal guardians for unaccompanied minors and ensuring access to education and psychosocial support. However, during

---

1430 Act No. 404/2011 Coll. on the Stay of Foreigners, as amended.

1431 UN General Assembly, Convention on the Rights of the Child, United Nations, Treaty Series, vol. 1577, 3, November 20, 1989.

times of crisis, implementation has faced delays due to limited staffing and administrative bottlenecks.

Special care is provided for children who arrive without their families. Slovak authorities assign guardians to represent the interests of these minors and ensure their access to safe housing and education. Emergency protocols during the war in Ukraine accelerated this process, but gaps remained, particularly in providing timely psychosocial evaluations and ensuring consistent long-term support.

Victims of human trafficking are entitled to immediate protection, including safe housing, medical care, and legal assistance. During emergencies, a surge in demand for shelters revealed the need for additional funding and interagency coordination to prevent further exploitation.

Women, particularly those fleeing conflict, are at heightened risk of gender-based violence. Slovakia's emergency shelters provided refuge, yet reports indicated overcrowding and insufficient resources in certain regions. Legal aid organizations have called for stronger preventive measures and enhanced training for first responders.

Vulnerable adults, especially those with mobility challenges or chronic illnesses, encountered significant barriers during the pandemic and migration surges. Accessibility to healthcare services and reception centers was inconsistent, which highlighted the need for disability-inclusive policies. Mobile health units and outreach programs were deployed in some cases but were not uniformly available across all regions.

NGOs and international agencies, such as UNHCR and IOM, played a critical role in supporting vulnerable populations, providing supplemental services when state resources were overwhelmed. However, these efforts emphasized the need for sustainable state-NGO partnerships and consistent funding to ensure that vulnerable groups receive comprehensive care.

Slovakia can improve compliance with its human rights obligations during emergencies by investing in targeted services for vulnerable groups.

2.6.2.2 Personal rights for third-country nationals

In the context of migration, the individual rights of third-country nationals (TCNs) in Slovakia encompass key aspects of their well-being and integration, such as access to health care, the right to personal freedom and privacy, data protection, and freedom of religion. During times of emergency, such as public health crises or security threats, these rights are often subject to restrictions that challenge the balance between individual liberties and the public interest.

Health care is a fundamental aspect of ensuring the dignity and well-being of TCNs. Upon entering Slovakia, asylum seekers and migrants must undergo mandatory health screenings for infectious diseases. These health checks, regulated by public health laws, are intended to safeguard the broader community but can impose significant procedural burdens on new arrivals. During the COVID-19 pandemic, Slovakia implemented quarantine protocols for TCNs at reception centers and border crossings. These included isolation requirements and periodic testing. While intended to curb the spread of the virus, these measures highlighted systemic vulnerabilities, including overcrowding at reception centers and delays in medical evaluations. Humanitarian organizations played a crucial role in filling gaps by providing essential medical support and mental health services.

Access to routine and emergency medical care for TCNs often depends on their residency status. While those with permanent or long-term residence permits are entitled to broader health care benefits, individuals with temporary or no legal status may only receive emergency care. Advocacy groups have stressed the importance of implementing inclusive health policies that ensure consistent access to preventive care and psychological support. The cornerstone of healthcare access in Slovakia is Act No. 580/2004 Coll. on Health Insurance,[1432] which defines the conditions under which individuals may participate in the public health insurance system. Migrants with long-term or permanent residence permits are typically required to enroll in public health insurance, which grants them access to a comprehensive range of services, including preventive care, diagnostics, and treatment. This ensures that legally residing migrants can benefit from the same healthcare entitlements as Slovak citizens.

However, for migrants holding temporary or short-term residence permits, access to public health insurance is not automatic. These individuals must secure private health insurance to cover their medical needs. Private policies often provide more limited coverage and may impose restrictions, highlighting a disparity in healthcare access based on legal status. Despite

---

1432 Act No. 580/2004 Coll. on Health Insurance.

these limitations, all migrants, regardless of their insurance status, are entitled to emergency healthcare services, which must be provided by healthcare institutions without discrimination or delay. Slovak healthcare legislation includes specific protections for patients, including the right to choose a healthcare provider, access information about one's health condition, and provide or withhold informed consent for medical treatment. These rights apply to all patients, including migrants, reinforcing Slovakia's commitment to upholding human dignity within its healthcare system. However, in practice, migrants may face challenges in exercising these rights due to language barriers, administrative complexities, or a lack of understanding of their legal entitlements.

The right to personal freedom and privacy is enshrined in the Slovak Constitution and international legal instruments, including the European Convention on Human Rights. However, during emergencies, the detention of irregular migrants is permitted under specific conditions regulated by Act No. 404/2011 Coll. on the Stay of Foreigners.

Detention centers are required to uphold humanitarian standards, but emergencies often exacerbate administrative backlogs and extend detention durations. Reports have documented instances where TCNs experienced prolonged stays due to delayed legal proceedings and restricted court operations during crisis periods. Civil society organizations have called for greater transparency in detention procedures and emphasized the need for consistent judicial oversight to ensure the rights of detainees are upheld.[1433]

The right to privacy is also affected by the living conditions in reception centers, where overcrowding can undermine personal space and privacy. Efforts to improve accommodation and provide private family spaces remain ongoing challenges, particularly during influxes of asylum seekers.

The collection and management of personal data, especially during public health emergencies, have been areas of heightened concern. Slovakia's data protection laws, aligned with the General Data Protection Regulation (GDPR),[1434] mandate that any collection of personal information must be

---

1433 Human Rights League, *Observations on Asylum Procedures in Slovakia* (European Union Agency for Asylum 2022).

1434 European Union, Regulation (EU) 2016/679 of the European Parliament and of the Council of April 27, 2016 on the protection of natural persons with regard to the processing of personal data and on the free movement of such data (General Data

lawful, necessary, and proportionate. Supplementing the GDPR, Act No. 18/2018 Coll. on the Protection of Personal Data[1435] aligns national regulations with EU standards, detailing obligations for data controllers and reinforcing individuals' rights to data access, correction and deletion. However, emergency legislation during the pandemic expanded data collection efforts to include contact tracing and health monitoring.

While these measures were justified on public health grounds, privacy advocates raised concerns about the potential for government overreach and inadequate safeguards for sensitive information. Independent oversight mechanisms are critical to ensure that data collected during emergencies is securely stored, used only for its intended purpose, and deleted once the emergency subsides.

In the context of migration, personal data collected may include sensitive information such as biometric data, health records, and details related to asylum claims or legal status. As such, Slovak authorities must apply heightened protections when processing such data to prevent unauthorized access and ensure compliance with the principles of data minimization and purpose limitation. The Slovak Office for Personal Data Protection plays a critical role in overseeing compliance with data protection regulations. Migrants who believe their personal data has been mishandled have the right to file complaints with the Office and seek legal remedies, including compensation for damages. However, access to these remedies may be limited for vulnerable individuals without adequate legal support, which highlights the need for accessible legal aid services and information in multiple languages.

Freedom of religion is a protected right under Article 24 of the Slovak Constitution and extends to all residents, including TCNs. This right includes the ability to practice religion individually or in community with others, as well as the right to establish places of worship. Migrants, whether temporary residents, asylum seekers, or beneficiaries of international protection, are entitled to exercise this right freely, individually or in community with others, through worship, religious observance, and the expression of their beliefs.

Protection Regulation—GDPR) (2016) L119 *Official Journal of the European Union*, 1–88.

1435 Act No. 18/2018 Coll. on the Protection of Personal Data.

Slovakia's legal system ensures the protection of religious freedoms in line with international obligations under the European Convention on Human Rights (Article 9) and the International Covenant on Civil and Political Rights (ICCPR). These instruments, alongside national laws, prohibit discrimination based on religion and guarantee migrants the right to practice their religion freely. The Act No. 308/1991 Coll. on Freedom of Religious Belief and the Status of Churches and Religious Societies[1436] regulates the registration and legal status of religious groups, allowing recognized churches and religious organizations to operate freely and support their communities, including migrants.

In Slovakia, registered religious communities play a significant role in supporting migrants, particularly those who have recently arrived or are seeking asylum. Religious organizations often provide essential social services, such as shelter, food and legal aid, in addition to spiritual support. Migrants and asylum seekers have the right to participate in religious ceremonies, access places of worship, and observe religious holidays without fear of reprisal or discrimination. Some reception centers for asylum seekers also accommodate religious practices by providing prayer spaces and respecting dietary requirements based on religious beliefs.

While the right to freedom of religion is broadly protected, it is not absolute and may be subject to certain limitations in specific circumstances. According to Article 24(4) of the Slovak Constitution, restrictions may be imposed for the protection of public order, health, morals, or the rights and freedoms of others. For example, during the COVID-19 pandemic, restrictions on public gatherings significantly impacted religious practices. Places of worship were closed or limited to small, socially distanced gatherings, which disrupted communal religious observances and ceremonies. While exemptions were granted for some religious gatherings under strict health protocols, the limitations prompted legal and social debates about the proportionality of such restrictions. Religious communities adapted by offering virtual services and small private gatherings, but these solutions were not universally accessible, particularly for asylum seekers living in reception centers with limited internet access. Faith-based organizations advocated

[1436] Act No. 308/1991 Coll. on Freedom of Religious Belief and the Status of Churches and Religious Societies.

for clearer guidelines and greater government support to maintain religious practice during emergencies.

Slovak law prohibits discrimination based on religion or belief in both public and private spheres, as outlined in Act No. 365/2004 Coll. on Equal Treatment (Antidiscrimination Act).[1437] Migrants who experience religious discrimination in accessing housing, employment, education, or public services have the right to seek legal remedies.

2.6.2.3 Political rights for third-country nationals

While political rights are often associated with the citizens of a state, Slovakia extends certain political freedoms to third-country nationals, recognizing their role in democratic participation and social cohesion. These rights include the freedom of assembly, the right to establish associations, the right to petition, and, to a more limited extent, the right to participate in civil service.

These rights are protected under the Slovak Constitution and relevant legislative provisions, ensuring that third-country nationals can engage in peaceful demonstrations, form organizations to represent their interests, and address public authorities through petitions. However, some restrictions apply, particularly regarding access to public employment and civil service roles, which remain largely reserved for Slovak and EU citizens.

The freedom of assembly is a fundamental democratic right enshrined in Article 28 of the Constitution of the Slovak Republic[1438] and protected under international human rights treaties, including the European Convention on Human Rights (Article 11)[1439] and the International Covenant on Civil and Political Rights (ICCPR).[1440] This right ensures that individuals, regardless of their nationality or migration status, can organize and participate in peaceful public gatherings, protests, and demonstrations to express their views and advocate for their interests. Migrants, including third-country nationals and asylum seekers, are entitled to exercise this right within the Slovak legal

1437 Act No. 365/2004 Coll. on Equal Treatment.

1438 Constitution of the Slovak Republic (No. 460/1992 Coll. as amended).

1439 Council of Europe, European Convention on Human Rights, as amended by Protocols Nos. 11, 14 and 15, ETS No. 005, November 4, 1950.

1440 UN General Assembly, International Covenant on Civil and Political Rights, United Nations, Treaty Series, vol. 999, 171, December 16, 1966.

framework, subject to specific legal limitations aimed at maintaining public order and security. In Slovakia, the Act No. 84/1990 Coll. on the Right of Assembly[1441] governs the organization and regulation of public assemblies. The Act affirms that all individuals, including migrants, have the right to assemble peacefully without prior authorization, although organizers are required to notify the local authorities in advance. Assemblies that are intended to be held in public spaces must be reported at least five working days before the planned event. This notification process enables public authorities to coordinate security measures and ensure that the assembly does not pose a risk to public safety.

However, the law also specifies circumstances in which assemblies may be restricted or prohibited. Assemblies that incite violence, promote hatred or discrimination, or threaten public health and safety can be lawfully dissolved. Restrictions may also apply during states of emergency, such as public health crises, where gatherings may be temporarily limited to prevent the spread of infectious diseases.

Migrants in Slovakia have increasingly used the freedom of assembly to advocate for their rights, raise awareness of social issues, and express solidarity with their communities. Public demonstrations in support of refugees, antidiscrimination protests, and events organized by migrant communities are examples of the exercise of this right. Slovak law provides safeguards to prevent arbitrary interference with the right to assemble. Law enforcement officers are required to ensure that assemblies remain peaceful and to intervene proportionately if disruptions occur.

The COVID-19 pandemic highlighted the tension between public health measures and the exercise of the freedom of assembly. Restrictions on gatherings, including limits on the number of participants and social distancing mandates, were imposed to contain the spread of the virus. Although these restrictions applied to all individuals, including Slovak citizens, migrants were particularly affected due to their reliance on public demonstrations as a means of visibility and advocacy.

The right to establish associations is a key component of democratic participation, enabling individuals to form and join organizations that represent their collective interests. In Slovakia, this right is protected under Article 29

1441 Act No. 84/1990 Coll. on the Right of Assembly.

of the Constitution of the Slovak Republic[1442] and further regulated by Act No. 83/1990 Coll. on the Association of Citizens.[1443] Migrants, including third-country nationals, are entitled to form associations and participate in civil society initiatives, provided they comply with the legal requirements governing the registration and operation of associations.

Slovak law allows all individuals, regardless of nationality, to form and join civic associations, provided their activities are lawful and aligned with democratic principles. Associations may be established to pursue a wide range of goals, including cultural, educational, charitable, and social objectives. The process for establishing an association involves submitting a formal application to the Ministry of Interior, which must include the association's statutes, objectives, and information about its founders. A minimum of three founding members is required, and the application is typically processed within 10 days. However, certain restrictions apply. Associations that promote violence, hatred or illegal activities, or that undermine public order, can be denied registration or disbanded by the authorities. Additionally, political parties and organizations with the intent to participate in the exercise of state power cannot be established by non-citizens, which limits the extent to which migrants can engage in formal political representation.

Migrant associations often provide essential services, such as language classes, legal aid, cultural events, and job placement support. They also create platforms for dialogue between migrant communities and public institutions. In some cases, associations founded by migrants have partnered with Slovak NGOs and governmental bodies to implement programs that address the specific needs of migrant populations.

The Act No. 365/2004 Coll. on Equal Treatment (Antidiscrimination Act) prohibits discrimination based on nationality, religion, or other personal characteristics in the establishment and operation of associations. Migrants who experience barriers to forming associations due to discriminatory treatment have the right to file complaints and seek legal remedies.

The right of petition is an important democratic instrument that enables individuals to formally address public authorities with requests, proposals, or complaints. In Slovakia, this right is protected under Article 27 of

1442 Constitution of the Slovak Republic (No. 460/1992 Coll. as amended).

1443 Act No. 83/1990 Coll. on the Association of Citizens.

the Constitution of the Slovak Republic[1444] and further regulated by Act No. 85/1990 Coll. on the Right of Petition.[1445] The law grants all individuals, including migrants and third-country nationals, the right to submit petitions on matters of public interest and to receive a response from relevant authorities within a reasonable timeframe.

Slovak law defines a petition as a written or electronic submission addressed to a government authority, calling for action or raising concerns about public policy, social issues, or individual rights. The petition process is accessible to all individuals, regardless of their citizenship or legal status, provided that the submission adheres to formal requirements, such as including the petitioner's identification and a clear statement of the request or complaint.

Petitions can be submitted individually or collectively and may address a wide range of issues, including housing, employment, healthcare, or legal protections. Collective petitions, which require signatures from a minimum number of individuals (typically 10,000 for parliamentary consideration), are a common tool used to raise awareness and advocate for systemic changes.

The authorities receiving petitions are obligated to process them transparently and provide a written response outlining any actions taken or reasons for rejecting the request. However, petitions that promote illegal activities, incite hatred, or disrupt public order are not admissible under the law.

Slovak law prohibits any form of retaliation or discrimination against individuals who exercise their right of petition. This protection ensures that migrants can raise concerns without fear of repercussions related to their immigration status, employment, or social standing. Nevertheless, fear of negative consequences may still deter some migrants, particularly those with precarious legal status, from submitting petitions.

The right to enter the civil service is an essential aspect of political rights that reflects an individual's ability to contribute to public administration and governance. In Slovakia, access to civil service roles is regulated by Act No. 55/2017 Coll. on the Civil Service,[1446] which outlines the conditions for employment in public institutions and defines who is eligible to hold such positions. Most civil service roles, especially those involving public authority,

---

1444 Constitution of the Slovak Republic (No. 460/1992 Coll. as amended).

1445 Act No. 85/1990 Coll. on the Right of Petition.

1446 Act No. 55/2017 Coll. on Civil Service.

remain inaccessible to non-citizens due to statutory restrictions. However, exceptions exist for certain non-citizen roles, particularly in areas such as education, research, and health care.

2.6.2.4 Economic, social and cultural rights for third-country nationals

Economic, social, and cultural rights are essential for ensuring the full inclusion and well-being of third-country nationals in Slovakia. These rights enable individuals to access fundamental resources and opportunities, contributing to their personal development and social integration. Key among these rights are the right to education, which facilitates access to learning and language acquisition; the right to work, which ensures economic self-sufficiency and dignity; and the right to social allowances, which provides a safety net for individuals facing economic hardship.

Slovakia's legal framework for these rights is shaped by both national policies and international commitments, such as the International Covenant on Economic, Social, and Cultural Rights (ICESCR)[1447] and EU directives on the treatment of third-country nationals.

Education is a fundamental human right that plays a crucial role in the integration and social mobility of third-country nationals. In Slovakia, the right to education is protected under Article 42 of the Constitution of the Slovak Republic,[1448] which guarantees free access to primary and secondary education for all children, regardless of nationality. Additionally, Slovakia's obligations under the International Covenant on Economic, Social, and Cultural Rights (ICESCR)[1449] and the Convention on the Rights of the Child (UNCRC)[1450] ensure that third-country nationals have the right to access education without discrimination.

Slovak legislation provides that all children residing in the country, including those of third-country nationals, have the right to enroll in primary and

1447 UN General Assembly, International Covenant on Economic, Social and Cultural Rights, United Nations, Treaty Series, vol. 993, 3, December 16, 1966.
1448 Constitution of the Slovak Republic (No. 460/1992 Coll. as amended).
1449 UN General Assembly, International Covenant on Economic, Social and Cultural Rights, United Nations, Treaty Series, vol. 993, 3, December 16, 1966.
1450 UN General Assembly, Convention on the Rights of the Child, United Nations, Treaty Series, vol. 1577, 3, November 20, 1989.

secondary schools. Act No. 245/2008 Coll. on Upbringing and Education (Education Act)[1451] stipulates that compulsory schooling applies equally to children of foreign nationals and Slovak citizens. Public primary and secondary schools are free of charge, and access to higher education is also available, though non-EU students may be subject to tuition fees.

In addition, Slovakia has implemented policies aimed at supporting third-country national children through language integration programs and educational support services. Specialized Slovak language classes are offered in many schools to help migrant children adapt to the curriculum and overcome language barriers.

While access to compulsory education is generally well-regulated, challenges persist in early childhood and higher education. Enrollment in preschool is not guaranteed due to capacity limitations, which can disproportionately affect migrant families with young children. In higher education, third-country nationals often face administrative hurdles, such as the recognition of prior qualifications and additional financial burdens related to tuition fees for non-EU students. These barriers can limit opportunities for academic advancement and professional development.

The right to work is a fundamental component of economic and social integration for third-country nationals, enabling individuals to achieve self-sufficiency, contribute to the economy, and participate in society. In Slovakia, this right is governed by Act No. 5/2004 Coll. on Employment Services,[1452] which sets out the conditions under which third-country nationals may access the labor market. While the Slovak Constitution recognizes the right to work as a universal principle, the legal framework imposes specific conditions on third-country nationals based on their residency status.

The employment of third-country nationals in Slovakia is regulated through work permits, temporary residence permits for employment purposes, and EU Blue Cards for highly skilled workers. Third-country nationals generally require both a work permit and a temporary residence permit for employment unless they qualify for an exemption. These exemptions may

---

1451 Act No. 245/2008 Coll. on Upbringing and Education.

1452 Act No. 5/2004 Coll. on Employment Services.

apply to individuals with long-term residence, beneficiaries of international protection, or family members of Slovak or EU citizens.

The Slovak government has introduced several initiatives to address labor shortages and facilitate the employment of third-country nationals. For example, the Foreign Nationals' Labour Mobility Strategy aims to streamline administrative procedures, improve language training, and support the integration of foreign workers into the labor market. Additionally, partnerships with NGOs and international organizations have helped provide legal assistance, job placement services, and vocational training to third-country nationals.

The right to social allowances plays a crucial role in ensuring that third-country nationals have access to basic financial support during periods of economic hardship. Social allowances help individuals meet their essential needs, such as housing, healthcare, and family support, promoting social cohesion and reducing vulnerability to poverty. In Slovakia, access to social benefits is governed by Act No. 417/2013 Coll. on Assistance in Material Need[1453] and Act No. 461/2003 Coll. on Social Insurance,[1454] which define the conditions for eligibility and the scope of support available.

The Slovak social protection system includes two primary categories of financial support:

1. Contributory Benefits: These are funded through the social insurance system and are accessible to individuals who have made sufficient contributions through employment. Examples include unemployment benefits, sickness benefits, and maternity allowances.
2. Non-Contributory Benefits: These are funded by the state and provided based on financial need, regardless of prior contributions. Examples include housing allowances, child benefits, and emergency financial assistance.

Third-country nationals' access to social allowances largely depends on their legal status and length of residence in Slovakia. Migrants with permanent

---

[1453] Act No. 417/2013 Coll. on Assistance in Material Need.

[1454] Act No. 461/2003 Coll. on Social Insurance.

residence have access to the full range of social benefits available to Slovak citizens. In contrast, those with temporary residence permits typically have more limited access, particularly to non-contributory benefits.

The Slovak government, in collaboration with NGOs and international organizations, has implemented programs aimed at improving access to social support for vulnerable groups, including third-country nationals. These initiatives include providing multilingual information on social benefits, offering legal counseling, and simplifying administrative procedures for beneficiaries of international protection. However, the effectiveness of these programs depends on consistent funding and efforts to address regional disparities in service availability.

The right to social allowances is an essential component of economic and social security for third-country nationals in Slovakia. While the legal framework provides access to a range of social benefits, eligibility is closely tied to legal status, creating disparities in support for different categories of migrants.

Cultural rights are a vital component of human rights, ensuring that individuals can participate in and contribute to cultural life while preserving their identity, language, and traditions. The protection and promotion of these rights are essential for successful integration and social cohesion. Cultural rights in Slovakia are safeguarded by both national and international legal instruments. Article 34 of the Constitution of the Slovak Republic guarantees the right of individuals belonging to national minorities and ethnic groups to preserve and develop their language, culture, and religious practices. These provisions apply to all individuals residing in Slovakia, including third-country nationals. Additionally, Slovakia is a signatory to the International Covenant on Economic, Social, and Cultural Rights (ICESCR),[1455] which affirms the right of everyone to participate freely in cultural life, enjoy the benefits of cultural heritage, and practice their cultural customs.

In the context of migration, cultural rights encompass not only the right to maintain one's cultural identity but also the right to access cultural institutions, participate in cultural events, and receive public support for cultural initiatives.

1455 UN General Assembly, International Covenant on Economic, Social and Cultural Rights, United Nations, Treaty Series, vol. 993, 3, December 16, 1966.

Language plays a central role in cultural expression and social integration. Slovak law mandates Slovak language courses for migrants as part of integration programs; however, these programs also encourage the preservation of migrants' native languages, recognizing that bilingualism can enrich cultural diversity. Migrant-led cultural associations often organize language and cultural heritage events that contribute to this dual goal.

Migrants have the right to access public cultural institutions, such as museums, theaters, and libraries, often at discounted rates or through community programs. These institutions play a critical role in promoting intercultural dialogue by organizing exhibitions and events that showcase the traditions and histories of migrant communities.

Cultural rights also include the right to participate in public celebrations, festivals, and artistic activities. Slovak cities have increasingly incorporated multicultural festivals, art exhibits, and culinary events that highlight the contributions of migrant communities.

Slovakia's cultural rights policies are influenced by its obligations under international frameworks, such as the UNESCO Convention on the Protection and Promotion of the Diversity of Cultural Expressions. Best practices from other EU countries, such as cultural ambassadors, intercultural festivals, and migrant inclusion in public broadcasting, can further enhance Slovakia's approach to cultural integration.

Cultural rights are a cornerstone of meaningful integration for third-country nationals in Slovakia, enabling them to maintain their cultural identity while actively participating in the cultural life of their host society. While the legal framework supports these rights, practical barriers such as limited funding, social prejudices, and geographic disparities can hinder full participation.

2.6.2.5 Solidarity rights for third-country nationals

Solidarity rights represent a collective dimension of human rights, emphasizing the shared responsibilities of states and societies in ensuring peace, security, and humanitarian support for all individuals, including third-country nationals. These rights reflect the interconnectedness of global challenges and the need for collective efforts to address issues such as forced displacement, conflict and poverty. For third-country nationals in Slovakia, solidarity rights encompass key protections such as the right to humanitarian aid in times of crisis and the right to live in peace free from violence, persecution and conflict.

Slovakia's legal and institutional framework for solidarity rights is influenced by international treaties, including the Universal Declaration of Human Rights (UDHR)[1456] and the European Convention on Human Rights (ECHR),[1457] as well as EU directives aimed at strengthening humanitarian support and promoting peaceful coexistence.

This section examines the legal foundations and practical implementation of solidarity rights for third-country nationals in Slovakia, focusing on access to humanitarian aid, peacebuilding initiatives, and the role of civil society.

The right to humanitarian aid is a fundamental expression of human solidarity, ensuring that individuals facing life-threatening circumstances receive the assistance necessary to safeguard their survival, dignity and well-being. For third-country nationals in Slovakia, this right is crucial in times of crises, such as natural disasters, armed conflicts, or forced displacement. Humanitarian aid encompasses access to shelter, food, medical care and essential services, with a particular focus on protecting vulnerable groups such as refugees, unaccompanied minors, and individuals affected by conflict. Slovakia's legal framework for humanitarian aid is grounded in its commitments under international and EU law. The 1951 Refugee Convention, the European Convention on Human Rights (ECHR), and the EU Temporary Protection Directive (2001/55/EC) obligate Slovakia to provide protection and assistance to individuals fleeing conflict or persecution. Domestically, Act No. 480/2002 Coll. on asylum[1458] and Act No. 417/2013 Coll. on assistance in material need[1459] outline the state's obligations to provide humanitarian support, including access to emergency shelter, healthcare and basic necessities.

The implementation of humanitarian aid is also supported by Slovakia's collaboration with international organizations such as the UNHCR, Red Cross, and IOM, as well as local NGOs that play a critical role in delivering assistance to vulnerable populations.

1456 UN General Assembly, Universal Declaration of Human Rights, 217 A (III), December 10, 1948.

1457 Council of Europe, European Convention on Human Rights, as amended by Protocols Nos. 11, 14 and 15, ETS No. 005, November 4, 1950.

1458 Act No. 480/2002 Coll. on Asylum.

1459 Act No. 417/2013 Coll. on Assistance in Material Need.

Slovakia provides temporary accommodation for asylum seekers, refugees, and individuals under temporary protection. Reception centers are designated to offer shelter, food and essential services during the processing of asylum applications or during crises. Access to emergency medical care is guaranteed to all individuals, regardless of legal status. This includes first aid, treatment for injuries, and care for individuals with chronic conditions or trauma. Humanitarian aid programs include the distribution of food, hygiene products and clothing to support individuals in need, particularly those residing in temporary facilities. Tailored assistance is provided to unaccompanied minors, pregnant women, elderly individuals and those with disabilities to address their specific needs and vulnerabilities.

The humanitarian response to the war in Ukraine highlighted Slovakia's capacity to mobilize resources and provide large-scale support to individuals fleeing conflict. The implementation of the EU Temporary Protection Mechanism allowed for expedited access to housing, healthcare and financial assistance.

NGOs and civil society organizations play a vital role in the delivery of humanitarian aid, often filling gaps left by state-run programs. Organizations such as People in Peril Slovakia, Mareena, and Caritas Slovakia provide direct support to migrants, including legal aid, counseling, and community integration services. Their work is essential in ensuring that humanitarian aid reaches those most in need, especially in remote or underserved areas.

The right to live in peace is a fundamental human right, which is an essential component of dignity and security, allowing individuals to live free from violence, persecution, and the fear of conflict. For third-country nationals in Slovakia, particularly refugees, asylum seekers and beneficiaries of subsidiary protection, the right to live in peace signifies not only safety from immediate harm but also the opportunity to rebuild their lives in an environment of stability and inclusion.

The right to live in peace is enshrined in international human rights instruments, such as the Charter of the United Nations,[1460] the Universal Declaration of Human Rights (UDHR), and the European Convention on Human Rights (ECHR). These frameworks obligate states to protect individuals fleeing conflict, persecution, or systemic violence. Slovakia's legal

1460 United Nations, Charter of the United Nations, 1 UNTS XVI, October 24, 1945.

commitments are further reflected in Act No. 480/2002 Coll. on asylum, which outlines the state's responsibilities in granting asylum, subsidiary protection and temporary protection to individuals whose safety is threatened in their home countries. Slovakia is also a signatory to the 1951 Refugee Convention and its 1967 Protocol, which affirm the principle of non-refoulement—the prohibition against returning individuals to countries where they face serious threats to their life or freedom. This principle ensures that third-country nationals seeking protection in Slovakia can remain in safe conditions, free from the risk of forced return to dangerous environments.

For third-country nationals, the right to live in peace extends beyond mere physical safety. It includes:

a. Protection from Persecution and Conflict: Ensuring that individuals who have fled war zones or oppressive regimes are safeguarded from harm and provided with legal status that recognizes their need for safety.
b. Legal Certainty and Long-Term Security: Providing clear and transparent asylum procedures that result in durable solutions, such as permanent residence or naturalization, rather than prolonged uncertainty and temporary legal statuses.
c. Freedom from Discrimination: Guaranteeing that migrants and refugees are not subject to violence, hate speech, or systemic discrimination within their host society.
d. Access to Social and Economic Integration: Ensuring that individuals have the opportunity to access employment, education and social services, which are essential for rebuilding stable and peaceful lives.

In recent years, the Slovak government has implemented measures to improve the living conditions of refugees and beneficiaries of protection, such as increasing funding for integration programs, expanding legal aid services, and partnering with NGOs to support social inclusion.

The right to live in peace is a foundational aspect of Slovakia's obligations toward third-country nationals. While the legal framework provides a strong basis for safeguarding this right, practical challenges related to social integration, economic security, and public attitudes must be addressed. Strengthening access to legal protections, promoting inclusive public narratives, and expanding mental health and social support services are key steps toward upholding the right to live in peace and building a more cohesive and resilient society.

2.6.2.6 Human rights of specific vulnerable groups

The protection of human rights for vulnerable groups is aimed at ensuring equality and human dignity. Vulnerable groups—such as children, women, older persons, and individuals with disabilities—often face unique challenges that require tailored legal safeguards to ensure their full participation in society. These individuals may encounter heightened risks of discrimination, exclusion, or exploitation, particularly in the context of migration, where displacement and legal uncertainty can exacerbate their vulnerabilities.

In Slovakia, the rights of these groups are protected through a combination of international commitments, such as the UN Convention on the Rights of the Child (CRC),[1461] the Convention on the Elimination of All Forms of Discrimination Against Women (CEDAW),[1462] and the Convention on the Rights of Persons with Disabilities (CRPD),[1463] as well as domestic legislation aimed at promoting equality and inclusion. However, the question remains whether these groups are treated equally under the law or afforded additional protections due to their specific vulnerabilities. Although Slovakia signed the Istanbul Convention[1464] in 2011, the country has not ratified it due to significant political and public debate. Opponents have expressed concerns about certain provisions of the Convention, particularly those related to the definition of gender and perceived impacts on national sovereignty and traditional family values.

This section explores the human rights of vulnerable groups within the context of migration, examining whether their status grants them enhanced

---

1461 UN General Assembly, Convention on the Rights of the Child, United Nations, Treaty Series, vol. 1577, 3, November 20, 1989.

1462 UN General Assembly, Convention on the Elimination of All Forms of Discrimination Against Women, United Nations, Treaty Series, vol. 1249, 13, December 18, 1979.

1463 UN General Assembly, Convention on the Rights of Persons with Disabilities: resolution / adopted by the General Assembly, A/RES/61/106, January 24, 2007.

1464 Council of Europe, Council of Europe Convention on preventing and combating violence against women and domestic violence, May 11, 2011.

protections or additional privileges and how these legal safeguards are implemented in practice. By focusing on the rights of children, women, older persons, and individuals with disabilities, the discussion highlights both the progress made and the persistent challenges that remain to be addressed.

Children are among the most vulnerable groups within the migration context, often facing heightened risks of exploitation, trauma and exclusion. Slovakia's legal framework for the protection of children's rights is shaped by international commitments, such as the UN Convention on the Rights of the Child, as well as domestic legislation, including Act No. 305/2005 Coll. on Social and Legal Protection of Children and Social Guardianship[1465] and Act No. 36/2005 Coll. on the Family.[1466] These laws ensure that the best interests of the child are a primary consideration in all legal and administrative proceedings involving children, regardless of their nationality or migration status.

Slovakia's child protection framework applies to all children within its jurisdiction, including those of third-country nationals, asylum seekers and unaccompanied minors. The following rights are particularly relevant:

a. Right to Family Unity: Migrant children have the right to be reunited with their family members whenever possible. Family reunification procedures are governed by national and EU regulations, such as Directive 2003/86/EC on Family Reunification.
b. Right to Education: Under Slovak law, all children, including those of asylum seekers and undocumented migrants, have access to free primary and secondary education. Language support programs are often provided to help migrant children integrate into the school system.
c. Right to Health Care: Children of third-country nationals, particularly those with legal residency or international protection status, are entitled to access essential healthcare services, including pediatric and preventive care. Emergency healthcare is guaranteed to all children, regardless of legal status.
d. Protection from Exploitation and Abuse: Slovakia's laws prohibit child labor, trafficking, and any form of violence or exploitation. Specialized

---

[1465] Act No. 305/2005 Coll. on Social and Legal Protection of Children and Social Guardianship.

[1466] Act No. 36/2005 Coll. on the Family.

agencies, such as the Centre for the Protection of Children and Social Guardianship, provide support and intervention services for at-risk children.

Unaccompanied minors—children who arrive in Slovakia without their parents or legal guardians—receive special legal protections. Under Act No. 480/2002 Coll. on asylum, unaccompanied minors must be assigned a legal guardian to represent their interests during asylum procedures. They are placed in specialized reception centers that provide age-appropriate care, education and psychological support. Efforts are made to reunite unaccompanied minors with their families when it is in the child's best interests.

The Commissioner for Children's Rights is an independent institution tasked with promoting and protecting the rights and well-being of all children in Slovakia, including migrant children. Established under Act No. 176/2015 Coll. on the Commissioner for Children and the Commissioner for Persons with Disabilities,[1467] the Commissioner operates as an advocate for children's rights and provides oversight to ensure that public authorities and institutions respect legal standards related to children's welfare.

Several government programs and civil society initiatives aim to address these challenges by supporting the integration and protection of migrant children. For example, NGOs such as Mareena and UNICEF Slovakia provide educational support, legal counseling and recreational activities for children from migrant backgrounds. The Slovak government has also partnered with international organizations to implement integration projects that focus on child-friendly spaces, inclusive education and access to mental health services.

Rights of Women: The protection and promotion of women's rights are essential components of Slovakia's legal and social framework. Women, including third-country nationals, are entitled to equal protection under the law, with specific guarantees aimed at preventing discrimination, ensuring access to opportunities, and protecting women from violence. These rights are enshrined in both international and domestic legal frameworks, including the Convention on the Elimination of All Forms of Discrimination Against Women, the European Convention on Human Rights, and Slovak

---

1467 Act No. 176/2015 Coll. on the Commissioner for Children and the Commissioner for Persons with Disabilities.

antidiscrimination legislation, such as Act No. 365/2004 Coll. on Equal Treatment (Antidiscrimination Act).[1468]

Women, particularly those fleeing conflict or persecution, face heightened risks of gender-based violence and exploitation. Slovak legal frameworks include measures aimed at preventing such abuses, including the provision of safe housing and access to legal and medical support. Slovak law prohibits discrimination based on gender in areas such as employment, education and healthcare. This protection extends to third-country nationals, ensuring equal access to services and opportunities. Under Act No. 311/2001 Coll. (Labor Code), women are entitled to equal pay for equal work and protection from workplace discrimination. Third-country national women employed in Slovakia are entitled to the same legal protections as Slovak citizens, though they may face additional challenges in practice. Women have the right to live free from violence and exploitation. Domestic and gender-based violence is addressed through criminal law provisions and support services, including crisis centers and helplines. Slovakia operates a network of shelters and crisis intervention centers that provide temporary housing, legal aid and psychological support to women experiencing domestic violence or homelessness.

Older individuals may face unique challenges related to health, economic security, and social participation, especially in the context of migration. Slovakia's legal framework, informed by international treaties such as the International Covenant on Economic, Social and Cultural Rights (ICESCR) and the European Convention on Human Rights (ECHR), provides important safeguards for the rights of older people, although gaps in access and implementation remain.

Slovakia's Constitution guarantees fundamental rights and freedoms to all individuals, including older people, without discrimination. Several national laws specifically address the needs and rights of older individuals:

Act No. 448/2008 Coll. on Social Services[1469]: This law governs the provision of social care services, including residential care, home care, and day care facilities for older individuals in need of assistance.

1468 Act No. 365/2004 Coll. on Equal Treatment.

1469 Act No. 448/2008 Coll. on Social Services.

Act No. 461/2003 Coll. on Social Insurance[1470]: This act provides for pensions, disability benefits, and other social insurance allowances for eligible residents, including older third-country nationals with legal status.

Act No. 365/2004 Coll. on Equal Treatment[1471] (Antidiscrimination Act): This act prohibits age-based discrimination in areas such as employment, healthcare, and access to social services.

Older third-country nationals with permanent residency or long-term legal status may be eligible for pensions and social security benefits, provided they have made sufficient contributions to Slovakia's social insurance system. Access to these benefits ensures economic security during retirement and reduces vulnerability to poverty. However, for those who have not contributed for the required period or whose status does not grant access to pensions, economic insecurity remains a significant concern.

Healthcare is another key right for older individuals, including migrants with legal status. Public healthcare services in Slovakia provide access to geriatric care, preventive screenings, and long-term medical support for chronic conditions. Importantly, emergency healthcare is available to all individuals, regardless of legal status, guaranteeing life-saving care to undocumented older migrants as well. Older migrants also have the right to social support services, such as in-home assistance, residential care homes, and community programs that improve their quality of life and foster social inclusion. These services aim to provide dignity and comfort for older people who require additional assistance in their daily lives.

Slovakia's policies for older people align with international human rights standards and EU directives that promote social protection and healthcare for older individuals. The Madrid International Plan of Action on Ageing emphasizes the need for inclusive aging policies that address the vulnerabilities of older migrants and support their active participation in society. However, best practices from other EU countries, such as the introduction of multilingual healthcare services and bilateral agreements for pension portability, could further enhance Slovakia's approach to supporting older third-country nationals.

[1470] Act No. 461/2003 Coll. on Social Insurance.

[1471] Act No. 365/2004 Coll. on Equal Treatment.

Slovakia's legal framework is informed by both domestic legislation and international conventions, particularly the Convention on the Rights of Persons with Disabilities (CRPD),[1472] which Slovakia ratified in 2010. Slovakia's Act No. 447/2008 Coll. on Cash Benefits for Compensation of Severe Disabilities[1473] outlines the state's obligations to provide financial support and assistance to individuals with disabilities to help them overcome social and physical barriers. In addition, Act No. 448/2008 Coll. on Social Services[1474] regulates access to essential services, such as personal assistance, rehabilitation and residential care. The Antidiscrimination Act (Act No. 365/2004 Coll.) prohibits discrimination based on disability and guarantees equal access to education, employment, healthcare and public services. These laws apply to all residents of Slovakia, including migrants with legal status. In addition to the general Public Defender of Rights (Ombudsman), Slovakia has a dedicated Commissioner for Persons with Disabilities, established under Act No. 176/2015 Coll. on the Commissioner for Persons with Disabilities and the Commissioner for Children. This independent institution is responsible for monitoring and advocating for the rights and well-being of individuals with disabilities, including third-country nationals. The Commissioner plays a crucial role in ensuring that public authorities comply with domestic and international obligations related to disability rights. The Commissioner monitors the implementation of disability-related laws and policies, ensuring that public institutions uphold their obligations under the CRPD and Slovak law. The Commissioner for Persons with Disabilities collaborates with domestic NGOs and international bodies, such as the UN Committee on the Rights of Persons with Disabilities, to strengthen advocacy efforts and ensure compliance with international human rights standards. Partnerships with organizations like Mareena and Caritas Slovakia help amplify the Commissioner's work, particularly in supporting vulnerable groups such as migrants and asylum seekers with disabilities.

1472 UN General Assembly, Convention on the Rights of Persons with Disabilities: resolution / adopted by the General Assembly, A/RES/61/106, January 24, 2007.

1473 Act No. 447/2008 Coll. on Cash Benefits for Compensation of Severe Disabilities.

1474 Act No. 448/2008 Coll. on Social Services.

2.6.3 Procedural law perspective

In migration law, procedural safeguards play a crucial role in ensuring fairness, transparency and accountability in decision-making processes related to the entry, residence and protection of third-country nationals. These safeguards uphold fundamental rights, such as the right to an effective remedy, the right to good administration, and the right to a fair hearing, as enshrined in the EU Charter of Fundamental Rights and international legal frameworks.

This section explores the procedural dimensions of migration law in Slovakia, focusing on how administrative and judicial processes are structured to balance national security with the protection of individual rights. It addresses the role of special procedures that apply during emergencies, such as public health crises and migration surges, and examines how legal obligations and institutional responses adapt to extraordinary circumstances. The allocation of competences to key actors, including Frontex, police, and border guards, is critically analyzed to assess whether their practices align with legal principles, particularly in light of key rulings such as Commission v. Hungary (C-808/18).

Another focal point of this section is the identification of procedural standards that govern administrative authorities and courts, including the principles of procedural fairness, impartiality, and the right to defend one's interests. The challenges posed by emergencies, such as increased caseloads and resource constraints, are examined to understand the legal and practical impacts on the administration of justice. In particular, the discussion highlights the importance of ensuring equal treatment for vulnerable groups, such as unaccompanied minors, persons with disabilities, and victims of trafficking, who face heightened barriers in navigating legal proceedings.

Lastly, the chapter considers the adoption of new technologies in administrative and court proceedings, assessing their potential to enhance efficiency while identifying associated risks, such as digital exclusion and privacy concerns. The integration of biometric systems, online applications, and automated translation tools is evaluated to determine their impact on procedural rights and access to justice for third-country nationals.

2.6.3.1 Special procedures on the entry and residence of the third-country nationals

In Slovakia, the management of migration during extraordinary circumstances is governed by special procedures on the entry and residence of third-country nationals. These procedures are grounded in both national legislation and EU regulatory frameworks and are designed to respond to events such as migration surges, public health crises and geopolitical conflicts. The primary legislative instruments underpinning Slovakia's approach include Act No. 480/2002 Coll. on Asylum[1475] and Act No. 404/2011 Coll. on the Stay of Foreigners.[1476] These acts define the structure of migration procedures and are supplemented by government decrees during emergencies. One notable example is the enactment of temporary protection measures during the Ukrainian refugee crisis, which provided immediate protection for displaced individuals. The special measures it included were:

a. Temporary Protection Status: This provision was implemented to allow displaced persons to remain in Slovakia without undergoing the full asylum process. This status provided immediate access to healthcare, housing and education.
b. Mandatory Health Screenings: In line with the Public Health Act, mandatory health checks were introduced during the COVID-19 pandemic, with designated quarantine facilities established at border points.
c. Expedited Residence Processing: During labor shortages, particularly in the healthcare sector, residence permits for essential workers were processed under streamlined procedures.

Specialized measures at Slovakia's borders were implemented to manage high volumes of entrants. These measures reflect a coordinated approach to balancing security concerns with humanitarian obligations.

Designated Border Checkpoints—Locations such as Vyšné Nemecké were reinforced with additional personnel, medical facilities and technological resources. During the peak of the Ukrainian refugee crisis, the checkpoint expanded its operational capacity by setting up modular shelters for temporary

---

1475 Act No. 480/2002 Coll. on Asylum.
1476 Act No. 404/2011 Coll. on the Stay of Foreigners.

processing and providing on-site interpreters to assist non-Slovak speakers. Health professionals from international organizations were stationed to perform medical screenings and ensure that vulnerable individuals received timely care.

Humanitarian Corridors—These safe routes were established through bilateral agreements and regional partnerships to ensure safe passage for refugees fleeing conflict zones. Humanitarian corridors prioritized vulnerable groups, including pregnant women, unaccompanied minors, and persons with disabilities. Coordination efforts included agreements with neighboring countries to ensure continuity of care, and temporary housing facilities along the corridors were equipped with essential supplies and psychosocial support services.

The Slovak government also established mobile units at border points to assist with rapid documentation and provide immediate information about rights and available services.

Special procedures differ from standard administrative processes in their objectives, timelines and practical implementation. The standard asylum and residence application process typically involves comprehensive background checks, in-person interviews and a detailed review of documentary evidence. Conversely, special procedures streamline these steps, prioritizing speed and safety. One example, outlined above, concerns the special procedures implemented during the Ukrainian refugee crisis. Another notable special measure was the creation of "simplified entry" for healthcare and essential workers during the COVID-19 pandemic, under Act No. 404/2011 Coll. on the stay of foreigners. While the standard process for residence permits includes multiple stages of approval and documentation submission, this emergency measure fast-tracked applications by limiting requirements to proof of employment and a clean medical record.

2.6.3.2 Identification of standards for the proper organization of administrative authorities and courts

The effective functioning of administrative authorities and courts in the context of migration law requires adherence to core procedural standards that ensure fairness, transparency and accountability.

In Slovakia, procedural fairness in migration-related cases is not only a legal necessity but also a reflection of the state's commitment to upholding the principles of justice, accountability and transparency. This concept is grounded in several foundational rights:

1. Right to a Court and Effective Remedy: Article 47 of the EU Charter of Fundamental Rights affirms that all individuals have the right to challenge administrative decisions before an independent and impartial tribunal. In Slovakia, this right is operationalized through the system of administrative courts that review migration-related decisions, such as asylum rejections and detention orders. For example, in 2022, administrative courts handled an unprecedented number of appeals following the influx of Ukrainian refugees, ensuring that temporary protection denials could be contested in a fair legal setting.
2. Right to Defend One's Interests: The right to defend one's interests is integral to ensuring that migrants can present evidence, challenge claims, and participate meaningfully in proceedings. Slovak legal provisions, such as those under Act No. 480/2002 Coll. on asylum, guarantee access to interpreters and legal representation. Nevertheless, civil society organizations have noted disparities in implementation, particularly for non-Slavic speakers and individuals with disabilities. In response, programs led by Mareena and Caritas Slovakia have provided essential support by facilitating language assistance and offering case-specific guidance. One notable case from 2021 involved a non-verbal applicant who was provided with augmented communication tools during a remote hearing, illustrating Slovakia's stance toward inclusive procedural standards. However, further investments in interpreter services and specialized legal training are necessary to ensure consistent access across all regions.
3. Right to Good Administration: Article 41 of the EU Charter stipulates that administrative processes must be conducted impartially, within reasonable timeframes, and with transparency. In practice, this means that migration-related procedures in Slovakia must adhere to clear timelines and avoid unnecessary delays. During the Ukrainian crisis, the Migration Office's introduction of an online application tracking system improved procedural transparency, allowing applicants to monitor the progress of their claims. However, reports from NGOs

indicate that applicants with limited digital literacy faced challenges in navigating this system.

Efforts to address these issues have included the establishment of in-person information desks at key reception centers near Košice and Michalovce. These centers provide step-by-step guidance and printed updates for individuals unable to use digital platforms.

Emergencies, such as public health crises, armed conflicts, or large-scale migration influxes, can place significant strain on administrative and judicial systems, necessitating temporary adjustments to procedural standards. In Slovakia, exceptional measures were adopted during the COVID-19 pandemic and the Ukrainian refugee crisis to address these pressures. During the COVID-19 pandemic, Slovakia introduced measures such as remote hearings, online application portals and electronic submissions to ensure continued access to legal processes. While these changes helped maintain functionality, they raised concerns about digital accessibility for vulnerable applicants lacking internet access or digital literacy. Under extreme circumstances, specific procedural rights may be temporarily limited. For example, in 2020, the government restricted in-person legal consultations to prevent the spread of COVID-19. Although necessary for public health, this restriction prompted criticism from legal advocacy groups, who argued that it disproportionately impacted unaccompanied minors and persons with disabilities.

Public authorities and courts in Slovakia have faced significant challenges when handling large volumes of international protection applications. During the Ukrainian refugee crisis in 2022, the government reported a threefold increase in asylum-related cases within months, with over 100,000 refugees processed within the first six months of the conflict. To date there have been over 270,000 Ukrainian refugees that have crossed the Slovak border.[1477] The Migration Office recorded that 90 % of temporary protection requests were approved within an average of three weeks, demonstrating the effectiveness of the accelerated procedures.

To address this surge, additional processing centers were established near border areas such as Vyšné Nemecké and Košice, with the Vyšné Nemecké

1477 Data provided by the Slovak Ministry of Interior.

checkpoint alone processing up to 5,000 individuals per day at the height of the crisis.

Courts also faced logistical hurdles in scheduling appeal hearings, leading to the introduction of remote hearings and a prioritized docket for vulnerable applicants.

Ensuring equal treatment for all parties in migration proceedings is fundamental to upholding the rule of law. Vulnerable groups, such as unaccompanied minors, elderly individuals, persons with disabilities, and victims of trafficking, require tailored support to meaningfully participate in legal processes.

Under Act No. 36/2005 Coll. on the Family, unaccompanied minors are assigned legal guardians to represent their interests. In practice, however, NGOs have reported that some regions face a shortage of trained guardians, delaying proceedings. To address this, emergency funding in 2022 allowed for the recruitment of temporary caseworkers and the provision of specialized training.

Accessibility remains a crucial concern. Persons with disabilities must be provided with accessible communication formats, such as large print documents or sign language interpreters, in line with Slovakia's obligations under the UN Convention on the Rights of Persons with Disabilities (CRPD). Language barriers also pose significant challenges. In 2022, it was reported that over 25 % of asylum applicants required interpreters for non-Slavic languages.[1478] NGOs such as Mareena stepped in to provide multilingual support, yet gaps remain, particularly for less common languages.

There are significant differences in the availability of services between urban centers and border regions. While facilities in Košice and Bratislava often benefit from NGO partnerships and infrastructure, smaller border towns have reported inconsistent access to legal and psychosocial support. Mobile legal clinics, established in partnership with international organizations, have attempted to bridge this gap by providing on-site consultations and case preparation services.

1478 Human Rights League, *Observations on Asylum Procedures in Slovakia* (European Union Agency for Asylum 2022).

Female asylum seekers, particularly survivors of gender-based violence, face unique vulnerabilities. Slovak authorities have introduced dedicated interview spaces and female caseworkers for such applicants to foster a supportive environment. However, advocacy groups have called for more trauma-informed training for personnel involved in these interviews.

2.6.3.3 Application of new technologies in administrative and courts proceedings

Slovakia, like many EU Member States, has embraced digital transformation in public administration and the judiciary. Key innovations include electronic filing systems, video conferencing tools, artificial intelligence for case management, and biometric authentication for identity verification. One notable example is the Slovak government's e-Government Portal, along with the e-Asylum Portal—introduced into our legislation in 2024 and set to launch March 1, 2025—which enables the electronic submission of asylum applications and other documents, thereby significantly reducing the need for physical visits to administrative offices. The portal has streamlined processes for residence permits, asylum applications and visa renewals.

Many major changes in the area of digitalization are set to take effect March 1, 2025, which is a future date at the time of writing this chapter. A central feature of the amendments is the introduction of electronic services for foreigners. Processes such as residence renewals, visa applications and status registrations can now be completed online, reducing the need for physical visits to immigration offices. This digital transformation streamlines communication between applicants and authorities, ensuring faster and more accessible services.

The reforms simplify procedural requirements for applicants and government agencies to further ease the administrative burden. These updates will make the immigration process more user-friendly, saving time and resources for all the stakeholders involved.

The amendments include security-focused updates for Ukrainian asylum holders. Holders of temporary asylum will receive new ID cards, improving both security and mobility within Slovakia. The government has also introduced updated accommodation rules for Ukrainian migrants, including a shorter stay period in asylum facilities and modified allowances to encourage faster integration into local communities.

Slovakia's immigration law amendments will benefit foreigners, asylum seekers and government authorities alike. Ukrainian asylum holders will benefit from secure ID cards and updated accommodation policies that balance humanitarian support with integration goals.

The reforms are expected to reduce processing times, streamline compliance, and enhance transparency in the immigration process.

In the judiciary, the use of video conferencing has grown substantially, particularly during the COVID-19 pandemic. Court hearings involving detained migrants or those with limited mobility have been conducted remotely, ensuring procedural continuity despite logistical challenges. Another technological innovation is the introduction of AI-driven systems to manage case distribution and predict procedural timelines, which helps optimize judicial workflows and reduce case backlogs.

Furthermore, e-identification and biometric systems have been implemented to verify identities quickly and securely. Migrants applying for residence or asylum status undergo biometric registration, which enhances border security but also raises concerns regarding data protection. Translation software and automated legal aid tools have also been integrated into court proceedings to assist non-Slovak speakers. For example, automated translation programs have been used to provide real-time interpretations during hearings, though their accuracy remains inconsistent.

Digital scheduling tools have also facilitated the organization of asylum interviews and legal hearings. Previously, administrative delays were common due to manual appointment systems. The new digital scheduling systems have improved coordination between migrants, their legal representatives, and administrative bodies, reducing procedural delays. Moreover, digital case tracking systems allow applicants to monitor the status of their applications in real time, fostering transparency and accountability.

The adoption of new technologies can significantly accelerate administrative and judicial proceedings for migrants. Automation of routine tasks, such as document verification and appointment scheduling, can reduce processing times. Digital communication tools, such as email notifications and online portals, ensure that migrants receive timely updates about their cases, minimizing the risk of missed deadlines.

Improved transparency is another notable benefit. Digital case tracking systems enable migrants to view the status of their applications, providing a clear timeline of procedural steps. This reduces uncertainty and enhances trust in public institutions. Moreover, the cost-efficiency of digital services benefits both migrants and the government. Migrants can avoid the financial burden of frequent travel to administrative offices, while government agencies can allocate resources more efficiently by digitizing routine processes.

Despite the advantages, the adoption of new technologies also presents several challenges. Digital exclusion is a significant concern, as not all migrants have access to the necessary devices or stable internet connections. Additionally, some migrants may lack digital literacy, making it difficult for them to navigate complex online systems. For example, rural areas in Slovakia may have limited technological infrastructure, exacerbating disparities in access to digital services.

Language barriers further complicate the use of digital tools. Many online portals are available only in Slovak, limiting their accessibility for non-native speakers. Although automated translation tools are often integrated into these systems, their accuracy can vary, leading to potential misunderstandings in critical legal proceedings.

Data privacy and cybersecurity risks are another major concern. Biometric data collection and the storage of sensitive personal information introduce vulnerabilities to data breaches and unauthorized surveillance. Compliance with the EU's General Data Protection Regulation (GDPR) is essential to safeguard migrants' privacy. Moreover, there is a risk of "algorithmic bias" in AI-based decision-making tools. If algorithms are trained on biased datasets, they may produce outcomes that disproportionately disadvantage certain groups of migrants.

Procedural fairness must also be considered when adopting new technologies. Automated systems can inadvertently reduce human oversight in decision-making processes, potentially leading to errors or unjust outcomes.

The integration of new technologies in administrative and court proceedings has the potential to enhance procedural efficiency and safeguard the rights of migrants in Slovakia. However, the implementation of these innovations must be approached with caution to avoid digital exclusion, data privacy breaches and automation biases.

2.6.4 Conclusions

Slovakia's migration framework presents an ongoing response to the realities of global displacement and mobility. Over the years, the legal landscape has adapted to a series of crises—from the European migration surge of 2015 to the COVID-19 pandemic and the recent influx of refugees from Ukraine. Each of these events tested the resilience of Slovakia's migration policies, highlighting both progress and persisting gaps in protecting the rights of third-country nationals.

Key reforms, such as the 2024 amendments to Act No. 480/2002 Coll. on Asylum, demonstrate Slovakia's intent to create a more efficient and humane system. By reducing the timeframe for asylum decisions and launching the e-Asylum Portal, the government has taken concrete steps toward enhancing transparency and access to justice. The digital platform allows applicants to track their cases in real time and receive updates in multiple languages, making the process more inclusive for non-Slovak speakers. However, while these reforms mark progress, implementation challenges—such as digital literacy barriers and uneven regional access to technology—remain pressing issues. Ensuring that no one is left behind in this digitized system, particularly vulnerable individuals such as unaccompanied minors and persons with disabilities, will require sustained investment and careful oversight.

One of the most notable features of Slovakia's recent reforms is its dual focus on security and inclusion. The introduction of secure identification cards for Ukrainian asylum holders and updated accommodation rules reflects a pragmatic approach aimed at balancing national security with humanitarian responsibilities. However, questions linger regarding the potential strain on already limited resources in reception centers and whether the new measures adequately address long-term integration. Effective integration is not merely about housing and legal documentation—it also requires meaningful social, economic, and cultural participation. Language acquisition, job training, and support for navigating everyday life are indispensable for reducing social isolation.

The report also highlights the critical role played by civil society organizations, such as Mareena and Caritas Slovakia, in filling gaps left by state institutions. These organizations have been instrumental in providing language courses, legal aid, and psychosocial support. However, relying heavily on NGOs without matching public sector capacity raises concerns about sustainability.

Moreover, the broader geopolitical and European context remains crucial. As an EU Member State, Slovakia cannot address migration challenges in isolation. Collaborative mechanisms, such as the EU relocation schemes and the work of the European Union Agency for Asylum, reinforce the need for solidarity among Member States.

Slovakia's legal framework provides a solid foundation, but the real measure of its success lies in its implementation. Policies must be matched with sufficient funding, clear communication, and accountability mechanisms to ensure that procedural safeguards are not only maintained but strengthened during times of crisis.

Looking ahead, Slovakia faces an opportunity to build on its achievements by addressing systemic inefficiencies. By continuing to prioritize non-discrimination, the principle of non-refoulement, and proportionality in its policies, Slovakia can enhance its role as a responsive and responsible host for those seeking safety.

Summary

Jacek Chlebny

The right of third-country nationals to enter and reside within the European Union is not absolute. Restrictions on this right are permissible, as Member States must also protect such values as state security, the safety of their citizens, and public order. At the same time, it is important that these restrictions and border controls do not lead to violations of fundamental rights, especially the right to life and the prohibitions on torture and inhuman or degrading treatment. The observance and protection of human rights pose major challenges for EU Member States at a time of mass migration and threats from armed conflict, terrorism, climate change and pandemics. The need to provide prompt and effective protection for migrants has become particularly evident in the context of the armed conflict between Russia and Ukraine, which has resulted in the mass migration of Ukrainian citizens to EU countries, especially Poland. In this case, it was necessary to enable refugees not only to enter and remain safely in the territory of EU countries but also to enjoy fundamental rights (particularly access to health care, education and social security). In addition, the situation on the eastern external border of the Union highlights the serious problem of the instrumentalization of migrants, which can destabilize security in Europe. This is also an issue that Member States must confront.

The research carried out in these case studies has clarified several sensitive issues related to the impact of third-country nationals' migration on the internal policy and legal order of EU Member States. The legal situation of third-country migrants is significantly affected by acts of EU law, the application of which may require the introduction of new procedures. The implementation of the Pact on Migration and Asylum is a current challenge for EU Member States, as they must ensure that the common European system of migration and asylum management functions smoothly from June 2026. However, it remains uncertain whether applying these new solutions will effectively reduce the risk of emergencies.

The past experience of individual states in migration policy confirms the importance of balancing, on the one hand, the need to protect human rights and, on the other, the security of the state, the safety of its citizens, and public order. In practice, mass migration, especially when crossing state borders at points not designated for this purpose, involves significant risks in this regard. At the same time, migrants, often with irregular status, including those awaiting international protection within EU Member States, should be guaranteed the protection of fundamental rights in accordance with international and EU law standards. As the COVID-19 pandemic demonstrated, a specific threat to human life and health justified entry bans, followed by stricter border controls. For migrants residing under a state's jurisdiction during the pandemic, it was necessary to ensure adequate protection and access to health care services.

The following specific conclusions arise from the considerations:

First, the term *emergency* does not have a single, fixed meaning. EU and national legislators use it in different contexts, referring to: 1) a threat from third-country nationals related to violations of security rules, public health or public policy; 2) a special situation related to a large number of third-country nationals, and the need to provide them with a special type of assistance, such as health care; 3) the situation (political, economic, health) in the refugee's country of origin that justifies granting international protection. For the purposes of this analysis, the first meaning of *emergency* was crucial.

Second, the crises triggering mass migration flows elicited a response from states and the European Union that was dynamic but inconsistent, often subordinated to ad hoc political interests and reliant on short-term countermeasures. Sudden influxes of migrants exposed weaknesses in coordination mechanisms and a lack of unanimity among Member States, leading to unilateral decisions, border closures and the selective application of humanitarian principles. EU institutions increasingly resorted to soft law, i.e., guidelines, recommendations and informal agreements, which provided flexibility in crisis response but at the same time weakened legal certainty and consistency of action. While soft law facilitated adaptation to changing conditions and bypassed lengthy legislative procedures, its non-binding nature allowed Member States to apply recommendations selectively and circumvented judicial review, depriving citizens and NGOs of effective legal tools to challenge them.

The externalization of migration policy, i.e., the transfer of responsibility for migration control to third countries through agreements and treaties, has also increased in importance, as it makes it possible to limit the influx of migrants but raises concerns over respect for human rights. The instrumentalization of migration, i.e., using migrants as a tool of political pressure and destabilization, became a mechanism of geopolitical influence, which showed that migration was no longer viewed solely in humanitarian terms but also as an element of security and state strategy. The strengthening of the Union's external borders and the tightening of asylum procedures reflect a growing tendency to treat migration primarily in security terms. The lack of institutional and legally binding mechanisms for sharing responsibility for the reception and relocation of migrants led to internal tensions between Member States and the selective treatment of different migrant groups. This, in turn, undermined the consistency of the values declared by the European Union and weakened its credibility as an entity guided by the principle of solidarity and committed to the protection of human rights.

Third, the protection of the human rights of migrants and asylum seekers in the EU is based on a complex legal framework that includes EU primary law, secondary law and international human rights conventions. The EU Charter of Fundamental Rights plays a key role, guaranteeing, among other things, the right to asylum, the principle of *non-refoulement* and the prohibition of discrimination. The new 2020 Pact on Migration and Asylum introduces comprehensive reforms to the EU's asylum system, aiming to create a fairer and more efficient approach to migration management. The Pact includes ten key legislative instruments designed to unify asylum procedures, improve reception conditions for migrants, and introduce a solidarity mechanism between Member States. Effective implementation of the Pact is challenging and will be key to truly improving the protection of migrants' and asylum seekers' rights in the EU. Despite significant progress in the creation of the legal framework, the ultimate success of these efforts will depend on the effective implementation of the new laws in practice, which may prove as difficult as the process of negotiating and adopting them.

Fourth, a phenomenon as widespread as population migration raises the crucial issue of ensuring effective protection of fundamental rights. Respect for and protection of human rights are fundamental obligations of states, both at the national level (through national constitutions and legislation) and at the international level (UDHR, ICCPR, ICESCR, ECHR) and EU level (CFR). International human rights law guarantees protection for all individuals, regardless of nationality and circumstances, and thus also in crisis situations. It thus also serves a guarantee function for migrants who are third-country nationals. The ECtHR currently plays a key role in setting standards related to the rights of foreigners, as reflected in the rather large number of complaints brought before the Court by foreigners.

The fundamental rights guarantees contained in the ECHR and its protocols are further developed in the Court's jurisprudence, which, in cases involving foreigners, also refers to universal sources of international law, such as the 1951 Geneva Convention Relating to the Status of Refugees and EU law. Interference with fundamental rights in situations of emergency, in accordance with the principles of legality and proportionality, requires states to carefully balance, on the one hand, the need to protect fundamental rights and respect for inherent human dignity, and on the other, the security of the state, the safety of its citizens, and public order. Some rights, such as the right to life or the prohibition of torture and inhuman or degrading treatment, are absolute and not subject to derogation in emergency situations.

At the same time, the ECtHR affirms the sovereign right of ECHR States Parties to control the entry and stay of foreigners on their territory. However, the protection of the state's borders and security must be carried out in a manner consistent with fundamental rights. Given the modern challenges posed by the increasing scale of third-country nationals migrating to the EU, it is essential to have a reliable and effective border procedure that ensures respect for the fundamental rights of the individual. The right to seek international protection should also be respected in emergency situations. Deportations should only be carried out in exceptional cases, such as when foreigners are in the country illegally, pose a threat to national security or public order, or are involved in illegal employment or violations of migration laws. At the same time, measures taken by national authorities against migrants should be subject to effective and independent judicial review, ensuring that foreigners have access to adequate legal remedies in national systems.

From the perspective of international human rights law, the fundamental importance of the principle of *non-refoulement* cannot be overlooked. Currently, this principle is being developed by the ECtHR, on the basis of Article 3 of the ECHR in conjunction with Article 4 of Protocol No. 4, forming an actual construction of European human rights law that protects foreigners to a greater extent than *non-refoulement* in international refugee law. Indeed, the 1951 Geneva Convention provides exceptions to the prohibition of *refoulement* (Article 33 in conjunction with Article 1). In contrast, the protection under Article 3 of the ECHR is absolute, meaning that a refoulement order that would create a risk of torture and inhuman or degrading treatment must be considered inadmissible. Moreover, the principle of *non-refoulement* should also be upheld in emergency situations. There is no doubt that human rights must remain central to any state response in emergency situations.

Fifth, the suspension of the application of obligations under the ECHR, the ICCPR and the CFR in a state of public emergency is a procedure distinct from the legal restriction of rights for the protection of public safety, order, health, public morals, or the fundamental rights and freedoms of others. As a special measure designed to safeguard the democratic order in situations of exceptional public danger threatening the existence of the nation, it is subject to a number of formal conditions.

The suspension of obligations under the ECHR, ICCPR and CFR is possible in the event of a threat to the life of the nation, including internal or external armed conflict, large-scale terrorist activities, natural disasters, epidemics, or industrial disasters of great magnitude. As indicated by an analysis of ECtHR jurisprudence and literature, this condition was also met in the case of the COVID-19 pandemic. However, each case required an assessment of the individual situation of the State Party, taking into account the stage of the pandemic cycle in which it found itself, and thus the degree of public health risk applicable to its territory. The measures applied had to be proportionate. There is therefore no room for an expansive interpretation of derogation clauses. This observation is particularly relevant to peremptory rights, including the prohibition of discrimination on the basis of race, color, sex, language, religion, or social origin. States Parties are obliged to use derogations only as an exception, first resorting to legal solutions available for "normal" circumstances—such as the possibility of statutory restrictions on particular rights for the protection of public security, order, health, public morals, or the fundamental rights and freedoms of others. The suspension obligations under the ECHR, the ICCPR and the CFR entail an obligation to immediately notify the competent authorities and officially declare an exceptional public emergency that threatens the existence of the nation. The notification itself must clearly indicate the provisions from which the state has derogated, the reasons for the derogation, the scope of the measures taken, and their duration. The termination of the derogation is also subject to the notification requirement.

Sixth, the Member States do not have a uniform policy for responding to a variety of emergency circumstances that may arise from both internal, external, or other factors. Nevertheless, an analysis of the legislation in force in the countries covered by this monograph reveals that each has regulations concerning specific forms of institutionalized response to emergencies affecting the functioning of the state and the society. The implementation of these measures may involve the restriction of individual rights and freedoms in order to protect values of broader significance, such as human health, life, and public safety and order. Their activation is most often dictated by the occurrence of events of an exceptional nature, the need to prevent such events, or efforts to minimize the negative effects of such events. This includes armed conflicts, or activities that may significantly disrupt the functioning of the state, its apparatus and society, due to internal unrest, natural disasters or disease outbreaks.

The legal basis for various forms of response to states of emergency, such as martial law, natural disaster or a state of emergency, is usually rooted in a country's constitution, though exceptions exist. For example, the Belgian Basic Law does not explicitly regulate "states of emergency," though some provisions refer to emergency situations, such as an ongoing armed conflict. In addition, the Belgian Constitution contains a clause preventing its suspension in whole or in part. While fundamental rights guaranteed by the Constitution cannot be suspended, they can be restricted under certain circumstances, so they are not absolute in nature. In the Czech legal system, on the other hand, states of emergency are not addressed directly in the Constitution, but are instead regulated in a separate constitutional act. In France, the Constitution formally provides for two mechanisms for responding to states of emergency, but these are very rarely used. These are the state of siege, triggered in cases of serious and imminent danger or conflict (such as severe internal unrest), and a mechanism activated in response to a serious and imminent threat to the independence of the nation or disruption of the normal functioning of public authorities, allowing the president to assume full state powers.

However, it turns out that the regulations for emergencies contained, as a rule, in constitutions are insufficient for states or overly restrict the functioning, freedom and scope of action of the executive branch. As a result, states either introduce additional response mechanisms at the level of ordinary legislation, or they introduce such mechanisms by acts of an even lower order, to avoid formally declaring a constitutionally regulated state of emergency. This allows them to limit certain rights and freedoms without triggering the constitutional consequences that such measures would otherwise entail.

For example, in response to the COVID-19 pandemic, an additional state of health emergency was regulated in French legislation. In addition, France has a system—based on the case law of the Council of State—that allows the administration, under judicial oversight, to disregard ordinary regulations and take emergency measures if special circumstances require it and there is a need to ensure the continuity of public services. In the Polish legal system, in turn, public authorities have resorted to introducing various restrictions typical of a state of emergency—such as limitations on freedom of residence and movement in the zone along the border with Belarus—without complying with the requirements imposed by the relevant provisions of the Polish Constitution.

It is difficult to unequivocally assess the reasons for the varied approaches to the legal regulation of state responses to emergencies. However, it can be hypothesized that this is due to a number of intertwining factors, ranging from the legal tradition and culture operating in a given state to its geopolitical situation, as well as strictly political and populist considerations aimed at influencing electoral outcomes.

Seventh, the COVID-19 pandemic was a state of emergency of global scope. States, including EU Member States, had to take measures during this period to balance the need to protect human life and health with the need to ensure the smooth functioning of the state and its institutions, including the administrative and judicial apparatus.

The pandemic also had a significant impact on freedom of movement, including the entry and stay of foreigners in the territories of EU Member States. However, it should be pointed out that most of the restrictions introduced during the pandemic period in the above regard did not specifically target third-country nationals arriving in an EU Member State or transiting through their territory, but applied to all individuals crossing state borders. The scale of restrictions introduced by states at the time varied, ranging from outright entry bans on foreigners (France) or prohibitions on travel for both foreigners and nationals (Czech Republic), to various forms of isolation aimed at limiting coronavirus transmission. The severity of these restrictions also varied and fluctuated over time.

This leads to the conclusion that no common approach was adopted across the EU, nor were uniform mechanisms developed for responding to a global threat to human life and health of pathogenic origin. On the one hand, allowing individual states discretion can be seen as appropriate, as it allowed them to tailor their response measures to the specific threat level in a given area. On the other hand, the establishment and implementation of common EU-wide instruments integrating and coordinating the activities of Member States in the sphere of combating epidemiological threats could have facilitated a faster and more efficient response to the pandemic, thereby enabling a swifter return to normal state functioning in all aspects.

It should be emphasized that in the Member States covered by the study, the outbreak of the coronavirus pandemic led to the adaptation of administrative and judicial-administrative procedures to the new realities. These adjustments aimed to ensure the relatively smooth functioning of the entire state apparatus while introducing procedural solutions that minimized the risk of infringing the procedural guarantees to which individuals are entitled. For example, in the area of the right to seek legal remedies, states adopted solutions allowing filings despite missed deadlines, or modified regulations on the time limits for certain procedural acts. Regarding foreigners residing on the territory of a Member State during the pandemic, solutions were usually introduced to extend the validity of certain residence permits by law. However, this does not mean that the pandemic had no negative effects in the administrative and judicial spheres. Particularly in its early stages, the closure of various public institutions resulted in a backlog of cases that had to be addressed later. In France, for example, the pandemic caused serious disruptions in the asylum procedure, which operates on the single-window principle, due to the complete suspension of the French Office of Immigration and Integration.

In turn, in order to streamline administrative court procedures, solutions were adopted to transfer the burden of hearing certain cases from multi-member panels to single-judge proceedings, while certain categories of cases were no longer heard at hearings and were instead adjudicated in closed sessions. To a large extent, the administrative judiciary began to use remote communication (online hearings), enabling parties to fully exercise their right to be heard and actively participate in proceedings without unnecessary exposure to the risk of coronavirus infection. This demonstrates that Member States managed to organize the administration and judiciary quite efficiently during the pandemic. Hence the crisis turned out to be a catalyst for change, accelerating the technological advancement of state structures by several generations—something that probably would not have happened so quickly under normal circumstances.

Eighth, the analysis of the legal conditions in the countries covered by the study showed that although they fully implemented general procedures related to the entry, stay and expulsion of foreigners into their national legal frameworks, they did not introduce specific solutions, such as border procedures under European law, to respond to crisis situations related to mass migration or its instrumentalization. In principle, only the introduction of mechanisms related to the granting of temporary protection to foreigners turned out to be a solution successfully implemented on a wider scale, a fact highlighted above all by the influx of Ukrainian citizens into EU countries following the invasion of Ukraine by Russian Federation troops.

However, returning to the issue of border procedures, it should be noted that although the analyzed EU Member States have so far not implemented them, some—particularly Poland and the Baltic states—have introduced mechanisms intended to serve as quasi-border procedures or as substitutes (push-back mechanism). However, due to the way they are regulated and, above all, the nature of their implementation in practice, these measures have generated significant controversy, especially from the point of view of respect for individual rights and guarantees derived from international, European and national law. Indeed, these procedures have been criticized for allegedly violating the principle of *non-refoulement*, the prohibition of collective expulsion, the right to make an effective application for international protection and many other rules and values.

Nevertheless, it is worth considering whether the criticism of these measures is fully justified, and whether their opponents acknowledge the various aspects underlying the crisis related to mass migratory movements. For there is no doubt that geopolitical conditions—namely, sharing borders with countries that are not only outside the Union but are also openly hostile to it and instrumentalize migrants for hybrid actions aimed at destabilizing individual states and the entire region, require looking at these mechanisms with greater understanding. After all, they do not serve only the particular interests of a given state, which should not be so readily condemned when the security of the country and its people is at stake. Rather, they de facto serve as a means of protecting all Member States, not just those whose borders also form the external wall of the European Union.

The use of restrictive migration policies and emergency border control measures, moreover, demonstrates the weakness of the Union as a whole and the mechanisms and principles on which it is based, at least in terms of the rules of entry and residence of foreigners in Member States. It is difficult to predict at present to what extent the New Pact on Migration and Asylum will address these weaknesses, but the reluctance expressed toward it, if only by the Polish authorities, and the tougher stance on migration policy, leads to the conclusion that this sphere requires further, in-depth consideration, and perhaps also a reassessment of certain principles related to migrants' rights, ensuring that guarantees intended to protect an individual—or even many individuals—do not stand in such stark contrast to the state's right to defend its integrity and security and its duty to protect its citizens.

Bibliography

Abraham M., "Pandemics," in D. Moeckli, S. Shah, S. Sivakumaran, and D. J. Harris (eds), *International Human Rights Law* (Oxford University Press 2022) 661–679.

Allain J., "The IUs Cogens Nature of Non-refoulement" (2001) 13 *International Journal of Refugee Law*, 533–558.

Antoš M., and Wintr J., (eds), Ústavní právo a koronavirus (Praha: Leges 2021).

Arnull A., "The Principle of Effective Judicial Protection in EU law: An Unruly Horse?" (2011) 1 *European Law Review*, 51–70.

Arowolo G. A., "Protecting the Rights of Migrants: the Challenges and the Prospects" (2021) 105 *Journal of Law, Policy and Globalization*, 92–105.

Auriel P., Beaud O., Wellman C. (eds), *The Rule of Crisis: Terrorism, Emergency Legislation and the Rule of Law* (Cham: Springer Verlag 2018).

Badar M. E., "Basic Principles Governing Limitations on Individual Rights and Freedoms in Human Rights Instruments" (2003) 7 *The International Journal of Human Rights*, 63–92.

Baranowska G., "Pushbacks in Poland: Grounding the Practice in Domestic Law in 2021" (2023) 41 *Polish Yearbook of International Law*.

Baranowska K., "Legalność i dopuszczalność procedury push-back (wywózek) i ocena prób ich legalizowania w Polsce," [w:] W. Klaus, *Poza prawem. Prawna ocena działań państwa polskiego w reakcji na kryzys humanitarny na granicy polsko-białoruskiej* (Warszawa 2022).

Bates E., "History," in D. Moeckli, S. Shah, S. Sivakumaran, and D. J. Harris (eds), *International Human Rights Law* (Oxford University Press 2022) 3–21.

Bilgorajski A., "Boundaries an Limitations of Human Rights: A Contribution to the Discussion" (2023) 27 *Scientific Journal of Bielsko-Biala School of Finance and Law*, 68–71.

Bílková V., *Koronavirová krize a lidská práva* (Praha: Ústav mezinárodních vztahů 2020).

Bílková V., Kysela J., and Šturma P. (eds), *Výjimečné stavy a lidská práva* (Praha: Auditorium 2016).

Bjornskov C., and Voight S. "The Architecture of Emergency Constitutions" (2018) 16(1) *International Journal of Constitutional Law*, p. 101–127.

Bodnar A., and Grzelak A., "The Polish–Belarusian Border Crisis and the (Lack of) European Union Response" (2023) 28(1) *Białostockie Studia Prawnicze—Bialystok Legal Studies* <https://doi.org/10.15290/bsp.2023.28.01.04>.

Bodnar A., and Grzelak A., "The Polish-Belarusian Border Crisis and the (Lack of) European Union Response" (2023) 28 *Białostockie Studia Prawnicze—Bialystok Legal Studies*, 83.

Bodziany M., and Kotasińska A., "Europejski kryzys migracyjny—włoskie studium przypadku" (2017) 5 *Pogranicze. Polish Borderlands Studies*, z. 2.

Boza Martínez D., "Procedural Rights Protecting Immigrants. Right to a Fair Trial (Article 6) and Right to an Effective Remedy (Article 13)," in D. Moya, and G. Milios (eds), *Aliens before the European Court of Human Rights. Ensuring Minimum Standards of Human Rights Protection* (Leiden: Brill 2021) 118–140.

Braithwaite B., Harby C., and Miletić G. (eds), *The Protection of Human Rights During Times of Emergency: An Analysis of the Relevant Jurisprudence of the European Court of Human Rights through the Lens of the Covid-19 Pandemic* (London: AIRE Centre 2022) 198–215.

Bruneau C., Plucinska J., and Abi Nader Y., *How Minsk Became a Destination for Migrants Travelling as Tourists* <https://www.reuters.com/world/europe/how-minsk-became-mecca-migrants-travelling-tourists-2021-11-15/>.

Bruun N., and Groussot X., "The Minimum Standards: The Role of the EU Charter of Fundamental Rights" (Swedish Institute for European Policy Studies (SIEPS) 2024) <https://www.sieps.se/en/publications/2024/the-minimum-standards/> accessed February 10, 2025.

Brzeziński M., "Wybrane zasady stanów nadzwyczajnych w konstytucji z dnia 2 kwietnia 1997 r.—uwagi de lege lata i de lege ferenda" (2017) 45 *Studia Politologiczne.*

Caicedo Camacho N., "Social Rights and Migrants before the European Court of Human Rights," in D. Moya, and G. Milios (eds), *Aliens before the European Court of Human Rights. Ensuring Minimum Standards of Human Rights Protection* (Leiden: Brill 2021) 191–210.

Çalı B., Bianku L., and Motoc I., "Migration and the European Convention on Human Rights," in B. Çalı, L. Bianku, and I. Motoc (eds), *Migration and the European Convention on Human Rights* (Oxford University Press 2021) 3–18.

della Cananea G., *The Common Core of European Administrative Laws; retrospective and prospective*, (Brill/Nijhoff 2023) 200.

Carrera S., The Strasbourg court judgment "N.D. and N.T. v Spain": a "carte blanche" to push backs at EU external borders?, EUI Working Paper RSCAS 2020/21.

Chetail V., *International Migration Law* (Oxford University Press 2019).

Chlebny J. (ed), Prawo o cudzoziemcach. Komentarz, (Warszawa 2020).

Chlebny J., *Postępowanie w sprawie nadania statusu uchodźcy* (Warszawa 2011).
Chlebny J., "Wyzwania dla procedury uchodźczej w czasie kryzysu na granicy," in *Współczesne problemy orzecznicze sądów administracyjnych Polski i Czech. Materiały ze spotkania polsko-czeskiej grupy roboczej sędziów sądów administracyjnych (Kraków, 11–13 czerwca 2023)* (2024) 20 (Special issue), *Zeszyty Naukowe Sądownictwa Administracyjnego.*
Chlebny J., "Zawrócenie cudzoziemca na granicy" (2023) 5 *Zeszyty Naukowe Sądownictwa Administracyjnego.*
Chlebny J., *Turning Back a Foreigner at the Border* (ZNSA 2023), No. 5, 13.
Chlebny J., "Konstytucyjny standard ochrony cudzoziemców w sprawach wjazd i pobytu w świetle orzecznictwa Naczelnego Sądu Administracyjnego," in J. Chlebny (ed), *Wolności i prawa człowieka i obywatela w orzecznictwie sądów administracyjnych. Jubilee book for the 100th anniversary of the establishment of the Supreme Administrative Court* (Warszawa 2022) 360.
Chlebny J., "Sądownictwo administracyjne w Polsce z perspektywy art. 47 KPP" (2022) 10 *Europejski Przegląd Sądowy*, p. 30.
Chlebny J., in A. Matan (ed), *System Prawa Administracyjnego Procesowego. Vol. IV. Postępowania autonomiczne i szczególne. Postępowania niejurysdykcyjne* (Warszawa 2021) 571.
Chlebny J., and Piątek W., "Ewolucja ustrojowa i kompetencyjna sądownictwa administracyjnego" (2021) 1–2, *Zeszyty Naukowe Sądownictwa Administracyjnego*, 32.
Chlebny J., "Crossing the Border by an Alien Intending to Submit an Application for International Protection. Gloss to the Judgment of the ECtHR of 23 July 2020, Joined Cases 40503/17, 42902/17 and 43643/17" (2020) 12 *Europejski Przegląd Sądowy*, 51.
Chlebny J., "Glosa to the ECHR Judgment of 15 October 2020, 80982/12" (2020) 6 *Zeszyty Naukowe Sądownictwa Administracyjnego*, 163–174.
Chlebny J., in J. Chlebny (ed), *Prawo cudzoziemców . Komentarz* (Warszawa 2020) 54–55.
Chlebny J., in W. Piątek, J. P. Tarno (eds), *System Prawa Administracyjnego Procesowego. Vol. II. Part 2. Zasady ogólne postępowania administracyjnego* (Warszawa 2018) 211–246.
Chlebny J., "Public Order, National Security and the Rights of Third-Country Nationals in Immigration Cases" (2018) 20 *European Journal of Migration and Law*, 117.
Chlebny J., in G. Łaszczyca, and A. Matan (eds), *System Prawa Administracyjnego Procesowego. Vol. I.* Zagadnienia ogólne (Warszawa 2017) 404.

Chlebny J., “Right to Information and Assistance of an Interpreter in the Case of Obliging a Foreigner to Leave the Territory of Poland,” in J. Sługocki (ed), *Dziesięć lat polskich doświadczeń w Unii Europejskiej. Problemy prawnoadministracyjne*, vol. 2 (Wrocław 2014) 618–619.

Chlebny J., *Postępowanie w sprawie o nadanie statusu uchodźcy* (Warszawa 2011) 265–266.

Chlebny J., “Refusal of Access to the File in an Administrative Case” (2014) 10 *Państwo i Prawo*, 107–108.

Chlebny J., “Protection of public interest and a foreigner’s right to stay in Poland” (2007), no. 10 *Europejski Przegląd Sądowy*, 18.

Chrostowska-Malak K., “Institutions of International Protection of Foreigners in Poland—Political and Legal Solutions,” *Nowa Polityka Wschodnia* (2023, No. 1) 91.

Chróścielewski W., and Chlebny J., “Z problematyki informacji udzielanej cudzoziemcom przez organy prowadzące postępowania administracyjne,” in M. Cherka, P. Gołaszewski, J. Piech, and M. Wierzbowski (eds), *Kryzys, stagnacja, renesans? Prawo administracyjne przyszłości. Księga jubileuszowa profesora dr hab. Jacka Jagielskiego* (Warszawa 2021) 1020–1021.

Chodorowska A., and Trylińska A., “The Concept of the Principle of Non-Refoulement in Refugee Law” (2021) 2 *Dyskurs Prawniczy i Administracyjny*, 7–23.

Chvojka Š., “Role Ústavního soudu v koronakrizi,” 30(2) *Jurispurdence*, 14–27.

Complak K., “Stany nadzwyczajne á la française oraz á la polonaise” (2014) 22 *Studia Iuridica Lublinensia*.

Ćorić V., and Knežević Bojović A., “European Court of Human Rights and COVID-19: What are Standards for Health Emergencies?,” in *New Legal Reality: Challenges and Perspectives* (Riga: University of Latvia Press) 380–398 <https://doi.org/10.22364/iscflul.8.2.26>.

Criddle E. (ed) *Human Rights in Emergencies* (Cambridge: CUP 2016).

Cvinerová B., and Čurdová M., *Residence of Foreigners after the State of Emergency* <https://danovky.cz/en/news/detail/page-4/663>.

Czarnota K., and Górczyńska M., *Gdzie prawo nie sięga. Raport Helsińskiej Fundacji Praw Człowieka z monitoringu sytuacji na polsko-białoruskiej granicy* <https://www.hfhr.pl/wp-content/uploads/2022/06/Raport_Gdzie_Prawo_Nie_Siega-HFPC-30062022.pdf>.

Czarnow S., “Między stanem epidemii a stanem klęski żywiołowej—COVID-19 a niektóre prawa człowieka” (2021) 3 *Radca Prawny. Zeszyty Naukowe*.

Czarnow S., "Próba refleksji nad reakcją państwa na pandemię COVID-19—uwagi o porządku prawnym czasu epidemii i jego wpływie na prawa i wolności człowieka" (2023) 1 *Radca Prawny. Zeszyty Naukowe*.

Czeszejko-Sochacki Z., *System konstytucyjny Szwajcarii* (Warszawa 2002).

Dąbrowski P., *Cudzoziemiec niepożądany w polskim prawie o cudzoziemcach* (Warszawa 2011).

Dąbrowski P., "Glosa do wyroku Naczelnego Sądu Administracyjnego z dnia 20 września 2018 r., II OSK 1025/18" (2019) 3 *Orzecznictwo Sądów Polskich*.

Dauvergne C., "Refugee Law as Perpetual Crisis," in C. Harvey, and S. S. Juss (eds), *Contemporary Issues in Refugee Law* (Edward Elgar 2013) 13–30.

Dean M., "Bridging the Gap: Humanitarian Protection and the Convergence of Laws in Europe" (2014) 20 *European Law Journal*, 34–65.

Delas O., "La création du principe de non-refoulement en droit international des droits de la personne par la Cour européenne des droits de l'homme : un chef-d'oeuvre à protéger" (2020) (Special Issue) *Revue québécoise de droit international /Quebec Journal of International Law / Revista quebequense de derecho internacional*, 395–416 <https://doi.org/10.7202/1078546ar>.

Díaz Morgado C., "Prohibition of Slavery and Forced Labour (Article 4). Human Trafficking," in D. Moya, and G. Milios (eds), *Aliens before the European Court of Human Rights. Ensuring Minimum Standards of Human Rights Protection* (Leiden: Brill 2021) 76–96.

Dolny J., "Realizacja zasady czynnego udziału stron i szybkości w postępowaniu administracyjnym prowadzonym przez organy jednostek samorządu terytorialnego w dobie epidemii. Uwagi praktyczne" (2020) 10 *Samorząd Terytorialny*.

Domagała P., "The Migration Crisis in the Case Law of the ECHR—Some Remarks on the Obligations of Countries to Refugees and Immigrants" (2020) 7(2) *Polish Review of International and European Law*, 173–192 <https://doi.org/10.21697/priel.2018.7.2.04>.

Domaradzki S., Khvostova M., and Pupovac D., "Karel Vasak's Generations of Rights and the Contemporary Human Rights Discourse" (2019) 20 *Human Rights Review*, 423–443 <https://doi.org/10.1007/s12142-019-00565-x>.

Donnelly J., and Whelan D. J., *International Human Rights* (London, New York: Routledge 2020).

Dorosz-Kruczyński J., "Case of El-Hassani v. Polish Minister of Foreign Affairs and judicial control of public administration activities in Poland" (2021) 1 *Krytyka Prawa*, 191–208.

Dov Bachmann S.-D., and Paphiti A., "Mass Migration as a Hybrid Threat?—A Legal Perspective" (2021) 50(1) *Polish Political Science Yearbook*, 125–129.

Drachal J., Jagielski J., and Gołaszewski P., in R. Hauser, and M. Wierzbowski (eds) *Prawo o postępowaniu przed sądami administracyjnymi. Commentary* (Warszawa 2023) 12–13.

Droscová, L., *How to Employ Foreigners During the State of Emergency* (<https://actlegal.com/cs/news/how-to-employ-foreigners-during-the-state-of-emergency/>).

Dzimińska-Mosio M., "Instytucja stanów nadzwyczajnych a stan wojenny" (2019) 3 *Biblioteka Nauki.*

Dubisz S. (ed), *Słownik języka polskiego* (Warszawa 2006) 332.

Duniewska Z., Jaworska-Dębska B., Olejniczak-Szałowska E., and Stahl M. (eds), *Prawo administracyjne materialne* (Warsaw 2020).

Durán Alba J. F., "Restrictions on the Political Activity of Aliens under Article 16 ECHR," in J. García Roca, and P. Santolaya (eds), *Europe of Rights: A Compendium on the European Convention of Human Rights* (Leiden: Brill 2012) 497–501.

Filipczyk H., "Rozpoznanie sprawy na posiedzeniu niejawnym na podstawie art. 15zzs^{4} ust. 3 specustawy w świetle zasady jawności postępowania sądowego" (2021) 5 *Przegląd Prawniczy.*

Florczak-Wątor M., "Niekonstytucyjność ograniczeń praw i wolności jednostki wprowadzonych w związku z epidemią COVID-19 jako przesłanka odpowiedzialności odszkodowawczej państwa" (2020) 12 *Państwo i Prawo.*

Florczak-Wątor M., "Konstytucyjna regulacja stanów nadzwyczajnych w świetle dotychczasowej praktyki jej (nie)stosowania" (2022) 10 *Państwo i Prawo.*

Florczak-Wątor M., *Konstytucja Rzeczpospolitej Polskiej. Komentarz* (Warsaw 2023).

Florczak-Wątor M., Gárdos-Orosz F., Malíř J., and Steuer M. (eds), *States of Emergency and Human Rights Protection. The Theory and Practice of the Visegrad Countries* (Routledge 2024).

Florczak-Wątor M., in M. Safjan, and L. Bosek (eds), *Konstytucja RP. Vol. I. Komentarz do art. 1–86* (Warszawa 2016) 916.

Furramani E., and Bushati R., "The Principle of "Non-Refoulement" and its Evolution in the Jurisprudence of the European Court of Human Rights" (2022) 11(3) *Academic Journal of Interdisciplinary Studies*, 107–120 <https://doi.org/10.36941/ajis-2022-007> accessed September 30, 2024.

Garlicki L., *Polskie prawo konstytucyjne* (Warsaw: Zarys wykładu 2022).

Gilbert G., "Human Rights, Refugees and Other Displaced Persons in International Law," in E. de Wer, and J. Vidmar (eds), *Hierarchy in International Law: The Place of Human Rights* (Oxford University Press 2012).

Ginsburg, Tom, and Versteeg, Mila, "The Bound Executive: Emergency Powers Druring the Pandemic" (2021) 19(5) *International Journal of Constitutional Law*, 1498–1535.

Goodwin-Gil G. S., McAdam J., and Dunlop E., *The Refugee in International Law* (Oxford University Press 2021).

Graca J., and Rodkiewicz W., *Russia Is Putting Migration Pressure on the Border with Finland, Analysis of the Centre for Eastern Studies* (November 17, 2023), <https://www.osw.waw.pl/en/publikacje/analyses/2023-11-17/russia-putting-migration-pressure-border-finland> accessed April 28, 2024 accessed April 28, 2024.

Greene A., *Permanent States of Emergency and the Rule of Law: Constitutions in an Age of Crisis* (Oxford: Hard Publishing 2018).

Greene A., *Emergency Powers in a Time of Pandemic* (Bristol University Press 2020).

Grześkowiak M., "Od aktywizmu do "polityki przyzwolenia." Komisja Europejska wobec nieregularnej migracji w latach 2015–2021 ze szczególnym uwzględnieniem kryzysu humanitarnego na granicy polsko-białoruskiej" (2023) 3 *Państwo i Prawo*.

Grześkowiak M., "Specustawa ukraińska jako szczególny przypadek formalizacji tzw. tymczasowego schronienia dla osób przymusowo migrujących" (2023) 8 *Europejski Przegląd Sądowy*.

Henčeková, S., and Drugda, Š., *Slovakia: Change of Government under COVID-19 Emergency* (Verfassungsblog 2020, May 22).

Hetnarowicz-Sikora J., and Walentowicz J., "Realistic Measures to Protect the Rights and Security of an Immigrant on the Belarus Border from the Perspective of the Law on Foreigners, the Law on the Protection of Foreigners and Acts of International Law" (2022) 3–4 *Journal of Criminal Law and Penal Studies*.

Hofmański P., and Wróbel A., in L. Garlicki (ed), *Konwencja o Ochronie Praw Człowieka i Podstawowych Wolności. Komentarz*, vol. I (Warsaw 2010).

Horvat M., Piątek W., Potesil L., and Rozsnyai K. F., "Public Administration's Adaptation to Covid-19 Pandemic—Czech, Hungarian, Polish and Slovak Experience" (2021) 1(19) *Central European Public Administration Review* <https://doi.org/10.17573/cepar.2021.1.06>.

Idrian P., "Zarządzanie kryzysowe a system bezpieczeństwa narodowego" (2015) 3 *Obronność—Zeszyty Naukowe Wydziału Zarządzania i Dowodzenia Akademii Obrony Narodowej*, 2.

Ineli-Ciger M., "Protecting Aliens with Article 3 of the ECHR. An Analysis with a Focus on Refugees and Migrants," in D. Moya, and

G. Milios (eds), *Aliens before the European Court of Human Rights. Ensuring Minimum Standards of Human Rights Protection* (Leiden: Brill 2021) 46–75.

Jagielski J., *Status prawny cudzoziemca w Polsce (problematyka administracyjno-prawna)* (Warszawa 1997) 112.

Jagielski J., in *Obywatelstwo polskie. Komentarz do ustawy* (Warszawa 2016) 106.

Jakubowski A., and Roszkiewicz J., "Glosa do wyroku Naczelnego Sądu Administracyjnego z 4 marca 2022 r., II GSK 38/22" (2023) 5 *Orzecznictwo Sądów Polskich*.

Jakulevičienė L., "Principle of Non-refoulement in the Context of Recent ECtHR Caselaw and the EU Migration and Asylum Pact" (2023) 24(3) *ERA Forum*, 379–396.

Jaskiernia J., "Challenges Posed by the COVID-19 Pandemic to the Protection of Human Rights" (2020) 4 *Stosunki Międzynarodowe—International Relations*, 65–78 <https://doi.org/10.7366/020909614202004>.

Jaźwińska M., Mickiewicz P., and Słubik K., in W. Klaus (ed), *Ustawa o pomocy obywatelom Ukrainy w związku z konfliktem zbrojnym na terytorium tego państwa oraz niektórych innych ustaw. Komentarz* (Warszawa 2022).

Kälin W., and Künzli J., *The Law of International Human Rights Protection* (Oxford University Press 2019).

Kapelańska-Pręgowska J., "The (Still) Unresolved Question of COVID-19 Passes Compatibility with the ECHR. Comments on the ECtHR Decision of October 7, 2021 in Zembrano v. France (Application no. 41994/21)" (2022) 11 *Polish Review of International and European Law*, 169–182.

Karska E., Morawska E. H., Czepek J., Dąbrowski Ł. D., Oręziak B., and Gałka K., *Human Rights in the European Paradigm of the Protection of Aliens* (Warsaw 2023).

Keisler I., Lobotka A., and Kotulková L., *Covid-19: přijatá opatření a náhrada újmy* (Praha: Wolters Kluwer 2020).

Kersten J., and Rixen S., *Der Verfassungsstaat in der Corona-Krise* (München: C.H. Beck 2020).

Klaus W. (ed), *Poza prawem. Prawna ocena działań państwa polskiego w reakcji na kryzys humanitarny na granicy polsko-białoruskiej* (Warszawa 2022).

Kmieciak Z., "Constitutional standard of administrative judiciary" (2022) 10 *Państwo i Prawo*, 120.

Kolendowska-Matejczuk M., and Mrowicki M., "Protection of Human Rights in States of Global Emergency—An Analysis on the Example of the COVID-19 Pandemic" (2021) 2 *Krakow International Studies*, 35–65.

Korzeniowski D., "General principles of the CAP as guidelines for public administration authorities" (2023) 2(80) *Ubezpieczenià w Rolnictwie—Materiały i Studia*, 209–230.

Kowalik-Bańczyk K., in A. Wróbel (ed), *Charter of Fundamental Rights of the European Union. Commentary* (Warszawa 2020) 1054–1055.

Kowalski M., "Between Openness and Efficiency of Administrative Court Proceedings (Some Reflections Related to the Pandemic and Its End" 2023) 12, *Państwo i Prawo*, 128.

Kowalski M., *Prawo do sądu administracyjnego. Standard międzynarodowy i konstytucyjny oraz jego realizacja* (Warszawa 2019).

Kowalski M., "Między jawnością a sprawnością postępowania przed sądem administracyjnym (kilka refleksji związanych z pandemią i jej zakończeniem" (2023) 12 *Państwo i Prawo.*

Krakała A., in B. JaworskaDębska (ed), *Kontrola legności pobytu cudzoziemców na terytorium RP, in: O prawie administracyjnym i administracji. Refleksje. Jubilee book dedicated to Professor Małgorzata Stahl* (Łódź 2017) 378–388.

Krzykowski P., "Rozprawa zdalna—wyjątek od reguły czy nowy model postępowania przed sądami administracyjnymi?" (2023) 2 *Studia Prawnicze KUL*.

Ktistakis Y., *Protecting Migrants under the European Convention on Human Rights and the European Social Charter. A Handbook for Legal Practitioners* (Council of Europe, February 2013).

Kumela-Romańska M., *Administracyjnoprawny status cudzoziemca w Polsce* (Warszawa 2017).

Kurzępa B., "Karnoprawne aspekty ochrony polskiej granicy państwowej. Wykroczenia graniczne" (2023) 2 *Prokuratura i Prawo.*

Kurzępa E., "Stan epidemii a stan klęski żywiołowej—rozważania w kontekście bezpieczeństwa państwa" (2021) 5 *Przegląd Prawa Publicznego*, 5–21.

Laaroussi M., Prawo cudzoziemców do równego traktowania i niedyskryminacji. Standard konstytucyjny i międzynarodowy oraz jego realizacja na przykładzie Belgii, Maroka i Polski, unpublished doctoral dissertation (Warszawa 2024).

Łachacz O., "Zasada non-refoulement w międzynarodowym prawie uchodźczym: zwyczaj międzynarodowy czy też peremptoryjna norma prawa międzynarodowego?" (2017) XV *Problemy Współczesnego Prawa Międzynarodowego, Europejskiego i Porównawczego* 134-142.

Lagrance P., "La protection internationale face aux nouveaux conflits," in T. Fleury Graff, and P. Jacob (eds), *Migrations et droit international* (Paris 2022) 439–454.

Lebret A., "COVID-19 Pandemic and Derogation to Human Rights" (2020) 7 *Journal of Law and the Biosciences*, 1–15 <https://doi.org/10.1093/jlb/lsaa015>.

Lenaerts K., "Exploring the Limits of the EU Charter of Fundamental Rights" (2012) 8 *European Constitutional Law Review*, 367.

Lewicki M., "Cudzoziemcy," in Z. Duniewska, B. Jaworska-Dębska, E. Olejniczak-Szałowska, and M. Stahl (eds), *Prawo administracyjne materialne* (Warszawa 2020).

López Baroni M. J., "Fourth Generation Human Rights in View of the Fourth Industrial Revolution" (2024) 9 *Philosophies*, 39–54 <https://doi.org/10.3390/philosophies9020039 https://www.mdpi.com/journal/philosophies>.

Mac B. Crorie, and Santomauro G., "The Margin of Appreciation of States in the European Convention on Human Rights and Additional Protocol No. *15*," in D. Moya, and G. Milios (eds), *Aliens before the European Court of Human Rights. Ensuring Minimum Standards of Human Rights Protection* (Leiden 2021) 249–276.

Mareš M., and Výborný Š., *Militantní demokracie ve Střední Evropě* (Brno: Centrum pro studium demokracie a kultury, 2013).

Marks S. P., "Poverty," in D. Moeckli, S. Shah, S. Sivakumaran, and D. J. Harris (eds), *International Human Rights Law* (Oxford University Press 2022) 622–642.

Matłacz A., and Horbaczewki R., "Od czwartku "stefa buforowa" przy granicy z Białorusią" <https://www.prawo.pl/samorzad/strefa-buforowa-przy-granicy-z-bialorusia,527405.html>.

Mikeš P., "Hledání cest soudní ochrany práv jednotlivců v době pandemie," in Šimíček, Vojtěch. Dělba moci (Praha: Leges 2022).

Milios G., "The Right to Family and Private Life in Migration and Asylum Cases (Article 8)," in D. Moya, and G. Milios (eds), *Aliens before the European Court of Human Rights. Ensuring Minimum Standards of Human Rights Protection* (Leiden: Brill 2021) 141–171.

Moran C. F., "Strengthening the Principle of Non-refoulement" (2020) 25 *The International Journal of Human Rights*, 1032–1052 <https://doi.org/10.1080/13642987.2020.1811690> accessed September 30, 2024.

Moreno-Lax V., *Accessing Asylum in Europe, Extraterritorial Border Controls and Refugee Rights under EU Law* (Oxford University Press 2017).

Mousmouti M., "Aliens' Right Not to Be Discriminated Against (Article 14 and Protocol 12 ECHR)," in D. Moya, and G. Milios (eds), *Aliens before the European Court of Human Rights. Ensuring Minimum Standards of Human Rights Protection* (Leiden: Brill 2021) 211–234.

Nowak M., *Introduction to the International Human Rights Regime* (Boston: Leiden 2003).

Nowicki M. A., "Potocka and Others v. Poland—ECHR judgment of 4 October 2001, Application No. 33776/96," in M. A. Nowicki (ed), *Nowy Europejski Trybunał Praw Człowieka. Wybór orzeczeń 1999–2004* (Kraków 2005) 573.

O'Boyle M., "Emergency Government and Derogation under the ECHR" (2016) 4 *European Human Rights Law Review*, 331–341.

Orosz L., Grabowska S., and Majerčák T. (eds), *Základné práva a slobody a ich ochrana v núdzovom stave a iných osobitných právnych režimoch* (Košice: Univerzita Pavla Joszefa Šafárika 2022).

Otwinowski W., "Crisis and Crisis Situation" (2010) 2 *Scientific and Methodical Review. Education for Security*, 86.

Oviedo Moreno C., *A Painful Slap from the ECtHR and an Urgent Opportunity for Spain* (Verfassungsblog, February 14, 2020) <https://verfassungsblog.de/a-painful-slap-from-the-ecthr-and-an-urgent-opportunity-for-spain/> accessed Septermber 30, 2024 <https://doi.org/10.17176/20200214-164222-0>.

Pannia P., "Questioning the Frontiers of Rights: the Case Law of the Italian Constitutional Court on Non-European Union Citizens Social Rights" (2022) 14(SI) *European Journal of LegalStudies*, 133–170.

Paśnik J., "Pozakonstytucyjne ustawodawstwo stanów nadzwyczajnych" (2023) 4 *Przegląd Prawa Publicznego*.

Perepolkin S. M., Perepolkin D. S., and Averianova M. V., "Typology of the Fourth Generation of Human Rights" (2021) 1 *Journal of International Legal Communication*, 91–101 <https://doi.org/10.32612/uw.27201643.2021.1> 91–101.

Piątek W., "Rozprawa w formie zdalnej przed sądem administracyjnym—nieuniknniona przyszłość czy rozwiązanie tymczasowe na czas pandemii?" (2022) 2 *Zeszyty Naukowe Sądownictwa Administracyjnego*.

Piątek W., "A Right to a Public Hearing in Times of Emergency—Online or Physical?" (2023) 14(2) *International Journal for Court Administration* <https://doi.org/10.36745/ijca.444>.

Piątek W., and Tarno J. P. (eds), *System Prawa Administracyjnego Procesowego. Vol. II. Part 2. Zasady ogólne postępowania administracyjnego* (Warszawa 2018).

Pichl M., and Schmalz D., *"Unlawful" may not mean rightless. The shocking ECtHR Grand Chamber judgment in case N.D. and N.T., Verfassungsblog*, February 14, 2020 <https://ver-fassungsblog.de/unlawful-may-not-mean-rightless/> accessed September 30, 2024 <https://doi.org/10.17176/20200214-164325-0>.

Pinto Oliveira A. S., "Aliens' Protection against Arbitrary Detention (Article 5 ECHR)," in D. Moya, and G. Milios (eds), *Aliens before the European Court of Human Rights. Ensuring Minimum Standards of Human Rights Protection* (Leiden: Brill 2021).

Pocar F., "Some Thoughts on the Universal Declaration of Human Rights and the "Generations" of Human Rights" (2015) 10 *Intercultural Human Rights Review*, 43–53.

de Pooter H., "Pandemie et migrations," in T. Fleury Graff, and P. Jacob (eds), *Migrations et droit international* (Paris 2022) 273–302.

Pořízek P., "Pokus o škálu výhrad veřejného pořádku v cizineckých a azylových věcech, aneb není výhrada jako výhrada," in Jílek, Dalibor, and Pořízek, Pavel (eds), *Ročenka uprchlického a cizineckého práva 2020/2021* (Praha: Wolters Kluwer 2021).

Pospíšil, I., "Právo na soudní a jinou právní ochranu," in Wagnerová, Eliška, Šimíček, Vojtěch, Langášek, and Tomáš, *Pospíšil, Ivo a kol. Listina základních práv a svobod. Komentář. 2. doplněné a aktualizované vydání* (Praha: Wolters Kluwer, 2023).

Radajewski M., "Prawa i wolności człowieka i obywatela w dobie pandemii," in T. Gardocka, and D. Jagiełło (eds), *Pandemia COVID-19 a prawa i wolności obywatela* (Warszawa 2020) 77–92.

Radziewicz P., in P. Tuleja (ed), *Konstytucja Rzeczypospolitej Polskiej. Komentarz* (Warszawa 2023).

Ragheboom H., *The International Legal Status and Protection of Environmentally Displaced Persons: A European Perspective* (Leiden: Boston 2017).

Raimondo G., *N. D. and N.T. v Spain: A Slippery Slope for the Protection of Irregular Migrants*, April 20, 2020 <https://www.law.ox.ac.uk/research-subject-groups/centre-criminology/centreborder-criminologies/blog/2020/04/nd-and-nt-v-spain>.

Rajamani L., "Climate Change," in D. Moeckli, S. Shah, S. Sivakumaran, and D. J. Harris (eds), *International Human Rights Law* (Oxford University Press 2022) 644–660.

Reynolds J., "The Margin of Appreciation Doctrine: Colonial Origins," in *Empire, Emergency and International Law* (Cambridge University Press 2017) 170–192.

Rogala R., in J. Chlebny (ed), *Prawo cudzoziemców* (Warszawa 2020) 1241.

Rogala R., *Prawo cudzoziemca do ubiegania na granicy o udzielenie ochrony międzynarodowej*, (EPS 2021), No. 11, 13–14.

Ruiz Ramos J., "The Right to Life of Migrants and Refugees under Article 2 ECHR. Outside, Inside and Along the Way," in D. Moya, and G. Milios (eds), *Aliens before the European Court of Human Rights. Ensuring Minimum Standards of Human Rights Protection*, (Leiden: Brill 2021) 16–45.

Rychetský P., "Změna ústavy," in Rychetský P., Langášek T., Herc, and T., Mlsna (eds), *Petr a kol. Ústava České republiky. Ústavní zákon o bezpečnosti ČR. Komentář* (Praha: Wolters Kluwer 2015).

Rząsa G., *Zastosowanie funkcji korygującej zasad ogólnych Kodeksu postępowania administracyjnego do sankcyjnych decyzji związanych—na przykładzie postępowania w sprawie zobowiązania cudzoziemca do powrotu*, in: *Determinanty prawa i postępowania administracyjnego oraz sądowoadministracyjnego. Księga Jubileuszowa dedykowana profesor Aleksandrze Wiktorowskiej* (Warszawa 2024) 159–170.

Rząsa G., in M. Wierzbowski, and Wiktorowska A. (eds), *Kodeks postępowania administracyjnego. Komentarz* (31st edn, Legalis 2023), Nb 3 to Article 6.

Rząsa G., "Skarga na bezczynność wniesiona po zakończeniu postępowania administracyjnego. Glosa to the resolution of the SAC of 22 June 2020" (2021) 1, *Orzecznictwo Sądów Polskich*, 157–158.

Rząsa G., *Nieważność postępowania sądowoadministracyjnego jako podstawa skargi kasacyjnej* (Warszawa 2011) 99.

Rząsa G., "Konstytucyjne aspekty pomocy prawnej udzielanej osób ubogim" (2005) 3–4 *Przegląd Legislacyjny*, 40–41.

Scheinin M., "Terrorism," in D. Moeckli, S. Shah, S. Sivakumaran, and D. J. Harris (eds), *International Human Rights Law* (Oxford University Press 2022) 605–621.

Scuto F., "Expulsion and Prohibition of Collective Expulsion of Migrants and Asylum Seekers. The Level of the ECtHR's Protection," in D. Moya, and G. Milios (eds), *Aliens before the European Court of Human Rights. Ensuring Minimum Standards of Human Rights Protection* (Leiden: Brill 2021) 235–248.

Smith R. K. M., *International Human Rights Law* (Oxford University Press 2022).

Svobodová M., "Omezování volného pohybu osob v EU v průběhu pandemie COVID-19: dopady na příhraniční pracovníky," in Jílek, Dalibor, and Pořízek, Pavel, *Ročenka uprchlického a cizineckého práva 2020/2021* (Praha: Wolters Kluwer 2021).

Świątkiewicz J., *Europejski Kodeks Dobrej Administracji. Introduction, text and commentary on the application of the code in the conditions of Polish administrative procedures* (Warszawa 2007).

Szewczyk E., "Modyfikacje postępowań administracyjnych prowadzonych w okresie stanu zagrożenia epidemicznego lub stanu epidemii" (2020) 6 *Samorząd Terytorialny*.

Tabaszewski R., "The Permissibility of Limiting Rights and Freedoms in the European and National Legal System Due to Health Protection" (2020) 3 *Review of European and Comparative Law*, 54–57.
Thym D., "The End of Human Rights Dynamism? Judgments of the ECtHR on "Hot Returns and Humanitarian Visas as a Focal Point of Contemporary European Asylum Law and Policy,"" (2020) 32(4) *International Journal of Refugee Law*, 569–596.
Trociuk S., "Legal Aid for the Poor as a Form of Ensuring Effective Access to National and European Justice, in H. Izdebski and H. Machińska (eds), *Access of citizens to European justice* (Warszawa 2005) 14.
Trykhlib, K., "The Principle of Proportionality in the Jurisprudence of the European Court of Human Rights" (2020) 4 *EU and Comparative Law Issues and Challenges Series (ECLIC)*, 128–154.
Tuleja P., "Pandemia COVID-19 a konstytucyjne stany nadzwyczajne" (2020) 9 *Palestra*.
Tuleja P., "Temporary Ban on Border Zone and Humanitarian Crisis" (2022) 3–4 *Journal of Criminal Law and Penal Studies*.
Tuleja P., *Konstytucja Rzeczpospolitej Polskiej—Komentarz* (Warszawa 2023).
Ura E., Pieprzny S., and Pado T., "Pojęcie bezpieczeństwa publicznego w prawie administracyjnym," in J. Zimmermann (ed), *Koncepcja systemu prawa administracyjnego* (Warszawa 2007) 161–177.
Uhl P., "Ústavní zákon o bezpečnosti České republiky," in Rychetský P., Langášek T., Herc, and T., Mlsna (eds), *Petr a kol. Ústava České republiky. Ústavní zákon o bezpečnosti ČR. Komentář* (Praha: Wolters Kluwer 2015).
Waisová Š., "Od národní bezpečnosti k mezinárodní bezpečnosti. Kodaňská škola na křižovatce strukturálního realismu, anglické školy a sociálního konstruktivismu" (2004) 39(3) *Mezinárodní vztahy*, Ústav mezinárodních vztahů.
Wegner J., Wróblewski B., "Prawo jednostki do nieodpłatnej pomocy prawnej" (2021) 6 *Przegląd Prawa Publicznego*, 5.
Wellman C., *An Approach to Rights: Studies in the Philosophy of Laws and Morals* (Dordrecht 1997).
Widdershoven R., "National Procedural Autonomy and General EU Law Limits" (2019) 2 *Review of European Administrative Law*, 5–15.
Wintr J., "Úvaha nad vhodným nastavením nouzového stavu v českém právním řádu," in Šimíček, Vojtěch (ed), *Dělba moci* (Praha: Leges 2022).
Wissing R., *Push Backs of "Badly Behaving" Migrants at Spanish Border Are Not Collective Expulsions (But Might Still be Illegal Refoulements)* (Ghent: Human Rights Centre 2020).

Wouters C. W., *International Legal Standards for the Protection from Refoulement: a Legal Analysis on the Prohibitions on Refoulement Contained in the Refugee Convention, the European Convention on Human Rights, the International Covenant on Civil and Political Rights, and the Convention Against Torture* (Leiden 2009).

Wróbel A., in A. Wróbel, *Charter of Fundamental Rights of the European Union. Commentary* (Warszawa 2020) 1117–1126.

Wróblewski R., *Zarys teorii kryzysu. Zagadnienia prewencji i zarządzania kryzysami* (Warszawa 1996) 10.

Zdanowicz M., "The Migration Crisis on the Polish–Belarusian Border" (2023) 28(1) *Białostockie Studia Prawnicze—Bialystok Legal Studies* <https://doi.org/10.15290/bsp.2023.28.01.06>.

Ziegler R., "Political Rights of Aliens. Articles 10, 11 and 16 of the ECHR and Article 3 of Additional Protocol I," in D. Moya, and G. Milios (eds), *Aliens before the European Court of Human Rights. Ensuring Minimum Standards of Human Rights Protection* (Leiden: Brill 2021) 172–190.

Zimmermann J., *Prawo administracyjne* (Kraków 2006) 92.

Notes on contributors

Jacek Chlebny – law professor at the Department of Administrative Procedure and Judicial Review of Administration, University of Lodz; President of the Supreme Administrative Court of Poland.

Anna Chmielarz-Grochal – doctor of law, assistant professor at the Department of Administrative Procedure and Judicial Review of Administration, University of Lodz; specialist in the office of the President of the Supreme Administrative Court.

Paweł Dańczak – doctor of law, assistant professor at the Department of Administrative Proceedings and Judicial Review of Administration, University of Lodz; judge of the Voivodeship Administrative Court in Lodz, Poland.

Geert Debersaques – law professor at the Vrije Universiteit of Brussels, President of Chamber at the Council of State of Belgium.

Lilla Garayova – associate professor at the Department of International Law, Faculty of Law, Pan-European University, Slovakia; Vice-Dean of the Faculty of Law.

Fanny Jacquelot – lecturer in public law at the Faculty of Law of Saint-Etienne, Jean-Monnet University; member of the Chair of Comparative Public Law and Politics.

Michał Kowalski – habilitated doctor of law professor at the Leon Koźmiński Academy in Warsaw; judge of the Supreme Administrative Court of Poland.

Anke Meskens – auditeur (investigative magistrate) at the Council of State of Belgium.

Barbara Opalska – attorney at law specializing in human rights; Senior Officer at the European Union Agency for Asylum.

Paola Pannia – assistant professor of comparative constitutional law at the Department of Italian and Supranational Public Law, University of Milan (la Statale).

Wojciech Piątek – law professor at the Institute of Administrative and Judicial Administrative Procedure, Adam Mickiewicz University in Poznań; specialist in the office of the President of the Supreme Administrative Court of Poland.

Ivo Pospíšil – doctor of law and master in political science, assistant professor at the Department of International Relations and European Studies at Faculty of Social Studies of Masaryk University in Brno; judge of the Supreme Administrative Court of the Czech Republic.

Rafał Rogala – lawyer, longtime Head of the Office for Foreigners, specialist in immigration law, currently leading the immigration team at EY Poland.

Grzegorz Rząsa – doctor of law; judge of the Voivodeship Administrative Court in Warsaw (delegated to adjudicate in the Supreme Administrative Court of Poland).

Index

al-Gaddafi, Mu'ammar 39
Aliens Act 458–63
Amnesty International 51–2
Amsterdam Treaty 135, 314
Antidiscrimination Act (Act No. 365/2004 Coll. on Equal Treatment) 513, 515, 528, 529–30
anti-trafficking directives 502
Application de Gestion des dossiers des ressortissants étrangers en France (AGDEF2) 329
Apulia Law, No. 563/1995 358
Arab Spring 39–40, 42, 135, 354, 379
  Directive 2001/55/EC 362
  extraordinary reception plan 361
  illegal crossings 39–40
  migrants coming from Sub-Saharan Africa or Asia 363
  National Civil Protection Fund 361
  National Civil Protection Service 360
  repatriation of Tunisian 362
  responses to the crisis, 2015 40
  SPRAR reception system 361
  Treaty on Friendship, Cooperation and Partnership with Libya 363
arbitrary deprivation of liberty 51, 214
ARGUS system 65
armed conflicts 23, 34–5, 39, 46, 111, 135, 140, 165, 168, 183, 197, 199, 202, 216, 220, 287, 296, 319, 385, 404, 407–9, 411, 435, 499, 522, 535, 543, 547, 548
asylum law regulations 17

Balkan emergencies
  Apulia Law, No. 563/1995 358
  ARGUS system 65
  closure of the Balkan route 59
  control of irregular migration 359
  Decree No. 60/1997 359
  disparity of treatment 359
  financial aid by EU Commission 360
  Law Decree 24.07.1992 No. 350 357
  National Asylum Plan 360
  Reception Directive 2003/9/CE 360
  Shared Action 360
  SPRAR (Protection System for Asylum Seekers and Refugees) 360
  temporary protection measure 358
Belgium, procedural law perspective
  administrative authorities and courts, 274–83
    adequacy of the justification 275–6
    applications for international protection 283
    approach of avoiding or processing backlogs 283
    breach of the right to be heard 279
    Convention on the Rights of the Child 280
    Council for asylum and immigration proceedings 281, 284–5exceptions 282
    non-refoulement principle 284
    obligation to hear a concerned party 277
    principle of "audi et alteram partem" 278
    principle of carefulness 275
    prioritization by the legislator on applications 284
    right to be heard 276–7
    standards for functioning 274
    standards for proper organization 282
  administrative detention 267
  coercive measures 270–1
  Council of Alien Law Litigation 286
  Decision 2004/573/ EC 273

deprivation and restriction of liberty 267–71
entry and residence
application of the "state of emergency" 265
Article 53 ECHR 264
illegally staying status 267
Law Decree 265
Schengen Borders Code 266
identity verification 267–8
law on foreign nationals 270
legal framework 264–6
pending removal from the territory 268–9
Police Service Act 267, 272
remote hearing 286
technologies 286
use of force by security drivers 272
violence, legitimate purpose for 273
Belgium, substantive law perspective
Adult Education Decree 252
authorization to stay, exceptional circumstances
Article *9bis* 224–8
Article 8 of the ECHR 226–7
extraordinary circumstances 225–6
refusal 228
Centre for Adult Education or a Centre for Basic Education 252
Council for asylum and immigration proceedings of Belgium 220–1
Council of State of Belgium 221
deathbed cases 238, 241
Directive 2004/83/EC 235–6
D v United Kingdom 240
economic, social, and cultural rights 249–50
expulsion of migrants
Article 74/13 of the Law on foreign nationals 228
balancing of interests 229–30
context of Article 3 ECHR 243–4
context of Article 8 ECHR 228–31
Makdoudi case 231
private life in Article 8 ECHR 230
private or family life, examinations by the Courts 231
inquiry on potential violation of Article 3 ECHR 244
legal framework 222–3
medical condition and medical support 238
migration
Abdida case 234
application of article 9ter of the law on foreign nationals 237–9
Article 9bis of the law on foreign nationals 222–3, 224–228, 238
Article 10 of the law on foreign nationals 222
Article 9ter of the law on foreign nationals 222, 223, 233–43
Mohamed M'Bodj v Belgian State 234
N. v. the United Kingdom 234–5, 240–1
Paposhvili v Belgium 232–3, 241–2
participation in European Union law 20
personal rights
Article 10, 11 and 191 Constitution 244–5
differential treatment disadvantaging a foreigner 245
political rights
right to civil service 246
statutory or contractual functions 247
Ponomaryovi v. Bulgaria 251
prohibition of torture, degrading treatment or punishment under Article 3 ECHR 232
protective measure against refoulement or involuntary deportation 224
public service for social welfare 250
right to education 250–4
right to residence
Article 3 ECHR 239–42

Article 9ter of the Law on foreign nationals 233–7
in the context of Article 8 ECHR 224–8
residence permit on medical grounds 233–42
right to social allowances 254–3
solidarity rights
concept of residence 257
inviolability of the home 257–63
proactive collaboration, return places and police services 263
regulatory conundrum in the Belgian legal order 259
right to live in peace 257–63
Sabani v. Belgium 258
standstill principle 255
state of emergency
Article 187 of the Constitution 220–1
regulatory, and punitive measures 221
system of formal restrictions 221
subsidiary protection in case of illness under Article 48/4 242–3
risk of serious harm 243
Berlin Wall, fall of 45
Bigo, D. 113–14
Bossi-Fini Law, Law No. 189/2002 353

Carrera, S. 72, 89, 135
The Charter of Fundamental Rights of the European Union (CFR) 88, 98, 146, 148–51, 215–16, 337, 453
Article 18 106
Equality between Women and Men, Article 23 153
Freedom of Expression and Information, Article 11 152
Freedom to Choose an Occupation and Right to Engage in Work, Article 15 152
healthcare, Article 35 154
Principle of Non-Refoulement, Article 19 153
Prohibition of Discrimination, Article 21 153
Prohibition of Torture, Inhuman, or Degrading Treatment or Punishment, Article 4 151
Rights of the Child, Article 24 154
Right to an Effective Remedy and a Fair Trial, Article 47 155
Right to Asylum, Article 18 152
Right to Education, Article 14 152
Right to Good Administration, Article 41 155
Right to Human Dignity, Article 1 151
Right to Respect for Private and Family Life including Family Reunification under EU Law, Article 7 151
Right to the Protection of Personal Data, Article 8 151
Social Security and Social Assistance, Article 34 154
clandestinity 353
climate change 23–4, 34, 164, 168, 197
climatic anomalies 23
protective measures 24
threat to fundamental values 24, 197
Code on the Entry and Residence of Foreigners and the Right of Asylum (CESEDA) 313–14, 320, 329
Common European Asylum System (CEAS) 123, 147, 150, 155, 157, 492
A common path to a safe and sustainable reopening 91
Common Security and Defense Policy (CSDP) 48
Community Customs Code 31
threats to public policy, internal security, or public health 31
Conseil d'Etat 309, 311, 317, 321, 322–4, 327–8, 332, 335, 336, 337, 341

Consolidated Law on Migration 345
Convention for the Protection of Human Rights and Fundamental Freedoms 28, 166–7, 328, 403, 420, 432, 466
  Article 15(1), possibility of restrictions (derogations) 28
Convention on the Elimination of All Forms of Discrimination Against Women (CEDAW) 525, 527
Convention on the Rights of Persons with Disabilities (CRPD) 525, 530, 536
Convention on the Rights of the Child (UNCRC) 280, 502, 507, 517, 525, 526
Court of Justice of the European Union (CJEU) 61–4, 71, 86, 216, 234–5, 247, 248, 260, 454, 464, 471–2
COVID-19 pandemic 18, 23–4, 68, 547, 548–9
  impact on freedom of movement 549
  law 107
  migration crisis, triggered by pandemic
    agricultural labor shortages 95
    Article 45 of TFEU 97
    Article 35 of the Charter of Fundamental Rights 88
    Article 72 TFEU 88
    borders closed to all EU and EFTA members 84
    Case C-128/22, judgement 86–7
    categories of cross-border workers 96
    concept of public order 88
    COVID-19 law 107
    crisis in migration flows in Europe 107
    Directive 2004/38/EC 87
    disruption, principle of free movement of people 83
    essential and non-essential travel 84
    EU guidelines 97
    first reactions to the pandemic crisis 83–9
    labor migrants 95–8
    marginalization 108
    Nordic Info ruling 87
    Poland's response *see* Poland's response to the pandemic
    reinforcement of orthodox approaches 108
  outbreak 280
  response from EU bodies
    challenges 95
    communication on the temporary restriction of non-essential travel 90
    Council Recommendation (EU) 2022/2548 91–2
    digital green certificates 91
    discretion, effects of 90
    ECDC 93
    EU Digital COVID Certificate 91–2
    exceptions to travel restrictions 94
    Instrument for Reconstruction and Enhanced Resilience 93
    list of safe third countries 93
    Next Generation EU, Recovery Plan for Europe 92–3
    REACT-EU program 93
    Recommendation (EU) 2020/912 91
    Regulation (EU) 2021/953 91
    testing and quarantine measures 94
    traffic light system 93–4
  restrictions on the movement 83
  SBC, mechanisms *see* Schengen Borders Code (SBC)
  selective approach to mobility 96
  selective border controls 84
  situation of applicants for international protection
    Common European Asylum System, fragmented nature 98–9
  soft law *see* soft law
  temporary reintroduction of border controls 87

temporary resumption of border controls 85
travel restrictions 84
violations of fundamental rights 107
weaknesses of the Schengen mechanism 144
COVID-19 Special Law 104
crimmigration 114
Crisis Act 289, 290, 300, 302–4
Czech Republic, states of emergency
Article 43(4) of the Constitution 26
concept of a defensive (or militant) democracy 287
Constitution 286–7, 288
Constitutional Security Act 289
COVID -19 outbreak 287
Crisis Act 290
description 288–9
during the floods 289
human rights, restrictions on
crisis measures 302–3
declared state of national emergency 303
emergency 301–2
freedom of movement and residence 301
legal regulation with the force of a sub-legislative regulation 302
limitation of rights in general 300–1
Pandemic Act 303
legal system 548
protection of rights, procedural guarantees 306–8
regulation of states of emergency 288–91
resolution Pl. ÚS 8/20 290
restrictions on rights and obligations 291
rights of foreigners, restrictions on
Act on the residence of foreigners 304
ban on the entry during COVID-19 305–6
control or prevention of an epidemic 305
Crisis Act 304
Public Health Protection Act 304–5
right to assemble 301
right to engage in business 301
right to inviolability 300
right to strike 301
state of national emergency 290
state of war 291
types of states of emergency 288
Czech Republic, substantive law perspective
Act No. 83/1990 Coll., on the Association of Citizens 293, 515
Act No. 325/1999 Coll., on Asylum 294, 304
Act No. 326/1999 Coll., on the Residence of Foreigners 286–7
Act No. 561/2004 Coll., on education 294, 304
Asylum Act 288–9
Charter of Fundamental Rights and Freedoms 299
concept of constitutional order 293
concept of vulnerable persons 298–9
Foreigners Residence Act 296
guarantee of property rights 296–7
institutional framework of protection 291–6
interests of the child 297–8
issues of human rights of migrants 296–300
migration policy 294
national humanitarian asylum 296
political rights and guarantee of social rights 299
protection of rights, procedural guarantees 299
measures to protect the health of the parties 308
participation in a hearing 307

rules of procedure to conduct hearings 308
1951 Refugee Convention and 1967 Protocol 291, 293
residence permits 295
right of a foreigner to private and family life 292
rights and obligations of the child as a child 298
right to adequate material security 300
right to asylum to foreigners 292
right to free healthcare 299
subsidiary protection 296
unlawful conduct 297
Visapoint system 295

Decreto Flussi 349, 382
defensive (or militant) democracy, concept of 287
Delhomme 88
den Hertog, L. 72
deportations 53, 55, 174, 180, 188, 195–6, 232, 239, 325, 338, 353
automatic 334
exceptional cases 546
hot returns 109
involuntary 224
Turkey criticized for 75
types of 333–4
derogations in time of emergency
application of derogation clause
assessment of compliance 203–4
ECHR 202–3
ECtHR 202
limitation clauses 202–3
measures taken during the COVID-19 208
mechanism, human rights conventions 172
public danger, life threatening
recognition of war 204–7
situation at particular time 205, 216
restriction of the rights and freedoms
Article 54 CFR 215–16
Article 52(3) of the CFR 215
limitation as an exception 215–16
rights of refugees and immigrants
Article 15(2) ECHR 208–9
measures relating to the right to liberty and security 210, 216–7
restrictions, COVID-19 pandemic 210
suspension
Article 2(3) ICCPR 214
Article 4(2) of the ICCPR, suspension of obligations 211–12
catalog of rights, absolute prohibition of derogation 213
concept of exceptional public danger 212–13
conditions for the suspension of obligations 212
most favoured nation clause 212
of obligations under the ICCPR, conditions 212–15
prohibition of discriminatory measures 213
of rights and freedoms in ICCPR 210
Terhes v. Romania 207
termination of derogation 548
discrimination
positive 388
prohibition of 547
dogmatic-legal method research 21

eastern border crisis, European Union's 144
e-Asylum Portal 503, 537, 540
Effective Protection of Human Rights in Situations of Crisis and Its Draft Explanatory Memorandum of 2024 208
e-Government Portal 537
e-identification and biometric systems 538
emergency
ad hoc responses to 27

assistance to third-country nationals 33
border control measures 128, 552
conditions in the refugee's country of origin 33
consequence of successive emergencies 27
constitutive features 24
contexts 544
and crisis 25
definitions 24
impact on life 25
interruption of public authorities functioning 26
joint response from countries 27
legal regulations 25–6
martial law 26
modern 24
need for essential health care and medical treatment 33
possibility of restrictions (derogations) 28
recognized state of 25
regulations for 548–9
risks 33
situations
Directive 2008/115/EC, EU legislator 32
state of emergency 27
threat arising from unexpected phenomenon 29
temporal constraints 25
temporary, recognized state 25
temporary deviation from the ordinary rules of law 56
threat arising from unexpected phenomenon 29
threat from third-country nationals 33
threat of human health or life 25
time of *see* time of emergency
emergency response mechanism
COVID-19 *see* COVID-19 pandemic
derogations *see* derogations in time of emergency
human rights *see* human rights, EU law perspective; human rights, international law perspective
migration *see* migration
equal treatment of parties 18
EU Dublin system 60
EU Med Group 157
EU migration policy 52, 54–5, 70, 73, 113, 132, 143, 145, 163
EU Pact on Migration and Asylum and Regulation on the European Border and Coast Guard 502
European Agenda on Migration 46, 49
fight against organized crime 46, 47
mechanisms for the relocation and resettlement 47
European Asylum Support Office (EASO) 48, 60–1, 90, 95, 97, 488, 493
European Border and Coast Guard Agency 97, 446–8
European Border Surveillance System (EUROSUR) 44–5
European Centre for Disease Prevention and Control (ECDC) 93
European Convention on Human Rights (ECHR) 51, 75, 124, 148–9, 170, 176, 221, 223–49, 280, 291, 314, 336, 349, 431, 433, 484, 501, 507, 510, 512, 513, 522, 523
European Court of Human Rights (ECtHR) 75, 109, 124, 148, 166, 186, 199, 229–32, 234, 241–2, 251, 258, 315, 322, 365, 377, 433, 435, 455, 458, 496, 546
European Fisheries Control Agency 78
European Free Trade Association (EFTA) 84, 400, 471
European Maritime Safety Agency 78
European Pact on Migration and Asylum 147–8, 155, 157, 161, 164
EU law perspective
The Asylum and Migration Management Regulation 160

The Asylum Procedures Regulation 158
Common European Asylum System 157
The Crisis and Force Majeure Regulation 161
EU Asylum Agency 156
The EU Asylum Agency Regulation 159
EU Med Group 157
The Eurodac Regulation 159
New Pact on Migration and Asylum 156
The Qualification Regulation 159
Reform of the CEAS 2016 155
The Return Border Procedure Regulation 158
The revised Reception Conditions Directive 158
The Screening Regulations 161
The Union Resettlement and Humanitarian Admission Framework Regulation 160–1
implementation plan
adequate reception conditions 162
Common Migration and Asylum Information System 162
effective and fair return procedures 163
enhanced safeguards for asylum applicants and vulnerable persons 163
fair, efficient and convergent asylum procedures 163
fair and efficient responsibility-sharing mechanism 163
new system for managing migration at the EU external borders 162
preparedness, contingency planning and crisis response 163
resettlement, inclusion, and integration 163
European Trust Fund
countering the root causes of irregular migration 76
drawbacks 76–7
Emergency Trust Fund for Africa 76
evidence-based targeting 77
Forced Displacement in Africa 76
implementation of short-term objectives 77
instrument of migration policy 78
European Union Agency for Asylum (EASO) 159–60, 488, 493, 541
European Union migration policy 55
Europol 48, 95, 114
EU-Turkey Agreement (Statement)
Article 218 TFEU 71
bilateral agreement between the EU and Turkey 66–7
changes by Council Decision 2016/1754 69
criticism 74–5
Directive 2013/32/ EU 69
intra-EU relocation mechanism 69
legality of 70
mechanism for the systematic and speedy return 69
non-refoulement obligation 70
operational approach 74
political declaration by representatives 71
Refugee Facility for Turkey 69
repercussions. 73
tensions between migration policy goals 73
two-phase financing plan 69
use of the “Community method” of cooperation 72
exceptional circumstances 26, 85, 121, 125, 172, 187, 222–8, 230, 240–1, 242, 288, 309, 506
exceptional public danger, concept of 210, 212–13, 215–16, 547

export act 430
expulsion
  of aliens 181–2
  Belgium
    Article 74/13 of the Law on foreign nationals 228
    balancing of interests 229
    context of Article 3 ECHR 243–4
    context of Article 8 ECHR 228–31
    Makdoudi case 231
    private life in Article 8 ECHR 230
    private or family life, examinations by the Courts 231
  measures, France 337
  obligation to leave French territory or expulsion 333–4
  prohibition of collective expulsion 169, 174, 181, 193, 551–2
  protection of foreigners against 431
  of a refugee, Geneva Convention, 1951 466
external borders, European Union's
  closure of 98
  essential travel 90
  response capabilities 44
  strengthening of 545
externalization of migration policy *see* migration crisis, 2015-2016
extraordinary legal measures 18
extraordinary reception centers 366, 369, 372, 375–6, 381

Forti, M. 131
Foschi Law 344
France, procedural law perspective
  2015 Code of Relations between the Public and the Administration 335
  Directorate-General for Foreigners in France 336
  emergency, special entry and residence procedures 334–5
    Article 25 of Regulation (EU) 2016/399 334
    internal border controls 335
  entering France
    Aliens Code 332, 333
    conditions for refusal 332
    residence permit 332
    Schengen Borders Code 333
    visa, regular entry 333
  health emergency adaptations
    administrative authorities/ administrative justice 338–9
    hearings 339
    Ordinance no. 2020-328 338
    validity of asylum application certificates 338
  new technologies
    in administrative and legal proceedings 339–40
    ANEF account 340–1
    digital transformation 340electronic registered letter 339–40
    online procedures 340–1
    specifically for third-country nationals 341
  pandemic, disruptions in the asylum procedure 550–1
  removal from French territory 333–4
    ban on leaving 334
    deportation, types 333–4
    obligation to leave French territory or expulsion 333–4
  right to a judge
    administrative court 336–7
    deportation order 338
    discretion when issuing visas 336
    expulsion measures 337
    OQTF 337
  special procedures on the entry and residence 332
  standard entry and residence procedure 333
  state of emergency is provided for by Article 16 26

third-country nationals and authorities, relations 335–6
two mechanisms 548–9
France, substantive law perspective
asylum, right to
Article L. 741-1 of the CESEDA 320
CESEDA 313–14
conditional freedom 310
domestic sources of asylum law 313–14
Emergency Health Law no. 2020-290 320
external sources of asylum law 314
law no. 2024-42 to control immigration 321
malfunctioning of the asylum system 319–21
National Court for the Right of Asylum 313
OFII platform 320
OFPPIR 313
OFPRA 313, 314, 315
Paris Administrative Tribunal 319, 320
refugee status 314–15
right to migrate 311
subsidiary protection 314–15
economic, social, and cultural rights
adaptations during emergency periods 331
"businesses get involved" portal 331
right to work 331
temporary worker or employee residence permit 330
work permit 330
emergency standards
Law no. 2020-290, COVID-19 crisis 310
Public Health Code 310
state of emergency 309–10
state of siege 309
exceptional circumstances 309
family reunification, restrictions on 322–3
family reunification visas 322
long-stay visa 322
individual freedom
administrative detention 324–5
Article L. 743-13 of the Foreign Nationals Code 325
Article L. 3115-10 of the Public Health Code 327
house arrest 325–6
Law no. 2011-467 326
personal freedom of foreign nationals 326–7
placing foreign nationals in isolation 327
problems during emergency under 1955 law 326
problems during health emergency 327
ordinance no. 2020-312 324
personal rights
Article R. 142-11 of the CESEDA 329
data protection 329
detention of illegal immigrants 324
French Data Protection Act no. 78-17 329
health 323–4
political rights, Law no. 81-908 329
privacy
issue of vaccines 328
Prime Ministerial Instruction no. 6268-SG 328
protection, types of
constitutional asylum 316–17
conventional asylum 317–18
Directive 2011/95/EU 318
fear of persecution 318
OFPRA, conditions 316–17
subsidiary protection, Directive 2002/90/EC 319

Protection Universelle Maladie (PUMA) 323
restrictions on freedom of movement 321–2
temporary protection 311–12
European Directive 2001/55/EC 311–12
status to Ukrainians 312
vulnerable groups, human rights
Immigration law no. 2024-42 332
unaccompanied minors, specific asylum rights 331–2
France Asylum 321
French Office for Immigration and Integration (OFPRA) 313, 314, 316–17, 320–21, 330, 332, 336
French Office for the Protection of Refugees and Stateless Persons (OFPPIR) 313
Frontex 44–5, 47–8, 52–3, 78, 95, 97, 163, 447–8, 488, 502, 504
Fundamental Rights Agency (FRA) 53

General Data Protection Regulation (GDPR) 510–11, 539
Geneva Convention, 1951 52, 71, 106, 115, 152, 159, 170, 345, 358, 547
Article 19 of the Charter of Fundamental Rights 432
exceptions to the prohibition of refoulement 175, 349, 547
exclusion clause in Article 1 318
expulsion of a refugee 466
inconsistency, Article 19 of the Charter of Fundamental Rights 432
international treaty 116
Refugees and EU treaties 154
Status of Refugees 124, 134, 170, 175, 198–9, 315, 317, 491–2, 546
Gerbaudo, M. 132
Germany
applications to 46
asylum applications 46, 59
border controls in emergency 59, 85
criticized for opening its borders 59
imposition of martial law 26
onward movement to other EU countries 41
Gkliati, M. 115, 132
Global Approach to Migration and Mobility 45
Goldner Lang, I. 122
Greenhill, K.M. 108–9, 112
Guild, E. 123, 126

Halilović 55
Helsinki Foundation for Human Rights 434
hot returns 109, 193
hotspots
absence of legal framework 49, 54–5
advanced intelligence mechanisms 53
anti-migrant security measures 53
Council Decisions 2015/1523 and 2015/1601 50
COVID-19 pandemic 55
criticisms 51–3
2015 European Agenda on Migration 49
heavy intelligence mechanisms 53
hotspot approach in Italy 50
to support frontline states in managing migration 51
lack of clear guidelines and standards 49, 54
Law No. 4375/2016 50
migrants as objects of risk 52
New Pact on Migration and Asylum 55
operation of 49, 51, 53–4
reception and identification centres 50
Screening Regulation 56
transformation of Greek hotspots 56
use of illegal pushback practices 52
see also migration

human rights, EU law perspective
Asady and Others v. Slovakia 194
Common European Asylum System 147, 150
ECHR 148
ECtHR 148
EU Charter of Fundamental Rights of the European Union 148
EU primary law 148
European Pact on Migration and Asylum 147, 155–61
building blocks 162–3
implementation plan 161–4
National Implementation Plan 161
fundamental rights of migrants in international law 167–72
guarantees of migrants' rights 176–82
Hirsi Jamaa and Others v. Italy 192
international law perspective 164–7
New Pact on Migration and Asylum 147
non-refoulement, principle of 147–8, 172–6
protection of migrants' rights 186–97
Treaty-based human rights protections 149
Treaty on European Union articles 148–9
Treaty on the Functioning of the European Union 147, 148
relevant Articles 149–50
human rights, international law perspective 164, 198
Convention for the Protection of Human Rights and Fundamental Freedoms 165
EU Pact on Migration and Asylum 198
European Court of Human Rights 165, 199
European law 165
fight against terrorism or illegal immigration 199–200
foreigners' rights, protection of 198
fundamental rights of migrants 165
civil and political rights 168
Convention relating to the Status of Refugees 167
derogation, act of/mechanism 169, 172
development of new technologies, bioethics 168
ECHR 169
economic, social and cultural rights 168
ECtHR 169
freedoms and solidarity rights 168
Geneva Convention Relating to the Status of Refugees 170
ICCPR 169
ICESCR 169
interference with fundamental rights, conditions 171
international agreements 167
limitations on human rights 169, 171
principle of non-discrimination 169
principle of non-refoulement 169
prohibition of collective expulsion 169
prohibition of inhuman or degrading treatment 171
prohibition of racism 170
prohibition of torture 171
UDHR 169
Universal Declaration of Human Rights 170
guarantees of migrant's rights 176
abolition of the death penalty 177–8
additional Protocols to the ECHR that apply to foreigners 181
Article 2 ECHR 177
Article 3 ECHR 178
Article 5 ECHR 178
Article 6 ECHR 179
Article 13 ECHR 180
Article 15(2) ECHR 177, 178

ECHR and its additional Protocols 176–7
expulsion of aliens 181–2
principle of non-discrimination 179
prohibition of collective expulsion of aliens 181
prohibition of deprivation of liberty 180
right to life 177
right to the free assistance of an interpreter 180
statutory restrictions 181
human rights instruments 165
international legal protection 164–5
mass migrations 164–5
M.K. and Others v. France 195
Muhammad and Muhammad v. Romania 195, 472–3
N.D. and N.T. v. Spain 193–5, 482
protection of migrants' rights 186–97, 545
allegations of violations 191
applicants' own behaviour, concept of 194
COVID-19 pandemic, exceptional circumstances 187
ECHR and ECtHR 189–90, 195
effective remedy 196
immigration status 190
interim measures 196–7
jurisprudence on migrants and refugees 195
legitimacy of the exclusion 196
migratory detention 188
principle of non-refoulement 188
private life, scope of 191
prohibition of arbitrary detention 188
prohibition of discrimination 190
risk of loss of life 188
standards for the protection of aliens 192
violation of the prohibition of collective expulsion 193
violations of the principle of non-refoulement 192
restrictions, permissibility of 183
ECHR's limitation clauses 184
freedom of expression 185
ICESCR 183
interference with rights or freedoms 183–4
legitimate objective for interference 185
pressing social need 185
restrictions through ICCPR, 186
UDHR 183
Shahzad v. Hungary 194
Human Rights Watch 51
hybrid war 127–8, 428, 431, 436, 480
hypocrisy trap 120

Idlib crisis 69
Ineli-Ciger, M. 135–9, 137
Integrated Political Crisis Response (IPCR) 65–6
interim measures 196
International Convention on the Protection of the Rights of All Migrant Workers and Members of Their Families 167
International Covenant on Civil and Political Rights (ICCPR) 165, 169, 174, 183–4, 186, 198, 207–17, 228, 284, 477, 487, 504–5, 547–8
Article 4 28
International Covenant on Economic, Social and Cultural Rights (ICESCR) 167, 169, 183, 198, 517, 520, 528
International human rights law 75, 165, 167–9, 171–5, 183, 192, 197–8, 546–7
Italy
Constitution 346
constitutional provisions 346–7
interpretation of the Constitutional Court 348

personalist principle of Article 2 346
rights of emigrants 346
emergency concept 342
emergency lexicon, ambiguities 382
ex post regularization schemes 382
extraordinary measures 382
immigration, recent history 343–5
geographical limitation 345
harsh immigration law 344
oil crisis 345
post-war economic boom 345
proportion of foreign residents 344
immigration law
Arab Spring 354
attempts to regulate migration (1980–1997) 352
back-and-forths movements 354
Common European Asylum System 354
Consolidated Law on Immigration 354–5
crime of clandestinity 353
D. Lgs. No. 142/2015 354
Decree-Law No. 78/2009 354
entropic phase (2018–2023) 354–5
Law Decree No. 1/2023 355
Law Decree No. 20/2023 355
Law Decree No. 46/2017 354
Law Decree No. 130/2020 355
Law No. 39/1990 352
Law No. 40/1998 352
Law No. 173/2020 355
Law No. 189/2002, Bossi-Fini Law 353
Laws No. 125/2008 and No. 94/2009, security packages 346
Legislative Decree No. 286/1998, Consolidated Law 353
normative changes (1998–2013) 352
policy of "closed port" 355
reformist phase (2014–2017) 354
stages 351
system of sponsorship 353
lacks national control room 379
Law Decrees, role of 380
legal status
Consolidated Law on Immigration 348
discretionary decision of Italian authorities 349
entry quota 350
EU Visa Code 349
legal treatments 350–1
selection of beneficiaries of social measures 3
system of quota 349–50
migrants, definition 342
migration crisis
agreement with Tunisia 40
Article 5 of Law No. 225/1992 on the Protection of Civilians 40
hotspots as centers for identification and redistribution 54
Lampedusa Crisis 40
smuggled migrants 342
Italy, substantial and procedural perspective of foreigners' rights
Apulia Law, No. 563/1995 358
Arab Spring *see* Arab Spring
Balkan, emergency *see* Balkan emergencies
Consolidated Law on Immigration: Article 35 356
COVID and regularization
Italian harbors as unsafe places 370
Quarantine ships 370
regularization of undocumented workers 371
restrictionist approach of the Salvini Decree 369
emergency, current state of
agreement Italy-Albania and safe third countries of origin 377–8
Albania Protocol 378

Civil Protection Ordinance 927/2022 372
declaration of a new state of emergency 374
Decree-Law No. 20/2023 374
Decree-Law No. 21 372
Decree-Law No. 50 372
Directive 55/2001 373
ethnicization 373
examination of asylum applications 377–8
extraordinary reception centers 372, 375
hypothesis of detentions 375–6
Law Decree No. 133 377
NGOs activities of search and rescue 374
ordinary system of reception 372
reforms and new state of emergency 374–7
residence permit for special protection 374–5
six-month state of emergency 376
socio-health assessments 377
temporary centers 375
widespread reception 372
infringement of a procedural right, consequences 357
Law Decree 356
refugee crisis
agreement with Tunisia 40
Article 5 of Law No. 225/1992 on the Protection of Civilians 40
"de facto" detention 364
extraordinary reception centers 366
hotspots as centers for identification and redistribution 54
illegitimate practices 364–5
Lampedusa Crisis 40
Law Decree No. 13/2017 368
Law Decree No. 130/2020 367
Legislative Decree No. 142/2015 365
management of arrivals and hotspots approach 363–5
photo-identification and fingerprinting 364
reforms for international protection procedure 368–9
reforms to restructure national reception system 365–8
Salvini Decree 367
system of hotspots 364
Territorial Commission 368

Johansson, Ylva 127, 128
jus sanguinis criterion 352

Klaus, W. 105
Kriesi, H. 81
Kurdi, Aylan 59

Lampedusa Crisis 40–1, 44, 46, 365
Landsbergis, Gabrielius 127
Lisbon Treaty 72, 150
Lukashenko, Alexander 106, 110, 118, 128, 143–4, 427

Malmström, Cecilia 42, 135
Malta Summit 48
Martelli Law 352
mass migration 17, 39, 143
crisis situations 544, 551
logistical challenges 504
means to achieve specific political goals 480
risks 544
Russia and Ukraine, conflict 523
social phenomenon 164–5
threat to state security 143
violations of fundamental rights 177
McLeod, M. 101
Mediterranean migration crisis 136
megatrends 488–9
Merkel, Angela 59

Middle East
  conflicts/hostilities 23–4, 37
  influx of refugees from 144, 363, 410, 427
  protection and development programs 48
  Regional Development and Protection Programs 48, 58
migration 545
  crisis, triggered by pandemic *see* COVID-19 pandemic
  Europe, examples in
    Belarus, pressure on EU 111
    Morocco, migration as a tool to pressure Spain 109
    Operation Sluice 111
    Spain, hot returns by 109
    Turkey, migration as a tool to pressure the EU 110
  EU's response 115
  2016 EU-Turkey agreement 112
  externalization *see* migration crisis, 2015-2016
  instrumentalization of
    ban-optics 113
    border controls 112
    broader securitization of migration 112
    communication 115
  intensified during COVID-19 pandemic 109
  as opportunity for development 146
  phenomenon of 112
  Polish-Belarusian border 127
    hotspot approach 132
    instrumentalization 129–30
    law on granting protection to foreigners 130–1
    new migration strategy 129
    state of emergency 128
  reason 23
  restrictive policies 552
  securitization
    crimmigration 114
    emergency measures 113
    threat, creating and escalating 114
  see also European Pact on Migration and Asylum; migration and asylum pacts
migration and asylum pacts
  alternative control measures 119
  Asylum Procedure Regulation 124
  asylum tourism 125
  Common European Asylum System 123
  cooperation between Member States 120
  creation of a European-level response mechanism 119
  definition of instrumentalization 118–9, 121
  ECHR 124
  EU Resettlement Framework Regulation 125
  Eurodac Regulation 125
  European Union Asylum Agency 126
  hypocrisy trap 120
  New Pact on Migration and Asylum, pillers 117–19, 123
  non-refoulement, adherence to 127
  Qualification Regulation 124
  Reception Conditions Directive 125
  Regulation (EU) 2021/1147 121
  Regulation on the Instrumentalization 120
  restrictive interpretations of asylum rights 126
  revised Schengen Borders Code 118
  Screening Regulation 124
  Temporary Protection Directive 122
migration crisis, 2015-2016
  actions prior to apogee
    European Agenda on Migration 46–7
    EUROSUR 44
    increased number of asylum applications 45–6

intensive migration in the Aegean Sea 46
Operation *EUNAVFOR MED* 47
Operation *Mare Nostrum* 44–5
Operations *Triton* and *Poseidon* 47
protection and development programs in North Africa 48
temporary relocation schemes 47–8
TFM, establishment of 44
2013 amendments to the Schengen Borders Code 43
Arab Spring and repercussions *see* Arab Spring
armed conflicts in Syria and Libya 39
civil war in Libya in 2011 41–2
controls at the French-Italian border 42
crisis management mechanisms
Integrated Political Crisis Response 65–6
Western Balkans Contact Group, the ARGUS system 65
"de facto" detention 364
Directive 2008/115/EC on the return of illegal migrants 41
escalation of international tensions 82
EU migration policies, shortcomings and limitations, 79–80
2015 *European Agenda on Migration* 49
European Border and coast guard, establishment of 78
European Trust Fund 76–8
EU-Turkey Agreement *see* EU-Turkey Agreement (Statement)
externalization of migration 545
externalization of border management 66–7
migration crisis 66
Migration Partnership Framework Mechanism 68
France, closure of southern border with Italy 41
freedom of movement and internal security 43
hotspots
approach in Italy 50–1
Greek, transformation of 56
management of arrivals 363–5
system of 364
see also hotspots
humanitarian approaches 82
illegitimate practices 364–5
internal border controls 42
Italy *see* Italy
lack of cohesion and solidarity 144
Law Decree No. 13/2017 368
Law Decree No. 130/2020 367
legal indeterminacy, state of 40
Legislative Decree No. 142/2015 365
Member States' response 81
migration as a political tool 81–2
New Pact on Migration and Asylum 55
photo-identification and fingerprinting 364
pushback practices 52
reception and identification centres (RICs) 50
reduced movement of Ukrainian refugees 79
reforms for international protection procedure 368–9
reforms to restructure national reception system 365–8
Regional Protection Program in North Africa 42
regulations on illegal migration 39
relocation and resettlement
Article 78(3) of the TFEU, use of 62
asylum applications of Syrians, process by Germany 59
challenges 60
2020 CJEU ruling, effects 63–4
differences between citizens and migrants 63
EU Council Decision 2015/1601 62
EU Dublin system 60
EU's response 58

EU's unpreparedness for the massive influx 57
joined cases C-715/17, C-718/17 and C-719/17, judgment 63
joined cases C-643/15 and C-647/15, judgment 61
legal analysis of the mechanism 60–1
mandatory relocation system 61
mechanism for 58
priority resettlement regions 58
Temporary Protection Directive 2001/55/ EC 57
temporary relocation mechanism 59–60, 63
response of states and the EU 38
restrictive practices 79–80
risk of human rights violations 80
Salvini Decree 367
Schengen border
code reform 42–3
Schengen Evaluation and Monitoring Mechanism 43
Schengen spirit 41
screening regulation 56
situation as migration crisis or asylum crisis 80
structure, EU-Turkey agreement or the coordination 79
Territorial Commission 368
Montaldo, S. 86
multifunctional pilot center at Niger 48

national humanitarian asylum 296
national regulations of selected legal orders 19
natural disaster, concept of 398
New Pact on Migration and Asylum 17, 55, 117–19, 123, 147, 156, 436, 438, 552
New York Protocol, 1967 314, 492
Next Generation EU 47
non-refoulement, principle of 73–4, 147–8, 169, 188, 545, 547, 551
adherence to 127, 176
Article 19 153
Article 33(1) of the Refugee Convention 173
Belgium 277
Convention against Torture and Other Cruel, Inhuman or Degrading Treatment or Punishment 174
description 173
ECtHR jurisprudence, developed through 174–5
EU-Turkey Agreement (statement) 70
in international human rights law 172–6
Poland 472–3
prohibition of extradition, deportation, expulsion 174
prohibition of refoulement 173
Slovakia 493
violations of 192

one-stop shop system for asylum seekers 321
openness of proceedings, principles of 18
Operation *EUNAVFOR MED* (Operation Sophia) 47
Operation *Mare Nostrum* 44–5
Operation Sluice 111
Operations *Triton* and *Poseidon* 47
Operation Terra 440
ordinary system of reception (SAI) 372

Pact on Migration and Asylum *see* European Pact on Migration and Asylum
Pandemic Act (No. 94/2021 Coll.,) 303
peremptory rights 216, 547
Pietras-Eichberger, M. 62
Poland, procedural law perspective
Consular Law 449
COVID-19 pandemic
preventing, counteracting and combating solutions 413–14
restrictions 414–15

crisis at the EU external border, Polish-Belarusian border *see* Polish-Belarusian border
direct coercion 443–6
bringing 445
enforcing the decision to oblige a foreigner to return 445
and firearms 444
placement in isolation room 445
principle of proportionality 444
use of physical force 444–5
entry and stay of a foreigner 453
acts of a soft-law 454
Aliens Act 461–3
Article 31(3) 465
Article 6 ECHR 468
Article 12(2) of Directive 2008/115/EC 459
Article 327(2) of the Aliens Act 459
Article 52(1) of the CFR 465
C-300/11, *ZZ v Secretary of State for the Home Department* 472
C-403/16, *El Hassani v Minister of Foreign Affairs* 471
C-949/19, *M.A. v Consul of the Republic of Poland* 471
Charter of Fundamental Rights of the European Union CFR 453
Convention for the Protection of Human Rights and Fundamental Freedoms 466
Convention relating to the Status of Refugees 466
Directive 2016/801 471
domestic law 465
ECtHR and ECHR 458
entry and stay 458–9
European Code of Good Administration 454
foreigner's access to a case file 466
independence and autonomy of judges 467
independent court, decision 472
instruction to a foreigner about his/her rights 459
international protection 460
2018 judgments of the SAC 458
Muhammad and Muhammad v. Romania 472
oral translations of procedural statements 460
participation of a translator 462
Poklikayew v. Poland 472
principle of equal treatment of the parties 456
principle of openness of proceedings 457
principle of proportionality 464
procedural justice 467
procedural rights of the parties, limitations 463
provisions of the CAP 453, 455–6
public order 464
public security 463
Recommendation CM/Rec (2007)7 454
Regner v Czech Republic 472
return decision, factual justification 465
right to a court, structural elements 467
right to effective judicial protection 469–70
right to good administration 453
right to participation in administrative proceedings 460
system of disciplinary responsibility 468
equal treatment of foreigners, principle of 451, 482
Article 37(1) and Article 37(2) 451–2
constitutional freedoms and rights, limitations 451–2
criterion of nationality 451
principles of equivalence 452

European Border and Coast Guard Agency, cooperation with 446–8
Operation Terra 447
physical and electronic barriers 448
selected border crossings, officers to 447
foreigners' rights, restrictions
Alien Act 480
Article 100d of the Law on assistance to citizens of Ukraine 479
Article 19(2) of the CFR 481
Article 15zzs4 of the COVID Law 474
Code of Civil Procedure 475
COVID-19 pandemic, restrictions related 474
crisis situation 473–474
migration cases 47
Mirovni Inštitut v Slovenia 476
N.D. and N.T. v. Spain 482
non-refoulement, principle of 480–1
PESEL number with the addition of UKR 477
principle of publishing the decisions 468
regulations in response to the mass influx of migrants 480
Schengen Borders Code 480
general procedure
accidental border crossing 424–5
border control 421–2
Border Guard, tasks 421–3
illegal crossing 424–5
refusal of entry 423
terrorist or espionage activities 426
judicial-administrative control 450
liberty, deprivation and restriction of 439–43
alternative measures 439
ban on staying in a specific area 443
detention measure 442
Directive 2008/15/EC 442
Law on granting protection to foreigners 440
measures limiting the foreigner's freedom of movement 441
non-isolation measures 442
placement in a guarded center or detention center 440
restriction and deprivation of freedom of foreigners 441
martial law 412
residence permits for humanitarian reasons 449
state of emergency 412–13
state of natural disaster 412
Ukrainians, inflow of
Articles 45(1) and 77(2) of the Constitution 420
Law on Assistance to Ukrainian Citizens in Connection with the Armed Conflict on the Territory of that State 416–17
negative effects of the mass influx 418
Ukrainian Special Law 417–18
see also Ukraine crisis
Poland, substantive law
active electoral right 384
constitutional standard
Article 56, 106
Article 37(1) Constitution RP 386
Article 31(3) of the Constitution 388
criminal responsibility, right to defense, presumption of innocence 391
direct or implicit reference to foreigners 386
duty to take care of the quality of the environment 397
establishment of compulsory education 389
freedom of artistic creation and scientific research 396

freedom of assembly 394
freedom of association 394
freedom of conscience and religion 392
freedom of expression 393
freedom of movement 392
freedom to choose occupation and place of work 395
freedom to teach and enjoy cultural goods 396
human freedom 387
inviolability, personal freedom and humane treatment 390
inviolability of the dwelling 392
martial law 398
natural disaster 398–9
obligation to pay public burdens and benefits 396
Ombudsman for the Rights of the Child 389
parental rights, limitation or termination of parental rights 391
participation in public life 394
positive discrimination 388
principle of compensating property losses 400
principle of equality 388
prohibition of extradition 393
prohibition of scientific experiments on human beings 390
prohibition of torture, inhuman or degrading treatment and punishment 390
restriction on individual freedoms and rights during emergency 399–400
restrictions on human and civil liberties and rights 399–400
restrictions on the exercise of constitutional freedoms 397
restrictions on the rights and freedoms 398
right of asylum and refugee status 393
rights of the child 389
right to a court 391
right to education 396
right to life 390
right to ownership, other property rights, right of inheritance 395
right to petitions, proposals and complaints 395
right to privacy 391
right to protection of personal data 391
right to safe and hygienic working conditions 396
right to strike 394
secrecy of communications 392
status of foreigners 389
illegal crossing, Polish-Belarusian border 410
legalizing stay of Ukrainian citizens, principles of 385
Polish legal order 383
prohibition of torture or cruel, inhuman or degrading treatment and punishment 384
states of emergency, Article 228(1) 26
statutory guarantees
Border Guard authority 404–6
cash and non-cash benefits and non-monetary benefits 409–10
categories of foreigners 401
Convention for the Protection of Human Rights and Fundamental Freedoms 403
foreigner, definition 401
law on assistance to Ukrainian citizens 407, 416
law on granting protection to foreigners 403–7
medical examination 405–6
Office of the UN High Commissioner for Refugees 405

persecution 403–4
PESEL number 408
protection to foreigners 403
regulation for minors 409
travel document, valid visa 402
Poland's response to the pandemic
Article 3(1)(2) of Law on the state of natural disaster 103
closure of key crossings 106
COVID-19 Special Law 104
divisive treatment of migrants 105
emergency measures 103
foreigners' access to the labor market 105
internal mobility, restrictions 104
residence/identity cards 105
restrictions 102–3, 107
Schengen visa or residence permit 104–5
Special Solutions Related to the Prevention 103
state of epidemic emergency 104
Polish-Belarusian border 127, 427–38
emergency asylum and return procedure 437
exploitation of migrants 428
export act 430
hotspot approach 132
hybrid attack or hybrid war 428, 431
instrumentalization 129–30
Law on granting protection to foreigners 130–1
new migration strategy 129
New Pact on Migration and Asylum 436, 438
Ordinance on temporary suspension or restriction of border traffic 429
Polish court rulings 434
Polish migration strategy 438
protection of foreigners against expulsion 431
push-back mechanism 428–9, 430
Schengen Borders Code 430
special border procedure 434
state of emergency 128
state sovereignty 431
protection standards
harmonizing 124, 126
international 75, 106, 174, 502, 504
stringent privacy 152
for third-country nationals 18
Protocol, 1967 124, 167, 291, 484, 492, 498, 524
public health threat, definition 30
pull factor effect 138
push-back procedure 192, 198, 428–30, 433–5, 481, 551
accused of using Greek government and Frontex 52
collective 359
controls at the borders 353

racism 170
Reception and Identification Centres (RICs) 50
Refugee Convention, 1951 152, 293, 484, 498, 522, 524
Article 33 173, 501
Czech Republic 288
grounds for Asylum 498–9
principle of non-refoulement 172–3, 484
significance 148
Refugee Facility for Turkey (FRiT) 69
refugee relocation mechanism 56
Reviglio, M. 67–8
Rodier, C. 66

Salvini Decree 355, 367, 369
SARSCoV- 2 virus 90, 200
Schengen Borders Code (SBC) 33, 118
2013 amendments to 43
freedom of movement and internal security, balance between 43
internal border controls 42
mechanisms

Article 25 85
concept of public order 86
exceptional circumstances 85
Member States approach 85–6
Schengen Evaluation and Monitoring Mechanism 43
threat to Member States 30
screening of foreigners 436
separation of powers, concept of 101
Shahzad v. Hungary 194
Skordas, A. 137
Slovakia, procedural law perspective
administrative authorities/courts, standards for
emergencies 535
right to a court and effective remedy 534
right to defend one's interests 534
right to good administration 534–5
entry and residence, special procedures
accessibility 536
Act No. 36/2005 Coll. on the Family 526, 536
Act No. 404/2011 Coll. on the stay of foreigners 532, 533
Act No. 480/2002 Coll. on Asylum 523, 540
Commission v. Hungary 531
designated border checkpoints, locations 532–3
equal treatment for all parties 536
expedited residence processing 532
female asylum seekers 537
humanitarian corridors 533
mandatory health screenings 532
standard asylum and residence application process 533
temporary protection status 532
urban centers and border regions, differences 536
technologies in administration and courts
AI-driven systems 538
data privacy and cybersecurity risks 539
digital exclusion 539
digitalization 537, 540
digital scheduling tools 538
e-Asylum Portal 537
e-Government Portal 537
e-identification and biometric systems 538
improved transparency 538–9
language barriers 539
security-focused updates for Ukrainian asylum holders. 537
Slovakia, substantive law perspective
Act No. 404/2011 Coll. on the Stay of Foreigners 485
Act No. 480/2002 Coll. on asylum 485
adequate housing, access to 494
causes of emigration 491
climate-neutral economy 488
Common European Asylum System 491
compliance with labor laws 490
cultural rights policies 520–1
digitalization, impact of 484
EASO 493
ECHR 484
economic, social and cultural rights
access to compulsory education 518
Act No. 5/2004 Coll. on Employment Services 518
Act No. 245/2008 Coll. on Upbringing and Education (Education Act) 518
Act No. 417/2013 Coll. on Assistance in Material Need 519
Act No. 461/2003 Coll. on Social Insurance 519
contributory/non-contributory benefits 519
education 517

employment 518–19
financial support, categories 519
Foreign Nationals' Labour Mobility Strategy 519
right to social allowances 519–20
e-Health Migration system 494
forced migration 492
healthcare
Act No. 176/2015 Coll. on the Commissioner for Persons with Disabilities and the Commissioner for Children 527, 530
Act No. 447/2008 Coll. on Cash Benefits for Compensation of Severe Disabilities 530
Antidiscrimination Act 530
Commissioner for Persons with Disabilities 530
Madrid International Plan of Action on Ageing 529
needs of foreigners 494–5
humanitarian solutions 491
ICCPR 484–5
illegal migration, fight against 486
inclusion and security 540
integration policy within migration policy 493–4
inter-institutional cooperation 489
internal EU migration management processes 488
international collaboration 490
international organizations and groupings 487
international protection strategy 492
language, role of 521
legal migration/labor mobility 488
migration
Act No. 144/2024 Coll. 502
Act No. 404/2011 Coll. on the Stay of Foreigners 495, 507
Act No. 480/2002 Coll. on Asylum 485, 495, 497, 502, 504, 522, 524, 527, 532, 534, 540
Article 23 of the Constitution 495–6
asylum shopping 498
care for children without family 508
challenges 501
digitalization of administrative processes 506
digital submission options 501
Dublin III Regulation 498, 502, 504
e-Asylum Portal 503
EU relocation schemes 504
European Court of Human Rights 496
gender-based violence 508
human trafficking 508
inclusion of subsidiary protection 499
multi-tiered system 500
policy 491
principle of non-refoulement 500
right to asylum 497
right to freedom of movement 505
Schengen Borders Code 506
significance of international 485–6
social group 499
special provisions for vulnerable groups 507–8
subsidiary protection 499
temporary travel bans 497
UNHCR and IOM 508
Migration Office of the Ministry of Interior, role of 485, 505
migration policy framework up to 2025 486
personal rights
Act No. 18/2018 Coll. on the Protection of Personal Data1415 511
Act No. 308/1991 Coll. on Freedom of Religious Belief and the Status of Churches and Religious Societies 512
Act No. 365/2004 Coll. on Equal Treatment 513

Act No. 404/2011 Coll. on the Stay of Foreigners 510
Act No. 580/2004 Coll. on Health Insurance 509
Article 24(4) of the Slovak Constitution 512
detention centers 510
faith-based organizations 512–13
freedom of religion 511
Slovak Office for Personal Data Protection 511
political rights
Act No. 55/2017 Coll. on the Civil Service, 516
Act No. 83/1990 Coll. on the Association of Citizens. 515
Act No. 84/1990 Coll. on the Right of Assembly 514
Act No. 85/1990 Coll. on the Right of Petition 516
Act No. 365/2004 Coll. on Equal Treatment 515
freedom of assembly 513
migrant associations 515
right of petition 515–16
right to enter the civil service 516–17
right to establish associations 514–15
public cultural institutions, right to access 521
quality education for the children of foreigners 494
security measures 489
solidarity rights
Act No. 480/2002 Coll. on asylum 485, 495, 497, 502, 504, 522, 524, 527, 534, 540
Charter of the United Nations 523
EU Temporary Protection Mechanism 523
legal and institutional framework for 522
right to humanitarian aid 522
right to live in peace 523
temporary accommodation 523
stabilization of asylum systems 493
vulnerable groups, human rights for
Act No. 176/2015 Coll. on the Commissioner for Children and the Commissioner for Persons with Disabilities 527
Act No. 305/2005 Coll. on Social and Legal Protection of Children and Social Guardianship 526
Act No. 311/2001 Coll. (Labor Code), women 528
Act No. 365/2004 Coll. on Equal Treatment 528, 529
Act No. 448/2008 Coll. on Social Services1449 528
Act No. 461/2003 Coll. on Social Insurance 519, 529
child protection framework 526
combination of CRC, CEDAW, CRPD 525
Istanbul Convention 52
unaccompanied minors 526
UN Convention on the Rights of the Child 526
violence, domestic and gender-based 528
women, rights of 527–8
social insurance 520
social services
Act No. 448/2008 Coll. on 528, 530
right to 255–6
right to social allowances for foreigners 255
soft law 67–8, 173, 454–5, 544
Article 288 (5) TFEU 99 dominance of 101
drawbacks 99–100
instruments 107
lack of transparency 101–2
legitimacy flaws 100
limited ability to enforce 101

SPRAR (Protection System for Asylum Seekers and Refugees) 360–1, 365–7
Stefan, M. 72
Swan, E. 145
Syrian conflict 136

Task Force Mediterranean (TFM) 44–5
terrorism 17, 83, 164, 168, 197, 199, 326, 335, 543
  counter 90
third-country nationals (TCNs) 483, 505–525
Thym, D. 85, 88, 100
time of emergency
  Directive 2003/109/EC, EU legislator
    types of threats 29
    withdrawal of resident status 29
  Directive 2008/115/EC 30
    Article 11(1) 30
    Article 11(2), 30
    Article 18 31
    threats, Article 7(4) in context of a justification 30
  legal sources 29–33
  Regulation 2024/1347 31
  Regulation 2024/1348 31
  Regulation 2024/1359 32
  safe third country, concept of 31
  threats to public policy, security, health
    Community Customs Code 31
    Directive 2003/109/EC 29
    Directive 2008/115/EC, Article 7(4) 30
    Schengen Borders Code 30
  types of emergency *see* emergency
Tokyo Convention 273–4
trauma-informed training 537
Treaty on Friendship, Cooperation and Partnership, Tunisia and Libya 363
Treaty on the Functioning of the European Union (TFEU)
  Article 45 97
  Article 45(3) 97
  Article 45(4) 247
  Article 67, Area of Freedom, Security and Justice 150
  Article 72 64, 88–9
  Article 78(3) 56, 61–2
  Article 218 71
  Article 258 64
  Article 288 (5), role in managing the COVID-19 99
  CFR *see* The Charter of Fundamental Rights of the European Union
  Common European Asylum System, Article 78 150
  legal framework for EU's common immigration policy, Article 79 150
  relevant Articles 150
  solidarity and fair sharing of responsibility, Article 80 150
Turco-Napolitano Law, Law No. 40/1998 352Turkey
  Akkad v. Turkey 75
  deportation and detention practices 75
  safe third country 70
Tusk, Donald 129
two-stage test, concept of 193

Ukraine crisis 498, 532–5
  border crossings from Ukraine to Poland 133, 145
  Decision (EU) 2022/382 139
  Directive 2001/55/EC 96, 134, 135, 138, 139
  invasion of Russian Federation troops 551
  mass influx, migrations as a threat 136–8, 143
  migration, European Union's response 82, 143

Poland's response to influx 143
Law on Assistance to Citizens of Ukraine 140
residence permit 141
rules for legalizing the stay of Ukrainians 141
pull factor effect 138
Russian aggression against 23–4, 128, 133–4, 385
temporary protection as emergency measures 134–9
Temporary Protection Directive (2001/55/EC) 136–7
UN Convention on the Rights of Persons with Disabilities (CRPD) 525, 530, 536
UN Convention on the Rights of the Child (UNCRC) 502–3, 507, 517, 525
UN High Commissioner for Refugees (UNHCR) 44, 47, 352, 508, 522
Office of 133
Universal Declaration of Human Rights (UDHR) 165, 169, 183, 196, 522, 523, 546

Valletta Summit 76
Visapoint system 288
Visegrad Group countries 94, 142
Vitiello, D. 142
von der Leyen, Ursula 110
vulnerable persons, concept of 298

Wessel, R.A. 67
World Health Organization (WHO) 30, 83, 106
Wroblewski, R. 473

Ius, Lex et Res Publica

Studies in Law, Philosophy and Political Cultures

Edited by
Barbara Janusz-Pohl

Vol. 1 Anna Jaron: Socio-Economic Constitutional Rights in Democratisation Processes. An Account of the Constitutional Dialogue Theory. 2012.

Vol. 2 Stanisław Filipowicz: Democracy – The Power of Illusion. 2013.

Vol. 3 Teresa Dukiet-Nagórska (ed.): The Postulates of Restorative Justice and the Continental Model of Criminal Law. As Illustrated by Polish Criminal Law 2014.

Vol. 4 Agnieszka Kupzok: Enforcement of Patents on Geographically Divisible Inventions. An Inquiry into the Standard of Substantive Patent Law Infringement in Cross-Border Constellations. 2015.

Vol. 5 Alicja Jagielska-Burduk / Wojciech Szafrański: Legal Issues in Cultural Heritage Management. A Polish Perspective. 2016.

Vol. 6 Maciej Mataczyński (ed.): The Takeover of Public Companies as a Mode of Exercising EU Treaty Freedoms. 2017.

Vol. 7 Maciej Barczewski (ed.): Value of Information. Intellectual Property, Privacy and Big Data. 2018.

Vol. 8 Pawel Smoleń, Marcin Burzec: Introduction to Polish Tax Law. 2018.

Vol. 9 Łukasz Pohl, Konrad Burdziak: Judicial Interpretation of the 1997 Criminal Code Provisions on Self-Defence. 2019.

Vol. 10 Adam Szot: Judicial Review of Administrative Discretion. The Influence of Court Decisions on Administrative Actions. 2019.

Vol. 11 Michał Peno / Konrad Burdziak (eds.): The Concept of Modern Law. Polish and Central European Tradition. 2019.

Vol. 12 Leszek Leszczyński / Bartosz Liṅewski / Adam Szot (eds.): Potential of Precedent in the Statutory Legal Order. 2019.

Vol. 13 Łukasz Bolesta: In Search of a Model for the Legal Protection of a Whistleblower in the Workplace in Poland. A legal and comparative study. 2020.

Vol. 14 Paweł Chmielnicki / Adam Sulikowski (eds.): New Perspectives on Legislation. A Comparative Approach. 2020.

Vol. 15 Marcin Burzec / Beata Kucia-Guściora / Paweł Smoleś: Agricultural Activity in Poland: A Fiscal and Legal Study. 2020.

Vol. 16 Magdalena Półtorak / Ilona Topa (eds.): Women, Children and (Other) Vulnerable Groups. Standards of Protection and Challenges for International Law. 2021.

Vol. 17 Josef Albert Fox: Die polnische Verfassung vom 3. Mai 1791. Hintergründe der Entstehung und der Außerkraftsetzung. Stellung Polens im Zeitalter der Aufklärung. 2021.

Vol. 18 Barbara Janusz-Pohl (ed.): Juvenile Justice Systems: Poland-Brazil-Portugal. 2021.

Vol. 19 Leszek Leszczyński: General Reference Clauses in the Judicial Process. Context of Legislative Intentions Interpretative Discretion. 2021.

Vol. 20 Francisco J. Campos Zamora: Das Problem der Begründung richterlicher Entscheidungen. Eine Analyse auf der Grundlage der Theorie der juristischen Argumentation. 2021.

Vol. 21 Aneta Skorupa-Wulczyńska: Language Rights of the Citizen of the European Union. 2022.

Vol. 22 Mateusz Osiecki: International Legal Aspects of Aerial Terrorism. Methods of Law Enforcement in Aviation. 2022.

Vol. 23 Vladimír Sharp / Gabriela Blahoudková / Jakub Handrlica (eds.): Law, Pandemics and Ownership Restrictions. 2022.

Vol. 24 Piotr Kasprzyk / Anna Konert: Drones – Future of Aviation Law? Interference of Public Law in Private Law. 2023.

Vol. 25 Szymon Pawelec (ed.): Consensual Mechanisms in Criminal Proceedings – Integrative and Comparative Perspective. 2023.

Vol. 26 Dorota Pudzianowska: Statelessness in Public Law. 2023.

Vol. 27 Boguslaw Przywora / Aleksander Wróbel: Formalised Access to Pre-jurisdictional Free Legal Aid. 2023.

Vol. 28 Ewa Dawidziuk / Patricia Panero / Anny Tarwacka (eds.): Family, Law, and Society: from Roman Law to the Present Day. 2024.

Vol. 29 Marian Grzybowsk / Boguslaw Przywora / Aleksandra Syryt (eds.): Free Legal Aid, Theory, Legal Basis and Practice. European Standards. 2024.

Vol. 30 Karolina Gmerek: Trial as a Social Communication Occurrence. 2024.

Vol. 31 Pawel Wiliński (ed.): Effective Legal Remedies in Criminal Justice System. European Perspective. 2024.

Vol. 32 Jakub Hanc / Olga Sitarz / Anna Jaworska-Wieloch: On the (non)existence of the right to religious freedom of persons deprived of liberty. 2024.

Vol. 33 Marian Grzybowsk / Boguslaw Przywora / Aleksandra Syryt (eds.): Free Legal Aid – A Comparative Approach. 2024.

Vol. 34 Dominik Gajewski (ed.): Functioning of Administrative Judiciary in the Context of Economic Changes. 2024.

Vol. 35 Mikołajczyk, Barbara: Older Migrants – Vulnerable and Excluded. 2024.

Vol. 36 Świder, Maciej: The Exercise of the Right to a Fair Trial in the Era of the COVID-19 Pandemic. 2024.

Vol. 37 Tomasz Barankiewicz / Boguslaw Przywora (eds.): Public and Civil Service in Poland. 2024.

Vol. 38 Daniele Vicoli (ed.): Effective Justice 1. Effective Justice. International and Comparative Approaches. 2025.

Vol. 39 Barbara Janusz-Pohl (ed.): Effective Justice 2. Effective Justice. International and Comparative Approaches. 2025.

Vol. 40 Kinga Anna Gajda / Marta Pietras-Eichberger / Małgorzata Skawińska (eds.): Mediation as an Inclusive and Sustainable Method of Resolving Conflicts. 2025.

Vol. 41 Ewa Dawidziuk / Anna Tarwacka / Sławomir Kursa (eds.): Historical and Contemporary Issues of Democracy, Person and Human Rights. 2025.

Vol. 42 Jakub Kępiński: The impact of Directive 2005/29/EC on Polish law on combating unfair competition. 2025.

Vol. 43 Paul Caesar von Chamier Cieminski: Hostile Cyber Operations between States and International Law. 2026.

Vol. 44 Monika Jagielska / Barbara Mikołajczyk / Piotr Pinior (eds.): Institutional Vulnerability in Law. 2026.

Vol. 45 Jacek Chlebny (ed.): Legal Restrictions on Third-Country Nationals in EU Emergencies. 2026.

www.peterlang.com

www.ingramcontent.com/pod-product-compliance
Ingram Content Group UK Ltd.
Pitfield, Milton Keynes, MK11 3LW, UK
UKHW021830100926
8556IPUK00004B/251

9 783631 925201